RHCE™ Red Hat® Certified Engineer Linux Study Guide, Fifth Edition

Exam (RH302)

RHCE™ Red Hat® Certified Engineer Linux Study Guide, Fifth Edition

Exam (RH302)

Michael Jang

New York   Chicago   San Francisco   Lisbon   London   Madrid
Mexico City   Milan   New Delhi   San Juan   Seoul   Singapore   Sydney   Toronto

The *McGraw·Hill* Companies

Cataloging-in-Publication Data is on file with the Library of Congress

McGraw-Hill books are available at special quantity discounts to use as premiums and sales promotions, or for use in corporate training programs. For more information, please write to the Director of Special Sales, Professional Publishing, McGraw-Hill, Two Penn Plaza, New York, NY 10121-2298. Or contact your local bookstore.

RHCE™ Red Hat® Certified Engineer Linux Study Guide (Exam RH302), Fifth Edition

234567890 CUS CUS 01987

ISBN-13: 978-0-07-226454-8
ISBN-10:   0-07-226454-3

Sponsoring Editor Timothy Green	**Copy Editor** Lisa Theobald	**Illustration** Apollo Publishing Services
Editorial Supervisor Janet Walden	**Proofreader** Paul Tyler	**Art Director, Cover** Jeff Weeks
Project Editor LeeAnn Pickrell	**Indexer** Rebecca Plunket	**Cover Designer** Pattie Lee
Acquisitions Coordinator Jennifer Housh	**Production Supervisor** Jim Kussow	
Technical Editor Elizabeth Zinkann	**Composition** Apollo Publishing Services	

For the young widows and widowers,
may they find the courage to face their fears,
to navigate their way through the pain,
and to find hope for a brighter future.

ABOUT THE CONTRIBUTORS

Author

Michael Jang (RHCE, LPIC-1, LCP, Linux+, MCP) is currently a full-time writer, specializing in operating systems and networks. His experience with computers goes back to the days of jumbled punch cards. He has written other books on Linux certification, including *Linux+ Exam Cram* and *Sair GNU/Linux Installation and Configuration Exam Cram*. His other Linux books include *Linux Annoyances for Geeks*, *Linux Patch Management*, and *Mastering Fedora Core Linux 5*. He has also written or contributed to books on Microsoft operating systems, including MCSE *Guide to Microsoft Windows 98* and *Mastering Windows XP Professional, Second Edition*.

Technical Editor

Elizabeth Zinkann is a logical Linux catalyst, a freelance technical editor, and an independent computer consultant. She was a contributing editor and review columnist for *Sys Admin Magazine* for ten years. As an editor, some of her projects have included *Mastering Fedora Core Linux 5*, *Ending Spam*, *Linux Patch Management*, and *Write Portable Code*. In a former life, she also programmed communications features, including ISDN at AT&T Network Systems.

CONTENTS AT A GLANCE

1	RHCE Prerequisites	1
2	Hardware and Installation	69
3	The Boot Process	143
4	Linux Filesystem Administration	183
5	Package Management	221
6	User Administration	271
7	System Administration Tools	329
8	Kernel Services and Configuration	375
9	Apache and Squid	443
10	Network File-Sharing Services	493
11	Domain Name Service	557
12	Electronic Mail	585
13	Other Networking Services	613
14	The X Window System	649
15	Securing Services	691
16	Troubleshooting	727
A	Sample Exam 1	767
B	Sample Exam 2	783
	Glossary	799
	Index	819

CONTENTS

About the Contributors . . . . *vii*

Acknowledgments . . . . *xxix*

Preface . . . . *xxxi*

Introduction . . . . *xxxix*

I RHCE Prerequisites . . . . **I**

Basic Hardware Knowledge 4

   Architectures 5

   Intel Communications Channels 5

   RAM Requirements 6

   Hard Drive Options 7

Basic Linux Knowledge 8

   The VIsual Editor 8

   Exercise 1-1: Using vi to Create a New User 10

   Other Text Editors 11

Linux Filesystem Hierarchy and Structure 11

   Linux Filesystems and Directories 12

   A Variety of Media Devices 12

   Making Reference to Devices in /dev 12

   Filesystem Formatting and Checking 14

   Configuring One Filesystem on Multiple Partitions 17

   Exercise 1-2: Creating a New LVM Partition 18

   Mounting Other Partitions 18

Basic File Operations and Manipulation 19

   Basic File Operations 19

   File Filters 23

   Administrative Commands 24

   Wildcards 25

Printing 25

   Adding Printers 26

   Print Commands 26

Shells 26

   Basic Shell Programming 27

Variables and Parameters 27
Exercise 1-3: Checking the PATH 28
Script Execution and Permissions 28
Inherited Environment 29
Piping, Input/Output, Error, and Redirection 29
Basic Security 30
File Permissions 30
Users, Groups, and umask 31
SUID and SGID 32
Shadow Passwords 33
Shadow Password Suite 33
System Administration 34
The Superuser 34
/etc/skel for Home Directories 35
Daemons 35
Controlling Network Services Through Daemons 35
cron 36
Backup and Restore 36
System Log File Management 38
Basic TCP/IP Networking 38
IP Numbers and Address Classes 39
IPv6 Addressing 39
How to Define a Network with IP Addresses 40
Tools and Commands 41
Configuring Name Resolution 42
Familiarity with Standard Network Services 44
Network File System, Locally and Remotely 44
sendmail and Postfix 45
POP, IMAP 45
File Transfer Protocol (FTP) 45
Domain Name Service (DNS) 45
Dynamic Host Configuration Protocol (DHCP) 46
Samba 46
Web Services 46
Network Information Service (NIS) 47
The Extended Internet Services Daemon (xinetd) 47
Basic Network Security 47
Allowing and Denying 48
Securing Ports 48

Network Address Translation 48

iptables 48

Other Basic Prerequisite Skills per the Red Hat Exam Prep Guide ... 49

Configuring an email Client 49

Using a Text and/or Graphical Browser to Access HTTP/HTTPs
URLs 50

Using lftp to Access URLs 51

Downloading the Red Hat Enterprise Linux Installation CDs 53

Downloading Red Hat Enterprise Linux 53

Red Hat Enterprise Linux Source RPMs 54

Third-Party Rebuilds 54

The Fedora Core 5/6 Prep Option 54

An Overview of the Download Process 55

✓ Two-Minute Drill 57

Q&A Self Test 61

Lab Questions 63

Self Test Answers 64

Lab Answers 65

2 Hardware and Installation **69**

Hardware Compatibility 70

Linux Hardware Documentation 72

Plug and Play and the Hardware Abstraction Layer 73

ACPI and APM 74

CPU and RAM 75

Compatible CPUs 75

CPUs and Virtualization 76

RAM Requirements 76

Hotswap Buses 77

Serial Ports 77

Parallel Ports 77

USB 78

IEEE 1394 78

PC Card (PCMCIA) 78

Hotswap Systems 79

Device Management 79

Configuring a Network Installation 81

Configuring a Network Installation Server 81

Creating an NFS Installation Server 81

Configuring Another Network Installation Server 83
Requirements for Network Installations 86
Setting Up Installation from a Local Hard Drive 87
The First Installation Steps 88
Boot Options 88
Booting from the First CD/DVD 89
If You Need an Installation USB or CD/DVD 89
Almost Ready to Install 90
CD/DVD or Boot USB Starts Installation 91
First Selections 92
Configuring Partitions, RAID, and LVM 96
RAID, Briefly 96
Logical Volumes, Briefly 97
Naming Conventions 97
Exercise 2-1: Partitioning 98
Exercise 2-2: Partitioning During Installation 99
Separate Filesystems 101
Stability and Security 102
Basic Storage Space Requirements 103
Linux Swap Space 104
BIOS Limits 105
Multiple Controllers 105
Post-partition Installation Steps 106
The Boot Loader 106
Networking 107
Time and Root Passwords 108
Baseline Packages 108
Package Groups 110
Post-installation, Security, and the First Boot Process 120
Licensing 122
Initial Firewall Configuration 122
Initial SELinux Configuration 122
kdump 123
Date and Time 123
Set Up Software Updates 124
The First Regular User 124
Password Security 125
Sound Card Configuration 125
Additional CDs 125

If You Haven't Configured the GUI 126
Caveat Emptor on Installation 126
Installation Validation 127
The Installation Log File 127
Installation Troubleshooting 127
Certification Summary 129
✓ Two-Minute Drill 131
Q&A Self Test 133
Lab Questions 134
Self Test Answers 140
Lab Answers 141

3   The Boot Process **143**
The BIOS Initialization Sequence 144
Basics of the BIOS 145
Using the BIOS Menu 145
The BIOS and the Boot Loader 146
The GRUB Boot Loader 147
GRUB, the GRand Unified Bootloader 147
GRUB Parameters 149
Updating GRUB 150
GRUB Error Effects 152
Exercise 3-1:   GRUB Error Effects 153
The GRUB Command Line 155
Exercise 3-2:   Using the GRUB Command Line 156
Kernel Initialization and the First Process 157
Kernel Message Analysis 158
Driver Loading 158
The First Process and /etc/inittab 159
The First Process 159
/etc/inittab 159
Virtual Consoles 160
Runlevels 161
Functionality of Each Runlevel 161
Runlevel Scripts 162
Booting into the Runlevel of Your Choice 164
Exercise 3-3:   Booting into a Different Runlevel 165
Controlling Services 167
Service Control from the Command Line 167

The Text Console Service Configuration Tool 168
The GUI Service Configuration Tool 168
System Configuration Files 169
Non-network /etc/sysconfig Files 170
GUI Configuration Utilities 171
✓ Two-Minute Drill 173
Q&A Self Test 175
Lab Questions 176
Self Test Answers 180
Lab Answers 181

4 Linux Filesystem Administration **183**
Partitioning Hard Disks 185
The fdisk Utility 186
The parted Utility 191
Managing Filesystems 196
Standard Formatting Filesystems 196
Understanding Journaling Filesystems 197
Creating Filesystems with mkfs 198
Managing ext2/ext3 Filesystem Attributes 199
Filesystem Management and the Automounter 200
Managing /etc/fstab 200
Mounting Filesystems, Actively 201
Mounting USB Keys and Removable Media 201
Mounting via the Automounter 203
Exercise 4-1:   Configuring the Automounter 206
A Floppy Drive and the Automounter 207
Access Control Lists and Other Security Attributes .. 208
Access Control Lists 208
Understanding SELinux 209
✓ Two-Minute Drill 211
Q&A Self Test 212
Lab Questions 213
Self Test Answers 215
Lab Answers 216

5 Package Management **221**
The Red Hat Package Manager 222
What Is a Package? 223

What Is an RPM? 223
Installing RPMs 224
Removing RPMs 225
Installing RPMs from Remote Systems 226
Updating a Kernel RPM 226
More RPM Commands 227
RPM Queries 227
Validating an RPM Package Signature 228
RPM Verification 229
Listing Installed RPMs 230
Using RPM Sources 230
Managing Updates with Pup and the Red Hat Network 234
RHN Registration 235
Updating with Pup 236
Automatic Dependency Resolution 237
RHN in the Enterprise 237
Adding and Removing RPM Packages with yum and pirut 238
The Basics of yum 238
Install Mode 241
Updates and Security Fixes 242
Third-Party Repositories 242
Managing with pirut 242
Exercise 5-1: Installing More with pirut 243
Using Kickstart to Automate Installation 244
Kickstart Concepts 245
Setting Up a Kickstart USB 245
Configuring a Kickstart Server 246
Starting the Installation with a Kickstart File 247
Sample Kickstart File 248
Kickstart Partitioning 251
Exercise 5-2: Creating a Sample Kickstart File 253
Modifying the Packages to be Installed 254
The Kickstart Configurator 254
✓ Two-Minute Drill 261
Q&A Self Test 263
Lab Questions 264
Self Test Answers 267
Lab Answers 268

6 User Administration **271**

User Account Management 273
    User Account Categories 273
    Basic Command Line Tools 274
    The Red Hat User Manager 277
    Exercise 6-1: Adding a User with the Red Hat User
        Manager 279
    User Account Management Tips 280
    Deleting a User Account 281
    Modifying a User Account 281
    Regular User Management Commands 283
    Limiting Access to su 284
    Limiting Access to sudo 284
The Basic User Environment 285
    Home Directories and /etc/skel 285
    Window Manager Configuration Files 287
Shell Configuration Files 287
    /etc/bashrc 287
    /etc/profile 288
    /etc/profile.d/ 289
    Exercise 6-2: Securing Your System 289
    User Shell Configuration Files 290
Setting Up and Managing Disk Quotas 290
    Quota Settings in the Kernel 291
    The Quota Package 292
    sysinit Quota Handling 293
    Quota Activation in /etc/fstab 293
    Quota Management Commands 294
    Using edquota to Set Up Disk Quotas 294
    Automating Quota Settings 298
    Quota Reports 298
    Quotas on NFS Directories 299
    Exercise 6-3: Configuring Quotas 300
Creating and Maintaining Special Groups 301
    Standard and Red Hat Groups 301
    Shared Directories 302
    Exercise 6-4: Controlling Group Ownership
        with the SGID Bit 303

Pluggable Authentication Modules 305
    Pluggable Authentication Modules (PAM)
      and Associated Files 306
    PAM Configuration Example: /etc/pam.d/login 308
    Exercise 6-5:   Configuring PAM 310
    Securing PAM by User 311
    Exercise 6-6:   Using PAM to Limit Access 312
Network Authentication Configuration: NIS and LDAP 313
    NIS Client Configuration 314
    LDAP Client Configuration 314
    The Name Service Switch File 315
    Configuring Clients with the Red Hat Authentication Tool 316
   ✓ Two-Minute Drill 319
Q&A   Self Test 321
    Lab Questions 322
    Self Test Answers 324
    Lab Answers 325

7   System Administration Tools **329**
Network Configuration 331
    The /etc/sysconfig/network-scripts Files 332
    Setting Up a Network Interface 333
    Exercise 7-1:   Modifying Network Interfaces
      with system-config-network 334
The CUPS Printing System 341
    Installing and Starting CUPS 341
    CUPS Configuration Files 342
    The Red Hat Printer Configuration Tool 342
    The Line Print Daemon Commands 347
    The CUPS Web-Based Interface 349
    Verifying CUPS Sharing 351
    CUPS and SELinux 354
Automating System Administration: cron and at 354
    The System crontab and Components 355
    Setting Up cron for Users 357
    Exercise 7-2:   Creating a cron Job 357
    Running a Job with the at System 358
    Securing cron and at 359

Understanding, Maintaining, and Monitoring System Logs 360

System Log Configuration File 360

Managing Logs 362

Exercise 7-3: Checking Logs 364

✓ Two-Minute Drill 365

Q&A Self Test 367

Lab Questions 368

Self Test Answers 371

Lab Answers 372

8 Kernel Services and Configuration **375**

The Basics of the Kernel 377

Best Practices 377

Kernel Concepts 378

Other RHEL Kernels 379

The /boot Partition 379

The /proc Filesystem 380

Understanding Kernel Modules 383

The /lib/modules/kernel_version/ Directory Structure 385

New Kernels, the Easy Way 388

Understanding Kernel Version Numbers 388

Upgrading Kernels 389

Kernel Patches 390

Updating GRUB 391

Kernel Sources 392

The Kernel Source Tree and Documentation 393

The Kernel RPMs 394

The Linux Kernel tar File 396

Recompiling a Kernel 396

The Kernel Configuration Scripts 396

Understanding Kernel Configuration Options 400

Exercise 8-1: Compiling and Installing a Custom Kernel ... 408

Advanced Partitioning: Software RAID 410

RAID 0 410

RAID 1 411

RAID 4 411

RAID 5 411

RAID 6 411

RAID 10 412

RAID in Practice 412

Exercise 8-2:   Mirroring the /home Partition
with Software RAID   415
Advanced Partitioning: Logical Volume Management   417
Creating a Physical Volume   418
Creating a Volume Group   419
Creating a Logical Volume   419
Using a Logical Volume   420
More LVM Commands   420
Adding Another Logical Volume   423
Removing a Logical Volume   424
Resizing Logical Volumes   424
The GUI LVM Management Tool   425
Converting LVM1 Filesystem to LVM2   430
✓   Two-Minute Drill   431
Q&A   Self Test   433
Lab Questions   434
Self Test Answers   437
Lab Answers   438

9   Apache and Squid **443**

The Apache Web Server   444
Apache 2.2   446
Installation   447
Starting on Reboot   447
Exercise 9-1:   Installing the Apache Server   449
The Apache Configuration Files   450
Analyzing the Default Apache Configuration   451
Analyzing httpd.conf   452
Basic Apache Configuration for a Simple Web Server   456
Apache Access Configuration   456
Basic Apache Security   456
Apache and Security Arrangements   458
Exercise 9-2:   Creating a List of Files   458
Host-Based Security   460
User-Based Security   460
Control Through .htaccess   463
Exercise 9-3:   Password Protection for a Web Directory   464
Virtual Hosts   466
Virtual Hosts   467
Secure Virtual Hosts   468

Checking Syntax 470
Executable Files in Apache 470
Apache Log Files 471
Apache Troubleshooting 472
Exercise 9-4: Updating a Home Page 473
Exercise 9-5: Setting Up a Virtual Web Server 474
The Red Hat httpd Configuration Tool 475
The Squid Web Proxy Cache 476
Key Squid Files and Directories 477
Starting Squid on Reboot 477
Basic Squid Configuration 478
Configuration Options 480
Security Options 482
Exercise 9-6: Configuring Squid to Act as a Proxy Server 482
✓ Two-Minute Drill 485
Q&A Self Test 486
Lab Questions 487
Self Test Answers 488
Lab Answers 489

10 Network File-Sharing Services **493**
Configuring a Network File System (NFS) Server 494
NFS Server Configuration and Operation 496
Required Packages 496
Configuring NFS to Start 496
Configuring NFS for Basic Operation 497
NFS Server Configuration Tool 499
Making NFS Work with SELinux 502
Quirks and Limitations of NFS 502
Performance Tips 504
NFS Security 505
Exercise 10-1; NFS 507
Exercise 10-2: Using the NFS Server Configuration Tool 508
Client-Side NFS 509
Mounting an NFS Directory from the Command Line 510
Client-Side Helper Processes 510
NFS and /etc/fstab 511
Diskless Clients 511
Soft Mounting 511

The File Transfer Protocol and vsFTPd 512
    Installing the Very Secure FTP Server 512
    Configuring SELinux Support for vsFTP 512
    Starting on Reboot 513
    vsFTP Server Security 513
    Exercise 10-3: Configuring a Basic vsFTP Server 515
Samba Services 516
    Installing Samba Services 517
    Configuring SELinux Support for Samba 518
    Configuring Samba to Start 518
    Some Samba Background 519
    Configuring Samba as a Client 520
    Configuring a Samba Server 523
    Joining a Domain 533
    Configuring Samba Users 533
    Exercise 10-4: Using Home Directories 535
    The Red Hat Samba Server Configuration Utility 536
    Testing Changes to /etc/samba/smb.conf 542
    Exercise 10-5: Configuring Samba with Shares 543
  ✓ Two-Minute Drill 546
  Q&A Self Test 548
    Lab Questions 549
    Self Test Answers 552
    Lab Answers 553

11 Domain Name Service **557**
Understanding DNS: Zones, Domains, and Delegation 559
    Basic Parameters 559
    Packages 559
    A DNS Client 560
The Berkeley Internet Name Domain (BIND) 561
    The DNS Configuration Files 561
    A Caching-Only Name Server 563
    A Slave Name Server 565
    A Forwarding-Only Name Server 565
    named.ca 566
    localhost.zone 567
    Reverse Lookups with named.local 567
    Configuring a Simple Domain 567
    Creating an RNDC Key 569

Creating a Zone File 570

The Reverse Zone 572

Starting named 573

Common DNS Pitfalls 573

BIND Utilities 574

BIND Commands 575

The DNS Configuration Tool 576

Exercise 11-1:   Setting up Your Own DNS Server 576

✓ Two-Minute Drill 578

Q&A Self Test 579

Lab Questions 580

Self Test Answers 581

Lab Answers 582

12 Electronic Mail 585

Mail Transport Agents, Mail Delivery Agents, and Mail User Agents ... 587

Definitions 587

Installing Mail Server Packages 588

Reception with Dovecot 589

POP 589

IMAP 589

Configuration File 590

Activating Dovecot 590

Dovecot Secure Certificates 591

sendmail Configuration 592

Configuring sendmail for Basic Operation 594

Configuring and Activating Postfix 598

Selecting an E-mail System 599

Using alternatives to Select an E-mail System 599

Switching with system-switch-mail 600

E-mail Clients 600

Testing the Results 602

Exercise 12-1:   Testing E-mail Services 602

✓ Two-Minute Drill 604

Q&A Self Test 605

Lab Questions 606

Self Test Answers 608

Lab Answers 609

13 Other Networking Services **613**

The Extended Internet Services Daemon (xinetd) 614
   Generic xinetd Configuration 616
   Sample xinetd Configuration 618
   Exercise 13-1:   Configuring xinetd 620
The Secure Shell Package 620
   Basic Encrypted Communication 621
   How to Generate Your Keys 623
   Why Use SSH? 623
   Configuring an SSH Server 625
   Configuring an SSH Client 626
Dynamic Host Configuration Protocol (DHCP) 627
   Installing DHCP Packages 627
   DHCP Server Configuration 628
   Client Configuration 632
   Exercise 13-3:   Configuring DHCP 633
The Network Time Protocol (NTP) 634
   NTP Client Configuration 634
   Basic Configuration 635
   Configuring a Local NTP Server 636
   ✓ Two-Minute Drill 638
   Q&A Self Test 640
   Lab Questions 641
   Self Test Answers 643
   Lab Answers 644

14 The X Window System **649**

X with Clients and Servers 651
   Different Meanings for Client and Server 652
   Supported Hardware 653
   Default X Clients 654
   Exercise 14-1:   Starting X Server 654
   X Clients and Command Line Options 655
   xterm 657
The X.org Server Configuration 658
   X.org Server Configuration Files 658
   Starting the X Window 659
   Exercise 14-2:   Starting Multiple X Servers 659

xorg.conf in Detail 660
Text or Graphical GUI Access 662
Text Login Mode 662
Display Managers: gdm and kdm 663
Analyzing startx 666
Exercise 14-3: Customizing the startx Process 668
Tools for X.org Configuration 670
Red Hat Display Settings Tool 670
Other Available Tools 673
X Font Server Issues 674
Running Remote X Applications 675
Exercise 14-4: Starting a Display from a Remote Client . . . 675
Troubleshooting 676
Desktops and Window Managers 677
The GNOME and KDE Desktops 677
Default Desktop 680
Exercise 14-5: Exploring Desktops 681
✓ Two-Minute Drill 683
Q&A Self Test 684
Lab Questions 685
Self Test Answers 687
Lab Answers 688

15 Securing Services **691**
Using tcp_wrappers to Secure Services 693
Security by User or Host 694
Exercise 15-1: Configuring tcp_wrappers 696
Firewalls and Packet Filtering Using netfilter 697
Configuring iptables 698
Maintaining Netfilter Rules 700
The Red Hat Firewall Configurator 701
Network Address Translation 703
IP Masquerading 703
IP Forwarding 705
Security Enhanced Linux 706
SELinux Status 707
Configuring Manually 708
Configuring with the SELinux Management Tool 709
The Setroubleshoot Browser 715

✓ Two-Minute Drill 718
Q&A Self Test 720
Lab Questions 721
Self Test Answers 723
Lab Answers 724

16 Troubleshooting **727**

Troubleshooting Strategies 728
Booting Into Different Runlevels 733
The linux rescue Environment 735
Required RHCT Troubleshooting Skills 742
Diagnosing and Correcting Network Problems 742
Exercise 16-1: Diagnosing and Correcting
Network Problems 743
Diagnosing and Correcting Hostname Resolution Problems . . . 744
Exercise 16-2: Diagnosing and Correcting Hostname
Resolution Problems 744
Configuring the X Window System 745
Exercise 16-3: Configuring the X Window System 745
Configuring a Desktop Environment 746
Exercise 16-4: Configuring a Desktop Environment 746
Adding New Partitions, Filesystems, and Swap 747
Exercise 16-5: Adding a New Partition 747
Important Command Line Tools 748
Required RHCE Troubleshooting Skills 748
Troubleshooting the Boot Loader 749
Exercise 16-6: Troubleshooting the Boot Loader 749
Module Errors 750
Exercise 16-7: Troubleshooting Boot Loader Modules 750
Filesystem Corruption and Checking 751
File Corruption 755
Network Service Issues 756
Add, Remove, and Resize Logical Volumes 756
Diagnosing SELinux-related Network Service Issues 759
✓ Two-Minute Drill 760
Q&A Self Test 761
Lab Questions 762
Self Test Answers 764
Lab Answers 765

A   Sample Exam I **767**

Troubleshooting and System Maintenance   768
   Troubleshooting and System Maintenance Exercise:
      RHCT Components   769
   Troubleshooting and System Maintenance:
      RHCE Components   770
   Troubleshooting and System Maintenance Discussion   772
Installation and Configuration   776
   Server Installation Problem: RHCT-Level Skills   777
   Server Installation Problem: RHCE-Level Skills   778
   Installation Discussion   779

B   Sample Exam 2 . . . . **783**

Troubleshooting and System Maintenance   784
   Troubleshooting and System Maintenance Exam:
      RHCT Components   785
   Troubleshooting and System Maintenance:
      RHCE Components   786
   Troubleshooting and System Maintenance Discussion   788
Installation and Configuration   793
   Server Installation Problem: RHCT-Level Skills   794
   Server Installation Problem: RHCE-Level Skills   795
   Installation Discussion   796

Glossary **799**

Index **819**

ACKNOWLEDGMENTS

I personally would like to thank the following people:

- **Nancy E. Cropley, R.N. (d. 2002)** It's now been over five years since you've left this world, but I continue to hold your spirit in my heart, and I hope you can still see the joy of the world through my eyes. You are my hero, even today. I hope you can see how happy I am with Donna, but I wish I could still be with you. I will always miss you.

  As a political activist, you fought for what you believed in: social justice, peace, and universal healthcare. You were never afraid to go to jail to support your beliefs. Your example is helping me find a backbone for life.

  As a nurse for the homeless, you helped so many who are less fortunate. You worked tirelessly in the clinics, in the shelters, and on the streets. Your efforts eased the pain of so many people. And you saved lives.

  As an Internet entrepreneur, you showed me how to be happy pursuing a life working from home. You made it possible for me to have the freedom to be, instead of getting stuck in the corporate world.

  Nancy, you were my partner, my lover, my soul mate. You helped me find joy in this world. I take your lessons with me. I thank you for the best seven years of my life.

- All the incredibly hard-working folks at McGraw-Hill: Tim Green, Jennifer Housh, LeeAnn Pickrell, Lisa Theobald, Paul Tyler, and Rebecca Plunket for their help in launching a great series and being solid team players.

PREFACE

L inux is thriving. Red Hat is at the forefront of the Linux revolution. And Red Hat Certified Engineers and Technicians are making it happen.

Even in the current economic recovery, business, education, and governments are cost conscious. They want control of their operating systems. Linux—even Red Hat Enterprise Linux—saves money. The open source nature of Linux allows users to control and customize their operating systems. While there is a price associated with Red Hat Enterprise Linux (RHEL), the cost includes updates and support. Now with Xen, it's possible to set up a cluster of virtual, independent installations of RHEL (and other operating systems) on a single physical computer. As I describe shortly, there are freely available "rebuilds" of RHEL that you can get without support from Red Hat, with features identical for most administrators.

on the
()ob

A "rebuild" is software that is built by a third party from the same source code as the original "build." On the other hand, a "clone" is built from different source code.

As this book is going to print, the New York Stock Exchange has just announced that it's moving to Linux. Major corporations, from Home Depot to Toyota, and governments such as Brazil, the Republic of Korea, and Switzerland have made the switch to Linux. When faced with a Microsoft audit for licenses, the Portland, Oregon, school system switched to Linux. Major movie studios such as Disney and Dreamworks use Linux to create the latest motion pictures. IBM has invested billions in Linux —and constantly features Linux in its advertising. HP has reported 2.5 billion dollars in Linux-related revenue in 2003, and it's still growing today (2007). Even though Linux is freely downloadable, Wall Street Technology just reported that Linux server revenue in 2006 was about 7 billion dollars, $1/3^{rd}$ that of Microsoft (up from $1/4^{th}$ in 2004), and is still gaining market share. Is Microsoft Vista motivating business to look more closely at Linux?

With the One Laptop Per Child (OLPC) initiative, a streamlined version of Fedora Core 6 will be placed in front of tens (or possibly hundreds) of millions of students worldwide. These students will learn Linux first. And Red Hat Enterprise Linux 5 is based on Fedora Core 6.

Security is another reason to move toward Linux. The U.S. National Security Agency has developed its own version of the Linux kernel to provide context-based security; RHEL has incorporated many of these improvements.

While there are Linux distributions available from a number of companies, Red Hat is far and away the market leader. Novell's acquisition of SUSE hasn't made a dent. Based on 2006 sales, Red Hat has apparently shrugged off the challenge of Oracle Linux (which is another "rebuild" of Red Hat Enterprise Linux). Incidentally, the RHCE was named #1 in CertCities.com's list of hottest certifications for 2006. Therefore, the RHCE provides the most credibility to you as a Linux professional.

The RHCT and RHCE exams are difficult. Available historical data suggests that less than 50 percent of first-time candidates pass the RHCE exam. But do not be intimidated. While there are no guarantees, this book can help you prepare for and pass the Red Hat Certified Technician and Red Hat Certified Engineer exams. And these same skills can help you in your career as a Linux administrator. Just remember, this book is not intended to be a substitute for Red Hat prep courses that I describe shortly.

To study for this exam, you should have a network of at least two Linux or Unix computers. (It's acceptable if these computers are on virtual machines such as VMware or Xen.) You need to install RHEL on at least one of these computers. That will allow you to configure Linux and test the results. After configuring a service, especially a network service, it's important to be able to check your work from another computer.

Getting Red Hat Enterprise Linux

The Red Hat exams are based on your knowledge of *Red Hat* Enterprise Linux. When you take the RHCE exam, it'll be on a "standard" PC with Intel 32-bit (or compatible) personal computers. The CPU should have a speed of at least 700MHz, and the PC should have at least 256MB of RAM. As Red Hat Network updates are not explicitly listed as a requirement in the Red Hat Exam Prep guide, a "trial" subscription or a rebuild distribution is probably sufficient. If you want a full subscription, which can help you test features associated with the Red Hat Network, the price depends on your hardware and the amount of support you need. I've emphasized *Red Hat* solely to focus on distributions that use Red Hat source code, including the "rebuilds" described in this section (and more).

With Red Hat Enterprise Linux 5, Red Hat has modified its offerings into two categories:

■ RHEL Server includes varying levels of support for entry-level to high-end and mission-critical systems.

■ The RHEL Server Advanced Platform supports unlimited virtualized guests, virtualized storage, high-availability clustering and failover, with support for more than two CPUs.

- RHEL Server subscriptions are available for IBM System Z mainframe systems on a per-processor basis.
- RHEL Server subscriptions are also available for High Performance Computing clusters.
- RHEL Desktop includes varying levels of support suitable for desktop computers and workstations. There are different options available for systems with one or more CPUs.

If you want to prepare for the RHCE exam with the official RHEL 5 server operating system, trial subscriptions are available (www.redhat.com/en_us/USA/home/developer/trial/). While they only support updates for 30 days, updates can also be tested using the mirror repositories associated with rebuild distributions. And you can download the same operating system (for the trial period) from the same sources as paying Red Hat users.

But you don't have to pay for the operating system or settle for a "trial subscription" to prepare for the RHCE exam. There are a wide variety of efforts to create "rebuilds" of Red Hat Enterprise Linux. The source code for almost all RHEL RPM packages is released under the Linux General Public License (GPL) or related licenses. This gives anyone the right to build Red Hat Enterprise Linux from the Red Hat released source code.

The source code is released in Source RPM package format, which means the RPM packages can be built using the **rpm** commands described in Chapter 5. The developers behind rebuild distributions have all revised the source code to remove Red Hat trademarks. Most, like CentOS-5, are freely available; others, like Oracle Linux, require a subscription.

on the ❗ **Job**
Oracle Linux has tried to undercut Red Hat by developing their own rebuild of Red Hat Enterprise Linux. Their subscriptions cost less at what I presume are similar support levels. As I have not tried Oracle Linux, I do not know if you get the same level of knowledge that you would get from Red Hat engineers.

You can select and download the rebuild that most closely meets your needs. I have tried several of the rebuilds, including those developed by Community Enterprise Linux (CentOS), Scientific Linux, and Lineox. All have proven reliable. In fact, they are so popular, some suggest that it has led to the demise of the Fedora Legacy project, which supported older versions of Fedora Core until December of 2006.

The rebuilds of RHEL are freely available; however, you should have a high-speed Internet connection. While these rebuilds do not use 100 percent RHEL software,

I have not seen any difference that would impair your ability to study for the
Red Hat exams.

- **Community Enterprise Linux** The Community Enterprise Operating
  System (CentOS) rebuild developed by the group at www.centos.org appears
  solid to me. This group probably has the largest community (or at least gets
  the most publicity) among the rebuilds.

- **Scientific Linux** Formerly known as Fermi Linux, it includes a lot of
  intellectual firepower associated with the Fermi National Accelerator Lab
  as well as CERN, the lab associated with Tim Berners-Lee, the person most
  commonly credited with the invention of the World Wide Web.

- **Lineox** Lineox is based in Finland and offers priority updates for a fee. It
  may be especially interesting for people in the European Union, as their
  prices are in Euros. You can find out more about Lineox at www.lineox.net.

Alternatively, you can work from RHEL Desktop, if you're willing to install
additional services from the source code. For more information on installing packages
from source code, see Chapters 1, 5, and 8. Using the techniques described in Chapter 5,
you can download the Red Hat Enterprise Linux Source RPMs at ftp.redhat.com, process
them into binary RPMs, and then install them on your computer.

For the RHCE exams based on Red Hat Enterprise Linux 5, you can *probably*
also work from Fedora Core 6, as RHEL 5 is based on this Red Hat community
distribution.

In This Book

The Red Hat RHCT and RHCE exams are designed to test candidate qualifications
as Linux systems technicians and engineers. If you pass either of these exams, it's not
because you've memorized a canned set of answers—it's because you have a set of
Linux administrative skills and know how to use them under pressure, whether it be
during an exam or in a real-world situation.

While this book is organized to serve as an in-depth review for the RHCT and
RHCE exams for both experienced Linux and Unix professionals, it is not intended
as a substitute for Red Hat courses, or more importantly, real-world experience.
Nevertheless, each chapter covers a major aspect of the exam, with an emphasis
on the "why" as well as the "how to" of working with and supporting RHEL as a
systems administrator or engineer. As the actual RHCT and RHCE Exam Prep
guide (www.redhat.com/rhce/examprep.html) changes with every release of RHEL
(and even sometimes between releases), refer to the noted URL for the latest
information. (Throughout the book, I often refer to the RHCT and RHCE Exam

Prep guide as the Red Hat Exam Prep guide, even though there are Red Hat exams for certifications other than the RHCT and RHCE.)

Red Hat says it's important to have real-world experience to pass their exams, and they're right! However, for the RHCT and RHCE exams, they do focus on a specific set of Linux administrative skills, as depicted in the Red Hat Exam Prep guide. This book is intended to help you take advantage of the skills you already have—and more importantly, brush up in those areas where you may have a bit less experience.

This book includes relevant information from Red Hat Enterprise Linux 5 (RHEL 5). There are significant changes from Red Hat Enterprise Linux 4; As of this writing, Red Hat even offers a course detailing the differences (RHUP 304 and RHUP 305). Several key differences between RHEL 4 and RHEL 5 include:

- A new hardware detection model. The udev system readily supports automatic mounting and configuration of a wide variety of devices.
- Multicore support. Fundamental to effective virtualization, multicore CPUs can help multiple operating systems run simultaneously on the same physical system. Red Hat includes Xen in RHEL 5 to take advantage of the latest multicore CPUs.
- Logical Volume Management (LVM), version 2, which supports smoother resizing of filesystems.
- Software RAID now supports more modes, including RAID 6. The associated tool is more flexible.
- NFS supports "stateless" network and loopback images.
- **yum** replaces Up2Date for repository and package management as well as updates.
- The Network Manager incorporates improvements in wireless networking and more, which eases administration on the desktop.
- SELinux is now easier to use and administer. The descriptions in the Security Level Configuration tool are improved, and **sealert -b** browser can help you diagnose many SELinux-related issues.

There are many more key features; those that I believe are relevant to the RHCT and RHCE exams, as defined by the publicly available course outlines and the Exam Prep guide, are also included in this book.

While it's a risky practice in service, it is fastest to administer RHEL during the exam by logging into the root user account. The command prompt and **PATH** assume use of that account. When you're logged into the root account, you'll see a command line prompt similar to:

```
[root@Enterprise root]#
```

As the length of this prompt would lead to a number of broken and wrapped code lines throughout this book, I've normally abbreviated the root account prompt as:

```
#
```

Be careful. The hash mark (#) is also used as a comment character in Linux scripts and programs; for example, here is an excerpt from /etc/inittab:

```
# Default runlevel. The runlevels used by RHS are:
```

When logged in as a regular user, the prompt is slightly different; for user michael, it would typically look like the following:

```
[michael@Enterprise michael]$
```

Similarly, I've abbreviated this as:

```
$
```

There are a number of command lines and code interspersed throughout the chapters.

Exam Readiness Checklist

At the end of the introduction, you will find an Exam Readiness Checklist. This table has been constructed to allow you to cross-reference the official exam objectives with the objectives as they are presented and covered in this book. The checklist also allows you to gage your level of expertise on each objective at the outset of your studies. This should allow you to check your progress and make sure you spend the time you need on more difficult or unfamiliar sections. References have been provided for the objective exactly as the vendor presents it, the section of the study guide that covers that objective, and a chapter and page reference.

In Every Chapter

For this series, we've created a set of chapter components that call your attention to important items, reinforce important points, and provide helpful exam-taking hints. Take a look at what you'll find in every chapter:

- Every chapter begins with the **Certification Objectives**—the skills you need to master in order to pass the section on the exam associated with the chapter topic. The Objective headings identify the objectives within the chapter, so you'll always know an objective when you see it.

- **Exam Watch** notes call attention to information about, and potential pitfalls in, the exam. These helpful hints are written by authors who have taken the exams and received their certification—who better to tell you what to worry about? They know what you're about to go through!

■ **Practice Exercises** are interspersed throughout the chapters. These are step-by-step exercises that allow you to get the hands-on experience you need in order to pass the exams. They help you master skills that are likely to be an area of focus on the exam. Don't just read through the exercises; they are hands-on practice that you should be comfortable completing. Learning by doing is an effective way to increase your competency with a product. Remember, the Red Hat exams are entirely "hands-on;" there are no multiple choice questions on these exams.

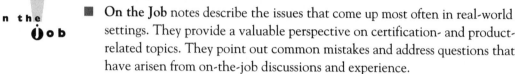

■ **On the Job** notes describe the issues that come up most often in real-world settings. They provide a valuable perspective on certification- and product-related topics. They point out common mistakes and address questions that have arisen from on-the-job discussions and experience.

■ **Inside the Exam** sidebars highlight some of the most common and confusing problems that students encounter when taking a live exam. Designed to anticipate what the exam will emphasize, getting inside the exam will help ensure you know what you need to know to pass the exam. You can get a leg up on how to respond to those difficult-to-understand labs by focusing extra attention on these sidebars.

■ **Scenario & Solution** sections lay out potential problems and solutions in a quick-to-read format.

■ The **Certification Summary** is a succinct review of the chapter and a restatement of salient skills regarding the exam.

■ The **Two-Minute Drill** at the end of every chapter is a checklist of the main points of the chapter. It can be used for last-minute review.

■ The **Self Test** offers "fill in the blank" questions designed to help test the practical knowledge associated with the certification exams. The answers to these questions, as well as explanations of the answers, can be found at the end of each chapter. By taking the Self Test after completing each chapter, you'll reinforce what you've learned from that chapter.

■ The **Lab Questions** at the end of the Self Test section offer a unique and challenging question format that requires the reader to understand multiple chapter concepts to answer correctly. These questions are more complex and more comprehensive than the other questions, as they test your ability to take all the knowledge you have gained from reading the chapter and apply it to complicated, real-world situations. Most importantly, the Red Hat exams contain *only* lab type questions. If you can answer these questions, you have proven that you know the subject!

Online Learning Center

If you'd rather take an electronic version of the Self Test questions and answers, these can also be accessed online through the book's Online Learning Center. These online exams should not stand in for an actual practice test and are not test simulations. You should complete the practice exams printed at the back of the book for a more accurate simulation of the live exam and the exam environment. The bonus content accompanying the book can also be located at the Online Learning Center.

All you need to access the Online Learning Center is an Internet connection and the following URL: http://highered.mhhe.com/sites/0072264543/.

The site also contains two Appendixes that accompany the book, available for download:

- "Installing Red Hat Enterprise Linux 5"
- "Studying with a Virtual Machine"

To access the bonus content once you have located the site, select View Student Content or click Returning Users and you should have access to all the available material. Use the drop-down menu to navigate the site.

Some Pointers

Once you've finished reading this book, set aside some time to do a thorough review. You might want to return to the book several times and make use of all the methods it offers for reviewing the material:

- *Reread all the Exam Watch notes.* Remember that these notes are written by authors who have taken the exam and passed. They know what you should expect—and what you should be on the lookout for.
- *Review all the Scenario & Solution sections* for quick problem solving.
- *Retake the Self Tests.* Focus on the labs, as there are no multiple choice (or even "fill in the blank") questions on the Red Hat exams. I've included "fill in the blank" questions just to test your mastery of the practical material in each chapter.
- *Complete the exercises.* Did you do the exercises when you read through each chapter? If not, do them! These exercises are designed to cover exam topics, and there's no better way to get to know this material than by practicing. Be sure you understand why you are performing each step in each exercise. If there is something you are not clear on, reread that section in the chapter.

The Red Hat Exam Challenge

This section covers the reasons for pursuing industry-recognized certification, explains the importance of your RHCE or RHCT certification, and prepares you for taking the actual examination. It gives you a few pointers on how to prepare, what to expect, and what to do on exam day.

Leaping Ahead of the Competition!

Red Hat's RHCT and RHCE certification exams are hands-on exams. As such, they are respected throughout the industry as a sign of genuine practical knowledge. If you pass, you will be head and shoulders above the candidate who has passed only a "standard" multiple-choice certification exam.

There are two parts to both RHCT and RHCE exams, as follows. The requirements are detailed in the Exam Readiness Checklist later in this introduction.

- **Section I** Troubleshooting and System Maintenance: (RHCE) 2.5 hours (RHCT) 1.0 hours. As described in the Red Hat Exam Prep guide, RHCE candidates need to meet the requirements for both Red Hat certifications. Both RHCT and RHCE candidates must complete *all five RHCT Troubleshooting and System Maintenance problems within the first hour*. As there are five "optional problems," RHCEs need to complete three of five of these RHCE-level problems for an overall score of 80 on this section.

- **Section II** Installation and Configuration: (RHCE) 3.0 hours (RHCT) 2.0 hours. As described in the Red Hat Exam Prep guide, RHCE candidates need to meet the requirements for both the RHCT and RHCE. RHCT candidates need a grade of 70 or higher on their section. RHCE candidates must get a grade of 70 or higher on *both* the RHCT and RHCE components of the Installation and Configuration section of your exam.

Why a Hands-On Exam?

Most certifications today are based on multiple-choice exams. These types of exams are relatively inexpensive to set up and easy to proctor. Unfortunately, many people without real-world skills are good at taking multiple-choice exams. This results in problems on the job with "certified" engineers, who have an image as "paper tigers" who do not have any real-world skills.

In response, Red Hat wanted to develop a certification program that matters. For the most part, they have succeeded with the RHCT, RHCE, and their other advanced certifications.

Linux administrators frequently debug computers with problems. The challenges in the Troubleshooting and System Maintenance sections are based on real-world problems. As the typical Linux administrator has to work through multiple challenges on a daily basis, the RHCE Troubleshooting and System Maintenance section provides a credible measure of real-world skills.

Linux administrators sometimes have to install Linux on a computer or virtual machine. Depending on the configuration, they may need to install Linux from a central source through a network. Installing Linux is not enough to make it useful. Administrators need to know how to configure Linux: add users, install and configure services, create firewalls, and more.

e x a m

ⓦ a t c h *The RHCT and RHCE exams are Red Hat exams. Knowledge of System V or BSD-based Unix is certainly helpful, as well as experience with services like Apache, SMB, NFS, DNS, iptables, and DHCP. But it is important to know how to* *set up, configure, install, and debug these services under Red Hat Enterprise Linux (or rebuild distributions that use the same source code, such as CentOS, Scientific Linux, or Lineox).*

Preparing for the RHCT and RHCE Exams

The RHCT is a complete subset of the RHCE. In other words, if you're studying for the RHCT, use this book, based on the guidelines listed in Table 2, at the end of this introduction. If you're studying for the RHCE, read the whole book. The RHCE exam includes every aspect of the RHCT exam.

Work with Red Hat Enterprise Linux. Install it on a computer (or virtual machine) that you don't need for any other purpose. Configure the services described in this book. Find ways to break network services and make Linux unbootable, study the characteristics of the problem, and find different ways to fix the problem.

As you go through this book, you'll have the opportunity to install RHEL several times. If you have more than one computer, you'll be able to install RHEL over a network. And you should, as network installations are explicitly listed in the Exam

Prep guide. Then you can work with the different network services. Test out each service as you configure it, preferably from another computer on your network. Testing your work becomes especially important when you start working with the security features of Linux.

Red Hat Certification Program

Red Hat offers several courses that can help you prepare for the RHCT and RHCE. Most of these courses are four or five days long. In some cases, you can take parts of an individual course on an electronic basis. Table 1 illustrates the available hands-on, instructor-led courses that can also help you prepare for the RHCE or RHCT exams.

These aren't the only Red Hat courses available; there are a number of others related to the Red Hat Certified Architect (RHCA) and Red Hat Certified Security Specialist (RHCSS) certifications. But study this first; the RHCE is a prerequisite for those certifications.

Should You Take an RHCT/RHCE Course?

This book is *not* intended as a substitute for the Red Hat RHCE "crash course" (RH300/301) or the RHCT prep course (RH131/RH133). However, the topics are based on the RHCE Rapid Track Course Outline and related RHCT/RHCE Exam

TABLE 1	Red Hat RHCT/RHCE Related Courses

Course	Description
RH033	Introduction to Linux: basic pre–system administration skills
RH131	Basic system administration skills for installation and configuration (RH133 without the RHCT exam)
RH133	Basic system administration skills for installation and configuration; includes the RHCT exam
RH202	The RHCT exam
RH253	Basic network and security administration; requires a basic knowledge of LANs/WANs and TCP/IP; when combined with RH133, prepares students for the RHCE exam
RH300	The crash course plus the RHCE exam
RH301	The crash course without the RHCE exam
RH302	The RHCE exam
RHUP304	Designed to update RHCEs certified on RHEL 3 and RHEL 4 to RHEL 5, plus the RHCE exam
RHUP305	The update course without the RHCE exam

Prep guide, both available at www.redhat.com. By design, these topics may help Linux users qualify as administrators and can also be used as such. Just remember, Red Hat can change these topics and course outlines at any time, so monitor www .redhat.com for the latest updates.

RH300 and RH133 are excellent courses. The Red Hat instructors who teach these courses are highly skilled. If you have the skills, it is the best way to prepare for the RHCT and RHCE exams. If you feel the need for classroom instruction, read this book, and then take the appropriate course.

If you're not sure if you're ready for the course or book, read Chapter 1. It is a rapid overview of the prerequisites for the Red Hat RHCT and RHCE certification courses. If you find the material in Chapter 1 to be overwhelming, consider one of the books noted near the start of the chapter, or one of the other Red Hat courses. However, if you are just less familiar with a few of the topics covered in Chapter 1, you're probably okay. Even experienced Linux administrators aren't familiar with everything. Just use the references noted at the beginning of Chapter 1 to fill in any gaps in your knowledge.

Alternatively, you may already be familiar with the material in this book. You may have the breadth and depth of knowledge required to pass the RHCT or RHCE exams. In that case, use this book as a refresher to help you focus on the skills and techniques you need to pass your exam.

Signing Up for the RHCT/RHCE Course and/or Exam

Red Hat provides convenient Web-based registration systems for the courses and test. To sign up for any of the Red Hat courses or exams, navigate to www.redhat.com, click the link for Training and the RHCE/RHCT Program, and select the desired course or exam. Alternatively, contact Red Hat Enrollment Central at (866) 626-2994.

Final Preparations

The Red Hat exams are grueling. Once you have the skills, the most important thing that you can take to the exam is a clear head. If you're tired or frantic, you may miss the easy solutions that are often available. Get the sleep you need the night before the exam. Eat a good breakfast. Bring snacks with you that can keep your mind in top condition.

Remember, the RHCE exam is five and a half hours long. Even the RHCT exam is three hours long. The time allotted for the RHCE exam is more than twice the length of a world-class marathon.

As I describe in Chapter 1, this is an advanced book. It is not designed for beginners to Unix or Linux. As Red Hat does not cover prerequisite skills in its prep course for the RHCT or RHCE exams, I've only covered the tools associated with these prerequisites briefly—mostly in Chapter 1. If you need more information on these prerequisite skills, Red Hat offers other courses (see www.redhat.com/apps/training/); alternatively, read the reference books I've cited in that chapter.

INSIDE THE EXAM

The RHCE exam requires that you master RHCT and RHCE skills, and assumes that you already have the prerequisite skills. I've cited them separately, as is done in the current version of the Red Hat Exam Prep guide. Watch for updates at www.redhat.com/training/rhce and www.redhat.com/training/rhce/examprep.html.

Exam RH302

| TABLE 2 | Coverage of Red Hat Exam Prep Guide Requirements |

Exam Readiness Checklist

Official Certification Objective	Study Guide Coverage	Ch #	Pg #	Prerequisite	RHCT	RHCE
Red Hat Exam Prerequisite Skills						
Use standard command line tools (e.g., **ls**, **cp**, **mv**, **rm**, **tail**, and **cat**, etc.) to create, remove, view, and investigate files and directories	Basic File Operations and Manipulation	1	19	*		
Use **grep**, **sed**, and **awk** to process text streams and file	Basic File Operations and Manipulation	1	19	*		
Use a terminal-based text editor, such as vim or nano, to modify text files	Basic Linux Knowledge	1	8	*		
Use input/output redirection	Shells	1	26	*		
Understand basic principles of TCP/IP networking, including IP addresses, netmasks, and gateways for IPv4 and IPv6	Basic TCP/IP Networking	1	38	*		
Use **su** to switch user accounts	System Administration	1	34	*		
Use **passwd** to set passwords	Basic Security	1	30	*		
Use **tar**, **gzip**, and **bzip2**	System Administration	1	34	*		
Configure an e-mail client on Red Hat Enterprise Linux	Other Basic Skills as Defined in the Exam Prep Guide	1	49	*		
Use text and/or graphical browser to access HTTP/HTTPS URLs	Other Basic Skills as Defined in the Exam Prep Guide	1	49	*		
Use lftp to access FTP URLs	Other Basic Skills as Defined in the Exam Prep Guide	1	49	*		
RHCT Troubleshooting and System Maintenance Skills					*	
Boot systems into different run levels for troubleshooting and system maintenance	Troubleshooting Strategies	16	728		*	
Diagnose and correct misconfigured networking	Network Configuration	7	331		*	
Diagnose and correct hostname resolution problems	Understanding DNS: Zones, Domains, and Delegation	11	559		*	
Configure the X Window System and a desktop environment	X Window System (entire chapter)	14	649		*	

Exam Readiness Checklist

Official Certification Objective	Study Guide Coverage	Ch	Pg #	Prerequisite	RHCT	RHCE
Add new partitions, filesystems, and swap to existing systems	Partitioning Hard Disks; Managing Filesystems; Advanced Partitioning: Software RAID; Advanced Partitioning: Logical Volume Management	4, 8	185, 196, 410, 417		*	
Use standard command-line tools to analyze problems and configure system	Entire book	all			*	
RHCE Troubleshooting and System Maintenance Skills						
Use the rescue environment provided by first installation CD	Troubleshooting Strategies	16	728			*
Diagnose and correct boot loader failures arising from boot loader, module, and filesystem errors	The GRUB Bootloader, Managing Filesystems, The Basics of the Kernel, Required RHCE Troubleshooting Skills	3, 4, 8, 16	147, 196, 377, 742			*
Diagnose and correct problems with network services (see the following Installation and Configuration skills for a list of these services)		7, 9, 10, 11, 12, 13, 14, 15	329, 443, 493, 557, 585, 613, 649, 691			*
Add, remove, and resize logical volumes	Configuring Partitions, RAID, and LVM; Advanced Partitioning: Logical Volume Management	2, 8	96, 417			*
Diagnose and correct networking service problems where SELinux contexts are interfering with proper operation		7, 9, 10, 11, 12, 13, 14, 15	329, 443, 493, 557, 585, 613, 649, 691			*
RHCT Installation and Configuration Skills						
Perform network OS installation	Configuring a Network Installation	2	81		*	
Implement a custom partitioning scheme	Configuring Partitions, RAID, and LVM	2	96		*	
Configure printing	The CUPS Printing System	7	341		*	

Exam Readiness Checklist

Official Certification Objective	Study Guide Coverage	Ch	Pg #	Prerequisite	RHCT	RHCE
Configure the scheduling of tasks using **cron** and **at**	Automating System Administration: cron and at	7	354		*	
Attach system to a network directory service, such as NIS or LDAP	Network Authentication Configuration: NIS and LDAP	6	313		*	
Configure **autofs**	Filesystem Management and the Automounter	4	200		*	
Add and manage users, groups, and quotas, and File Access Control Lists	User Account Management, The Basic User Environment, Setting Up and Managing Disk Quotas	6	273, 285, 290		*	
Configure filesystem permissions for collaboration	Creating and Maintaining Special Groups	6	301		*	
Install and update packages using **rpm**	The Red Hat Package Manager, More RPM Commands	5	222, 227		*	
Properly update the kernel package	New Kernels, the Easy Way	8	388		*	
Configure the system to update/install packages from remote repositories using yum or pup	Adding and Removing RPM Packages with yum and pirut, Managing Updates with Pup and the Red Hat Network (RHN)	5	238, 234		*	
Modify the system boot loader	New Kernels, the Easy Way; Kernel Sources	8	388, 392		*	
Implement software RAID at install-time and runtime	Configuring Partitions, RAID, and LVM; Advanced Partitioning: Software RAID	2, 8	96, 410		*	
Use /proc/sys and **sysctl** to modify and set kernel runtime parameters	The Basics of the Kernel	8	377		*	
Use scripting to automate system maintenance tasks	Automating System Administration: cron and at	7	329		*	
RHCE Installation and Configuration Skills						
For HTTP/HTTPS, install, configure SELinux support, configure to start on reboot for basic operation and host- and user-based security	The Apache Web Server, Virtual Hosts, Apache Access Configuration	9	444, 466, 456			*

Exam Readiness Checklist

Official Certification Objective	Study Guide Coverage	Ch	Pg #	Prerequisite	RHCT	RHCE
For SMB, install, configure SELinux support, configure to start on reboot for basic operation and host- and user-based security	Samba Services	10	516			*
For NFS, install, configure SELinux support, configure to start on reboot for basic operation and host- and user-based security	Configuring a Network File System (NFS) Server, Client-side NFS	10	494, 509			*
For FTP, install, configure SELinux support, configure to start on reboot for basic operation and host- and user-based security	The File Transfer Protocol and vsFTPd	10	512			*
For Web proxy, install, configure SELinux support, configure to start on reboot for basic operation and host- and user-based security	The Squid Web Cache Proxy	9	476			*
For SMTP, install, configure SELinux support, configure to start on reboot for basic operation and host- and user-based security	Electronic Mail (entire chapter)	12	585			*
For IMAP/IMAPS/POP3, install, configure SELinux support, configure to start on reboot for basic operation and host- and user-based security	Reception with Dovecot	12	589			*
For SSH, install, configure SELinux support, configure to start on reboot for basic operation and host- and user-based security	The Secure Shell Package	13	620			*
For DNS (caching name server, slave name server), install, configure SELinux support, configure to start on reboot for basic operation and host- and user-based security	Domain Name Service (entire chapter)	11	557			*
For NTP, install, configure SELinux support, configure to start on reboot for basic operation and host- and user-based security	The Network Time Protocol (NTP)	13	634			*
Configure hands-free installation using Kickstart	Using Kickstart to Automate Installation	5	244			*
Implement logical volumes at install-time	Configuring Partitions, RAID, and LVM	2	96			*
Use **iptables** to implement packet filtering and/or NAT	Firewalls and Packet Filtering using netfilter, Network Address Translation	15	697, 703			*
Use PAM to implement user-level restrictions	Pluggable Authentication Modules	6	305			*

1
RHCE
Prerequisites

CERTIFICATION OBJECTIVES

1.01	Basic Hardware Knowledge
1.02	Basic Linux Knowledge
1.03	Linux Filesystem Hierarchy and Structure
1.04	Basic File Operations and Manipulation
1.05	Printing
1.06	Shells
1.07	Basic Security
1.08	System Administration
1.09	Basic TCP/IP Networking
1.10	Familiarity with Standard Network Services
1.11	Basic Network Security
1.12	Other Basic Prerequisite Skills per the Red Hat Exam Prep Guide
1.13	Downloading the Red Hat Enterprise Linux Installation CDs
✓	Two-Minute Drill
Q&A	Self Test

The Red Hat exams are an advanced challenge. As both the RHCE and RHCT courses specify a number of prerequisite skills, this book assumes that you know some basics about Linux. This chapter covers the prerequisite topics for Red Hat's RH300 course in a minimum of detail, with references to other books and sources for more information. It also covers the related prerequisites as defined in the Red Hat Exam Prep guide. Unlike those in other chapters and other books in this series, the questions in this chapter include a number of "zingers" that go beyond the chapter's content. These questions will help determine whether you have the prerequisite skills necessary to handle the remaining chapters.

If you're serious about the RHCE and RHCT exams, this chapter should be just a review. In fact, for any user serious about Linux, this chapter should be trivial. Linux gurus should recognize that I've "oversimplified" a number of explanations; my intention is to keep this chapter as short as possible. However, it is okay if you do not feel comfortable with a few topics in this chapter. In fact, it's quite natural that many experienced Linux administrators don't use every one of the prerequisite topics in their everyday work. Many candidates are able to fill in the gaps in their knowledge with some self-study and practice.

If you're new to Linux or Unix, this chapter will not be enough for you. It's not possible to provide sufficient detail, at least in a way that can be understood by newcomers to Linux and other Unix-based operating systems. If, after reading this chapter, you find gaps in your knowledge, refer to one of the following guides:

- The *Red Hat Enterprise Linux 5* documentation guides, available online from http://www.redhat.com/docs/manuals/enterprise/.
- *Hacking Linux Exposed, Third Edition: Linux Security Secrets and Solutions*, by Casarik, Hatch, Lee, and Kurtz, gives you a detailed look at how to secure your Linux system and networks in every possible way.
- *Mastering Fedora Core 5*, by Michael Jang, covers the distribution that Red Hat used as one of the testbeds for RHEL 5.

Critical to a Linux administrator is knowledge of one or more text editors to manage the many configuration files on a Linux system. The Linux filesystem hierarchy organizes hardware, drivers, directories, and, of course, files. You need to master a number of basic commands to manage Linux. Printer configuration can be a complex topic. Shell scripts enable you to automate many everyday processes. Security is now a huge issue that Linux can handle better than other operating systems, both locally and on larger networks such as the Internet.

As an administrator, you need a good knowledge of basic system administration commands, TCP/IP configuration requirements, and standard network services. While the RHCE and RHCT exams are by and large not hardware exams, some basic hardware knowledge is a fundamental requirement for any Linux administrator.

This is not a book for beginners to Linux/Unix-type operating systems. Some of what you read in this chapter may be unfamiliar. Use this chapter to create a list of topics that you may need to study further. In some cases, you'll be able to get up to speed with the material in other chapters. But if you have less experience with Linux or another Unix-type operating system, you may want to refer to the aforementioned books.

If you're experienced with other Unix-type operating systems such as Solaris, AIX, or HP-UX, you may need to leave some defaults at the door. When Red Hat developed its Linux distribution, it included a number of things that are not consistent with the standards of Unix (or even other Linux distributions). When I took the RH300 course, some students with these backgrounds had difficulties with the course and the RHCE exam.

In this book, most commands are run as the Linux administrative user, root. Logging in as the root user is normally discouraged unless you're administering a computer. However, since the RHCE and RHCT exams test your administrative skills, it's appropriate to run commands in this book as the root user.

While this chapter is based on the prerequisites described at https://www .redhat.com/training/rhce/courses/rh300_prereq.html, there are several additional prerequisite skills defined in the Red Hat Exam Prep guide at https://www.redhat .com/training/rhce/examprep.html.

INSIDE THE EXAM

Prerequisite Skills

For the RHCE and RHCT exams, the skills outlined in this chapter are generally minimum requirements. For example, while you may prefer to use an editor other than vi, you may not have access to the GUI, and therefore need to know how to use a console-based text editor on at least the Troubleshooting and System Maintenance section of the exam. While you're not required to know how to pipe the output of **dmesg** to the **less** command, this is a useful tool that can help you identify problems.

Remember that there are more ways than one to do most everything in Linux. While it's best if you learn all of these "prerequisite" skills, you don't have to know everything in this chapter. In most cases, it's okay if you use other methods of editing or otherwise configuring your RHEL 5 system. As the Red Hat exams no longer include multiple choice questions, don't worry about memorizing the dozens of switches used for certain commands. Focus on results, not trivia.

Using Other Versions of Red Hat

For those of you with more advanced hardware experience, the Red Hat exams are based on PCs built with Intel 32-bit CPUs. That means you'll be using the Linux kernel and associated software that has been customized for this CPU.

For the purpose of this chapter, you can use Fedora Core 6 or one of the rebuild distributions to test your knowledge of basic commands. In fact, the rebuild distributions are excellent, freely available options, as they use the same source code as Red Hat uses to build RHEL 5. One list of rebuild options is available at http://linuxmafia.com/faq/RedHat/rhel-forks.html.

CERTIFICATION OBJECTIVE 1.01

Basic Hardware Knowledge

The architecture of a PC defines the components that it uses as well as the way that they are connected. In other words, the Intel-based architecture describes much more than just the CPU. It includes standards for other hardware such as the hard drive, the network card, the keyboard, the graphics adapter, and more. All software is written for a specific computer architecture, such as the Intel-based 32-bit architecture.

Even when a manufacturer creates a device for the Intel platform, it may not work with Linux. Therefore, it's important to know the basic architecture of an Intel-based computer.

Architectures

While different versions of RHEL 5 are available for a variety of architectures, you need to be concerned about only one for the Red Hat exams, the basic Intel 32-bit or i386 architecture. As of this writing, the Red Hat exams are offered only on computers with such CPUs, so you need not worry about special architecture-specific issues such as ELILO bootloaders or lib64 module directories.

Intel Communications Channels

Three basic channels are used to communicate in a basic PC: interrupt request (IRQ) ports, input/output (I/O) addresses, and direct memory address (DMA) channels. An IRQ allows a component such as a keyboard or printer to request service from the CPU. An I/O address is a memory storage location for communication between the CPU and different parts of a computer. A DMA channel is used when a device such as a sound card has an independent processor and can bypass the CPU.

With the plug and play features built into RHEL 5, these channels are generally not a problem but are included because they are on the prerequisite list for the RH300 course.

IRQ Settings

An *IRQ* is a signal that is sent by a peripheral device (such as a network card, graphics adapter, mouse, modem, or serial port) to the CPU to request processing time. Each device you attach to a computer may need its own IRQ port. Normally, each device needs a dedicated IRQ (except for USB and some PCI devices).

If you run out of IRQs, some PCI devices can share IRQs. USB devices can share IRQs. This support is available in most PCs manufactured after the year 2000.

on the
job
If you're having a problem with your USB ports or PCI cards, check your BIOS first. Many BIOS menus include options that enable PCI sharing and support USB connections.

Planning the IRQ Layout: Standard IRQs

IRQs are a precious commodity on some PCs. IRQ conflicts are common when you're connecting a lot of devices. If your printer doesn't work after you've connected a second network card, it can help to know the standard IRQ for printers. You can then assign a different IRQ to that network card. If you don't have any free IRQs to assign to that network card, you may be able to sacrifice a component that uses a standard IRQ. For example, if you always connect to a server remotely, that server PC may not need a keyboard. If you can boot a computer with a CD-ROM, you may not need a floppy drive.

Some IRQs are essential to the operation of a PC and just can't be changed. These are reserved by the motherboard to control devices such as the hard disk controller and the real-time clock. Do not use these interrupts for other devices or there will be conflicts! Other IRQs are normally assigned to common devices such as a floppy drive and a printer. In Linux, you can check /proc/interrupts to see which interrupts are being used and which are free for new devices.

Input/Output Addresses

Every computer device requires an *input/output (I/O) address*. It's a place where data can wait in line for service from your CPU. I/O addresses are listed in hexadecimal notation, where the "numbers" are 0, 1, 2, 3, 4, 5, 6, 7, 8, 9, a, b, c, d, e, and f. Some typical I/O addresses include those for the basic serial ports, known in the Microsoft world as COM1, COM2, COM3, and COM4. These ports normally use the following I/O addresses: 03f8, 02f8, 03e8, and 02e8.

You can find a list of assigned I/O addresses in your /proc/ioports file.

Direct Memory Addresses

A *direct memory address (DMA)* is normally used to transfer information directly between devices, bypassing the CPU. Many components don't need a CPU. For example, many sound cards include their own processor. This allows your PC to set up a DMA channel between a hard drive and a sound card to process and play any music files that you may have stored.

While DMA channels bypass the CPU, devices that use DMA are still configured with IRQ ports. There are eight standard DMA channels (0–7); DMA 4 is reserved and cannot be used by any device.

You can find a list of assigned DMA addresses in your /proc/dma file.

RAM Requirements

While I've installed RHEL 5 on computers with less RAM, 256MB is a good practical minimum.

The maximum amount of memory your system will use is the sum of all of the memory requirements of every program that you will ever run at once. That's hard to compute. Therefore, you should buy as much memory as you can afford. Extra RAM is usually cost effective when compared to the time you would spend trying to tune an underpowered system. Limitations are few; on Red Hat Enterprise Linux 5 Advanced Platform (with PAE support), RAM is limited only by the ability of the hardware to handle it.

on the
① o b

If you're setting up Linux as a server, RAM requirements increase with the number of users who may need to log in simultaneously. The same may be true if you're running a large number of programs or have memory-intensive data such as that required by a database.

Hard Drive Options

Before your computer can load Linux, the BIOS has to recognize the active primary partition on the hard drive. This partition should include the Linux boot files. The BIOS can then set up and initialize that hard drive, and then load Linux boot files from that active primary partition. You should know the following about hard drives and Linux:

- The standard PC is configured to manage up to four IDE (Integrated Drive Electronics) hard drives, now known as PATA (Parallel Advanced Technology Attachment) drives.

- Newer PCs can handle more SATA (Serial ATA) drives.

- Depending on the SCSI (Small Computer Systems Interface) hardware that you have, you can attach up to 31 different SCSI hard drives.

- While you can use as many PATA, SATA, or SCSI drives as your hardware can handle, you need to install the Linux boot files from the /boot directory on one of the first two hard drives. If Linux is installed on a later drive, you'll need a boot floppy.

- Although you can install Linux on USB (Universal Serial Bus) or IEEE 1394 (Institute of Electrical and Electronics Engineers standard 1394, also known as FireWire or iLink) hard drives, as of this writing, you can't load Linux boot files directly from these drives. However, it is possible to set up a boot floppy or CD/DVD to start Linux from these drives.

CERTIFICATION OBJECTIVE 1.02

Basic Linux Knowledge

Linux and Unix are managed through a series of text files. Linux administrators do not normally use graphical editors to manage these configuration files. Editors such as WordPerfect, OpenOffice.org Writer, and yes, even Microsoft Word normally save files in a binary format that Linux can't read.

Popular text editors for Linux configuration files include nano, pico, joe, and vi. If you already know one of these editors, feel free to skip this section. If you have to rescue an RHEL 5 system (as may be required during the exam), you'll have access to these editors when booting your system from RHEL 5 rescue media.

The VIsual Editor

While emacs may be the most popular and flexible text editor in the world of Linux, I believe every administrator needs at least a basic knowledge of vi, which may help you save a broken system. If you ever have to restore a critical configuration file using an emergency boot floppy, vi is probably the only editor that you'll have available.

In reality, RHEL 5 uses an enhanced version of the vi editor, known as vim. And as RHEL emergency boot media access installation packages, it supports more console-based editors. I describe vi here simply because it's the editor I know best.

on the **ĴOb**

If you boot in rescue mode and try to start emacs or pico, that starts the joe editor instead.

You should know how to use the two basic modes of vi: command and insert. When you use vi to open a file, it opens in command mode. Some of the commands start insert mode. Opening a file is easy: just use the **vi** *filename* command. By default, this starts vi in command mode. An example of vi with the /etc/inittab file is shown in Figure 1-1.

The following is only the briefest of introductions to the vi editor. For more information, there are a number of books available, as well as an extensive manual formatted as a HOWTO available from the Linux Documentation Project at www .tldp.org. Alternatively, a tutorial is available through the **vimtutor** command.

FIGURE 1-1

The vi editor with
/etc/inittab

```
#
# inittab       This file describes how the INIT process should set up
#               the system in a certain run-level.
#
# Author:       Miquel van Smoorenburg, <miquels@drinkel.nl.mugnet.org>
#               Modified for RHS Linux by Marc Ewing and Donnie Barnes
#

# Default runlevel. The runlevels used by RHS are:
#   0 - halt (Do NOT set initdefault to this)
#   1 - Single user mode
#   2 - Multiuser, without NFS (The same as 3, if you do not have networking)
#   3 - Full multiuser mode
#   4 - unused
#   5 - X11
#   6 - reboot (Do NOT set initdefault to this)
#
id:5:initdefault:

# System initialization.
si::sysinit:/etc/rc.d/rc.sysinit

l0:0:wait:/etc/rc.d/rc 0
"/etc/inittab" [readonly] 53L, 1663C
```

vi Command Mode

In command mode, you can do everything you need to a text file except edit it.
The options in command mode are broad and varied, and they are the subject of a
number of book-length texts. In summary, vi requires seven critical command skills:

- **Open** To open a file in the vi editor from the command line interface, run
  the **vi** *filename* command.
- **Search** Start with a backslash, followed by the search term. Remember,
  Linux is case-sensitive, so if you're searching for "Michael" in /etc/passwd,
  use the **/Michael** (not **/michael**) command.
- **Write** To save your changes, use the **w** command. You can combine
  commands: for example, **:wq** writes the file and exits vi.
- **Close** To leave vi, use the **:q** command.
- **Abandon** If you want to abandon any changes that you've made, use the **:q!**
  command.
- **Edit** You can use a number of commands to edit files through vi, such as
  x, which deletes the currently highlighted character; **dw**, which deletes the
  currently highlighted word; and **dd**, which deletes the current line. Remember,
  p places text from a buffer, and **U** restores text from a previous change.
- **Insert** A number of commands allow you to start insert mode, including **i**
  to start inserting text at the current position of the editor, and **o** to open up
  a new line immediately below the current position of the cursor.

Basic Text Editing

In modern Linux systems, editing files with vi is easy. Just use the normal navigation keys (arrow keys, PAGE UP, and PAGE DOWN), and then one of the basic commands such as **i** or **o** to start vi's insert mode, and type your changes directly into the file.

When you're finished with insert mode, press the ESC key to return to command mode. You can then save your changes or abandon them and exit vi.

on the
Job

There are several specialized variations on the vi command. Three are vipw, vigw, and visudo, which edit /etc/passwd, /etc/group, and /etc/sudoers, respectively.

EXERCISE 1-1

Using vi to Create a New User

In this exercise, you'll create a new user by editing the /etc/passwd file with the vi text editor. While you could create new Linux users in other ways, this exercise helps you verify your skills with vi and at the command line interface.

1. Open a Linux command line interface. Log in as the root user, and type the **vipw** command. This command uses the vi editor to open /etc/passwd.

2. Navigate to the last line in the file. As you should already know, there are several ways to navigate in command mode, including the DOWN ARROW key, the PAGE DOWN key, the **G** command, or even the K key.

3. Make one copy of this line. If you're already comfortable with vi, you should know that you can copy an entire line to the buffer with the **yy** command. This "yanks" the line into buffer. You can then restore or "put" that line as many times as desired with the **p** command.

4. Change the username, user ID, group ID, user comment, and home directory for the new user. If you understand the basics of Linux or Unix, you'll understand their locations on each line in the /etc/passwd file. For example, in Figure 1-2, this corresponds to gb, 501, 501, Gordon Brown, and /home/gb. Make sure the username also corresponds to the home directory.

5. Return to command mode by pressing the ESC key. Save the file with the **:w** command, and then exit with the **:q** command. (You can combine the two commands in vi; the next time you make a change and want to save and exit, run the **:wq** command.)

6. As the root user, run the **passwd** *newuser* command. Assign the password of your choice to the new user.

FIGURE 1-2

Adding a new
user in /etc/
passwd

```
netdump:x:34:34:Network Crash Dump user:/var/crash:/bin/bash
avahi:x:70:70:Avahi daemon:/:/sbin/nologin
named:x:25:25:Named:/var/named:/sbin/nologin
mailnull:x:47:47::/var/spool/mqueue:/sbin/nologin
smmsp:x:51:51::/var/spool/mqueue:/sbin/nologin
haldaemon:x:68:68:HAL daemon:/:/sbin/nologin
rpc:x:32:32:Portmapper RPC user:/:/sbin/nologin
rpcuser:x:29:29:RPC Service User:/var/lib/nfs:/sbin/nologin
nfsnobody:x:4294967294:4294967294:Anonymous NFS User:/var/lib/nfs:/sbin/nologin
sshd:x:74:74:Privilege-separated SSH:/var/empty/sshd:/sbin/nologin
xfs:x:43:43:X Font Server:/etc/X11/fs:/sbin/nologin
beagleindex:x:58:58:User for Beagle indexing:/var/cache/beagle:/bin/false
distcache:x:94:94:Distcache:/:/sbin/nologin
ntp:x:38:38::/etc/ntp:/sbin/nologin
squid:x:23:23::/var/spool/squid:/sbin/nologin
dovecot:x:97:97:dovecot:/usr/libexec/dovecot:/sbin/nologin
mysql:x:27:27:MySQL Server:/var/lib/mysql:/bin/bash
webalizer:x:67:67:Webalizer:/var/www/usage:/sbin/nologin
hsqldb:x:96:96::/var/lib/hsqldb:/sbin/nologin
gdm:x:42:42::/var/gdm:/sbin/nologin
postfix:x:89:89::/var/spool/postfix:/sbin/nologin
michael:x:500:500::/home/michael:/bin/bash
gb:x:501:501:Gordon Brown:/home/gb:/bin/bash
```

```
                                                        23,1          Bot
```

Other Text Editors

You can use any available text editor during the Red Hat exams. But do not count
on any GUI text editors, as the GUI may not be available for troubleshooting during
the exam, or in real life.

CERTIFICATION OBJECTIVE 1.03

Linux Filesystem Hierarchy and Structure

Everything in Linux can be reduced to a file. Partitions are associated with *filesystem
device nodes* such as /dev/hda1. Hardware components are associated with node files
such as /dev/dvd. Detected devices are documented as files in the /proc directory.
The Filesystem Hierarchy Standard (FHS) is the official way to organize files in
Unix and Linux directories. As with the other sections, this introduction provides
only the most basic overview of the FHS. More information is available from the
official FHS homepage at www.pathname.com/fhs.

Linux Filesystems and Directories

Several major directories are associated with all modern Unix/Linux operating systems. These directories organize user files, drivers, kernels, logs, programs, utilities, and more into different categories. The standardization of the FHS makes it easier for users of other Unix-based operating systems to understand the basics of Linux.

Every FHS starts with the root directory, also known by its symbol, the single forward slash (/). All of the other directories shown in Table 1-1 are subdirectories of the root directory. Unless they are mounted separately, you can also find their files on the same partition as the root directory. You may not see some of the directories shown in the table if you have not installed associated packages. Not all directories shown are officially part of the FHS.

Mounted directories are often known as *volumes*, which can span multiple partitions. However, while the root directory (/) is the top-level directory in the FHS, the root user's home directory (/root) is just a subdirectory.

In Linux, the word filesystem *has several different meanings. For example, a* filesystem *can refer to the FHS, an individual partition, or a format such as ext3. A filesystem device node such as /dev/sda1 represents the partition on which you can mount a directory.*

A Variety of Media Devices

Several basic types of media are accessible to most PCs, including PATA, SATA, and SCSI hard disks; floppy drives; DVD/CD drives; and more. Other media are accessible through other PC ports, including serial, parallel, USB, and IEEE 1394 systems. You can use Linux to manage all of these types of media.

Most media devices are detected automatically. Linux may require a bit of help for some devices described in Chapter 2. But in the context of the Linux FHS, media devices, like all others, are part of the /dev directory. Typical media devices are described in Table 1-2.

Making Reference to Devices in /dev

Take a look at the files in the /dev directory. Use the **ls -l /dev | more** command. Scroll through the list for a while. The list actually used to be longer. Well, there's a method to this madness. Some devices are linked to others, and that actually makes it easier to understand what is connected to what. For example, the virtual device files /dev/cdrom and /dev/dvd are easier to identify than the true device files. Generally, these devices are automatically linked to the actual device files during

TABLE 1-1   Basic Filesystem Hierarchy Standard Directories

Directory	Description
/	The root directory, the top-level directory in the FHS. All other directories are subdirectories of root, which is always mounted on some partition.
/bin	Essential command line utilities. Should not be mounted separately; otherwise, it could be difficult to get to these utilities when using a rescue disk.
/boot	Includes Linux startup files, including the Linux kernel. The default, 100MB, is usually sufficient for a typical modular kernel and additional kernels that you might install during the RHCE or RHCT exam.
/dev	Hardware and software device drivers for everything from floppy drives to terminals. Do not mount this directory on a separate partition.
/etc	Most basic configuration files.
/home	Home directories for almost every user.
/lib	Program libraries for the kernel and various command line utilities. Do not mount this directory on a separate partition.
/media	The mount point for removable media, including floppy drives, DVDs, and Zip disks.
/misc	The standard mount point for local directories mounted via the automounter.
/mnt	A legacy mount point; formerly used for removable media.
/net	The standard mount point for network directories mounted via the automounter.
/opt	Common location for third-party application files.
/proc	Currently running kernel-related processes, including device assignments such as IRQ ports, I/O addresses, and DMA channels, as well as kernel configuration settings such as IP forwarding.
/root	The home directory of the root user.
/sbin	System administration commands. Don't mount this directory separately.
/selinux	Currently configured settings associated with Security Enhanced Linux.
/smb	The standard mount point for remote shared Microsoft network directories mounted via the automounter.
/srv	Commonly used by various network servers on non–Red Hat distributions.
/tftpboot	Included if the TFTP server is installed.
/tmp	Temporary files. By default, Red Hat Enterprise Linux deletes all files in this directory periodically.
/usr	Small programs accessible to all users. Includes many system administration commands and utilities.
/var	Variable data, including log files and printer spools.

TABLE 1-2	Media Devices

Media Device	Device File
Floppy drive	First floppy (Microsoft A: drive) = /dev/fd0 Second floppy (Microsoft B: drive) = /dev/fd1
PATA (IDE) hard drive PATA (IDE) CD/DVD drive	First drive = /dev/hda Second drive = /dev/hdb Third drive = /dev/hdc Fourth drive = /dev/hdd
SATA or SCSI hard drive SATA or SCSI CD/DVD drive	First drive = /dev/sda Second drive = /dev/sdb ... Twenty-seventh drive = /dev/sdaa and so on
Parallel port drives	First drive = /dev/pd1 First tape drive: /dev/pt1
USB drives	Varies widely
IEEE 1394 drives	IEEE 1394 (a.k.a. FireWire, iLink) is actually a SCSI standard, so these are controlled in Linux as SCSI devices.

Linux installation. For example, if you have a printer and DVD writer installed, the following commands illustrate possible links between these components and the actual device files:

```
# ls -l /dev/par0
lrwxrwxrwx  1 root   root   3 Mar 29 09:37 /dev/par0 -> lp0
# ls -l /dev/dvd
lrwxrwxrwx  1 root   root   3 Mar 29 09:37 /dev/dvd -> hdd
```

These commands show that /dev/par0 is linked directly to the first printer port, and that /dev/dvd is linked directly to the fourth PATA drive.

Filesystem Formatting and Checking

Three basic tools are available to manage the filesystem on various partitions: **fdisk**, **mkfs**, and **fsck**. They can help you configure partitions as well as create, check, and repair different filesystems.

Yes, there are more options, such as **parted**. But this chapter covers only the very basics as described in the Red Hat prerequisites; for more information, see the man page associated with each respective command tool.

INSIDE THE EXAM

Running as Root

Throughout the book, I'm assuming that you're running commands after having logged in as the root user. While it may not be the best practice on the job, it can save you a little bit of time on the RHCT and RHCE exams. For example, if you've logged in as a regular user, you'd start **fdisk** with the **/sbin/fdisk** command. This applies even if you've taken administrative privileges with the **su** command. (I know, you could take administrative privileges with the root user PATH with the **su - root** command, but time is of the essence on these exams.) On the other hand, if you log in as the root user, you can take advantage of a different **$PATH**, which means all you need to type is **fdisk**.

fdisk

The Linux **fdisk** utility is a lot more versatile than its Microsoft counterpart. But to open it, you need to know the device file associated with the hard drive that you want to change. Identifying the hard disk device file is covered in Chapter 2. Assuming you want to manage the partitions on the first SCSI hard disk, enter the following command:

```
# fdisk /dev/sda
```

As you can see in Figure 1-3, the **fdisk** utility is flexible. Some key **fdisk** commands are described in Table 1-3.

mkfs

To format a Linux partition, apply the **mkfs** command. It allows you to format a partition to a number of different filesystems. To format a typical partition such as /dev/hda2 to the current Red Hat standard, the third extended filesystem, run the following command:

```
# mkfs -t ext3 /dev/hda2
```

The **mkfs** command also serves as a "front end," depending on the filesystem format. For example, if you're formatting a Red Hat standard ext3 filesystem, **mkfs** automatically calls the **mkfs.ext3** command. Therefore, if you're reformatting an ext3 filesystem, the following command is sufficient:

```
# mkfs /dev/hda2
```

FIGURE 1-3

Linux **fdisk** commands; **p** returns the partition table

```
Command (m for help): m
Command action
   a   toggle a bootable flag
   b   edit bsd disklabel
   c   toggle the dos compatibility flag
   d   delete a partition
   l   list known partition types
   m   print this menu
   n   add a new partition
   o   create a new empty DOS partition table
   p   print the partition table
   q   quit without saving changes
   s   create a new empty Sun disklabel
   t   change a partition's system id
   u   change display/entry units
   v   verify the partition table
   w   write table to disk and exit
   x   extra functionality (experts only)

Command (m for help): p

Disk /dev/sda: 82.3 GB, 82348277760 bytes
255 heads, 63 sectors/track, 10011 cylinders
Units = cylinders of 16065 * 512 = 8225280 bytes

   Device Boot     Start        End      Blocks   Id  System
/dev/sda1   *          1         24      192748+  83  Linux
/dev/sda2             25       1848    14651280   83  Linux
/dev/sda3           1849       1970      979965   82  Linux swap / Solaris
/dev/sda4           1971      10011    64589332+   5  Extended
/dev/sda5           1971       1983      104391   83  Linux
/dev/sda6           1984       3258    10241406   83  Linux
/dev/sda7           3259       5083    14659281    c  W95 FAT32 (LBA)
/dev/sda8           5084       6300     9775521   83  Linux
/dev/sda9           6301      10011    29808576   83  Linux

Command (m for help):
```

TABLE 1-3

Important **fdisk** Options

fdisk Command	Description
a	Allows you to specify the bootable Linux partition (with /boot).
l	Lists known partition types; **fdisk** can create partitions that conform to any of these filesystems.
n	Adds a new partition; works only if there is free space on the disk that hasn't already been allocated to an existing partition.
q	Quits without saving any changes.
t	Changes the partition filesystem; you'll still need to format appropriately.

on the Job *Be careful with the mkfs command. Back up any data on the subject partition and computer, as this command erases all data on the specified partition.*

fsck

The **fsck** command is functionally similar to the Microsoft **chkdsk** command. It analyzes the specified filesystem and performs repairs as required. Assume, for example, you're having problems with files in the /var directory, which happens to be mounted on /dev/hda7. If you want to run fsck, unmount that filesystem first. In some cases, you may need to go into single-user mode with the **init 1** command before you can unmount a filesystem. To unmount, analyze, and then remount the filesystem noted in this section, run the following commands:

```
# umount /var
# fsck -t ext3 /dev/hda7
# mount /dev/hda7 /var
```

The **fsck** command also serves as a "front end," depending on the filesystem format. For example, if you're formatting an ext2 or ext3 filesystem, **fsck** by itself automatically calls the **e2fsck** command (which works for both filesystems). Therefore, if you're checking an ext3 filesystem, once you unmount it with the **umount** command, the following command is sufficient:

```
# fsck /dev/hda7
```

Configuring One Filesystem on Multiple Partitions

The Logical Volume Manager (LVM) enables you to set up one filesystem on multiple partitions. For example, assume you're adding more users and are running out of room in your /home directory. You don't have any unpartitioned space available on your current hard disk.

With the LVM, all you need to do is add another hard disk, configure some partitions, back up /home, and use the LVM tools to combine the new partition and the one used by /home into a volume set. You may need to install the LVM RPM package. Once it is installed, the steps are fairly straightforward, as described in the following exercise.

![EXERCISE 1-2]

Creating a New LVM Partition

LVM is more important than the prerequisite skills covered in most of this chapter. The latest available Red Hat Exam Prep guide includes LVM requirements on both parts of the RHCE exam. For more information on LVM, see Chapters 2 and 8.

1. Add a new hard disk.
2. Create new partitions. Assign the Linux LVM filesystem to one or more of these partitions. This can be easily done with the Linux fdisk utility.
3. Back up /home. Assign the LVM filesystem to that partition.
4. Scan for Linux LVM filesystems with the vgscan utility to create a database for other LVM commands.
5. Create volumes for the set with the **pvcreate /dev/partition** command.
6. Add the desired volumes to a specific volume group with the **vgcreate** *groupname /dev/partition1 /dev/partition2 ...* command.
7. Now you can create a logical volume. Use the **lvcreate -L xyM -n** *volname groupname* command, where *xy* is the size of the volume and *groupname* is the volume group name from the previous step.
8. Finally, you can format the logical volume with the **mkfs** command for the desired filesystem (usually ext2 or ext3), using the device name returned by the **lvcreate** command.

I describe this process in more detail in Chapter 8.

Mounting Other Partitions

The **mount** command can be used to attach local and network partitions to specified directories. Mount points are not fixed; you can mount a CD drive or even a Samba share to any empty directory where you have appropriate permissions.

There are standard mount points based on the FHS. The following commands mount a floppy with the VFAT filesystem, a CD formatted to the ISO 9660 filesystem, and a Zip drive. The devices may be different on your system; if in doubt, look though the startup messages with **dmesg | less**.

```
# mount -t vfat /dev/fd0 /mnt/floppy
# mount -t iso9660 /dev/cdrom /mnt/cdrom
# mount /dev/sdc
```

Other mount points are available through the automounter. Once configured, other systems and even shared network directories can be mounted as needed. For more information, see Chapter 4.

Basic File Operations and Manipulation

Linux was developed as a clone of Unix, which means that Linux has the same functionality with different source code. The essence of both operating systems is at the command line. Basic commands for file manipulation and filters are available to help you do more with a file.

This section covers only the most basic of commands that you can use in Linux. It describes only a few of the things that you can do with each	*command. Unfortunately, a full discussion would require several hundred more pages. Expect to know considerably more about commands for the RHCE and RHCT exams.*

Basic File Operations

Two basic groups of commands are used to manage Linux files. One group helps you get around Linux files and directories. The other group actually does something creative with the files. Remember that in any Linux file operation, you can take advantage of the **HISTORY** (this is capitalized because it's a standard environment variable) of previous commands, as well as the characteristics of command completion, which allow you to use the TAB key almost as a wildcard to complete a command or a filename or give you the options available in terms of the absolute path.

Almost all Linux commands include *switches*, options that allow you to do more. Few are covered in this chapter. If you're less familiar with any of these commands, use their man pages. Study the switches. Try them out! Only with practice, practice, and more practice can you really understand the power behind some of these commands.

Basic Navigation

Everything in Linux can be reduced to a file. Directories are special types of files that serve as containers for other files. Drivers are files. As discussed earlier, devices are special types of files. The nodes associated with USB hardware are just files, and so on. To navigate around these files, you need some basic commands to tell you where you are, what is there with you, and how to move around.

The Tilde (~)   But first, every Linux user has a home directory. You can use the tilde (~) to represent the home directory of any currently active user. For example, if your username is tb, your home directory is /home/tb. If you've logged in as the root user, your home directory is /root. Thus, the effect of the **cd ~** command depends on your username. For example, if you've logged in as user mj, the **cd ~** command brings you to the /home/mj directory. If you've logged in as the root user, this command brings you to the /root directory. You can list the contents of your home directory from anywhere in the directory tree with the **ls ~** command.

Paths   There are two path concepts associated with Linux directories: absolute paths and relative paths. An absolute path describes the complete directory structure based on the top level directory, root (/). A relative path is based on the current directory.

Relative paths do not include the slash in front.

The difference between an absolute path and a relative one is important. Especially when you're creating a script, absolute paths are essential. Otherwise, scripts executed from other directories may lead to unintended consequences.

pwd   In many configurations, you may not know where you are relative to the root (/) directory. The **pwd** command, which is short for print working directory, can tell you, relative to root (/). Once you know where you are, you can determine whether you need to move to a different directory.

cd   It's easy to change directories in Linux. Just use **cd** and cite the absolute path of the desired directory. If you use the relative path, just remember that your final destination depends on the present working directory.

ls   The most basic of commands lists the files in the current directory. But the Linux **ls** command, with the right switches, can be quite powerful. The right kind of **ls** can tell you everything about a file, such as creation date, last access date, and size. It can help you organize the listing of files in just about any desired order. Important variations on this command include **ls -a** to reveal hidden files, **ls -l** for long listings, **ls -t** for a time-based list, and **ls -i** for inode numbers. You can combine switches; I often use the **ls -ltr** command to display the most recently changed files last.

Looking for Files

There are two basic commands used for file searches: **find** and **locate**.

find   The **find** command searches through directories and subdirectories for a desired file. For example, if you wanted to find the directory with the xorg.conf GUI configuration file, you could use the following command, which would start the search in the top-level root (/) directory:

```
# find / -name xorg.conf
```

But this search on my old laptop computer (on an older version of Linux) with a 200 MHz CPU took several minutes. Alternatively, if you know that this file is located in the /etc subdirectory tree, you could start in that directory with the following command:

```
# find /etc -name xorg.conf
```

locate   If this is all too time-consuming, RHEL 5 includes a default database of all files and directories. Searches with the **locate** command are almost instantaneous. And **locate** searches don't require the full file name. The drawback is that the **locate** command database is normally updated only once each day, as documented in the /etc/cron.daily/mlocate.cron script.

Getting into the Files

Now that you see how to find and get around different files, it's time to start reading, copying, and moving the files around. Most Linux configuration files are text files. Linux editors are text editors. Linux commands are designed to read text files. If in doubt, you can check the file types in the current directory with the **file *** command.

cat   The most basic command for reading files is **cat**. The **cat** *filename* command scrolls the text within the *filename* file. It also works with multiple file names; it concatenates the file names that you might list as one continuous output to your screen. You can redirect the output to the file name of your choice.

more and less   Larger files demand a command that can help you scroll through the file text at your leisure. Linux has two of these commands: **more** and **less**. With the **more** *filename* command, you can scroll through the text of a file, from start to finish, one screen at a time. With the **less** *filename* command, you can scroll in both directions through the same text with the PAGE UP and PAGE DOWN keys. Both commands support vi-style searches.

head and tail   The **head** and **tail** commands are separate commands that work in essentially the same way. By default, the **head** *filename* command looks at the first 10 lines of a file; the **tail** *filename* command looks at the last 10 lines of a file. You can specify the number of lines shown with the **-n***x* switch. Just remember to avoid the space when specifying the number of lines; for example, the **tail -n15 /etc/passwd** command lists the last 15 lines of the /etc/passwd file.

Creating Files

A number of commands are used to create new files. Alternatively, you can let a text editor such as vi create a new file for you.

cp   The **cp** (copy) command allows you to take the contents of one file and place a copy with the same or different name in the directory of your choice. For example, the **cp** *file1 file2* command takes the contents of *file1* and saves the contents in *file2*. One of the dangers of **cp** is that it can easily overwrite files in different directories, without prompting you to make sure that's what you really wanted to do.

mv   While you can't rename a file in Linux, you can move it. The **mv** command essentially puts a different label on a file. For example, the **mv** *file1 file2* command changes the name of *file1* to *file2*. Unless you're moving the file to a different partition, everything about the file, including the inode number, remains the same.

ln   You can create a linked file. As discussed earlier, linked files are common with device files such as /dev/dvdwriter and /dev/par0. They're also useful for making sure that multiple users have a copy of the same file in their directories. Hard links include a copy of the file. As long as the hard link is made within the same partition, the inode numbers are identical. You could delete a hard-linked file in one directory, and it would still exist in the other directory. For example, the following command creates a hard link from the actual Samba configuration file to smb.conf in the local directory:

```
# ln smb.conf /etc/samba/smb.conf
```

On the other hand, a soft link serves as a redirect; when you open up a file created with a soft link, you're directed to the original file. If you delete the original file, the file is lost. While the soft link is still there, it has nowhere to go. The following command is an example of how you can create a soft link:

```
# ln -s smb.conf /etc/samba/smb.conf
```

File Filters

Linux is rich in commands that can help you filter the contents of a file. Simple commands can help you search, check, or sort the contents of a file. And there are special types of files that contain others, colloquially known as a "tarball."

Tarballs are a common way to distribute Linux packages. They are normally distributed in a compressed format, with a .tar.gz or .tar.bz2 file extension, consolidated as a package in a single file. In this respect, they are similar to Microsoft-style compressed zip files.

sort

You can sort the contents of a file in a number of ways. By default, the **sort** command sorts the contents in alphabetical order depending on the first letter in each line. For example, the **sort /etc/passwd** command would sort all users (including those associated with specific services and such) by username.

grep and egrep

The **grep** command uses a search term to look through a file. It returns the full line that contains the search term. For example, **grep 'Michael Jang' /etc/passwd** looks for my name in the /etc/passwd file.

The **egrep** command is more forgiving; it allows you to use some unusual characters in your search, including +, ?, |, (, and). While it's possible to set up **grep** to search for these characters with the help of the backslash, the command can be awkward to use.

The locate command is essentially a specialized version of the grep command, which uses the updatedb command–based database of files on your Linux computer.

wc

The **wc** command, short for word count, can return the number of lines, words, and characters in a file. The **wc** options are straightforward: for example, **wc -w** *filename* returns the number of words in that file.

sed

The **sed** command, short for stream editor, allows you to search for and change specified words or even text streams in a file. For example, the following command changes the *first* instance of the word *Windows* to the word *Linux* in each line of the file opsys, and writes the result to the file newopsys:

```
# sed 's/Windows/Linux/' opsys > newopsys
```

However, this may not be enough. If a line contains more than one instance of *Windows*, the above **sed** command does not change the second instance of that word. But you can make it change every appearance of *Windows* by adding a "global" suffix:

```
# sed 's/Windows/Linux/g' opsys > newopsys
```

awk

The **awk** command, named for its developers (Aho, Weinberger, and Kernighan), is more of a database manipulation utility. It can identify lines with a keyword and read out the text from a specified column in that line. Again, using the /etc/passwd file, for example, the following command will read out the username of every user with a *Mike* in the comment column:

```
# awk '/Mike/ {print $1}' /etc/passwd
```

Administrative Commands

You'll work with a number of administrative commands in this book. But every budding Linux administrator should be familiar with at least two basic administrative commands: **ps** and **who**.

ps

It's important to know what's running on your Linux computer. The **ps** command has a number of critical switches. When trying to diagnose a problem, it's common to get the fullest possible list of running processes, and then look for a specific program. For example, if the Firefox Web browser were to suddenly crash, you'd want to kill any associated processes. The **ps aux | grep firefox** command could then help you identify the process(es) that you need to kill.

who and w

If you want to know what users are currently logged into your system, use the **who** command or the **w** command. This can help you identify the usernames of those who are logged in, their terminal connections, their times of login, and the processes that they are running.

If you suspect that a username has been compromised, use the w command to check currently logged on users. Look at the terminal. If the user is in the office but the terminal indicates a remote shell connection, be concerned. The w command can also identify the current process being run by that user.

Wildcards

Sometimes you may not know the exact name of the file or the exact search term. This is when a wildcard is handy. The basic wildcards are shown in Table 1-4.

The use of wildcards is sometimes known as globbing.

CERTIFICATION OBJECTIVE 1.05

Printing

As of this writing, printers are not always connected or configured during the installation of Red Hat Enterprise Linux. You may have to install printers yourself. The default Red Hat Enterprise Linux print daemon is CUPS, the Common Unix Printing System.

There are three basic ways to configure a printer: first, you can edit the configuration files in the /etc/cups directory with a text editor, which can be a difficult process. These files are long, and the language is somewhat obscure, at least on the surface.

TABLE 1-4	Wildcard	Description
Wildcards in the Shell	*	Any number of alphanumeric characters (or no characters at all). For example, the **ls ab*** command would return the following file names, assuming they exist in the current directory: ab, abc, abcd.
	?	One single alphanumeric character. For example, the **ls ab?** command would return the following file names, assuming they exist in the current directory: abc, abd, abe.
	[]	A range of options. For example, the **ls ab[123]** command would return the following file names, assuming they exist in the current directory: ab1, ab2, ab3. Alternatively, the **ls ab[X-Z]** command would return the following file names, assuming they exist in the current directory: abX, abY, abZ.

Through its support of the Internet Printing Protocol (IPP), CUPS provides another way toward managing printers on a network: a Web-based configuration tool using TCP/IP port 631.

The third method in RHEL 5 is with the Red Hat Printer Configuration tool, which is described in Chapter 7.

Adding Printers

The easy way to add a printer is with the Red Hat Printer Configuration tool, which is also known by the command used to start it from a terminal, **system-config-printer**. I recommend that you learn to use this GUI tool. Unless you're a CUPS expert, it's a faster way to configure printers on the RHCT and RHCE exams. I show you how to use this utility in Chapter 7.

Print Commands

Three basic commands are associated with printing in Linux, as described in Table 1-5.

CERTIFICATION OBJECTIVE 1.06

Shells

A *shell* is a user interface. The Linux command shell is the prompt that allows you to interact with your computer with various system commands. With the right file permissions, you can set up commands in scripts to run when you want, even in the middle of the night. Linux shells can process commands in various sequences, depending on how you manage the input and output of each command. The way commands are interpreted is in part determined by variables and parameters associated with each shell. Some of these variables make up the environment that is carried over even if you change from one shell to another.

TABLE 1-5	Command	Description
	lpr	The basic print command; **lpr** *filename* prints that file.
Linux Print Commands	lpq	Query the print queue for status; **lpr -l** lists print job numbers.
	lprm	Remove a specific job, usually specified by job number, from the printer queue.

The default shell in Linux is bash, also known as the Bourne Again Shell. A number of other shells are popular with many users. As long as you have installed the appropriate RPMs, users can start any of these shells. As desired, you can change the default shell for individual users in the /etc/passwd file.

Basic Shell Programming

"Real" Linux administrators program their own scripts. They create scripts because they don't want to sit at their computers all the time. Scripts can allow Linux to back up directories automatically when nobody is in the office. Scripts can help Linux process databases when few people are using the system.

If you're not a programmer, don't worry—this is not as difficult as it sounds. For example, utilities related to the **crontab** command automate the creation of a number of different scripts. The cron system is discussed in more detail in Chapter 6.

If you're at all familiar with shell commands and programming expressions, you can find some examples of Red Hat Enterprise Linux shell programs in the /etc/cron .daily directory.

Variables and Parameters

Variables can change. Parameters are set. The bash shell includes a number of standard environment variables. Their default values are shown in the output to the **env** command. One critical variable is the value of PATH, which you can check at the command line with the **echo $PATH** command. The directories listed in PATH are automatically searched when you try to run a command. For example, if you want to run the **fdisk** command from the /sbin directory, you could do it with the following command:

```
$ /sbin/fdisk
```

However, if the /sbin directory were in your PATH, you don't need the leading **/sbin** to call out the command; the following would work:

```
$ fdisk
```

You can easily change the PATH variable. For example, if you want to add the /sbin directory to your PATH, just run the following commands:

```
# PATH=$PATH:/sbin
# export PATH
```

The /sbin directory is already in the default PATH for the root user. The most common parameters are the settings associated with Linux configuration files, which are mostly located in the /etc directory. For example, the /etc/resolv.conf file uses the **nameserver** parameter to represent the DNS servers for your network. This is normally set to the IP address for that DNS server.

EXERCISE 1-3

Checking the PATH

In this exercise, you'll examine the PATH for a regular and the root user.

1. Log into the Linux command line interface as a regular user. If you're in the GUI, you can get to a command line login by pressing CTRL-ALT-F2. From the command prompt, run the following command and note the result:

```
$ echo $PATH
```

2. From the regular user command line interface, log in as the superuser. You'll need the root user's password.

```
$ su
Password:
#
```

3. Run the following command again and note the result. Compare it to the result as a regular user. Is there a difference?

```
# echo $PATH
```

4. Log out of Linux. If you followed steps 1, 2, and 3, you'll need to type the **exit** command twice to log out.

5. Now log into Linux as the root user. At the command prompt, run the following command again and note the result:

```
# echo $PATH
```

6. Observe the difference. You'll see more directories in the PATH for the root user. Now you can see why many Linux gurus who are doing heavy-duty administrative work log in as the root user. And that is why I also recommend that you log in as the root user during the RHCE and RHCT exams.

Script Execution and Permissions

Any Linux file can be set up as an executable file. Then if the file includes a series of commands that can be interpreted by the shell, the commands in that file are executed. If you want Linux to run a script that you've created, you need to assign executable permissions. For additional information on executable files, read the information under the "Basic Security" objective later in this chapter.

Inherited Environment

It's easy to move from shell to shell. While the default Linux shell is bash, many experienced Unix users prefer the Korn shell. Once set with the **set** command, environment variables stay the same from shell to shell. In contrast, shell variables such as **umask** may change when you move from shell to shell, or even from user to user. For example, **umask** is typically different for regular users and the root user.

Piping, Input/Output, Error, and Redirection

Linux uses three basic data streams. Data goes in, data comes out, and errors are sent in a different direction. These streams are known as standard input (stdin), standard output (stdout), and standard error (stderr). Normally, input comes from the keyboard and goes out to the screen, while errors are sent to a buffer. Error messages are also sent to the display (as text stream 2). In the following example, *filename* is stdin to the **cat** command:

```
# cat filename
```

When you run **cat *filename***, the contents of that file are sent to the screen as standard output.

You can redirect each of these streams to or from a file. For example, if you have a program named *database* and a datafile with a lot of data, the contents of that datafile can be sent to the database program with a left redirection arrow (**<**). As shown here, datafile is taken as standard input:

```
# database < datafile
```

Standard input can come from the left side of a command as well. For example, if you need to scroll through the boot messages, you can combine the **dmesg** and **less** commands with a pipe:

```
# dmesg | less
```

The output from **dmesg** is redirected as standard input to **less**, which then allows you to scroll through that output as if it were a separate file.

Standard output is just as easy to redirect. For example, the following command uses the right redirection arrow (**>**) to send the standard output of the **ls** command to the *filelist* file.

```
# ls > filelist
```

You can add standard output to the end of an existing file with a double redirection arrow with a command such as **ls >> filelist**.

If you believe that a particular program is generating errors, redirect the error stream from it with a command like the following:

```
# program 2> err-list
```

CERTIFICATION OBJECTIVE 1.07

Basic Security

The basic security of a Linux computer is based on file permissions. Default file permissions are set through the **umask** shell variable. SUID and SGID permissions can give all users access to specific files. Ownership is based on the default user and group IDs of the person who created a file. Managing permissions and ownership involves commands such as **chmod, chown,** and **chgrp.**

Users and groups own files. Users and groups have passwords. Security can be enhanced if you configure users and groups in the Shadow Password Suite. Obviously, more levels of security are available, but security options such as Access Control Lists and Security Enhanced Linux (SELinux) are not included in the Red Hat exam prerequisites.

File Permissions

Linux file permissions are straightforward. Consider the following output from **ls -l /sbin/fdisk**:

```
-rwxr-xr-x  1 root   root      95572 Jan   11   08:10    /sbin/fdisk
```

The permissions are shown on the left side of the listing. Ten characters are shown. The first character determines whether it's a regular or a special file. The remaining nine characters are grouped in threes, applicable to the file owner (user), the group owner, and everyone else on that Linux system. The letters are straightforward: r = read, w = write, x = execute. These permissions are described in Table 1-6.

Key commands that can help you manage the permissions and ownership of a file are **chmod, chown,** and **chgrp.** The **chmod** command uses the numeric value of permissions associated with the owner, group, and others. In Linux, permissions are assigned the following numeric values: r = 4, w = 2, and x = 1. For example, if

TABLE 1-6	Position	Description
	1	Type of file; - = regular file, *d* = directory, *b* = device, *l* = linked file
Description of	234	Permissions granted to the owner of the file
File Permissions	567	Permissions granted to the group owner of the file
	890	Permissions granted to all other users on the Linux system

you were crazy enough to give read, write, and execute permissions on **fdisk** to all users, you would run the **chmod 777 /sbin/fdisk** command. The **chown** and **chgrp** commands adjust the user and group owners associated with the cited file.

on the
Ĵob

*Red Hat now includes security contexts in file listings, in support of SELinux. To preview this feature, run the **ls -Z** command. For more information, see Chapter 4.*

Users, Groups, and umask

Linux, like Unix, is configured with users and groups. Everyone who uses Linux is set up with a username, even if it's just "guest." Take a look at /etc/passwd. One version of this file is shown in Figure 1-4.

FIGURE 1-4

/etc/passwd

```
                              michael@Enterprise5a:~
root:x:0:0:root:/root:/bin/bash
bin:x:1:1:bin:/bin:/sbin/nologin
daemon:x:2:2:daemon:/sbin:/sbin/nologin
adm:x:3:4:adm:/var/adm:/sbin/nologin
lp:x:4:7:lp:/var/spool/lpd:/sbin/nologin
sync:x:5:0:sync:/sbin:/bin/sync
shutdown:x:6:0:shutdown:/sbin:/sbin/shutdown
halt:x:7:0:halt:/sbin:/sbin/halt
mail:x:8:12:mail:/var/spool/mail:/sbin/nologin
news:x:9:13:news:/etc/news:
uucp:x:10:14:uucp:/var/spool/uucp:/sbin/nologin
operator:x:11:0:operator:/root:/sbin/nologin
games:x:12:100:games:/usr/games:/sbin/nologin
gopher:x:13:30:gopher:/var/gopher:/sbin/nologin
ftp:x:14:50:FTP User:/var/ftp:/sbin/nologin
nobody:x:99:99:Nobody:/:/sbin/nologin
dbus:x:81:81:System message bus:/:/sbin/nologin
rpm:x:37:37::/var/lib/rpm:/sbin/nologin
nscd:x:28:28:NSCD Daemon:/:/sbin/nologin
vcsa:x:69:69:virtual console memory owner:/dev:/sbin/nologin
apache:x:48:48:Apache:/var/www:/sbin/nologin
pcap:x:77:77::/var/arpwatch:/sbin/nologin
netdump:x:34:34:Network Crash Dump user:/var/crash:/bin/bash
"/etc/passwd" [readonly] 46L, 2148C                    23,1          Top
```

As you can see, all kinds of usernames are listed in the /etc/passwd file. Even a number of Linux services such as mail, news, ftp, and apache have their own usernames. In any case, the /etc/passwd file follows a specific format, described in more detail in Chapter 6. For now, note that the only users shown in this file are mj and tb, their user IDs (UID) and group IDs (GID) are 500 and 501, and their home directories match their usernames. The next user gets UID and GID 502, and so on.

Users can change their own passwords with the **passwd** command. The root user can change the password of any user. For example, the **passwd mj** command allows the root user to change user mj's password.

umask

The way **umask** works in Red Hat Enterprise Linux may surprise you, especially if you're coming from a different Unix-style environment. You cannot configure **umask** to allow you to create new files automatically with executable permissions. This promotes security: if fewer files have executable permissions, fewer files are available for a cracker to use to run programs to break through your system.

on the

job

In the world of Linux, a **hacker** *is a good person who simply wants to create better software. A* **cracker** *is someone who wants to break into your system for malicious purposes.*

Every time you create a new file, the default permissions are based on the value of **umask**. In the past, the value of **umask** canceled out the value of numeric permissions on a file. For example, if the value of **umask** is 000, the default permissions for any file created by that user were once 777 – 000 = 777, which corresponds to read, write, and execute permissions for all users. They're now 666, as new files can no longer get executable permissions.

When you type the **umask** command, you get a four-number output such as 0245. As of this writing, the first number in the **umask** output is always 0 and is not used. In the future, this first number may be usable to allow for new files that automatically include the SUID or SGID bits.

Also, no matter what the value of **umask**, new files in Red Hat Enterprise Linux can no longer be automatically created with executable permissions. In other words, a **umask** value of 0454 leads to identical permissions on new files as a **umask** value of 0545. You need to use commands such as **chmod** to set executable permissions on a specific file.

SUID and SGID

Permissions can be a risky business, but you need to give all users access to some programs. Setting full read, write, and execute permissions for all users on a Linux system can be dangerous. One alternative is setting the SUID and the SGID permission bits for a file. When active, these bits allow you to configure appropriate permissions on the subject file. For example, one common practice is to set the SUID bit for the KPPP Internet Connection Utility so users who require telephone modems can use KPPP to dial in to the Internet. You can set the SUID bit on this utility with the following command:

```
# chmod u+s /usr/sbin/kppp
```

SGID permissions can be useful when you're setting up a special group of users who need to share files on a specific task or project. This process is discussed in more detail in Chapter 6.

Shadow Passwords

When you look at the default /etc/passwd file, you should see an "x" in the second column. Older versions of Linux had an encrypted version of user passwords in this column. As /etc/passwd is accessible to all users, a cracker could copy this file and decrypt everyone's password on a Linux computer. This problem led to the development of the Shadow Password Suite.

Shadow Password Suite

Historically, all that was needed to manage Linux users and groups was the information included in the /etc/passwd and /etc/group files. These files included passwords and are by default readable by all users.

The Shadow Password Suite was created to provide an additional layer of protection. It is used to encrypt user and group passwords in shadow files (/etc/shadow and /etc/gshadow) that are readable only by users with root privileges.

The Shadow Password Suite is now enabled by default in Red Hat Enterprise Linux. Standard commands for creating new users and groups automatically set up encrypted passwords in the Shadow Password Suite files. These commands are described in more detail in Chapter 6.

But if you're restoring a system, you may not have access to these special commands. The old way of creating new users and groups is by editing the /etc/passwd and /etc/group files directly. Four commands allow you to convert passwords to and from the /etc/shadow and /etc/gshadow files:

- **pwconv**   Converts passwords from /etc/passwd to /etc/shadow. This command works even if some of the passwords are already encrypted in /etc/shadow.
- **pwunconv**   Opposite of **pwconv**.

■ **grpconv** Converts passwords from /etc/group to /etc/gshadow. This command works even if some of the passwords are already encrypted in /etc/gshadow.

■ **grpunconv** Opposite of **grpconv**.

CERTIFICATION OBJECTIVE 1.08

System Administration

Most system administration tasks require root or superuser privileges. You should already be familiar with a number of basic Linux system administration commands and files. Standard user files are stored in /etc/skel. Daemons are processes that run in the background and run various Linux services. cron is a specialized daemon that can run scripts when you want. It's especially useful for setting up backup jobs in the middle of the night. Logging is a key part of monitoring Linux and any services that you choose to run.

The Superuser

Generally in Linux, a system administrator does everything possible as a normal user. It's a good practice to use superuser privileges only when absolutely necessary. But one time when it's appropriate is during the Red Hat exams. Good administrators will return to being normal users when they're done with their tasks. Mistakes as the root user can disable your Linux system.

There are two basic ways to make this work:

■ **su** The superuser command, **su**, prompts you for the root password before logging you in with root privileges. A variation, **su -c**, sets up root privileges for one specific command. Many Red Hat GUI utilities are set up to prompt for the root password before they can be started using Pluggable Authentication Modules (see Chapter 6). One more variation, **su - root**, sets up root privileges with the root user **PATH**. (Remember to use a space on both sides of the dash in this command.)

■ **sudo** The **sudo** command allows users listed in /etc/sudoers to run administrative commands. You can configure /etc/sudoers to set limits on the root privileges granted to a specific user.

However, Red Hat Enterprise Linux provides some features that make working as root somewhat safer. For example, logins using the **ftp** and **telnet** commands to remote computers are disabled by default.

/etc/skel for Home Directories

Basic configuration files for individual users are available in the /etc/skel directory. This directory includes a number of hidden files. For a full list, run the **ls -a /etc/skel** command. If you want all future users to get specific files in their home directories, include them here.

The next time you create a regular user, check that person's home directory. For example, if you just created a user named elizabeth, run the **ls -a /home/elizabeth** command. Compare the results to the previous command on the /etc/skel directory.

Daemons

A *daemon* is a process that runs in the background. It is resident in your computer's RAM and watches for signals before it goes into action. For example, a network daemon such as httpd, the Linux Web server known as Apache, waits for a request from a browser before it actually serves a Web page.

Daemons are often configured to start automatically when you start Linux. This process is documented at various runlevels in the /etc/rc.d directory. Alternatively, you can use a tool such as ntsysv to identify and manage the daemons that are started at various Linux runlevels. This is discussed in more detail in Chapter 4.

Controlling Network Services Through Daemons

Networks don't always work. Sometimes you need to restart a network daemon to implement a configuration change. Red Hat Enterprise Linux provides an easy way to control network service daemons through the scripts in /etc/rc.d/init.d. This directory includes scripts that can control installed Linux network services (and more) for everything from the Network File System (NFS) to sendmail. The actual daemon itself is usually located in the /sbin or /usr/sbin directory.

With these scripts, it's easy to start, stop, status, reload, or restart a network daemon. This is useful to implement or test changes that you make to a specific configuration file. For example, if you make a change to the Postfix mail server configuration file in /etc/postfix/main.cf, you can implement the change right away with the **/etc/init.d/postfix reload** command. Other switches to these scripts allow you to stop, start, or status these services. Service management is discussed in more detail in Chapter 3.

e x a m

w a t c h *In Red Hat Enterprise Linux, a simpler way to reload or restart a service in the /etc/init.d directory is with the service command. For example, to restart the vsftpd service, you could run the service vsftpd restart command. (And that's one more reason to log in as the root user; if you invoke root privileges with su, based on the default $PATH, you'd have to type /sbin/service vsftpd restart.)*

cron

Perhaps the most important daemon is **cron**, which can be used to execute a command or a series of commands in a script, on a schedule. Red Hat Enterprise Linux already includes a series of scripts that are executed by **cron** on committed schedules in the /etc/cron.hourly, /etc/cron.daily, /etc/cron.weekly, and /etc/cron .monthly directories.

System crontab

The easiest way to set up your own cron jobs is through the crontab file, which can be managed through the **crontab** command. Users can edit their own crontab files with the **crontab -e** command; the root user can configure the crontab for a specific user with the **crontab -u** *username* **-e** command.

The general format for a crontab file can be found in the /etc/crontab script, which is used to run the scripts in the aforementioned schedule-related directories. A typical crontab entry from that file is

```
42 4 1 * * root run-parts /etc/cron.monthly
```

Five schedule fields appear on the left side of each crontab entry: minute, hour, day of month, month, and day of week. This line executes the scripts in the /etc/cron .monthly directory at 4:42 A.M. on the first of every month, no matter what day of the week it is.

Backup and Restore

Hard drives include spinning disks and magnetic media. These are mechanical parts. By definition, all mechanical hard drives will eventually fail. If you're administering a Linux system with multiple users, you do not want to have to hear the complaints of people who "know" that their data is more important than yours, because you'll know that they are "right."

Configuring backups involves a number of strategic choices that go beyond Linux.

Using full backups, you can back up the entire drive; using incremental backups, you back up just the data that has changed since the last backup. A wide variety of media are available for backups, including tape drives, writable CD/DVDs, and other hard drives in various RAID configurations. You can back up data locally or over a network. Linux includes a number of quality tools for backups.

It's common to back up through a network to a dedicated backup server. Since you're transferring at least substantial portions of a hard drive during a backup, backups can degrade network performance for other users. So it is best to perform backups when few people are using your Linux system, which in most cases is during the middle of the night. For this reason, it's a common practice to automate backups using the **cron** daemon.

Tape Backups

Using magnetic tape in Linux depends on the ftape system using tarballs to group directories into single compressed backup files. Once it is mounted, it's easy to test a tape drive; just use the **mt -f /dev/*tapedevice*** command to status, rewind, or eject the tape. If it's a SCSI tape drive, use the **st** command instead.

You don't mount a tape as you would when using regular media; you can actually use switches with the **tar** command to write or restore directly from the tape device. Just cite the appropriate **/dev/*tapedevice*** in the command. Make sure you can also restore from the backup you've made.

DVD/CD Backups

Backups to DVDs and CDs can be made in a similar fashion, using "iso" files instead of tarballs. The **mkisofs -J -r -T -o /tmp/backhome.iso /home** command can consolidate regular users' home directories from /home onto a single file—or it can be easily saved to a remote system. You can then record this file onto the media with a command such as this:

```
# cdrecord -v /tmp/backhome.iso
```

You can then store the DVD/CD and later restore the files from it by mounting it as you would any regular DVD/CD.

Hard Drive (RAID) Backups

Hard drive backups are based on the system known as the Redundant Array of Independent Disks (RAID), which is covered in more detail in Chapter 8. There are several versions of RAID that can automatically restore data once you've replaced a broken hard disk.

gzip and bzip2

The **gzip** and **bzip2** commands are similar—they compress and decompress files, using different algorithms. If you wanted to compress a big picture file, you could do so with one of the following commands:

```
# gzip big.jpg
# bzip2 big.jpg
```

It adds a .gz or a .bz2 suffix to the file, compressed to the associated algorithms.

You can uncompress from these files with the **-d** switch:

```
# gzip -d big.jpg.gz
# bzip2 -d big.jpg.bz2
```

tar

The **tar** command was originally developed for archiving data to tape drives. However, it's commonly used today for collecting a series of files, especially from a directory. For example, the following command backs up the information from the /home directory in the home.tar.gz file:

```
# tar czvf home.tar.gz /home
```

This is one of the few commands that does not require a dash in front of the switch. This particular command creates (**c**) an archive, compresses (**z**) it, in verbose (**v**) mode, with the filename (**f**) that follows. Alternatively, you can extract (**x**) from that file with the following command:

```
# tar xzvf home.tar.gz /home
```

The compression specified (**z**) is associated with the **gzip** command; if you wanted to use bzip2 compression, substitute the **j** switch.

System Log File Management

Log files are controlled by the **syslogd** daemon and organized in the /etc/syslog.conf file. It is important to use log files to understand the behavior of your Linux system; deviations may be a sign of problems with a recently installed service or a security breach. Basic log files are organized in the /var/log directory. For more information on system logs, see Chapter 7.

CERTIFICATION OBJECTIVE 1.09

Basic TCP/IP Networking

TCP/IP is a series of protocols organized in layers, known as a protocol suite. It was developed for Unix and eventually adopted as the standard for communication on the Internet. With IP addresses, it can help you organize your network. There are a number of TCP/IP tools and configurations that can help you manage your network.

As with the previous sections in this chapter, the statements here are oversimplifications. So if you find this section overwhelming, read the references cited at the beginning of the chapter. Linux is built for networking, and there is no practical way to pass either the RHCT or the RHCE exam unless you understand networking in some detail.

IP Numbers and Address Classes

Every computer that communicates on a network needs its own IP address. Some addresses are assigned permanently to a particular computer; these are known as *static* addresses. Others are leased from a DHCP server, associated with the Dynamic Host Configuration Protocol, for a limited amount of time; these are also known as *dynamic* IP addresses.

Two standards for IP addresses are in use today: IP version 4 (IPv4) and IP version 6 (IPv6). IPv4 addresses have 32 bits and are set up in octets in dotted decimal notation. The range of possible IPv4 addresses is between 0.0.0.0 to 255.255.255.255. While this range includes more than 4 billion IP addresses, that is not nearly enough for the current Internet.

IPv6 addresses have 128 bits and are set up in hexadecimal notation. An IPv6 address is normally organized in eight groups of four hexadecimal numbers each, and it may look like *4abe:03e2:c132:69fa:0000:0000:c0b8:2148*. This is a range of over 340,000,000,000,000,000,000,000,000,000,000,000,000 IPv6 addresses.

To ease the transition, specific IPv6 addresses have been assigned for every one of the 4 billion IPv4 addresses. There are still more than 3.4×10^{38} addresses left over. While actual routing on the Internet now commonly uses IPv6, network configuration in Linux is still normally based on IPv4 addresses.

IPv4 addresses are organized into five different classes, as shown in Table 1-7. The academics among you may note that this is different from the official addresses in each IPv4 class as specified in RFC 1518 from the Internet Engineering Task Force (www.ietf.org). The *assignable* address range includes those IP addresses that can be assigned to a specific computer on a network.

In addition, there are several private IP address ranges available for computers and networks. They are associated with network addresses 10.0.0.0, 172.168.0.0, and 192.168.0.0 through 192.168.255.0.

IPv6 Addressing

There are 128 bits in an IPv6 address. That's 96 more bits than IPv4. A typical IPv6 address might look like this:

```
63.51.33.167.110.50.0.0.0.0.153.53.68.98.31.235
```

TABLE 1-7	IP Address Classes

Class	Assignable Address Range	Note
A	1.1.1.1–126.255.255.254	Allows networks of up to 16 million computers
B	128.0.0.1–191.255.255.254	Allows networks of up to 65,000 computers
C	192.0.0.1–223.255.255.254	Allows networks of up to 254 computers
D	224.0.0.1–239.255.255.254	Reserved for multicasts
E	240.0.0.1–255.255.255.254	Reserved for experimental use

The best way to understand an IPv6 address is to break it down, bit by bit. When routing to individual computers, the first three bits are set to

```
001
```

which is associated with "unicast" or one computer routing. Note how "unicast" contrasts to "multicast" routing, which would address multiple systems. Of course, a multicast IPv6 address has a different first three bits.

The following bits depend on the functionality of the network. Generally, IPv6 addresses to most networks will be assigned 47 or 48 of the 128 bits. The first three bits are included in the 47 or 48 bits. The remaining (80 or 81) bits are available for addressing on the local network.

In contrast, private IP addresses on a single physical network include the following first 10 bits, also known as the Local Link Unicast:

```
1111 1110 10
```

Translated to hexidecimal notation, that's also known as fe80, which is what you'll see in the output to the **ifconfig** command for most Ethernet cards in the *inet6 addr* line.

To ease the transition from IPv4 to IPv6, IPv4 addresses can be embedded at the end of every IPv6 address. In other words, the IPv4 address embedded above is

```
68.98.31.235
```

How to Define a Network with IP Addresses

Three key IP addresses define a network: the network address, the broadcast address, and the subnet mask. The network address is always the first IP address in a range; the broadcast address is always the last address in the same range. The subnet mask helps your computer define the difference between the two addresses. You can assign IP addresses between the network and broadcast addresses (not including these addresses) to any computer on the network.

As an example, let's define the range of addresses for a private network. Start with the private network address 192.168.122.0. Use the standard subnet mask for a class C network, 255.255.255.0. Based on these two addresses, the broadcast address is 192.168.122.255, and the range of IP addresses that you can assign on that particular network is 192.168.122.1 through 192.168.122.254.

If you're working with IPv6, remember there are 128 bits. Private IPv6 addresses are defined by the first nine bits, specifically 1111 1110 1. Any address that starts with these bits is reserved and cannot be used on the Internet, just like the aforementioned private IPv4 addresses.

If this is confusing to you in any way, please refer to the IP Sub-Networking Mini-HOWTO of the Linux Documentation Project at www.tldp.org.

Tools and Commands

A substantial number of commands are available to manage the TCP/IP suite on your Linux computer. Three of the more important commands are **ping**, **ifconfig**, and **netstat**.

ping

The **ping** command allows you to test connectivity—locally, within your network, and on the Internet. For the purpose of this section, assume your IP address is 192.168.122.43 and the gateway address on your network is 192.168.122.99. If you're having problems connecting to a network, you should use the **ping** command in the following order.

First test the integrity of TCP/IP on your computer:

```
# ping 127.0.0.1
```

Normally, **ping** works continuously on Linux; you'll need to press CTRL-C to stop this command. If you need to see if you're properly connected to your LAN, you should **ping** your own IP address:

```
# ping 192.168.122.43
```

If that works, **ping** the address of another computer on your network. Then start tracing the route to the Internet. **ping** the address for your gateway, in this case, 192.168.122.99. If possible, **ping** the address of your network's connection to the Internet. And finally, **ping** the address of a computer that you know is *active* on the Internet.

You can substitute host names such as www.google.com for an IP address. If the host name doesn't work, there's a problem with the database of host names and IP addresses, more commonly known as a DNS, BIND, or **nameserver**.

If you're working with IPv6, the **ping** command is **ping6**; the loopback address is known as 0:0:0:0:0:0:0:1, sometimes expressed by compressing zeros as ::1. To see how this works, try the following command:

```
# ping6 ::1
```

ifconfig

The **ifconfig** command can help you check and configure network adapters. Run the **ifconfig** command by itself to see the detected adapters on your computer. You can also use **ifconfig** to assign IP address or hardware port information as well. For example, if you want to assign IRQ 10 to the second Ethernet adapter, run the following command:

```
# ifconfig eth1 irq 10
```

For more information on **ifconfig**, refer to Chapter 7.

netstat

The **netstat** command is versatile; it can help you see the channels available for network connections, interface statistics, and more. One important version of this command, **netstat -r**, displays routing tables that can tell you if your computer knows where to send a message. More information on this command is available in Chapter 7.

Configuring Name Resolution

When I used a static IP address on my high-speed Internet connection, I could sometimes memorize those numbers. But how can anyone memorize the IP addresses of every Web site you need on the Internet? Using four configuration files, Linux can help you translate computer host names to IP addresses.

/etc/sysconfig/network

Red Hat distributions include basic networking parameters in /etc/sysconfig/network. In most cases, this file activates networking and specifies the host name with directives such as this:

```
NETWORKING=yes
HOSTNAME=Enterprise5.example.com
```

/etc/hosts

The first database of host names and IP addresses was set up in a static text file, /etc/hosts. When there were just a few nodes on the network that eventually turned into the Internet, it was possible to maintain identical /etc/hosts files on each computer.

Here's a typical line in /etc/hosts, which lists the IP address, fully qualified domain name, and alias for one computer connection:

```
192.168.132.32    linux1.mommabears.com   laptop
```

/etc/resolv.conf

There are millions of hosts on the Internet. Even if it were possible to collect all domain names and IP addresses into a /etc/hosts file, the file would overwhelm every computer. And it would overwhelm every network administrator who would have to make sure that all the /etc/hosts files on the Internet match—and get updated every time a new Web site appears. That's why the Domain Name System (DNS) was developed, based on the Berkeley Internet Name Domain (BIND). In /etc/resolv.conf, the IP address of each DNS server is listed with a simple line similar to this:

```
nameserver 192.168.0.1
```

/etc/host.conf

Many networks configure an /etc/hosts file for the local network and a DNS server for other networks and/or the Internet. When your computer looks for an IP address, this file determines whether it searches through /etc/hosts or DNS first. This is usually a one-line file:

```
order hosts,bind
```

A computer with this line looks through /etc/hosts first. If it can't find the computer name that you want in that file, it next looks to the DNS server (bind) for the computer name.

But in most cases, this file has been superseded by /etc/nsswitch.conf.

/etc/nsswitch.conf

This file relates to the configuration on a network of Linux- and Unix-type computers, which are configured to communicate using the Network File System (NFS). When it is used in concert with the Network Information Service (NIS), networks can maintain a single database of usernames and passwords for all NFS-enabled computers on that network.

The key directive in this file, with respect to name resolution, is

```
hosts:    files dns
```

This is a more straightforward expression of where Linux looks for an IP address when it sees a host name. First, it looks at the file, /etc/hosts, and then it looks at the available DNS server, as defined in /etc/resolv.conf.

CERTIFICATION OBJECTIVE 1.10

Familiarity with Standard Network Services

Linux is built for networking. The code associated with many standard networking services is integrated into the Linux kernel. A basic understanding of the functionality of standard Linux networking services is essential. Many themes throughout this book assume that you already understand the purposes of network communication protocols, mail services, host name and IP address management, Web services, and more.

In Red Hat Enterprise Linux, network services are often installed separately. Some include different packages for clients and servers. Some network services are activated through /etc/xinetd.conf, which reads activation files in the /etc/xinetd.d directory. Others are activated directly with scripts in the /etc/init.d directory. Some key RHEL network services are briefly examined in the following sections.

Network File System, Locally and Remotely

The first network system on Unix and Linux computers is NFS. Ideally, this leads to a seamless Linux interface; for example, you can set up one /home directory for all users on your network on one server. Remember that you need NFS on both server and client computers on your network.

First, make sure NFS support is part of the kernel, as documented in /proc/filesystems. If it isn't there, you may need to activate the nfs and related modules (nfsd, lockd, sunprc) in the kernel. Inspect installed modules with the following command:

```
# lsmod | more
```

Make a list of the modules that aren't included in the list. Run a **modprobe** command (for example, **modprobe nfs**) on any missing modules. With a standard Red Hat Enterprise Linux installation, this should add the modules to the lsmod list, and then add them to the kernel, as listed in /proc/filesystems.

Once you've shared an NFS directory, you can then activate the NFS daemon with the **service nfs start** command. You'll see an example of sharing the Red Hat Enterprise Linux installation files through NFS in Chapter 2.

Once NFS is configured, you can find shared directories on the server's /etc/exports file, and then mount them with a command similar to the following:

```
# mount -t nfs nfsserver:/home /mhome
```

For more information on NFS, see Chapter 10.

sendmail and Postfix

Some people suggest that sendmail is the biggest test (or perhaps headache) for Linux system administrators. While the sendmail configuration files, sendmail.cf and submit.cf, are complex, they should not be intimidating. With the help of the corresponding .mc files, it's easier to define the features you want, the protocols you need, and the way mail is sent and received on your network.

More information on sendmail and the alternative Postfix mail server is available in Chapter 12.

POP, IMAP

The Post Office Protocol (POP) and the Internet Mail Access Protocol (IMAP) each provide a set of rules for delivering e-mail from a server such as sendmail to an e-mail client such as Netscape, mutt, or pine. While POP3 is the current standard for e-mail that is sent to clients, IMAP4 is more flexible for users such as those who access their mail using different computers. POP3 and IMAP4 configuration, using the Dovecot service, is addressed in Chapter 12.

File Transfer Protocol (FTP)

Perhaps the most basic file sharing protocol still in common use is the File Transfer Protocol (FTP). It is set up specifically for file transfers; you might already know that file transfers using FTP are generally faster than those with any other protocol.

As with NFS and Samba, this protocol requires a server and a client. FTP servers can be anonymous, which means they accept connections from anyone, or they can be configured to require a specific username and password. Generally, Linux FTP servers share files from the /var/ftp directory. Red Hat Enterprise Linux now comes with the Very Secure FTP daemon (vsFTPd) as the only FTP server.

The original FTP client works from the command line. Most Linux navigational commands work for FTP; just remember that the **get** and **put** commands download and upload specific files. FTP is covered in more detail in Chapter 10.

Domain Name Service (DNS)

If there were a practical way to list all of the domain names and IP addresses of every Web site on the Internet in a single file, we would not need the Domain Name Service (DNS). The DNS system allows us to set up different parts of this database on different servers around the world. If a DNS server does not have the answer, you can configure it to ask other DNS servers for help. DNS is covered in more detail in Chapter 11.

Dynamic Host Configuration Protocol (DHCP)

IP version 4 addresses are scarce. The Dynamic Host Configuration Protocol (DHCP) was designed to help ration IP addresses. A DHCP server leases a specific IP address to a computer network card for a limited, but renewable, amount of time. DHCP servers can lease IP addresses on different LANs using the BOOTP protocol. More information on setting up DHCP clients and servers is available in Chapter 13.

Samba

The network system originally developed for networks with Microsoft and IBM computers is based on the Server Message Block (SMB) format. Developers originally created Samba to allow Linux to communicate in the SMB format, to participate in Microsoft Windows Workgroups and Domains. It can share files just like any other peer in a workgroup. It can act as a server. Current versions of Samba can even be configured as a Windows NT–style Primary Domain Controller or an Active Directory Services member server on a Windows 2000/XP/2003/Vista–based network.

As Microsoft has moved beyond SMB to the Common Internet File System (CIFS), Samba has evolved as well. To this end, future versions of Samba (starting hopefully with version 4.0) will be able to act as Active Directory Domain Controllers.

Separate packages are available to set up your Linux computer as a Samba client and as a Samba server. Once shares are configured in /etc/samba/smb.conf, other Samba-enabled Linux clients can mount these directories with a command similar to the following:

```
# mount -t cifs -o username=user //servername/sharename /mountpoint
```

But that command is generally limited to the root user. You can also set up the **mount.cifs** command to allow regular users to mount shared Samba directories. Samba and the associated configuration tools are discussed extensively in Chapter 10.

Web Services

Apache is by far the most popular Web server in use on the Internet. It's a standard part of the Red Hat Enterprise Linux server installation. The main configuration file is /etc/httpd/conf/httpd.conf. Configuration is based on an extensive array of modules in the /etc/httpd directory. Basic HTML files, icons, and CGI applets are installed in the /var/www directory. The main Apache log files are part of the /var/log/httpd directory. Daily log files for the largest Web sites can grow into the gigabyte range. Apache is covered in more detail in Chapter 9.

A substantial number of other Web servers are available for Red Hat Enterprise Linux, such as Sun's iPlanet and Zeus's Web Server.

Network Information Service (NIS)

The Network Information Service (NIS) was formerly known as the "yellow pages," as it is a centralized database of usernames and passwords on a network with Linux and other Unix-style computers. NIS can be configured as a centralized database for a number of other configuration files in the /etc directory. Anything that can standardize the configuration of different computers on a network helps the system administrator. For more information on NIS, see Chapter 6.

The Extended Internet Services Daemon (xinetd)

Several less frequently used networking services do not use their own daemons but are configured as part of the Extended Internet Services Daemon, also known as xinetd. You can review installed xinetd services in the /etc/xinetd.d directory. If installed, you'll see services such as rsync, time, swat, and the Kerberos-based Telnet in that directory. All are controlled by the /etc/init.d/xinetd script, using defaults defined in the script and in /etc/xinetd.conf.

Other Linux distributions may configure additional services in this directory. For example, SUSE Linux includes the vsFTPd service in /etc/xinetd.d.

CERTIFICATION OBJECTIVE 1.11

Basic Network Security

Network security in Linux has five basic components. Security by computer can help you manage what computers can send messages into and out of your network. Security by port can help you manage the services that others can use to break into your network. Security by address translation can help you hide the computers inside your network. Security by rule can help you manage the type of data allowed into your network in excruciating detail. And finally, security by SELinux can help manage network services on an entirely different level. Red Hat Enterprise Linux includes tools that can help you configure a firewall and SELinux on your computer: **system-config-securitylevel** (also known as the Red Hat Security Level Configuration tool) and **system-config-selinux** (also known as the SELinux Management Tool). Firewalls are covered in Chapter 15 and SELinux configuration is covered in Chapters 4 and 15. As SELinux is not a "prerequisite" skill, it is not covered in this chapter.

Allowing and Denying

The /etc/hosts.allow and /etc/hosts.deny files can help you manage what computers are allowed into your network. You can specify computers by name, IP address, network, or domain name in each file. This can help you limit access to a trusted few computers such as those within your company, or it can protect you from computers that you know may pose a problem.

Securing Ports

TCP/IP has 65,536 ports, which work sort of like TV channels. If you leave all ports open, you're leaving a lot of options for a cracker who wants to break into your network. With a firewall, you can create a solid barrier and then open only the ports that you need.

Network Address Translation

Most LAN administrators set up Network Address Translation (NAT) as a matter of course on an IPv4 network. Since IPv4 addresses are scarce, it is typical to use private IP addresses inside a LAN, with a regular IP address only on the gateway computer that is directly connected to an outside network such as the Internet.

For example, when a computer inside a LAN wants access to a Web page, NAT sends the IP address of the gateway to the Internet. Nobody outside the LAN need know the real source of the Web page request.

iptables

The **iptables** command has three basic ways to look at a data packet: input, output, or forward. Within these and other parameters, you can set up your firewall with instructions to let the packet pass, let it drop, or direct it someplace else. If you're working with IPv6, the corresponding command is **ip6tables**.

Once you've configured a firewall and loaded it, the rules are stored in the /etc/sysconfig/iptables file. **iptables** is covered in more detail in Chapter 15.

Other Basic Prerequisite Skills per the Red Hat Exam Prep Guide

There are more prerequisite skills defined in the Red Hat Exam Prep guide at https://www.redhat.com/training/rhce/examprep.html. These are over and above the RH300 prerequisites as defined by https://www.redhat.com/training/rhce/courses/rh300_prereq.html. Word for word from the current Exam Prep guide, they specify that you know how to:

- Configure an e-mail client on Red Hat Enterprise Linux
- Use a text and/or graphical browser to access HTTP/HTTPS URLs
- Use lftp to access FTP URLs

Configuring an email Client

The configuration process for a GUI e-mail client should be trivial for any candidate for Red Hat certification. However, the same may not necessarily be true for command line clients, and it's certainly possible that you'll have to configure RHEL 5 solely on the command line.

Command Line Mail

To test your mail system, you can use the built-in command line **mail** utility, a simple text-based interface. The system keeps each user's mail in a system directory. Once users read a message, they can reply, forward, or delete it. If they do not delete the message before quitting the mail utility, the system stores the message in the /var/mail directory, in a file named after the applicable username.

You can certainly use any of the other mail readers, such as mutt, or the e-mail managers associated with different GUI Web browsers to test your system. Other mail readers store messages in different directories. For example, pine would create and store messages for user mj in the /home/mj/mail directory.

To send mail to another user, you can use the mail command line utility. There are two basic methods for using mail. First, you can enter the subject and then the text of your message. When you're done, press CTRL-D and then enter another addressee in the Cc: line, if desired. When you press ENTER, the message is sent and the mail utility stops and sends you back to the command line:

```
$ mail Michael
Subject: Test Message
Sent and received
Cc: mjang@example.com
$
```

Alternatively, you can redirect a file as the text of an e-mail to another user. For example, the following command sends a copy of /etc/hosts to the root user, with the subject name "hosts file":

```
$ mail root@localhost -s 'hosts file' < /etc/hosts
```

Reading Mail Messages

By default, the mail system doesn't open unless you actually have e-mail in your inbox. Once it is open, you'll see a list of new and already read messages. To read a specific message, enter the number of the message and press ENTER. If you press ENTER with no argument, the mail utility assumes you want to read the next unread message. To delete a mail message, use the **d** command after reading the message, or use **d#** to delete the message numbered #.

Mail Group "Alias" Lists

If you have a distribution list of people for the same e-mail, you can set it up in the /etc/aliases file. By default, it's set up to forward e-mail from pseudo-accounts such as system and apache to root. You can change it by adding a group list similar to the following:

```
groupname:  user01, user02, othergroupname
```

You can then run the **newaliases** command to compile this database. Then all you need to do is name the group of users as addressees for your e-mail.

Using a Text and/or Graphical Browser to Access HTTP/HTTPs URLs

First, the prerequisite specifies the use of a text and/or graphical browser. RHEL 5 uses the Mozilla Firefox browser, known popularly as Firefox. This prerequisite should be trivial for any serious user of Linux. However, it's possible that you'll have access only to the command line interface during the Red Hat exams; therefore, you may want to learn how to use a text-based browser such as **elinks**. Once the package is installed, you can use it from the command line to open the Web site of your choice. For example, Figure 1-5 illustrates a view of www.osborne.com.

If you configure a Web server, the easiest way to make sure it works is with a simple text home page. No HTML coding is required. For example, if you added the following text to home.html:

```
This is my home page
```

you could then run the **elinks home.html** command to view this text in the elinks browser.

Using lftp to Access URLs

The original FTP client software was a basic command line, text-oriented client application that offered a simple but efficient interface. Most Web browsers offer a graphical interface and can also be used as an FTP client.

Any FTP client allows you to view the directory tree and files. Using FTP as a client is easy. You could use the **ftp** command to connect to a server such as ftp .redhat.com with the following command:

```
# ftp ftp.redhat.com
```

The FTP client listed in the Red Hat Exam Prep guide is **lftp**. You can use it to connect to the FTP server of your choice. It automatically attempts an anonymous login. It also supports command completion, which can especially help you access files and directories with longer names.

Figure 1-6 illustrates a typical **lftp** session to ftp.redhat.com. As you can see, **lftp** uses a number of typical bash commands. The command completion feature lists

---

FIGURE 1-5   Using **elinks**

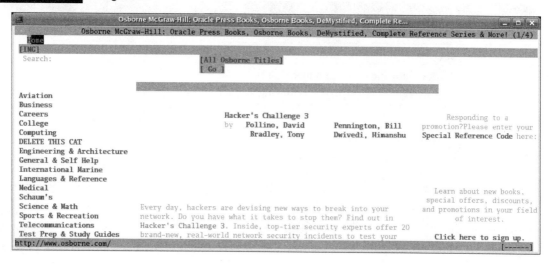

FIGURE 1-6

Using lftp

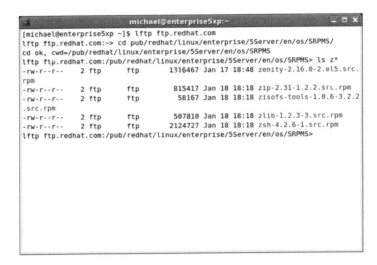

```
                              michael@enterprise5xp:~                    _ □ ✕
[michael@enterprise5xp ~]$ lftp ftp.redhat.com
lftp ftp.redhat.com:~> cd pub/redhat/linux/enterprise/5Server/en/os/SRPMS/
cd ok, cwd=/pub/redhat/linux/enterprise/5Server/en/os/SRPMS
lftp ftp.redhat.com:/pub/redhat/linux/enterprise/5Server/en/os/SRPMS> ls z*
-rw-r--r--    2 ftp       ftp         1316467 Jan 17 18:48 zenity-2.16.0-2.el5.src.
rpm
-rw-r--r--    2 ftp       ftp          815417 Jan 18 18:18 zip-2.31-1.2.2.src.rpm
-rw-r--r--    2 ftp       ftp           58167 Jan 18 18:18 zisofs-tools-1.0.6-3.2.2
.src.rpm
-rw-r--r--    2 ftp       ftp          507810 Jan 18 18:18 zlib-1.2.3-3.src.rpm
-rw-r--r--    2 ftp       ftp         2124727 Jan 18 18:18 zsh-4.2.6-1.src.rpm
lftp ftp.redhat.com:/pub/redhat/linux/enterprise/5Server/en/os/SRPMS>
```

available subdirectories. I've navigated to the directory with RHEL 5 Source RPMs
(RHEL Source RPMs are released to the public under the GPL—the GNU General
Public License from www.fsf.org), and this doesn't require any subscription to the
Red Hat Network.

Another advantage of **lftp** is that it can handle all of the basic upload and download
commands of a regular FTP client. Some of these commands are described in Table 1-8.

Almost all commands from the FTP prompt are run at the remote host, similar
to a Telnet session. To run a regular shell command on the local system, start the
command with an exclamation point (!).

TABLE 1-8   Standard **lftp** Client Commands

Command	Description
cd	Changes the current working directory at the remote host
ls	Lists files at the remote host
get	Retrieves one file from the remote host
mget	Retrieves many files from the remote host with wildcards or full filenames
put	Uploads one file from your computer to the remote host
mput	Uploads a group of files to the remote host
pwd	Lists the current working directory on the remote host
quit	Ends the FTP session
!ls	Lists files on your host computer in the current directory
lcd	Changes the local host directory for upload/download
!pwd	Lists the current working directory on the local host computer

This is only a subset of the commands available through **lftp**. Typing the **help** command at the **lftp** prompt gives you a full list of the available commands. The command **help** *cmd* yields a brief description of the command itself.

CERTIFICATION OBJECTIVE 1.13

Downloading the Red Hat Enterprise Linux Installation CDs

First, this section is not directly related to the Red Hat exams. There is no evidence from the Red Hat Exam Prep guide or course outlines that you need to know how to download and write the RHEL 5 CDs during either exam.

Nevertheless, you need some Red Hat–style Linux distribution to prepare for the Red Hat exams, and this section focuses on whatever steps you need to take to download the relevant media. Obviously, it's best if you have an official subscription to the Red Hat Network, as you may get support for your installation and configuration. However, subscriptions are expensive, and courtesy of the GPL, alternatives are available.

The main alternatives are Fedora Core (versions 5 and 6), as well as the third-party "rebuilds" described earlier. Fedora Core 5/6 is the "testbed" for RHEL 5. While Fedora Core 5 is the "pre-alpha," Fedora Core 6 was used to develop the beta for RHEL 5. In other words, it's what Red Hat used to test many of the features now seen in RHEL 5. In my opinion, the better alternative is one of the rebuild distributions. As described earlier, these distributions are based on the source code for RHEL 5, which Red Hat has released under the GPL.

Several of these groups provide regular updates. As Red Hat releases updates to RHEL 5, these groups rebuild the updated source code into repositories. Most are compatible with the **yum** update tool. (Starting with release 7, Red Hat has dropped the "Core" from the name of the Fedora distribution.) You can keep these rebuild distributions up to date using **yum** or another update tool such as **smart** or **apt**.

Downloading Red Hat Enterprise Linux

Naturally, if you have a subscription to the Red Hat Network, it's best if you download RHEL 5 CDs directly from the network. Of course, you can purchase a subscription from Red Hat. But if you do not want to spend the money, Red Hat offers a trial subscription to RHEL 5. For more information, see www.redhat.com/rhel/details/eval/. As of this writing, it requires a quick telephone call from a Red Hat sales representative. If approved, you should be able to create a trial account on the Red Hat Network, from where you can download the installation CDs for RHEL 5 and receive updates for the 30-day evaluation period (though Red Hat may revoke this offer at any time). Once you have a Red Hat Network account, navigate to https://rhn.redhat.com, log into your account, click the Channels link on the top bar, and click the link associated with the following statement: *download ISO images of channel content*. (As Red Hat updates its systems, these URLs and links are subject to change.)

With an authorized Red Hat Network account, you should then be able to download the installation CDs for RHEL 5 in ISO format, using the instructions therein.

As of this writing, Red Hat Enterprise Linux is not available on DVDs, but I believe will be sometime in the near future.

Red Hat Enterprise Linux Source RPMs

As of this writing, you can navigate to the Red Hat FTP server, log in anonymously, and download the source code associated with RHEL 5. You can use commands such as **rpmbuild** to build the source code packages into binary RPMs that can then be installed.

Unfortunately, it is rather difficult to take these steps with all RHEL 5 source RPMs. Fortunately, a number of third parties have "rebuilt" these source RPMs into working distributions.

Third-Party Rebuilds

When third parties rebuild the RHEL 5 source RPMs, they do so under the GPL. However, they still have to respect various trademark laws that prohibit copying without permission. So when third parties rebuild RHEL 5 packages, they create their own icons, logos, and backgrounds.

However, several rebuild distributions have done more. For example, CentOS (www.centos.org) include installation DVDs and even live CDs similar to those associated with the Ubuntu and Knoppix distributions. They may even be available at the same servers from which you can download other Linux distributions. For example, the CentOS list of mirrors for their (and I say their, because CentOS is a community of developers) rebuild is available from www.centos.org/modules/tinycontent/index.php?id=13.

The Fedora Core 5/6 Prep Option

It's possible to prepare for the Red Hat exams using Fedora Core 5 or 6. Red Hat developed RHEL 5 from this distribution. Fedora Core 5/6 is freely available online and is easily downloadable. It's also available from many other sources, including my book *Mastering Fedora Core 5*, published by Sybex.

However, Fedora Core 5 is essentially a pre-alpha version of RHEL 5, and as such it may not reflect the RHEL 5 you work with during the Red Hat exams or on the job. While Fedora Core 6 is a bit closer, the software packages will vary. For that reason, I believe if you can't afford a subscription to the Red Hat Network, the best option is one of the third-party rebuild distributions.

An Overview of the Download Process

Whether you download RHEL 5, a rebuild, or Fedora Core 5/6, the basic download process is the same and follows these basic steps:

1. Select a distribution to download.
2. Find the download server with ISO files.
3. Proceed with the download, using a high-speed connection.

Other options are possible; for example, you can install Fedora Core 5/6 or some of the rebuild distributions directly from their Internet servers. As Red Hat supports downloads from HTTP and FTP servers, all you need is a boot disk and a sufficiently high-speed Internet connection. But when you download installation media, you can use that media to install RHEL 5 again and again on multiple computers.

You can then use a command such as **cdrecord**, or a GUI tool such as GnomeBaker, K3b, or even many Microsoft Windows–based tools to write the ISO file to appropriate blank CDs. The use of GUI tools to write ISO files to CDs (or even DVDs) is fairly trivial. Just look for the menu command that writes the ISO directly to the CD or DVD.

Downloads are not practical without a high-speed connection. (I once tried downloading a Red Hat CD over a telephone modem. After three days, the download file was corrupt and unusable.) If you don't have a high-speed connection, RHEL 5 CDs are available from Red Hat (though they're expensive), or CDs associated with some of the rebuild distributions are available from third parties. For example, the rebuilds created by CentOS and Scientific Linux (www.scientificlinux.org) are available for a modest fee from CheapBytes (www.cheapbytes.com).

CERTIFICATION SUMMARY

The RHCE and RHCT exams are not for beginners. This chapter covers the prerequisites for the RHCE exam and thus the elementary skills that you need for the remainder of this book. If the explanations in this chapter are too brief, you may need to refer to sources such as those I cite at the beginning of this chapter. While these exams are based on RHEL 5, you can use Fedora Core 5/6 or a third-party rebuild of RHEL 5 to study for these exams.

This chapter provides an overview of many Linux fundamentals. While the RHCE and RHCT hands-on exams may not explicitly test the skills you learn in this chapter, you need to know many of these fundamentals to solve the problems presented on those exams.

Before you start planning your Linux installation, you need a basic degree of knowledge of PC hardware, specifically the Intel-based architecture. A basic understanding of IRQ ports, I/O addresses, DMA channels, and hard drive systems can help you plan how Linux manages and connects every component in your PC.

But not all hardware is supported by Linux. You should now have enough information to find the hardware that fits your needs. Alternatively, you now know about the resources that help you determine what other hardware you need that also works with Linux. Planning your Linux installation makes it easier to handle a wide variety of hardware.

TWO-MINUTE DRILL

Here are some of the key points from the certification objectives in Chapter 1.

Basic Hardware Knowledge

❑ The Red Hat exams are given on computers built for an Intel-based 32-bit architecture.

❑ An Intel-architecture PC has three basic communications channels: IRQ ports, I/O addresses, and DMA channels.

❑ The latest version of Red Hat Enterprise Linux as certified should have at least 256MB of RAM.

❑ You can set up Linux on IDE, SCSI, USB, or IEEE 1394 hard drives. However, the BIOS of a PC can load Linux boot files only from the first two PATA, SATA, or SCSI drives.

Basic Linux Knowledge

❑ Linux is managed through a series of text configuration files.

❑ Understanding text editors is a critical skill. If you ever have to recover your system with a rescue CD, you may not have access to the GUI and will need to know how to use a console-based text editor such as vi.

Linux Filesystem Hierarchy and Structure

❑ Linux directories are organized to the Filesystem Hierarchy Standard (FHS).

❑ In the FHS, devices such as mice and hard drives are grouped in the /dev directory. Some /dev files have logical names such as dvdwriter and are linked to the actual device files.

❑ FHS partitions can be managed and formatted with the **fdisk**, **fsck**, and **mkfs** commands.

❑ The Logical Volume Manager allows you to consolidate multiple partitions in one filesystem, on one directory.

❑ Once configured, Linux directories can be mounted on a partition through /etc/fstab or directly with the **mount** command.

Basic File Operations and Manipulation

❑ Linux administrators need to know how to use the command line interface.

❑ Basic commands allow you to navigate, find the files that you need, read file contents, create new files, and more.

❑ File filters allow you to search through the files themselves for specific citations or other file characteristics.

❑ Administrative commands allow you to manage Linux in a number of ways, including running processes and managing logged-in users.

Printing

❑ The default Red Hat Enterprise Linux print system is CUPS.

❑ You can configure printers by directly editing the files in the /etc/cups directory or by opening the Red Hat Printer Configuration tool with the **system-config-printer** command.

Shells

❑ Command lines are based on a shell.

❑ With the right permissions, you can set up shell programs in executable scripts.

❑ The way a shell works depends on the settings in its variables and parameters. Some variables and parameters are grouped in the inherited environment, which maintains settings from shell to shell.

❑ With stdin, stdout, and stderr, you can manage different data streams.

Basic Security

❑ Basic security within Linux is based on file permissions, users, groups, and **umask**.

❑ The SUID and SGID bits allow you to share owner-level permissions with different users and groups.

❑ Shadow passwords hide user authentication data. The Shadow Password Suite protects user and group passwords in files that should be accessible only to the root user.

System Administration

❑ While it's normally best to log in as a regular user, it's faster to log in as the root user for the RHCE and RHCT exams.

❑ Standard files for new users are kept in /etc/skel.

❑ Daemons are processes that run in the background.

❑ Network service can be controlled through scripts in the /etc/init.d and /etc/xinetd.d directories.

❑ The **cron** daemon helps you schedule different jobs, including backup and restore jobs, which should be done when network use is at a minimum.

❑ When you have problems, system log files, as organized by /etc/syslog.conf, provide important clues to the causes.

Basic TCP/IP Networking

❑ Most of the work in TCP/IP networking is in configuring IP addresses.

❑ There are three different sets of private IPv4 addresses suitable for setting up TCP/IP on a LAN.

❑ IPv6 addresses include all available IPv4 addresses. If the first three bits of an IPv6 address are 001, that is a unicast address—in other words, one that is associated with a specific computer or other device.

❑ The first 48 bits of an IPv6 address are typically associated with a specific network.

❑ Tools such as **ping**, **ping6**, **ifconfig**, and **netstat** can help you diagnose problems on that LAN.

❑ Name resolution configuration files determine how your computer finds the right IP address.

Familiarity with Standard Network Services

❑ There are a number of standard network services, including NFS, sendmail, POP, IMAP, FTP, DNS, DHCP, Samba, Apache, and NIS.

❑ Each of these services, when installed, can be configured to start and stop through the scripts located in the /etc/rc.d/init.d or /etc/xinetd.d directories.

Basic Network Security

❑ Basic network security settings can depend on allowing or denying access to different computers by their IP addresses or by the desired TCP/IP port.

❑ Computers behind a firewall can be protected through Network Address Translation or various **iptables** commands.

Other Basic Prerequisite Skills per the Red Hat Exam Prep Guide

❑ While GUI e-mail clients should be trivial, it's important to know how to configure a command line e-mail client.

❑ While GUI Web browsers should be trivial for serious Red Hat exam candidates, it can help to know a text-based browser such as **elinks**.

❑ While GUI FTP clients should be trivial for serious Red Hat exam candidates, it can help to understand a text-based FTP client such as **lftp**.

Downloading the Red Hat Enterprise Linux Installation CDs

❑ There is no evidence that you need to know how to download the Red Hat installation CDs for the Red Hat exams.

❑ While the best option is to download the RHEL 5 CDs from the Red Hat Network, excellent options are available.

❑ You can use the rebuild distributions to prepare for the Red Hat exams. Their distributions are built on the same source code used by Red Hat for RHEL 5.

SELF TEST

The following questions will help you measure your understanding of the material presented in this chapter. As there are no multiple choice questions on the Red Hat exams, there are no multiple choice questions in this book. These questions exclusively test your understanding of the chapter. While the topics in this chapter are "prerequisites," it is okay if you know another way of performing a task. Getting results, not memorizing trivia, is what counts on the Red Hat exams. There may be more than one answer for many of these questions.

Basic Hardware Knowledge

1. Once Linux is booted, what file can tell you all about the CPU(s) on your system?

   _____

Basic Linux Knowledge

2. If you're editing the /etc/inittab file in vi, what command would you use to copy the currently highlighted line? _____

Linux Filesystem Hierarchy and Structure

3. What command would you use to find currently mounted drives? _____

Basic File Operations and Manipulation

4. If you want to find the actual number of times user mj is logged into your Linux computer, what command would you use? _____

Printing

5. You're maintaining a large queue of print jobs on your network, and you need some job numbers to make sure the engineers get highest priority on the printer. What command would you use to list print job numbers? _____

Shells

6. What command would you use to add the /usr/sbin directory to your PATH?

   _____

Basic Security

7. When you run the **umask** command, you see the following result: 0000. The next time you create a file, what will be the permissions? _____

System Administration

8. Based on the following line from a user's crontab file, when will the Berkeleylives program be run?

```
0 1 2 3 * Berkeleylives
```

_____

Basic TCP/IP Networking

9. Provide an example of an appropriate IPv4 network address, subnet mask, and broadcast address for a network of less than 300 computers on the 10.0.0.0 private network.

Network address: _____

Subnet mask: _____

Broadcast address: _____

Familiarity with Standard Network Services

10. What is the protocol associated with the service used to connect Linux to a Microsoft Windows–based network? _____

Basic Network Security

11. What command would you use to start the basic Red Hat Enterprise Linux firewall configuration utility? _____

Other Basic Prerequisite Skills per the Red Hat Exam Prep Guide

12. Name one of the major e-mail clients available on Red Hat Enterprise Linux 5.

_____

Downloading the Red Hat Enterprise Linux Installation CDs

13. Name one alternative distribution that uses the same source code as RHEL 5.

_____

LAB QUESTIONS

The first lab is fairly elementary, designed to get you thinking in terms of networks and networking. The last two labs both work with the /etc/inittab configuration file. Before working with that file, make sure to back it up first.

Lab 1

You have 18 computers on a LAN behind a firewall. Diagram your computers on a sheet of paper. Connect them together in a "star" configuration. Assign a private IP address to each computer. Take one computer and draw a second connection to the Internet.

   While this is a fairly simple exercise, Linux is built for networking. To understand what you can do with Red Hat Enterprise Linux, you need to think in terms of the role of your computer on a network.

Lab 2

In this lab, you'll start your experiments with the /etc/inittab file. So before you begin, back it up to a file such as /etc/inittab.bak or back up a copy to your home directory.

   1.   Use the vi editor to open the /etc/inittab file in your computer.

   2.   Take a look at your id variable. If it's set to 3, change it to 5; if it's 5 set it to 3.

   3.   Reboot your computer and see what happens.

   4.   Restore your original /etc/inittab file.

Lab 3

In this lab, you'll experiment a bit more with the /etc/inittab configuration file.

   1.   If you haven't already done so, create a backup for /etc/inittab.

   2.   Press CTRL-ALT-F2. You should see a virtual console text login screen.

   3.   Return to the original text console by pressing CTRL-ALT-F1 or the GUI console by pressing CTRL-ALT-F7.

   4.   In the /etc/inittab file, identify the lines related to the virtual login consoles.

   5.   Try experimenting with these lines with the **mingetty** commands. Add a comment character (#) in front of the second line with the **mingetty** command.

   6.   Run the **init q** command to make Linux reread this file.

   7.   Try pressing CTRL-ALT-F2 again. What happens?

   8.   Restore your original /etc/inittab configuration file.

SELF TEST ANSWERS

Basic Hardware Knowledge

1. The key Linux file associated with the CPU is /proc/cpuinfo. However, other files can tell you about how Linux detected the CPU, including /var/log/dmesg. The more you know about such files, the more problems you can diagnose with your hardware.

Basic Linux Knowledge

2. The yy command in vi yanks a copy of the current line into the buffer.

Linux Filesystem Hierarchy and Structure

3. To find currently mounted drives, the simplest method is to use the **mount** command; other commands that can tell you about mounted drives are **cat /etc/mtab** and **df**.

Basic File Operations and Manipulation

4. The most elegant way to find the actual number of times user mj is logged in is to use the **who | grep mj | wc -l** command. However, for these purposes, it's usually good enough to count from the list associated with the **who** command. Remember that results are what matter on the Red Hat exams.

Printing

5. The simplest method to check print queues is to use the **lpq** command. If you want more information, try **lpq -l** for a long listing format. If you have more than one printer, the **lpq -a** command checks all configured printers.

Shells

6. The simplest way to add /usr/sbin to your **$PATH** is to use the **PATH=$PATH:/usr/sbin** command. But to make sure this command takes effect the next time you log in, you should add this command to the hidden .bash_profile file in your home directory.

Basic Security

7. The answer is read and write permissions for all users, or _rw_rw_rw. Even if you try to set it to allow execute permissions, Red Hat won't let you do this anymore. You'll need to set execute permissions on each file after creation.

System Administration

8. The convention for the first five entries in a crontab line is minute, hour, day of month, month, and day of week, so this particular job will run at 1 A.M. on March 2.

Basic TCP/IP Networking

9. The answer to this question will vary widely. If you can't provide many answers to this question, you may need to learn more about basic IPv4 addressing. One example is a network address of 10.11.12.0, a subnet mask of 255.255.255.0, and a broadcast address of 10.11.12.255.

Familiarity with Standard Network Services

10. The basic protocol is Samba (SMB), associated with the Common Internet File System (CIFS). Any of these answers are correct; however, as described in Chapter 10, it's important to know that the CIFS module has superseded the SMBFS module for RHEL 5.

Basic Network Security

11. The basic Red Hat firewall configuration utility can be started with the **system-config-securitylevel** command.

Other Basic Prerequisite Skills as per the Red Hat Exam Prep Guide

12. Several different e-mail clients are available in RHEL 5, including mutt, mail, Kmail, and Evolution.

Downloading the Red Hat Enterprise Linux Installation CDs

13. There are several different rebuild distributions available, including CentOS, Lineox, Scientific Linux, and more. One list of available rebuild distributions can be found at http://linuxmafia.com/faq/RedHat/rhel-forks.html. The answer is correct only if the group you've cited has rebuilt the source code for RHEL 5.

LAB ANSWERS

Lab I

There are many ways to configure the IP addresses on a LAN. But it is generally best to do it by setting up a network from one of the private IP address ranges. When you configure networking on your LAN, pay particular attention to the computer that also has a connection to the Internet. The IP address of its connection to your network will be the gateway address for every other computer on your LAN. It's also the logical location for any firewall that you may wish to configure.

Lab 2

When you troubleshoot a Red Hat Enterprise Linux computer, one of the things you'll be checking are critical configuration files. One key file in the boot process is /etc/inittab. One thing that I can do in this book is to illustrate the behavior of potential problems. The more problems you're familiar with, the easier it will be to troubleshoot or debug a problem during the RHCT and RHCE exams. However, there is often more than one way to solve a problem. I present one method, but you may be able to find others.

To go through this lab, I'd take the following steps:

1. Log in as the root user. You can do this from either the GUI or the text login interface.

2. Run the **cp /etc/inittab /root/inittab** command. This backs up the subject configuration file in the root user's home directory.

3. Open the subject file with the **vi /etc/inittab** command.

4. Scroll down to until you see the following line:

   ```
   id:3:initdefault
   ```

5. The number after the **id** command identifies your starting runlevel. If it's 3, Linux starts in text mode; if it's 5, Linux starts in the GUI.

6. Change this number from 3 to 5 (or from 5 to 3).

7. Save your changes and exit from the vi editor with the **:wq** command.

8. Reboot your computer with the **reboot** command.

9. Linux should now start in your new runlevel (3 or 5).

10. Restore your original settings in /etc/inittab. You can do this by opening /etc/inittab with the vi editor. Alternatively, you can copy your backup from the /root directory with the **cp /root/inittab /etc/inittab** command.

Lab 3

In this lab, experiment with deactivating a specific virtual console. By default, six virtual text login consoles are configured in the /etc/inittab configuration file. You'll deactivate the second of the six consoles.

1. Log in as the root user. You can do this from either the GUI or the text login interface. If you're in the GUI, open a text console. Right-click the desktop and choose New Terminal in the pop-up menu.

2. Run the **cp /etc/inittab /root/inittab** command. This backs up the subject configuration file in the root user's home directory.

3. Open the subject file with the **vi /etc/inittab** command.

4. Scroll down until you see the following line:

   ```
   2:2345:respawn:/sbin/mingetty tty2
   ```

5. Press CTRL-ALT-F2. This should start a text login interface. You should be able to log in at the prompt with your username and password. (If you've started at a text console, you don't need to use the CTRL button.)

6. If you logged into the GUI, press CTRL-ALT-F7 to return to the GUI. If you logged into the text interface, press CTRL-ALT-F1 to return to your original screen.

7. Turn the **subject** command in /etc/inittab into a comment. Add a comment character in front of the line as shown:

   ```
   #2:2345:respawn:/sbin/mingetty tty2
   ```

8. Close and save this change to /etc/inittab using the **:wq** command.

9. Make Linux reread /etc/inittab with the **init q** command.

10. Press CTRL-ALT-F2. This should start a text login interface. Try logging in again. You'll see that it's not possible. Now you can see how adding a comment character to the right line in /etc/inittab deactivates the second virtual console.

11. If you logged into the GUI, press CTRL-ALT-F7 to return to the GUI. If you logged into the text interface, press CTRL-ALT-F1 to return to your original screen.

12. Restore your original settings in the /etc/inittab file.

2

Hardware and Installation

CERTIFICATION OBJECTIVES

2.01   Hardware Compatibility

2.02   CPU and RAM

2.03   Hotswap Buses

2.04   Configuring a Network Installation

2.05   The First Installation Steps

2.06   Configuring Partitions, RAID, and LVM

2.07   Post-partition Installation Steps

2.08   Post-installation, Security, and the First Boot Process

2.09   Installation Validation

✓   Two-Minute Drill

Q&A   Self Test

I nstallation is one of the two parts of both the RHCE and the RHCT exams. To pass this part of each exam, you'll need to know a lot more than just the basic GUI installation process for a single computer! Once you've studied the installation chapters (Chapters 2 and 5), you'll be able to install Red Hat Enterprise Linux (RHEL) in a number of ways: over a network, directly from the CD, using boot disks, and with automated kickstart–based tools.

While this chapter covers the "basics," they are important. Naturally, you need compatible hardware, as well as sufficient processing power and RAM. The latest Linux tools help detect portable and network devices.

Generally, unless you've copied the installation DVD or CDs to the local system, network installations are fastest. To help you learn all installation methods, we'll show you how to configure a network installation server.

on the
job

While Red Hat does not provide an installation DVD, it is available for some of the "rebuild" distributions such as CentOS and Scientific Linux.

Then you'll learn how to install RHEL on your system, step by step. The installation program is known as Anaconda. You'll see how you can create regular (software) RAID and Logical Volume Management (LVM)–based partitions. Then you'll be guided through the First Boot process to see how to continue the RHEL configuration process after installation is complete.

You may be asked to install and configure some or all of the services described on the Red Hat Exam Prep guide (www.redhat.com/training/rhce/examprep.html). This chapter will help you understand the services that you can install with RHEL. The fastest way to install RHEL is in text mode.

However, you may wish to install RHEL via the regular graphical screen as you can't customize LVM partitions in text mode. If the test system and network is up to date (for example, Fast Ethernet is probably sufficient), the time penalty associated with GUI installations may be trivial.

CERTIFICATION OBJECTIVE 2.01

Hardware Compatibility

Now it's time to explore the hardware that RHEL can handle. While some manufacturers now include their own Linux hardware drivers, most Linux hardware support comes from third parties. Fortunately, a vast community of Linux users

INSIDE THE EXAM

Focus During Installation

Both the RHCE and RHCT exams include an Installation and Configuration section. You'll have to do more than just install Linux. You'll follow a series of instructions, configure custom partitions, and configure certain services.

Time limits are severe on these exams. Install and configure as much as you can when you install RHEL on your computer. Although you can configure and install almost anything after Linux is installed, that can take more time than you have.

On the other hand, don't install everything. It takes time to install gigabytes of software over a network. If you're spending time installing software that you don't need, that's time you can't get back during the exam.

As you read this chapter, learn every part of the installation process. Know what you need to install. For example, if you see a requirement to set up Apache and Samba servers, you'll want to install the Web Server and Windows File Server package groups when you install RHEL.

Studying for the Installation and Configuration Section

You can use one of the "rebuilds" of RHEL 5 or even Fedora Core 6 to study for the Installation portion of the RHCE and RHCT exams. The steps required are essentially identical to those for RHEL 5. To assure you that the steps are the same, consult "Installing Red Hat Enterprise Linux 5" in the Online Learning Center (http://highered.mhhe.com/sites/0072264543), which provides a pictorial-only guide to the RHEL 5 installation process.

are hard at work, producing Linux drivers and more, even distributing them freely on the Internet. If a certain piece of hardware is popular, you can be certain that Linux support for that hardware will pop up somewhere on the Internet and will be incorporated into various Linux distributions, including RHEL.

Be careful when purchasing a new computer to use with Linux. Though Linux has come a long way the last few years, and you should have little problem installing it on most modern PCs, you shouldn't assume Linux will install or run flawlessly on *any* PC, especially if the PC in question is a state-of-the-art laptop computer (though several major laptop manufacturers seem determined to maintain good relationships with the Linux community). Laptops are often designed with proprietary configurations that work with Linux only after some reverse-engineering. For example, when I installed Red Hat Enterprise Linux on a new widescreen laptop, I could install only in text mode.

Other types of hardware, such as "winmodems" and "winprinters," are designed to use Microsoft Windows driver libraries. Integrated hardware (such as video chips that share system RAM) and parallel port devices can also be problematic. While Linux drivers exist for many of these devices, do your research.

Linux runs very well on lower-end computers. This is one of Linux's strong points over other operating systems, especially Microsoft Windows Vista. Linux runs fine on 64MB of RAM, although more is always better, especially if you want to run any graphical applications. RHEL 5 does require a minimum of 192MB of memory to start the graphical installer. However, the latest versions of Linux do have limits; modern distributions don't run on anything less than a Pentium-class system.

e x a m

ⓦ a t c h   *While it is important that you know how to select and configure hardware components to get to a smoothly running Linux computer, the RHCE and RHCT exams are not hardware exams.*

Linux Hardware Documentation

Many resources are available to help you select the best hardware for Linux. Thousands of Linux gurus are available online via mailing lists, IRC rooms, and newsgroups. Perhaps the best places to look are the Linux Documentation Project (LDP) or the Red Hat Hardware Compatibility List (HCL). The LDP is a global effort to produce reliable documentation for all aspects of the Linux operating system, including hardware compatibility.

Linux Hardware HOWTO

The Linux Hardware HOWTO is a document listing most of the hardware components supported by Linux. It's updated irregularly with added hardware support, so it is a relatively up-to-date source of information, available at www.tldp.org.

The Red Hat Hardware Compatibility List

The Red Hat HCL is different from the one you'll find in the Linux Hardware HOWTO. It specifies name brand hardware that has been tested with various versions of RHEL. If you've purchased RHEL, Red Hat will provide some level of installation support for any certified or compatible hardware. Some hardware that has been tested by Red Hat has specifically been found not to work with Red Hat Linux or RHEL and is therefore not supported. Red Hat doesn't have the resources to test more than a limited range of hardware; most PCs and servers built today work well with RHEL. For that information, refer to the aforementioned Linux Hardware HOWTO.

Plug and Play and the Hardware Abstraction Layer

Plug and play (PnP) refers to the ability of an operating system to allocate hardware ports or addresses automatically to specific devices such as hard drives, sound cards, or modems. Linux's ability to work with PnP devices is finally up to speed, courtesy of the Linux implementation of the Hardware Abstraction Layer (HAL). Conceptually different from the Microsoft version, HAL provides a constant list of detected components. Some distributions can now automatically detect and mount the smart cards associated with digital cameras and fingerprint readers.

If you want to see the full list of detected hardware, run the **lshal** command. It's a long list; you may need to pipe the output to a pager with a command like:

```
# lshal | less
```

which allows you to scroll through the output.

Channel Conflicts

In rare cases, the Linux HAL subsystem may have problems with the newest computer devices or some very old ones. If you're having problems with the newest computer equipment, various Web sites are dedicated to offering help. For example, www.linmodems.org can help you configure many so-called "winmodems," and www .linux-usb.org can help you configure the latest USB equipment on Linux.

Many hardware conflicts with relatively old equipment are fairly simple to eliminate. There are three possible areas of conflict:

- A physical hardware jumper is conflicting with another card.
- Your ISA cards are not properly configured.
- You are out of IRQs or other resources to add to your new device.

You can use the /proc files to check the currently used IRQ ports, I/O addresses, and DMA channels. For example, to check the occupied IRQs, the following command lists the devices that *are* loaded by the kernel:

```
# cat /proc/interrupts
```

If there is a conflict, the device is not loaded. You can quickly scan over the left side to see what interrupts are available. To get a list of used I/O addresses and DMA channels, issue the following commands:

```
# cat /proc/ioports
# cat /proc/dma
```

The kernel included with RHEL 5 and above should keep HAL configuration problems to a minimum. When problems arise, two or more devices are probably trying to use the same IRQ, I/O, and/or DMA. In that case, one or both devices may not be loaded. It may take a little detective work to identify the troubled hardware; conflicts may prevent it from being listed in one of the associated /proc directory files. Then select one of the devices, and change its IRQ, I/O, and/or DMA to a free location.

This is usually a two-step process: first, change the settings on the card itself through physical jumpers or a diagnostic disk, as described in the next section. If Linux doesn't detect your changes, use the appropriate configuration tool, such as **system-config-keyboard**, **ifconfig**, **modprobe**, or **system-config-network**, to change the settings on your device.

Generally, Linux should not have problems with PCI cards, USB devices, or even many IEEE 1394 (also known as FireWire or iLink) systems. Linux should recognize them and set them up with appropriate IRQ ports, I/O addresses, and DMA channels. If you cannot see what your PCI cards are set to, type **cat /proc/pci**. If a PCI card that you're concerned about does not show up here, you may be out of IRQs. If you run out of IRQs, you may want to look into alternatives such as IEEE 1394 or USB devices.

Some Linux distributions may not detect multiple CPUs, or the different CPUs associated with dual-core systems (unless you've installed the right kernel). To know what CPUs are detected, check /proc/cpuinfo.

ACPI and APM

Closely related to HAL are the computer power management standards, known as Advanced Configuration and Power Interface (ACPI) and Advanced Power Management (APM). Both are efforts to manage PC power consumption. As such, they are important tools to extend the lifetime of battery-operated devices such as laptop computers.

Microsoft has driven developments in both areas toward computers that can be easily suspended and reactivated from a minimum power state. On Linux systems, some customization may be required, especially for laptops. For this purpose, the experience of others as documented on sites such as www.tuxmobil .org are most valuable. The experiences of others, as documented on that Web site, helped me customize the functionality of multimedia buttons on my dual-core laptop system.

If you have problems with an ACPI computer, you can deactivate ACPI support with the **acpi=off** command to the kernel during the RHEL boot or installation process.

CERTIFICATION OBJECTIVE 2.02

CPU and RAM

Red Hat Enterprise Linux supports computers with Intel and compatible 32-bit and 64-bit processors.

Linux is commonly used as a server operating system. Many server applications can take advantage of the flexibility provided by multiple CPUs. This is known as *symmetric multiprocessing (SMP)* support. Linux began supporting multiple CPUs with the release of the 2.4 kernel back in 2001. RHEL 5 also supports virtual machines with a customized Xen-based kernel. If you have a newer "dual-core" type CPU, RHEL 5 can even support hardware virtualization, which allows dedicated installations of Microsoft Windows (and other Intel-compatible operating systems) within Linux.

Compatible CPUs

You can install RHEL 5 on systems with a wide variety of CPUs. Red Hat supports six different CPU architectures:

- x86
- Athlon/AMD64 (x86_64)
- Itanium (ia64)
- IBM zSeries
- IBM iSeries
- IBM pSeries

e x a m

w a t c h
As of this writing, we assume that Red Hat tests and will continue to test based on the most popular architecture, x86. Other architectures such as Itanium use a different boot loader (ELILO), which is not covered in the Red Hat Exam Prep guide or associated course outlines.

on the job Some developers hope to increase the SMP limit to 128 CPUs. If you're running Linux on an SMP computer, keep up to date with the latest kernel developments at www.kernel.org.

CPUs and Virtualization

Red Hat is in the process of incorporating virtualization in its operating systems. Both Fedora Core 6 and RHEL 5 include Xen, which is a "free virtual machine monitor," which includes QEMU-based emulation to support virtualization similar to VMware.

on the
Job

QEMU is one more alternative for virtualization, licensed under the GPL and the closely related Lesser GPL. Kernel-based Virtual Machine (KVM) technologies require Linux kernel version 2.6.19; RHEL 5 uses 2.6.18. Paravirtualization for VMWare isn't expected until 2.6.21.

There are two kinds of virtualization associated with Xen. Paravirtualization provides a software interface that allows you to install specially ported operating systems (with a Xen-enabled kernel) within software-based virtual machines. Full, or hardware-assisted, virtualization supports direct hardware access; it is limited to certain Intel Dual Core and AMD X2 CPUs.

on the
Job

Not all Intel Dual Core or AMD X2 CPUs support hardware-assisted virtualization. AMD X2 CPUs need to be TL-50 and above; Intel Dual Core CPUs need to be T2300 (or T5600) and above. Furthermore, Intel-based systems are often disabled in the BIOS and may not support hardware-assisted virtualization unless specifically activated through the BIOS menu. If you see the vmx (Intel) or svm (AMD) flags in /proc/cpuinfo, your system supports hardware virtualization.

RAM Requirements

The minimum RAM requirements for RHEL 5 are trivial for today's computers. While you need at least 192MB to install in graphical mode, 64MB is sufficient to install in text mode—and to run this distribution with a text-based login. One advantage of this small footprint is that it allows you to configure more virtual machines using Xen.

on the
Job

In reality, the minimum amount of RAM depends on the amount of shared video RAM. For example, if 64MB of RAM is used for your video system, you need at least 256MB of RAM to install RHEL 5 in graphical mode.

CERTIFICATION OBJECTIVE 2.03

Hotswap Buses

After a lot of work over the years, Linux handles hotswappable devices well. If everything works as it should, you can plug a device into a hotswap system, and Linux automatically detects the device, loads drivers, and, if appropriate, mounts the data from that device on an appropriate filesystem. There are several commands available to help manage these devices.

You can install many devices externally to your computer. These devices are sometimes known as peripherals, which fall into six categories: serial, parallel, USB, IEEE 1394, smart cards, and PC Cards. A device attached to a serial port, such as a mouse or a modem, uses the device associated with that port. Devices attached to parallel, smart cards, USB, or IEEE 1394 ports normally use their own device files. PC Cards are a special case normally associated with laptop computers.

While Linux normally recognizes basic devices attached to these ports, configuring a few devices may take additional work.

Serial Ports

In many cases, configuring a device for a serial port is as simple as linking to the driver of the associated port. For example, if you have an external modem connected to the only serial port on your computer, the Linux HAL subsystem may have already linked the device for that port with the device for your modem. Run the **ls -l /dev/modem** command. If it shows something like the following output, you know that Linux has already linked your modem driver with the second serial port:

```
lrwxrwxrwx   1 root    root    10 Apr 1 13:17 /dev/modem -> ttyS1
```

Otherwise, you can use the **ln** command to create a link to the appropriate port. If you have a CD/DVD drive, you should find the same type of link from /dev/cdrom.

Parallel Ports

Configuring devices attached to a parallel port can be more complex. For example, Linux doesn't always recognize printers that are attached to a parallel port such as /dev/lp0. Further configuration with tools such as the CUPS Web-based tool or the Red Hat Printer Configuration tool may be required. If there's a local printer you can find the device associated with it in the /etc/cups/printers.conf file.

.. you're connecting an external hard drive to a parallel port, you'll want to install the paride module and the module associated with your device, whether it is a hard drive, a tape drive, or a CD-ROM. Similar steps are required for other parallel port devices. Detailed information on configuring parallel port devices is available from the Linux Parallel Port Web site at www.torque.net/linux-pp.html.

USB

Linux support for USB is growing with the evolution of the latest kernels, including most devices associated with the higher speed USB 2.0 standard. For the latest information, see the Linux USB Web site at www.linux-usb.org.

IEEE 1394

The Institute of Electrical and Electronics Engineers (IEEE) has developed the IEEE 1394 specifications for very high speed data transfer applications, such as digital movies. Equipment designed to these standards is often known by the trade names FireWire and iLink. The current status is similar to USB; in other words, a lot of IEEE 1394 equipment works with Linux, and development continues. For the latest information, see the Linux IEEE 1394 Web site at www.linux1394.org.

PC Card (PCMCIA)

Linux has a package known as Card Services that deals exclusively with PC Cards. This package includes all the kernel modules you'll need to manage PCMCIA cards and a set of drivers for specific cards. The package also includes a daemon that handles hotswapping for most PC Cards.

While development of the Card Services package is ongoing, there is often a period in which there is limited support for the proprietary configurations especially common on laptops. For this reason, the latest laptop is often not the best choice for a Linux installation. However, support for Linux on most name-brand laptops is now common even when the laptop is first released. In fact, several companies sell laptops with Linux installed.

Development of PC Cards continues to evolve with the Express Card, which is not backward-compatible with the CardBus PCMCIA card. It's narrower; and one version of the Express Card is shaped with a notch.

Supported PCMCIA Controllers

According to the Linux PCMCIA Information page at http://pcmcia-cs.sourceforge .net, Linux now supports all common PCMCIA controllers. If you have a problem with a specific PCMCIA card, focus on finding a driver for the card itself. A current list of supported PCMCIA controllers can be found on the Hardware HOWTO.

Express Cards

The Express Card is physically different. The current version supports two form factors. In other words, there are Express Cards designed for 34mm- and 54mm-width cards. Older CardBus cards won't work in these slots. (Imagine my surprise when I tried installing a CardBus modem in a newer laptop. If I pushed too hard, I would have had to call for a hardware repair on my laptop.)

Express Cards are smaller and are shipping with laptops from several of the major manufacturers.

on the **job**

During your career as a computer professional, there will be times where you'll be asked to research a specific product or technology. To get an idea of how hard or easy this can be, call a major computer retailer or manufacturer and inquire about their latest laptop. Ask them if it supports Linux. What kind of answers do you get? Ask whether they have any earlier models that will support Linux. Do you believe the answers you receive are reliable? Check out the company's Web page, if you can, and find out if they provide any information about the product on the Internet. Doing this kind of research can be trying, with or without success. Before deciding on what kind of hardware you want to install Linux, you should have a good understanding of what will and will not work. Start early and build a good base of reliable references you can use to find out new computer information. Web sites, such as the Linux Documentation Project, as well as magazines such as **Linux Journal,** **Linux Format** *(UK),* **Sys Admin Magazine,** *and* **Linux Magazine,** *will help you stay informed.*

Hotswap Systems

To summarize what we know, there are several different types of hotswap systems, including:

- USB
- IEEE 1394 (a.k.a. FireWire, iLink)
- PC Cards (PCMCIA, CardBus, Express Card)

Device Management

There are a number of useful commands that can help you manage hardware devices. The first of these commands is associated with Linux's implementation of the Hardware Abstraction Layer, **lshal**. The output is long, and can tell you a lot about each device. Here's a partial excerpt associated with my CD/DVD drive:

```
udi = '/org/freedesktop/Hal/devices/storage_model_QSI_CD_RW/DVD_ROM_SBW_241'
  org.freedesktop.Hal.Device.Storage.method_execpaths = {'hal-storage-eject',
'hal-storage-closetray'} (string list)
```

Note how the functions are included in the list:

```
  org.freedesktop.Hal.Device.Storage.method_names = {'Eject', 'CloseTray'}
(string list)
  info.interfaces = {'org.freedesktop.Hal.Device.Storage',
'org.freedesktop.Hal.Device.Storage'} (string list)
  info.addons = {'hald-addon-storage'} (string list)
  block.storage_device =
'/org/freedesktop/Hal/devices/storage_model_QSI_CD_RW/DVD_ROM_SBW_241'  (string)
```

The **lsmod** command lists loaded hardware modules. For more information, see Chapter 8. The **lspci** command can tell you more about components attached to the PCI bus. For example, the following output from my laptop tells me more about the wireless card, which is enough for me to find third-party drivers:

```
# lspci
00:00.0 Host bridge: ATI Technologies Inc RS200/RS200M AGP Bridge [IGP 340M]
  (rev 02)
00:01.0 PCI bridge: ATI Technologies Inc PCI Bridge [IGP 340M]
00:02.0 USB Controller: ALi Corporation USB 1.1 Controller (rev 03)
00:06.0 Multimedia audio controller: ALi Corporation M5451
  PCI AC-Link Controller Audio Device (rev 02)
00:07.0 ISA bridge: ALi Corporation M1533/M1535 PCI to ISA Bridge
  [Aladdin IV/V/V+]
00:08.0 Modem: ALi Corporation M5457 AC'97 Modem Controller
00:09.0 Network controller: Intel Corporation PRO/Wireless 2200BG
  Network Connection (rev 05)
```

Note the last line, which displays more information about my internal wireless card. I can get even more information about all of these components by using the **lspci -v** (or even the **lspci -vv**) command. It's more than enough information for me to find Linux drivers, and even packages that allow me to use this wireless card on RHEL 5. For USB devices, the **lsusb** command can help. If you haven't attached anything to a USB port, all you'll see are USB buses:

```
# lsusb
Bus 001 Device 001: ID 0000:0000
```

Once Linux detects a connected USB device, you'll get more information; for example, this is what I see after I insert a USB key drive:

```
# lsusb
Bus 001 Device 002: ID 04e8:1623 Samsung Electronics Co., Ltd
Bus 001 Device 001: ID 0000:0000
```

The **lspcmcia** command is supposed to be the successor to **cardctl** for PC Cards.

CERTIFICATION OBJECTIVE 2.04

Configuring a Network Installation

Most Linux users can install RHEL from a CD/DVD. During the installation portion of the Red Hat exam, you'll save time by installing RHEL over a network from an NFS, HTTP, or FTP server. As you'll want to practice with network installations, you should set up a network server. For completeness, while it's not a "network installation" per se, you can also install RHEL from ISO images on a local hard disk.

on the **job**

SELinux is an excellent system that provides a different level of security for Linux. In this book, I describe many ways that you can work with SELinux enabled. However, users do report trouble making SELinux work with Linux and services such as NFS, HTTP, and FTP. While SELinux has just been included in the Red Hat Exam Prep guide, the exams don't test how you've configured a network installation server. So, if necessary, disable SELinux for a specific service, or disable it completely with the Security Level Configuration tool described in Chapter 15.

Configuring a Network Installation Server

Once you have the Red Hat installation media, configuring a network installation server is a fairly easy process. All you need to do is copy the files from each CD to a common directory, configure sharing on the directory, and then activate the NFS, FTP, or HTTP network. Naturally, if you've downloaded a rebuild installation DVD, the process is simpler.

Before you set up a network installation source, you'll need a partition with at least 2.7GB of free space (3.5 if you're installing the RHEL 5 Client, appropriate for the RHCT exam). I'll illustrate the process for an NFS server and explain the variations for FTP and HTTP servers.

Creating an NFS Installation Server

In the following steps, you'll learn how to create a shared directory, copy the Red Hat installation files, and then set up the share through NFS. As NFS is the most efficient way to share files between Linux and Unix computers, I suspect it's the most likely option for network installations during the exam. You'll need the Red Hat Enterprise Linux installation CDs, or at least the ISO files associated with those CDs.

1. Create a directory for your installation files. With the following command, create the /inst directory:

   ```
   # mkdir /inst
   ```

2. Insert the first Red Hat Enterprise Linux installation CD/DVD into its drive. If you're running the default GNOME desktop, it'll get mounted automatically, using the name of the media; for example, my first RHEL installation CD is automounted in the /media/RHEL-5 i386 Disc 1 directory (including all of those spaces). Otherwise, you can mount the CD with a command such as **mount /dev/cdrom /media**. (If all you have are the ISO files, say in the /tmp directory, substitute **mount -ro loop /tmp/firstcd.iso /media**.)

3. Copy the required files from the first Red Hat Enterprise Linux installation CD. Use the **cp -ar /source/. /inst** command, where *source* is the mount directory (such as /media/RHEL 5 i386 Disc 1). Don't forget the dot (.); it copies hidden files, including the .discinfo file from the first Red Hat Enterprise Linux installation CD.

4. Unmount the first Red Hat Enterprise Linux installation CD. If it's an installation DVD, skip to step 6. Use the **umount /source** command.

5. Repeat steps 2, 3, and 4 with the remaining Red Hat Enterprise Linux installation CDs.

6. Set up an NFS share. Add the following line to /etc/exports. You can do it with a text editor such as vi or the **system-config-nfs** utility (also known as the NFS Server Configuration tool) described in Chapter 10.

   ```
   /inst        *(ro,sync)
   ```

7. Export the shared directory.

   ```
   # exportfs -a
   ```

8. Make sure there's nothing blocking access to NFS. The default Red Hat Enterprise Linux firewall blocks access to an NFS server. While inelegant, the following command "flushes," or turns off, the standard Linux firewall from the local computer. If you've enabled SELinux, you'll also have to use the SELinux Management Tool to change the associated NFS boolean variable to "Allow the reading on any NFS file system". Don't forget to restart NFS to activate all of your changes. I'll describe the **iptables** command and the SELinux Management Tool in more detail in Chapter 15.

on the
job

As of this writing, if SELinux is disabled, RHEL 5 won't let you open the SELinux Management Tool. For the latest information, see bug 232544 at http://bugzilla.redhat.com.

```
# iptables -F
```

9. Now you can activate the NFS service. The following commands assume that it's already running (which you can check using the **service nfs status** command):

```
# service nfs stop
# service nfs start
```

10. Finally, you can check the status of your share. If it's working, you should see the contents of the /etc/exports directory when you run the following command:

```
# showmount -e
```

When you install Red Hat Enterprise Linux from an NFS server, you'll need the name of the installation directory—in this case, /inst.

on the
job

For an NFS connection, you don't need to copy the files from a CD. If you've downloaded ISOs of the RHEL (or rebuild) installation DVD/CDs, all you need to do is copy them to the shared NFS directory—in this case, /inst. However, this does not work for FTP or HTTP servers, and you won't be able to use the share as an installation source for individual packages.

Configuring Another Network Installation Server

The Red Hat exams test your knowledge of Linux. The most efficient way to share files between Linux computers is via NFS. If you have a choice on the exams, install Red Hat Enterprise Linux over a network connection, using NFS. However, it's possible that you'll want or need to install Red Hat Enterprise Linux using one of the two other available protocols: HTTP or FTP.

As some users may install only one kind of installation server, some of the instructions in this section may be repetitive.

HTTP Installation Server

The most popular Web server on the Internet is Apache, which you can easily install with Red Hat Enterprise Linux. The basic steps are the same as those for the NFS server. The details are slightly different. I'm assuming that you've already installed the Apache Web server; for more information, see Chapter 9.

The basic Apache share directory corresponds to the **DocumentRoot** variable, which is by default the /var/www/html directory. In other words, you'd copy the Red Hat installation files to a subdirectory of this directory. For the purpose of this chapter, I've already created the /var/www/html/test directory. Here are the detailed steps:

1. Create a directory for your installation files. Using the following command, create the /var/www/html/inst directory. (If you get an error message, Apache may not be properly installed.)

   ```
   # mkdir /var/www/html/inst
   ```

2. Insert the first Red Hat Enterprise Linux installation CD/DVD into its drive. In many cases, it'll get mounted automatically, using the name of the media; for example, my RHEL DVD is automounted in the /media/RHEL-5 i386 Disc 1 directory. Otherwise, you can run a command such as **mount /dev/cdrom /media**. (If all you have are the ISO files, say in the /tmp directory, substitute **mount -ro loop /tmp/firstcd.iso /media**.)

3. Copy the required files from the first Red Hat Enterprise Linux installation CD. Use the **cp -ar /source/. /var/www/html/inst** command, where *source* is the mount directory (such as /media/RHEL 5 i386 Disc 1). Don't forget the dot (.); it makes sure to copy hidden files, including the .discinfo file from the first Red Hat Enterprise Linux installation CD.

4. Unmount the first Red Hat Enterprise Linux installation CD. If it's an installation DVD, skip to step 6. Use the **umount /source** command.

5. Repeat steps 2, 3, and 4 with the remaining Red Hat Enterprise Linux installation CDs.

6. Make sure there's nothing blocking access to your Apache server. If you're using SELinux, you'll also have to use the SELinux Management Tool to allow access to appropriate directories—use **chcon** to change the security context of the target subdirectory (see Chapter 9), and reboot your system to activate the changes. While inelegant, the following command "flushes," or turns off, the standard Linux firewall from the local computer. I'll describe the **iptables** command in more detail in Chapter 15.

   ```
   # iptables -F
   ```

7. Now you can activate the Apache service, **httpd**. The following commands assume that it's already running (which you can check using the **service httpd status** command):

```
# service httpd stop
# service httpd start
```

When you install Red Hat Enterprise Linux from an Apache HTTP server, you'll need to remember the directory with the Red Hat installation files. For an HTTP server, the right directory is relative to the **DocumentRoot** variable, /var/www/html. With these steps, the installation files are in /var/www/html/inst; therefore, the correct directory is /inst.

FTP Installation Server

One of the oldest protocols still in common use on the Internet is FTP, the File Transfer Protocol. It's efficient and easy to use, and now that Red Hat has implemented the Very Secure FTP (vsFTP) service on its systems, it's relatively secure.

The basic steps are the same as those for the NFS server. I'm assuming that you've already installed the vsFTP server as described in Chapter 10. The basic FTP share directory is /var/ftp/pub. In other words, you'd copy the Red Hat installation files to a subdirectory of this directory. For the purpose of this chapter, I've created the /var/ftp/pub/test directory. Here are the detailed steps:

1. Create a directory for your installation files. With the following command, create the /var/ftp/pub/inst directory. (If you get an error message, vsFTP may not be properly installed.)

```
# mkdir /var/ftp/pub/inst
```

2. Insert the first Red Hat Enterprise Linux installation CD/DVD into its drive. In many cases, it'll get mounted automatically, using the name of the media; for example, my RHEL DVD is automounted in the /media/RHEL-5 i386 Disc 1 directory. Otherwise, you can run a command such as **mount /dev/cdrom /media**. (If all you have are the ISO files, say in the /tmp directory, substitute **mount -ro loop /tmp/firstcd.iso /media**.)

3. Copy the required files from the first Red Hat Enterprise Linux installation CD. Use the **cp -ar /source/. /var/ftp/pub/inst** command, where *source* is the mount directory (such as /media/RHEL 5 i386 Disc 1). Don't forget the dot (.); it makes sure to copy hidden files, including the .discinfo file from the first Red Hat Enterprise Linux installation CD.

4. Unmount the first Red Hat Enterprise Linux installation CD. If it's an installation DVD, skip to step 6. Use the **umount /source** command.

5. Repeat steps 2, 3, and 4 with the remaining Red Hat Enterprise Linux installation CDs.

6. Make sure there's nothing blocking access to your vsFTP server. If you're using SELinux, you'll also have to use the SELinux Management Tool to allow access to appropriate directories, and reboot your system to activate the changes. While inelegant, the following command "flushes," or turns off, the standard Linux firewall from the local computer. I'll describe the **iptables** command in more detail in Chapter 15.

```
# iptables -F
```

7. Now you can activate the FTP server, vsFTP. The following commands assume that it's already running (which you can check using the **service vsftpd status** command):

```
# service vsftpd stop
# service vsftpd start
```

When you install Red Hat Enterprise Linux from an FTP server, you'll need to remember the directory with the Red Hat installation files. For an FTP server, the right directory is relative to the basic /var/ftp directory. With these steps, the installation files are in /var/ftp/pub/inst; therefore, the correct directory is /pub/inst.

Requirements for Network Installations

Now that you've set up the Red Hat Enterprise Linux installation files on a network server, let's look at what else you'll need on the computer where you'll be installing Linux. Once Linux detects your network card, you'll need to configure that card to be a part of your network. It'll be done by a DHCP (Dynamic Host Configuration Protocol) server or by static IP addressing.

on the
job

Naturally, if there's no native driver for your network card (as is the case with many wireless cards), you'll need to examine alternative installation methods such as from CD/DVD or from ISO files copied to a local hard drive.

If a DHCP server is on your network, this process is easy. All you'll need to do is set the Linux installation program to ask for your IP address information from that DHCP server. As long as no active firewalls are between your computer and the DHCP server, you should have no problems.

Otherwise, you'll need to configure your computer with static IP addresses. In this case, you'll need a valid, unused IP address; the local network mask; the default gateway IP address (if the installation files are on a different LAN); and, optionally, the primary DNS IP address, which is a domain name such as example.com and the host name to use for the local computer.

As you can see in Figures 2-1 and 2-2, Anaconda allows you to get your IP address information (for IPv4 and/or IPv6) from a DHCP server or enter the static IP address information yourself.

You'll also need the host name or IP address of the Red Hat Enterprise Linux installation server, whether it uses NFS, HTTP, or FTP.

If you're installing RHEL from files on a network server, check the firewall on that server. The standard RHEL firewalls cut off network communication to whatever FTP, HTTP, or NFS server you might be using to store the installation directory tree.

Setting Up Installation from a Local Hard Drive

There are cases where it's most convenient to install RHEL from a local hard drive. I do this when I download the ISO files to the system where I want to install RHEL, and then boot more than one system on that computer.

For example, on my laptop system, I boot RHEL 5, Ubuntu Linux, and (don't tell anyone!) Microsoft Windows XP. I downloaded the ISO files to the main Ubuntu Linux partition, /dev/sda10, in my /home/michael directory.

I don't need to burn these ISO files to a CD or DVD. All I need to do is create a boot CD or USB key and then boot my system accordingly. Details are provided in the next section. Of course, I need a record of my current partitions so I know where the ISO files are stored and what partitions I want to keep.

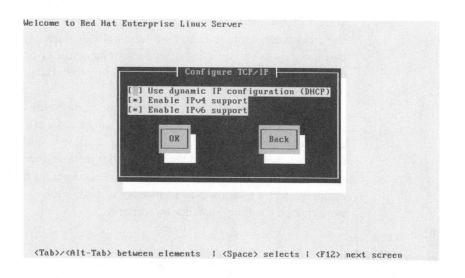

FIGURE 2-1

Configuring
TCP/IP on your
network card
during installation

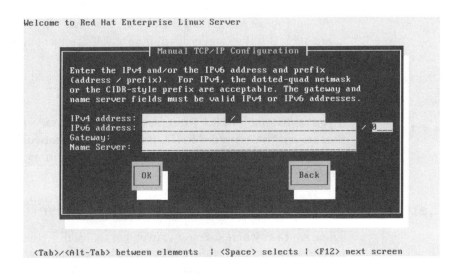

FIGURE 2-2

Manual TCP/IP
network card
configuration

CERTIFICATION OBJECTIVE 2.05

The First Installation Steps

Before installing Red Hat Enterprise Linux, let's examine some critical decisions that you'll make during the Red Hat exams. Time is of the essence on the exams. While you could just install everything, that could easily cost you 15 minutes or more. On the other hand, while you can customize individual packages to be installed, that can also steal the time that you need to configure the critical services required to pass the exam. By the time you're done reading this chapter, you'll know how to select just what you need.

You have to answer many interrelated questions during installation, just as you have many ways to access installation files, and many options on how to install the operating system. The following installation outline is designed to get you through the process as simply as possible. While other sections and chapters address the special situations that you're more likely to encounter on the RHCE and RHCT exams, you need to know how to install Red Hat Enterprise Linux before you can work though the other installation scenarios.

Boot Options

During the RHCE or RHCT exams, you'll have access to the installation files. There are four methods available to start the RHEL Desktop or Server installation process:

- Boot from a copy of the Red Hat Enterprise Linux installation CDs or DVD
- Boot from the first RHEL installation CD or DVD
- Boot from a special RHEL boot CD or USB key
- Boot from a kickstart server using a PXE network boot card

ⓦatch

During the exam, avoid installing RHEL from the CDs if at all possible. The basic installation takes longer, and you don't want to waste time removing and reinserting CDs.

The last three options generally assume that you're going to install RHEL over a network. It's possible that you'll see one of these options during the exam, which is why I described how to create a network installation server earlier in this chapter.

Booting from the First CD/DVD

Most current Intel-based PC hardware systems allow you to boot directly from the CD drive. You can start the installation process by booting from the first Red Hat Enterprise Linux CD or DVD.

If You Need an Installation USB or CD/DVD

If you don't have the first installation CD/DVD, you can start a network installation from a specialized boot USB key or CD. While one may be provided for you for the RHCE or RHCT exams, you'll need to know how to create one so you can practice for the exam.

It's easy to create an installation USB key or CD from one of the files on the /images directory on the first installation CD:

- **diskboot.img** For a boot USB key
- **boot.iso** For a boot CD

The boot.iso file is small enough to fit on a credit card–sized CD. It contains all the information in the diskboot.img file. Alternatively, if your systems have USB ports and can boot from that media, you can create the installation media from the diskboot.img file.

For the purpose of this section, assume you've inserted the first installation CD/DVD into its drive, and it's automatically mounted in the /media/disk directory. (In practice, the /media subdirectory is named after the label on the CD/DVD; you may end up with a directory such as /media/RHEL-5 i386 Disc 1.) If automounting does not work, you may need to mount the CD/DVD yourself.

Creating a Boot USB Key

You can also create images on a USB key with the **dd** command from any running Unix or Linux computer. Find a USB key, save anything important that you've stored onto it, and insert it into your system. Run the **fdisk -l** command to find the device associated with the USB key. Assuming it's /dev/sdc, run the following commands:

```
# dd  if=/media/disk/images/diskboot.img  of=/dev/sdc
```

Be careful—if /dev/sdc/ is a hard drive with data, these commands will overwrite all data on that drive.

Alternatively, you can just run the **cat** command to read the disk image of your choice directly to a floppy drive or USB device. For example, the following command reads the laptop driver disk directly to the USB key:

```
# cat /media/disk/images/diskboot.img  > /dev/sdc
```

You can also create a boot CD from the boot.iso file in the images/ subdirectory. Assuming you don't have two CD/DVD drives, you'll first have to copy the boot.iso file to a directory such as /tmp. You can then burn the boot CD using the following command:

```
# cdrecord dev=/dev/hdc -v -eject /tmp/boot.iso
```

Naturally, this command may vary; for example, a system with a SATA-based drive may require that you substitute the appropriate device name, such as **dev=/dev/scd0**.

Know how to create the right boot disk for your system. If you have a problem, the installation boot CD or USB key can also serve as a rescue disk. (I do not have a system that supports booting from a SD card, so I have not considered that option.) At the boot prompt, the linux rescue command will eventually bring you to a rescue mode that can help you mount your partitions or recover specific files or directories. I describe this process in Chapter 16.

Almost Ready to Install

Most newer computers can be set to boot directly from the CD/DVD drive. Many systems allow direct access to a boot menu by pressing a key such as ESC or F12. Alternatively, just after your computer reboots, go into the BIOS menu. You should be able to change the boot order to look to the CD/DVD or USB drive first.

Some older systems can start only from a boot floppy. You'll still need to boot the RHEL installation system from a CD/DVD or USB key. In that case, a universal boot floppy such as the Smart Boot Manager http://sourceforge .net/projects/btmgr/ may be helpful.

CD/DVD or Boot USB Starts Installation

Now your PC should boot from the CD/DVD or the installation USB key. After a few files are opened and decompressed, an RHEL installation screen should appear with the following prompt:

```
[F1-Main] [F2-Options] [F3-General] [F4-Kernel] [F5-Rescue]
boot: _
```

You are finally beginning to install Red Hat Enterprise Linux! Press the F2 key. As you can see in Figure 2-3, a number of options are available when you start the process.

If you're working from installation CDs that you downloaded online, your first step should be to check the media. While Red Hat provides secure hash checksums that you can use for this purpose, the easiest way to check your CDs is with the **linux mediacheck** option. (Alternatively, you can verify the secure hash checksums by applying the **sha1sum** command to a downloaded ISO file.) Type in that command at the boot: prompt, and you'll see an option to test the media, as shown back in Figure 2-1. Follow the prompts to check your CDs or DVD.

on the !
Ⓙⓞⓑ

*If you have a problem with your graphics hardware, press F3 from the first screen. As described under the General Boot Help screen, you can try to force installation with a specific resolution using a command such as **linux resolution=800x600.***

FIGURE 2-3

Red Hat Installer
boot options

```
                           Installer Boot Options
  -  To disable hardware probing, type: linux noprobe <ENTER>.

  -  To test the install media you are using, type: linux mediacheck <ENTER>.

  -  To enable rescue mode, type: linux rescue <ENTER>.
     Press <F5> for more information about rescue mode.

  -  If you have a driver disk, type: linux dd <ENTER>.

  -  To prompt for the use of other install methods such as network
     install when booting from a CD, type: linux askmethod <ENTER>.

  -  If you have an installer update disk, type: linux updates <ENTER>.

  -  To test the memory in your system type: memtest86 <ENTER>.
     (This option is only available when booting from CD.)

[F1-Main] [F2-Options] [F3-General] [F4-Kernel] [F5-Rescue]
boot: _
```

To start the installation process from the boot: prompt, there are three basic options:

- **Graphical mode** By default, Red Hat is installed from the CDs (or DVD), or even over a network, in graphical mode. Just press the ENTER key at the boot: prompt. Graphical mode starts after a few simple questions.

- **Text mode** The **linux text** option starts a low-intensity graphical installation known as text mode that all but the most graphically challenged computers can handle.

- **Network installation** You can use the installation CD or boot floppy to install RHEL over a network connection. If you're booting from the installation CD, enter **linux askmethod** at the boot: prompt. This tells the RHEL installation CD to ask you whether you want to install from a CD, a local hard drive partition, or from a network server. This option is automatic if you're booting from a boot CD or USB.

The Exam Prep guide suggests that you'll install RHEL over a network during the exam.

on the
Job

It's also possible to install from files or ISOs on the local hard drive. For example, if you're dual-booting with another version of Linux, you can copy the files or ISOs to a specific directory on a specific partition. You can then use the linux askmethod command to get Anaconda to look for files on a certain directory on that partition. If you don't know the partition device, such as /dev/hda8, some trial and error may be required.

First Selections

The basic RHEL installation is straightforward and should already be well understood by any RHCT/RHCE candidate. The differences between the RHEL and Fedora Core 6 installation processes are almost trivial. Most of the steps are described here for reference; it's useful to remember this process as you work on advanced configuration situations such as kickstart files, which are described in Chapter 5. I've detailed the RHEL installation process in screenshots in "Installing Red Hat Enterprise Linux 5" in the Online Learning Center (http://highered.mhhe.com/sites/0072264543/).

I'm assuming that you'll be installing RHEL as the only operating system on the local computer (in other words, no dual-boots with Microsoft Windows). If you don't have a separate computer that you can use for testing purposes (that is, one on which you don't need any data), a very useful option is VMware Server, which you can download without charge from www.vmware.com. It allows you to set up RHEL on a virtual machine, configured on a Linux or a Microsoft Windows Vista/XP/2000 computer. A second option, if your hardware supports it, is Xen. It's included with

RHEL 5 and Fedora Core 6. If your hardware (and BIOS) supports full virtualization as described earlier in this chapter, you can install RHEL 5 within Xen, just like installing RHEL 5 within VMware Server.

The most efficient, and thus (in my opinion) the most likely, way to install Red Hat Enterprise Linux during the RHCE and RHCT exams is via a text or graphical installation from a remote NFS server. Therefore, the instructions presented here are based on that scenario. While text mode may save you a little time up front, graphical mode supports configuration of custom LVM volumes, which is listed as a RHCE requirement in the Exam Prep guide. You'll have the opportunity of installing RHEL from a CD and from remote FTP or HTTP servers in exercises or labs later in this chapter. A complete step-by-step review of the installation process is available in the Online Learning Center.

1. Boot your computer from the first RHEL CD, from a boot CD, or from a boot USB key.

2. When you see the boot: prompt, enter the **linux askmethod** command. This temporarily starts the installation process in text mode (which is actually a low-resolution graphical mode), as shown in Figure 2-4. Use the TAB key to switch between options.

on the job *While the* **linux askmethod** *command isn't required to start a network installation from a boot CD or USB key, it still works as described.*

3. Select a language to use during the installation process. English is the default; nearly 50 options are available.

FIGURE 2-4

Starting the installation process

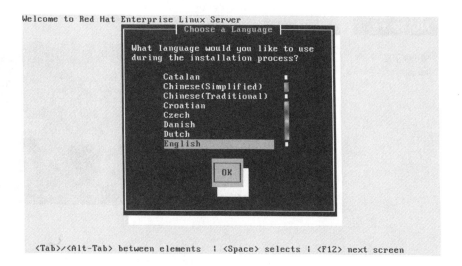

4. Select a keyboard type; the default depends on the language you selected.

5. Choose your installation method. Earlier in this chapter, I described how to configure an NFS installation server. Therefore, select the NFS image option (the steps for installing from an HTTP or FTP server vary slightly).

6. Choose how you want IP addressing configured. Your options are to enable support as a DHCP client, for IPv4 and/or IPv6 addresses. (If your DHCP server does not support IPv6, enabling this option with DHCP slows the installation process.)

   If you enable DHCP, the installation looks for a DHCP server for IPv4 and/or IPv6 addresses. Otherwise, you'll need to enter the information manually, along with appropriate gateway and nameserver (DNS) addresses. (I recommend that you review installation with and without DHCP, so you know what to do in either case.)

7. Direct your computer to the remote NFS server. As shown in Figure 2-5, you can enter the host name or IP address of the NFS server, as well as the shared directory. (If you enter a host name, you'll need a working DNS server on your network.) If you set up an NFS installation server with the instructions earlier in this chapter, enter **/inst** in the Red Hat Enterprise Linux Server Directory text box. (The corresponding HTTP and FTP configurations are shown in Figures 2-6 and 2-7, respectively.)

8. If a proper connection is made, you'll see the first Red Hat Enterprise Linux graphical installation screen. Click Next to continue. Since you've already selected a keyboard type and language, RHEL skips those graphical screens that you'd otherwise see when installing from a CD/DVD.

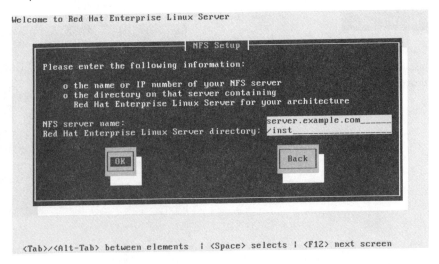

FIGURE 2-5

Connecting to an NFS server

FIGURE 2-6

Connecting to an
HTTP server

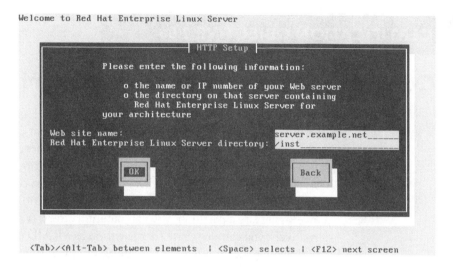

If you encounter problems, examine the third and fourth consoles; to do so, press ALT-F3 or ALT-F4.

9. If you have a subscription, you should see an installation number that automatically specifies a set of supported packages. Enter the number here if desired (or if so prompted by the person overseeing your exam). You can still customize the package groups to be installed.

10. If you've installed Red Hat Enterprise Linux on this system before, you're given the chance to upgrade the existing installation.

Additional steps are described in upcoming sections, starting with Exercise 2-2.

FIGURE 2-7

Connecting to an
FTP server

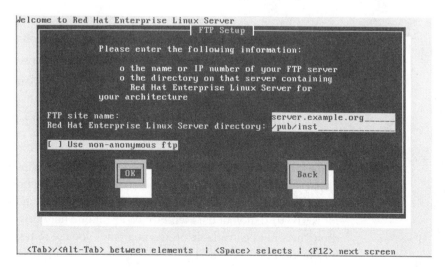

CERTIFICATION OBJECTIVE 2.06

Configuring Partitions, RAID, and LVM

A disk drive requires a partition table. The *partition* is a logical sequence of cylinders on the disk, while a *cylinder* represents all the sectors that can be read by all heads with one movement of the arm that contains all these heads. Although it's possible to create more, RHEL will recognize only up to 16 partitions on any individual SATA/SCSI or an ATA/IDE hard drive. But don't be too concerned about these details; you probably won't have to create so many partitions on either exam.

Once you create a partition, you can mount a directory directly on that partition. Alternatively, you can designate that partition as a RAID device or as part of a logical volume. Both systems are described briefly in this chapter; for more information, see Chapter 8.

The main Linux partition utilities are fdisk and parted. As you'll see in Chapter 4, although you can create more than 16 partitions on each physical hard disk, you'll find that you can't write more than 16 partitions on each hard disk.

RAID, Briefly

RAID is short for a Redundant Array of Independent (or Inexpensive) Devices, and it can help you create a filesystem on more than one partition, with or without redundancy. Red Hat supports the software version of this scheme at four different levels.

- RAID 0 stripes a filesystem across multiple partitions for faster reads and writes.
- RAID 1 mirrors all data in a filesystem between two partitions.
- RAID 5 uses parity bits (striping) for data redundancy over three or more partitions.
- RAID 6 uses double parity bits (striping) for data redundancy over four or more partitions.

To take full advantage of RAID, you'll want to configure partitions on different physical hard drives, preferably connected to different hard drive controllers. That maximizes the ability to read and write to a RAID filesystem, and it means (except for RAID 0) that your data will not be lost if one hard drive fails. But multiple hard drives may not be available on the computer you use to take an exam. (For more information on RAID and how you can manage it after installation, see Chapter 8.)

Logical Volumes, Briefly

Logical volumes give you flexibility with your filesystems. You can expand and contract the space associated with different directories. If you need more space, say for the /home directory, you can add a new hard drive, partition it as a logical volume, and use it to add more space to the /home directory.

The Red Hat installation process, by default, configures all but the /boot directory as part of a logical volume, with the configuration described in Table 2-1. Chances are good that won't match the requirements on your RHCE or RHCT installation exam. We'll explore how you can customize it shortly.

It's faster and easier to configure LVM during the installation process. While Red Hat provides the Logical Volume Management GUI tool, it takes time to use it. It may be faster to use regular command line–based commands to reconfigure LVM. But requirements change and mistakes are made, during the installation process and in real life. So for more information on logical volumes and how you can manage them after installation, see Chapter 8.

Naming Conventions

Linux has a simple naming standard for disk partitions: three letters followed by a number. The first letter identifies the type of drive (h is for IDE/EIDE, s is for SATA or SCSI). The second letter is d for disk, and the third letter represents the relative position of that disk, starting with a. In other words, the first ATA/IDE drive is hda, followed by hdb, hdc, and hdd.

The number that follows is based on the relative position of the primary, extended, or logical partition. Primary partitions can contain the boot files for an operating system. Hard drives can also be configured with one extended partition, which can then contain up to 12 logical partitions.

You are limited to four primary partitions on each hard disk. But four partitions are often not enough. If you need more partitions on a hard drive, substitute an extended partition for one primary partition. You can then configure the logical partitions that you need within the extended partition.

You can't install files directly in an extended partition. You must first allocate some extended partition space to at least one logical partition. You can then configure logical partitions within that extended partition. In all cases, the first logical partition on the first PATA/IDE drive is hda5.

TABLE 2-1	Location	Size
Result When You Partition Automatically	/boot	100MB
	Swap	Twice available RAM (assuming sufficient hard drive space)
	/	Remaining space on the drive, mounted on a Logical Volume Group

Each partition is associated with a Linux device file. At least this is straightforward; for example, the device filename associated with the first logical partition on the first PATA/IDE drive is /dev/hda5.

e x a m

ⓦatch *You should know the device name associated with each partition, as well as the starting names and numbers of any logical partitions created on any* *basic disk drive. Also remember that logical partitions on a hard drive always start with number 5; on the first PATA/IDE hard drive on a PC, that is hda5.*

EXERCISE 2-1

Partitioning

You may never have had to plan partitions on a basic Microsoft Windows desktop computer. On a real server, whether you're using Windows or Linux, you should preplan your disk usage and partitions very carefully. This is a preliminary exercise; be prepared to think more deeply about partitions later in this chapter and in Chapter 4.

1. On a piece of paper, draw a rectangle to represent each hard drive on your computer.

2. Label them in order just as Linux would (Hard Drive 1: /dev/hda, Hard Drive 2: /dev/sda, Hard Drive 3: /dev/sdb).

3. Use this diagram to plan how you are going to partition each drive. While this is a preview of future chapters, you should already know that Linux is set up in multiple directories. Each of these directories can be set up in its own partition. Think about how much space you want to allocate to several major directories, such as /home, /var, /usr, /boot. Don't forget to allocate some area for a swap partition.

Using this method, you can organize your data, keeping system or users' files together, as well as strategically plan where to place your swap partition(s). Now in the second exercise, let's examine how you can create and configure partitions during the installation process. We'll also examine how you can allocate a filesystem to a partition, a logical volume, or a RAID array.

EXERCISE 2-2

Partitioning During Installation

To follow along in this chapter, you presumably are installing RHEL 5 on some system. It's easiest if you practice using a virtual machine based on VMware or Xen. If you make a mistake, you can restart the installation process and return to these partitioning steps. This exercise starts with Figure 2-8, which is the first partitioning step, and assumes you're testing with the graphical installation.

The Advanced Storage Configuration option is associated with network connections using the TCP/IP iSCSI network protocol. As this option is not part of the Red Hat Exam Prep guide, we won't cover it here. For more information, start with the Linux-iSCSI project, described at http://linux-iscsi.sourceforge.net.

1. Click the top drop-down text box, and you'll see four options. In the following steps, you'll examine each option in turn with the associated default partitioning layout.

2. Check the Review And Modify Partitioning Layout checkbox near the bottom of the window.

3. Select Remove All Partitions On Selected Drives And Create Default Layout, and click Next.

FIGURE 2-8

Basic partitioning

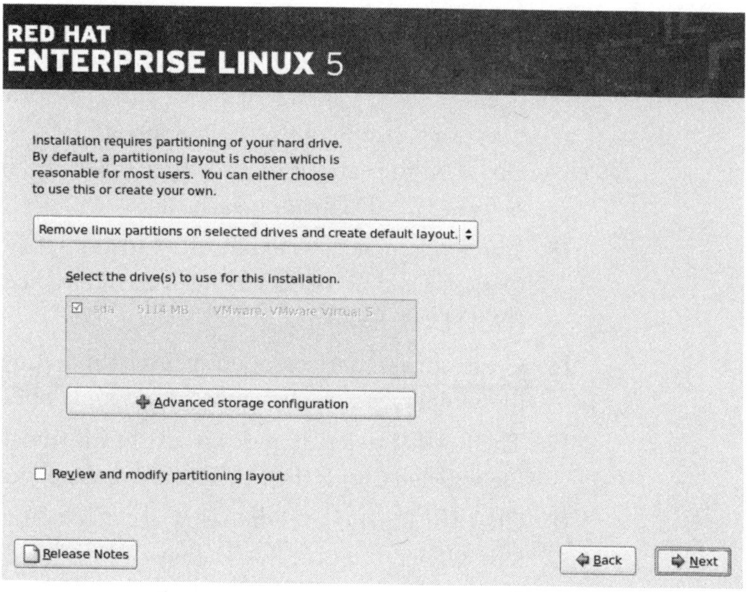

4. If more than one drive is available, deselect drives where you want to save the data.

5. If you see the warning about removing partitions from specified drives, click Yes to continue.

6. Review the default partitioning layout, and click Back to return.

7. Select Remove Linux Partitions On Selected Drives And Create Default Layout, and click Next to continue. Repeat steps 4 to 6.

8. Select Use Free Space On Selected Drives And Create Default Layout, and click Next to continue. Repeat steps 4 to 6.

9. Select Create Custom Layout, and click Next to continue.

10. Start creating your own custom layout. If you're starting with blank hard disks, no partitions will be configured. Delete configured partitions if no space is available.

11. Try creating a regular partition. Click New. Create an appropriate mount point, such as /home/user. Click the File System Type drop-down text box and review the available formats.

12. Create one partition with an unused filesystem type, and click OK to continue.

13. Repeat steps 11 and 12. For the purpose of this exercise, the default 100MB is sufficient.

14. Create five RAID partitions. Click RAID; this opens the RAID Options window. If you don't have any other RAID partitions, only one of the three options can be selected: Create A Software RAID Partition. Click OK; this opens the Add Partition window, with a Software RAID File System Type. Create a partition of the desired size (100MB is OK for this exercise) and click OK. Repeat this process three times, making sure to select Create A Software RAID Partition each time.

15. You should now have five RAID partitions. Click RAID, and in the RAID Options window, select Create A RAID Device. Click OK to open the Make RAID Device window.

16. Create an appropriate mount point such as /home/raidtest. Check available filesystem types; you'll see the same format options you saw in step 11.

17. The RAID Device drop-down text box is trivial; it just specifies the device file associated with the RAID array you're about to create.

18. Click the RAID Level drop-down text box. You'll see that you can configure four different types of RAID arrays: RAID0, RAID1, RAID5, and RAID6. (For more information on each level, see Chapter 8.) Select RAID6.

19. Enter **1** in Number of Spares, and click OK. This works because RAID 6 requires a minimum of four RAID partitions and as many spares as available. Review the resulting RAID device. How much space is available in the device? How does that compare to the space used by the five different RAID partitions?

20. Now click New again, and create a partition of the Physical Volume (LVM) filesystem type. Repeat the process to create a second LVM partition.

21. Click LVM. This opens the Make LVM Volume Group window. Review the available options.

22. In the Make LVM Volume Group window, click the Physical Extent drop-down text box. Review the available Physical Extents, which are units associated with volume groups.

23. Make sure all available Physical Volumes To Choose are active.

24. Click Add; this opens the Make Logical Volume window.

25. Create an appropriate mount point such as /home/volume. Note that the available filesystem types are more limited. The Logical Volume Name shown is just the default; you can use any legal filename for your logical volume. Set a size that does *not* use all available space. Click OK.

26. Review the result in the Make LVM Volume Group window. Click OK and review the result in the original partition window.

27. Changes are not permanent; you should be able to click Back a couple of times and return to restore the original partition configuration.

Separate Filesystems

Normally, you should create several partitions when preparing your hard drive to install Linux. This is a good idea for various reasons. First, RHEL is normally configured with at least two filesystems: a Linux native filesystem and a Linux swap filesystem. Second, if you want to install RHEL and another operating system on the same computer, you should configure separate partitions for each operating system. You can and should configure software RAID partitions on different physical hard drives (if available) during the RHEL installation process. However, if you have a hardware RAID system, you'll need to configure it after RHEL is installed.

Stability and Security

Linux is organized in a Filesystem Hierarchy Standard (FHS) that includes a number of directories described in Chapter 1. You can organize these directories into a few or many hard drive partitions. During the installation process, RHEL is by default organized into three partitions: the root directory /, the /boot directory, and a swap partition. One recommended configuration for a Linux server includes separate partitions for each of the following directories: /, /boot, /usr, /tmp, /var, and /home. Other partitions may be appropriate for corporate data, database services, and even directories associated with Web (/var/www/html) and FTP (/var/ftp/pub) sites if you need them to hold a lot of data.

Partitioning the hard drive in this manner keeps system, application, and user files isolated from each other. This helps protect the disk space used by the Linux kernel and various applications. Files cannot grow across partitions. For example, an application such as a Web server that uses huge amounts of disk space can't crowd out space needed by the Linux kernel. Another advantage is that if a bad spot develops on the hard drive, the risk to your data is reduced, as is recovery time. Stability is improved.

Security is also improved. Multiple partitions give you the ability to set up certain directories as read-only filesystems. For example, if there is no reason for any user (including root) to write to the /usr directory, mounting that partition as read-only will help protect those files from tampering.

While there are many advantages to creating more disk partitions, it isn't always the best solution. When hard drive space is limited, the number of partitions should be kept to a minimum. For example, if you have a 4GB hard drive and want to install 3000MB of packages during RHEL installation, you may not want to dedicate extra space to the /var directory. You need room for swap space, additional programs, and your own personal files on other directories.

It can take considerable time to set up LVM partitions. Unless you know the process very well, the fastest way is through the RHEL installation program in graphical mode, which is available when installing from CD/DVD or over a network from an NFS server. (LVM configuration is not available via text mode RHEL installation.) Learn the process well, just in case you need to set up LVM during the Installation and Configuration part of your exam.

Basic Storage Space Requirements

Linux is a flexible operating system. While a full installation of RHEL requires several gigabytes of space, slightly older versions of Linux fit even on a 1.44MB floppy disk. Depending on your needs, you can install RHEL, with a couple of services, *without the GUI*, on any hard drive larger than 2GB.

on the
ⓙob

There are also complete Linux distributions that you can boot and load directly from a CD or DVD, which can be used to diagnose hard disk failures on Microsoft Windows PCs. For more information, see www.knoppix.net. Even Fedora Core now has a so-called "live" DVD. But you won't be able to use live CDs or DVDs on the Red Hat exams.

You should size your Linux partitions according to your needs and the function of the computer. For example, a mail server will require more space in /var, because mail files are stored in /var/spool/mail. You could create a separate partition for /var or even /var/spool/mail. In almost every case, it's a good idea to configure at least the /boot directory on a separate partition.

On the other hand, if you install everything, including support for various languages, you could require 10GB or more.

Example: File Server

If the Linux system you are installing is to be a file server, then you could configure your partitions as shown in Table 2-2.

The /usr filesystem is large enough to include key services such as Samba and the Linux graphical user interface. Most of the disk space has been allocated to /var for the log files and for FTP and Web services, to /home for individual user files, and to /home/shared for common files. If there's room left over, you can configure these directories on logical volumes and add to them as your needs evolve. Of course,

TABLE 2-2	Filesystem	Size (MB)	Mounted Directory
	/dev/sda1	100	/boot
Example Partition	/dev/sda2	6000	/
Configuration	/dev/sda5	4000	/var
for a Linux File	/dev/sda6	8000	/usr
Server	/dev/sda7	2000	Swap space
	/dev/sda8	20000	/home
	/dev/sda9	6000	/home/shared

this is only an example. The amount of disk space you allocate for file sharing will depend on factors such as the number of users and the type of files they use.

Linux Swap Space

Linux uses the swap space configured on one or more hard drive partitions to store infrequently used programs and data. Swap space can extend the amount of effective RAM on your system. However, if you don't have enough actual RAM, Linux may use the swap space on your hard drive as virtual memory for currently running programs. Because hard drive access can be 1/1,000,000th the speed of RAM, this can cause significant performance problems.

on the Job

The relative speeds of RAM and hard drives are evolving; in many cases, hard drive access times are fast enough that large amounts of swap space have lower performance penalties. However, the rule of thumb still applies: RAM is much faster than hard drives.

But you can't just buy extra RAM and eliminate swap space. Linux moves infrequently used programs and data to swap space even if you have gigabytes of RAM.

Normally, Linux (on a 32-bit Intel-style computer) can use a maximum 4GB of swap space in partitions no larger than 2GB. This 4GB can be spread over a maximum of eight partitions. The typical rule of thumb suggests that swap space should be two to three times the amount of RAM. However, at larger amounts of RAM, the amount of swap space that you need is debatable.

The way Red Hat assigns default swap space is based on the amount of RAM on your system and the space available in your hard drive. As discussed earlier, graphical installations of RHEL require at least 192MB of RAM. If your system has the minimum amount of RAM and there's room available on your hard drives, Anaconda configures a swap partition of twice this size (384MB). For Intel 32-bit systems, Red Hat suggests a swap partition at least equal to the amount of RAM on your system. But it isn't required; I have a couple of 2GB systems for which 1GB of swap space is more than sufficient.

on the
job

Red Hat RAM and swap space requirements vary if you're installing RHEL on computers with non-Intel 32-bit CPUs.

In any case, you want to make the swap space you create as efficient as possible. Swap partitions near the front of a hard disk, thus on a primary partition, have faster access times. Swap partitions on different hard drives attached to separate disk controllers give Linux flexibility as to where to send swap data. Linux can start a program through one hard drive controller and move files to and from swap space on a separate hard drive controller simultaneously.

BIOS Limits

Some computers built before 1998 may have a BIOS that limits access to hard disks beyond the 1024th cylinder. Some older BIOSs report only 1024 cylinders on a hard drive no matter how many actual cylinders are present. Computers that are subject to this limit can't see partitions beyond this cylinder. In this case, you should configure the Linux /boot directory on its own partition. Make sure that partition is located within the first 1024 cylinders of the hard drive. Otherwise, the BIOS won't be able to find the partition with the Linux kernel.

Most PCs manufactured for a few years after 1998 have a built-in fix called *logical block addressing,* or *LBA*. A system that can report LBA will adjust the cylinder, head, and sector numbers such that the entire disk is available using these logical addresses. This has been superseded by the Enhanced BIOS, which virtualizes this form of addressing.

Multiple Controllers

It is possible and desirable to use more than one disk controller interface card at the same time on the same PC. This is a common method to increase throughput on your system by reducing your read/write bottlenecks to the only disk.

You can use both SATA/SCSI and ATA/IDE controllers in the same machine (which is the situation on my desktop system), but you should be aware of a few snags. Older BIOS may have access only to the first two IDE hard drives. Also, SCSI disks may not be accessible if IDE drives are installed. The BIOS might have a setting to allow you to boot from SCSI hard disks—or even USB keys. Make sure you understand which drives the BIOS will be able to access, because if you install /boot on an inaccessible drive, the BIOS won't be able to find your Linux boot files.

CERTIFICATION OBJECTIVE 2.07

Post-partition Installation Steps

Naturally, there's more to installation than partitioning. You'll need to configure networking, set the root password, set the current timezone, select basic package groups, and customize additional package groups if desired. And after installation, you have to deal with the First Boot process, but that's for later in this chapter.

If you've accepted the default and haven't selected the Review And Modify Partitioning Layout option described earlier, you won't see a boot loader configuration step and should skip to the "Networking" section a bit later in the chapter.

The Boot Loader

Next, you'll be able to configure the boot loader, as shown in Figure 2-9. This can help you configure how your BIOS finds Linux (and possibly other operating systems) on your computer. GRUB is the default, which is described in more detail in Chapter 3.

In this screen, you'll need to make several decisions:

1. If you already have another boot loader (such as the one associated with VCOM System Commander or Symantec Partition Magic), click No Boot Loader Will Be Installed.

FIGURE 2-9

Configuring a boot loader

RED HAT
ENTERPRISE LINUX 5

○ The GRUB boot loader will be installed on /dev/sda.

○ No boot loader will be installed.

You can configure the boot loader to boot other operating systems. It will allow you to select an operating system to boot from the list. To add additional operating systems, which are not automatically detected, click 'Add.' To change the operating system booted by default, select 'Default' by the desired operating system.

Default	Label	Device	
☑	Red Hat Enterprise Linux Server	/dev/VolGroup00/LogVol00	Add
			Edit
			Delete

A boot loader password prevents users from changing options passed to the kernel. For greater system security, it is recommended that you set a password.

☐ Use a boot loader password   Change password

☐ Configure advanced boot loader options

☐ Release Notes   ⬅ Back   ➡ Next

2. If you want to change how an operating system appears in the GRUB menu, select it and click Edit. For example, when I'm dual-booting with Microsoft Windows XP, that boot option is shown as "Other." In that case, I click Other, click Edit, and change the Label name to Windows XP.

3. If you select Use A Boot Loader Password, it immediately opens the Enter Boot Loader Password window, where you can set up this option.

4. If you select Configure Advanced Boot Loader Options, you're taken to a different menu before the next step, where you can place the boot loader on the first sector of the boot partition and force LBA32 addressing, needed for some older hard drives.

5. You can also add kernel parameters of your choice with the Advanced Boot Loader Configuration menu.

Networking

Now you'll be able to configure this computer on your network. Assuming you've set up installation from a remote computer on the network, you'll see the settings you entered previously, as shown in Figure 2-10. You can either configure the IP address information shown manually, or you can leave this task to a DHCP server.

If you want to change the characteristics of a network card (many computers have more than one), select it and click Edit. This opens the Edit Interface window associated with the network card. You can even enable IPv4 and/or IPv6 address support. Some DHCP servers can assign host names as well. Make your selections and click Next to continue.

FIGURE 2-10

Configuring
networking

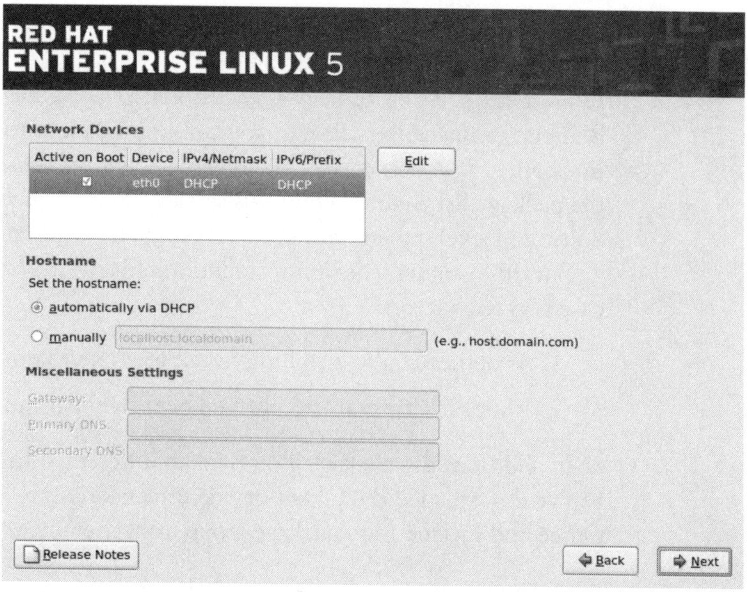

e x a m

⒲ a t c h   For the RHCE and RHCT installation exams, follow the IP address instructions carefully. It's possible that you may be told to leave configuration   to a DHCP server and set up a specific host name; alternatively, you might set a static IP address for the network gateway and DNS servers.

Time and Root Passwords

Setting a timezone is more important than just making sure you have the right time. Web sites with servers in different timezones may have to synchronize clocks. Accuracy in e-mail timestamps can help your users keep their correspondence straight.

There are two questions associated with the timezone section of the installation process. First, you need to identify what timezone you're in. Even though there are only 24 hours in a day, there are many more than 24 different timezones. Some areas move to and from daylight savings time on different dates, or sometimes not at all.

Unless you're dual-booting with an operating system such as Microsoft Windows, you should activate the System Clock Uses UTC option. UTC is a French acronym, which is the atomic realization of what is slightly inaccurately known as Greenwich Mean Time (or Zulu Time).

After you set the timezone, the next step is to set the root password. Don't forget it, or you'll have to use one of the techniques described in Chapter 16 to rescue your system and restore your root password.

Baseline Packages

In most cases, it's best to *modestly* customize the packages that you install during the Red Hat exams. Alternatively, you can use the **pirut** tool, described in more detail in Chapter 5. When you see the screen shown in Figure 2-11, you'll get to customize the package list slightly. From this screen, you can choose whether to install the Software Development and Web Server package groups.

But this assumes a default installation of RHEL. What you actually do install is based on two factors:

1. Whether you're installing from Server or Client installation media.

2. Your subscription key, entered near the beginning of the installation process.

In addition, the package groups mean different things depending on whether you've downloaded the Client or Server versions of RHEL. For example, while the Office and Productivity package group from the Client includes the OpenOffice.org

FIGURE 2-11

Basic package
customization

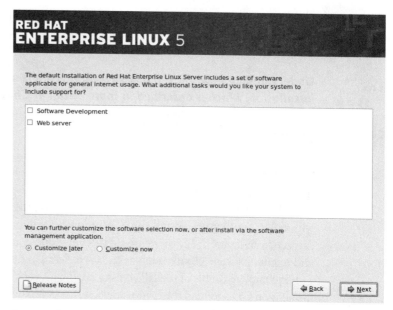

suite, the package group of the same name from the Server includes only a couple of
document readers.

We won't examine every iteration; suffice to say that some logic lies behind the
subscriptions. For example, if your subscription key includes Virtualization, the
default package groups installs the Xen kernel. However, surprisingly, the standard
Server installation does not install standard servers such as those associated with the
Web Server or FTP Server package groups.

e x a m

🐶 a t c h   *Unless you have a specific
requirement for Xen-based virtualization,
don't install the Virtualization package
group. As of this writing, it leads to very
different settings in the boot loader;
Xen-based kernels cannot yet handle all
of the hardware of a standard Linux kernel.*

The next two sections focus on package
groups. If you see requirements on the exam
for a mail server, graphics applications such as
The GIMP, and recompiling the kernel, you'll
want to select the Mail Server, Graphics, and
Development Tools package groups.

But don't overdo it. During the GUI
installation process, you can customize optional
packages to be installed one by one, but the
time it takes to read and choose these packages
is usually not worth the time saved during the
actual installation.

Red Hat package groups are organized logically; for example, all the packages
associated with the GNOME desktop environment belong to one Red Hat package
group. It's important to choose only the package groups you need. Fewer installed
packages means more room for personal files for you and your users, as well as the

log files you need to monitor your system and actually get some use from your applications. On the exam, fewer installed packages leaves more time to configure the required services.

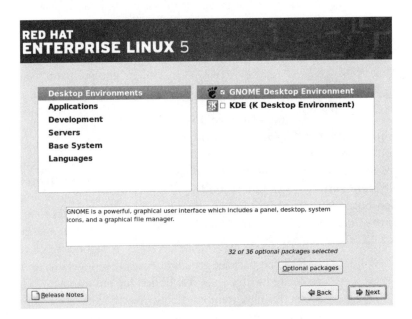

on the **Job** *Understanding how these package groups work is important in a kickstart installation, which is described in more detail in Chapter 5.*

Package Groups

This section includes the briefest possible overview of each of the packages you can select during the RHEL installation process. Remember that installation of some of these packages depends on installation of others; for example, if you want to install the GNOME Desktop Environment package group, the Red Hat installation program will make sure that you install the X Window System package group as well. As you can see from Figure 2-12, there are high-level groups, such as Desktop Environments, and regular package groups, such as the GNOME Desktop Environment.

For complete details of the RPMs associated with each package, go to the first RHEL installation CD and read the comps-rhel5-server-core.xml file in the /Server/repodata directory in the text editor or Web browser of your choice. If you're installing the RHEL 5 client, substitute the comps-rhel5-client-core.xml file in the /Client/repodata directory.

These packages, as well as the order in which they are presented, are based on RHEL. If you're using Fedora Core or one of the third-party rebuilds, the packages

FIGURE 2-12

Red Hat Enterprise Linux package groups

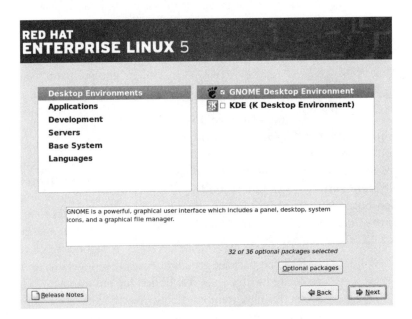

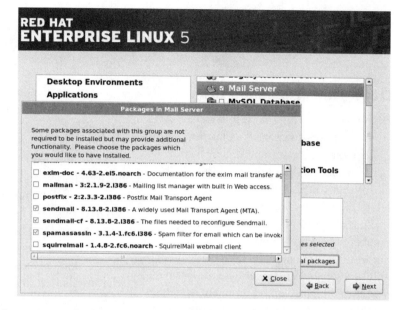

FIGURE 2-13

Red Hat
Enterprise Linux
Mail Server
package group
details

may vary. In any case, the best way to study what's in each package group is through the graphical installation.

For example, Figure 2-13 illustrates the RHEL installation, with a focus on the Mail Server package group. As you can see, sendmail is installed by default; if you need to install postfix, you'll need to make changes.

Take some time studying this screen. Examine the packages within each package group. You'll learn about the kinds of packages that are installed by default. If you don't add them during the installation process, it isn't the end of the world. You can still add them with the **rpm** commands or the **pirut** tool both described in Chapter 5. What you learn here can help you select the package groups to install during the RHCE or RHCT exam. But don't overdo it; I've seen people spend (waste?) an hour customizing every last package when they can connect to the installation source to install more after installation.

In the following sections, I describe each package group in more detail, based on what you see during the RHEL Server graphical installation process. If you're installing the RHEL Client, what you see will vary in many cases.

Desktop Environments

There are two package groups in this category, the GNOME and KDE Desktop Environments. Naturally, these install the two major desktop environments associated with Linux. And if you install one, it'll install the X Window System package group, which is described shortly as one of the Base packages.

INSIDE THE EXAM

During the Installation Exam

Even if you're taking the RHCE exam, pay attention to the software associated with the Linux Desktop Environment. The RHCE exam includes RHCT components, which means that you also need to know how to set up Linux as a client.

That also means you'll be installing a number of package groups that you would not install on a computer that's being used only as a server. When you take the exam, read the configuration requirements carefully. Don't be surprised if you see a requirement to install software such as video players and the OpenOffice.org suite.

Whatever you do, don't install everything. If you don't need to install the OpenOffice.org suite and are installing from the Client CDs/DVD, you can deselect the Office/Productivity package group and save several minutes during the Installation and Configuration portion of either exam. The time you save could allow you to configure a few more services, which could determine whether you pass.

If you make a mistake during the installation process, don't panic. You can use the **pirut** tool after installation to add any package groups that you missed.

GNOME Desktop Environment The GNOME group includes the basic packages required to install the GNOME Network Object Model Environment. While GNOME is the default GUI for RHEL, read the instructions on your exam carefully. It's possible that you'll be asked to install the other major GUI, the KDE Desktop Environment.

When you choose to install the GNOME Desktop Environment package group, all but a few GNOME packages are installed by default.

KDE Desktop Environment The KDE group includes the basic packages required to install the K Desktop Environment, which is the main alternative GUI for RHEL. It is the default GUI for a number of other Linux distributions.

When you choose to install the KDE Desktop Environment package group, all but one of the KDE packages are installed by default.

Applications

There are a number of package groups associated with applications. The groups range from Authoring and Publishing to Graphics to Text-based Internet.

Authoring and Publishing   The Authoring and Publishing group includes support for several documentation systems, such as LinuxDoc, DocBook, and TeX.

Editors   This group include the basic text editors associated with Linux: vi and emacs. While it's essential that you know vi to use the Linux rescue mode, the emacs text editor may be the most popular text editor in the world of Linux and Unix.

Engineering and Scientific   RHEL includes a group of packages for mathematical and scientific purposes, such as gnuplot, pvm, and units.

Games and Entertainment   Be careful with this package group. Do you really want to install games on a business computing system? Some believe that computer games are useful to help newer users become comfortable with Linux. While I doubt that you'll ever have to install this package group during the RHCE or RHCT exams, read the instructions that come with your exam.

Graphical Internet   The Graphical Internet package group includes the Firefox Web browser, the GNOME-based gFTP client, and XChat.

Graphics   This package group automatically incorporates the X Window package and a number of graphical applications. This includes the most prominent Linux graphics application, The GIMP.

Office/Productivity   If you're installing from an RHEL Server source, this group includes a PDF reader (evince) and a DVI reader (tetex-xdvi). If you're installing from an RHEL Client source, this package group includes OpenOffice.org as well as related packages.

Sound and Video   Not surprisingly, the Sound and Video group installs the packages required to allow you to use sound cards and interconnect the basic components of your sound and video system: sound card, speakers, microphone, and CD/DVD drive.

   Don't dismiss this package group out of hand; I've heard that some people are asked to configure a sound card during the RHCE exam. Therefore, it's possible that you'll want to install this package group when you configure the Linux Desktop Environment.

Text-based Internet   Linux includes a number of different text-based clients for Internet access, including the **elinks** Web browser; and the fetchmail and mutt e-mail readers. This is closely related to the Graphical Internet package group.

Development

Red Hat has organized all development package groups into this category. They're not just for developers; if you need to recompile the kernel, you'll need the Development Tools package group.

Additional development tools are included when you install other packages such as GNOME Development, Graphics, Web Server, News Server, and more. Unless you need to use development tools to recompile the kernel, I don't believe that you'll have to install this package group during either exam.

Development Libraries   The Development Libraries package group includes systems that can help you add or modify features for a wide range of programs such as those associated with PCI utilities and even the **rpm** command.

Development Tools   This group includes a large number of development tools, such as make, gcc, perl, and python, useful for compiling such things as the kernel.

GNOME Software Development   The GNOME group includes the basic packages required to develop additional GTK+ and GNOME GUI applications. Some of these packages can help work with a GUI tool that can help compile the kernel. For more information, see Chapter 8.

Java Development   This group includes packages that can help you develop programs in Java.

KDE Software Development   The KDE group includes the basic packages required to develop additional QT and KDE GUI applications. Some of these packages can help work with a GUI tool that can help compile the kernel. For more information, see Chapter 8.

Legacy Software Development   Red Hat makes it possible to develop software on RHEL for older versions of Red Hat Linux. The Legacy Software Development group includes support for older C and C++ language compilers. As there is no reference to these software development packages in any materials related to the RHCT or RHCE exams, I don't believe that you'll have to install this package group during either exam.

Ruby The Ruby programming language is becoming more popular, especially for Web development. The associated package group adds a development environment for this language.

X Software Development The X Software Development group includes the basic packages required to develop additional GUI applications. No reference to X Software Development packages appears in any materials related to the RHCT or RHCE exams; therefore, I don't believe that you'll have to install this package group during either exam.

Servers

Naturally, there are a number of servers associated with Linux. They're all available from the Servers group. As none are selected by default, you'll want to pay careful attention here. For example, if your exam requires you to install sendmail, bind, and Samba, you'll want to install the Mail Server, DNS Server, and Windows File Server package groups.

DNS Name Server The DNS Name Server group includes the tools you need to configure and maintain a Domain Name System server on the local Linux computer. In the Linux world, a DNS server is also known as a nameserver, based on the Berkeley Internet Name Domain (BIND). While it is not installed by default, the Red Hat Exam Prep guide suggests that you may have to configure a DNS caching or slave server during the RHCE exam.

FTP Server This includes the default Red Hat FTP server, the Very Secure FTP daemon (**vsftpd**). While it is not installed by default, it is possible that you'll have to configure an FTP server during the RHCE exam. It also happens to be the server that Red Hat uses for its own FTP sites.

Legacy Network Servers Some Linux gurus discourage use of the several legacy network servers due to security concerns. Nevertheless, they remain popular. They include packages that allow you to install an RSH (Remote Shell), Telnet, and TFTP (Trivial File Transfer Protocol) server. However, it's possible that TFTP servers will become more popular in the future, as they are used for automated PXE-based installations of RHEL.

Mail Server This group includes the packages required to configure a sendmail-based IMAP or a postfix mail server. While a mail server is not installed by default, it is possible that you'll have to configure a mail server such as sendmail or postfix during the RHCE exam.

MySQL Database   The Structured Query Language (SQL) is one of the basic database languages. This group includes support for the MySQL database system. It is not installed by default. As there is no reference to SQL or databases in any materials related to the RHCT or RHCE exams, I don't believe you'll have to install this package group during either exam.

News Server   This is a simple group, incorporating the Internet Network News (INN) server. It is not installed by default, and there is no reference to a News Server in the Red Hat Exam Prep guide.

Network Servers   This package group includes a number of smaller servers that are useful for running a network, including those associated with DHCP and Network Information Service (NIS). It is not installed by default. When you select this package group during the RHEL installation process, Red Hat installs DHCP and the NIS server.

However, if you're asked to install other components of this package group during the RHCE Installation exam, you may want to customize details during the Anaconda installation process; for example, a DHCP server is not installed unless you so specify, such as is shown in Figure 2-14. Alternatively, you can just use the **rpm** or **yum** command as described in Chapter 5 to install the appropriate packages after RHEL is installed. Servers with similar functionality are included in the Legacy Network Servers package group.

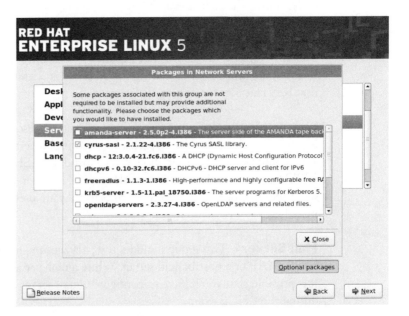

FIGURE 2-14

Network Servers package group

PostgreSQL Database   SQL is one of the basic database languages. This package group includes support for the PostgreSQL database system. It is not installed by default. As no reference is made to SQL or databases in any materials related to the RHCT or RHCE exams, I don't believe that you'll have to install this package group during either exam.

Printing Support   RHEL currently includes support for the Common Unix Printing System (CUPS). It supports the next-generation printing protocol, known as Internet Printing Protocol (IPP). Once installed, CUPS can help detect network printers, with the help of the **system-config-printer** tool.

Printing Support is the only package group installed by default with most RHEL installations.

Red Hat no longer includes the Line Print Daemon (LPD) in its latest Linux distributions.

Server Configuration Tools   Red Hat has developed a series of GUI server configuration tools. For expert users, it's faster to configure most services from the command line interface. In fact, I encourage you to learn to configure all Linux services in this way; in the long run, you'll be a better administrator.

These tools are not installed by default in RHEL. As the RHCE exam requires you to configure servers, I encourage you to install this package group for that exam. It includes about 6MB of files, so the time penalty during the installation process is trivial. If you're less certain about your skills in one or more of these services—or if nerves affect your skills during an exam—these GUI tools can be a lifesaver.

- **system-config-bind**   DNS—The Red Hat BIND DNS Configuration tool
- **system-config-boot**   A graphical interface for configuring the boot loader
- **system-config-httpd**   Apache configuration tool
- **system-config-nfs**   NFS Server Configuration tool
- **system-config-samba**   Samba Server Configuration tool
- **system-config-securitylevel**   Security Level Configuration tool
- **system-config-services**   Service Configuration tool
- **system-switch-mail-gnome**   A GUI Interface for the Mail Agent Transfer Switcher

Web Server   The Web Server group installs Apache, Squid, and the extensive array of supporting modules and configuration files. It's quite possible that you'll have to configure at least a Web server for the RHCE exam.

Windows File Server   This group includes the Samba packages required to set up Linux as a client and as a server on a Microsoft Windows–based network. It is installed by default, and it's possible that you'll have to configure Samba during the RHCE exam. RHEL includes a stable version of the Samba 3 file server.

While I haven't seen any Microsoft Windows computers at Red Hat, it is possible to configure and test Samba clients and servers using a second Linux computer as a client.

Base System

The Base System includes standard packages associated with Linux. Not all package groups in this category are installed by default.

Administration Tools   Red Hat has developed a series of GUI administration tools. For expert users, it's faster to configure most services from the command line interface. In fact, I encourage you to learn to configure all Linux services in this way; in the long run, you'll be a better administrator.

However, these tools are installed by default in RHEL. For the purposes of the RHCE and RHCT exams, I encourage you to accept the default to install this package group. If you're less certain about your skills in one or more of these services—or if nerves affect your skills during an exam—these GUI tools can be a lifesaver:

- **authconfig-gtk**   Supports configuration of NIS, LDAP, and Samba clients and more; also known as the Authentication Configuration tool. It can help you connect to these network directory services, as described in the Exam Prep guide. It can also be started with the **system-config-authentication** command.

- **pirut**   Lets you install packages after RHEL is installed. Also known as the Package Management tool; it can also be started with the **system-config-packages** command.

- **sabayon**   Helps maintain user profiles in the GNOME Desktop Environment.

- **setroubleshoot**   Helps diagnose problems associated with SELinux.

- **system-config-date**   Allows you to configure the time and date of your system; also known as the Date/Time Properties tool.

- **system-config-kdump**   Supports GUI-based configuration of what happens in the event of a kernel crash dump.

- **system-config-keyboard**   Lets you select a different keyboard; also known as the Keyboard Configuration tool.

- **system-config-kickstart** Opens a GUI for customizing a kickstart file; also known as the Kickstart Configurator.
- **system-config-language** Supports configuration of the GUI in different languages; also known as the Language Selection tool.
- **system-config-lvm** Supports configuration of and changes to logical volumes, which can help "add, remove, and resize logical volumes," as described in the Exam Prep guide.
- **system-config-network** Allows detailed configuration of network devices.
- **system-config-rootpassword** Allows you to change the root password.
- **system-config-soundcard** Automatically configures most sound cards.
- **system-config-users** Supports creating and modifying users and groups; also known as the Red Hat User Manager.

Closely related to Pirut is Pup, the package updater. As described in Chapter 5, Pup is used to keep systems up to date. Pup is explicitly cited in the Red Hat Exam Prep guide as a tool to keep RHEL systems up to date.

Base The Base package group includes the fundamentals required for Linux. Naturally, it's a large group with more than 100 packages. If you're installing Linux, don't deselect this group.

Dialup Networking Support The Dialup Networking Support package group includes the packages required to support connections over telephone and ISDN modems, as well as other PPP connections. Some DSL connections also require PPP.

Java Now that Sun Microsystems has released Java under the GPL, this programming language is set to become more important in Linux.

Legacy Software Support The Legacy Software Support package group is not installed by default. If you install systems that require the support of older programming libraries, you may find them here.

System Tools This package group includes a varied array of tools, from the ethereal network traffic reader to the zsh shell. This package group is not installed by default, and it's unlikely that you'll have to install this package group during either exam. While the Samba client is part of this package group, you can also install it through the Windows File Server package group. If you need to create a local repository, you'll need the createrepo RPM package.

While this package group is not installed by default, it's a good idea to review the details of this package group during your studies, just in case you need one of these packages during your exam.

X Window System   This package group includes a number of basic Linux GUI fonts, libraries, and critical tools such as the Red Hat Display Settings tool, which you can start using the **system-config-display** command. It's required if you install the GNOME or KDE Desktop Environments.

As a Linux administrator, you may have confidence in your ability to configure Linux from the command line. In practice, you may install Linux on a number of computers without the GUI. However, even the RHCE exam includes an RHCT component, which tests your ability to "Configure the X Window system and a Desktop Environment," which by definition includes a GUI.

<table>
<tr><td>

e **x a m**

ⓦa t c h   *Since the RHCT exam requires you to configure a workstation, and you have to meet all RHCT requirements during the RHCE exam, expect to install the GUI.*

</td></tr>
</table>

<table>
<tr><td>

e **x a m**

ⓦa t c h   *While installation proceeds, you'll have a bit of "dead time." You can use this time to start configuring your RHEL system. Just press the CTRL-ALT-F2 command, and you'll see a shell. You'll find*

</td><td>

the standard root directory (/) mounted on the /mnt/sysimage subdirectory during the installation process. You can edit the files of your choice as soon as they're installed.

</td></tr>
</table>

CERTIFICATION OBJECTIVE 2.08

Post-installation, Security, and the First Boot Process

Now you've selected the package groups you need. The installation program takes a moment (or even a few minutes) to collect the list of packages and installs any other packages on which they depend (also known as dependencies). Once complete, Linux reboots. The first time RHEL boots, it starts the First Boot process shown in Figure 2-15, which takes you through the license agreement, firewall configuration, SELinux activation, kdump configuration for kernel crashes, the date and time,

FIGURE 2-15

First Boot
configuration

software updates from the Red Hat Network, creating a user, configuring a sound card, and installing from additional CDs if required. You may not see all of the options shown in the figure; for example, if your computer does not have a sound card, you won't see that option.

If you haven't installed the GUI, what you see is quite different, as shown in Figure 2-16. We'll describe the text-mode First Boot process at the end of this section.

FIGURE 2-16

Text-mode
First Boot
configuration

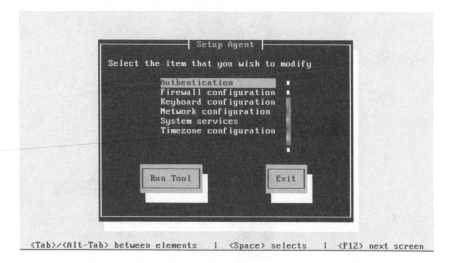

Licensing

If you're running RHEL, you'll need to agree to the license agreement. If you do not agree, you're prompted to shut down your system and uninstall the operating system.

Initial Firewall Configuration

Next, you'll be able to configure a standard firewall for your computer. Generally, you won't need to configure a firewall for a workstation inside a LAN. Firewalls are generally located on computers that serve as junctions, or routers between networks such as a LAN and the Internet. Figure 2-17 illustrates a configuration with two network cards that are presumably connected to different networks. The options you see here are identical to those shown in the **system-config-securitylevel** (Security Level Configuration) tool, which is described in Chapter 15.

Initial SELinux Configuration

After configuring a firewall, you can set up basic SELinux protections on your system. It provides a different layer of defense to protect a wide variety of systems on your computer. If you don't know SELinux well, you may want to disable its protection temporarily. It's easy to do here, as shown in Figure 2-18; you can change it and customize it further using the new SELinux Management Tool described in Chapter 15.

FIGURE 2-17

Configuring a
firewall

FIGURE 2-18

Configuring
SELinux

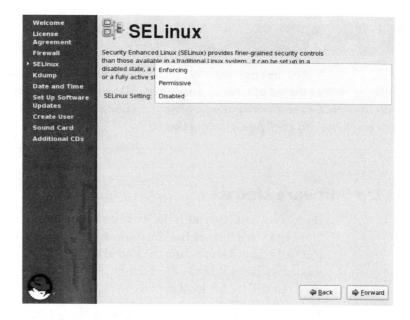

kdump

The kdump service allows you to configure what happens in the event of a kernel crash. In the associated First Boot screen, you can dedicate a specific amount of RAM to the process. Be aware that any such RAM is then unavailable for other processes.

Date and Time

In the Date and Time screen, you can set the date and time for your system. Under the Network Time Protocol tab, if you select the Enable Network Time Protocol option, you can synchronize your computer with a Network Time Protocol server. Red Hat provides three: 0.rhel.pool.ntp.org, 1.rhel.pool.ntp.org, and 2.rhel.pool.ntp.org. If you're not sure, you can return to this configuration screen with the **system-config-time** utility. Make any selections required by your exam, and click Next.

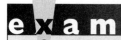

e x a m

⚠ a t c h   *Red Hat has recently*   *a time server. For more information, see the*
included NTP in the list of services associated   *Date/Time Configuration tool as described in*
with the RHCE exam, so it's quite possible   *Chapter 13.*
that you'll have to configure a connection to

Set Up Software Updates

If you want to register with the Red Hat Network, select Yes, I'd Like To Register
Now, and you'll first see the Choose Server screen. You can select whether you
receive updates directly from the Red Hat Network or from a local Red Hat caching
service, such as a Red Hat Network Proxy or Satellite Server. If it's the latter, you'll
need the URL of the local server.

o n t h e   *Naturally, if you're using a rebuild distribution, the information on this screen*
🛈 o b   *will be different—or may not even exist.*

If you click the Advanced Network Configuration button, you can set your
system to read through any installed local proxy server.

Then you'll see a Red Hat Network configuration screen where you can set up a
connection. You'll either need the username and password of your Red Hat Network
account or you'll want to click Create A New Account.

The First Boot process then collects a profile of your hardware and currently
installed packages and assumes that the current IP address is the name of your
system. You can review what it will send to the Red Hat Network, change the
system name, and disable transmission of the hardware or software profiles. If you
do not want to register at this time, you can set up a Red Hat Network connection
using the **rhn_register** command (or in the GNOME Desktop Environment, select
Applications | System Tools | Software Updater, which registers your system before
checking for available updates).

The First Regular User

Generally, you should configure at least one regular user account on every Linux
system. Using the root account for everything is considered dangerous. In the User
Account screen, you can configure a regular account. You may be required to create
regular users with a specific password during your exam. You can create additional users
with the system-config-users (Red Hat User Manager) tool described in Chapter 6.
Create a user if required. Don't click Next yet; first review the next section.

Password Security

First, when you create a password, Red Hat has some protections. The First Boot process won't accept a password of less than six characters. In real life, it's best to use a password with a mixture of numbers and upper- and lowercase letters, and even punctuation. I like to create passwords from a favorite phrase or sentence. For example, a user could use **Ieic3teT.** because he told you "**I** eat ice cream **3** times every **T**hursday." (The period at the end is part of the password.)

In First Boot's Create User screen, there's a Use Network Login button. This opens the same window and tabs associated with the Authentication Configuration tool described in Chapter 6. Briefly, you can use it to configure connections to a NIS, LDAP, or Samba user database, encryption support such as that associated with Kerberos, Hesiod, or MD5 support, and more.

Sound Card Configuration

Normally, Red Hat automatically detects sound cards. If successful, you can click the Play Test Sound button to confirm. If more than one sound card is installed, you may see them in different tabs; you can click the tab for the other sound card and repeat the process. Click Next to continue.

Additional CDs

Finally, if you have more software to install, such as software from a Red Hat supplementary CD, you'll get to do so in the Additional CDs window. Don't do this unless required by your particular exam. Click Next to continue.

You'll now see the Finish Setup screen, which tells you that "Your system is now set up and ready to use." Click Next to finish the process.

Congratulations! Installation is now complete. As the basic installation process for Rebuilds such as CentOS (and even Fedora Core 6) is almost identical to RHEL, you can use that freely available operating system to practice for the exam. In addition to the trademarks, the only major substantive difference is the lack of access to the Red Hat Network (RHN). And there is no mention of the RHN in the Exam Prep guide.

If You Haven't Configured the GUI

The text-mode First Boot process does not require a lot. As shown back in Figure 2-16, it starts the Setup Agent, which supports access to the following text-based configuration tools:

1. Authentication
2. Firewall Configuration (no access to SELinux configuration)
3. Keyboard Configuration
4. Network Configuration
5. System Services
6. Timezone Configuration

While I encourage you to learn to configure Linux from the command line, these tools are not as capable as their GUI-based cousins. (Of course, if you want the most capable tools, learn to edit appropriate configuration files directly from the command line.) You can learn more about the GUI versions of these tools throughout this book.

Caveat Emptor on Installation

Do not worry if you make a mistake the first time you practice installing Linux on a test computer. Just redo the installation; it will be significantly faster and easier than trying to correct a problem. With so many installation options and possibilities available, it is not possible to name them all or take them all into account here. In most cases, the default is sufficient if you do not understand the question posed. Move on and get it installed, and then read the FAQs, HOWTOs, and other related documents once you are up and running. You can always reinstall. The second and third installs are actually a good thing, considering you need to know this process very well for the Red Hat exam.

If you have to reinstall Linux on the Installation and Configuration part of the exam, you may not have time to configure services as required.

You are not allowed to reinstall Linux during the RHCE or RHCT   *Troubleshooting and System Maintenance portion of those exams*

CERTIFICATION OBJECTIVE 2.09

Installation Validation

RHEL creates a number of files during the installation process. These files essentially document what happened. The basic installation log file, /root/install.log, lists the packages that Anaconda installed on your system. The commands used by Anaconda to install Linux are stored in the /root/anaconda-ks.cfg file. This can serve as a template for the kickstart process, which you can use to install RHEL automatically on different computers. I describe this process in more detail in Chapter 5.

The Installation Log File

The installation log file, /root/install.log, provides a baseline. After you run Linux for some time, you'll probably have installed and upgraded a number of additional packages. You can refer back to this file to find the packages installed when Linux was installed on this computer.

Installation Troubleshooting

Installation involves many running processes and many parts. The system logs everything to an installation log file and separates related information among four of the five virtual console screens supported during the installation.

e x a m

ⓦ a t c h
If your installation is trouble-free, you'll have a few minutes on your hands during the Installation part of the exam. Use that time to plan how you'll configure the services per the requirements of your particular exam. But pay attention to the following sections. If your installation gets stuck, the console screens described can quickly help you diagnose the problem.

The Console Installation Output Screens

Six consoles are available during the installation process, and each tells a different story. What you see depends on whether you install in text or graphical mode. A network graphical installation is something of a hybrid; it starts in text mode before connecting to the network source and proceeding to the graphical installation.

Text mode starts in the first virtual console. Graphical mode runs in the sixth virtual console (it used to be the seventh console). You can switch between virtual consoles using the commands defined in Table 2-3. If you're in text mode, you don't

TABLE 2-3	Installation Virtual Console Commands and Functions

Command	Console and Function
CTRL-ALT-F1	Text installation display; if you're running in graphical mode, it includes the basic commands to start graphics drivers.
CTRL-ALT-F2	Accesses a bash shell prompt; available after the first few installation steps.
CTRL-ALT-F3	Lists the log of installation messages; if network problems occur, you may see related messages here.
CTRL-ALT-F4	Displays all kernel messages, including detected hardware and drivers.
CTRL-ALT-F5	Installation displays partition formatting; nothing is shown here until Anaconda formats the actual partitions.
CTRL-ALT-F6	Graphical installation display; active only if you're running the installation program in graphical mode (was formerly available from CTRL-ALT-F7). Naturally, if you're installing in text mode, nothing is shown in this console.

need to use the CTRL key (but it does no harm). As you can see in the table, each console is associated with a function key.

The messages on the third and fourth consoles can scroll by quickly; fortunately they're collected in dedicated files, which are described shortly.

Installation bash   You can find a bash shell on the second console, which can help you review what has been installed so far. Check it out for yourself with the CTRL-ALT-F2 command. You'll see the following installation boot prompt during the installation process:

```
sh-3.1#
```

This prompt allows you to run standard bash commands on the system as configured so far. Before Anaconda starts installing packages, you can inspect a number of things at this prompt. The installation files from the CD or network source will be mounted on the /mnt/source directory. You can also find a number of interesting files in the /tmp directory; the significant ones are described in Table 2-4.

on the **!** **()**ob

The files listed in this section are deleted or moved after installation is complete.

Other Consoles   The third console primarily lists detected hardware. If your computer is having problems with something critical such as the CD drive or network card, you'll see it here.

The fourth console tells you more about detected hardware. However, you may need to be a detective to understand these messages. For example, you might see the following message:

```
<6>pcnet32: 1 cards_found.
```

| TABLE 2-4 | /tmp Directory Configuration Files During the Installation Process |

File from Installation /tmp	Description
anaconda.log	Contains a log of installation messages (from the third console).
ks.cfg	If you're installing from a kickstart configuration file, it's stored in the /tmp directory; otherwise, this doesn't exist.
modprobe.conf	Includes detected hardware that requires a driver module (frequently includes network cards).
netinfo	Contains IP address information for configured network cards; if no cards are configured (e.g., during a local installation, this file does not exist).
syslog	Includes a log of kernel messages (from the fourth console).
XConfig.test	Contains a temporary X Window configuration file.

You might not know there's a problem unless you remember that two network cards are on this computer.

On the fifth console, you can see what happens to your partitions; it lists the output of the **mke2fs** command, which can tell you if there's a problem with your partitions. This console will be empty until Anaconda starts formatting partitions.

While Installing Software   Once Anaconda starts installing software, you'll see the Installing Packages screen, where you can watch as it actually installs Linux on your computer. Once this process starts, press CTRL-ALT-F2 to return to the bash console. Then run the following command:

```
sh-3.1# cd /mnt/sysimage
```

You can browse around the directory tree as it's being built. Even better, once enough packages are installed, you can change the root directory to /mnt/sysimage with the following command:

```
# chroot /mnt/sysimage
```

You can return to the installation console with the **exit** command.

CERTIFICATION SUMMARY

One of the two parts of the Red Hat RHCE and RHCT certification exams tests your ability to install Linux in different situations. In this chapter, you learned to install RHEL over a network. You also worked with the major configuration tools that are part of the installation process.

Linux works well on most current computer hardware, and RHEL is no exception. Plug and play, ACPI, and APM systems are integrated into Linux. If you want support from Red Hat, use hardware that they've tested and certified.

RHEL 5 requires a minimum of 192MB of RAM for a graphical installation, and 512MB of hard drive space. That does not include the space required for a swap partition, user files, and more. It's possible to create a functional system (for a simple server) in a 2GB hard drive. If you install everything associated with RHEL 5, including support for various languages, you could need 10GB or more.

Linux represents hardware with devices, whether they're attached by serial or parallel ports, or hotswapped through USB or IEEE 1394 devices. In most cases, Linux can automatically mount devices such as USB keys, IEEE 1394 drives, and even digital media cards once installed.

You'll usually install Red Hat Enterprise Linux over a network. I've shown you how to set up a network installation server in this chapter. The same basic lessons apply if you're studying for the RHCE or RHCT exams.

Hard drive partition planning is quite important. How you assign partitions to directories depends on the size of your hard drives, what you plan to install, and the demands on the system. Appropriately configured partitions can prevent overloads on key systems, allow for appropriate swap space, and improve security on key files.

There are a number of ways to customize your installation. The distribution is organized in package groups. Red Hat starts with baseline package groups, which are the minimum requirements for the operating system. These include default packages for a functional client or server. You can customize by adding or subtracting the package groups of your choice. The selections you make are critical during the Red Hat installation exams.

After installation comes the First Boot process, which varies depending on whether you've installed a GUI, which can help you configure a firewall, SELinux protection, date and time, the first user, password security, and sound cards. The standard First Boot process assumes a GUI. If you haven't installed a GUI, RHEL uses a Setup Agent in its place.

The Linux installation is extremely flexible. You can troubleshoot the installation process with several different consoles. Some provide useful messages: one console provides a bash shell prompt where you can inspect the current detailed status of the installation. After Linux is installed, you can find out what happened. The /var/log/dmesg file helps you figure out what hardware was detected. The /root/install.log file lists the packages that were installed.

Understanding the installation process is one of the keys to success on the RHCE exam. Find a spare computer. Practice every installation scenario that you can imagine.

TWO-MINUTE DRILL

The following are some of the key points from the certification objectives in Chapter 2.

Hardware Compatibility

❑ If you have a subscription to Red Hat Enterprise Linux, it's best to use hardware tested and documented by Red Hat. Alternative sources of documentation include the Hardware Compatibility List of the Linux Documentation Project.

❑ Linux has made excellent progress with plug and play; if conflicts occur, you may be able to diagnose them with the help of files in the /proc directory.

CPU and RAM

❑ Typically, swap space should be two to three times the amount of RAM. However, the amount of swap space you need is debatable when you have larger amounts of RAM.

❑ Depending on your requirements, Red Hat Enterprise Linux installs between approximately 512MB and 10GB of files. This does not include swap space requirements.

❑ When you plan space for any RHEL installation, remember to leave room for user data, additional applications, services, and a swap partition.

Hotswap Buses

❑ Linux plug and play works well; in most cases, when you plug a device into a serial, parallel, USB, IEEE 1394, or PC Card port, Linux detects and adds the drivers automatically. If an external disk is present, it is automatically mounted.

❑ Device Management includes a number of commands that can help you find detected devices and modules, including **lsusb**, **lspci**, and **lshal**.

Configuring a Network Installation

❑ When practicing for the exam, you may need to install over a network.

❑ You can create a network installation server using NFS, HTTP, or FTP.

❑ You can even install locally from a hard drive partition.

The First Installation Steps

❑ You can usually start the RHEL installation process directly from a bootable CD or USB key.

❑ The installation process is fairly straightforward and self-explanatory. Default package groups depend on the installation subscription number.

❑ When you practice installing RHEL, don't worry if you make a mistake during the process. It is usually easiest to restart the process from the beginning.

Configuring Partitions, RAID, and LVM

❑ Linux has a simple naming standard for disk partitions: three letters followed by a number. The first letter reflects the type of drive (*h* for PATA/IDE, *s* for SATA or SCSI). The second letter is *d* for drive. The third letter represents the relative position of the disk. The number that follows is based on the relative position of the partition on the disk.

❑ The first PATA/IDE drive would be hda and the next hdb, then hdc, and hdd.

❑ It's helpful to configure separate partitions for important data such as Web services, databases, FTP sites, and e-mail.

❑ Unless you use LVM, there is no easy way to resize Linux partitions. Therefore, you need to consider your partition scheme carefully.

Post-partition Installation Steps

❑ After configuring partitions, you'll need to set up network devices and assign a root password.

❑ The baseline packages associated with different subscriptions vary; you can customize them during the post-partition installation steps.

Post-installation, Security, and the First Boot Process

❑ After installation is complete, RHEL reboots and starts the First Boot process.

❑ The First Boot process takes you through licensing, configuring firewalls, enabling or disabling SELinux, configuring date and time, adding the first regular user, setting up sound cards, and more.

❑ If you didn't install the GUI, the First Boot process is the setup tool that is a front end to a number of other text-based tools.

Installation Validation

❑ If you have trouble during the installation process, a number of log files can help.

❑ There are several virtual consoles that can help you validate the installation.

SELF TEST

The following questions will help you measure your understanding of the material presented in this chapter. As no multiple choice questions appear on the Red Hat exams, no multiple choice questions appear in this book. These questions exclusively test your understanding of the chapter. Getting results, not memorizing trivia, is what counts on the Red Hat exams. There may be more than one answer to many of these questions.

Hardware Compatibility

1. In what file can you find more information associated with your CPU?

   _____

CPU and RAM

2. Name three different architectures on which you can install RHEL 5.

   _____

Hotswap Buses

3. What command lists all PCI devices connected to your system?

   _____

Configuring a Network Installation

4. Name three network servers that you use to serve Red Hat Enterprise Linux installation files.

   _____

   _____

   _____

5. If you're unsure on how to customize a firewall, what can you run from the command line to eliminate all current firewall rules?

   _____

The First Installation Steps

6. If you need to check the integrity of the installation CDs in a purchased Red Hat boxed set, what command should you run from the boot: prompt when starting the installation process?

   _____

Configuring Partitions, RAID, and LVM

7. Which device file is associated with the fourth logical partition on the second SATA drive?

_____

8. To configure a RAID 6 array, what is the minimum number of partitions you need?

_____

Post-partition Installation Steps

9. List three names for package groups associated with servers.

_____

_____

_____

Post-installation, Security, and the First Boot Process

10. You've just installed RHEL 5 and have just rebooted your system. Why might you not see the GUI First Boot process?

_____

Installation Validation

11. If you want access to a command line during the installation process, what keys would you press?

_____

12. If you suspect a networking problem freezing the installation process, what console can you access to confirm?

_____

LAB QUESTIONS

Several of these labs involve installation exercises. You should do these exercises on test machines only. The instructions in these labs delete all of the data on a system. As suggested earlier, one option is to use a virtual machine that can simulate a computer inside your operating system. An example of this is VMware, available from www.vmware.com; or Xen, which is included with RHEL 5.

Lab 1

You need to test Red Hat Enterprise Linux as a replacement for your current RHL 9 installed Web server. But you do not want to lose the current RHL 9 Web setup just yet. You just want to test

RHEL 5 using the Web pages and CGI scripts to see if they will work. What can you do? (Note: Fresh installations from Red Hat Linux to RHEL 5 are recommended.)

Lab 2

You want to practice network installations. To do so, set up an FTP installation server on a different Linux computer using the instructions described earlier in this chapter. These instructions also work if you want to create an FTP installation server on Fedora Core.

If you don't have another Linux computer, you can set up an FTP server on Microsoft Windows 2000/XP Professional/2003/Vista for this purpose.

For the purpose of this exercise, assume that you've been asked to install a Web server, a DNS server, an FTP server, and a mail server during the RHEL installation process.

Lab 3

You want to practice network installations. To do so, set up an HTTP installation server on a Linux computer using the instructions described earlier in this chapter. These instructions also work if you want to create an FTP installation server on Fedora Core.

If you don't have another Linux computer, you can set up an HTTP server on Microsoft Windows 2000/XP Professional/2003/Vista for this purpose.

For the purpose of this exercise, assume that you've been asked to install a Samba server and a print server, and you will need to recompile the kernel.

Lab 4

In this lab, you will distribute your filesystem over more than just one partition—as a workstation. You will need to create the partitions on a 20GB or larger PATA/IDE hard disk (see Table 2-5). If your hard drive is larger, don't use the extra space. If your system has a SATA or SCSI drive, substitute device names (e.g., sda2 for hda2) accordingly.

1. Create a Linux boot CD from the boot.iso image file, and then reboot the system.
2. Select manual partitioning at the appropriate step.
3. Use Disk Druid to reconfigure the partition table.
4. Delete all partitions.
5. Create the first partition with 100MB of disk space, ext3, and assign to /boot.
6. Create the next primary partition, hda2, as Linux Swap, and assign to ID 83.
7. Create a third partition with about 5500MB of disk space, ext3, and assign it to the root directory, /.
8. Create an extended partition containing all the rest of the disk space. Make it *growable*.
9. Create the first logical partition, fifth in number, with about 4GB, and assign it to /var.

10. Create two more logical partitions, hda6 and hda7. Split the remaining space between these two partitions (about 5GB each). Set it up with to a software RAID filesystem.

11. Make a RAID 1 device from the two new software RAID partitions, formatted to ext3, and assign it to /home.

on the *Job*

In the real world, you should never configure different parts of a RAID array on the same hard drive. If you do this, the failure of any single hard drive can lead to the loss of all of your data on that array. However, you may have to do so if the computer on your exam has only one physical hard drive.

12. Continue with the installation process, using your best judgment.

13. When asked to select packages, make sure that the Office/Productivity, Graphics, Graphical Internet, and Games package groups are selected.

14. Finish the installation normally.

15. Reboot the computer and log in as the root user.

Lab 5

In this lab, you will install RHEL to create a basic server. You will need to create the partitions on a 10GB or larger hard disk (see Table 2-6). If your hard drive is larger, don't use the extra space. If your system has a SATA or SCSI drive, substitute device names (e.g., sda2 for hda2) accordingly.

1. Create a Linux installation USB from the diskboot.img image file or a boot CD from the boot .iso file, and then reboot the system.

2. Make sure to boot from the new media.

TABLE 2-5   Custom Installation as a Workstation (No Other OS), 1.2 GHz Pentium, 20GB Single Disk, 256MB of Memory

Partition	Size	Use	Comment
hda1	100MB	/boot	Maintains boot files
hda2	512MB	swap	Plenty of space
hda3	5.5GB	/	The root directory
hda4	14GB	Extended partition	Solely a container for logical partitions
hda5	4GB	/var	For print spool files
hda6	5GB	/home	User directories—RAID 1
hda7	5GB	/home	User directories—RAID 1

3. Select custom partitioning at the appropriate time.

4. Delete all partitions.

5. Create the first partition with 100MB of disk space, formatted to ext3, and assign it to /boot.

6. Create the next primary partition, hda2, with about 500MB of disk space, as Linux Swap.

7. Create the third partition with about 5GB disk space, Linux Native, and assign to the root directory, /.

8. Create an extended partition containing all the rest of the disk space, 4500MB.

9. Create the first logical partition, hda5, with about 500MB, formatted to ext3, and assign it to /var.

10. Create the next logical partition, hda6, with about 1000MB, formatted to ext3, and assign it to /var/www.

11. Create the next logical partition, hda7, with about 2000MB, formatted to ext3, and assign it to /home.

12. Create the next logical partition, hda8, with about 1000MB, formatted to ext3, and assign it to /usr.

13. Continue with the installation process, using your best judgment.

14. Choose to customize the package groups to be installed. On an exam, you may see a requirement to install a number of different services such as a Web server, communication with Windows PCs, and an FTP server, as well as servers for DNS and DHCP.

15. Finish the installation normally.

16. Reboot when prompted and log in as the root user.

TABLE 2-6 Custom Installation as a Server, 2 GHz Pentium, 10GB Single Disk, 256MB RAM

Partition	Size	Use	Comment
hda1	100MB	/boot	Maintains boot files
hda2	500MB	swap	Probably plenty of space
hda3	5GB	/	The root directory
hda4	4500MB	Extended partition	Solely a container for logical partitions
hda5	500MB	/var	For print spool files
hda6	1000MB	/var/www	Web services
hda7	2000MB	/home	No interactive users
hda8	1000MB	/usr	Additional network services

Lab 6

In this exercise, you will install RHEL to configure the partitions for an imaginary database server. You will need to create the partitions on a 25GB or larger hard disk (see Table 2-7). The main use for such a system is as a database, file, and print server, with few interactive users. If your hard drive is larger, don't use the extra space. If your system has a SATA or SCSI drive, substitute device names (e.g., sda2 for hda2) accordingly.

1. Create a Linux installation USB from the diskboot.img image file (assuming you can boot from the USB key) or a boot CD from the boot.iso file, and then reboot the system.

2. Make sure to boot from the new media.

3. Select custom partitioning at the appropriate time.

4. When prompted, select Disk Druid to edit partitions.

5. Delete all partitions.

6. Create the first partition with 100MB of disk space, formatted to ext3, and assign it to /boot.

7. Create the next primary partition, hda2, with about 1000MB of disk space, as Linux Swap.

8. Create the third partition with about 10GB disk space, Linux Native, and assign it to / (root).

9. Create an extended partition containing all the rest of the disk space, about 14GB.

10. Create the first logical partition, hda5, with about 3GB, formatted to ext3, and assign it to /var.

11. Create the next two logical partitions, hda6 and hda7, with about 3.5GB each. Format each to the software RAID filesystem.

on the
Job

In the real world, you should never configure different parts of a RAID array on the same hard drive. If you do this, the failure of any single hard drive can lead to the loss of all of your data on that array. However, it may be necessary to do so if the test computer you're using has only one physical hard drive.

12. Use the Make RAID option to set up a RAID 1 array from these two partitions. Format it to ext3 and assign it to /opt.

13. Create the next two logical partitions, hda8 and hda9, with about 2GB each. Format each to the software RAID filesystem.

14. Use the Make RAID option to set up a RAID 0 array from these two partitions. Format it to ext3 and assign it to /usr.

15. Continue with the installation process, using your best judgment.

16. When asked to select packages, make sure to include the MySQL Database Server package group.

17. Finish the installation normally.

18. Reboot and log in as the root user.

TABLE 2-7   Custom Installation as a Server (No Other OS), 2.4 GHz Pentium II, 25GB Single Disk, 512MB RAM

Partition	Size	Use	Comment
hda1	100MB	/boot	Maintains boot files
hda2	1000MB	swap	Probably plenty of space
hda3	10GB	/	The root directory
hda4	14GB	Extended partition	Solely a container for logical partitions
hda5	3GB	/var	For print spool files
hda6	3.5GB	/opt	Database system using RAID 1
hda7	3.5GB	/opt	Database system using RAID 1
hda8	2GB	/usr	File services using RAID 0
hda9	2GB	/usr	File services using RAID 0

SELF TEST ANSWERS

Hardware Compatibility

1. The file most closely associated with information on the CPU is /proc/cpuinfo. Less information on the CPU is available from other files, such as /var/log/dmesg.

CPU and RAM

2. There are versions of RHEL 5 available for at least six different architectures (depending on interpretations): i386, x86_64 (AMD Athlon and AMD64), ia64, IBM zSeries, IBM pSeries, and IBM iSeries.

Hotswap Buses

3. The **lspci** command lists all PCI devices connected to your system. If you want more information, you can run **lspci -v** or even **lspci -vv**.

Configuring a Network Installation

4. Three network servers that you can use to serve Red Hat Enterprise Linux installation files are FTP, HTTP, and NFS.

5. If you're unsure how to customize a firewall, the simplest way to flush out the rules is with the **iptables -F** command.

The First Installation Steps

6. The **linux mediacheck** command at the boot: prompt adds a step to the installation process that allows you to check the integrity of installation CDs.

Configuring Partitions, RAID, and LVM

7. The device file associated with the fourth logical partition on the second SATA drive is /dev/sdb8. The first logical partition is /dev/sda5.

8. To configure a RAID 6 array, you need at least four RAID partitions.

Post-partition Installation Steps

9. The names of package groups within the Server group that install servers are DNS Name Server, FTP Server, Legacy Network Server, Mail Server, MySQL Database, Network Servers, News Server, PostgreSQL Database, Printing Support, Web Server, and Windows File Server.

While there's no requirement to memorize these names, if you've installed RHEL a few times, you should be quite familiar with at least the names of a few of these groups.

Post-installation, Security, and the First Boot Process

10. If you don't see the GUI First Boot process after RHEL reboots for the first time, you probably haven't installed the GUI. (It's also possible that you have a configuration problem, such as a full partition associated with /home, that prevents the GUI from booting normally.)

Installation Validation

11. If you want access to a command line during the installation process, press ALT-F2 (or if you're installing via the GUI, press CTRL-ALT-F2).

12. If you want to see any error messages associated with access to a network installation server during the installation process, press ALT-F3 (or if you're installing via the GUI, press CTRL-ALT-F3).

LAB ANSWERS

Lab 1

Scenario 1: Buy a new disk and add it to the system. Then do a custom install to create a new installation of RHEL to partitions on the new disk, adding an entry to /boot/grub/grub.conf to provide a boot option to both versions of Linux.

Scenario 2: No space on server. Hmm…. You've got to get creative and either find a test computer on which you can do the test install or back up everything on the main server after taking it off line. Perform a new installation of RHEL. Copy your httpd.conf configuration file and see how it works. If it fails, you can restore everything back to the way it was. Note: Test your backups first before overwriting an existing operating system.

Lab 2

As described earlier in this chapter, the standard Red Hat FTP server is vsFTP; the default location for download files is the /var/ftp/pub directory. You'll want to specify a subdirectory to copy the files from the root directory of the installation CDs.

As this is a book on RHEL, I do not describe the steps needed to create an alternative FTP server on a Microsoft Windows computer.

To install a Web server, a DNS server, an FTP server, and a mail server during the RHEL installation process, you need to select the DNS Name Server, Web Server, FTP Server, and Mail Server package groups.

Lab 3

As described earlier in this chapter, the standard Red Hat HTTP server is Apache. The default location for download files is the /var/www/html directory. You'll want to specify a subdirectory to copy the files from the root directory of the installation CDs.

As this is a book on RHEL, I do not describe the steps needed to create an alternative HTTP server on a Microsoft Windows computer.

To install a Samba server, a print server, and the packages associated with recompiling the kernel during the RHEL installation process, you need to select the Windows File Server, Printing Support, and Kernel Development package groups.

Labs 4–6

No special solutions are required for these labs; they're simply intended to help you practice installing Linux in a variety of different situations. The more you practice different configurations, the faster you can set up Linux during the Installation and Configuration portion of your exam.

3

The Boot Process

CERTIFICATION OBJECTIVES

3.01	The BIOS Initialization Sequence	3.06	Controlling Services
3.02	The GRUB Boot Loader	3.07	System Configuration Files
3.03	Kernel Initialization and the First Process	✓	Two-Minute Drill
3.04	The First Process and /etc/inittab	Q&A	Self Test
3.05	Runlevels		

W

hen you've finished reading this chapter, you'll know the fundamentals of the boot process. When RHEL 5 is properly installed, the BIOS points to the GRUB boot loader, normally on the appropriate master boot record (MBR). GRUB points to and initializes the Linux kernel, which then starts **init**, the first Linux process. The **init** process then initializes the system and moves into appropriate runlevels. When Linux boots into a specific runlevel, it starts a series of services. You can customize this process.

CERTIFICATION OBJECTIVE 3.01

The BIOS Initialization Sequence

While not officially a Red Hat exam prerequisite or requirement, a basic understanding of the BIOS is a fundamental skill for all serious computer users. While many modern computers allow you to boot directly from the media of your choice, such as an RHEL 5 installation CD or a rescue USB key, that may not be possible during your Red Hat exam. Therefore, you need to know how to modify the BIOS menu to boot from the media of your choice.

INSIDE THE EXAM

Understanding the Boot Process

Both Red Hat (RHCT and RHCE) exams require intimate knowledge of the boot process. If you have problems booting into the default GUI, you need to know how to boot into a different runlevel—and what you can do in key runlevels. From the Red Hat Exam Prep guide, the associated RHCT skill is

■ Boot systems into different runlevels for troubleshooting and maintenance.

When you know GRUB, you can use it to boot RHEL into the runlevel of your choice, which can boot the system into a

configuration in which you can address other issues described in this book. When you know how to modify the GRUB boot loader, you can change the way Linux boots on your system.

From the Red Hat Exam Prep guide, the associated RHCE skill is

■ Diagnose and correct boot failures arising from bootloader, module, and filesystem errors.

The focus in this chapter is the boot process, and therefore the boot loader. Problems associated with kernel modules and filesystems are addressed in Chapters 4, 8, and 16.

Because of the variety of BIOS software available, this discussion is general. It's not possible to provide any sort of step-by-step instructions for modifying the wide array of available BIOS menus.

Basics of the BIOS

When you power up a computer successfully, the first thing that starts is the BIOS. Based on settings stored in stable, read-only memory, BIOS performs a series of diagnostics to detect and connect the CPU and key controllers. This is known as the Power On Self Test (POST). If you hear beeps during this process, you may have a hardware problem such as an improperly connected hard drive controller. The BIOS then looks for attached devices such as the graphics card. After the graphics hardware is detected, you may see a screen similar to Figure 3-1, which displays other hardware as detected, tested, and verified.

Once complete, the BIOS passes control to the MBR of the boot device, normally the first hard drive. At this point, you should see a boot loader screen.

Using the BIOS Menu

Generally, the only reason to go into the BIOS menu during the Red Hat exams is to boot from different media, such as a CD, floppy, or USB key. In many cases, you can bypass this process. Return to Figure 3-1. The options for this particular system are shown in the bottom of the screen. In this case, pressing F2 enters SETUP, the BIOS menu; pressing F12 boots directly from a network device; and pressing ESC starts a boot menu. The actual keys may vary on your system.

FIGURE 3-1

The BIOS
initialization
process

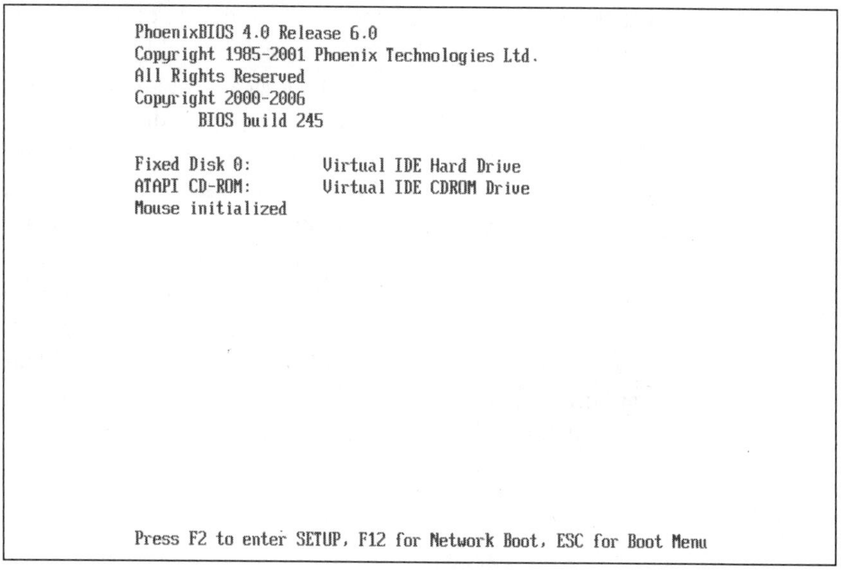

```
PhoenixBIOS 4.0 Release 6.0
Copyright 1985-2001 Phoenix Technologies Ltd.
All Rights Reserved
Copyright 2000-2006
        BIOS build 245

Fixed Disk 0:        Virtual IDE Hard Drive
ATAPI CD-ROM:        Virtual IDE CDROM Drive
Mouse initialized




         Press F2 to enter SETUP, F12 for Network Boot, ESC for Boot Menu
```

In many cases, all you see after POST is a blank screen. The BIOS is often configured in this way. In that case, you'll need to do some guessing based on your experience on how to reveal the screen shown in Figure 3-1 and access the boot or BIOS menu.

If you're fortunate, the computer you use on your exam has a boot menu accessible by pressing a key such as ESC, DEL, F2, or F12, with entries similar to:

```
    Boot Menu
1. Removable Devices
2. Hard Drive
3. CD-ROM Drive
4. USB Drive
5. Built-In LAN
```

If you see such a menu, you should be able to select the desired boot device using the arrow and ENTER keys. If that doesn't work, you'll have to use the BIOS menu to boot from the desired drive.

The BIOS and the Boot Loader

As described in Chapter 2, the default boot loader is GRUB, and the first part of it is installed in the MBR of the default drive. Normally, the BIOS should automatically start the boot loader, with a message similar to:

```
Booting Red Hat Enterprise Linux Server (2.6.18-8.el5) in 5 seconds...
```

If you're working with an older PC, the BIOS can't find your boot loader unless it's located within the first 1024 cylinders of the hard disk, which is why the /boot partition installed in Chapter 2 is normally a primary partition.

BIOSs overcome this problem with logical block addressing, which is also known as LBA mode. LBA mode reads "logical" values for the cylinder, head, and sector, which allows the BIOS to "see" a larger disk drive.

If you have multiple hard drives, there is one more caveat. If your drives are IDE (PATA) hard drives, the /boot directory must be on a hard drive attached to the primary IDE controller. If your drives are all SCSI hard drives, the /boot directory must be located on a hard drive with SCSI ID 0 or ID 1. If you have a mix of hard drives, the /boot directory must be located on either the first IDE drive or a SCSI drive with ID 0.

However, I believe most computers used for the Red Hat exams have only one hard drive. This saves costs for the exam site and means you probably won't have to worry about which hard drive contains the /boot directory.

CERTIFICATION OBJECTIVE 3.02

The GRUB Boot Loader

The standard boot loader associated with Red Hat Enterprise Linux (RHEL) is GRUB, the GRand Unified Boot loader. LILO, the Linux Loader, is no longer supported. As suggested by the Red Hat exam requirements, for the RHCT exam, you need to know how to use the GRUB menu to boot into different runlevels, and diagnose and correct boot failures arising from boot loader errors.

GRUB, the GRand Unified Bootloader

Red Hat has implemented GRUB as the only boot loader for its Linux distributions. When you start your computer, your BIOS looks for the /boot directory and finds the GRUB menu, which will look similar to Figure 3-2. If you've configured your computer with multiple operating systems, you can use the GRUB menu to boot any operating system detected during the Linux installation process.

If you need to do something special with GRUB, you can edit the commands. If GRUB is password protected, you'll need to start with the **p** command. Use the

FIGURE 3-2

The GRand
Unified
Bootloader
(GRUB)

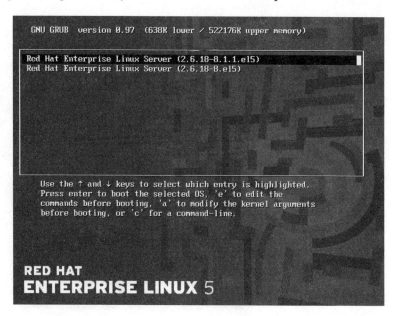

e command to temporarily edit the file. You'll see a number of basic commands that you can use to modify GRUB, as shown in Figure 3-3 and Table 3-1. You can use these commands to test different GRUB configurations. They can help you troubleshoot problems with the GRUB configuration file, without booting, editing, and rebooting your system. That could possibly help you save time during the Troubleshooting exam. But once you find the solution, make sure to record the change in the GRUB configuration file, /boot/grub/grub.conf.

on the job

Other Linux distributions store the GRUB menu in /boot/grub/menu.lst. Red Hat links that file to its GRUB menu file, /boot/grub/grub.conf.

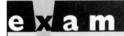

e x a m

⟨w⟩ a t c h   *If you're troubleshooting GRUB, the GRUB menu can help you experiment with changes quickly. However,* *if you find the solution in this way, you'll still need to change (and test) the GRUB configuration file, /boot/grub/grub.conf.*

FIGURE 3-3

Details of GRUB

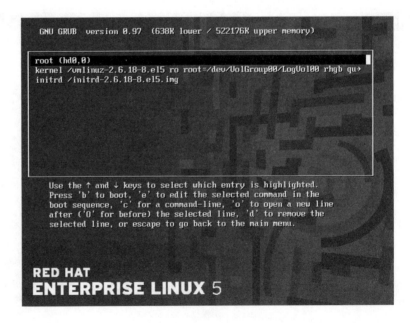

```
GNU GRUB  version 0.97  (638K lower / 522176K upper memory)

root (hd0,0)
kernel /vmlinuz-2.6.18-8.el5 ro root=/dev/VolGroup00/LogVol00 rhgb qu→
initrd /initrd-2.6.18-8.el5.img

      Use the ↑ and ↓ keys to select which entry is highlighted.
      Press 'b' to boot, 'e' to edit the selected command in the
      boot sequence, 'c' for a command-line, 'o' to open a new line
      after ('O' for before) the selected line, 'd' to remove the
      selected line, or escape to go back to the main menu.
```

RED HAT
ENTERPRISE LINUX 5

TABLE 3-1	Command	Description
	b	Boot the currently listed operating system
GRUB Editing	d	Delete the current line
Commands	e	Edit the current line
	o	Create an empty line underneath the current line
	O	Create an empty line above the current line

exam

watch *If you find a problem with GRUB during the Troubleshooting and System Maintenance part of your exam and are unsure about the solution, testing changes through the GRUB menu could* *save you time. However, until you record the change in the GRUB configuration file (which requires that you boot Linux into some runlevel), you won't get credit for the work that you've done.*

You can also use GRUB to boot other operating systems, including various versions of Microsoft Windows, as shown in Figure 3-3.

on the job *The /etc/grub.conf file is linked to the actual GRUB configuration file, /boot/grub/grub.conf. If you edit /etc/grub.conf, changes are automatically reflected in /boot/grub/grub.conf.*

GRUB Parameters

To pass a parameter to GRUB, type the **a** command in the first GRUB menu. This allows you to append the command sent to the kernel. After typing the **a** command, you might see a command line similar to the following:

```
grub append> ro root=LABEL=/ rhgb quiet
```

You can add the command of your choice to the end of this command. For example, if you add **single** at the end of this line, Linux starts in single-user mode. If you're having trouble getting Linux to recognize all of the RAM on your computer, try adding **mem=xyzM** (where xyzM represents the amount of memory on your computer) at the end of the line.

In short, you can boot your system into runlevels 1, single (or s), emergency, 2, 3, 4, or 5. If you have trouble booting into any runlevel, try **init=/bin/sh**. While it's possible to boot into runlevels 0 or 6, those runlevels would automatically halt or reboot your system. For more information, see the runlevels section later in this chapter.

Updating GRUB

If you're going to diagnose GRUB problems, you need to know how GRUB works. The best place to start is with a typical GRUB configuration file.

```
# grub.conf generated by anaconda
#
# Note that you do not have to rerun grub after making changes to this file
# NOTICE:  You have a /boot partition. This means that
#          all kernel and initrd paths are relative to /boot/, eg.
#          root (hd0,4)
#          kernel /vmlinuz-version ro root=/dev/sdb2
#          initrd /initrd-version.img
# boot=/dev/sda
default=0
timeout=5
splashimage=(hd0,4)/grub/splash.xpm.gz
hiddenmenu
password --md5 $1$2Srxmp06%KSkbeE#7deIrX8ucnCFzn/
title Red Hat Enterprise Linux (2.6.17-1.EL)
        root (hd0,4)
        kernel /vmlinuz-2.6.17-1.EL ro root=LABEL=/ rhgb quiet
        initrd /initrd-2.6.17-1.EL.img
title Windows XP Professional
        rootnoverify (hd0,0)
        chainloader +1
```

As you can see, even the comments are significant. The first line suggests that this file was created by Anaconda, the RHEL installation program. The next line notes that changes do not have to be written to the MBR; this file is automatically linked to the GRUB pointer that is probably already installed in the MBR.

If you've previously installed a different boot loader to the MBR, such as Microsoft's NTLDR, you can make your MBR look for the GRUB configuration file. Just run the grub-install command.

The commented "Notice" in the configuration file appears if you have created a separate partition for the /boot directory. Now this is really weird—there are two definitions for the word **root** in this file. First, the /boot directory in the GRUB configuration file is associated with root, in this case, **root(hd0,4)**. But the actual Linux top-level root directory is associated with a different partition, as defined by this comment:

```
root=/dev/sdb2
```

The **root(hd0,4)** directive uses numbers starting with 0. In other words, this directive points to the fifth partition on the first hard drive. The /boot directory is mounted on this partition. If it were the first partition on the first hard drive, for example, this directive would read *root(hd0,0)*.

The last commented line indicates the hard drive with the MBR—in this case, /dev/sda. Now examine the actual commands in this file:

```
default=0
timeout=5
splashimage=(hd0,4)/grub/splash.xpm.gz
hiddenmenu
password --md5 $1$2Srxmp06%KSkbeE#7deIrX8ucnCFzn/
title Red Hat Enterprise Linux Server(2.6.18-1.EL)
        root (hd0,4)
        kernel /vmlinuz-2.6.18-1.EL ro root=LABEL=/ rhgb quiet
        initrd /initrd-2.6.18-1.EL.img
title Windows XP Professional
        rootnoverify (hd0,0)
        chainloader +1
```

The **default=0** directive points to the first stanza. In other words, based on the remaining commands in this file, GRUB boots RHEL 5 by default. If you changed this to **default=1**, GRUB would boot the second stanza (in this case, Windows XP Professional) by default.

The **timeout=5** directive specifies the time, in seconds, before GRUB automatically boots the default operating system. The **splashimage** directive locates the graphical GRUB screen you see in Figure 3-3. In this case, you can find it on the fifth partition of the first hard drive, in the /grub/splash.xpm.gz file. As **(hd0,4)** has been previously defined as the /boot directory, you can find the splash screen file in /boot/grub/splash .xpm.gz. The **hiddenmenu** directive means that the GRUB options are hidden, with the message shown here:

```
Booting Red Hat Enterprise Linux Server (2.6.18-8.el5) in 4 seconds...
```

The **password --md5** directive specifies a password, hashed to the MD5 (Message-Digest algorithm 5) format, which protects GRUB from modification during the boot process. As described earlier, when you see the GRUB menu, you can enter the password after pressing **p**. If you want to create your own MD5 password for this file, run the **grub-md5-crypt** command. You'll be prompted for a password that is converted to an MD5 hash. You can then copy this hash to the GRUB configuration file.

Each of the next two stanzas has a title normally associated with the operating system, such as:

```
title Red Hat Enterprise Linux Server (2.6.18-1.EL)
```

This is a standard, based on the currently installed kernel. If you've configured more than one kernel, you'll probably see more than one stanza. Both would boot RHEL 5, using a different kernel.

The next three lines specify the location of the /boot directory, the kernel, and the initial RAM disk, respectively:

```
root (hd0,4)
kernel /vmlinuz-2.6.18-1.EL ro root=LABEL=/ rhgb quiet
initrd /initrd-2.6.18-1.EL.img
```

In this case, the /boot directory, as described earlier, is on the fifth partition of the first hard drive, as specified by **root (hd0,4)**. The kernel is specified by the vmlinuz-2.6.18-1.EL file, which you can find in the /boot directory. It's opened as read only (**ro**) to protect it from any accidental writes from the initial RAM disk; the actual top-level root directory is associated with the / label (**root=LABEL=/**). Finally, the **rhgb quiet** directive hides the boot messages by default.

You may see other directives on this line, such as **selinux=0**, which disables Security Enhanced Linux (SELinux). But remember, SELinux is now part of the RHCE exam requirements.

The initial RAM disk creates a temporary filesystem during the boot process. It includes kernel modules and user space programs needed to mount actual filesystems and run the first initialization programs.

The final three lines are trivial with respect to the Red Hat exams; however, many users see them when they configure their computers in a dual-boot with Microsoft Windows. In most cases, you'll actually see the first line as:

```
title Other
```

I've modified it to specify the actual operating system on the other partition. In this case, Microsoft Windows XP is installed on the first partition on the first hard drive, as specified by:

```
rootnoverify (hd0,0)
```

This is different from the aforementioned **root (hd0,4)** directive, as **rootnoverify** does not attempt to mount the noted partition in a Linux fashion.

Finally, the **chainloader +1** directive points to the first sector of the noted partition, where Microsoft Windows continues the boot process:

```
chainloader +1
```

GRUB Error Effects

Now that you've analyzed the GRUB configuration file, you can probably visualize some of the effects of errors in this file. If some of the filenames or partitions are wrong, GRUB won't be able to find critical files such as the Linux kernel. Here's an example of the error you'll see if the **root (hd0,4)** directive points to something other than the /boot directory:

```
    Booting command-list

root (hd0,4)
   Filesystem type unknown, partition type 0x8e
kernel /vmlinuz-2.6.18-1.EL ro root=LABEL=/ rhgb quiet

Error 17: Cannot mount selected partition

Press any key to continue...
```

If the GRUB configuration file is completely missing, you'll see a prompt similar to this:

```
grub>
```

You'll see more of these issues in Chapter 16.

EXERCISE 3-1

GRUB Error Effects

It's important to know what can happen when there are errors in the GRUB configuration file. In this exercise, you'll first back up and print out the GRUB configuration file, change it during the boot process, and see what happens. Save the printout for Exercise 3-2.

If you make a mistake during the process, you'll have to refer to the techniques described in Chapter 16 to rescue the system from the backup grub.conf that you created. However, the steps used here should make no permanent changes in grub .conf. All you need to do to restore the original settings is reboot your system.

1. Boot into Linux, and back up the default GRUB configuration file with a command such as:

```
# cp /boot/grub/grub.conf ~
```

This particular command, run as the root user, saves a copy of grub.conf in the root user's home directory, /root. Print out a copy; if your printer is connected, all you need to run is **lpr /boot/grub/grub.conf**.

2. Reboot your system. When you see the following line at the top of the screen, press a key to access the GRUB menu:

```
Press any key to enter the menu
```

3. If your GRUB configuration file is password protected, you'll have to press **p** to enter the password.

4. Highlight a RHEL 5 kernel (if you haven't installed new kernels, there will be only one in the menu), and press **e** to edit the associated stanza.

5. Highlight and press **e** to edit the first line in the stanza, which should look similar to:

```
root (hd0,0)
```

6. Change the root directive—misspell it in some way. For this exercise, I deleted a letter:

```
roo (hd0,0)
```

7. Press ENTER to save the change temporarily, and press **b** to boot this stanza. You'll see messages similar to:

```
    Booting command-list

roo (hd0,0)

Error 27: Unrecognized command

Press any key to continue...
```

8. Observe the result. You can see what happens when you try to boot from a stanza with a misspelled command. Repeat the process in steps 5 through 7, but try different changes, such as (what you do depends on your specific configuration):

```
root (h0,0)
root (hd1,0)
root (hd0,1)
```

9. You should see messages such as "Error while parsing number" and "Cannot mount selected partition."

10. Now restore the first line. If you don't remember what you did, reboot or reset your system; that should restore the original line.

11. Repeat steps 2 through 4, and now try creating errors in the second line. Misspell the **kernel** command. What kind of error do you see? What do you see before the error? Does this provide a clue?

12. When you get to the **ro** in the second line, delete it, and try to boot. What happens? Why did it work? Why is the **ro** important?

13. Normally, the second line will include a directive that points to a LABEL or a logical volume. Here are two examples:

    ```
    root=/dev/VolGroup00/LogVol00
    root=LABEL=/1
    ```

    See what happens when you misspell the **root** directive. Would this be fault tolerance? And again, see what happens if you change the LABEL or logical volume number. What happens if you delete the directive completely? If there's an error in this directive, remember that you can check /etc/fstab to restore it.

    However, you should be careful. If you happen to change the LABEL to another existing partition, you may end up booting RHEL 5 on a different root directory tree.

14. Observe the kernel panic error. Note the **setuproot** directives, such as:

    ```
    setuproot: error mounting /proc: No such file or directory
    ```

    This particular error means that the GRUB directives can't find your top-level root directory; in other words, the root directive on the second line points to a bad partition or volume. Whenever you see a kernel panic, a reboot may not be possible; you may have to reset the power on your system.

15. Note what happens when you delete the **rhgb** or **quiet** directive. Does it make a difference to the system once booted?

16. Repeat steps 2 through 4, and now try creating errors in the third line. What kinds of errors result? Compare the result with step 11, with respect to the line before "Error 15: File not found."

17. Reboot your system. Check the details of your GRUB configuration file against your backup or printout.

The GRUB Command Line

If you see a GRUB command line, you may feel lost. To see a list of available commands, press the TAB key at the **grub>** prompt.

Some trial and error may be required. You should be able to find all detected hard drives on a standard PC from the BIOS menu (SCSI drives can be a different story). Assuming you have just one, you can use the **find** command to identify the partition with the GRUB configuration file. For example, to find grub.conf on this particular system, start with the following command:

```
grub> find (hd0,0)/grub/grub.conf
```

This returns an "Error 15: File not found" error message. Repeat this process with the other partitions on this drive,

```
grub> find (hd0,1)/grub/grub.conf
grub> find (hd0,2)/grub/grub.conf
grub> find (hd0,3)/grub/grub.conf
grub> find (hd0,4)/grub/grub.conf
```

and so on, until you see output associated with your partition, such as:

```
(hd0,4)
```

In this case, the /boot directory is on the fifth partition on the first hard drive. Just to confirm, use the **cat** command to read the contents of the GRUB configuration file:

```
grub> cat (hd0,4)/grub/grub.conf
```

Now use these commands from the GRUB configuration file to boot Linux from the **grub>** command line. But what if your GRUB configuration file is missing? In Chapter 16, you'll create a GRUB configuration file from scratch, using documentation available on your system via a rescue disk.

Note that a shortcut is available. From the **grub>** command line, look for the stage1 boot loader file. The command is simple:

```
grub> find /grub/stage1
```

If the stage1 boot loader file is still there, you'll see output specifying the partition with the /boot directory, such as:

```
(hd0,4)
```

But wait, it can be even simpler. Just run **root** at the **grub>** command line:

```
grub> root
(hd0,4): Filesystem type is ext2fs, partition type 0x83
```

Command completion works from the GRUB command line. For example, if you don't remember the name of the Kernel file, type kernel / and then press the TAB key to review the available files in the /boot directory.

EXERCISE 3-2

Using the GRUB Command Line

In this exercise, you'll use the printout of the GRUB configuration file from Exercise 3-1 to boot RHEL 5 manually. Look at the printout and identify the desired commands in the stanza. Now follow these steps:

1. Boot your system. When you see the following line at the top of the screen, press any key to access the GRUB menu:

   ```
   Press any key to enter the menu
   ```

2. If your GRUB configuration file is password protected, you'll have to press **p** to enter the password.

3. Press **c** for a GRUB-based command line interface. You should see the **grub>** prompt.

   Type in the commands listed in the selected stanza. Start by issuing the first **root** directive. If the command is successful, you should see output similar to:

   ```
   Filesystem type is ext2fs, partition type 0x83
   ```

   Note that if you've configured a different filesystem such as XFS, you'll see a slightly different result.

4. Enter the second command from your selected GRUB configuration file stanza, which specifies the kernel and root directory partition. Yes, this is a long line; however, you can use command completion (press the TAB key) to make it faster. If successful, you'll see the following message (the setup and size numbers may vary):

   ```
   [Linux-bzImage, setup=0x1e00, size=0x16eb71]
   ```

5. Enter the third command from the stanza, which specifies the initial RAM disk command and file location. If successful, you'll see the following message (the numbers may vary):

   ```
   [Linux-initrd @ 0x16544000, 0x19b6c7 bytes]
   ```

6. Now enter the **boot** command. If successful, Linux should now boot your desired kernel and initial RAM disk just as if you selected that option from the GRUB configuration menu.

CERTIFICATION OBJECTIVE 3.03

Kernel Initialization and the First Process

This section provides a basic overview of the boot process that occurs after the GRUB boot loader finds the kernel. Understanding what happens here can help you diagnose a wide variety of boot problems, some of which you might see during a Red Hat exam.

Kernel Message Analysis

Just a few messages after you boot a kernel from the GRUB configuration menu, Linux hands over boot responsibilities to the kernel. If you've disabled the **quiet** directive in the GRUB configuration file, you can watch as the messages pass quickly through the screen. To review these messages, open /var/log/dmesg or run the **dmesg** command.

What you see depends on the hardware and configuration of your computer. Key messages include:

- The version of the kernel
- Amount of recognized RAM (which does not necessarily match the actual amount of installed RAM)
- CPUs (labeled as CPU 0, CPU 1, and so on)
- SELinux status, if active
- Kernel command line, specifying the logical volume or root filesystem label
- Freeing of memory associated with the initial RAM disk (initramfs)
- Hard drives and partitions (as defined by their device file names, such as /dev/sda or /dev/hda1)
- Network cards, as defined by their device names, such as eth0
- Active filesystems
- Swap partitions

This file is filled with potential clues. If you've booted from the wrong kernel, you'll see it here. If Linux isn't using a partition that you've configured, you'll also see it here (indirectly). If you don't see an active network card and don't see it in the dmesg file, it may signal either a missing driver or a hardware problem with your computer.

e x a m

ⓦ a t c h *Remember that the Red Hat exams are not hardware exams. If you identify a problem with a key hardware component, such as a network card (which cannot be solved by some Linux command), inform your instructor/ exam proctor.*

Driver Loading

While it's possible to create and install a "monolithic" kernel without drivers, that's not the way it's done on RHEL. Most kernels on modern PCs are modular. That means when you boot, kernels are loaded, followed by drivers. While many drivers are associated with hardware components, others include key software modules, such as the ext3 filesystem. You can review loaded modules using the **lsmod** command.

CERTIFICATION OBJECTIVE 3.04

The First Process and /etc/inittab

Once kernels and drivers are loaded, Linux starts loading the rest of the system. This all starts with the First Process, known as **init**. It loads based on the parameters defined in /etc/inittab, which specifies runlevels, the system initialization script, virtual consoles, and more.

The First Process

The Linux kernel continues the boot process by calling **init**. The **init** process in turn runs /etc/rc.d/rc.sysinit, which performs a number of tasks, including network configuration, SELinux status, keyboard maps, system clock, partition mounts, and host names. It also loads the modules described in the previous section. It does even more: the default version of this file contains more than 500 lines.

/etc/inittab

The **init** process then determines which runlevel it should be in by looking at the **initdefault** directive in /etc/inittab. A runlevel is defined as a group of activities. For example, the entry

```
id:5:initdefault:
```

shows a default starting point in runlevel 5, which is associated with the GUI. For more information on runlevels, read the "Runlevels" section later in this chapter. The virtual console commands are described in the "Virtual Consoles" section toward the end of the chapter.

There are four other default commands in /etc/inittab. The first of these commands captures the CTRL-ALT-DELETE key combination and associates it with the **shutdown** command shown, which executes the command after 3 seconds, in reboot mode, starting the 3-second countdown immediately:

```
# Trap CTRL-ALT-DELETE
ca::ctrlaltdel:/sbin/shutdown -t3 -r now
```

The next two commands are associated with the signal from an uninterruptible power supply (UPS). If you have a UPS connected to your system and a power failure occurs, the UPS should take over powering your computers. But as a UPS can keep your system running for only a limited amount of time, the following command starts the shutdown process in 2 minutes and warns your users as such:

```
pf::powerfail:/sbin/shutdown -f -h +2 "Power Failure; System Shutting Down"
```

This specific command skips running **fsck** on reboot and powers down (halts) the system. If the power is restored before shutdown is executed, the next command cancels the shutdown sequence:

```
pr:12345:powerokwait:/sbin/shutdown -c "Power Restored; Shutdown Cancelled"
```

Finally, the last command refers to the /etc/X11/prefdm file, which is run if the default runlevel is 5. As you'll see in Chapter 14, the default GUI login manager is configured in this and related files.

Virtual Consoles

A *virtual console* is a command line where you can log into and control Linux. As RHEL is a multiterminal operating system, you can log into Linux, even with the same user ID, several times.

It's easy to open a new virtual console. Just use the appropriate ALT-function key combination. For example, pressing ALT-F2 brings you to the second virtual console. You can switch between adjacent virtual consoles by pressing ALT-RIGHT ARROW or ALT-LEFT ARROW. For example, to move from virtual console 2 to virtual console 3, press ALT-RIGHT ARROW.

Virtual Consoles in /etc/inittab

Virtual consoles are configured in /etc/inittab. By default, RHEL is configured with six virtual consoles. You can configure up to twelve virtual consoles in /etc/inittab. Here are the default /etc/inittab entries for the first six virtual consoles:

```
1:2345:respawn:/sbin/mingetty tty1
2:2345:respawn:/sbin/mingetty tty2
3:2345:respawn:/sbin/mingetty tty3
4:2345:respawn:/sbin/mingetty tty4
5:2345:respawn:/sbin/mingetty tty5
6:2345:respawn:/sbin/mingetty tty6
```

Virtual consoles really bring the multiuser capabilities of Linux to life. You can be viewing a man page on one console, compiling a program in another, and editing a document in a third virtual console. Other users who are connected through a network can do the same thing at the same time.

Virtual Consoles in the GUI

The GUI is, in one way, just another console. By default, six virtual consoles are configured with Linux, so the GUI is next in line, at console 7. To switch from the GUI to a regular virtual console, press CTRL-ALT-Fx, where x represents one of the other virtual consoles.

CERTIFICATION OBJECTIVE 3.05

Runlevels

Linux services are organized by runlevel. Some runlevels can reboot and halt Linux. Other runlevels can boot Linux with or without networking. The default runlevel for RHEL 5 boots Linux into the GUI.

Runlevels are controlled by scripts, organized in runlevel-based directories. While the default runlevel is defined in /etc/inittab, you can override the default during the boot process from the GRUB menu.

Functionality of Each Runlevel

RHEL has six basic runlevels, as defined in /etc/inittab. Each runlevel is associated with a level of functionality. For example, in single-user mode, also known as runlevel 1, only one user is allowed to connect to that Linux system. X11 mode, also known as runlevel 5, starts Linux into a GUI login screen. The Red Hat definitions for System V init runlevels are shown in Table 3-2.

Making each runlevel work is the province of a substantial number of scripts. Each script can start or stop fundamental Linux processes such as printing (**cupsd**), scheduling (**crond**), Apache (**httpd**), Samba (**smbd**), and more. The starting and stopping of the right scripts becomes part of the boot process.

It should go without saying that if you set your **initdefault** to 0, your system will shut down when Linux tries to boot. Likewise, if you set the **initdefault** to 6, Linux will enter a continuous reboot cycle.

The default runlevel when you boot RHEL 5 is 5, GUI with networking. If you don't install the GUI on RHEL 5, the default is 3. If you have problems with one runlevel, consider booting into another. For example, if the GUI isn't working,

TABLE 3-2	Runlevel	Description
	0	Halt
Red Hat Runlevels	1	Single-user mode, for maintenance (backups/restores) and repairs
	2	Multiuser, with some network services
	3	Multiuser, with networking
	4	Unused
	5	X11, defaults to a GUI login screen; logins bring the user to a GUI desktop, with networking
	6	Reboot (never set **initdefault** in /etc/inittab to this value)

e x a m

ⓦ a t c h

To practice for the Troubleshooting and System Maintenance part of each exam, it can be useful to back up and then modify critical configuration files such as /etc/inittab. But remember to do this on a test computer; if you can't solve the problem, you may lose the data on that computer. Before you proceed, learn the rescue mode techniques described in Chapter 16.

consider booting into runlevel 1, 2, or 3. It allows you to boot into Linux, examine appropriate logs, and address related problems.

Different runlevels can be customized. For example, if you boot into runlevel 1 and have an appropriate network connection, all you need to do is run a command such as **dhclient eth0** to activate that network connection.

Runlevel Scripts

There are a series of scripts associated with each runlevel. For example, the default runlevel is 5, and the scripts associated with this runlevel can be found in the /etc/rc.d/rc5.d directory.

Naturally, the scripts associated with other runlevels can be found in other /etc/rc.d directories:

```
rc0.d
rc1.d
rc2.d
rc3.d
rc4.d
rc5.d
rc6.d
```

If the default runlevel is 5, init will look in /etc/rc.d/rc5.d and run each "kill" and "start" script it finds in that directory. A kill script is any file or symbolically linked file with a name that begins with a K. Likewise, start scripts start with S. If you run an **ls -l** command in this directory, you'll see only symbolic links to the actual scripts in /etc/rc.d/init.d. Observe current examples of kill and start scripts at runlevel 5 in Figure 3-4.

on the

⚫o b

init *scripts in the /etc/rc.d directories are hard linked to /etc. In other words, you'll see the same script files in the /etc/rc.d/rc5.d and /etc/rc5.d directories. You can confirm this by running the* ls -i *command on both directories, which displays the same inodes for each matching script file. For brevity, I normally refer to the shorter directory name in this book.*

What's going on here? The **init** process knows to go to the directory associated with a particular runlevel. Once there, **init** runs the scripts in that directory that start with a K and then the scripts starting with an S. The K scripts stop processes

FIGURE 3-4

Sample kill and
start scripts in
runlevel 5

```
[root@Enterprise5a ~]# \ls /etc/rc5.d/
K01rgmanager          K74ypserv              S25bluetooth
K01yum                K74ypxfrd              S25netfs
K02avahi-dnsconfd     K77fenced              S26hidd
K02dhcdbd             K78lock_gulmd          S26lm_sensors
K02NetworkManager     K79cman                S28autofs
K02NetworkManagerDispatcher  K80ccsd         S40smartd
K05innd               K84btseed              S44acpid
K05saslauthd          K84bttrack             S50hplip
K10dc_server          K85mdmpd               S55cups
K10psacct             K87multipathd          S55sshd
K12dc_client          K87named               S56xinetd
K20rwhod              K88wpa_supplicant      S58ntpd
K24irda               K89iscsi               S60nfs
K25squid              K89netplugd            S80sendmail
K30spamassassin       K89rdisc               S85gpm
K34dhcrelay           K91capi                S85httpd
K34yppasswdd          K94diskdump            S90crond
K35dhcpd              S04readahead_early     S90xfs
K35dovecot            S05kudzu               S91smb
K35vncserver          S06cpuspeed            S95anacron
K35winbind            S08iptables            S95atd
K36lisa               S09isdn                S95firstboot
K36mysqld             S10network             S96readahead
K50netdump            S12syslog              S98avahi-daemon
K50tux                S13irqbalance          S98cups-config-daemon
K50vsftpd             S13portmap             S98haldaemon
K69rpcsvcgssd         S14nfslock             S98xend
K73ldap               S15mdmonitor           S99local
K73ypbind             S18rpcidmapd           S99xendomains
K74gfs                S19rpcgssd
K74nscd               S22messagebus
[root@Enterprise5a ~]# █
```

that aren't supposed to operate in that runlevel. The S scripts start the processes associated with that runlevel. Within each category, scripts are run in numeric order; for example, K01yum is run before K35dhcpd, which is run before S10network.

Red Hat configures six different runlevels: 0, 1, 2, 3, 5, and 6. (Runlevel 4 is unused.) Hard links allow the configuration of the same scripts in the /etc/rc.d/init.d and /etc/init.d directories. For example, if you modify /etc/init.d/smb, the changes are automatically shown in /etc/rc.d/init.d/smb.

You can run a start script yourself, with some key switches. For example, you can run the smbd (Samba) and sshd (secure shell daemon) scripts with the following options:

```
# /etc/init.d/smb
Usage: /etc/init.d/smb {start|stop|restart|reload|status|condrestart}
# service smb     # service is a shortcut to the management scripts
Usage: /etc/init.d/smb {start|stop|restart|reload|status|condrestart}
# service sshd
Usage: /etc/init.d/sshd {start|stop|restart|reload|condrestart|status}
#
```

The **/etc/init.d/smb restart** command stops and starts Samba. See from the code how you can substitute the **service** command for /etc/init.d. It's one more timesaver that you can use on the Red Hat exams.

This is used by the scripts at each runlevel. In other words, if a K script exists for the smbd daemon, **init** runs **/etc/init.d/smb stop**. And naturally, an S script for the ssh daemon runs **/etc/init.d/sshd start**.

Examine the scripts at each runlevel, as defined in the /etc/rcx directory, where x is the runlevel. Make a note of the differences. The default difference between runlevels 3 and 5 is subtle. However, runlevel 2 includes fewer network-related scripts than 3; runlevel 1 starts only a couple of services. In contrast, runlevels 0 and 6 start the killall script and execute the halt or reboot services.

e x a m

ⓦ a t c h   *Make sure you go through the /etc/rc.d hierarchy as well as the /etc/inittab and /etc/rc.d/rc.sysinit files (as specified in /etc/inittab), and understand what's happening along the way. This is the key to understanding what's happening during the boot process.*

Booting into the Runlevel of Your Choice

You should know how to boot into different runlevels during the boot process. As defined in the Red Hat Exam Prep guide, this is explicitly described as an RHCT (and therefore also an RHCE) requirement:

Boot systems into different runlevels for troubleshooting and maintenance.

In other words, you need to know how to boot into a different runlevel from the main GRUB menu. If you do nothing during the boot process, GRUB automatically boots the default operating system and kernel. If you want to see and possibly select from available kernels (and even operating systems), press any key before the following message expires (normally in 5 seconds)

```
Press any key to enter the menu
```

You'll then see a menu similar to Figure 3-5, from where you can modify how GRUB boots into Linux.

If you have problems booting into the GUI, first try to boot into runlevel 3, which boots into Linux with all services except the GUI. You can then use the techniques described in Chapter 14 to examine typical problems that can prevent the GUI from starting.

The GRUB boot
loader

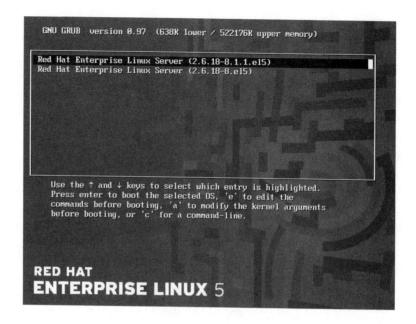

EXERCISE 3-3

Booting into a Different Runlevel

One key skill is understanding how to boot into a different runlevel. This exercise assumes you've configured RHEL 5 per the defaults, which sets the default runlevel as 5. Check your /etc/inittab file. If your system reflects the defaults, it should read as follows:

```
id:5:initdefault:
```

Change this directive if needed and reboot your system. Now you can start the exercise.

1. When you see the following message, make sure to press any key to access the GRUB menu:

```
Press any key to enter the menu
```

2. If the menu is password protected, you'll have to press **p** before entering the GRUB password. Then you can press **a** to access the kernel command line.

3. At the end of the kernel command line, type a space followed by the runlevel of your choice. First, enter **3**, and press **b** to boot this kernel.

4. Watch the boot messages. What kind of login screen do you see?

5. Log into this system. You can use any existing user account.

6. Run the **reboot** command to restart this system.

7. Repeat steps 1 through 3, but boot this system into runlevel **1**.

8. Watch the boot messages. What kind of login screen do you see? Do you have to log in at all?

9. Repeat steps 1 through 3, but boot this system into runlevel **s**.

10. Watch the boot messages. What kind of login screen do you see? Do you have to log in at all?

11. Run the **reboot** command to restart this system.

12. Repeat steps 1 through 3, but boot this system into runlevel **emergency**.

13. Watch the boot messages. What kind of login screen do you see? What password do you need?

14. Repeat steps 1 through 3, but boot this system into runlevel **init=/bin/sh**.

15. Watch the boot messages. What kind of login screen do you see?

16. Run the **halt** command to stop this system.

More serious problems can be addressed by booting into other runlevels. The standard is to boot into "single-user mode," also known as runlevel 1. Check the scripts in the /etc/rc1.d directory. Note that these scripts typically start only a couple of services.

There are three command alternatives to runlevel 1: **s**, **init=bin/sh**, and **emergency**. To boot Linux at these levels, reboot your system. When you see the GRUB configuration menu described earlier in this chapter, enter the GRUB password if required, and then press **a** to modify the kernel arguments.

Except for a normal boot of Linux, single-user mode is the most commonly used option. This is the system maintenance mode for experienced Linux administrators. It allows you to perform clean backups and restores to any partitions as needed from local hardware. It also allows you to run administration commands, recover or repair password and shadow password files, run filesystem checks, and so forth.

From single-user mode, type **exit** and your system will go into multiuser mode. If you have made changes or repairs to any partitions, you should reboot the computer with the **reboot** command. If you've made changes during your exam, you'll want to test those changes with a reboot.

Controlling Services

Whenever you install a service on the Red Hat exams, you'll generally want to make sure that they're active when the person grading your exam boots your system. There are three basic tools used to control services: text commands, text-based tools, and the Red Hat GUI Service Configuration tool.

Service Control from the Command Line

It's generally fastest to control services at the command line. The **chkconfig** command gives you a simple way to maintain different runlevels within the /etc/rc.d directory structure. With **chkconfig**, you can add, remove, and change services; list startup information; and check the state of a particular service. For example, you can check the runlevels where the sendmail service is set to start with the following command:

```
# chkconfig --list sendmail
sendmail 0:off 1:off 2:on 3:on 4:on 5:on 6:off
```

This indicates that sendmail is configured to start in runlevels 2, 3, 4, and 5. If you want to turn the sendmail service off for runlevel 4, execute the following command:

```
# chkconfig --level 4 sendmail off
```

Now sendmail is configured to run only on runlevels 2, 3, and 5. To turn it back on for runlevel 4, run the same command, substituting **on** for **off**. With **chkconfig**, you can also add or delete services with the **--add** and **--del** switches. Installing a service sets up the appropriate links within the /etc/rc.d directory hierarchy. Uninstalling that service removes the associated links from the same hierarchy.

The commands need not even be that complex. If you leave out the runlevel, the following commands automatically deactivate the sendmail service in all runlevels and then activate it in runlevels 2, 3, 4, and 5.

```
# chkconfig sendmail off
# chkconfig sendmail on
```

The Text Console Service Configuration Tool

If you're managing a substantial number of services, the command line can be less efficient. You don't need a GUI, just the **ntsysv** tool, which you can open with the command of the same name. However, it's a bit tricky; it affects only services in the current runlevel unless you add an appropriate switch.

For example, if you want to activate several services in runlevels 3 and 5, start **ntsysv** with the following command (don't forget the double-dash):

```
# ntsysv --level 35
```

For this section, I've started **ntsysv** with the noted command and activated the sendmail service (and deactivated spamassassin), as shown in Figure 3-6.

Once I complete my changes, I can then check the result with the following command:

```
# chkconfig --list sendmail
sendmail 0:off 1:off 2:off 3:on 4:off 5:on 6:off
```

The GUI Service Configuration Tool

The Service Configuration tool shown in Figure 3-7 allows you to select the services that are to be activated in runlevel 3 (text login) and runlevel 5 (GUI login), one level at a time. You can start it in one of two ways in the GUI: run the **system-config-services** command or choose System | Administration | Server Settings | Services.

FIGURE 3-6

Controlling services with **ntsysv**

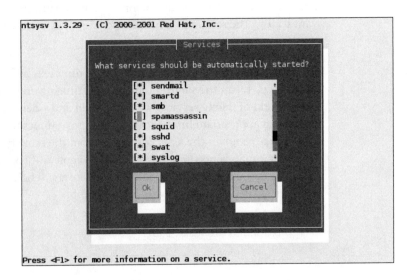

FIGURE 3-7

The Service
Configuration
tool

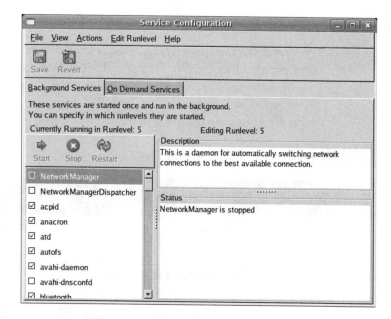

When you configure or repair a service, use chkconfig (or a related utility such as ntsysv or system-config-services) to make sure that the service *is activated at the appropriate runlevels. Otherwise, you may not get full credit for your work.*

CERTIFICATION OBJECTIVE 3.07

System Configuration Files

Red Hat sets up a number of key configuration files in the /etc/sysconfig directory. You can configure them with a text editor, with text commands, or in many cases with a Red Hat graphical tool. Many of the non-network system configuration files are discussed in this section.

It's fastest if you know how to configure these systems directly using text commands or by directly editing the key configuration file. However, if you forget how to manage one or two configuration commands or files, the Red Hat graphical tools can be a lifesaver.

I address only those systems not already covered in other chapters.

Non-network /etc/sysconfig Files

Let's return to the /etc/sysconfig directory and discuss some of the non-network configuration files listed in Table 3-3. This section covers only those files that are less likely to be of interest on the Red Hat exams. More important files are covered in other chapters. Some files can be edited directly; others can be configured with other Red Hat tools discussed in the following section.

TABLE 3-3   Key Non-network /etc/sysconfig Files

File in the /etc/sysconfig Directory	Description
clock	Contains defaults for the system clock, including time zone, UTC, and ARC (Alpha CPU-based) settings. If **UTC=true**, the BIOS is set to the atomic realization of Greenwich Mean Time.
firstboot	If **RUN_FIRSTBOOT=YES**, then you can start the First Boot process with the **firstboot** command, if you're in runlevel 5.
grub	Lists the hard disk with your /boot drive, assuming you're using the GRUB boot loader.
hwconf	Lists peripherals detected by **kudzu**. Do *not* edit this file!
i18n	Sets the default language.
init	Specifies the graphics and associated colors during the boot process.
iptables	Includes the **iptables** firewall commands that run when you boot Linux.
iptables-config	Adds configuration for adding **iptables** rules.
irda	Controls infrared devices.
kernel	Specifies defaults when you update the kernel.
keyboard	Contains keyboard configuration data: **KEYBOARDTYPE**, usually **pc**, and **KEYTABLE**, usually **us**.
kudzu	Configures hardware detection during the boot process, as it relates to serial ports, DDC (Display Data Channel) between the monitor and video card, and PS/2 ports.
ntpd	Specifies synchronization with the hardware clock after synchronizing with a remote NTP (network time protocol) server.
pcmcia	Contains PCMCIA configuration data. If **PCMCIA=yes**, Linux loads PCMCIA modules on boot.
pm	Configures hibernation characteristics.
rhn/	Directory with Red Hat Network configuration.

GUI Configuration Utilities

It's important to know how to configure RHEL 5 by hand, because it's the most efficient way to control everything on your Linux system. It's faster on the Red Hat exams, where time is of the essence. There are a number of good GUI configuration tools available; almost all of them are "front ends" that edit text configuration files, which you could edit directly.

However, there's a lot to learn about Linux. Learning how to edit *all* key Linux configuration files can be more than some RHCT/RHCE candidates can handle. While you should learn how to edit these files by hand, you may not have time. You may get nervous during the Red Hat exams and forget details. In these cases, the Red Hat GUI tools can be a lifesaver.

on the job

The text mode setup tool is a front end to a number of other tools you can view from the text console: authentication, firewall, keyboard, network, printer, service, time zone, and GUI display configuration. You can start the tool with the setup command. While they may be faster than GUI tools, some of these tools do not have the same capabilities as GUI tools.

Date/Time Properties

With the Date/Time Properties configuration tool, you can set the date, time, timezone, and NTP server for your system. You can start it in one of three ways in the GUI: run the **system-config-date** or **system-config-time** command, or choose System | Administration | Date and Time. This opens the Date/Time Properties window shown in Figure 3-8.

exam

ⓦatch *If you're studying for the RHCE, Red Hat has just added NTP configuration and troubleshooting to the Exam Prep guide. For more information, see Chapter 13.*

Keyboard Configuration Tool

The Keyboard Configuration tool allows you to reselect the keyboard associated with your system. You can start it in one of two ways in the GUI: run the **system-config-keyboard** command or choose System | Administration | Keyboard. The options are the same as those you saw during the installation process. Results are recorded in /etc/sysconfig/keyboard.

FIGURE 3-8

The Date/Time
Properties
window

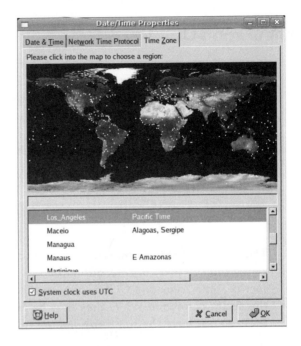

CERTIFICATION SUMMARY

This chapter covered the basic boot process of an RHEL system. You learned the basics of the BIOS and what happens when it hands control to the GRUB boot loader. You experimented with GRUB, observing the results of various errors.

Once GRUB boots your system successfully, it hands control to the kernel. You can find out more about what happens through /var/log/dmesg and the drivers it loads. It hands control to the First Process, also known as **init**, as configured in /etc/inittab. It then starts various services, which you can control with various text or graphical service configuration tools.

The non-network configuration files in the /etc/sysconfig hierarchy affect basic parameters such as the system clock, kernel updates, and the keyboard. There are Red Hat GUI tools available for those who forget how to configure some key configuration files by hand during the Red Hat exams.

TWO-MINUTE DRILL

Here are some of the key points from the certification objectives in Chapter 3.

The BIOS Initialization Sequence

❑ While not strictly a part of the exam, it's important to know the basics of the BIOS.

❑ You can change the boot sequence from the BIOS menu.

❑ Once the BIOS detects your drives, it hands control to GRUB via the master boot record (MBR).

The GRUB Boot Loader

❑ GRUB, the GRand Unified Boot loader, is the default for RHEL 5.

❑ Errors in the GRUB configuration file can lead to a number of boot problems, including kernel panics.

❑ You can read the GRUB configuration file from the GRUB command line.

Kernel Initialization and the First Process

❑ You can analyze how the kernel booted your system through /var/log/dmesg.

❑ As the kernel initializes your system, it loads important modules such as the ext3 filesystem.

The First Process and /etc/inittab

❑ Once the kernel boots, it hands control to **init**, also known as the First Process.

❑ The init process starts your system as configured in /etc/inittab.

❑ One of the key configuration files started by the First Process is /etc/rc.sysinit.

Runlevels

❑ There are six different runlevels available; the default is configured in /etc/inittab.

❑ Don't configure a default runlevel of 0 or 6.

❏ The default runlevel configured in /etc/inittab starts scripts in the associated /etc/rcx.d directory, where *x* is the runlevel.

❏ You can boot to the runlevel of your choice from the GRUB configuration menu.

❏ Study the /etc/rc.d hierarchy and the /etc/inittab and /etc/rc.d/rc.sysinit files. This is the key to understanding what's happening during the boot process.

Controlling Services

❏ The **chkconfig** command gives you a simple way to maintain the /etc/rc.d directory structure.

❏ The **ntsysv** and **system-config-services** commands provide console and GUI tools for the same purpose.

System Configuration Files

❏ There are a number of non-network configuration files in the /etc/sysconfig directory.

❏ You can edit many of these files directly or use GUI tools, which you can start with commands such as **system-config-date**, **system-config-keyboard**, and **system-config-services**.

SELF TEST

The following questions will help you measure your understanding of the material presented in this chapter. As no multiple choice questions appear on the Red Hat exams, no multiple choice questions appear in this book. These questions exclusively test your understanding of the chapter. While the topics in this chapter are "prerequisites," it is okay if you have another way of performing a task. Getting results, not memorizing trivia, is what counts on the Red Hat exams. There may be more than one answer to many of these questions.

The BIOS Initialization Sequence

1. If you want to boot from the CD/DVD drive, what two ways might you work with the BIOS?

   _____

   _____

The GRUB Boot Loader

2. When you see the GRUB configuration menu, what command would you use to modify the kernel arguments? Assume a regular (non-Xen) kernel and that GRUB is not password protected. _____

3. If you've run the proper commands at the **grub>** command line, what command would you use to start booting Linux? _____

Kernel Initialization and the First Process

4. What file contains the kernel initialization messages? _____

5. What one-word command can you use to read the kernel initialization messages?

   _____

The First Process and /etc/inittab

6. What configuration file is associated with the First Process?

   _____

7. What is normally the default runlevel for RHEL 5?

   _____

Runlevels

8. If you can't boot into the GUI, what runlevel should you try first from the GRUB menu?

   _____

9. What alternatives are available from the GRUB menu to runlevel 1 if you want to boot directly into the root account? _____

Controlling Services

10. The FTP server is **vsFTPd**. If you want to make sure it starts the next time you boot into a standard runlevel, what command should you run?

_____

11. What command would you use to open the console-based Service Configuration tool in runlevels 3 and 5?

_____

System Configuration Files

12. What directory contains most Red Hat system configuration files?

_____

LAB QUESTIONS

The Red Hat exams are unique based on their reliance on labs and hands-on demonstrations. With these questions, you're practicing the skills you need on both Red Hat exams.

Lab I

In this exercise, you are going to experiment with two ways of managing services at different runlevels: the **chkconfig** command and the **system-config-services** utility, also known as the Service Configuration utility. The commands in this lab don't start or stop scripts immediately, just the next time you move your Linux system into runlevel 3.

1. Open the GUI. From a text command line interface, run the **system-config-services &** command. This allows you to use the same terminal window for other commands. Alternatively, in the GNOME desktop, choose System | Administration | Server Settings | Services.

2. The Service Configuration utility is a graphical tool for controlling the services that Linux starts and stops at each runlevel.

3. These next steps assume that the NFS service, as controlled by the /etc/init.d/nfs script, is already running and installed. If not, pick another service to add and remove (it does not matter which as long as you restore the original condition when you're done).

4. At the command line, run the **ls /etc/rc3.d/*nfs** command to find the priority number.

5. Remove the NFS service from runlevel 3 using the Service Configuration utility.

6. Switch back to the command line window and run the **chkconfig --list nfs** command to see if it has been deactivated in runlevel 3.

7. Restore the **nfs** start script with the following command:

   ```
   # chkconfig --level 3 nfs on
   ```

8. Switch back to the console window and run the **chkconfig --list nfs** command to verify that the NFS service is activated.

9. Return to the Service Configuration utility, and choose View | Refresh Service List to confirm that **nfs** is once again active in runlevel 3.

10. Although the Red Hat Service Configuration utility provides a nice graphical interface, the **chkconfig** command is faster and more reliable, especially since X (also known imprecisely as the GUI) is not always available in an emergency or through remote login.

Lab 2

In this lab, you'll move the GRUB configuration file and examine its effects on the boot process.

1. Boot into Linux, and print out the contents of the GRUB configuration file.

2. Move the GRUB configuration file, /boot/grub/grub.conf, to the administrative home directory. One way to do this is with the following command:

   ```
   # mv /boot/grub/grub.conf /root
   ```

3. Reboot your system. When you do, you should see the following entry:

   ```
   [Minimal BASH-like line editing is supported. For the first word, TAB lists
   possible command completions. Anywhere else, TAB lists the possible
   completions of a device/filename.]

   grub>
   ```

4. Refer to the printout of the GRUB configuration file. Select the stanza that you want to boot. Enter the first command at the GRUB command line. The command should be something like:

   ```
   grub> root (hd0,0)
   ```

   If successful, you'll see output similar to:

   ```
   Filesystem type is ext2fs, partition type 0x83
   ```

   If you've configured the ext3 filesystem, this output is still correct.

5. Enter the kernel command directive. Leave out the second part of the directive that refers to the root directory.

6. Enter the second part of the directive with the **root** command reference. What happens?

7. Try the second GRUB configuration line again, this time entering the whole kernel command directive. If successful, you'll see output similar to:

   ```
   [Linux-bzImage, setup=0x1e00, size=0x16eb71]
   ```

8. Enter the final GRUB configuration line associated with the Initial RAM disk. If successful, you'll see output similar to:

```
[Linux-initrd, setup=0x10d44000, 0x19b13c bytes]
```

9. Now you should be ready to start Linux with the following command at the **grub>** prompt:

```
grub> boot
```

10. Don't forget to restore the GRUB configuration file. If you followed the instructions earlier in this lab, you can do so with the following command:

```
# mv /root/grub.conf /boot/grub/
```

Lab 3

In this lab, you'll see what happens without the **init** service. As you did in Lab 2, you'll move a key file, in this case, /etc/inittab, to the root user's home directory, and then reboot your system.

1. Move your /etc/inittab configuration file to the root user home directory. You can do so with a command such as:

```
# mv /etc/inittab /root/
```

2. Reboot your system. Observe the messages carefully. Note that RHEL 5 is very specific when the /etc/inittab file is not where expected.

```
INIT: No inittab file found

Enter runlevel:
```

3. At the prompt, enter runlevel **5**. See what happens. You'll see messages similar to:

```
INIT: Entering runlevel: 5
INIT: no more processes left in this runlevel
```

4. Because the system stops at this point, you'll have to cycle power on your system. Try any of the other standard runlevels. You'll see the same results even in runlevels 0 and 6. Remember to cycle power after entering each standard runlevel.

5. Try the emergency runlevel; enter the **emergency** command at the **Enter runlevel:** prompt. See what happens.

6. Finally, try the single runlevel with the **s** command at the **Enter runlevel:** prompt. What do you see?

7. At the prompt, you'll be in the top level root directory. Try restoring the /etc/inittab file from the root user's home directory. The easiest way is with the following command:

```
# mv /root/inittab /etc/
```

But this command doesn't work. You'll see a message like:

```
mv: cannot move '/root/inittab' to '/etc/inittab': Read-only file system
```

8. Now you'll have to remount the top-level root directory, using a command you'll learn more about in Chapter 4. But first, before you know what you're remounting, you need to confirm the partition where the root directory is mounted, from the contents of /etc/fstab.

In my particular configuration, a cat /etc/fstab confirms the root directory mounted on a logical volume, /dev/VolGroup00/LogVol00.

Based on that data, I can remount with the following command:

```
# mount -o remount /dev/VolGroup00/LogVol00 /
```

Substitute accordingly, based on the output from your /etc/fstab configuration file.

9. Now try restoring the inittab file again:

```
# mv /root/inittab /etc/
```

You should now be successful. You can now run the **reboot** command to restart your system.

SELF TEST ANSWERS

The BIOS Initialization Sequence

1. There are two basic ways to boot directly from a CD/DVD. First, you can change the boot order within the BIOS menu. Second, in many cases, you can access a boot order menu directly with a key command such as pressing ESC or DEL, which may be shown onscreen as the computer starts up. Not all computers have a boot order menu, but if the one you're using on the Red Hat exam has such a menu, using it can save you a bit of time.

The GRUB Boot Loader

2. By default, you need to press any key within 5 seconds before the default operating system is booted. When you do, you'll see the GRUB configuration menu. Press **a** to see the kernel command line; you can then modify the line adding commands. As described in this chapter, you can use this line to supersede the default runlevel.

3. The proper commands at the **grub>** command line specify the /boot directory, the kernel, the partition with the top-level root directory, and the initial RAM disk. Once executed, you can start Linux with the **boot** command.

Kernel Initialization and the First Process

4. The file with the kernel initialization messages is /var/log/dmesg.

5. The one-word command that you can use to read the kernel initialization messages is **dmesg**.

The First Process and /etc/inittab

6. The configuration file associated with the First Process is /etc/inittab.

7. The default runlevel for RHEL 5 is 5.

Runlevels

8. If you can't boot into the GUI, the first runlevel you should run from the GRUB menu is 3, which is the standard command line runlevel with all standard services except the GUI.

9. The alternatives to runlevel 1 from the GRUB menu are **s** for single-user mode and **emergency** for a boot without any mounted directories or services.

Controlling Services

10. If you want to make sure the **vsftpd** service starts the next time you boot into a standard runlevel, run the **chkconfig vsftpd on** command. The **chkconfig --level 35 vsftpd on** command also works.

11. If you want to open the console-based service configuration tool in runlevels 3 and 5, run the **ntsysv --level 35** command.

System Configuration Files

12. The directory that contains most Red Hat *system* configuration files is /etc/sysconfig.

LAB ANSWERS

Lab 1

1. To open a command line interface in the default Red Hat GNOME desktop, choose Applications | Accessories | Terminal.

2. In the new terminal, open the Service Configuration utility. Run the applicable graphical tool in the background so you can still use this terminal window with the following command:

```
# system-config-services &
```

3. Run the **ls /etc/rc3.d** command. Look for the **nfs** start script and record the current order number, **60**. If you see only a kill script for nfs, it is not active in runlevel 3. If you don't see it at all, you need to install the nfs-utils RPM.

4. Deactivate the **nfs** service from runlevel 3. It's easy to do so in the Service Configuration utility. But you need to remember to save your changes by choosing File | Save Changes.

5. Switch back to the console window and run **chkconfig** to see if it has been deactivated in runlevel 3. If it has, you should see the following result:

```
# chkconfig --list nfs
nfs    0:off   1:off   2:off   3:off   4:on   5:on   6:off
```

6. Now run the **chkconfig** command to reactivate the **nfs** service. Return to the Service Configuration utility. Add the **nfs** service back to runlevel 3 with the following command:

```
# chkconfig --level 3 nfs on
```

7. Now run the following **chkconfig** command to verify that **nfs** is active again in runlevel 3:

```
# chkconfig --list nfs
nfs    0:off   1:off   2:off   3:on   4:on   5:on   6:off
```

This should show that the **nfs** service is started in runlevel 3. You practice using the **chkconfig** command. One way is to redo this lab. Use the service of your choice. Make sure what you see in the GUI Service Configuration utility matches. After each change with the **chkconfig** command, run the View | Refresh Service List command to make sure the GUI tool reflects your change.

Lab 2

This lab should be somewhat self-explanatory. It examines what happens when a configuration file related to the boot process is missing. You'll see more examples of this in Chapter 16.

While it's an excellent idea to experiment with other key configuration files, don't do so haphazardly. Remember to back up your configuration. And if you want to rescue your system, you may need to learn how to use **linux rescue** mode as discussed in Chapter 16.

However, if you want to experiment with other key configuration files, back up /etc/fstab. You can change it and even move it from the /etc/ directory, in the manner described with the GRUB and /etc/inittab configuration files in this chapter. If /etc/fstab is missing, it looks like everything still works. RHEL 5 even boots into the GUI. However, the problems you'll see are subtle. No filesystem is mounted. However, you can still restore the fstab file from backup. You'll learn about mounts and /etc/fstab in more detail in Chapter 4.

Lab 3

One of the required skills in the Red Hat Exam Prep guide is booting into different runlevels. This lab sets up a scenario in which you need to learn how to boot into a specialized runlevel, **s**, also known as single-user mode. If you want to learn more, try the **init=/bin/sh** runlevel, and see what you need to do to restore the /etc/inittab file.

4

Linux Filesystem Administration

CERTIFICATION OBJECTIVES

4.01   Partitioning Hard Disks

4.02   Managing Filesystems

4.03   Filesystem Management and
        the Automounter

4.04   Access Control Lists and Other
        Security Attributes

✓   Two-Minute Drill

Q&A   Self Test

A fter installation has completed, you still have work to do. To customize the system to meet your needs, you may need to add partitions, new filesystems, automounted directories, and more. Much of this depends on the security attributes on files and directories.

While it's easier to use Disk Druid during the installation process, the **fdisk** and **parted** tools can help you create new partitions. Once created, filesystems can be configured on these partitions with format commands and more. Once created, you can configure mounting during the boot process in /etc/fstab or over a network using the automounter.

What you create can be protected with Security Enhanced Linux (SELinux). To that end, in this chapter you'll examine basic access control lists and set SELinux characteristics from the command line. (If you're interested in controlling SELinux using the SELinux Management Tool, see Chapter 15.)

INSIDE THE EXAM

Administrative Skills

As in the real world, it is the results that matter. It doesn't matter whether you use Disk Druid, **fdisk**, or **parted** to create partitions. You can create new partitions at the command line or use GUI front ends to these tools such as GParted (if it's ever included with RHEL). Make sure that your partitions meet the requirements of the exam. Just remember Disk Druid is available only during the installation process.

The current Red Hat Exam Prep guide suggests that RHCTs need to know how to *Add new partitions, filesystems, and swap to existing systems* for the Troubleshooting and System Maintenance part of their exams. It also suggests that RHCTs need to know how to

■ Add and manage users, groups, quotas, and File Access Control Lists.

Remember that RHCEs also need to be prepared to do anything from the RHCT requirements.

The Exam Prep guide also suggests that RHCEs need to be prepared, during their Troubleshooting and System Maintenance sections, to

■ Add, remove, and resize logical volumes.

As of this writing, SELinux has just been added to the Red Hat Exam Prep guide; in most cases, you'll need to know how to configure services to work while SELinux is running in targeted mode. However, this is a skill associated with RHCEs, not RHCTs. While the services are primarily covered in Chapters 9–15, the basic skills associated with controlling SELinux are covered near the end of this chapter.

CERTIFICATION OBJECTIVE 4.01

Partitioning Hard Disks

It's best to create partitions using Disk Druid during the installation process. This can save you grief as an administrator, and especially during the Red Hat exams. However, mistakes are made. You might forget to create a critical partition during the Installation and Configuration part of the exam, for example.

As suggested by the Red Hat Exam Prep guide, you may need to do more with partitions on an installed system. In the real world, you might need to create a larger /home directory partition for your users. For this purpose, the standard is still the **fdisk** utility, which is described shortly along with the emerging alternative, **parted**.

Before you use **fdisk** to create or revise partitions, you should check your free space and the partitions that are currently mounted. You can do this with the **df** and **mount** commands. The following example illustrates how the **df** command displays the total, used, and available free space on all currently mounted filesystems.

Note the numbers under the 1k-blocks column. In this case (except for the mounted DVD), they add up to about 35GB of allocated space. If your hard drive is larger, you may have unallocated space that you can use for another partition. Just remember to leave room for expansion in appropriate directories, such as /home, /tmp, and /var.

```
[root@Enterprise root]# df
Filesystem 1k-blocks        Used Available Use% Mounted on
/dev/mapper/VolGroup00-LogVol00
             9903432     2333948   7058304   25% /
/dev/hda3      101105       19821     76063   21% /boot
tmpfs          451200           0    451200    0% /dev/shm
/dev/mapper/VolGroup00-LogVol02
             4951688      149164   4546936    4% /home
/dev/md0       302684       10326    276730    4% /tmp
/dev/mapper/VolGroup00-LogVol03
             4951688      194308   4501792    5% /var
/dev/hdc         7384        7384         0  100%
                         /media/Red Hat Enterprise Linux Server
/dev/hda2    11715984     9509432   2206552   82% /DosD
[root@Enterprise root]#
```

The second command, **mount**, includes the filesystem type. In this case, examine the partition represented by device /dev/hda2 mounted with the VFAT file type on the /DosD directory. It provides direct access to the D: drive of the Windows operating system. For the following example, I've set up the data shown from the **mount** command in columns for clarity; what you actually see from the RHEL command line is less organized.

```
[root@Enterprise root]# mount
/dev/mapper/VolGroup00-LogVol00 on / type ext3          (rw)
proc       on /proc type proc                           (rw)
sysfs      on /sys type sysfs                            (rw)
devpts     on /dev/pts type devpts                       (rw,gid=5,mode=620)
/dev/hda3 on /boot type ext3                             (rw)
tmpfs      on /dev/shm type tmpfs                         (rw)
/dev/mapper/VolGroup00-LogVol02 on /home type ext3      (rw)
/dev/md0   on /tmp type ext3                             (rw)
/dev/mapper/VolGroup00-LogVol01 on /var type ext3       (rw)
none       on /proc/sys/fs/binfmt_misc type binfmt_misc (rw)
sunrpc     on /var/lib/nfs/rpc_pipefs type rpc_pipefs   (rw)
/dev/hdc   on /media/RHEL-5 i386 Disc 1type iso9660     (ro,noexec,nosuid,nodev,uid=500)
/dev/hda2 on DosD type vfat                              (rw)
[root@Enterprise root]#
```

One of the benefits is that you can move and copy files between the Linux and the DOS partitions using standard Linux commands. You cannot, however, run any Windows applications within Linux unless you run a DOS or Windows emulation package such as Wine (www.winehq.org) or CrossOver Office (www.codeweavers.com). Options such as VMware and Xen fall into a different category and are covered in "Studying with a Virtual Machine" in the Online Learning Center (http://highered .mhhe.com/sites/0072264543).

The fdisk Utility

The **fdisk** utility is a universally available tool that you should know well. There are many commands within **fdisk**, more in expert mode, but you need to know only the few discussed here.

Though you can modify the physical disk partition layout using many programs, this section explores the Linux implementation of **fdisk**. FDISK.EXE from DOS has the same name and is also used for creating partitions, but it doesn't incorporate any Linux-compatible features. It also uses a different interface.

Using fdisk: Starting, Getting Help, and Quitting

The following screen output lists commands that show how to start the **fdisk** program, how to get help, and how to quit the program. The /dev/hda drive is associated with the first PATA/IDE drive on a regular PC. Your computer may have a different hard drive; you can check the output from the **df** and **mount** commands for clues.

As you can see, once you start **fdisk**, it opens its own command line prompt:

```
# fdisk /dev/hda
Command (m for help): m
Command action
   a   toggle a bootable flag
   b   edit bsd disklabel
   c   toggle the dos compatibility flag
   d   delete a partition
   l   list known partition types
   m   print this menu
   n   add a new partition
   o   create a new empty DOS partition table
   p   print the partition table
   q   quit without saving changes
   s   create a new empty Sun disklabel
   t   change a partition's system id
   u   change display/entry units
   v   verify the partition table
   w   write table to disk and exit
   x   extra functionality (experts only)

Command (m for help): q
```

There are a wide variety of commands associated with **fdisk**—and more when you run the **x** command to access **fdisk**'s extra functionality.

Using fdisk: In a Nutshell

At the **fdisk** command line prompt, start with the print command (**p**) to print the partition table. This allows you to review the current entries in the partition table. Assuming you have free space, you then create a new (**n**) partition, either primary (**p**) or logical (**l**). If it doesn't already exist, you can also create an extended partition (**e**) to contain your logical partitions. Remember that you can have up to four primary partitions, which would correspond to numbers 1 through 4. One of the primary partitions can be redesignated as an extended partition. The remaining partitions are logical partitions, numbered 5 and above. The Linux **fdisk** utility won't allow you to create more than 16 partitions on the drive.

When you assign space to a partition, you're assigning a block of cylinders on that hard disk. If you have free space, the **fdisk** default starts the new partition at the first available cylinder. The actual size of the partition depends on disk geometry; do not worry about exact size here.

Using fdisk: Deleting Partitions

The following example removes the only configured partition. The sample output
screen first starts **fdisk**. Then you print (**p**) the current partition table, delete (**d**) the
partition by number (**1** in this case), write (**w**) the changes to the disk, and quit (**q**)
from the program. Needless to say, *do not perform this action on any partition where you
need the data.*

```
# fdisk /dev/hdb
Command (m for help): p
Disk /dev/hdb: 255 heads, 63 sectors, 525 cylinders
Units = cylinders of 16065 * 512 bytes

Device     Boot     Start     End     Blocks    Id  System
/dev/hdb1    *          1     525    4217031     6  FAT16
Command (m for help): d
Partition number (1-1): 1
```

This is the last chance to change your mind before deleting the current partition.
If you want to change your mind, exit from **fdisk** with the **q** command. If you're
pleased with the changes that you've made and want to make them permanent,
proceed with the **w** command:

```
Command (m for help): w
```

You did it! Now you have an empty hard disk or hard disk area where you can create
the partitions you need.

You no longer have to reboot to get Linux to read the new partition table. Now,
the **partprobe** command rereads the partition table without a reboot.

Using fdisk: Creating Partitions

The following screen output sample shows the steps used to create (**n**) the first
(/boot) partition, make it bootable (**a**), and then finally write (**w**) the partition
information to the disk. (Note that although you may ask for a 100MB partition,
the geometry of the disk may not allow that precise size, as shown in the example.)

```
# fdisk /dev/hdb

Command (m for help): n
Command action
   e   extended
   p   primary partition (1-4)
p
Partition number (1-4):
```

```
First cylinder (1-256, default 1): 1
Last cylinder or +size or +sizeM or +sizeK (2-256,def 256): +100M

Command (m for help): a
Partition number (1-4): 1

Command (m for help): p
Disk /dev/hdb: 255 heads, 63 sectors, 256 cylinders
Units = cylinders of 16065 * 512 bytes
   Device Boot     Start       End     Blocks   Id  System
/dev/hdb1    *           1        12     98163   83  Linux

Command (m for help):
```

Repeat the commands to create any other partitions that you might need. One possible group of partitions is illustrated here:

```
Command (m for help): p

Disk /dev/hdb: 255 heads, 63 sectors, 256 cylinders
Units = cylinders of 16065 * 512 bytes
     Device Boot  Start  End    Blocks  Id  System
/dev/hdb1    *        1    2     16044  83  Linux
/dev/hdb2             3   18     64176  82  Linux swap / Solaris
/dev/hdb3            19  169   1203300  83  Linux
/dev/hdb4           170  250    649782   5  Extended
/dev/hdb5           170  201    248682  83  Linux
/dev/hdb6           202  257    449232  83  Linux

Command (m for help): w
```

on the **Job**

The number of blocks that you see may vary slightly depending on the size of your hard disk; the number of heads, sectors, and cylinders on that disk; as well as the version of fdisk that you're using.

Using fdisk: A New PC with No Partitions

After installing Linux on a new PC, you'll want to use **fdisk** to configure additional physical disks attached to the system. For example, if the additional disk is the first disk attached to the secondary IDE controller, run the **fdisk /dev/hdc** command. Remember the limitations on partitions. If you need more than four partitions on the new physical disk, configure type **Primary** for the first three partitions, and then **Extended** for the rest of the disk as partition 4. You can then creating logical partitions 5–16 within the extended partition.

Using fdisk: Creating a Swap Partition

You need to create a partition before you can reassign it as a swap partition. At the **fdisk** prompt, run the l command. You'll see a large number of file types, listed as hex codes. When you create a partition, **fdisk** creates a Linux Native type partition by default. As you can see from the output of the l command, the associated hex code is (83).

It's easy to reassign a partition as a swap partition. Run the **p** command. Remember the number of the partition you want to change. Make sure that partition doesn't contain data that you want to save.

Now run the **t** command. Type in the number associated with the partition that you want to change. Type in the hex code for the type you want—in this case, **82** for a Linux swap partition. For example, I could run the following sequence of commands to set up a new swap partition on the second IDE hard drive. The commands that I type are in boldface. The details of what you see depend on the partitions that you may have created. It'll be a 1GB swap space on the first primary partition (/dev/hdb1).

```
# fdisk /dev/hdb
Command (m for help): n
Command action
    e   extended
    p   primary partition (1-4)
p
Partition number (1-4): 1
First cylinder (1-10402, default 1):
Using default value 1
Last cylinder or +size or +sizeM or +sizeK (1-10402, default 10402): +1000M

Command (m for help): p

Disk /dev/hdb: 5368 MB, 5368709120 bytes
16 heads, 63 sectors/track, 10402 cylinders
Units = cylinders of 1008 * 512 = 516096 bytes

   Device Boot     Start       End      Blocks   Id  System
/dev/hdb1              1      1939      977224+   83  Linux

Command (m for help): t
Selected partition 1
Hex code (type L to list codes): 82
Changed system type of partition 1 to 82 (Linux swap / Solaris)

Command (m for help): w
The partition table has been altered!
```

```
Calling ioctl() to re-read partition table.
Syncing disks.
#
```

The **fdisk** utility doesn't actually write the changes to your hard disk until you run the write (**w**) command. You have a chance to cancel your changes with the quit (**q**) command. To make sure Linux rereads the partition table after **fdisk** writes it, run the **partprobe** command.

The parted Utility

The **parted** utility is becoming increasingly popular. It's an excellent tool developed by the GNU foundation. As with **fdisk**, you can use it to create, check, and destroy partitions, but it can do more. You can also use it to resize and copy partitions, as well as the filesystems contained therein. For the latest information, see www.gnu .org/software/parted.

on the job

It's much easier to make a mistake with **parted**. *For example, I accidentally ran the* **mklabel** *command from the (parted) prompt on an existing RHEL system. It deleted all existing partitions. Fortunately, I had a snapshot of this system on a VMware server and was able to recover quickly with little trouble.*

During our discussion of **parted**, we'll proceed from section to section assuming that **parted** is still open with the following prompt:

```
(parted)
```

If you use **parted** and then check your partitions with **fdisk**, you might get errors such as:

```
Partition 1 does not end on cylinder boundary.
```

Don't worry about it. While **fdisk** partitions are associated with hard drive cylinders, **parted** is not so limited.

Using parted: Starting, Getting Help, and Quitting

The next screen output lists commands that show how to start the **parted** utility, how to get help, and how to quit the program. In this case, the /dev/sdb drive is associated with the second SATA drive on a regular PC. Your computer may have a different hard drive; you can check the output from the **df** and **mount** commands for clues.

As you can see in Figure 4-1, once you start **parted**, it opens its own command line prompt. The explanations are line-wrapped due to limitations in formatting in this book.

FIGURE 4-1

parted
Command
Options

```
[root@enterprise5dl ~]# parted /dev/sdb
GNU Parted 1.8.1
Using /dev/sdb
Welcome to GNU Parted! Type 'help' to view a list of commands.
(parted) help
  check NUMBER                               do a simple check on the file system
  cp [FROM-DEVICE] FROM-NUMBER TO-NUMBER     copy file system to another partition
  help [COMMAND]                             prints general help, or help on
        COMMAND
  mklabel,mktable LABEL-TYPE                 create a new disklabel (partition
        table)
  mkfs NUMBER FS-TYPE                        make a FS-TYPE file system on
        partititon NUMBER
  mkpart PART-TYPE [FS-TYPE] START END       make a partition
  mkpartfs PART-TYPE FS-TYPE START END       make a partition with a file system
  move NUMBER START END                      move partition NUMBER
  name NUMBER NAME                           name partition NUMBER as NAME
  print [free|NUMBER|all]                    display the partition table, a
        partition, or all devices
  quit                                       exit program
  rescue START END                           rescue a lost partition near START
        and END
  resize NUMBER START END                    resize partition NUMBER and its file
        system
  rm NUMBER                                  delete partition NUMBER
  select DEVICE                              choose the device to edit
  set NUMBER FLAG STATE                      change the FLAG on partition NUMBER
  toggle [NUMBER [FLAG]]                     toggle the state of FLAG on partition
        NUMBER
  unit UNIT                                  set the default unit to UNIT
  version                                    displays the current version of GNU
        Parted and copyright information
(parted)
```

As you can see, a wide variety of commands are available within the **parted** interface. If you're familiar with **fdisk**, you can see that **parted** can do more: you can even format and resize partitions from **parted**. Unfortunately, the format functionality is limited and does not allow you to create or resize ext3 partitions, at least as of this writing. The current Exam Prep guide lists only resizing logical volumes as an RHCE requirement.

Using parted: In a Nutshell

At the **parted** command line prompt, start with the **print** the partition table command. This allows you to review the current entries in the partition table, assuming one exists. Assuming you have free space, you then make a new (**mkpart**) partition or even make and format the filesystem (**mkpartfs**). If you need more information about command options, use the **help** command with it; here's an example:

```
(parted) help mkpart
  mkpart PART-TYPE [FS-TYPE] START END     make a partition

        PART-TYPE is one of: primary, logical, extended
        FS-TYPE is one of: ext3, ext2, fat32, fat16, hfsx,
        hfs+, hfs, jfs, linux-swap,ntfs, reiserfs, hp-ufs,
```

```
sun-ufs, xfs, apfs2, apfs1, asfs, amufs5, amufs4,
amufs3, amufs2, amufs1, amufs0, amufs, affs7, affs6,
affs5, affs4, affs3, affs2, affs1, affs0
START and END are disk locations, such as 4GB or 10%.
Negative values count from the end of the disk.
For example, -1s specifies exactly the last sector.

mkpart makes a partition without creating a new
file system on the partition.
FS-TYPE may be specified to set an appropriate
partition ID.
```

If that's too much for you, just run the command. You'll be prompted for the necessary information. Remember that you can have up to four primary partitions, corresponding to numbers 1 through 4. One of the primary partitions can be redesignated as an extended partition. The remaining partitions are logical partitions, numbered 5 and above. While the Linux **parted** utility allows you to create more than 15 partitions, in this case, anything beyond /dev/sdb15 is not recognized by Linux.

Using parted: Deleting Partitions

Deleting partitions is easy. All you need to do from the **(parted)** prompt is use the **rm** command to delete the partition that you no longer need.

Of course, before deleting any partition, you should:

- Save any data you need from that partition.
- Unmount the partition.
- Make sure it isn't configured in /etc/fstab, so Linux doesn't try to mount it the next time you boot.
- After starting **parted**, run the **print** command to identify the partition you want to delete, as well as its ID number.

For example, if you want to delete partition /dev/sdb10 from the **(parted)** prompt, run the following command:

```
(parted) rm 10
```

Using parted: A New PC (or Hard Drive) with No Partitions

Whenever you install a new hard drive, you may need to create a new partition table. For example, after I add a new hard drive to my virtual RHEL system, just about any command I run in **parted** leads to the following message:

```
Error: Unable to open /dev/sdb - unrecognised disk label.
```

Before I can do anything else with this drive, I need to create a label. As shown from the list of available commands, I can do so with the **mklabel** command. As strange as it sounds, the default label to be used for Linux is **msdos**; here are the commands I run:

```
(parted) mklabel
New disk label type? msdos
```

on the **Job**

Be careful! Never run mklabel *from the* (parted) *prompt on a hard drive that stores data that you need.*

Now you can create a new partition. Let me show you how **mkpart** works on the new hard drive. Naturally, if an extended partition already exists, you'll be able to create a logical partition.

```
(parted) mkpart
Partition type? primary/extended? primary
File system type? [ext2]? ext3
Start? 0
End? 100MB
```

Now you can review the results:

```
(parted) print

Disk /dev/sdb: 10.7GB
Sector size (logical/physical): 512B/512B
Partition Table: msdos

Number   Start     End      Size     Type      File system   Flags
  1      0.51kB   100MB    100MB    primary    ext2
```

If this is the first partition you've created, the filesystem type is empty; otherwise it's ext2, even if you've specified another format such as ext3. Unfortunately, **parted** does not work perfectly, and it does not always create ext3 filesystems from the command line interface. (It works if an ext3 filesystem is already on the hard drive.)

If you now exit from **parted**, you can reboot or run the **partprobe** command to get Linux to read the new partition table. For the purpose of this chapter, don't exit from **parted** just yet.

on the **Job**

The GUI parted tools (GParted, QTParted) do support formatting to a wider variety of filesystem formats, even though they're just "front ends" to parted. They may be available from third-party repositories such as those described in Chapter 5.

Using parted: Creating a Swap Partition

Now let's repeat the process to create a swap partition. Make the start of the new partition 1MB after the end of the previous partition. You can still use the same commands, just substitute the **linux-swap** file system type as appropriate:

```
(parted) mkpart
Partition type? primary/extended? primary
File system type? [ext2]? linux-swap
Start? 101MB
End? 1100MB
```

Now you can review the result:

```
(parted) print

Disk /dev/sdb: 10.7GB
Sector size (logical/physical): 512B/512B
Partition Table: msdos

Number  Start    End     Size    Type     File system  Flags
  1     0.51kB   100MB   100MB   primary  ext2
  2     101MB    1100MB  1000MB  primary
```

Let's repeat the process, creating a regular partition after the swap partition:

```
(parted) mkpart
Partition type? primary/extended? primary
File system type? [ext2]? ext2
Start? 1101MB
End? 2100MB
```

If you exit from **parted**, you can reboot, or run the **partprobe** command to make sure Linux reads the new partition table. Now go ahead and exit from **parted**. After exiting, you can implement your changes; format and then activate the swap partition on /dev/sdb2 using the following commands:

```
(parted) quit

# partprobe
# mkswap /dev/sdb2
# swapon /dev/sdb2
```

on the
job

Sometimes you'll see errors when you run the partprobe *command, even on a correctly configured system. For example, if you haven't put a disk in a floppy drive, you'll see errors related to the associated device (usually fd0). If the disk in your CD/DVD drive is read-only (as are most CD/DVD disks), you'll see an error message about being unable to open read-write.*

Now the new regular Linux partition is formatted to ext2. You can change it to ext3 with the following command:

```
# tune2fs -j  /dev/sdb2
```

CERTIFICATION OBJECTIVE 4.02

Managing Filesystems

There are as many, if not more, filesystem types as there are operating systems. While RHEL can work with many of these formats, the default is ext3. While many users enable other filesystems such as ReiserFS, Red Hat may not support them.

Linux supports a rich variety of filesystems. Linux filesystems can be somewhat inaccurately divided into two categories: "standard" formatting and journaling. While this is an oversimplification, it suffices to describe the filesystems important to Linux. To me, a standard filesystem is an older Linux filesystem which does not log changes.

on the job

There are a large number of filesystem types well described in the Filesystems HOWTO at www.tldp.org. Strictly speaking, there is no "standard" filesystem.

The filesystems I describe in this book are just a small list of those available for RHEL. If you have the kernel source RPMs loaded on your system, you can find a list of the filesystems supported by your kernel. For x86 systems, navigate to the /usr/src/redhat/BUILD/kernel-2.6.18/linux-2.6.18.i386 directory. Run the **make menuconfig** command and use your arrow keys to navigate to the filesystems section.

Standard Formatting Filesystems

Linux is a clone of Unix. The Linux filesystems were developed from the Unix filesystems available at the time. The first Linux operating systems used the Extended Filesystem (ext). Until the past few years, Red Hat Linux operating systems formatted their partitions by default to the Second Extended Filesystem (ext2).

There are other filesystems available for RHEL, a sample of which are included in Table 4-1. These "standard" filesystems don't include journaling features.

TABLE 4-1	Some Linux Standard Filesystem Types

Filesystem Type	Description
ext	The first Linux filesystem, used only on early versions of that operating system.
ext2 (Second Extended)	The foundation for ext3, the default RHEL filesystem. The ext3 filesystem is essentially ext2 with journaling.
swap	The Linux swap filesystem is associated with dedicated swap partitions. You've probably created at least one swap partition when you installed RHEL.
MS-DOS and VFAT	These filesystems allow you to read MS-DOS-formatted filesystems. MS-DOS lets you read pre–Windows 95 partitions, or regular Windows partitions within the limits of short file names. VFAT lets you read Windows 9x/NT/2000/XP/Vista partitions formatted to the FAT16 or FAT32 filesystems.
ISO 9660	The standard filesystem for CD-ROMs. It is also known as the High Sierra File System, or HSFS, on other Unix systems.
NTFS	The Microsoft Windows NT/2000/XP/2003 filesystem designed for username/password security. Currently supported as a read-only system.
/proc	A Linux *virtual* filesystem. Virtual means that it doesn't occupy real disk space. Instead, files are created as needed. Used to provide information on kernel configuration and device status.
/dev/pts	The Linux implementation of the Open Group's Unix98 PTY support.
NFS	The Network File System, the system most commonly used to share files and printers between Linux and Unix computers.
CIFS	The Common Internet File System (CIFS) is the successor to the Samba/ Server Message Block (SMB) system based on Microsoft and IBM network protocols. Linux can use CIFS and SMB to share files and printers with Microsoft Windows operating systems.

Understanding Journaling Filesystems

As hard disks and partitions grow in size, Linux users are moving toward filesystems with journaling features. Journaling filesystems have two main advantages. First, it's faster for Linux to check during the boot process. Second, if a crash occurs, a journaling filesystem has a log (also known as a journal) that can be used to restore the metadata for the files on the relevant partition.

The default RHEL filesystem is the Third Extended Filesystem, also known as ext3. However, it isn't the only journaling filesystem option available. I list a few of the options commonly used for RHEL in Table 4-2. From this list, Red Hat officially supports only ext3.

TABLE 4-2	Journaling Filesystems

Filesystem Type	Description
ext3	The default filesystem for RHEL.
JFS	IBM's journaled filesystem, commonly used on IBM enterprise servers.
ReiserFS	The Reiser File System is resizable and supports fast journaling. It's more efficient when most of the files are very small and very large. It's based on the concept of "balanced trees." It is no longer supported by RHEL, or even by its main proponent, SUSE. For more information, see www.namesys.com.
xfs	Developed by Silicon Graphics as a journaling filesystem, it supports very large files; as of this writing, xfs files are limited to 9×10^{18} bytes. Do not confuse this filesystem with the X Font Server; both use the same acronym.

Creating Filesystems with mkfs

There are several commands that can help you create a Linux filesystem. They're all based on the **mkfs** command. As described in Chapter 1, the **mkfs** command works as a front-end to filesystem-specific commands such as **mkfs.ext2** and **mkfs.ext3**.

If you want to reformat an existing partition, take the following precautions:

- Back up any existing data on the partition.
- Unmount the partition.

There are two ways to apply formatting on a partition. For example, if you've just created a partition on /dev/sdb5, you can format it to the ext3 filesystem using one of the following commands:

```
# mkfs -t ext3 /dev/sdb5
# mkfs.ext3 /dev/sdb5
```

Alternatively, you can use the **mke2fs** command; the first of the following two commands formats the noted partition to the ext2 filesystem, and the second adds a journal that formats the partition to the ext3 filesystem:

```
# mke2fs /dev/sdb5
# mke2fs -j /dev/sdb5
```

You can format partitions to other filesystems. The options available in RHEL 5 include:

- **mkfs.cramfs** creates a compressed ROM filesystem.
- **mkfs.ext2** formats a partition to the ext2 filesystem.
- **mkfs.ext3** formats a partition to the Red Hat default ext3 filesystem.

- **mkfs.msdos** (or **mkfs.vfat** or **mkdosfs**) formats a partition to the Microsoft-compatible VFAT filesystem; it does not create bootable filesystems. (The inode numbers for all three files are the same; in other words, they are three different names for the same command.)

- **mkswap** formats a partition to the Linux swap filesystem.

These commands assume that you've created an appropriate partition in the first place; for example, if you've used **fdisk** to create a swap partition, you'll need to change the filesystem type before you can save it and format it appropriately with the **mkswap** command.

Managing ext2/ext3 Filesystem Attributes

Filesystem attributes can help you control what anyone can do with different files. The key commands in this area are **lsattr** and **chattr**. The use I'm most familiar with protects a file from deletion, even by the root user. For example, you could protect /etc/inittab from tinkering by other administrators with the following command:

```
# chattr +i /etc/inittab
```

Then when I try to delete the file, I get the following result:

```
# rm /etc/inittab
rm: remove write-protected regular file `/etc/inittab'? y
rm: cannot remove `/etc/inittab': Operation not permitted
```

As you can see, this adds the immutable attribute to /etc/inittab:

```
# lsattr /etc/inittab
----i-------- /etc/inittab
```

To me, the man pages for these commands are somewhat confusing, so I summarize three key attributes that you can change in Table 4-3. The **c** (compressed), **s** (secure deletion), and **u** (undeletable) attributes don't work for files in the ext2 and ext3 filesystems.

TABLE 4-3   File Attributes

Attribute	Description
append only (**a**)	Prevents deletion, but allows appending to a file—for example, if you've run **chatter +a tester, cat /etc/fstab >> tester** would add the contents of /etc/fstab to the end of the tester file.
no dump (**d**)	Does not allow backups of the configured file with the **dump** command.
immutable (**i**)	Prevents deletion or any other kind of change to a file.

CERTIFICATION OBJECTIVE 4.03

Filesystem Management and the Automounter

Before you can use the files in a directory, you need to mount that directory on a partition formatted to some readable filesystem. Linux normally automates this process using the /etc/fstab configuration file. When you boot Linux, specified directories are mounted on configured partitions. The mount options require some explanation, especially for removable media.

You may encounter problems if connections are lost or media is removed. When you configure a server, you could be mounting directories from a number of remote computers. You could also want temporary access to removable media such as USB keys or Zip drives. The automount daemon, also known as the automounter or autofs, can help. It can automatically mount specific directories as needed. It can unmount a directory automatically after a fixed period of time.

Managing /etc/fstab

Linux stores information about your local and remotely mounted filesystems in /etc/fstab. Open this file in the text editor of your choice. As you can see, different filesystems are configured on each line. A sample /etc/fstab might look like the following:

```
LABEL=/          /            ext3      defaults            1   1
LABEL=/boot      /boot        ext3      defaults            1   2
none             /dev/pts     devpts    gid=5,mode=620      0   0
none             /proc        proc      defaults            0   0
none             /dev/shm     proc      tmpfs               0   0
/dev/hda3        swap         swap      defaults            0   0
LABEL=/usr       /usr         ext3      defaults            1   2
LABEL=/tmp       /tmp         ext3      defaults            1   2
LABEL=/var       /var         ext3      defaults            1   2
LABEL=/home      /home        ext3      defaults            1   2
```

As you can see, there are six fields associated with each filesystem, which are described from left to right in Table 4-4. Remember, this is a configuration file. You can verify partitions that are actually mounted in /etc/mtab.

| TABLE 4-4 | Description of /etc/fstab by Column, Left to Right |

Field Name	Description
Label	Lists the device to be mounted. If mounted, you can find the associated partition in /etc/mtab. For example, if you see /dev/hda2 in this file, you can verify its LABEL with the **e2label /dev/hda2** command.
Mount Point	Notes the directory where the filesystem will be mounted.
Filesystem Format	Describes the filesystem type. Valid filesystem types include ext, ext2, ext3, msdos, vfat, devpts, proc, tmpfs, udf, iso9660, nfs, smb, and swap.
Mount Options	Covered in the following section.
Dump Value	Either 0 or 1. A value of 1 means that data is automatically saved to disk by the dump(8) command when you exit Linux.
Filesystem Check Order	Determines the order that filesystems are checked by fsck(8) during the boot process. The root directory (/) filesystem should be set to 1, and other local filesystems should be set to 2. Removable filesystems such as /mnt/cdrom should be set to 0, which means that they are not checked during the Linux boot process.

Mounting Filesystems, Actively

Although **defaults** is the appropriate mount option for most /etc/fstab filesystems, there are other options, such as those listed in Table 4-5. If you want to use multiple options, separate them by commas. Don't use spaces between options. The list in Table 4-5 is not comprehensive. You can find out more from the mount manual, which you can read by running the following command:

```
# man mount
```

There are more options available, including **noatime**, **noauto**, **nodev**, **noexec**, **nosuid**, and **nouser**, which are the opposites of **atime**, **auto**, **dev**, **exec**, **suid**, and **user**, respectively.

Mounting USB Keys and Removable Media

To read USB keys and other removable media, RHEL now automatically mounts most devices (if you're running the GNOME or KDE Desktop Environments). While the details of this process are not part of the Red Hat Exam Prep guide, the process is based on configuration files in the /etc/udev/rules.d directory. If RHEL detects your hardware, it mounts the drive in the /media directory.

| TABLE 4-5 | /etc/fstab Mount Options |

Mount Option	Description
async	Data is read and written asynchronously.
atime	The inode associated with each file is updated each time the file is accessed.
auto	Searches through /etc/filesystems for the appropriate format for the partition; normally associated with a floppy or removable drive.
defaults	Uses default mount options **rw**, **suid**, **dev**, **exec**, **auto**, **nouser**, and **async**.
dev	Permits access to character devices such as terminals or consoles and block devices such as drives.
exec	Allows binaries (compiled programs) to be run on this filesystem.
noatime	The inode associated with each file is not updated when accessed.
noauto	Requires explicit mounting. Common option for CD and floppy drives.
nodev	Devices on this filesystem are not read or interpreted.
noexec	Binaries (compiled programs) cannot be run on this filesystem.
nosuid	Disallows **setuid** or **setgid** permissions on this filesystem.
nouser	Only root users are allowed to mount the specified filesystem.
remount	Remounts a currently mounted filesystem. Also an option for the **mount** command.
ro	Mounts the filesystem as read-only.
rw	Mounts the filesystem as read/write.
suid	Allows **setuid** or **setgid** permissions on programs on this filesystem.
sync	Reads and writes are done at the same speed (synchronously) on this filesystem.
user	Allows nonroot users to mount this filesystem. By default, this also sets the **noexec**, **nosuid**, and **nodev** options.

Here's relevant output from the **mount** command after I inserted a DVD and USB key on my system:

```
/dev/sda on /media/disk type vfat
                 (rw,noexec,nosuid,nodev,shortname=winnt,uid=500)
/dev/hdc on /media/RHEL-5 i386 Disc 1 type iso9660
                 (ro,noexec,nosuid,nodev,uid=500)
```

If it doesn't work for some reason, you can use the **mount** command directly. For example, the following command mounts a floppy in a drive:

```
# mount -t vfat /dev/fd0 /mnt
```

The -t switch specifies the type of filesystem (vfat). The device file /dev/fd0 represents the first floppy drive; /mnt/ is the directory through which you can access the files on the floppy after mounting. Just remember that it is important to unmount floppy disks before removing them. Otherwise, the data that you thought you wrote to the disk might still be in the cache. In that case, you would lose that data.

on the job

Here's another example that I suspect you're unlikely to see on the Red Hat exams. Assume you're working with a Zip drive of 100MB. The device is set as /dev/hdd and formatted as a single partition (/dev/hdd1) with the Linux Native (ext3) filesystem. If properly detected, it'll be automounted as a subdirectory of /media. But remember that you have to eject a Zip drive with a command such as # eject /dev/hdd1.

Mounting via the Automounter

Once you run the **mount** command on a partition, it stays mounted until you unmount it or shut down or reboot your computer. This can cause problems. For example, if you've mounted a floppy and then physically removed the disk, Linux may not have had a chance to write the file to the disk. This situation also applies to Zip or other hotswappable removable drives.

Another example, with mounted NFS directories, occurs if the remote computer fails or the connection is lost; your system may become slow or even hang as it looks for the mounted directory.

This is where the automounter can help. It relies on the **autofs** daemon to mount configured directories as needed, on a temporary basis. In RHEL, the relevant configuration files are /etc/auto.master, /etc/auto.misc, and /etc/auto.net. If you use the automounter, keep the /misc and /net directories free. Red Hat configures automounts on these directories by default, and they won't work if local files or directories are stored there.

on the job

You won't even see the /misc or /net directories unless you properly configure /etc/auto.master and activate the autofs daemon. The /etc/auto.smb configuration file does not work for CIFS shares, such as from Windows XP/ Vista. One option for CIFS shares is an /etc/auto.cifs configuration, described at www.howtoforge.com/accessing_windows_or_samba_shares_using_autofs.

Default automounter settings are configured in /etc/sysconfig/autofs. The default settings include a timeout of 300 seconds; in other words, if nothing happens on an automount within that time, the share is automatically unmounted:

```
DEFAULT_TIMEOUT=300
```

The **DEFAULT_BROWSE_MODE** can allow you to search from available mounts. The following directive disables it by default:

```
DEFAULT_BROWSE_MODE="no"
```

There are a wide variety of additional settings available, as commented in the /etc/sysconfig/autofs file, which also assumes that the **autofs** daemon is active. To check, run the following command:

```
# /etc/init.d/autofs status
```

Make sure to run this command with administrative privileges; otherwise, you'll get the misleading message "automount is stopped".

/etc/auto.master

The standard /etc/auto.master file includes a series of comments, with three default commands. The first refers to the /etc/auto.misc file as the configuration file for this directory. The **/net -hosts** command allows you to specify the host to automount a network directory, as specified in /etc/auto.net.

```
/misc /etc/auto.misc
/net  -hosts
+auto.master
```

In any case, these commands point to configuration files for each service. Shared directories from each service are automatically mounted, on demand, on the given directory (/misc and /net).

You can set up the automounter on other directories. One popular option is to set up the automounter on the /home directory. In this way, you can configure user home directories on remote servers, mounted on demand. Users are given access to their home directories upon login, and based on the **DEFAULT_TIMEOUT** directive in the /etc/sysconfig/autofs file, all mounted directories are automatically unmounted 300 seconds after that user logs off the system.

```
# /home /etc/auto.home
```

This works only if you don't already have a /home directory on your computer.

/etc/auto.misc

Red Hat conveniently provides standard automount commands in comments in the /etc/auto.misc file. It's helpful to analyze this file in detail. I use the default RHEL version of this file. The first four lines are comments, which I skip. The first command is:

```
cd   -fstype=iso9660,ro,nosuid,nodev   :/dev/cdrom
```

In RHEL, this command is active by default—assuming you've activated the **autofs** service. In other words, if you have a CD in the /dev/cdrom drive, you can access its files through the automounter with the **ls /misc/cd** command. The automounter accesses it using the ISO9660 filesystem. It's mounted read-only (**ro**); set user ID permissions are not allowed (**nosuid**), and devices on this filesystem are not used (**nodev**).

With the command from /etc/auto.master, the CD is unmounted 300 seconds after the last time it's accessed. There are a number of other sample commands, commented out, ready for use. Of course, you would have to delete the comment character (#) before using any of these commands. The first of these commented commands allows you to set up a /misc/linux mount point from a shared NFS directory, /pub/linux, on the ftp.example.org computer:

```
#linux    -ro,soft,intr      ftp.example.org:/pub/linux
```

The next command assumes that the /boot directory is stored on the /dev/hda1 partition. With this command, you don't need to mount /boot when you start Linux. Instead, this command allows you to automount it with the **mount /misc/boot** command.

```
#boot     -fstype=ext2      :/dev/hda1
```

The following three commands apply to a floppy disk drive on your computer. The first command, set to an "auto" filesystem type, searches through /etc/filesystems to try to match what's on your floppy. The next two commands assume that the floppy is formatted to the ext2 filesystem.

```
#floppy        -fstype=auto     :/dev/fd0
#floppy        -fstype=ext2     :/dev/fd0
#e2floppy      -fstype=ext2     :/dev/fd0
```

The next command points to the first partition on the third SCSI drive. The **jaz** at the beginning suggests this is suitable for an Iomega-type Jaz drive.

```
#jaz          -fstype=ext2      :/dev/sdc1
```

Finally, the last command assumes that you want to apply the automounter to the IDE drive connected as the slave on the secondary controller. The **removable** at the beginning suggests this is suitable for removable hard drives.

```
#removable    -fstype=ext2       :/dev/hdd
```

With the possible exception of the **floppy** commands, you'll need to modify these lines for your own hardware.

/etc/auto.net

With the /etc/auto.net configuration script, you can review and read shared NFS directories. As IP addresses don't work with this script, you'll need either a DNS server or at least an appropriate database entry in /etc/hosts that associates the host name with the IP address of the NFS server.

To make this work, make sure execute permissions are enabled on this file. If necessary, run the following command:

```
# chmod 755 /etc/auto.net
```

Activate the automounter as described in the next section. Then to review available shares on my enterprise5fc6d system, I run the following command:

```
# /etc/auto.net enterprise5fc6d
-fstype=nfs,hard,intr,nodev,nosuid \
        /inst enterprise5fc6d:/inst
```

This tells me that the /inst directory on the enterprise5fc6d system is shared via NFS. Based on the directives in /etc/auto.master, I can access this share (assuming appropriate firewall and SELinux settings) with the following command:

```
# ls /net/enterprise5fc6d/inst
```

Activating the Automounter

Once you've configured the desired configuration files, you can activate the automounter. As it is governed by the **autofs** daemon, you can activate it (and make it reread your configuration files) with the following command:

```
# service autofs restart
```

With the default command in the /etc/auto.misc file, you should now be able to mount a CD on the /misc/cd directory, automatically, just by accessing the configured directory. Once you have a CD in the drive, the following command should work:

```
# ls /misc/cd
```

If you were to make /misc/cd your current directory, the automounter would ignore any timeouts. Otherwise, /misc/cd is automatically unmounted according to the timeout, which according to the command in /etc/auto.master is 60 seconds.

EXERCISE 4-1

Configuring the Automounter

In this exercise, you'll test the automounter. You'll need at least a CD. Ideally, you should also have a USB key, or possibly a floppy disk. First, however, you need to make sure that the **autofs** daemon is in operation, modify the appropriate configuration files, and then restart **autofs**. You can then test the automounter for yourself.

1. From the command line interface, run the following command to make sure the **autofs** daemon is running:

   ```
   # service autofs start
   ```

2. Review the /etc/auto.master configuration file in a text editor. The defaults are sufficient if you want to activate the settings in /etc/auto.misc and /etc/auto.net.

3. Check the /etc/auto.misc configuration file in a text editor. Make sure it includes the following line (which should already be there by default). Save and exit from /etc/auto.misc.

   ```
   cd      -fstype=iso9660,ro,nosuid,nodev   :/dev/cdrom
   ```

4. Now restart the **autofs** daemon. (I know, this isn't the most efficient method, but it's a good habit to check the status of a service.)

   ```
   # service autofs restart
   ```

5. The automounter service is now active. Insert a CD into the drive on your computer and when you run the following command, you should see the contents of your CD:

   ```
   # ls /misc/cd
   ```

6. Run the **ls /misc** command immediately. You should see the CD directory in the output.

7. Wait at least five minutes, and repeat the previous command. What do you see?

OPTIONAL EXERCISE 4-2

A Floppy Drive and the Automounter

Now that you're more familiar with the automounter, try using it on a USB key. If you don't have one, try it with a floppy drive, or experiment with some of the other commented commands in /etc/auto.misc.

CERTIFICATION OBJECTIVE 4.04

Access Control Lists and Other Security Attributes

Three of the methods for protecting individual files in Linux are based on file permissions, access control lists, and SELinux. File permissions are the standard method for security control, regulating access by user, group, and others. It's a basic prerequisite described in Chapter 1. With access control lists, file owners can regulate permissions for specific users. You can control SELinux from the command line; however, as described in Chapter 15, it's easier to control with the SELinux Management tool.

Although ACLs and SELinux have just been added to the Red Hat Exam Prep guide, they have already been part of the course outline associated with both the RHCT and RHCE exams.

Access Control Lists

There was a time where users had read access to the files of all other users. But by default, users have permissions only in their own directories. Before you can configure ACLs, you'll need to set up execute permissions on the associated directories. For example, when I want to configure access to Donna's home directory, I first need to set appropriate permissions with the following command:

```
# chmod 701 /home/donna
```

The control associated with regular permissions is limited; the right ACLs can allow administrators to grant read, write, and execute access to a variety of users and groups.

Configuring a Filesystem for ACLs

Before you can configure a file or directory with ACLs, you need to mount the associated filesystem with the same attribute. If you're just testing a system for ACL, you can remount an existing partition appropriately. For example, if /home is mounted on /dev/sda3, I can remount it with ACL using the following command:

```
# mount -o remount -o acl /dev/sda3 /home
```

Naturally, to make sure this is the way /home is mounted on the next reboot requires editing /etc/fstab; for the noted parameters, the applicable line might read:

```
/dev/sda3      /home      ext3      defaults,acl      1,2
```

Depending on your configuration, you might see **LABEL=/home** in place of **/dev/sda3**.

Working with ACLs

Now with a properly mounted filesystem and appropriate permissions, you can manage ACLs on your system. To review default ACLs, run the **getfacl** *filename* command. For this example, I've created a text file named abc in Donna's home directory, and I get the following result:

```
# getfacl /home/donna/abc
# file: home/donna/abc
# owner: donna
# group: donna
user::rw-
group::rw-
other::r--
```

Now when I assign ACLs for the file named abc for myself (user Michael), I first need to assign appropriate ACLs for the /home/donna directory. The following command sets the ACLs, which support read and execute permissions for myself on Donna's home directory, as well as an effective rights mask that should equal or exceed the user ACLs.

```
# setfacl -m user:michael:r-x /home/donna
# setfacl -m mask:r-x /home/donna
```

Now I can configure individual files with ACLs. First, I deny access to all users but the owner:

```
# chmod 700 /home/donna/abc
```

To check the result, I log into my own account and try opening abc from Donna's home directory. I get the **[permission denied]** message.

Now I set the ACLs for file abc with the following commands:

```
# setfacl -m user:michael:r-- /home/donna/abc
# setfacl -m mask:r-x /home/donna/abc
```

Now I can open /home/donna/abc from my own account. Now here's a question for you—what change would you make to the previous commands to make abc writable from the user michael account?

Understanding SELinux

The controls associated with SELinux are described in more detail in Chapter 15. This chapter serves as a basic overview of SELinux and describes what associated policies can do.

SELinux was first developed by the US National Security Agency (NSA) as patches to the Linux kernel to provide a different level of "mandatory access control." Once it was released under an open-source license, Linux developers integrated SELinux into every process.

Red Hat implements SELinux with a *targeted* level of enforcement. In other words, SELinux in RHEL protects targeted network daemons. Thus, when you run SELinux and a firewall, you'll need to configure access through the firewall and create SELinux settings that enable the daemon (and probably more distinct settings such as access to certain directories).

To review SELinux security contexts in the current directory, run the **ls -Z** command. When I run it in my home directory, I get the following output:

```
drwxr-xr-x   mike mike user_u:object_r:user_home_t   Desktop
-rw-r--r--   mike mike user_u:object_r:user_home_t   f1505.tif
```

If you're familiar with the output to **ls -l**, you should recognize some of the output from the **ls -Z** command; the first bits specify permissions and ownership, and the last bits specify the name of the file or directory. The SELinux context is:

```
user_u:object_r:user_home_t
```

This specifies the identity, role, and domain associated with the file. Typical options for identity are **user_u**, **root**, and **system_u**, which naturally correspond to generic users, the root user, and system users, respectively. Every file I've checked on my Red Hat system is associated with the **object_r** role. The domain is most variable and is most closely associated with the settings used to control SELinux. This domain is different from any sort of DNS or Microsoft domain and can be very specific: for example, the domain for the **ping** command is **ping_exec_t**; the domain associated with the default FTP server directory (/var/ftp/pub) is **public_context_t**. If you want to support FTP write access to that directory, you'll need to change the domain to **public_context_rw_t**.

For a more complete discussion of how RHEL implements SELinux, see the Security and Authentication manual available from www.redhat.com.

CERTIFICATION SUMMARY

This chapter covers basic filesystem administration techniques on a Red Hat Enterprise Linux system. It also covers the different types of filesystems Linux uses, discusses how to mount them, and describes what mount options to use with them.

Creating a new filesystem means knowing how to create and manage partitions. Two excellent tools for this purpose are **fdisk** and **parted**.

You can automate this process for regular users with the automounter. Properly configured, it allows users to access shared network directories, removable media, and more through paths defined in /etc/auto.master.

Filesystems can be secured through attributes on individual files, access control lists, and settings available through Security Enhanced Linux.

TWO-MINUTE DRILL

Here are some of the key points from the certification objectives in Chapter 4.

Partitioning Hard Disks

- ❏ It's easiest if you can partition hard disks during the installation process.
- ❏ The **fdisk** tool can help you create and delete partitions, as well as change partition types.
- ❏ The **parted** tool can do everything that **fdisk** can do, and it can help you resize a partition.

Managing Filesystems

- ❏ Linux filesystems can be loosely defined as regular and journaling filesystems. While there are other filesystems available, this chapter describes the essential differences between the older ext2 and the current default ext3 filesystems.
- ❏ If you have the kernel source RPMs installed, you can review supported filesystems.
- ❏ A number of mount options are available for /etc/fstab. The **defaults** option sets up a partition as **rw** (read/write), **suid** (superuser ID and super group ID files allowed), **dev** (device files read), **exec** (binaries can be run), **auto** (automatic mounting), **nouser** (mountable only by root), and **async** (data is read asynchronously).

Filesystem Management and the Automounter

- ❏ Standard filesystems are mounted as defined in /etc/fstab.
- ❏ Portable filesystems such as CDs and USB keys are usually mounted automatically when installed.
- ❏ With the automounter, you can configure automatic mounts of removable media and shared network drives.

Access Control Lists and Other Security Attributes

- ❏ With Access Control Lists, you can allow specific users access to the files of your choice with the **setfacl** command.
- ❏ With SELinux, Red Hat has implemented targeted control that protects network daemons, using fine-grained controls.

SELF TEST

The following questions will help you measure your understanding of the material presented in this chapter. As no multiple choice questions appear on the Red Hat exams, no multiple choice questions appear in this book. These questions exclusively test your understanding of the chapter. While the topics in this chapter are "prerequisites," it is okay if you have another way of performing a task. Getting results, not memorizing trivia, is what counts on the Red Hat exams. There may be more than one answer to many of these questions.

Partitioning Hard Disks

1. What **fdisk** command lists configured partitions from all attached hard drives?

   _____

2. What command from the **parted** prompt lists all created partitions?

   _____

3. If you've just installed a new hard drive and are configuring it in **parted**, what command do you need to run first?

   _____

4. After creating a swap partition, what command activates it?

   _____

Managing Filesystems

5. What is the primary advantage of a journaling filesystem such as ext3?

   _____

6. What can you run on /etc/samba/smb.conf to make sure even the administrative user can't delete it just using the **rm** command? The command must still allow the file to be readable.

   _____

7. What command formats /dev/sdb3 to the default Red Hat filesystem format?

   _____

Filesystem Management and the Automounter

8. To change the mount options for a local filesystem, what file would you edit?

   _____

9. If you've started the **autofs** daemon and want to read the list of shared NFS directories from the first.example.com computer, what automounter-related command would you use?

_____

10. What daemon do you need to activate before using the automounter?

_____

Access Control Lists and Other Security Attributes

11. What setting do you need to add to /etc/fstab to make sure a filesystem is mounted with ACLs the next time you boot Linux?

_____

12. What is the default policy associated with SELinux on Red Hat distributions?

_____

LAB QUESTIONS

The Red Hat exams are unique based on their reliance on labs and hands-on demonstrations. With these questions, you're practicing the skills you need on both Red Hat exams.

Lab 1

This lab assumes you have a new hard disk (or at least empty space on a current hard drive where you can add a new partition). You can simulate a new hard disk by adding appropriate settings to a VMware or Xen virtual machine. In this lab, you'll create a new partition using **parted**, format it, transfer the files currently on your /home (or if you don't have a lot of space, /tmp) directory to that partition, and revise /etc/fstab so the new partition is properly mounted the next time you boot Linux.

    If you have a limited amount of available space, dedicate only half of it to this lab and leave the other half empty for Lab 2.

Lab 2

In this lab, you'll add a new swap partition using the **fdisk** utility. Remember to make the partition work with the appropriate file type, and then format and activate it. Make sure it's properly included in /etc/fstab so this partition is used the next time you boot Linux.

Lab 3

In this lab, you'll configure the automounter on your computer on an NFS connection, using two different methods. You'll need a second computer with Linux or Unix installed, and a shared NFS directory. You can use the shared NFS installation source created in Chapter 2 or any other shared NFS directory described in Chapter 10. A virtual machine such as a VMware computer qualifies as a second computer.

1. Back up your current /etc/auto.master and /etc/auto.net configuration files.

2. Open the /etc/auto.master configuration file in the text editor of your choice. Add or activate the command that applies the automounter to the /net directory.

3. Open the /etc/auto.misc configuration file. Use the example shown in this file to create an NFS entry that points to the shared NFS directory on the second computer. For the purpose of this lab, I'll assume the name of the directory to test. Substitute accordingly.

4. Restart the **autofs** server.

5. Try your connection. Run the following command:

   ```
   # ls /misc/test
   ```

6. You should see the contents of the shared NFS directory. Run the following command. What do you see?

   ```
   # ls /misc
   ```

7. Wait a while, at least the *timeout* specified in the /etc/auto.master configuration file.

8. Run the **ls /misc** command again. What happens?

9. Once you're satisfied with the result, restore the files you backed up in step 1.

10. Use the **/etc/auto.net** *servername* command to see NFS shares on the NFS server. Substitute the hostname or IP address for *servername* here and in the following steps.

11. Run the **ls /net/**servername command. You should see the NFS shares listed, including test.

12. Run the **ls /net/**servername**/test** command. You should see the contents of the NFS share named test.

Lab 4

In this lab, you'll configure access for the supervisor named Donna to the project.odt OpenOffice .org writer file in John's home directory, /home/john. Remember that you'll need to remount the appropriate partition, revise /etc/fstab, change permissions to /home/john, and set the ACL permissions to allow access by Donna.

SELF TEST ANSWERS

Partitioning Hard Disks

1. The **fdisk** command that lists configured partitions from all attached hard drives is **fdisk -l**.

2. The command from the **parted** prompt that lists all created partitions is **print all**. The **print** command by itself just prints active partitions.

3. If you've just installed a new hard drive and are configuring it in **parted**, the command you need to run first is **mklabel**.

4. After creating a swap partition, the **swapon *partitionname*** activates it; just substitute the device file associated with the partition (such as /dev/sda10 or /dev/VolGroup00/LogVol03) for *partitionname*.

Managing Filesystems

5. The primary advantage of a journaling filesystem such as ext3 is faster data recovery if power is suddenly cut.

6. To make sure even the administrative user can't delete /etc/samba/smb.conf just using the **rm** command, run **chattr +i /etc/samba/smb.conf**. Other commands such as **chmod 000 /etc/samba/smb.conf** provide some level of protection, but the file would no longer be readable.

7. The command that formats /dev/sdb3 to the default Red Hat filesystem format is **mkfs.ext3 /dev/sdb3**. Since ext3 is atop the list in /etc/filesystems, the **mkfs /dev/sdb3** command works as well.

Filesystem Management and the Automounter

8. To change the mount options for a local filesystem, edit /etc/fstab.

9. If you've started the **autofs** daemon and want to read the list of shared NFS directories from the first.example.com computer, the automounter-related command you'd use to list those directories is **/etc/auto.net first.example.com**.

10. The daemon you need to activate before using the automounter is **autofs**.

Access Control Lists and Other Security Attributes

11. The setting you need to add to /etc/fstab to make sure a filesystem is mounted with ACLs the next time you boot Linux is **acl**. For example, if you want to support ACL options, you can add the setting to the desired line in that file. The following would add ACL options to the directory labeled /home:

```
LABEL=/home    /home    ext3    defaults,acl    1,2
```

12. The default policy associated with SELinux on Red Hat distributions is *targeted*.

LAB ANSWERS

Lab I

1. If you've been able to add a new hard drive, you should be able to review it from the **(parted)** prompt. But make sure to open the appropriate drive. For example, if it's the second SATA drive, do so with the **parted /dev/sdb** command.

2. Run the **print** command from the **(parted)** prompt. If it's a new drive, you'll see an "unrecognized disk label" message and can run **mklabel** to add an **msdos** label as described in the chapter. Otherwise don't run **mklabel**!

3. Make a note of available space in your partitions.

4. Create the new partition. The **mkpart** command provides prompts that help you define the new partition. If the partition is on a new hard drive, create a primary partition. Otherwise, you may be able to create only a logical partition.

5. Use the prompts to define the size of the partition from the start and ending MB location on the drive. As noted in the lab, make sure the size of the partition is half the available free space.

6. Run **print** again to confirm your changes. Make a note of the partition number. For example, if you've created partition 1 on /dev/sdb, the partition device file is /dev/sdb1.

7. Run **quit** to exit from **parted**. Run the **partprobe** command to make Linux reread the partition table (without rebooting).

8. Format the partition. Assuming you're using the default Red Hat format, use the **mkfs.ext3** *partitionname* command; substitute the device file for *partitionname*.

9. Mount the new partition on a temporary directory; I often create a /test directory for this purpose. For the aforementioned partition, the command would be **mount /dev/sdb1 /test**.

10. Copy all of the files recursively from the directory that you're going to mount on the new partition. For example, if you're moving the files from the /home directory using the noted partitions, the command would be **cp -ar /home/* /test**.

11. Unmount **/test** from the new partition with a command like **umount /test**.

12. Mount the new partition such as /dev/sdb1 on the /home directory.

13. Review the results. Are the files you transferred on the new partition?

14. When you're confident of your new configuration, unmount /home from the new partition. You can then delete the files from the /home directory mounted on the old partition, allowing you to use the space for other directories.

Lab 2

In this lab, you'll add a new swap partition using the **fdisk** utility. Remember to make the partition work with the appropriate file type, format, and activate it. Make sure it's properly included in /etc/fstab so this partition is used the next time you boot Linux.

1. If you've completed Lab 1, you presumably have half the free space—from either an existing or a newly installed drive—still available.

2. Use **fdisk** to open the drive with free space. You may need to be specific. The **fdisk -l** command can help you define the drive with free space, such as /dev/hdc. In that case, run the **fdisk /dev/hdc** command to edit that drive's partition table.

3. Add a new partition using existing free space. From the **fdisk** prompt, the **p** command prints defined partitions, including the one you just created. Make sure to change the partition type; the **t** command from the **fdisk** prompt allows you to change the partition number you just created to the Linux swap system ID (82).

4. Write your changes from **fdisk**; if you want to reread the partition table without rebooting, use the **partprobe** command.

5. Format the new partition to the Linux swap filesystem: for example, if the new partition is on /dev/hdc3, you'd run the **mkswap /dev/hdc3** command.

6. Once the format process is complete, you can immediately activate this partition with the **swapon /dev/hdc3** command.

7. But that's not it. You need to make sure that swap partition is activated the next time you boot. To do so, you need to add information associated with that partition to /etc/fstab. One line that would work in this case is:

```
/dev/hdc3   swap   swap   defaults   0 0
```

In many cases, this may look different from the first swap partition, probably created when you first installed RHEL. If the swap filesystem is on a logical volume, it might look like:

```
/dev/VolGroup00/LogVol01   swap   swap   defaults   0 0
```

Alternatively, a swap partition on a different location such as /dev/hda3 might have a directive such as:

```
LABEL=SWAP-hda3   swap   swap   defaults   0 0
```

The differences don't matter with respect to the Red Hat exams (unless otherwise specified), as the result is what matters.

Lab 3

Configuring the automounter on a shared NFS directory is easier than it looks. Before you begin, make sure that you can mount the shared NFS directory from the remote computer. Resolve those problems first before beginning this lab. Refer to Chapter 2 on creating an NFS installation server or Chapter 10 on NFS for more information. If there's no problem with a source on an NFS server with an IP address of 192.168.30.4, you should be able to mount it locally. For example, you can mount a shared remote NFS /inst directory on an existing empty local /test directory as follows:

```
# mount -t nfs 192.168.30.4:/inst /test
```

Whatever you do, it's important to back up any files that you're about to edit. In this case, there are two configuration files that should be backed up: /etc/auto.master and /etc/auto.misc. Make sure the following directives are active in /etc/auto.master:

```
/misc /etc/auto.misc
/net  -hosts
```

In /etc/auto.misc, the following commented directive provides a template for one way to connect to a shared NFS directory:

```
#linux    -ro,soft,intr    ftp.example.org:/pub/linux
```

When active (remove the **#**), this would mount the NFS share /pub/linux from ftp.example.org on the /misc/linux directory. Substitute accordingly. Based on the conditions described in the lab, you would substitute *test* for *linux*, **192.168.30.4** for **ftp.example.org**, and *test* for **/pub/linux**.

Now you can restart the **autofs** server; the quickest way is with the following command:

```
# service autofs restart
```

Now when you test the result, you should be able to see the contents of the shared NFS directory from the remote system with both of these commands:

```
# ls /misc/test
# ls /net/192.168.30.4/
```

You can test the result in a different way. Once you've connected to all available systems, the following command should reveal the systems with available NFS shares:

```
# ls /net
192.168.30.4
```

Please, retry this lab with other shared NFS directories.

Lab 4

As described in this chapter, you'll first have to change the mount of the filesystem with the /home directory to include ACL settings. For example, if /home isn't mounted separately from the top level root (/) directory and is part of /dev/VolGroup00/LogVol00, you can remount the filesystem with the /home directory with the following command:

```
# mount -o remount -o acl /dev/VolGroup00/LogVol00 /
```

Needless to say, you'll also want to add **acl** to the appropriate line in /etc/fstab; it might look like this (obviously, it varies with the partition, mounted directory, and **LABEL**):

```
/dev/VolGroup00/LogVol00   /    ext3    defaults,acl   1 1
```

Now with these settings, allow others to execute in John's home directory:

```
# chmod 701 /home/john
```

Now you can set ACLs to allow Donna access to John's home directory:

```
# setfacl -m user:donna:r-x /home/john/
# setfacl -m mask:r-x /home/john/
```

Next, configure individual files with ACLs. The file in question is project.odt in John's home directory. Deny access to all users but the owner:

```
# chmod 700 /home/john/project.odt
```

To check the result, log into your own account and try opening abc from Donna's home directory. You should see the **[permission denied]** message.

Now set read-write permissions in the ACLs for the project.odt file with the following commands:

```
# setfacl -m user:donna:rwx /home/john/project.odt
# setfacl -m mask:r-x /home/john/project.odt
```

Now user Donna can do what she needs with the project.odt file in John's home directory. You can confirm the changes with the **getfacl /home/john/project.odt** command.

To simplify the test process, you can use a separate console to log into Donna's account. If you're working from the administrative root account, you can log into Donna's account with the **su - donna** command.

5

Package Management

CERTIFICATION OBJECTIVES

5.01 The Red Hat Package Manager

5.02 More RPM Commands

5.03 Managing Updates with Pup and the Red Hat Network

5.04 Adding and Removing RPM Packages with yum and pirut

5.05 Using Kickstart to Automate Installation

✓ Two-Minute Drill

Q&A Self Test

After installation is complete, you still have administrative work to do. To customize the system to meet your needs, you may need to add or remove packages and more. To make sure you get the right updates, you need to know how to get your system working with the Red Hat Network (or the repository associated with your distribution). If you're satisfied with your configuration, you may want to use kickstart to automate future installations.

CERTIFICATION OBJECTIVE 5.01

The Red Hat Package Manager

One of the major duties of a system administrator is software management. New applications are installed. Services are updated. Kernels are patched. Without the right tools, it can be difficult to figure out what software is on a system, what is the

INSIDE THE EXAM

Administrative Skills

The management of RPM packages is a fundamental skill for Red Hat administrators, so it's reasonable to expect to use the **rpm** and related commands on both parts of the RHCT or RHCE exam. While the requirements are listed in the Installation and Configuration part of each exam, these skills may also help you during the Troubleshooting and System Maintenance part of each exam. The Red Hat Exam Prep guide includes two specific references to the **rpm** command:

■ Install and update packages using **rpm**.

■ Properly update the kernel package.

And there's a related reference, as update tools such as **yum** and Pup are essentially front-ends to the **rpm** command:

■ Configure the system to update/install packages from remote repositories using **yum** or Pup.

But whenever you install a new package, you need to know how to use the **rpm** command. You need to know how to use it to find the files you need. You need to know how the **yum** command helps manage dependencies, including any additional packages that might be required.

Finally, this chapter will also help you meet the Exam Prep guide requirement associated with Kickstart, which suggests that RHCEs must also be able to

■ Configure hands-free installation using Kickstart.

latest update, and what applications depend on other software. Worse, you may install a new software package only to find it has overwritten a crucial file from a currently installed package.

The Red Hat Package Manager (RPM) was designed to alleviate these problems. With RPM, software is managed in discrete *packages*. An RPM package includes the software with instructions for adding, removing, and upgrading those files. When properly used, the RPM system can back up key configuration files before proceeding with upgrades and removals. It can also help you identify the currently installed version of any RPM-based application.

RPMs and the **rpm** command are far from perfect, which is why it has been supplemented with the **yum** command. With a connection to a repository such as that available from the Red Hat Network or third-party "rebuilds" such as CentOS, you'll be able to use **yum** to satisfy dependencies.

What Is a Package?

In the generic sense, an RPM package is a container of files. It includes the group of files associated with a specific program or application, which normally includes binary installation scripts as well as configuration and documentation files. It also includes instructions on how and where these files should be installed and uninstalled.

An RPM package name usually includes the version, the release, and the architecture for which it was built. For example, the fictional penguin-3.4.5-26.i386 .rpm package is version 3.4.5, build 26, and the i386 indicates that it is suitable for computers built to the Intel 32-bit architecture.

on the **job** *Many RPM packages are CPU-specific. You can identify the CPU type for your computer in the /proc/cpuinfo file. Some RPM packages with the noarch label can be installed on computers with all types of CPUs.*

What Is an RPM?

At the heart of this system is the RPM database. Among other things, this database tracks the version and location of each file in each RPM. The RPM database also maintains an MD5 checksum of each file. With the checksum, you can use the **rpm -V** *package* command to determine whether any file from that RPM package has changed. The RPM database makes adding, removing, and upgrading packages easy, because RPM knows which files to handle and where to put them.

RPM also manages conflicts between packages. For example, assume you have two different packages that use configuration files with the same name. Call the original configuration file */etc/someconfig.conf*. You've already installed package X. If you then try to install package Y, RPM packages are designed to back up the original */etc/someconfig.conf* file (with a file name like */etc/someconfig.conf.rpmsave*) before installing package Y.

on the **J o b**

While RPM upgrades are supposed to preserve or save existing configuration files, there are no guarantees. It's best to back up all applicable configuration files before upgrading any associated RPM package.

Installing RPMs

There are three basic commands *that may* install an RPM. They won't work if there are dependencies (packages that need to be installed first). For example, if you haven't installed Samba and try to install the system-config-samba package, you'll get the following message (your version numbers may be different):

```
# rpm -i system-config-samba-*
error: Failed dependencies:
        samba is needed by system-config-samba-1.2.39-1.1.noarch
```

When dependency messages are shown, **rpm** does not install the given package.

on the **J o b**

Sure, you can use the --force option to make rpm ignore dependencies, but that can lead to other problems, unless you install those dependencies as soon as possible. The best option is to use an appropriate yum command, described later in this chapter. In this case, a yum install system-config-samba command would automatically install the Samba RPM as well.

If you're not stopped by dependencies, there are three basic commands that can install RPM packages:

```
# rpm -i packagename
```

```
# rpm -U packagename
```

```
# rpm -F packagename
```

The **rpm -i** option installs the package, if it isn't already installed. The **rpm -U** option upgrades any existing package or installs it if an earlier version isn't already installed. The **rpm -F** option upgrades only existing packages. It does not install a package if it wasn't previously installed.

I like to add the **-vh** options whenever I use the **rpm** command. These options add verbose mode and use hash marks to help you monitor the progress of the installation. So when I use **rpm** to install a package, I run

```
# rpm -ivh packagename
```

There's one more thing the **rpm** command does before installing a package: it checks to see whether it would overwrite any configuration files. The **rpm** command tries to make intelligent decisions about what to do in this situation. As suggested earlier, if the **rpm** command chooses to replace an existing configuration file, it gives you a warning (in most cases) like:

```
# rpm -i penguin-3.26.i386.rpm
warning: /etc/someconfig.conf saved as /etc/someconfig.conf.rpmsave
```

It's up to you to look at both files and determine what, if any, modifications need to be made.

If you've already customized a package and upgraded it with rpm, go to the saved configuration file. Use it as a guide to change the settings in the new configuration file. Since you may need to make different changes to the new configuration file, you should test the result for every situation in which the package may be used in a production environment.

Removing RPMs

The **rpm -e** command removes a package from your system. But before removing a package, RPM checks a few things. It does a dependency check to make sure no other packages need what you're trying to remove. If it finds dependent packages, **rpm -e** fails with an error message identifying these packages.

If you have modified most any of the configuration files, RPM makes a copy of the file, adds an .rpmsave extension to the end of the file name, and then erases the original. Finally, after removing all files from your system and the RPM database, it removes the package name from the database.

Be very careful about which packages you remove from your system. Like many other Linux utilities, RPM may silently let you shoot yourself in the foot. For example, if you were to remove the packages that include /etc/passwd or the kernel, it would devastate your system.

Installing RPMs from Remote Systems

With the RPM system, you can even specify package locations similar to an Internet address, in URL format. For example, if you want to apply the **rpm** command to the foo.rpm package on the /pub directory of the ftp.rpmdownloads.com FTP server, you can install this package with a command such as:

```
# rpm -ivh ftp://ftp.rpmdownloads.com/pub/foo.rpm
```

Assuming you're connected to the Internet, this particular **rpm** command logs onto the FTP server anonymously and downloads the file.

If the FTP server requires a username and password, you can use the following format: ftp://*username:password @hostname:port/path/to/remote/package/file*.rpm, where *username* and *password* are the username and password you need to log on to this system, and *port*, if required, specifies a nonstandard port used on the remote FTP server. Naturally, transmitting passwords in clear text over a network is discouraged, so anonymous FTP servers may be preferred.

Based on the preceding example, if the username is *mjang* and the password is *Ila451MS*, you could install an RPM directly from a server with the following command:

```
rpm -ivh ftp://mjang:Ila451MS@ftp.rpmdownloads.com/pub/foo.rpm
```

The key to this system is the **rpm** command. Even over a network, it works with globbing; in other words, if you don't know the version number, you can replace it with a *:

```
rpm -ivh ftp://mjang:Ila451MS@ftp.rpmdownloads.com/pub/foo-*
```

Later, in this age of insecure downloads, you'll see how to validate the signature associated with an RPM and verify the files in a specific package.

Updating a Kernel RPM

Kernel updates incorporate new features, address security issues, and generally help your Linux system work better. However, kernel updates can also be a pain in the rear end, especially if you have specialized packages that depend on an existing version of a kernel.

In other words, don't upgrade a kernel if you're not ready to repeat everything you've done with the existing kernel, whether it's specialized drivers, recompiling to incorporate additional filesystems, or more.

If you're told to update a kernel RPM, the temptation is to run the **rpm -U newkernel** command. Don't do it! It overwrites your existing kernel, and if the new kernel doesn't work with your system, you're out of luck. (Well, not completely out of luck, but if you reboot and have problems, you'll have to use **linux rescue** mode to boot your system and reinstall the existing kernel, which might make for an interesting test scenario.)

The best option for upgrading to a new kernel is to install it, specifically with a command such as:

```
# rpm -ivh newkernel
```

If you're connected to an appropriate repository, the following command works just as well:

```
# yum install kernel
```

This installs the new kernel, side by side with the current working kernel. It adds options to boot the new kernel in the boot loader menu (through the GRUB configuration file), without erasing existing options. If you use the **yum** command (described later in this chapter), make sure you use **yum install kernel** to ensure the kernel is installed and the previous kernel (and associated configuration options) is not overwritten.

CERTIFICATION OBJECTIVE 5.02

More RPM Commands

The **rpm** command is rich with details, and learning to use this command can and does fill entire books, including the *Red Hat RPM Guide*, by Eric Foster-Johnson. All this book can do is cover some of the basic ways **rpm** can help you manage your systems. You've already read about how **rpm** can install and upgrade packages in various ways. Queries can help you identify what's installed, in detail. Validation tools can help you check the integrity of packages and individual files. You can use related tools to help you find the RPM that meets specific needs as well as a full list of what's already installed.

RPM Queries

The simplest RPM query verifies whether a specific package is installed. The following command verifies the installation of the Samba package:

```
# rpm -q samba
samba-3.0.23c-2.el5.2
```

You can do more with RPM queries, as described in Table 5-1. Note how queries are associated with **-q** or **--query**; full word switches such as **--query** are usually associated with a double-dash.

Validating an RPM Package Signature

RPM uses two methods for checking the integrity of a package: the MD5 checksum and the GPG signature. You can use the MD5 checksum to verify that the file is intact (no data was lost or corrupted while copying or downloading the file). You can then use the GPG signature to make sure the file is authentic. For example, you can use it to confirm that an RPM file is indeed an official Red Hat RPM. Red Hat provides a GNU Privacy Guard (GPG) public key for its RPM files; you can find it on each installation CD in the appropriate RPM-GPG-KEY-* file or in the /etc/pki/rpm-gpg/ directory.

To authenticate your RPMs using the GPG system, assuming it was released after November 2006, import the key file using the following command (assuming it's a CD-based keyfile, mounted on the /media/disk directory):

```
# rpm --import /media/disk/RPM-GPG-KEY-redhat-release
```

on the Job

There are six GPG keys associated with RHEL 5. The RPM-GPG-KEY-redhat-release and RPM-GPG-KEY-redhat-auxilliary keys are used for packages released after November 2006; the RPM-GPG-KEY-redhat-former key is used for packages released before that date.

Now if you wanted to check the integrity of some RPM such as pkg-1.2.3-4.noarch.rpm on a CD, you'd run the following command:

```
# rpm --checksig /media/disk/Server/pkg-1.2.3-4.noarch.rpm
```

This allows you to verify both the integrity and the authenticity of the RPM.

TABLE 5-1	rpm Query Command	Meaning
	rpm -qa	Lists all installed packages.
rpm --query Options	rpm -qf /path/to/file	Identifies the package associated with /path/to/file.
	rpm -qc *packagename*	Lists only configuration files from *packagename*.
	rpm -qi *packagename*	Displays basic information for *packagename*.
	rpm -ql *packagename*	Lists all files from *packagename*.
	rpm -qR *packagename*	Notes all dependencies; you can't install *packagename* without them.

RPM Verification

Verifying an installed package compares information about that package with information from the RPM database on your system. The **--verify** (or **-v**) switch checks the size, MD5 checksum, permissions, type, owner, and group of each file in the package. Here are a few examples:

- Verify all files. Naturally, this may take a long time on your system. (Of course, the **rpm -va** command performs the same function.)

  ```
  # rpm --verify -a
  ```

- Verify all files within a package against a downloaded RPM.

  ```
  # rpm --verify -p /root/Desktop/inn-2.4.3-6.i386.rpm
  ```

- Verify a file associated with a particular package.

  ```
  # rpm --verify --file /bin/ls
  ```

If the files or packages check out, you will see no output. Any output means that a file or package is different from the original. There's no need to panic if you see a few changes; after all, you do change configuration files. There are eight tests. If there's been a change, the output is a string of up to eight characters, each of which tells you what happened during each test.

If you see a dot (.), that test passed. The following example shows /bin/vi with an incorrect group ID assignment:

```
# rpm --verify --file /bin/vi
......G.   /bin/vi
```

Table 5-2 lists the failure codes and their meanings.

TABLE 5-2	Failure Code	Meaning
rpm --verify Codes	5	MD5 checksum
	S	File size
	L	Symbolic link
	T	File modification time
	D	Device
	U	User
	G	Group
	M	Mode

Listing Installed RPMs

There are two basic ways to list all installed RPMs. The basic list is stored in /var/log/rpmpkgs. However, this is updated only once a day. If you want the most current list, run the following command:

```
# rpm -qa
```

The /root/install.log file includes all packages installed when RHEL was installed on this system. It's not updated after installation.

Using RPM Sources

The RPMs described so far are already in binary format. In other words, they're compiled and ready to install just like "tarballs" or Microsoft-style installation packages. But Linux goes back to the source code. Courtesy of the GPL, the source code is readily available.

In fact, if you're studying for the Red Hat exams using Fedora Core 6 and don't have an RHN subscription, you still have access to the RHEL source code packages through ftp.redhat.com.

---

e x a m

⚥ a t c h *You can also build RPM sources from a tar archive. However, as of this writing, no requirements in the RHCE and RHCT related course outlines are related to building source RPMs from* *tar archives. But an obsolete version of the RHCE Exam Prep guide suggests that you need to be "familiar with the basic elements of" source RPMs.*

Creating Custom RPMs from Source

A source RPM is, as the name indicates, a package of source code used to build architecture-specific packages. Properly labeled source RPMs include the **src** identifier as part of the file name, like so:

```
polarbear-2.07-2.src.rpm
```

Binary RPMs are built from source RPMs. The source RPM contains the source code and specifications necessary to create the binary RPM.

Before you continue with this section, make sure your system includes the rpm-build RPM package, for access to the **rpmbuild** command.

In RHEL, the rpmbuild *command has superseded the older* rpm *commands associated with building RPM packages from source code.*

Installing Source RPMs

Like normal RPMs, a source RPM (SRPM) is installed with the **rpm -i** *rpmname* **.src.rpm** command. However, this command installs only the contents of the SRPM in various /usr/src/redhat subdirectories, which you can then use to create a binary RPM. For the purpose of this section, I've installed the source for the Linux kernel from the freely available RHEL source RPMs, which you can download for yourself from ftp.redhat.com.

Once downloaded from the source of your choice, proceed to install it as if it were a regular RPM, in this case with the following command:

```
# rpm -ivh kernel-*.src.rpm
```

As noted earlier, you can now use the source code and spec files in various /usr/ src/redhat/ subdirectories to build and install the package.

The /usr/src/redhat/ Directory Structure

There are five subdirectories located under the /usr/src/redhat directory, as described in Table 5-3.

When you build a source RPM, you build it within this structure. If you install a source RPM, it is extracted into this structure. The kernel source RPM that you installed in the previous section should have unpacked a kernel-2.6.spec file in the /usr/src/redhat/SPECS directory.

Changing Compile Options for a Source RPM

While most precompiled RPMs will serve your needs, at times you will want to modify the source code or compile options in the corresponding SRPMs. You can do so in the spec file that you get when you installed the source RPM.

| **TABLE 5-3** | Build Directories from RPM Sources |

Directory	Purpose
/usr/src/redhat/SOURCES	Contains the original program source code.
/usr/src/redhat/SPECS	Contains spec files, which control the RPM build process.
/usr/src/redhat/BUILD	Source code is unpacked and built here.
/usr/src/redhat/RPMS	Contains the output binary RPM.
/usr/src/redhat/SRPMS	Contains the SRPM created by the build process.

To change the compile options in an SRPM, you must understand spec files. The spec file is stored in /usr/src/redhat/SPECS/*packagename*.spec. The spec file controls the way a package is built and what actions are performed when it is installed or removed from a system. A spec file has 10 different sections, as described in Table 5-4. Several of the sections include commands that can be run as individual shell scripts. You won't see all of these sections in every spec file. For more information, see the RPM HOWTO at www.rpm.org.

You can change the compile-time options for a package in the build section of the spec file. Here's a sample **%clean** section from a different spec file (this is not from the vsftpd source RPM):

```
%build
rm -rf $RPM_BUILD_ROOT
mkdir -p $RPM_BUILD_ROOT/usr/bin $RPM_BUILD_ROOT/etc
./configure --prefix=/usr --exec-prefix=/
make CFLAGS="$RPM_OPT_FLAGS" LDFLAGS=-s
```

This section, a shell script, begins with some housekeeping, removing any files that may be left over from a previous build. A directory structure is created for the source files. Then the package is configured and compiled with the **make** command.

For a different package, you might modify the **make** command line to compile other components after **LDFLAGS**. The compile options from **$RPM_OPT_FLAGS** are defaults, set by RPM. Alternatively, you could use this variable to set other compile-time options such as a different CPU.

on the **job**

Perhaps the essential reference guide to the RPM system is Red Hat's book Maximum RPM. An older version is available online from Red Hat at www. redhat.com/docs/books/max-rpm.

Building Custom Source and Binary RPMs

By now, you should understand where you should modify a source RPM spec file to change compile-time options in the **%build** section. However, there's much more to building customized RPMs. Once you have modified the spec file, you need to tell RPM to build a new binary and source RPM.

You can build an RPM using the **rpmbuild** command, with the build switch, **-b**. By itself, **rpmbuild -b** calls the scripts specified in the %prep, %build, and %install sections of the spec file. Normally, you'll modify the **-b** with **a**, which makes RPM go through the build process, step by step. The **rpmbuild** command is directed at a spec file. For example, this command

```
# rpmbuild -ba vsftpd.spec
```

TABLE 5-4	Build Directories for Source RPM Files

Section	Description
%preamble	Includes information shown with an **rpm -qi** command. This normally includes a summary, version, and group. It also includes a list of dependent packages.
%description	A basic package description.
%pre	Adds a macro for preinstallation scripts.
%prep	Includes any preparatory commands required before building the source code, such as unpacking.
%build	Commands to compile the spec file and build sources.
%install	Commands to install the software on a system.
Install and uninstall scripts	Spec files usually contain scripts that will be run on the end user's system to install or remove the software. RPM can execute a script before the package is installed, after the package is installed, before the package is removed, and after the package is removed.
%verify	Although RPM takes care of most verification tasks, a script can be inserted here for any desired extra checks.
%clean	A script can be specified here to perform any necessary cleanup tasks.
%post	Adds a macro that cleans up after installation.
%preun	Scripts that prepare for uninstallation.
%postun	Adds a macro that cleans up after uninstallation.
%files	A list of files in the package.
%changelog	A list of revisions.

directs RPM to create binary and source RPMs from this spec file. Alternatively, if you just want the binary RPM, use the following command:

```
# rpmbuild -bb vsftpd.spec
```

Naturally, the RPMs are created in the RPMS/ and SRPMS/ subdirectories.

Building Red Hat Enterprise RPMs

Red Hat makes source RPMs freely available at ftp.redhat.com. You can find the SRPMs for RHEL 5 Server in the /pub/redhat/linux/enterprise/5Server/en/os/SRPMS directory. If you're working with RHEL 5 Desktop, substitute 5Client for 5Server.

If you're studying for the Red Hat exams using a "rebuild," you don't have to buy RHEL. Alternatively, you can build Red Hat Enterprise RPMs from the source code. For example, you can learn more about the Samba server from the Samba source code. To do so, take the following steps. First navigate to ftp.redhat.com (or a mirror site) and navigate to the directory with RHEL 5 source RPMs. (The source code for the RHEL 5 Client and Server are identical, as of this writing.) Then you can

1. Download the RHEL 5 version of the package that contains the Samba server, samba-*.src.rpm.

2. Install the source RPM package. The **rpm** command described earlier sets up the source code in your /usr/src/redhat tree.

3. Build the RPM from source. The **rpmbuild** commands use the code loaded in the /usr/src/redhat directories to create RPM packages in the /usr/src/redhat/ RPMS directory, in the subdirectory associated with your architecture.

CERTIFICATION OBJECTIVE 5.03

Managing Updates with Pup and the Red Hat Network

One key advantage of RHEL is access to the Red Hat Network (RHN). With the RHN, you can keep all of your registered systems up to date from one Web-based interface. You can even configure RHN to run commands remotely, on a schedule. Naturally, this can be a terrific convenience for remote administrators. But before any of this is possible, you'll need to register your system on the RHN.

If you're running a "rebuild" distribution such as CentOS-5, you don't need access to the RHN. If this applies to you, feel free to skim until reaching the "Updating with Pup" section.

ⓦatch *While the Red Hat Network is covered per the public syllabus for the prep courses for both the RHCT and RHCE, it is not included in the Red Hat Exam Prep guide. And I don't think you'll have Internet access during the Red Hat exams.*

As the RHN requires subscriptions, Red Hat does not have any public mirrors for RHEL updates. If you have a group of RHEL systems, it's possible to download the updates once and store them locally. You can then use those RPMs to update the other RHEL systems on your network. Red Hat facilitates this kind of communication with the RHN Proxy Server and Satellite Server products.

While you can configure your own local proxy of updates, it won't come with Red Hat support. I've written a guide to this process, *Linux Patch Management*, published by Prentice-Hall.

RHN Registration

Before you can administer your system on the RHN, you have to register. You'll need either a registration code associated with your subscription or available entitlements for your RHN account.

You may have already registered during the First Boot process described in Chapter 2. But if you've installed the system in text-mode, or using kickstart (common on many servers), you may not have gone through the First Boot process, at least the version that supports registration. Naturally, you can still register after installation. This section covers text-mode registration, which is how most administrators work with servers. If you want to register your system from the GNOME Desktop Environment, you're prompted to do so during the first update. Choose Applications | System Tools | Package Updater, and follow the wizard. If you don't see the wizard, your system is already registered (or you're using a rebuild distribution).

To register from the command line, take the following steps:

1. Run **rhn_register** from the command line.
2. You'll see a Setting Up Software Updates window. If you need more information about the RHN, select Why Should I Connect To RHN; otherwise, select Next to continue.
3. You'll see a screen where you can enter your login information for the RHN. If you don't have an RHN account, select Create A New Login, and follow the instructions there before moving on to step 4. Otherwise, enter your RHN account information and select Next.
4. Now you can choose whether to register a system profile. First, you can choose whether to send basic hardware information about your system; make a decision and select Next to continue.
5. Next, you can choose to include a list of installed packages, which helps the RHN check whether you need software and security updates. Make any desired changes and select Next to continue.

6. Finally, you can choose whether to send your system profile to the RHN. If you click Cancel, the tool stops, and your system is not registered. I assume you want to register; if so, select Next to continue.

7. Your system attempts to contact the RHN server (or possibly your RHN Satellite Server). After additional prompts, you should see a message that you've successfully registered your system with the RHN.

Updating with Pup

Red Hat has adapted the Package Updater, also known as Pup, to manage updates for RHEL systems. If you're properly registered on the RHN, you can use Pup to list available updates and download them as needed. It runs only in the GUI. To start it, choose Applications | System Tools | Software Updater. As shown in Figure 5-1, it's a simple tool; it lists only those packages for which later versions are available, which you can deselect as desired before newer packages are downloaded and installed. If you select Update Details, you can review the version numbers of the packages being changed.

on the **Ó o b**

If you haven't already registered your system, starting Pup first starts the Red Hat Network Registration steps just described.

When you've made your selections, click Apply Updates.

Automatic Dependency Resolution

Red Hat has incorporated dependency resolution into the update process. Through RHEL 4, this was done with **up2date**. Red Hat has now incorporated **yum** into RHEL 5. The **yum** command uses subscribed RHN channels and any other repositories that you may have configured in the /etc/yum.repos.d directory.

Before **yum** and **up2date**, dependencies were a serious annoyance. For example, if you hadn't installed the Samba RPM and tried to install the system-config-samba RPM, the installation would fail with a message like this:

```
error: Failed Dependencies:
      samba is needed by system-config-samba-1.2.39-1.el5.noarch
```

With **yum**, you can install the system-config-samba RPM, and the samba RPM is automatically installed together with it. In this case, all you need to run is

```
# yum install system-config-samba
```

And dependencies—in this case, the Samba RPM—are installed automatically.

You can use a single **yum** command to install as many packages as you want; just add each package name to the end of the command. The **yum** command is described in more detail later in this chapter.

There are a number of third-party repositories available for RHEL. They include several popular applications that are not supported by Red Hat. For example, I use one to install packages associated with my laptop wireless network card.

While the owners of these repositories work closely with some Red Hat developers, there are some reports where dependencies required from one repository are unavailable from other repositories, leading to a different form of what is known as "dependency hell." However, at least the more popular third-party repositories are excellent; I've never encountered "dependency hell" from using these repositories.

on the
ⓞ o b

There are two main reasons why Red Hat does not include most proven and popular packages available from third-party repositories. Some are not released under open-source licenses, and others are packages that Red Hat simply chooses not to support.

RHN in the Enterprise

One of the benefits of the RHN is that it allows you to manage all your registered RHEL systems remotely, over a Web-based interface. You can manage and even run remote commands on all of your systems on any schedule you can configure. To ease administrative issues, you can group systems together and apply your changes to every system in a group.

Naturally, the RHN allows you to do a number of things remotely, including:

- Schedule commands.
- Install packages.
- Edit and add custom configuration files.
- Create kickstart installations.
- Create snapshots.

It also allows you to configure different subscription channels for each of your systems, and much more. For more information on the RHN, see the latest version of the reference guide, available from https://rhn.redhat.com/rhn/help/reference/.

CERTIFICATION OBJECTIVE 5.04

Adding and Removing RPM Packages with yum and pirut

The **yum** command makes it easy to add and remove software packages to your system. It maintains a database regarding the proper way to add, upgrade, and remove packages. This makes it relatively simple to add and remove software with a single command.

The Basics of yum

If you want to know all that you can do with **yum**, run the command by itself:

```
# yum
Loading "rhnplugin" plugin
Loading "installonlyn" plugin
You need to give some command

usage: yum [options] < grouplist, localinstall, groupinfo,
localupdate, resolvedep, erase, deplist, groupremove,
makecache, upgrade, provides, shell, install, whatprovides,
groupinstall, update, groupupdate, info, search,
check-update, list, remove, clean, grouperase >

options:
  -h, --help          show this help message and exit
  -t, --tolerant      be tolerant of errors
  -C                  run entirely from cache, don't update
                      cache
```

```
-c  [config file]      config file location
-R  [minutes]          maximum command wait time
-d  [debug level]      debugging output level
-e  [error level]      error output level
-y                     answer yes for all questions
--version              show Yum version and exit
--installroot=[path]   set install root
--enablerepo=[repo]    enable one or more repositories
                       (wildcards allowed)
--disablerepo=[repo]   disable one or more repositories
                       (wildcards allowed)
-x [package], --exclude=[package]
                       exclude package(s) by name or glob
--obsoletes            enable obsoletes processing during
                       updates
--noplugins            disable Yum plugins
```

You'll examine how a few of these options work in the following sections. While it's unlikely that you'll have an Internet connection during the exam, you could have a network connection to a local repository. So you should be ready to use the **yum** command during either Red Hat exam. Besides, it's an excellent tool for administering Red Hat systems.

If you run the yum command as a regular user, you'll get a message to the effect that the local system is not registered on the RHN (even if you've already done so). The only way to use yum is through the administrative (root) account.

The basic **yum** configuration is shown in /etc/yum.conf. The first line shows that it's the main configuration file for this service:

```
[main]
```

The **cachedir** directive specifies the directory where **yum** downloads are stored:

```
cachedir=/var/cache/yum
```

If you change the **keepcache** setting, you can save downloaded RPMs in a /var/cache/yum subdirectory associated with the RHN software channel or repository:

```
keepcache=0
```

The **debuglevel** directive specifies the level of messages specified in the file associated with the **logfile** directive. Since multiple packages may be associated with each version of RHEL, the **pkgpolicy** directive specifies that **yum** uses the latest version:

```
debuglevel=2
logfile=/var/log/yum.log
pkgpolicy=newest
```

The **distroverpkg** directive shown takes the version number from the /etc/redhat-release file:

```
distroverpkg=redhat-release
```

The **tolerant** directive shown allows **yum** to work even with minor errors. For example, if you run **yum install** on a list of packages, and one is already installed, the command still proceeds.

```
tolerant=1
```

Most Linux distributions are architecture-dependent; the following directive makes sure that **yum** downloads correspond to your CPU architecture:

```
exactarch=1
```

During a **yum update** command, the following directive checks for and uninstalls any obsolete packages:

```
obsoletes=1
```

Naturally, to confirm appropriate packages, it's important for **yum** to check the GPG key, as determined by the following directive:

```
gpgcheck=1
```

The following directive includes plug-ins as defined in the /etc/yum/pluginconf.d/ and /usr/lib/yum-plugins/ directories as part of the **yum** configuration:

```
plugins=1
```

To make sure the header data downloaded from the RHN (and any other repositories) are up to date, the **metadata_expire** directive specifies a lifetime for headers. In other words, if you haven't used the **yum** command in 30 minutes (1800 seconds), the next use of the **yum** command downloads the latest header information.

```
metadata_expire=1800
```

Finally, the following notes the default location for configuring other repositories. Even though it's in comments, the /etc/yum.repos.d directory is the default location for these third-party repository configuration files.

```
# PUT YOUR REPOS HERE OR IN separate files named file.repo
# in /etc/yum.repos.d
```

Regular RHN repositories are defined in various python-based configuration files in the /usr/lib/yum-plugins directory.

Install Mode

There are two basic installation commands. If you haven't installed a package before, or if you want to update it to the latest stable version, run the **yum install** *packagename* command. For example, if you're checking for the latest version of the Samba RPM, the following command will update it or add it if it isn't already installed on your system.

```
# yum install samba
```

If you just want to keep the packages on your system up to date, run the **yum update** *packagename* command. For example, if you already have the Samba RPM installed, the following command makes sure it's updated to the latest version:

```
# yum update samba
```

If you haven't installed Samba, this command doesn't add it to your installed packages.

The **yum update** command by itself is powerful; if you want to make sure that all installed packages are updated to the latest stable versions, run the following command:

```
# yum update
```

The **yum update** command may take some time as it communicates with the RHN, with all dependencies.

But what if you don't know what you want to install? For example, if you want to install the Evince document reader, the **yum whatprovides** *filename* command can help. To search for all instances of the Evince document reader, you can run the following command:

```
# yum whatprovides evince
```

It lists all instances of the *evince* file name, with the associated RPM package. It works like the **locate** command; in other words, partial file names also work with the **yum whatprovides** command. Once you identify the package you need to install, you can proceed with the **yum install** *packagename* command.

on the **Job**

If you have problems with yum, try yum clean all. If there are recent updates to RHN packages (or third-party repositories), this command flushes the current cache of headers, allowing you to resynchronize headers with configured repositories, without having to wait the default 30 minutes before the cache is automatically flushed (as defined by the metadata_expire directive in /etc/yum.conf).

Updates and Security Fixes

Red Hat maintains a public list of errata at http://rhn.redhat.com/errata/. It's divided by RHEL versions and now by repositories. If you have an RHEL subscription, you generally don't need to watch this, as long as you keep your packages up to date using Pup or by running periodic **yum update** commands. This list is useful for those third parties who use RHEL source code, such as CentOS, Scientific Linux, or even the new Oracle Linux.

Third-Party Repositories

To add third-party repositories to your system, you'll need to add appropriate directives to a .repo file in the /etc/yum.repos.d directory. For example, I often use Axel Thimm's third-party repository for my RHEL and Fedora Core systems. It's available from http://ATrpms.net. To make it work with my RHEL system, I use the instructions available from that Web site and add the following information to atrpms.repo in the /etc/yum .repos.d/ directory:

```
[atrpms]
baseurl=http://dl.atrpms.net/el5-i386/atrpms/stable
gpgkey=http://atrpms.net/RPM-GPG-KEY.atrpms
gpgcheck=1
```

If you want to disable any repository in the /etc/yum.repos.d/ directory, add the following directive to the applicable repository file:

```
enabled=0
```

Managing with pirut

You can update packages with a graphical tool. The **pirut** tool, also known as the Package Manager utility, has several advantages: It includes an interface similar to the Anaconda Custom Installation screen. It allows you to install more than one package at a time. It automatically installs any other dependent packages that may be needed.

There are two ways to start the Package Manager utility. From the GNOME desktop, choose Applications | Add/Remove Software. Alternatively, in a GUI text command window, run the **pirut** command. Either action opens the Package Manager shown in Figure 5-2. (If you're running RHEL 5 and haven't registered this system, or have trouble with your Internet connection, the windows in the Browse tab will be blank.)

FIGURE 5-2

The Package
Manager

You can use the Package Manager to add the packages or package groups of your choice. As you can see in Figure 5-2, there are three tabs. The Browse tab displays package groups in a format similar to what you saw during the GUI installation process.

The Search tab allows you to search for a specific package and identify whether or not it's currently installed. When you search, partial matches are okay; for example, a search for *system-config* returns all packages associated with **system-config-*** tools.

The List tab lists all packages; they can be filtered by installed and available packages.

EXERCISE 5-1

Installing More with pirut

This exercise requires a network connection to a remote repository. If you're using a rebuild of RHEL 5, you'll need to make sure your connection to the core repository for your rebuild is working. If you've already connected to the RHN, you can skip a couple of steps in this exercise.

1. Run the **yum list** command. If you're properly connected to a repository, you'll see a full list of available packages, including those already installed.

Note the label in the right column; it will either show the repository where a package is available or note that the package is already installed.

2. Try the **pirut** command in a GUI; alternatively, in GNOME, choose Applications (or in KDE, choose Main Menu | System) | Add / Remove Software. It's more informative if you start **pirut** from a GUI command line, as errors are shown in the command line terminal.

3. Under the Browse tab, you'll see the same package groups that you saw in Chapter 2 if you customized the packages to be installed.

4. Review available package groups on the Browse tab. Select an active package group, and click Optional Packages. For this exercise, select a package of your choice, which will be installed when you click Apply.

5. Click the List tab. Review the list of available packages. Packages that are already selected are currently installed. If you select or deselect a package, it will be installed or removed (with dependencies) when you click Apply.

6. Click the Search tab. Use a common search term such as *gnome* and watch as a long list of packages are shown. Use a less common search term such as *iptables*. Highlight a package and review it in the Package Details window.

7. Once you've selected some packages, click Apply. You'll see a window with a list of packages that you've selected for installation and removal. Click Continue.

8. If there are dependencies, you'll see a Dependencies Added window that lists those dependent packages that will also be installed or removed. Review the Details, and click Continue.

9. Wait as **pirut** downloads packages to be installed.

10. When the process is complete, you'll see a confirmation. Click OK, and then choose File | Quit to exit **pirut**.

CERTIFICATION OBJECTIVE 5.05

Using Kickstart to Automate Installation

Kickstart is Red Hat's solution for an automated installation of Red Hat. All the questions asked during setup can be automatically supplied with one text file. You can easily set up nearly identical systems very quickly. Kickstart files are useful for quick deployment and distribution of Linux systems.

INSIDE THE EXAM

Kickstart and the Red Hat Exams

For the Troubleshooting and System Maintenance portion of the exam, it's possible that the exam proctor might configure your computer using a customized kickstart configuration file. (It's possible that she might use another method such as a VMware snapshot.) The file might be local or it might be stored on the server. Understanding kickstart is a very useful skill that can help you install Linux on a number of different computers simultaneously. You can start the process and walk away. The options are rich and varied. The Red Hat Exam Prep guide suggests that you know how to configure "hands-free installation using Kickstart."

Whether or not you see kickstart labs on your exam, understanding how it works is an important administrative skill that I think Red Hat should include on its exams. You can check the bug status for yourself at https://bugzilla.redhat.com.

Kickstart Concepts

There are two methods for creating the required kickstart configuration file:

- Start with the anaconda-ks.cfg file from the root user's home directory, /root.
- Use the graphical Kickstart Configurator, accessible via the **system-config-kickstart** command.

The first option lets you use the kickstart template file created for your computer by Anaconda, the Red Hat Enterprise Linux installation program. The second option, the Kickstart Configurator, is discussed in detail later in this chapter.

If you're installing RHEL on a number of computers, the anaconda-ks.cfg file is handy. You can install RHEL the way you want on one computer. You can then use the anaconda-ks.cfg file from that computer as a template to install RHEL on the other identical computers on your network. If the computers aren't identical, you can customize each anaconda-ks.cfg file as required for elements such as a different hard disk size, host name, and so on.

Setting Up a Kickstart USB

Once the kickstart file is configured, the easiest way to use it is through the RHEL installation USB drive. Similar steps can be used if your system has a floppy drive. To do so, follow these basic steps:

1. Configure and edit the anaconda-ks.cfg file as desired. I'll describe this process in more detail shortly.

2. Insert and mount the image file for an installation boot CD or USB drive. These options are described in more detail in Chapter 2. If the drive doesn't mount automatically, you can then mount the drive with a command such as **mount /dev/cdrom /mnt**.

3. If you mounted a CD, insert a USB drive. Find the associated device with the **fdisk -l** command. Make a note of the device, such as /dev/sdb. You'll need it shortly.

4. If it doesn't mount automatically (as it should if you're in the GNOME desktop), mount it with a command such as **mount /dev/sdb /net**.

5. Copy the kickstart file to the top level directory of the USB drive. Make sure the file name on the USB drive is ks.cfg.

6. You should now be ready to try out the installation boot USB on a different computer. You'll get to try this again shortly in an exercise.

7. When you try the boot USB, you can start the kickstart installation from the aforementioned USB drive, possibly with the following command (some trial and error may be required):

```
boot: linux ks=hd:sdb1:/ks.cfg
```

Alternatively, if the kickstart file is on the boot CD, try

```
boot: linux ks=cdrom:/ks.cfg
```

Or if it's on the first floppy drive, try

```
boot: linux ks=hd:fd0:/ks.cfg
```

As long as you have a DHCP server on your network, you may be able to use the same USB key or even a 1.44MB floppy drive. Just boot each new Linux computer, type in the associated command such as **linux ks=floppy** at the boot prompt, give the computer a moment to read the ks.cfg file, and insert the same device in the next new Linux computer.

Configuring a Kickstart Server

Alternatively, you can configure a kickstart configuration file on the DHCP/BOOTP server for your network. If you want to put the file on a DHCP/BOOTP server, open the /etc/dhcpd.conf configuration file on that server. Specify the kickstart file. For example, if you've stored the appropriate kickstart file in the /usr/install directory on the DHCP server, add the **filename "/usr/install/"** command to dhcpd.conf. That prompts Anaconda to look on the server in the /usr/install directory for a *client_ip*-kickstart file, where the assigned IP address is substituted for *client_ip*.

For example, if the DHCP server assigns IP address 192.168.0.55, the installation looks for the kickstart file named 192.168.0.55-kickstart. If necessary, you can associate a specific IP address with a certain network card in the DHCP configuration file, as described in Chapter 13.

If the kickstart file is stored on a different server, add the **next-server** *servername* option to the dhcpd.conf configuration file. In this case, the *servername* is the name of the computer with the kickstart file.

on the **Job**

Red Hat is working on making it easier to create a kickstart-based installation server. For more information, see the Cobbler project at http://cobbler.et .redhat.com/.

Starting the Installation with a Kickstart File

No matter where you choose to put the kickstart file, you can boot with a USB key or a specialized installation CD. You can put the kickstart file on the boot media. Just copy the configuration file as ks.cfg from wherever you've saved your kickstart configuration file.

If you're booting from a CD, and the kickstart file is also on that CD, enter the following command at the **boot:** prompt. This assumes the ks.cfg file is in the top level directory of the CD.

```
boot: linux ks=cdrom:/ks.cfg
```

If you're booting from the Red Hat installation CD, you can still refer to a kickstart configuration file on a USB key or hard disk, respectively, possibly with one of the following commands:

```
boot: linux ks=hd:sdb:/ks.cfg
boot: linux ks=hd:hda2:/home/mj/ks.cfg
```

This assumes the kickstart configuration file is called ks.cfg and is located on the USB key detected as /dev/sdb, or the second partition of the first IDE drive in the /home/mj directory.

You don't need to get a kickstart file from a DHCP server. To boot from a specific NFS or HTTP server on the network, say with an IP address of 192.168.17.18, from the /kicks/ks.cfg file, type one of the following commands:

```
boot: linux ks=nfs:192.168.17.18:/kicks/ks.cfg
boot: linux ks=http:192.168.17.18:/kicks/ks.cfg
```

However, even if you've specified a static IP address in ks.cfg, this installation looks for IP address information from a DHCP server. If the information is not found, Anaconda continues with a standard installation, not using the kickstart file.

Sample Kickstart File

I've based this section on the anaconda-ks.cfg file created when I installed my RHEL Server. I've added a number of comments. While you're welcome to use it as a sample file, be sure to customize it for your hardware and network. This section just scratches the surface on what you can do with a kickstart file; your version of this file may vary.

While most of the options are self-explanatory, I've interspersed my explanation of each command within the file. This file illustrates just a small portion of available commands. For more information on each command (and options) in this file, read the latest RHEL System Administration Guide, which is available online at www .redhat.com/docs/manuals/enterprise.

Follow these ground rules and guidelines when setting up a kickstart file:

■ Do *not* change the order of the options.

■ You do not need to use all the options.

■ If you leave out a required option, the user will be prompted for the answer.

on the
job

If you leave out an option, you will be prompted to complete it. This is an easy way to see if your kickstart file is properly configured. But as some kickstart options change the partitions on your hard drive, even testing this file can delete all of the data on your computer. So it's safest to have a test computer (with no important data) such as a Xen or VMware machine available to test your kickstart configuration file.

Here is the code from my kickstart file. The first line is a comment that tells me that this file was created during the installation process:

```
# Kickstart file automatically generated by anaconda.
```

The first command is simple; it starts the installation process. It defaults to the first available local media; in this case, the first RHEL installation DVD/CD or USB key.

```
install
```

However, if you want to specify an installation, you could add the source of your choice on the next line. It could be **cdrom**, or if you're installing from an NFS server, you can specify it as follows. If you have the name of the server (and a reliable DNS), you can substitute it for the IP address.

```
nfs --server=192.168.0.4 --dir=/inst
```

You can also configure a connection to an FTP or HTTP server by substituting one of the commands shown here. The directories I specify are based on the FTP and HTTP installation servers created in Chapter 2:

```
url --url http://192.168.0.4/inst
```

or

```
url --url ftp://192.168.0.4/pub/inst
```

If the installation files (or even the ISOs) are on a local hard drive, you can specify that as well. For example, when I downloaded the RHEL CDs to my home directory on the /dev/sda10 drive and installed on a separate partition, it added the following directive to my anaconda-ks.cfg file:

```
harddrive --partition=/dev/sda10 --dir=/home/michael/
```

The **lang** command specifies the language to use during the installation process. It matters if the installation stops due to a missing command in this file. The **keyboard** command is self-explanatory, as it specifies the keyboard to configure on this computer.

```
lang en_US.UTF-8
keyboard us
```

The **network** command is a lot more straightforward if you have a DHCP server for your network; it would read **network --device eth0 --bootproto dhcp**. This particular line configures static IP address information, with the specified network mask (**--netmask**), gateway address (**--gateway**), DNS servers (**--nameserver**), and computer name (**--hostname**).

```
network --device eth0 --bootproto static --ip 192.168.0.44 --netmask 255.255.255.0
--gateway 192.168.0.1 --nameserver 192.168.0.1 --hostname enterprise5
```

Please note that all options for the **network** command *must* be on *one* line. Line wrapping, if the options exceed the space in your editor, is acceptable.

The **xconfig** command specifies the graphical configuration for this system. The switches are nearly self-explanatory. The **--driver** switch specifies the graphics card driver. The **--resolution** switch sets the default resolution for the monitor, with a given color **--depth** in bits. If you see **--startxonboot**, the system starts the GUI by default when you boot Linux.

```
xconfig --driver "i810" --resolution 800x600 --depth 24
```

You need to specify the root user password during the installation process. This line specifies the password in encrypted format. You don't have to encrypt the root password in this line. If needed, you can copy this password from /etc/shadow.

```
rootpw --iscrypted $1$5UrLfXTk$CsCW0nQytrUuvycuLT317/
```

As for security, the firewall is either **--enabled** or **--disabled**. If a port is to be open, it's also specified on this line; for example, **--port=22:tcp** specifies an open SSH port.

```
firewall --enabled
```

Open by default, the **authconfig** command sets up the Shadow Password Suite (**--enableshadow**) and MD5 encryption (**--enablemd5**).

```
authconfig --enableshadow --enablemd5
```

The **selinux** command can be set to **--enforcing**, **--permissive**, or **--disabled**.

```
selinux --enforcing
```

The **timezone** command is associated with a long list of timezones. If you've installed the SquirrelMail RPM, you can find a full list in /usr/share/squirrelmail/locale/timezones.cfg. If you want to set the hardware clock to the equivalent of Greenwich Mean Time, add the **--utc** switch.

```
timezone America/Los_Angeles
```

The default bootloader is GRUB. Naturally, it should normally be installed on the Master Boot Record (MBR) of a hard drive. You can include a **--driveorder** switch to specify the drive with the bootloader and an **--append** switch to specify commands for the kernel.

```
bootloader --location=mbr --driveorder=sda --append="rhgb quiet"

# The following is the partition information you requested
# Note that any partitions you deleted are not expressed
# here so unless you clear all partitions first, this is
# not guaranteed to work
#clearpart --linux --drives=sda
#part /boot --fstype ext3 --size=100 --ondisk=sda
#part raid.53 --size=1000
#part raid.51 --size=1000
#part raid.49 --size=1000
#part raid.45 --size=1000
#part raid.43 --size=1000
#part raid.41 --size=1000
#part raid.39 --size=1000
#part raid.37 --size=1000
#part raid.35 --size=1000
#part pv.25 --size=0 --grow --ondisk=sda
#raid /tmp --fstype ext3 --level=RAID6 --device=md0
    raid.45 raid.43 raid.41 raid.37 raid.35
#volgroup VolGroup00 --noformat --pesize=32768 pv.25
```

```
#logvol swap --fstype swap --name=LogVol01
    --vgname=VolGroup00 --size=960 --grow --maxsize=1920
#logvol /home --fstype ext3 --name=LogVol02
    --vgname=VolGroup00 --size=4992
#logvol / --fstype ext3 --name=LogVol00
    --vgname=VolGroup00 --size=9984
#logvol /var --fstype ext3 --name=LogVol03
    --vgname=VolGroup00 --size=4992
```

The following is a list of package groups that are installed through this kickstart configuration file. These names correspond to the names that you can find in the comps-rhel5-server-core.xml file described in Chapter 2.

By default, the commands that partition your hard drives are commented out of the anaconda-ks.cfg file. These options are a bit more complex, so I discuss them in more detail in the next section. If the commands work for you, don't forget to delete the comment character (**#**) to activate these commands. (Note that the directives that start with **raid** and **logvol** are line-wrapped.)

```
%packages
@ dialup
@ system-tools
```

After the package groups are installed, you can specify post-installation commands (**%post**) in the kickstart installation file:

```
%post
```

Kickstart Partitioning

The partitioning options in the kickstart file are a bit complex. They can give you full control of the partitioning options, too. You can clear all partitions with **clearpart --all**, or just clear any Linux-type partitions with **clearpart --linux**, or just add partitions to existing free hard drive space. You can create partitions on more than one drive, but you need to identify each device specifically.

To add Linux partitions, use the **part** command with the following syntax:

```
part mount_dir --size=size [--grow] [--maxsize=size]
```

The *size* is in megabytes. You can use the **--grow** option to allow the partition to expand and fill all remaining disk space (or share it with any other partitions marked **grow** on the same disk). This will not expand on the fly, but instead, when all fixed-size partitions are added, these "growable" partitions will use the remaining free space.

If you specify multiple partitions with the **--grow** option, their space will be divided evenly. You can also specify a **--maxsize**, which will allow the partition to grow only to the size specified in megabytes.

The following commands from my kickstart configuration file (with comment characters remove) perform the following tasks.

The **clearpart** command removes all of the partitions on the first SATA or SCSI hard drive:

```
clearpart --all --drives=sda
```

This first **part** command configures the /boot directory to the ext3 filesystem with 100MB of space on the first SATA/SCSI hard drive:

```
part /boot --fstype ext3 --size=100 --ondisk=sda
```

The next several **part** commands specify RAID devices. The **raid.53** is an arbitrary number. The **--size** designation is straightforward, in MB.

```
#part raid.53 --size=1000
```

After the RAID partitions, an LVM partition is specified as growable (**--grow**) on the first IDE drive:

```
#part pv.25 --size=0 --grow --ondisk=hda
```

Now I configure a RAID device for the /tmp directory, configured to RAID 6 (**--level=RAID6**), set to **--device** name **md0**, using RAID partitions **raid.45**, **raid.43**, **raid.41**, **raid.37**, and **raid.35**.

```
#raid /tmp --fstype ext3 --level=RAID6
    --device=md0 raid.45 raid.43 raid.41 raid.37 raid.35
```

Next, I configure a volume group, followed by configuring logical volumes for a swap, /home, root (/), and /var partitions of the noted sizes:

```
#volgroup VolGroup00 --noformat --pesize=32768 pv.25
#logvol swap --fstype swap --name=LogVol01
    --vgname=VolGroup00 --size=960 --grow --maxsize=1920
#logvol /home --fstype ext3 --name=LogVol02
    --vgname=VolGroup00 --size=4992
#logvol / --fstype ext3 --name=LogVol100
    --vgname=VolGroup00 --size=9984
#logvol /var --fstype ext3 --name=LogVol03
    --vgname=VolGroup00 --size=4992
```

Alternatively, I could specify a **part** command for the root directory (/), formatted to the ext3 filesystem, on partition /dev/sda5. If more room is available, this partition expands to fill the available space.

```
part / --fstype ext3 --onpart=sda5
```

EXERCISE 5-2

Creating a Sample Kickstart File

In this exercise, you will use the anaconda-ks.cfg file to duplicate the installation from one computer to another with identical hardware. This exercise installs all the exact same packages with the same partition configuration on the second computer. Assume that both computers use DHCP to set up their IP addresses. To the existing partitions, add one /home partition of 2000MB and a 512MB swap partition. In other words, on the second computer, you'll need at least 2.5GB *more* free space than on the first computer.

You want to install all the same packages as your current installation, so you do not need to make any package changes to the default anaconda kickstart file in the /root directory. This assumes you can boot from a CD and have a USB drive. If you do not have multiple computers for this exercise, alternatives include VMware and Xen. If you don't have a USB drive, you can substitute a floppy drive.

1. Review the /root/anaconda-ks.cfg file. Copy it to ks.cfg.
2. Insert the USB key. Run the **fdisk -l** command to find the USB device, such as /dev/hdb. If it isn't automatically mounted, use the device file to mount it.
3. Copy the ks.cfg file to the mounted USB key.
4. Prepare the second computer so that it has at least 2.5GB more unused and unpartitioned space than the first computer. Reboot the second computer with the Linux boot file with the kickstart file in the USB key and the first binary CD (or boot CD) in the CD-ROM drive.
5. At the Red Hat Installation menu boot prompt, enter the following startup command. If the device file associated with the USB key is different, or if you're using a floppy drive, substitute accordingly.

```
boot: linux ks=hd:hdb:/ks.cfg
```

You should now see the system installation creating the same basic setup as the first system. The difference should correspond to the different partitions. Depending on how you installed Linux on the original computer, you may need a network connection to the same installation source or the other installation CDs.

OPTIONAL EXERCISE 5-3

Modifying the Packages to be Installed

Edit the ks.cfg file on the USB key and add one more package group. For a list
of package group names, consult the comps-rhel5-server-core.xml file in the first
installation CD's /Server/repodata subdirectory. (If you're working with the RHEL 5
desktop, substitute *Client* for *Server*.) Alternatively, set up an interactive installation
so that you can test and observe the result on another computer.

---

on the *job*   *In the KDE desktop, the default command line terminal is* **konsole,** *which has
modest differences from* **gnome-terminal.**

The Kickstart Configurator

Now that you understand the basics of what goes into a kickstart file, it's time to
solidify your understanding through the graphical Kickstart Configurator. When
you experiment with this GUI tool, you can learn more about what happens in the
kickstart configuration file.

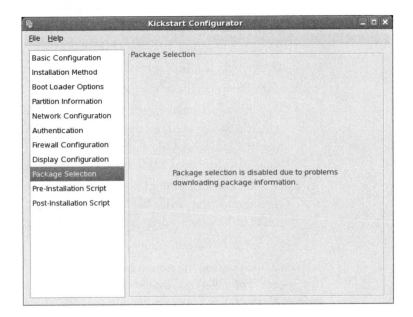

FIGURE 5-3

The Kickstart
Configurator
doesn't quite
work.

INSIDE THE EXAM

For Administrators from Other Unix-style Distributions

Linux is not the only operating system developed in the style of Unix. There are a number of other important Unix-style operating systems in the computing world, including, but not limited to, Solaris, HP-UX, AIX, IRIX, or even SCO UNIX. A substantial number of candidates for the Red Hat exams learn their skills on these operating systems.

The Red Hat exams test your skills on *Red Hat* Enterprise Linux. While many Unix skills are transferable to the exam, many features are unique to RHEL. While you can configure anything in Linux from the command line interface, Red Hat has created a number of administrative tools that you can use only in the GUI.

Based on the nature of the published Red Hat Exam Prep guide, you'll almost certainly be installing a GUI during the installation portion of the exam. When you install the GUI, you'll also have access to the tools developed by Red Hat. You can also access the command line interface in the GUI with a right-click, which opens a pop-up menu. In GNOME, you can click Open Terminal; in KDE, you can click Konsole. Alternatively, you can choose KDE

Main Menu | System | Terminal or GNOME Applications | Accessories | Terminal to open the same command line interface.

You can then start the Red Hat tool of your choice from the command line; most of these utilities start with **system-config-***. To see a full list, type **system-** at the command line and press the TAB key twice. Alternatively, from the GNOME desktop, you can start a number of these tools from the GNOME System menu (or KDE Main Menu), under the Administration submenu.

On the other hand, the GUI may not be available during the Troubleshooting and System Maintenance portion of either exam. So while the GUI tools can be helpful, you still need to know what to do from the command line interface.

If you're confident in your skills editing the Linux text configuration files, don't bother with the GUI tools. It's faster to edit Linux text configuration files directly in any Unix-style operating system. However, if you get nervous on exams or are uncertain of your skills and a GUI tool is available, learn to use the appropriate GUI tools. This can be a lifesaver during the exam.

As of this writing, I recommend that you *do not* use the Kickstart Configurator, at least until Package Selection is no longer disabled, as shown in Figure 5-3. I believe it's one of the problems left over in the transition from **up2date** to **yum**.

To start the Kickstart Configurator, go into the Linux GUI. Open a command line interface shell. Start the Kickstart Configurator with the **system-config-kickstart** command. (If the command is not found, you'll need to install the RPM of the same name.) Alternatively, in the GNOME desktop, choose Applications | System Tools | Kickstart. The following sections should look familiar, as they are closely related to the RHEL installation menus.

The first screen in Figure 5-4 illustrates a number of basic installation steps. If you've installed RHEL or Red Hat Linux, all of these steps should look familiar.

As you can see, a number of other options appear in the left-hand pane, each associated with different kickstart commands. To learn more about kickstart, experiment with some of these settings. Use the File | Save command to save these settings with the file name of your choice, which you can then review in a text editor. Alternatively, you can choose File | Preview to see the effect of different settings on the kickstart file.

The following sections provide a brief overview of each option shown in the left-hand pane. I'm guessing it's unlikely that you'll have to know kickstart in this level of detail on the Red Hat exams, at least until bug 217165 is addressed. However, an understanding of the Kickstart Configurator can help you understand the installation process, which is important on the installation part of each exam.

FIGURE 5-4

The Kickstart Configurator

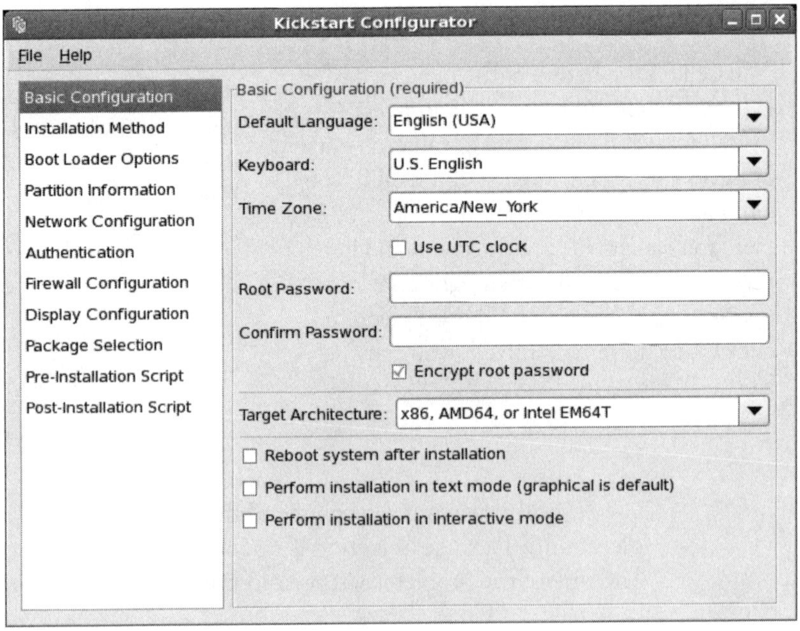

on the **job**

If you need to customize package groups, don't use a GUI Kickstart Configurator version before RHEL 5.1 (update 1) is released. As of this writing, bug 217165 (https://bugzilla.redhat.com) won't be addressed until that release. If you use a Kickstart Configurator version before that, it will overwrite the kickstart file that you've previously created.

Basic Configuration

In the Basic Configuration screen, you can assign settings for the following components:

- **Default Language**   The default language for the installation and operating system.
- **Keyboard**   Also normally associated with language.
- **Time Zone**   Supports computers in which the hardware clock is set to the atomic realization of UTC, which corresponds closely to Greenwich Mean Time.
- **Root Password**   Can be encrypted in the kickstart file.
- **Target Architecture**   Can help you customize a kickstart file for different systems.
- **Reboot System After Installation**   Adds the **reboot** command to the end of the kickstart file.
- **Perform System Installation In Text Mode**   Supports automated installation in text mode.
- **Perform Installation In Interactive Mode**   Allows you to test the steps associated with a kickstart installation.

Installation Method

The Installation Method options are straightforward. You're either installing Linux for the first time or upgrading a previous installation. The installation method, and your entries, are based on the location of the installation files. For example, if you select an NFS installation method, the Kickstart Configurator prompts you for the name or IP address of the NFS server and the shared directory with the RHEL installation files.

You can set up your kickstart file to install RHEL from a CD/DVD, a local hard drive partition, or one of the standard network servers: NFS, HTTP, or FTP.

Boot Loader Options

The next section lists boot loader options. The default boot loader is GRUB, which supports passwords for an additional level of security during the boot process.

Linux boot loaders are normally installed on the MBR. If you're dual-booting Linux and Microsoft Windows with GRUB, you *can* set up the Windows boot loader (or an alternate boot loader such as Partition Magic or System Commander) to point to GRUB on the first sector of the Linux partition with the /boot directory. Kernel parameters allow you to pass commands to the kernel through the GRUB configuration file as described earlier in this chapter.

Partition Information

The Partition Information options determine how this installation configures the hard disks on the affected computers. While it supports the configuration of standard and RAID partitions, it does not yet support the configuration of LVM groups. The Clear Master Boot Record option allows you to wipe the MBR from an older hard disk that might have a problem there; it sets up the **zerombr yes** command in the kickstart file.

on the job

Don't use the **zerombr yes** *option if you want to keep an alternate bootloader on the MBR such as Partition Magic or the NT Boot Loader.*

You can remove partitions depending on whether they've been created to a Linux filesystem. If you're using a new hard drive, you'll want to Initialize the Disk Label as well. Click the Add command; it opens the Partition Options dialog box. As you can see in Figure 5-5, this corresponds to the Anaconda Add Partition dialog box shown back in Chapter 2.

FIGURE 5-5

Using the Kickstart Configurator to set up partitions

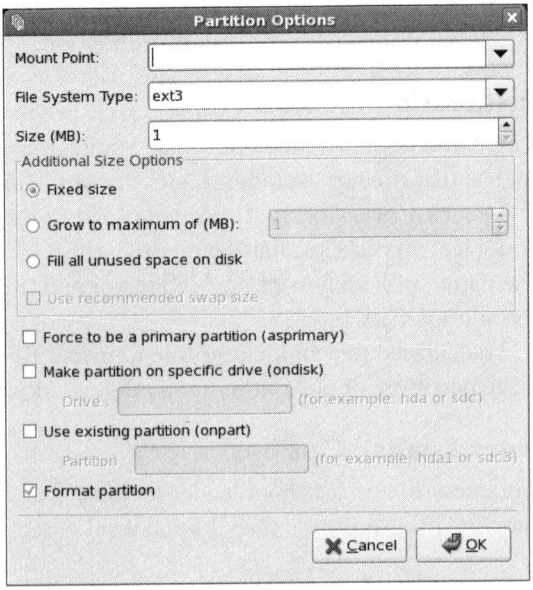

Network Configuration

The Network Configuration section enables you to set up IP addressing on the network cards on a target computer. You can customize static IP addressing for a specific computer, or you can configure the use of a DHCP server. You can also make kickstart look for a BOOTP server, which is a specially configured DHCP server on a remote network.

Authentication

The Authentication section lets you set up two forms of security for user passwords: Shadow Passwords, which encrypts user passwords in the /etc/shadow file, and MD5 encryption. This section also allows you to set up authentication information for various protocols:

- **NIS** Network Information Service for one login database on a network with Unix and Linux computers on a network.
- **LDAP** The Lightweight Directory Assistance Protocol is used for certain types of databases such as directories.
- **Kerberos 5** The MIT system for strong cryptography to authenticate users on a network.
- **Hesiod** Associated with Kerberos 5.
- **SMB** Samba (CIFS) allows configuration of your Linux computer on a Microsoft Windows–based network.
- **Name Switch Cache** Associated with NIS for looking up passwords and groups.

Firewall Configuration

The Firewall Configuration section allows you to configure a default firewall for the subject computer. Generally, you'll want a firewall only for those computers that are connected to outside networks such as the Internet.

In this section, you can also configure basic SELinux settings. The Active and Disabled options are straightforward; the Warn option corresponds to a Permissive implementation of SELinux. For more information, see Chapter 15.

Display Configuration

The Display Configuration section allows you to configure the Linux GUI. While there is a lot of debate on the superiority of GUI- or text-based administrative tools, text-based tools are more stable. For this reason (and more), many Linux administrators don't even install a GUI. However, if you're installing Linux on a series of computers, it's likely that most of the users won't be administrators.

In this section are three tabs. Under the General tab, you can set a default color depth and resolution, indicate a default desktop (GNOME or KDE), configure the X Window to start by default, and disable or enable the Setup Agent (the First Boot process). Under the Video Card and Monitor tabs, you can set Linux to probe your hardware or specify the hardware from a list. If you want to do something fancy such as specifying multiple resolutions, you'll need to modify the ks.cfg file directly.

Package Selection

The Package Selection section allows you to choose the package groups that are installed through this kickstart file. You should recognize it as the custom installation screens shown during the installation process.

Package Selection doesn't work in the GUI Kickstart Configurator for RHEL 5 and isn't scheduled to be fixed until the first update, scheduled three months after the first release of RHEL 5.

Installation Scripts

You can add preinstallation and post-installation scripts to the kickstart file. Post-installation scripts are more common, and they can help you configure other parts of a Linux operating system in a common way. For example, if you wanted to install a directory with employee benefits information, you could add a post-installation script that adds the appropriate cp commands to copy files from a network server.

CERTIFICATION SUMMARY

This chapter covered the management of RPM packages. You learned how to add, remove, and upgrade packages, and how to add updates—locally and remotely. It's important to upgrade kernels by installing them, side by side with currently working kernels.

You also learned how to query packages, examine to which package a file belongs, the steps necessary to validate a package signature, and how to find the current list of installed RPMs. You also read about installing and building source RPMs.

If you have an RHEL subscription, you can keep your system up to date through the RHN. You can install more packages from the RHN or configured repositories using **yum**. Alternatively, you can connect to the same repositories using tools such as **pirut**. In either case, **yum** provides automatic dependency resolution, which simplifies the installation and update process.

You can automate your entire installation with kickstart. Every RHEL system has a kickstart template file in the /root directory, which you can modify and use to install RHEL on other systems automatically. Alternatively, you can use the GUI Kickstart Configurator to create an appropriate kickstart file.

TWO-MINUTE DRILL

Here are some of the key points from the certification objectives in Chapter 5.

The Red Hat Package Manager

❏ The RPM database tracks where each file in a package is located, its version, and much more.

❏ Verifying an installed package confirms the integrity based on the RPM database.

❏ The Install mode of RPM installs RPM packages on your system; a newly installed kernel is loaded side by side with a previously installed kernel.

❏ The Upgrade mode of RPM replaces the old version of the package with the new one.

More RPM Commands

❏ The **rpm -e** command (erase) removes a package from your system.

❏ The **rpm** command query mode (**-q**) determines whether packages are installed on your system or files are associated with a particular package.

❏ Source RPMs, as the name indicates, contain the source code used to build architecture-specific packages.

❏ The spec file loaded in /usr/src/redhat/SPECS/packagename.spec controls the way a package is built and what actions are performed when it is installed or removed from a system.

❏ Run **rpmbuild -ba** *packagename*.**spec** to build your binary and source RPM.

Managing Updates with Pup and the Red Hat Network

❏ Before connecting to the RHN, you need to register your system.

❏ The Package Updater, Pup, can help you keep systems up to date.

❏ With automatic dependency resolution, **yum** and the RHN help install dependencies along with desired packages.

❏ The RHN can help you manage subscribed systems remotely using a Web-based interface.

Adding and Removing RPM Packages with yum and pirut

❏ The **yum** command can help install a group of packages from the RHN or repositories configured in the /etc/yum.repos.d directory.

❑ The **pirut** tool can help you add and remove packages and complete package groups from your system.

Using Kickstart to Automate Installation

❑ Kickstart is Red Hat's solution for an automated simultaneous installation on several computers.

❑ Kickstart installations can be configured to take installation files from a CD-ROM, a local drive, an NFS, an FTP, or an HTTP server.

❑ There are two ways to create a kickstart file: from the configuration when you installed Linux as documented in the /root/anaconda-ks.cfg file, or from the GUI Kickstart Configurator.

SELF TEST

The following questions will help you measure your understanding of the material presented in this chapter. As no multiple choice questions appear on the Red Hat exams, no multiple choice questions appear in this book. These questions exclusively test your understanding of the chapter. It is okay if you have another way of performing a task. Getting results, not memorizing trivia, is what counts on the Red Hat exams. There may be more than one answer to many of these questions.

The Red Hat Package Manager

1. What command would you use to install the penguin-3.26.i386.rpm package, with extra messages in case of errors? The package is on the local directory.

   _____

2. What command would you use to upgrade the penguin RPM with the penguin-3.27.i386.rpm package? The package is on the ftp.remotemj02.abc server.

   _____

3. If you've downloaded a later version of the Linux kernel to the local directory, and it's kernel-2.6.19.el5.i386.rpm, what's the best way to make it a part of your system?

   _____

More RPM Commands

4. What command lists all installed RPMs? What about the RPMs installed when you first installed the local system?

   _____
   _____

5. Assume you have the rpm-build RPM installed. When you install a source RPM, in what directory (and subdirectories) will you find key files?

   _____

6. If you've downloaded an RPM from a third party and called it third.i386.rpm, how would you validate the associated package signature?

   _____

Managing with Pup and the Red Hat Network

7. If you want official updates for RHEL, to where should you connect your RHEL system?

   _____

Adding and Removing RPM Packages with yum and pirut

8. Name at least two tools that can help you download and install updates from the RHN.

_____

_____

9. What **yum** command installs the latest Linux kernel?

_____

Using Kickstart to Automate Installation

10. You're using the Kickstart Configurator to create a ks.cfg file for several computers. Interpret the following directive:

```
part /var --size 1000 --grow yes
```

11. If your kickstart installation file is on the local CD, and you boot from the USB drive, what would you type at the **boot:** prompt to start the kickstart installation?

_____

12. If your kickstart installation file is on the local hard drive in /dev/sda7, on the top-level directory on that partition, and you boot from the USB drive, what would you type at the **boot:** prompt to start the kickstart installation?

_____

LAB QUESTIONS

The Red Hat exams are unique based on their reliance on labs and hands-on demonstrations. With these questions, you're practicing the skills you need on both Red Hat exams.

Lab 1

In this lab, you'll examine what happens when you update a kernel RPM by installing it side by side with an existing kernel. If a newer kernel is not available, the kernel-xen package, or even an older kernel, will serve the purpose for this lab. Just remember, if you don't want the kernel that you install during this lab, make sure to remove the package properly from your system.

1. Make a copy of your existing GRUB configuration file, /boot/grub/grub.conf. Print it out or copy it to your home directory.

2. Make a copy of the current file list in the /boot directory. One method uses the **ls /boot > bootlist** command, which writes the file list to the bootlist file.

3. If a newer kernel is available, and you're connected to the RHN or another appropriate repository, run the following command:

```
# yum install kernel
```

Alternatively, if you want to install the Xen-based kernel (which requires access to a Virtualization repository, through the RHN or an appropriate file in the /etc/yum.repos.d/ directory), you can run

```
# yum install kernel-xen
```

Another alternative is to download and install the RPM. Just be sure to use the **-i** switch to install the new kernel; otherwise, the command overwrites the existing kernel. (If you're installing an older kernel, you'll have to add the **--force** switch.)

4. Check the results in your GRUB configuration file, /boot/grub/grub.conf. Observe the differences versus the old GRUB configuration file, which you saved in step 1. What is the default kernel? If you happened to install an older kernel, is the default what you expected?

5. Check the results in your /boot directory. Observe the differences with the original list of files in the /boot directory.

Lab 2

Generally, the only reason you need to install a kernel source RPM is if you absolutely need to recompile the kernel. Drivers can often be compiled using the kernel-devel package. However, if you need the source code, you may have to download it directly from the repository associated with your distribution. If you're running RHEL 5, that's available through your RHN subscription or ftp .redhat.com. If you're running Fedora Core, you'll need to activate the applicable source repository. If you're running a rebuild, you may need to download the kernel-*versionnum*.src.rpm directly from the repositories associated with that rebuild.

While "rebuilds" are supposed to use the same source code as Red Hat, there is no guarantee as such. I've run into trouble when mixing the source code released with different rebuild distributions. So it's best if you download the source code from the associated repositories.

Once you download the source RPM, you can install it with the **rpm -ivh kernel-*versionnum*.src .rpm** command, but that just starts the process of unpacking the source code. You'll need the **rpmbuild** command, available from the rpm-build RPM. You can then navigate to the /usr/src/redhat/SPECS directory, and use the **rpmbuild -bb** command to unpack the source code to different directories in the /usr/src/redhat/BUILD/ directory tree.

But wait, the kernel source code already seems to be in the /usr/src/kernels directory, in a subdirectory named for the kernel version. However, this source code is not complete; it's intended only for building drivers, and if you want to recompile a kernel, you still need to apply the **rpmbuild -bb** command to the kernel-2.6.spec file in the /usr/src/redhat/SPECS directory.

Lab 3

This lab may not be possible unless updates are available from your repository or the RHN. In this lab, you'll examine what happens when you run an update to upgrade to newer versions of packages available for new features, to address security issues, and more. Before you start, run the following command to clear the cache, so you get the full set of messages:

```
# yum clean all
```

Run the following command to send the messages to a text file:

```
# yum update > update.txt
```

If a lot of updates are available, this process may take some time. If you want to watch, you can run the following command:

```
# tail -f update.txt
```

If you want to download and install the updates, use the **-y** switch, which answers "yes" to all prompts. The complete command becomes

```
# yum update -y > update.txt
```

After the download and installation is complete, review the update.txt file. Note the first messages, how plug-ins are installed from the /etc/yum/pluginconf.d/ directory. Note how it loads information from the repositories, downloads headers, and resolves dependencies.

Once dependencies are resolved, examine where the downloads come from. Note how some packages are installed and how others are updated.

Lab 4

In this lab, you'll get a chance to use the configuration for your current system to kickstart an installation of a second system. Ideally, you'll have a VMware or Xen virtual machine available for the process, with an identical amount of free space and hardware as the current system. Otherwise, this lab may not work.

Open the anaconda-ks.cfg file in the current installation of RHEL. Remove the comments as appropriate from the directives associated with partitions and filesystems. Configure an installation boot CD or USB key, depending on what you can boot from your system. Copy the revised kickstart file to ks.cfg, and write it to appropriate media, even a floppy drive if available.

Make sure the same source you used for the original installation (network, hard drive, CD/DVD) is still available. Boot the new system to test the installation.

SELF TEST ANSWERS

The Red Hat Package Manager

1. The command that installs the penguin-3.26.i386.rpm package, with extra messages in case of errors, from the local directory, is

```
# rpm -iv penguin-3.26.i386.rpm
```

2. The command that upgrades the aforementioned penguin RPM with the penguin-3.27.i386.rpm package from the ftp.remotemj02.abc server is

```
# rpm -Uv ftp://ftp.remotemj02.abc/penguin-3.26.i386.rpm
```

If you use the default vsFTP server, the package may be in the pub/ subdirectory. In other words, the command would be

```
# rpm -Uv ftp://ftp.remotemj02.abc/pub/penguin-3.26.i386.rpm
```

Yes, the question is not precise. But that's what you see in real life.

3. If you've downloaded a later version of the Linux kernel to the local directory, and it's kernel-2.6.18-8.4.4.el5.i386.rpm, the best way to make it a part of your system is to install it—and not upgrade the current kernel. Kernel upgrades overwrite existing kernels. Kernel installations allow kernels to exist side by side; if the new kernel doesn't work, you can still boot into the working kernel. So you'd use a command like this:

```
# rpm -iv kernel-2.6.18-8.4.4.el5.i386.rpm
```

More RPM Commands

4. The command that lists all installed RPMs is

```
# rpm -qa
```

The file that lists the RPMs installed when you first installed the local system is /root/install.log. The /var/log/rpmpkgs file is complete but is updated only once per day.

5. When you install a source RPM, the directory in which key files are stored is /usr/src/redhat. One important file is the spec file associated with the RPM in the /usr/src/redhat/SPECS directory.

6. If you've downloaded an RPM from a third party, call it third.i386.rpm, you'll first need to download and install the RPM-GPG-KEY file associated with that repository. You can then validate the associated package signature with a command like (note the uppercase **-V**):

```
# rpm -V third.i386.rpm
```

Managing with Pup and the Red Hat Network

7. If you want official updates for RHEL, you should connect your RHEL system to the Red Hat Network.

Adding and Removing RPM Packages with yum and Pirut

8. Three tools can help you download and install updates from the RHN: Pup, **pirut**, and **yum**.

9. This **yum** command installs a later available version of the Linux kernel:

```
# yum install kernel
```

If you're working with a Xen-based kernel, the command is slightly different:

```
# yum install kernel-xen
```

Using Kickstart to Automate Installation

10. The following directive in ks.cfg configures a partition for the /var directory, of at least 1000MB, but growable—which means it can take up the remaining free space.

```
part /var --size 1000 --grow yes
```

11. If your kickstart installation file is on the local CD, and you boot from the USB drive, type the following at the **boot:** prompt to start the kickstart installation:

```
linux ks=cdrom:/ks.cfg
```

12. If your kickstart installation file is on the local hard drive in /dev/sda7, on the top-level directory, and you boot from the USB drive, type the following command at the **boot:** prompt to start the kickstart installation:

```
linux ks=hd:sda7:/ks.cfg
```

LAB ANSWERS

Lab 1

This lab is somewhat self-explanatory and is intended to help you explore what happens when you properly install a new kernel RPM. As with other Linux distributions, when you install (and do not use upgrade mode) for a new kernel, two areas are affected.

The new kernel is added as a new option in the GRUB configuration menu. Unless you've installed an older kernel, the default boot option does not change. However, when you reboot, you'll be able to select the new kernel from the GRUB menu.

When you review the /boot directory, all of the previously installed boot files should be there. The new kernel RPM should add matching versions of all of the same files—with different revision numbers (unless it's a Xen-based kernel).

To keep this all straight, it helps if you made copies of the original versions of the GRUB configuration file and the file list in the /boot directory.

Lab 2

This lab can help you prepare for Chapter 8, where you'll recompile the Linux kernel. Red Hat no longer provides a binary RPM for the source code. The process for installing a kernel source code RPM is subtly different from other source code RPMs, as it loads the source code into unique directories.

Lab 3

This lab is intended to help you examine what the **yum update** command can do. It's the essential front end to other update tools, namely Pup. As you can see from the update.txt file created in this lab, the messages show you how **yum** looks for all newer packages from configured repositories or the RHN, downloads their headers, and uses them to check for dependencies that also need to be downloaded and installed.

Lab 4

For a lab like this, it's critical that you have a *second* system in which you don't mind losing all data. VMware and Xen are excellent options for this purpose. If successful, the kickstart installation you create and run will erase all data on that second system (unless specially configured). If space is limited, you can certainly delete the virtual machine files associated with this second system after installation.

6

User Administration

CERTIFICATION OBJECTIVES

6.01   User Account Management

6.02   The Basic User Environment

6.03   Shell Configuration Files

6.04   Setting Up and Managing Disk Quotas

6.05   Creating and Maintaining Special Groups

6.06   Pluggable Authentication Modules

6.07   Network Authentication Configuration: NIS and LDAP

✓   Two-Minute Drill

Q&A   Self Test

For the Red Hat exams, the skills you learn in this chapter are important for the Installation and Configuration portion of each exam. As described in the Red Hat Exam Prep guide, you need to know how to manage accounts and set up the user environment.

As part of learning how to set up the user environment, you will learn how to set up the Linux startup shell configuration scripts so that users' sessions are configured according to your (and their) requirements. You will learn how to create and implement policies for managing disk usage—by user or by group. Special groups can help users share files securely.

There are different ways to secure your system and network. The PAM (Pluggable Authentication Modules) system lets you configure how users are allowed to log in or access different services. The Network Information Service (NIS) and the Lightweight Directory Access Protocol (LDAP) can provide a common database of authentication and configuration files for your network.

INSIDE THE EXAM

This chapter addresses four items as listed in the Red Hat Exam Prep guide. Three are associated with the Installation and Configuration section of the RHCT exam requirements:

- Attach system to a network directory service, such as NIS or LDAP.
- Add and manage users, groups, and quotas, and File Access Control Lists.
- Configure filesystem permissions for collaboration.

(File Access Control Lists were already addressed in Chapter 4.)

Remember that if you're studying for the RHCE, you have to know all the RHCT

requirements. In addition, one item in this chapter is associated with the Installation and Configuration section of the RHCE exam requirements:

- Use PAM to implement user-level restrictions.

When you take the Red Hat exams, as long as you don't cheat, it generally does not matter how you come to a solution. For example, you get the same credit whether you add users by directly editing /etc/passwd using commands such as **useradd** or by using GUI tools such as the Red Hat User Manager (**system-config-users**). As in the real world, it is the results that matter.

CERTIFICATION OBJECTIVE 6.01

User Account Management

You need to know how to create and configure users for the Red Hat exams. This means that you need to know how to configure the environment associated with each user account—in configuration files and in user settings. You also need to know how to specify the configuration files associated with the default bash shell. Finally, you need to know how to limit the resources allocated to each user through quotas. These requirements are all explicitly cited in the Red Hat course outlines associated with the RHCT exam and are applicable to both exams.

If you've installed RHEL 5 via kickstart or in text mode, the default Red Hat installation gives you just a single login account: root. You should set up some regular user accounts. You may have already done so through the First Boot process described in Chapter 2. Even if you're going to be the only user on the system, it's a good idea to create at least one nonadministrative account to do your day-to-day work. Then you can use the root account only when it's necessary to administer the system. Accounts can be added to Red Hat Enterprise Linux systems using various utilities, including application of the vi text editor (and related specialized commands) on password configuration files (the manual method), the **useradd** command (the command line method), and the Red Hat User Manager utility (the graphical method).

exam

ⓦatch

As discussed earlier, it's faster to log in as root (and not just the superuser). While you'll be doing most of the work on the Red Hat exams as root, it's quite possible that you'll be asked to create accounts for regular users (and groups) to configure a workstation.

User Account Categories

There are three basic types of Linux user accounts: administrative (root), regular, and service. The administrative root account is automatically created when you install Linux, and it has administrative privileges for all services on your Linux computer. A cracker who has a chance to take control of this account can take full control of your system.

Nevertheless, it is sometimes appropriate to log in as an administrator (that is, as the root user), such as during most of the Red Hat exams. Red Hat Enterprise Linux builds in safeguards for root users. Log in as the root user, and then run the **alias** command. You'll see entries such as this,

```
alias rm='rm -i'
```

which prompt for confirmation before the **rm** command deletes a file. Unfortunately, a command such as **rm -rf** *directoryname* supersedes this safety setting.

Regular users have the necessary privileges to perform standard tasks on a Linux computer. They can access programs such as word processors, databases, and Web browsers. They can store files in their own home directories. Since regular users do not normally have administrative privileges, they cannot accidentally delete critical operating system configuration files. You can assign a regular account to most users, safe in the knowledge that they can't disrupt your system with the privileges they have on that account.

Services such as Apache, Squid, mail, games, and printing have their own individual service accounts. These accounts exist to allow each of these services to interact with your computer. Normally, you won't need to change any service account, but if you see that someone has logged in through one of these accounts, be wary. Someone may have broken into your system.

One resource for checking whether your system has been cracked is the Distributed Intrusion Detection System at www.dsheild.org. Check your public IP address against its database. If your system has been cracked, it's likely that someone is using it to attack other systems. When this is the case, your public IP address will be logged in the www.dsheild.org database.

To review recent logins, run the utmpdump /var/log/wtmp | less command. If the login is from a remote location, it will be associated with a specific IP address outside your network.

Basic Command Line Tools

There are two basic ways to add users through the command line interface. You can add users directly by editing the /etc/passwd file in a text editor such as vi. Alternatively, you can use text commands customized for the purpose.

Adding Users Directly

Open the /etc/passwd file in the text editor of your choice. If you choose to open it in the vi editor, you can do so with the **vipw** command. If you've added regular users to your system, you'll normally see them listed at the bottom of this file. Scroll around this file, and you should see a series of lines like the following:

```
mj:x:500:500:Michael Jang:/home/mj:/bin/bash
```

Each column in /etc/passwd, delineated by a colon, has a purpose, which is described in Table 6-1.

You can create a new user in /etc/passwd by copying and then editing a line associated with an existing user. Just substitute the information of your choice to create the new user. Make sure that you at least assign a new username and user ID.

Assuming you've assigned a new home directory for your new user, you have to remember to create that directory. For example, if your new user is ez, you'll probably want to create the /home/ez directory. You'll also need to make sure that ez has ownership permissions on that directory and all the files that you're going to put in that directory.

You can then populate that new user's home directory. A default environment is available in the /etc/skel directory. You can copy the contents of that directory to the new user's home directory. The /etc/skel directory is covered in more detail later in this chapter.

Adding Users to a Group

Every Linux user is assigned to a group. By default in RHEL 5, every user gets his own private group. The user is the only member of that group, as defined in the /etc/

| TABLE 6-1 | The Anatomy of /etc/passwd |

Field	Example	Purpose
Username	mj	The user logs in with this name. Usernames can include hyphens (-) or underscores (_). However, they should not start with a number or include uppercase letters.
Password	x	The password. You should see either an *x*, an asterisk (*), or a seemingly random group of letters and numbers. An *x* points to /etc/shadow for the actual password. An asterisk means the account is disabled. A random group of letters and numbers represents the encrypted password.
User ID	500	The unique numeric user ID (UID) for that user. By default, Red Hat starts user IDs at 500.
Group ID	500	The numeric group ID (GID) associated with that user. By default, RHEL creates a new group for every new user, and the number matches the UID. Some other Linux and Unix systems assign all users to the default Users group (GID=100).
User info	Michael Jang	You can enter any information of your choice in this field. Standard options include the user's full name, telephone number, e-mail address, or physical location. You can leave this blank.
Home Directory	/home/mj	By default, RHEL places new home directories in /home/*username*.
Login Shell	/bin/bash	By default, RHEL assigns users to the bash shell. You can change this to any legal shell that you have installed.

group configuration file. Open that file in the editor of your choice. If want to use the vi editor, use the **vipw** command. You should see lines similar to the following:

```
mj:x:500:
vp:x:501:
managers:x:1000:mj,vp
```

The contents are straightforward. The users mj and vp are members of their own groups as well as the managers group. The four columns in each /etc/group line are described in Table 6-2.

Adding Users at the Command Line

Alternatively, you can automate this process with the **useradd** command. If you wanted to add a new user named pm, you could just type **useradd pm** to add this user to the /etc/passwd file. By default, it creates a home directory, /home/pm; adds the standard files from the /etc/skel directory; and assigns the default shell, /bin/bash. But **useradd** is versatile. It includes a number of command options shown in Table 6-3.

Assigning a Password

You can now use the **passwd** *username* command to assign a new password to that user. For example, the **passwd pm** command lets you assign a new password to user pm. You're prompted to enter a password twice. RHEL is configured to discourage passwords that are based on dictionary words or that are shorter than six characters for security reasons. Nevertheless, such passwords are legal, and such a password is accepted by the **passwd** command when you type it in a second time.

TABLE 6-2   The Anatomy of /etc/group

Field	Example	Purpose
Groupname	mj	Each user gets his own group, with the same name as his username. You can also create unique groupnames.
Password	x	The password. You should see either an x or a seemingly random group of letters and numbers. An x points to /etc/gshadow for the actual password. A random group of letters and numbers represents the encrypted password.
Group ID	500	The numeric group ID (GID) associated with that user. By default, RHEL creates a new group for every new user. If you want to create a special group such as managers, you should assign a GID number outside the standard range; otherwise, Red Hat GIDs and UIDs would probably get out of sequence.
Group members	mj,vp	Lists the usernames that are members of the group. If it's blank, and there is a username that is identical to the groupname, that user is the only member of that group.

TABLE 6-3	**useradd** Command Options

Option	Purpose
-u *UID*	Overrides the default assigned *UID*. By default, in RHEL this starts at 500 and can continue sequentially the maximum number of users supported by kernel 2.6, which is 2^{32}.
-g *GID*	Overrides the default assigned *GID*. By default, RHEL uses the same *GID* and *UID* numbers to each user. If you assign a *GID*, it must be either 100 (users) or already otherwise exist.
-c *info*	Enters the comment of your choice about the user, such as her name.
-d *dir*	Overrides the default home directory for the user, /home/*username*.
-s *shell*	Overrides the default shell for the user, /bin/bash.

on the

Öob

Good passwords are important. Any cracker who may have tapped into your network can try to match the password of any of your users. A password-cracking program may be able to find dictionary word passwords in a matter of minutes. In contrast, it may take hours to crack a more complex password such as IIa451MS (which could stand for "I live at 451 Main Street").

The Red Hat User Manager

As of this writing, the Red Hat User Manager can be run only from the Linux GUI. If you're running a command line console and have installed the needed software, the **startx** command moves you into the GUI. The default GNOME desktop is shown here.

The look of the alternative KDE desktop is slightly closer to that of Microsoft Windows; if you're using KDE, pay attention to the icon of the Red Hat Fedora in the lower-left corner of the desktop; it starts program menus similar to those associated with the Microsoft Windows Start button. When referring to the KDE desktop shown next, I'll refer to it as the Main Menu button.

If you're in the GNOME Desktop Environment, you can access almost all administrative tools from the System | Administration menu from the top taskbar. If you're in the KDE Desktop Environment, you can access the same tools from the Main Menu | Administration submenu.

Because of the variations, this discussion focuses on starting GUI tools using a text command. You can access a text console in the GNOME desktop by choosing Applications | Accessories | Terminal. You can access a text console in the KDE desktop by selecting Main Menu | System | Terminal. Alternatively, you can run a standard text command from either GUI by pressing ALT-F2 and entering the command in the window that appears.

Now from the Linux GUI, you can start the Red Hat User Manager in one of three ways: Enter **system-config-users** from a command line interface in the

GUI, choose System | Administration | Users and Groups in GNOME, or choose Main Menu | Administration | Users and Groups in KDE. The next screen shows the Red Hat User Manager window.

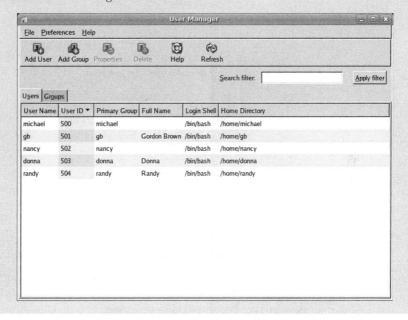

If you have not logged in as the root user, you'll be prompted for a root password before opening administrative tools such as the Red Hat User Manager (system-config-users).

EXERCISE 6-1

Adding a User with the Red Hat User Manager

To add a user with the Red Hat User Manager, open it. If it isn't already open, press ALT-F2. Type **system-config-users** in the text box that appears.

1. In the Red Hat User Manager, click the Add User button, or choose File |
   Add User. This will open the Create New User window, as shown here:

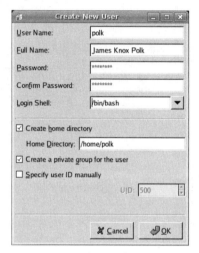

2. Complete the form. All entries are required, except Full Name. The entries
   are fairly self-explanatory (see the earlier discussions of each field). The
   password should be at least six characters and should contain a mix of upper-
   and lowercase letters, numbers, and symbols to keep it more secure from the
   standard password-cracking programs.

3. Enter the identical password in the Confirm Password field.

4. Click OK when you are done.

5. Repeat the process as desired for any additional new users you're expected to
   support.

User Account Management Tips

Although creating user accounts may seem to be a straightforward process, there are
a few things to consider when configuring new users:

- By default, RHEL 5 configures individual private group IDs (GIDs) for each user.
  As this associates each user with her own exclusive group, this is also known as
  the Red Hat user private group scheme. In the default Red Hat scenario, each
  user has a unique private GID (which corresponds to her UID), and regular users
  do not have access to other users' home directories. These users can still share
  access to special directories, as described later in this chapter.

- If your configuration doesn't require each user to have her own GID, or if you have no need for the security associated with the user private group scheme, you can assign all of your users to the Users group, with a GID of 100. In many cases, this can make system administration easier, but it may expose every user's files to every other regular user.

- Discourage the use of shared accounts, where several people use a single account. Shared accounts are almost always unnecessary and are easily compromised.

- If you'll be using the Network File System (NFS), make sure all users have the same UID on every system on the network. But this can be problematic. One alternative is the NIS, which supports a centralized database of users and passwords for users on all participating computers, as described later in this chapter.

Deleting a User Account

Removing user accounts is a pretty straightforward process. The easiest way to delete a user account is with the **userdel** command. By default, this command does not delete that user's home directory. Alternatively, the **userdel -r** *username* command deletes that user's home directory along with all of the files stored in that home directory.

If you know both the text and GUI tools to perform a task, use the text method. It almost always saves time.

This is a lot faster than the GUI method, for which you start the X Window System, open the Red Hat User Manager, select the user, and then click Delete. While it's probably easier for a less experienced user to remember the GUI method, text commands are faster.

Modifying a User Account

As a Linux administrator, you may want to add some limitations to your user accounts. The easiest way to illustrate some of what you can do is through the Red Hat User Manager. Start the Red Hat User Manager, select a currently configured user, and then click Properties to open the User Properties dialog box.

Click the Account Info tab for the account expiration information shown in Figure 6-1. As shown in the figure, you can limit the life of an account so that it expires on a specific date, or you can disable an account by locking it.

Click the Password Info tab. As shown in Figure 6-2, you can set several characteristics related to an individual user's password. Even when you set good passwords, frequent password changes can help provide additional security. The

Managing user
account life

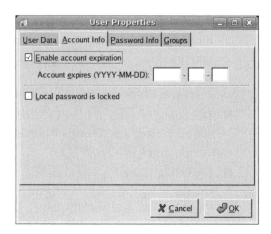

categories shown in the figure are self-explanatory; a 0 in any of these text boxes
means that the limit does not apply.

e x a m

w a t c h   *You may not have access*
to a GUI during the Troubleshooting
portion of either Red Hat exam. Therefore,
you need to know how to manage users
independent of GUI tools such as the Red
Hat User Manager. In any case, text-based
tools are almost always faster.

Click the Groups tab. Users can belong
to more than one group in Linux. Under the
Groups properties tab shown in Figure 6-3,
you can assign the target user to other groups.
For example, if you want to collect the files
supporting the managers in your company into
one directory, you can assign appropriate users to
the group named managers. Alternatively, you
can then assign members of that project team
to the project group through the Groups tab.

Configuring
password
information

User last changed password on: Tue 06 Jun 2006 12:00:00 AM PST

FIGURE 6-3

Assigning groups

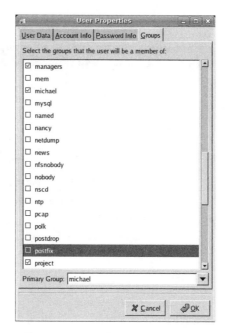

Regular User Management Commands

While the Red Hat User Manager GUI utility is convenient, it's often faster to perform the associated administrative functions at the command line interface. I've described some of these commands such as **useradd** and **userdel**. Two other key user administration commands are **usermod** and **chage**.

usermod

The **usermod** command modifies various settings in /etc/passwd. It also allows you to set an expiration date for an account or an additional group. For example, the following command sets the account associated with user test1 to expire on June 8, 2007:

```
# usermod -e 2007-06-08 test1
```

The following command makes user test1 a member of the special group:

```
# usermod -G special test1
```

chage

You can use the **chage** command to manage the expiration date of a password. Password aging information is stored in the /etc/shadow file. In order, the columns in /etc/shadow are shown in Table 6-4. The associated **chage** switch, where available, is shown with each description entry. For example, if you wanted to require that user test1 keep a password for at least two days, use the **chage test1 -m 2** command.

TABLE 6-4   The Anatomy of /etc/shadow

Column	Field	Description
1	Username	Username
2	Password	Encrypted password; requires an *x* in the second column of /etc/passwd
3	Password history	Date of the last password change, in number of days after January 1, 1970
4	mindays	Minimum number of days that you must keep a password (**-m**)
5	maxdays	Maximum number of days after which a password must be changed (**-M**)
6	warndays	Number of days before password expiration when a warning is given (**-W**)
7	inactive	Number of days after password expiration when an account is made inactive (**-I**)
8	disabled	Number of days after password expiration when an account is disabled (**-E**)

Limiting Access to su

As described earlier, I recommended that you use the root account during the Red Hat exams. However, I assume you still need to configure Linux computers in real life. One security measure that can help is to limit regular users who can access the root account via the **su** command. This takes two basic steps.

First, you'll need to add the users who you want to allow access to the **su** command. Make them a part of the wheel group. By default, this line in /etc/group looks like:

```
wheel:x:10:root
```

You can add the users of your choice to the end of this line directly, with the **usermod -G wheel *username*** command, or with the Red Hat User Manager.

Next, you'll need to make your Pluggable Authentication Modules (PAM) look for this group. You can do so by activating the following command in your /etc/pam.d/su file:

```
# auth   required pam_wheel.so use_uid
```

You'll learn more about how this works later in this chapter.

Limiting Access to sudo

Alternatively, you can limit access to the **sudo** command. Regular users who are authorized in /etc/sudoers can access administrative commands with their own password. You don't need to give out the administrative password to everyone who thinks they know as much as you do about Linux.

To access /etc/sudoers in the vi editor, run the **visudo** command. From the following directive, the root user is allowed full access to administrative commands:

```
root     ALL=(ALL) ALL
```

For example, if you want to allow user boris full administrative access, add the following directive to /etc/sudoers:

```
boris    ALL=(ALL) ALL
```

In this case, all boris needs to do to run an administrative command such as starting the vsFTPd service from his regular account is to run the following command, entering his own user password (note the regular user prompt, $):

```
$ sudo /sbin/service vsftpd start
Password:
```

You can even allow special users administrative access without a password. As suggested by the comments, the following directive in /etc/sudoers would allow all users in the wheel group to run administrative commands without a password:

```
%wheel   ALL=(ALL)   NOPASSWD: ALL
```

But you don't have to allow full administrative access. For example, if you want to allow those in the %users group to shut down the local system, you can activate the following directive:

```
%users  localhost=/sbin/shutdown -h now
```

CERTIFICATION OBJECTIVE 6.02

The Basic User Environment

Each user on any Red Hat Enterprise Linux system has an *environment* when logged on to the system. The environment defines directories where Linux looks for programs to run, the look of the login prompt, the terminal type, and more. This section explains how you can configure the default environment for your users.

Home Directories and /etc/skel

By default, when you create a new user, a default set of configuration files is created in the user's home directory. These defaults are hidden files stored in the /etc/skel directory.

Home Directory

The home directory is where a user starts when he first logs on to a RHEL system. The home directory for most users is /home/*username*, where *username* is the user's login name. Every user should normally have write permission in his own home directory, so each user is free to read and write his own files. Later in this chapter, you'll learn how to configure disk quotas, so users don't take more than their fair share of disk space.

/etc/skel

The /etc/skel directory contains default environment files for new accounts. The **useradd** command and the Red Hat User Manager copy these files to the home directory when you create a new account. The contents of /etc/skel may vary depending on what you have installed. Standard files from my copy of /etc/skel are described in Table 6-5.

If you've installed more than the default software on RHEL, you may see additional configuration files in the /etc/skel directory. For example, if you've installed the appropriate RPMs, you may see configuration files associated with emacs and the z shell (zsh) in this directory.

on the
Job

Linux includes many hidden files that start with a dot (.). To list these files, run the ls -a command. For example, if you want to list all of the files in the /etc/skel directory, run the ls -a /etc/skel command.

As the system administrator, you can edit these files or place your own customized files in /etc/skel. When new users are created, these files are propagated to the new users' home directories.

| TABLE 6-5 | Default Home Directory Files from /etc/skel |

File	Purpose
.bashrc	This basic bash configuration file may include a reference to the general /etc/bashrc configuration file. Can include commands you want to run when you start the bash shell, appropriate for aliases such as **rm='rm -i'**.
.bash_logout	This file is executed when you exit a bash shell and can include commands appropriate for this purpose, such as commands for clearing your screen.
.bash_profile	Configures the bash startup environment. Appropriate place to add environment variables or modify the directories in your PATH.
.gtkrc	Adds the Bluecurve theme for the default Red Hat GUI.
.kde	This directory includes autostart settings for the K Desktop Environment. Not added to /etc/skel and not copied to user home directories if you haven't installed KDE on this computer.

Adding files to /etc/skel may be a convenient way to distribute files such as corporate policies to new users.

Window Manager Configuration Files

RHEL comes with several window managers. At some point you will want to configure one or more of them for use on your system. In the past, window manager configuration files were stored in the /etc/X11/*windowmanager* directory, where *windowmanager* is the name of the specific window manager. This directory still includes twm (Tom's Window Manager). The X Display Manager is no longer available for RHEL 5. The GNOME and KDE Display Managers are stored in their own directories, /etc/gdm and /usr/share/config/kdm.

CERTIFICATION OBJECTIVE 6.03

Shell Configuration Files

All system-wide shell configuration files are kept in the /etc directory. These files are bashrc, profile, and the scripts in the /etc/profile.d directory. These files and scripts are supplemented by hidden files in each user's home directory, as just described. Let's take a look at these files.

/etc/bashrc

The /etc/bashrc file is used for aliases and functions, on a system-wide basis. Open this file in the text editor of your choice. Read each line in this file. Even if you don't understand the programming commands, you can see that this file sets the following bash shell parameters for each user. For example:

- ▨ It assigns a value of **umask**, which creates the default permissions for newly created files. It supports one set of permissions for root and system users (with user IDs below 100), and another for regular users. (Officially, RHEL reserves all user IDs above 500 for regular users but that is not reflected in /etc/bashrc.)
- ▨ It assigns a prompt, which is what you see just before the cursor at the command prompt.
- ▨ It includes settings from *.sh files in the /etc/profile.d/ directory.

The settings here are called by the .bashrc file in each user's home directory. The settings are supplemented by the .bash_history and .bash_logout files in each user's home directory.

/etc/profile

The /etc/profile file is used for system-wide environments and startup files. The following is the profile script from my copy of the operating system. The first part of the file sets the PATH for searching for commands, adding more directories using the **pathmunge** command. (Unless you use the Korn shell, ignore the **ksh workaround** stanza.) Then it sets the **PATH, USER, LOGNAME, MAIL, HOSTNAME, HISTSIZE,** and **INPUTRC** variables and finally runs the scripts in the /etc/profile .d directory. You can check the current value of any of these variables with the **echo $***variable* command.

```
# /etc/profile

# System wide environment and startup programs, for login setup
# Functions and aliases go in /etc/bashrc

pathmunge () {
  if ! echo $PATH | /bin/egrep -q "(^|:)$1($|:)" ; then
    if [ "$2" = "after" ] ; then
        PATH=$PATH:$1
    else
        PATH=$1:$PATH
    fi
  fi
}

# ksh workaround
if [ -z "$EUID" -a -x /usr/bin/id ]; then
        EUID=`id -u`
        UID=`id -ru`
fi

# Path manipulation
if [ `id -u` = 0 ]; then
  pathmunge /sbin
  pathmunge /usr/sbin
  pathmunge /usr/local/sbin
fi

# No core files by default
ulimit -S -c 0 > /dev/null 2>&1

if [ -x /usr/bin/id ]; then
    USER="`id -un`"
    LOGNAME=$USER
    MAIL="/var/spool/mail/$USER"
fi
```

```
HOSTNAME=`/bin/hostname`
HISTSIZE=1000

if [ -z "$INPUTRC" -a ! -f "$HOME/.inputrc" ]; then
    INPUTRC=/etc/inputrc
fi

export PATH USER LOGNAME MAIL HOSTNAME HISTSIZE INPUTRC

for i in /etc/profile.d/*.sh ; do
    if [ -r "$i" ]; then
      . $i
    fi
done

unset i
unset pathmunge
```

/etc/profile.d/

Actually, /etc/profile.d is not a script, but a directory of scripts. As I just noted, /etc/profile runs the scripts in this directory. Here is a partial listing of the files; those with .sh extensions apply to the default bash shell:

```
colorls.csh              kde.sh                    less.sh
colorls.sh               krb5-devel.csh            qt.csh
cvs.sh                   krb5-devel.sh             qt.sh
glib2.csh                krb5-workstation.csh      vim.csh
glib2.sh                 krb5-workstation.sh       vim.sh
gnome-ssh-askpass.csh    lang.csh                  which-2.sh
gnome-ssh-askpass.sh     lang.sh
kde.csh                  less.csh
```

By looking at the /etc/profile script, you can see that any script in this directory that ends with an .sh and is set as an executable will be run when /etc/profile is executed. Scripts with other extensions, such as .csh, relate to a different command shell.

EXERCISE 6-2

Securing Your System

It's important to keep your system as secure as possible. One approach is to change the default permissions users have for new files and directories they make. In this exercise, you'll set all new files and directories to prevent access from other users or groups.

1. Back up your current /etc/bashrc file. If you want to cancel any changes that you make during this exercise, restore from the backup after the final step.

2. Edit the /etc/bashrc file. Two lines in the file set the **umask**. One of the two lines is selected depending on the **if** statement above them. See if you can determine which line gets executed for an average (nonroot) user.

3. The **if** statement tests to see whether the user ID (**UID**) and group ID (**GID**) are the same, and that the **UID** is greater than 99. (On RHEL 5, you can—but don't have to—change this to 499.) If this is true, then the first **umask** is executed; otherwise, the second is executed. The second **umask** is for root and other key system accounts. The first is for users.

4. Change the first **umask** statement to exclude all permissions for groups and others. Use **umask 077** to do the job.

5. Save and exit the file.

6. Log in as a nonprivileged user. Use the **touch** command to make a new empty file. Use **ls -l** to verify the permissions on that file.

7. Log in as root. Again, use the **touch** command to make a new empty file and use **ls -l** to verify the permissions on that new file.

You have just changed the default umask for all shell users. If you backed up your /etc/bashrc in step 1, you can now restore the original version of this file.

User Shell Configuration Files

As described earlier, each user gets a copy of the hidden files from the /etc/skel directory. As your users start working with their accounts, more configuration files are added to their home directories. Some are based on shells such as bash (.bash*); others draw their settings from the GUI desktops, typically GNOME and KDE. I'll describe the GUIs in more detail in Chapter 14.

The default Linux shell is bash, and it's the only shell described in the Red Hat Exam Prep guide and associated courses. However, if you or your users work with other shells, you'll find configuration files associated with those shells hidden in each user's home directory.

CERTIFICATION OBJECTIVE 6.04

Setting Up and Managing Disk Quotas

Quotas are used to limit a user's or a group of users' ability to consume disk space. This prevents a small group of users from monopolizing disk capacity and potentially interfering with other users or the entire system. Disk quotas are commonly used by Internet Service Providers (ISPs), by Web hosting companies, on FTP sites, and on corporate file servers to ensure continued availability of their systems.

Without quotas, one or more users can upload files on an FTP server and occupy all free space on a partition. Once the affected partition is full, other users are effectively denied upload access to the disk. This is also a reason to mount different filesystem directories on different partitions. For example, if you only had partitions for your root (/) directory and swap space, someone uploading to your computer could fill up all of the space in your root directory (/). Without at least a little free space in the root directory (/), your system could become unstable or even crash.

You have two ways to set quotas for users. You can limit users by inodes or by kilobyte-sized disk blocks. Every Linux file requires an inode. Therefore, you can limit users by the number of files or by absolute space. You can set up different quotas for different filesystems. For example, you can set different quotas for users on the /home and /tmp directories if they are mounted on their own partitions.

Limits on disk blocks restrict the amount of disk space available to a user on your system. Older versions of Red Hat Linux included LinuxConf, which included a graphical tool to configure quotas. As of this writing, Red Hat no longer has a graphical quota configuration tool. Today, you can configure quotas on RHEL only through the command line interface.

on the **!**
job *Learn to focus on command line tools. Red Hat used to make LinuxConf available as a graphical and console tool for a number of system administration functions, including quotas. While Red Hat may eventually create another GUI quota manager, don't count on it.*

Quota Settings in the Kernel

By default, the Linux kernel as configured by Red Hat supports quotas. However, if you install and compile a new kernel from a remote source, you should make sure that this feature is active. The basic kernel configuration is stored in the /boot directory. For the default RHEL system, you'll find the configuration in the config-*versionumber* file. If you've configured a custom kernel file, you'll find it listed under a different name.

To verify that quotas are enabled in the default kernel, run the following command (the shell substitutes the actual version number of the kernel for `uname -r`):

```
# grep CONFIG_QUOTA /boot/config-`uname -r`
```

There are two possible results. The following means quota support is enabled:

```
CONFIG_QUOTA=y
```

Alternatively, if you see either of the following, quota support is not enabled:

```
CONFIG_QUOTA=n
CONFIG_QUOTACTL=n
```

CONFIG_QUOTA enables limits on usage; **CONFIG_QUOTACTL** is associated with disk quota manipulation.

If you have a custom or upgraded kernel, use either the **make menuconfig, make gconfig**, or **make xconfig** command to make sure support is enabled for quotas. The quota support option is located in the filesystem section. All you need to do is turn on quota support and then rebuild and install your new kernel. I'll describe this process in more detail in Chapter 8.

The Quota Package

The quota RPM package is installed by default. You can find out more about RPMs such as quota with the following command:

```
# rpm -qi quota
```

Assuming you haven't removed the quota RPM, you'll see the following description of the package, which tells you that it includes a number of tools:

```
The quota package contains system administration tools for monitoring and limit-
ing user and or group disk usage per filesystem.
```

You can find out more about these tools by reviewing a list of associated files. You can find a list of files installed through the quota RPM with the following command:

```
# rpm -ql quota
```

As you can see for yourself, the quota package includes the following commands:

- **/sbin/quotaon** */fs*   Enables quotas for the specified filesystem.
- **/sbin/quotaoff** */fs*   Disables quota tracking.
- **/usr/sbin/edquota** *name*   Edits the quota settings for the specified username. Can also be used to set defaults or to copy quota settings from one user to another.
- **/usr/bin/quota**   Allows users to see their current resource consumption and limits.
- **/usr/sbin/repquota**   Generates a report of disk consumption by all users for a quota-enabled filesystem.
- **/sbin/quotacheck**   Scans a filesystem for quota usage. Initializes the quota databases.

I've included the entire path to each command for your reference. But as discussed earlier in this book, I recommend that you normally work as the root user during the Red Hat exams. As the noted directories are all part of the root user's PATH, you don't need to specify the full path to each command. (You can verify the directories in your path with the **echo $PATH** command.)

The next step is to ensure the quotas are active and checked when Linux boots on your system.

sysinit Quota Handling

The /etc/rc.sysinit script noted in Chapter 3 initializes Linux system services during the boot process. This script includes commands that start quota services. Specifically, this script runs both the **quotacheck** (to ensure that disk consumption usage records are accurate) and **quotaon** (to enable quotas on all filesystems indicated in /etc/fstab) commands. You don't have to run these commands manually.

Quota Activation in /etc/fstab

As described in Chapter 4, the file /etc/fstab tells Linux which filesystems to mount during the boot process. The options column of this file configures how Linux mounts a directory. You can include quota settings in /etc/fstab for users and/or groups.

on the job

Before you edit a key configuration file such as /etc/fstab, it's a good idea to back it up and save it to any boot or rescue disks that you may have. If your changes lead to a catastrophic failure, you can boot your system from a rescue disk and then restore the original configuration file.

Here is a sample /etc/fstab before editing:

```
Device              Mount point     Filesys     Options             dump  Fsck
LABEL=/             /               ext3        defaults              1    1
LABEL=/boot         /boot           ext3        defaults              1    2
/dev/sdb1           /home           ext3        defaults              1    2
devpts              /dev/pts        devpts      gid=5,mode=620        0    0
tmpfs               /dev/shm        proc        tmpfs                 0    0
proc                /proc           proc        defaults              0    0
sysfs               /sys            proc        sysfs                 0    0
/dev/sda3           swap            swap        defaults              0    0
```

In this configuration, it may make sense to enable quotas on the root (/) and /home directory filesystems. You can tell Linux to start tracking user quotas by adding the keyword **usrquota** under the options column. Similarly, you can tell Linux to start tracking group quotas with the **grpquota** option. Use vi or your favorite text editor to update /etc/fstab.

In this example, I add both user and group quotas to the /home directory filesystem:

```
/dev/sdb1    /home    ext3    exec,dev,suid,rw,usrquota,grpquota    1    2
```

If you edit the /etc/fstab file by hand, you'll need to ensure that the line you are editing does not wrap to the next line. If it does, the format for your /etc/fstab will be invalid and the boot process may be affected.

If you don't have a separate /home directory partition, you can apply the quota settings to the top-level root directory (/) partition.

on the
job

You can test changes to /etc/fstab by rebooting your computer or remounting a filesystem. For example, if you've just added usrquota and grpquota entries as shown to the /home directory filesystem, you can test it with the mount -o remount /home command. Check the result in the /etc/mtab file.

Quota Management Commands

The next step is to create quota files. For user and group quotas, you'll need the aquota .user and aquota.group files in the selected filesystem before you can activate actual quotas. You no longer need to create those files manually; once you've remounted the desired directory, the appropriate **quotacheck** command creates them automatically. For the /home directory described earlier, you'd use the following commands:

```
# mount -o remount /home
# quotacheck -cugm /home
```

The options for **quotacheck** are

- ■ **-c** Performs a new scan.
- ■ **-v** Performs a verbose scan.
- ■ **-u** Scans for user quotas.
- ■ **-g** Scans for group quotas.
- ■ **-m** Remounts the scanned filesystem.

This will check the current quota information for all users, groups, and partitions. It stores this information in the appropriate quota partitions. Once the command is run, you should be able to find the aquota.user and aquota.group files in the configured directory.

Using edquota to Set Up Disk Quotas

To specify disk quotas, you need to run the **edquota** command. This edits the aquota .user or aquota.group file with the vi editor. In this example, pretend you have a user named nancy, and you want to restrict how much disk space she is allowed to use. You'd type the following command to edit nancy's quota records:

```
# edquota -u nancy
```

This command launches the vi editor and opens the quota information for user nancy, as shown in Figure 6-4.

On a standard command line terminal, the quota information is formatted strangely, with seven columns. (If you're running a command line terminal in the GUI, you can remove the line wrapping by increasing the width of the window; the terminals used to create Figures 6-4 through 6-7 include 90 columns.) The lines are wrapped. In this case, the filesystem with the quota is mounted on partition /dev/sdb2. Soft and hard limits are included for both blocks and inodes. By default, soft and hard limits of 0 means that there are no limits for user nancy.

We can see that nancy is currently using 22,692 blocks and has 24 files (inodes) on this partition. Each block takes up 1KB of space; thus user nancy's files total approximately 22MB. In this example, we'll show you how to set a limit so that nancy does not take more than 100MB of space with her files.

First, it's important to understand the meaning of soft and hard limits.

- **Soft limit** This is the maximum amount of space a user can have on that partition. If you have set a grace period, this will act as an alarm. The user will then be notified she is in quota violation. If you have set a grace period, you will also need to set a hard limit. A grace period is the number of days a user is allowed to be above the given quota. After the grace period is over, the user must get under the soft limit to continue.

FIGURE 6-4

Quota
information

```
Disk quotas for user nancy (uid 502):
  Filesystem                   blocks       soft       hard     inodes       soft       hard
  /dev/sdb2                     22692          0          0         24          0          0
~
~
~
~
~
~
~
~
~
~
~
~
~
~
~
~
~
~
~
"/tmp//EdP.aSaBqYv" 3L, 216C
```

■ **Hard limit** Hard limits are necessary only when you are using grace periods. If grace periods are enabled, this will be the absolute limit a user can use. Any attempt to consume resources beyond this limit will be denied. If you are not using grace periods, the soft limit is the maximum amount of available space for each user.

In this example, set an 100MB soft limit and a 120MB hard limit for the user. As shown in Figure 6-5, this is written as a number of 1KB blocks in the quota file.

Note that nancy's use of inodes is not limited. She is still able to use as many inodes (thus as many files) as she likes. To implement these quotas, these settings must be saved. In the default vi editor, the **:wq** command does this job nicely.

In addition, give user nancy a seven-day grace period. If and when she exceeds the soft limit, she has that amount of time to get back under the soft limit. To set the grace period for all users, run the **edquota -t** command. The result should look similar to what you see in Figure 6-6.

Here, Linux has provided the default of seven days for both inodes and block usage. That is, a user may exceed the soft limit on either resource for up to seven days. After that, further requests by that user to use files will be denied. Our user nancy would have to delete files to get her total disk block consumption under 100MB before she could create new files or expand existing files. You can edit the grace period directly, using vi commands. To activate the new grace period, just save the file.

There is a quirk associated with quota grace periods. When you use **edquota** and specify the grace period, you cannot include a space between the number and the unit (for example, **7days**, not 7 days). Fortunately, the quota system in RHEL 5 automatically fixes this problem.

FIGURE 6-5

Quotas with hard and soft limits

```
Disk quotas for user nancy (uid 502):
  Filesystem         blocks      soft       hard     inodes      soft       hard
  /dev/sdb2          22692     100000     120000         24         0          0
~
~
~
~
~
~
~
~
~
~
~
~
~
~
~
~
~
~
~
```

Quota grace
period

```
Grace period before enforcing soft limits for users:
Time units may be: days, hours, minutes, or seconds
  Filesystem                Block grace period    Inode grace period
  /dev/sdb2                      7days                 7days
  ~
  ~
  ~
  ~
  ~
  ~
  ~
  ~
  ~
  ~
  ~
  ~
  ~
  ~
  ~
"/tmp//EdP.aYWpYJC" 4L, 233C
```

on the **Job**
In older versions of Red Hat distributions, a space between the quota number and the unit would lead to a quota error. In RHEL 5, that space is automatically removed when the appropriate quota setting is saved.

The **edquota** command allows you to use an already configured user's quota as a template for new users. To use this feature, you need to run the command with the **-p** switch and **configured_user arguments** options:

```
# edquota -up nancy michael randy donna
```

This command will not provide any output, but it will take the quota configuration settings of user nancy and apply them to michael, randy, and donna. You can include as many users as you want to edit or to which you want to apply templates.

You can also set up quotas on a per-group basis. To do this, simply run **edquota** with the **-g** *group_name* argument. Here, *group_name* would need to be a valid group as specified in the /etc/group file.

```
# edquota -g nancy
```

This opens the block and inode quota for group nancy, as shown in Figure 6-7.

on the **Job**
When testing quotas, there is one useful technique that creates a blank file of the desired size. For example, if you want to create a 100MB file named bigfile in the local directory, run the dd if=/dev/zero of=bigfile bs=1k count=100000 command.

FIGURE 6-7

Group quota

```
Disk quotas for group nancy (gid 502):
 Filesystem                  blocks     soft       hard     inodes     soft       hard
  /dev/sdb2                    22692        0          0         24        0          0
~
~
~
~
~
~
~
~
~
~
~
~
~
~
~
~
~
"/tmp//EdP.awJznje" 3L, 217C
```

Automating Quota Settings

As an administrator, you'll want to maintain any quotas that you create. For that purpose, it's useful to run the aforementioned **quotacheck** command on a regular basis. As you'll see later in this chapter, it is easy to do through the cron system. A simple command in the right cron file automatically runs the **quotacheck** command on a regular basis. For example, the following command in the right cron file runs the **quotacheck** command at 2:00 A.M. every Saturday:

```
0 2 * * 6 /sbin/quotacheck -avug
```

You can also use the **edquota** command to apply quotas to all users on your system. For example, the following command applies the quotas that you've already set on user mj to all other real users on the system (the **awk** command was described briefly in Chapter 1):

```
edquota -p mj `awk -F: '$3 > 499 {print $1}' /etc/passwd`
```

Note that this command lists the first column ($1) of /etc/passwd, which is the username. And in keeping with the UIDs for regular Red Hat users (from the third column, $3, of /etc/passwd), this is limited to users with UIDs of 500 or higher. You can add this type of command to the appropriate cron file as well, which makes sure that the quotas are applied to all existing and new users.

Quota Reports

As an administrator, it can be useful to see reports on who is using the most disk space. You can generate reports on users, groups, or everybody on every partition. To view a report showing quota information for all users, run the **repquota -a** command. You'll see a list of quotas for all users similar to that shown in Figure 6-8.

A quota report

```
                          Block limits              File limits
User              used    soft    hard  grace   used  soft  hard  grace
---------------------------------------------------------------------------
root          -- 37231124    0      0          316506    0     0
daemon        --       20    0      0               3    0     0
lp            --       16    0      0               2    0     0
news          --     7388    0      0             183    0     0
uucp          --      168    0      0               1    0     0
games         --      344    0      0              86    0     0
rpm           --    84636    0      0             111    0     0
apache        --       96    0      0               8    0     0
netdump       --       16    0      0               2    0     0
avahi         --       32    0      0               5    0     0
named         --       56    0      0               7    0     0
smmsp         --       24    0      0               3    0     0
rpcuser       --       48    0      0               6    0     0
xfs           --        8    0      0               2    0     0
beagleindex   --    26644         0      0          27         0      0
ntp           --       16    0      0               2    0     0
squid         --       16    0      0               2    0     0
mysql         --       36    0      0               7    0     0
webalizer     --       32    0      0               4    0     0
hsqldb        --       20    0      0               2    0     0
gdm           --       32    0      0               2    0     0
postfix       --      104    0      0              13    0     0
michael       --  7015340    0      0           15179    0     0
ldap          --       16    0      0               2    0     0
gb            --       68    0      0               9    0     0
nancy         --    22692 100000 120000            24    0     0
donna         --       68    0      0               9    0     0
randy         --       68    0      0               9    0     0
polk          --       68    0      0               9    0     0
#100          --       24    0      0               3    0     0
#537          --  2680116    0      0            3523    0     0

[root@Enterprise5a ~]#
```

If you have multiple filesystems with quotas, you can use the **repquota** command to isolate a specific filesystem. For example, if you wanted to view the quota report for the partition with the /home directory, run the following command:

```
# repquota -u /home
```

Alternatively, if you wanted to view quota information on user nancy, run the following **quota** command:

```
# quota -uv  nancy
Disk quotas for user nancy(uid 507):
Filesystem  blocks   quota   limit   grace   files   quota   limit  grace
/dev/hdd1    22692  100000  120000              24       0       0
```

An individual user can check his own usage with the **quota** command, but only the administrative root user can examine the quotas for other users.

Quotas on NFS Directories

The Network File System (NFS) allows users to share files and directories on a network with Linux and Unix computers. Users across the network mount a shared NFS directory from a specific computer. Users are normally in a single database in an NFS setup. Disk quotas can be applied to these users in virtually the same way as they are to users on a regular Linux computer. For example, if you create a local user called nfsuser, and you translate all remote requests to this user, then you need to set up quota restrictions for nfsuser on the mounted partition. This will limit the disk consumption of all incoming NFS users. See Chapter 10 for more about NFS.

EXERCISE 6-3

Configuring Quotas

In this exercise, you will set up user quotas for one user on your system. These quotas will allow a soft limit of 80MB and a hard limit of 100MB for each user. No limits are to be placed on the number of inodes. Assume the /home directory is mounted on a separate partition. (If /home is not mounted separately, apply the commands to the top-level root directory /.) The first couple of steps should be formalities, as quotas should be active and installed by default. However, it's a good habit to check. To set up quotas in this exercise, follow these steps:

1. Check your kernel configuration for the **CONFIG_QUOTA** variable, using the /boot/config-`uname -r` file. It should be set to "Y." If not, proceed to Chapter 8 for general instructions on how to revise your kernel.

2. Check to make sure that the quota package is installed. Install it from the RHEL 5 installation source if required.

3. Add quotas to /etc/fstab. Add the **usrquota** directive to the Options column for the partition with the /home directory. Make sure the info stays on one line in /etc/fstab.

4. Activate the quotas. You can unmount and remount the /home directory, reboot Linux, or use the following command:

   ```
   # mount -o remount /home
   ```

5. Use the **quotacheck -cum /home** command to activate the user quota file in the /home directory.

6. Make sure this command worked. Look for the aquota.user file in the /home directory.

7. Now you're ready to set up quotas for a specific user. If necessary, look up usernames in /etc/passwd. Use the **edquota -u *username*** command to edit the quotas for the user of your choice.

8. Under the soft and hard columns, change the 0 to **80000** and **100000**, respectively. Remember that these files are set up for 1KB blocks. Save the file.

9. Restore any previous settings that existed before this exercise.

CERTIFICATION OBJECTIVE 6.05

Creating and Maintaining Special Groups

One major difference between Red Hat Enterprise Linux and non–Red Hat Linux or Unix distributions is how new users are assigned to groups. A Linux group allows its members to share files. Unfortunately, that also means everyone in the same primary group has access to the home directories of all other group members. Users may not always want to share the files in their home directories with others. For example, if you're setting up an ISP, your users pay for their privacy.

On the other hand, RHEL gives each user a unique user ID and group ID in /etc/passwd. This is known as the *user private group* scheme. Users get exclusive access to their own groups and don't have to worry about other users reading the files in their home directories.

on the job

There are other ways to provide access to other users, as discussed in Chapter 4's "Access Control Lists."

Standard and Red Hat Groups

Traditionally, users are assigned to one or more groups such as users in /etc/group. For example, you might configure accgrp for the accounting department and infosys for the information systems department in your company.

If you have access to one of these other versions of Unix or Linux, check the third and fourth fields in /etc/passwd. Many users will have the same fourth field, which represents their *primary* group. Then, when you create a new user, each account receives a unique user ID but shares the same group ID with other users in the acct group. Users can also belong to other groups.

In RHEL, each user gets her own special private group by default. As you probably noticed earlier, user IDs and group IDs by default start at 500, match, and proceed in ascending order.

By default in RHEL, all regular users have a **umask** of 0002. If you are coming from a traditional Unix environment, you may be concerned. With the traditional user/group scheme, any member of that user's primary group will automatically have write access to any file that the user creates in his home directory.

This is the advantage behind the user private group scheme. Since every user account is the only member in its own private group, having the **umask** set to 0002 does not affect file security. This provides advantages for systems such as ISPs, where you don't want users to have access to each other's files.

Shared Directories

Most people work in groups. They may share files. You can give a group of users access to a specific user's home directory or you can set up a shared directory for a group.

When you configure a shared directory, you can set up a group owner and then add the users to that group through the /etc/group configuration file. When you set the group ID bit (SGID) on this directory, any file created in this directory inherits the group ID. Assuming you have set appropriate permissions, all members of this group can then access files in that directory.

There are several basic steps required to create a useful shared directory. For example, assume you want to set up a shared directory, /home/accshared, for the accountants in your organization. To set this up, take the following steps:

1. Create the shared directory:

   ```
   # mkdir /home/accshared
   ```

2. Create a group with the users in your accounting department. Give it a group ID that doesn't interfere with existing group or user IDs. One way to do this is to add a line such as the following to your /etc/group file. You could also create this kind of group using the Red Hat User Manager. Note that the name of this new group is accgrp. Substitute the usernames of your choice.

   ```
   accgrp:x:5000:robertc,alanm,victorb,roberta,alano,charliew
   ```

3. Set up appropriate ownership for the new shared directory. The following commands prevent any specific user from taking control of the directory and assign group ownership to accgrp:

   ```
   # chown nobody.accgrp /home/accshared
   # chmod 2770 /home/accshared
   ```

Any user who is a member of the accgrp group can now create files in the /home/accshared directory. Any files generated within that directory will then be associated with the accgrp group ID, and all users listed as members of accgrp in the /etc/group file will have read, write, and execute access to the /home/accshared directory.

What makes this possible are the permissions that you've assigned to the /home/accshared directory: 2770. Let's break this down into its component parts.

The first digit (2) is the *set group ID bit*, also known as the *SGID bit*. When you set the SGID bit for a directory, any files created in that directory automatically have their group ownership set to be the same as the group owner of the directory. There are two ways to set the SGID bit for the /home/accshared directory:

```
chmod g+s /home/accshared
```

or alternatively, the following command sets the SGID bit and sets appropriate permissions for a shared directory:

```
chmod 2770 /home/accshared
```

Setting the SGID bit solves the problem of making sure all files created in a shared directory belong to the correct group—as long as the **umask** is set properly.

The remaining digits are basic knowledge for any experienced Linux or Unix user. The **770** sets read, write, and execute permissions for the user and group that own the directory. But since the user owner is nobody, the group owner is what counts. In other words, members of the accgrp group gain read, write, and execute permissions to files created in this directory.

Otherwise, users who are members of accgrp and belong to another primary group would have to remember to use the **chgrp** command on every file they put in /home/accshared. While clumsy, that command allows other users in that group to access the file.

EXERCISE 6-4

Controlling Group Ownership with the SGID Bit

In this exercise, you will create new files in a directory where the SGID bit is set.

1. Add users called test1, test2, and test3. Specify passwords when prompted. Check the /etc/passwd and /etc/group files to verify that each user's private group was created:

```
# useradd test1; passwd test1
# useradd test2; passwd test2
# useradd test3; passwd test3
```

2. Edit the /etc/group file and add a group called tg1. Make the test1 and test2 accounts a member of this group. You could add the following line to /etc/group directly or use the Red Hat User Manager:

```
tg1:x:9999:test1,test2
```

Before you proceed, make sure the group ID you assign to group tg1 (in this case, 9999) is not already in use.

3. Create a shared directory for the tg1 group:

```
# mkdir   /home/testshared
```

4. Change the user and group ownership of the shared directory:

```
# chown   nobody.tg1   /home/testshared
```

5. Log in as test1 and test2 separately. Change the directory to the testshared directory and try to create a file. Two ways to do so are with the following commands. What happens?

```
$ date   >>test.txt
$ touch abcd
```

6. Now as the root user, set group write permissions on the testshared directory.

```
# chmod 770 /home/testshared
```

7. Log in again as user test1, and then try to create a file in the new directory. So far, so good.

```
$ cd /home/testshared
$ date   >> test.txt
$ ls -l test.txt
```

8. Now check the ownership on the new file. Do you think other users in the tg1 group can access this file?

```
$ ls -l
```

9. From the root account, set the SGID bit on the directory:

```
# chmod g+s   /home/testshared
```

(Yes, the efficient among you may know that the **chmod 2770 /home/testshared** command combines steps 6 and 9.)

10. Switch back to the test1 account and create another file. Check the ownership on this file. Do you think that user test2 can now access this file? (To see for yourself, try it from the test2 account.)

```
$ date >> testb.txt
$ ls   -l
```

11. Now log in as the test2 account. Go into the /home/testshared directory, create a different file, and use **ls -l** to check permissions and ownership again. (To see that it worked, try accessing this file from the test1 account.)

12. Switch to the test3 account and check whether you can or cannot create files in this directory, and whether you can or cannot view the files in this directory.

CERTIFICATION OBJECTIVE 6.06

Pluggable Authentication Modules

RHEL uses the Pluggable Authentication Modules (PAM) system to check for authorized users. PAM includes a group of dynamically loadable library modules that govern how individual applications verify their users. You can modify PAM configuration files to suit your needs.

PAM modules are documented in the /usr/share/doc/pam-versionnumber/txts directory. For example, *the functionality of the pam_securetty .so module is described in the README .pam_securetty file.*

PAM was developed to standardize the user authentication process. For example, the login program uses PAM to require usernames and passwords at login. Open the /etc/pam.d/login file. Take a look at the first line:

```
auth [user_unknown=ignore success=ok ignore=ignore default=bad] \
  pam_securetty.so
```

This line means that root users can log in only from secure terminals as defined in the /etc/securetty file, and unknown users are ignored.

on the job
A backslash in a command line "escapes" the meaning of the next character; in the preceding command, pam_securetty.so is added to the end of the command line. Due to limits in the format of this series, I've had to change the spacing of some lines and add backslashes to others.

on the job

In older Red Hat distributions, the full path to the PAM module was required. It is now understood that these modules are stored in the /lib/security directory.

The configuration files shown in the /etc/pam.d directory are named after applications. These applications are "PAM aware." In other words, you can change the way users are verified for applications such as the console login program. Just modify the appropriate configuration file in the /etc/pam.d directory.

Pluggable Authentication Modules (PAM) and Associated Files

The PAM system divides the process of verifying users into four separate tasks. These are the four different types of PAM modules:

■ **Authentication management (auth)**   Establishes the identity of a user. For example, a PAM **auth** command decides whether to prompt for a username and/or a password.

■ **Account management (account)**   Allows or denies access according to the account policies. For example, a PAM **account** command may deny access according to time, password expiration, or a specific list of restricted users.

■ **Password management (password)**   Manages other password policies. For example, a PAM **password** command may limit the number of times a user can try to log in before a console is reset.

■ **Session management (session)**   Applies settings for an application. For example, the PAM **session** command may set default settings for a login console.

The code shown in Figure 6-9 is an example PAM configuration file, /etc/pam .d/login. Every line in all PAM configuration files is written in the following format:

```
module_type   control_flag   module_path   [arguments]
```

The **module_type**, as described previously, can be **auth, account, password,** or **session**. The **control_flag** determines what PAM does if the module succeeds or fails. The **module_path** specifies the location of the actual PAM module file. Finally, as with regular shell commands, you can specify arguments for each module.

The **control_flag** field requires additional explanation. It determines how the configuration file reacts when a module flags success or failure. The five different control flags are described in Table 6-6.

To see how control flags work, take a look at the commands from the /etc/pam .d/reboot configuration file:

```
auth    sufficient    pam_rootok.so
```

FIGURE 6-9

The PAM
/etc/pam.d/login
module

```
#%PAM-1.0
auth [user_unknown=ignore success=ok ignore=ignore default=bad] pam_securetty.so
auth       include     system-auth
account    required    pam_nologin.so
account    include     system-auth
password   include     system-auth
# pam_selinux.so close should be the first session rule
session    required    pam_selinux.so close
session    include     system-auth
session    required    pam_loginuid.so
session    optional  █ pam_console.so
# pam_selinux.so open should only be followed by sessions to be executed in the
user context
session    required    pam_selinux.so open
session    optional    pam_keyinit.so force revoke
~
~
~
~
~
~
~
"/etc/pam.d/login" [readonly] 14L, 643C
```

The first **auth** command checks the pam_rootok.so module. In other words, if
the root user runs the **reboot** command, the **control_flag** is **sufficient**, and the
other **auth** commands in this file are ignored. Linux runs the **reboot** command.
This is explained in the README.pam_rootok file in the /usr/share/doc/pam-
versionnumber/txts directory.

```
auth   required    pam_console.so
```

The second **auth** command is run only for nonroot users; it just governs permissions
within the console. As described in the README.pam_console file, you can find
more information about this module with the **man pam_console** command.

```
#auth   include    system-auth
```

TABLE 6-6   PAM Control Flags

control_flag	Description
required	If the module works, the command proceeds. If it fails, PAM proceeds to the next command in the configuration file—but the command controlled by PAM will still fail.
requisite	Stops the process if the module fails.
sufficient	If the module works, the login or other authentication proceeds. No other commands need be processed.
optional	PAM ignores module success or failure.
include	Includes all **module_type** directives from the noted configuration file; for example, if the directive is **password include system-auth**, this includes all password directives from the PAM system-auth file.

The third line is commented out by default. If you make this line active, it includes the commands from the system-auth configuration file, which requires root user privileges. Remote users who know your root password are still allowed to reboot your computer.

```
account    required    pam_permit.so
```

The module associated with the **account** command (pam_permit.so) accepts all users, even those who've logged in remotely. In other words, this configuration file would allow any root user, local or remote, to reboot your Linux computer.

Alternatively, you might add the pam_securetty.so module, which would keep remote users from rebooting your system. This module is described in more detail earlier in this chapter.

While it's not normal to allow just any user to shut down a corporate server, you may want to do so on a Linux workstation. In this way, users can shut down their own laptops or desktops without having access to the root account.

PAM Configuration Example: /etc/pam.d/login

This section refers back to the /etc/pam.d/login configuration file shown in Figure 6-9. When a user opens a text console and logs in, Linux goes through this configuration file line by line. As previously noted, the first line in /etc/pam.d/login limits root user access to secure terminals as defined in the /etc/securetty file:

```
auth [user_unknown=ignore success=ok ignore=ignore default=bad] \
  pam_securetty.so
```

The next line includes the commands from the system-auth PAM configuration file:

```
auth  include     system-auth
```

The system-auth configuration file shown in Figure 6-10 sets up environment variables and allows different users to log in. The next **auth** line from /etc/pam.d/login checks for accounts not allowed to log in as listed in the /etc/nologin file:

```
account  required    pam_nologin.so
```

e**x**a m

ⓦatch   *If the /etc/nologin file exists,   tries to log in gets to read the contents of*
regular users are not allowed to log into   /etc/nologin as a message.
the local console. Any regular user that

The /etc/pam
.d/system-auth
configuration file

```
#%PAM-1.0
# This file is auto-generated.
# User changes will be destroyed the next time authconfig is run.
auth        required      pam_env.so
auth        sufficient    pam_unix.so nullok try_first_pass
auth        requisite     pam_succeed_if.so uid >= 500 quiet
auth        required      pam_deny.so

account     required      pam_unix.so
account     sufficient    pam_succeed_if.so uid < 500 quiet
account     required      pam_permit.so

password    requisite     pam_cracklib.so try_first_pass retry=3
password    sufficient    pam_unix.so md5 shadow nullok try_first_pass use_autht
ok
password    required      pam_deny.so

session     optional      pam_keyinit.so revoke
session     required      pam_limits.so
session     [success=1 default=ignore] pam_succeed_if.so service in crond quiet
use_uid
session     required      pam_unix.so
~
"/etc/pam.d/system-auth" [readonly] 20L, 844C
```

The **account** and **password** commands in /etc/pam.d/login also refer to the /etc/
pam.d/system-auth configuration file:

```
account    include    system-auth
password   include    system-auth
```

For more information, refer to the following **account** directives in /etc/pam.d/
system-auth:

```
account   required    pam_unix.so
account   sufficient  pam_succeed_if.so uid < 500 quiet
account   required    pam_permit.so
```

This refers to the pam_unix.so module in the /lib/security directory, which brings up
the normal username and password prompts. Service users (with user IDs less than

500) are automatically logged in, without messages (which is why they have the /sbin/ nologin shell in /etc/passwd). The pam_permit.so module always returns success.

For more information on the /etc/pam.d/login password directives, you'll need to refer to the three **password** commands in /etc/pam.d/system-auth:

```
password requisite    pam_cracklib.so try_first_pass retry=3
password sufficient   pam_unix.so md5 shadow nullok try_first_pass \
use_authok
password required     pam_deny.so
```

The first command from this list allows the use of a previously successful password (**try_first_pass**) and then sets a maximum of three retries. The next command encrypts passwords using the MD5 algorithm, supports the Shadow Password Suite described in Chapter 1, allows the use of null (zero-length) passwords, allows the use of a previously successful password (**try_first_pass**), and prompts the user for a password (**use_authok**). If you've configured NIS, you'll see **nis** in this list as well. The **password required pam_deny.so** directive is trivial; as noted in README .pam_deny in the /usr/share/doc/pam-*versionlevel*/txt directory, that module always fails, so PAM moves on to the next directive.

Finally, there are six **session** commands in the /etc/pam.d/login file:

```
session    required    pam_selinux.so close
session    include     system-auth
session    required    pam_loginuid.so
session    optional    pam_console.so
session    required    pam_selinux.so open
session    optional    pam_keyinit.so force revoke
```

The first and fifth commands deactivate and reactivate SELinux, just for this part of the login process. The second command includes **session** directives from system-auth, which can allow you to set limits on individual users through /etc/security/ limits.conf. The third command logs the user ID for audits. The fourth command manages file permissions while users are logged onto your Linux computer. The final command forces a unique session keyring, and revokes it when the session is closed (to close one more potential security hole).

EXERCISE 6-5

Configuring PAM

In this exercise, you can experiment with some of the PAM security features of Red Hat Enterprise Linux 5.

1. Make a backup copy of /etc/securetty with the following command:

   ```
   # cp /etc/securetty /etc/securetty.sav
   ```

2. Edit /etc/securetty and remove the lines for tty3 through tty11. Save the changes and exit.

3. Use ALT-F3 (CTRL-ALT-F3 if you're running X Window) to switch to virtual console number 3. Try to log in as root. What happens?

4. Repeat step 3 as a regular user. What happens? Do you know why?

5. Use ALT-F2 to switch to virtual console number 2 and try to log in as root.

6. Review the messages in /var/log/secure. Do you see where you tried to log in as root in virtual console number 3?

7. Restore your original /etc/securetty file with the following command:

   ```
   # mv /etc/securetty.sav /etc/securetty
   ```

One thing to remember is that the /etc/securetty file governs the consoles from where you can log into Linux as the root user. Therefore, the changes that were made do not affect regular (nonroot) users.

Securing PAM by User

In this section, you'll learn how to configure PAM to limit access to specific users. The key to this security feature is the pam_listfile.so module in the /lib/security directory. As described earlier, four settings are available for each PAM configuration command. To make sure that the command respects what you do with this module, you should use this directive first:

```
auth required pam_listfile.so
```

The way PAM limits user access is in the last part of the command—in the details. For example, if you added the following line to a PAM configuration file, access to the associated tool would be limited to any users listed in /etc/special:

```
auth required pam_listfile.so onerr=succeed item=user \
sense=allow file=/etc/special
```

To understand how this works, break this command into its component parts. You already know the first three parts of the command from the previous section. The switches that are shown are associated with the pam_listfile.so module, as described in Table 6-7.

TABLE 6-7	Switches for the pam_listfile.so Module

pam_listfile Switch	Description
onerr	If there is a problem, tell the module what to do. The options are **onerr=succeed** or **onerr=fail**.
item	You can use this switch to limit access to a terminal (**tty**), users in a specific file (**user**), groups (**group**), or more.
sense	If the item is found in the specified **file**, take the noted action. For example, if the user is in /etc/special, and **sense=allow**, then this command allows use of the specified tool.
file	Configures a file with a list, such as **file = /etc/special**.

on the Job

Based on the topic matter for the exam, this information in Table 6-7 is limited; for full details, see README.pam_listfile in the /usr/share/doc/pam-versionnumber/txts directory.

Thus, for the specified command (**onerr=succeed**), an error, strangely enough, returns success (**item=user**), based on a specific list of users. If the user is in the specified list (**file=/etc/special**), allow that user (**sense=allow**) to access the specified tool. To see how this works, run through the steps in Exercise 6-6.

exam
watch
Make sure you understand how Red Hat Enterprise Linux handles user authorization through the /etc/pam.d configuration files. When you test these files, make sure you create a backup of everything in PAM before making any changes, because any errors that you make to a PAM configuration file can disable your system completely (PAM is that secure).

EXERCISE 6-6

Using PAM to Limit Access

You can also use the PAM system to limit access to regular users. In this exercise, you'll limit access by adding one or more users to the /etc/nologin file. It should work hand-in-hand with the default /etc/pam.d/login security configuration file, specifically the following line:

```
account   required   pam_nologin.so
```

1. Look for an /etc/nologin file. If it doesn't already exist, create one with a message such as:

   ```
   I'm sorry, access is limited to the root user
   ```

2. Access another terminal with a command such as CTRL-ALT-F2. Try logging in as a regular user. What do you see?

3. If the message flashes by too quickly for you, log in as the root user. You'll see the same message; but as the root user, you're allowed access.

4. Inspect the /var/log/secure file. Did your system reject the attempted login from the regular user? What were the associated messages for the root user?

CERTIFICATION OBJECTIVE 6.07

Network Authentication Configuration: NIS and LDAP

By default, access to a Linux computer requires a valid username and password. One problem with a large network of Linux systems is that "normally," each user requires an account on every Linux computer.

The two services that allow you to set up one centrally managed database of usernames and passwords for Linux and Unix computers are NIS and LDAP. With each of these services, you can maintain one password database on an NIS or LDAP server and configure the other systems on the network as clients. When a user logs into an NIS or LDAP client, that system first checks its local password file, usually /etc/passwd. If it can't find your username, it looks up the corresponding file on the server.

exam

ⓦatch   *In the Red Hat Exam Prep guide, the only requirement is to be able to connect a client to a network directory service, such as NIS or LDAP. As of this writing, the prep course outline for the RHCE (RH300) no longer includes NIS server configuration requirements. I therefore focus on NIS and LDAP clients in this section.*

First, I'll show you how you can configure NIS and LDAP clients using the command line interface and then use the Red Hat Authentication Configuration tool.

NIS Client Configuration

It's fairly simple to configure an NIS client on a network. Assuming you have an NIS server, you need to do three things. First, specify the server and domain name in /etc/yp.conf. Next, make sure the **ypbind** client service starts the next time you boot Linux. Finally, make sure the /etc/nsswitch.conf file looks to the NIS service for at least the username and password database.

The change to the /etc/yp.conf configuration file is simple. All you need is a command such as the following, which specifies the name of the NIS domain as **nisdomain**, and the name of the NIS server as **enterprise5a**:

```
domain nisdomain server enterprise5a
```

Making sure that the **ypbind** client service starts the next time you boot Linux is a simple matter. Just as with other Linux services, you can make sure it starts at the appropriate runlevels with a command such as the following:

```
# chkconfig ypbind on
```

If you want to start the service immediately, the following command should be familiar:

```
# service ypbind start
```

Finally, making sure your computer looks for the NIS server for key files means modifying the /etc/nsswitch.conf configuration file. For example, to make sure your computer looks to the NIS server for the username and password database, you'll want to configure the following commands in that file (you can add other services such as **ldap** to the list):

```
passwd:    files nis
shadow:    files nis
group:     files nis
```

This assumes that you're using the NIS server that's included with RHEL 5, NIS version 2.

One command you need to know about when running an NIS client is **yppasswd**. All users can manage their NIS password with this command.

LDAP Client Configuration

If you want to configure your RHEL computer as an LDAP client, you'll need the openldap-clients, openldap, and nss_ldap RPM packages. The openldap-clients RPM is a default part of the System Tools package group. The other two packages should be installed by default on your RHEL system.

To configure an LDAP client, you'll need to configure two different ldap.conf configuration files in the /etc and the /etc/openldap directories. While both files can get quite complex, for the purposes of the exam, I'll keep the definitions simple.

/etc/ldap.conf

The default version of the /etc/ldap.conf file includes a number of different commands and comments. To set up your LDAP client, you'll need to be concerned with several commands in this file, including those described in Table 6-8.

/etc/openldap/ldap.conf

You'll need to specify the **HOST** and **BASE** variables in this file, just as you did in the /etc/ldap.conf configuration file. Based on the parameters in the previous section, this leads to the following two commands:

```
BASE dc=example,dc=com
URI ldap://127.0.0.1
```

If your LDAP server is not on the local computer, and your domain is not example .com, you'll need to substitute accordingly. Individual users can supersede this file in a hidden .ldaprc file in their home directories.

The Name Service Switch File

The Name Service Switch file, /etc/nsswitch.conf, governs how your computer searches for key files such as password databases. You can configure it to look through

| TABLE 6-8 | Some /etc/ldap.conf Parameters |

Command	Description
host 127.0.0.1	Specifies the IP address for the LDAP server. This command assumes the LDAP server is on the local computer.
base dc=example,dc=com	Sets the default **base** distinguished name, in this case, example.com.
ssl start_tls	Required if you want Transport Layer Security (TLS) support to encrypt passwords that are sent to the LDAP server.
pam_password	Supports encryption schemes for passwords; options include **crypt**, **nds** (Novell Directory Services), and **ad** (Active Directory).
nss_init, groups_ignoreusers root, ldap	Assumes no supplemental groups in the LDAP directory server.

NIS and LDAP server databases. For example, when an NIS client looks for a computer host name, it might start with the following entry from /etc/nsswitch.conf:

```
hosts: files nisplus nis dns
```

This line tells your computer to search through name databases in the following order:

1. Start with the database of host names and IP addresses in /etc/hosts.
2. Next, search for the host name in a map file based on NIS+ (NIS Version 3).
3. Next, search for the host name in a map file based on NIS (Version 2).
4. If none of these databases includes the desired host name, refer to the DNS server.

You can configure the /etc/nsswitch.conf configuration file to look at an LDAP server for the desired databases. For example, if you want to set up a centralized username and password database for your network, you'll need to configure at least the following commands in /etc/nsswitch.conf:

```
passwd:    files ldap
shadow:    files ldap
group:     files ldap
```

You can configure a number of additional files in an LDAP or NIS centralized database; however, the details are beyond the scope of this book.

Configuring Clients with the Red Hat Authentication Tool

If you're not familiar with NIS or LDAP, it may be simpler to configure your computer as a client using the Red Hat Authentication Configuration tool. In RHEL 5, you can start it in the GUI with the **system-config-authentication** command or in the console with the **authconfig-tui** command. This opens an Authentication Configuration tool; the GUI version is shown in Figure 6-11.

If you've gone through the First Boot process described in Chapter 2, you may have already configured your computer using this tool. You can set your computer to check an NIS and an LDAP server for usernames and passwords.

If you choose to activate the Enable NIS Support option, click the Configure NIS button. You'll need to enter the name of the NIS domain, as well as the name or IP address of the computer with the NIS server. Make any desired changes and click OK.

If you choose to activate the Enable LDAP Support option, click the Configure LDAP button. Make any desired changes and click OK. You'll need to enter the following information:

1. If you want to use Transport Layer Security to encrypt the passwords sent to the LDAP server, activate the Use TLS To Encrypt Connections option. If

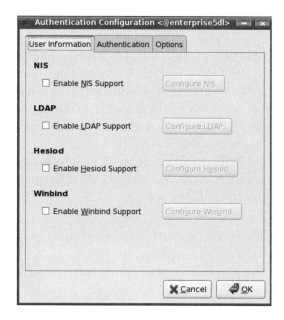

FIGURE 6-11

Authentication
Configuration

you do so, you can also click Download CA Certificate, which allows you to specify the URL with the CA Certificate associated with the LDAP domain or realm.

2. Enter the domain name for your server in LDAP format in the LDAP Search Base DN text box. For example, if your domain is my-domain.com, enter the following:

```
dc=my-domain,dc=com
```

3. Specify the location of the LDAP server. If it's the local computer, you can use the 127.0.0.1 IP address.

Once you've made your changes, click OK; it may take a few seconds for the Authentication Configuration tool to write the changes to the noted configuration files before it closes. If you've set up an NIS client, it automatically sets the **ypbind** service to start at appropriate runlevels the next time you boot Linux.

CERTIFICATION SUMMARY

You can have great control over how your Linux installation is set up and configured. You can configure users and groups and control almost all aspects of the user environment. Any variables or system-wide functions you may need to run can be kept in the /etc/bashrc or /etc/profile script.

You can set up quotas to limit the user's disk usage. You can set up one quota per partition and set soft and hard limits for users. With grace periods, you can set up a soft limit to give users an appropriate warning.

By default, Red Hat Enterprise Linux assigns unique user and group ID numbers to each new user. This is known as the user private group scheme. This scheme allows you to configure special groups for a specific set of users. The users in the group can be configured with read and write privileges in a dedicated directory, courtesy of the SGID bit.

RHEL 5 includes powerful tools for securing critical commands, using Pluggable Authentication Modules (PAM). You can use centralized account management with an NIS or LDAP service.

TWO-MINUTE DRILL

Here are some of the key points from the certification objectives in Chapter 6.

User Account Management

❑ After installation, your system may have only a single login account: root. For most installations, you'll want to create more accounts, if only for everyday use.

❑ Accounts can be added by directly editing /etc/passwd or with the **useradd** command. The advantage of **useradd** is that it automatically adds the new home directory as well as configuration files from /etc/skel.

❑ Accounts can be added with the Red Hat User Manager tool. You can also use this tool or related commands such as **chage** and **usermod** to configure an account further with parameters such as a password lifetime or a time limit on the account.

❑ Discourage the use of shared accounts, where several people use a single account. Shared accounts are almost always unnecessary, and they are easily compromised.

❑ If you're using the Network File System (NFS), it can help establish user accounts with the same UID across systems.

❑ The Network Information System (NIS) can serve the same purpose by establishing one database for all systems on your network.

The Basic User Environment

❑ Each user on your system has an environment when logged on to the system.

❑ The home directory for each login account is the initial directory in which users are placed when they first log on. They start with hidden files configured in the /etc/skel/ directory.

Shell Configuration Files

❑ All system-wide shell configuration files are kept in the /etc directory.

❑ /etc/profile is the system-wide startup shell script for bash users.

❑ All users have hidden shell configuration files in their home directories.

Setting Up and Managing Disk Quotas

❑ Quotas are used to limit a user's or a group of users' ability to consume disk space.

❑ Quotas are set on specific filesystems mounted to standard Linux formats.

❑ Quota support must be enabled in the kernel. By default, quotas are enabled in RHEL kernels.

❑ Quotas have soft limits and hard limits. If both soft and hard limits are set, a user can exceed his or her soft limit for a modest period of time.

❑ Users and groups may never exceed their hard quota limits.

Creating and Maintaining Special Groups

❑ Red Hat's user private group scheme configures users with their own unique user and group ID numbers.

❑ With appropriate SGID permissions, you can configure a shared directory for a specific group of users.

❑ Setting the SGID bit ensures that all files created in a shared directory belong to the correct group.

❑ Setting the SGID bit is easy; use **chown** to set nobody as the user owner and the name of the group as the group owner. Then run the **chmod 2770** command on the shared directory.

Pluggable Authentication Modules

❑ Red Hat Enterprise Linux uses the Pluggable Authentication Modules (PAM) system to check for authorized users.

❑ PAM modules are called by configuration files in the /etc/pam.d directory. These configuration files are usually named after the service or command that they control.

❑ There are four types of PAM modules: authentication, account, password, and session management.

❑ PAM configuration files include lines that list the module_type, the control_flag, and the path to the actual module, followed by arguments.

❑ PAM modules are well documented in the /usr/share/doc/pam-*versionnumber*/ txts directory.

Network Authentication Configuration: NIS and LDAP

❑ NIS allows you to configure one centrally managed username and password database with other Linux and Unix systems on your LAN.

❑ LDAP provides similar support to NIS, and it supports various forms of encryption.

SELF TEST

The following questions will help you measure your understanding of the material presented in this chapter. As no multiple choice questions appear on the Red Hat exams, no multiple choice questions appear in this book. These questions exclusively test your understanding of the chapter. It is okay if you have another way of performing a task. Getting results, not memorizing trivia, is what counts on the Red Hat exams. There may be more than one answer to many of these questions.

User Account Management

1. What's the standard minimum user ID number for regular users on Red Hat distributions?
   _____

2. What command at a GUI-based text console starts the Red Hat User Manager?
   _____

The Basic User Environment

3. If you want to add files to every new user account, what directory should you use?
   _____

Shell Configuration Files

4. The system-wide file associated with the bash shell is _____.

Setting Up and Managing Disk Quotas

5. You are running an ISP and provide space for users' Web pages. You want them to use no more than 40MB of space, but you will allow up to 50MB until they can clean up their stuff. How could you use quotas to enforce this policy?

   Set the hard limit to _____

   Set the soft limit to _____

   Enable grace periods with the following command:_____

6. If you wanted to configure quotas for every user on the /home directory, you'd add the following option to the /home directory line in /etc/fstab:
   _____

Creating and Maintaining Special Groups

7. What command would set the SGID bit on the /home/developer directory?

_____

8. When creating a special group, should you use the default Group ID for a regular user?

_____

Pluggable Authentication Modules

9. What are the four basic Pluggable Authentication Modules types?

_____

_____

_____

_____

10. You are editing the PAM configuration file by adding a module. Which control flag immediately terminates the authentication process if the module succeeds?

_____

Network Authentication Configuration: NIS and LDAP

11. What two pieces of information do you need to connect to an NIS server?

_____

_____

12. If your domain is example.org, what is your LDAP Search Base DN?

dc=_____

dc=_____

LAB QUESTIONS

Lab 1

In this first lab, you'll look at setting up automatic connections to a shared network directory. While this lab uses files described in Chapter 10, it is focused on shell configuration files. For the purpose of this lab, assume your username is vaclav and you're mounting a shared NFS /inst directory from a remote computer with an IP address of 192.168.30.4. You're going to mount it in vaclav's home directory, in a blank directory named inst.

1. Select the regular user of your choice. That user should have files such as .bashrc and .bash_logout.

2. Find a shared directory on a remote computer.

3. Set up a local directory for that user as a mount point.

4. Configure commands for that user to **mount** and **umount** that remote directory. Make sure those commands run only when that user logs into his or her account.

Lab 2

In this lab, you will test the quotas created in this chapter. You'll use the basic quota settings described in this chapter and then copy files to fill up the home directory of a user who has a quota applied. The steps required for this lab are straightforward.

1. Set up quotas on the local computer. Use the criteria described earlier in this chapter. If you don't have a separate /home directory partition, you can set up quotas on the top-level root directory (/).

2. Once you've set quotas in your /etc/fstab configuration file, remember to remount the partition where you've created a quota. Alternatively, you could reboot Linux, but that would take time that you may not be able to spare during either of the Red Hat exams.

3. Set up a quota for the user of your choice. Remember that when you use the **edquota** command on a specific user, you can edit the quota file directly using vi editor commands. Configure a hard and a soft limit for that user.

4. Log in as the user with the quota. Copy some large files to the home directory of that user. To speed up this process, if you want to create an arbitrary large file, say 179MB, run the following command:

```
# dd if=/dev/zero of=testfile bs=1k count=179000
```

5. Continue the copying process until you see a warning message. When you do, run the **quota** command. What do you see? Does anything in the output give you a warning that you've exceeded the quota?

6. Copy some additional files until you see a "Disk quota exceeded" message. Run the **quota** command again. What do you see?

7. Delete some files from that user's home directory—at least enough to get the files under the quota limits.

Lab 3

In this lab, you'll create a private directory for a group of engineers designing some galleys. You'll want to create a group named galley for the engineers named mike, rick, terri, and maryam. They'll want to share files in the /home/galley directory. What do you need to do?

Lab 4

You want to make sure even the root user has to enter the root password when opening Red Hat administrative tools. You can do this by modifying the appropriate file in the /etc/pam.d directory.

SELF TEST ANSWERS

User Account Management

1. The minimum user ID number for regular users on Red Hat distributions is 500. It's 100 on many other Linux distributions.

2. The command in a GUI-based text console that starts the Red Hat User Manager is **system-config-users**.

The Basic User Environment

3. The directory of files that is automatically added to every new user account is /etc/skel.

Shell Configuration Files

4. The system-wide configuration file associated with the bash shell is /etc/bashrc.

Setting Up and Managing Disk Quotas

5. Set the hard limit to 40MB; set the soft limit to 50MB. You can set these limits on user1 with the **edquota -u** command; once created, you can apply them to all users with the following command:

   ```
   # edquota -p user1 `awk -F: '$3 > 499 {print $1}' /etc/passwd`
   ```

   Then if you want to enable grace periods for all users, run the **edquota -t** command.

6. If you wanted to configure quotas for every user on the /home directory, you'd add the **usrquota** option to the /home directory partition directive in /etc/fstab.

Creating and Maintaining Special Groups

7. There are two different commands available to set the SGID bit on the /home/developer directory. If that's all you want to do, run the following command:

   ```
   # chmod g+s /home/developer
   ```

   Alternatively, if you're also assigning full user and group permissions to /home/developer, you could run the following command:

   ```
   # chmod 2770 /home/developer
   ```

8. When creating a special group, you should not use the default Group ID for a regular user, unless you want to allow others in the group access to all files of that user.

Pluggable Authentication Modules

9. The four basic Pluggable Authentication Modules types are: **auth**, **account**, **password**, and **session**.

10. You are editing the PAM configuration file by adding a module. The **sufficient** control flag immediately terminates the authentication process if the module succeeds.

Network Authentication Configuration: NIS and LDAP

11. The two pieces of information you need to connect to an NIS server are the NIS domain name and NIS server (IP address or FQDN).

12. If your LDAP domain is example.org, your LDAP Search Base DN is **dc=example, dc=org**.

LAB ANSWERS

Lab 1

This lab has two purposes: it is designed to help you understand mounted network directories and the login process. You can substitute the user, the shared network directory, and directories of your choice. To some extent, the automounter described in Chapter 4 provides an alternative. If you have problems, more information on NFS is available in Chapter 10. But based on the premises in this lab, I would take the following steps:

1. Log in as user vaclav. Create the specified directory. For this lab, you would use the **mkdir /home/vaclav/inst** command.

2. Test the network connection. Mount the remote NFS directory on the directory that you just created. For this lab, use the following command (substitute the appropriate IP address or host name for your network):

```
# mount -t nfs 192.168.30.4:/inst /home/vaclav/inst
```

If you have problems, review SELinux settings. If you're trying to connect from the root account, make sure **no_root_squash** is configured in the /etc/exports file of the NFS server. For more information, see Chapter 10. Firewalls and nonstandard ports can also be a problem.

3. Run the **mount** command by itself. If you've successfully mounted to the shared directory, you should see it at the end of the list of mounted directories.

4. Unmount the network connection. For this lab, you would use the following command:

   ```
   # umount /home/vaclav/inst
   ```

5. Add the commands specified from steps 2 and 4 to the local .bashrc and .bash_logout configuration files. Remember that since these files start with a dot, they are hidden.

6. Test the result. Log out, and log back in. Check your mounted directories. If the command in .bash_logout does not work, you'll probably see the shared directory mounted multiple times.

Lab 2

The purpose of this lab is to practice creating quotas for users. It's quite possible that you'll have to configure quotas on the Red Hat exams. While you may not have to test quotas in the way described in this lab, it will help you become familiar with the error messages that you'll see when you exceed a hard and then a soft quota limit.

Lab 3

This is a straightforward process, using the following basic steps:

1. Create accounts for mike, rick, terri, and maryam if required. You can use the **useradd** command, edit the /etc/passwd file directly, or work through the Red Hat User Manager.

2. Set up a group for these users. Configure a group ID outside the range of your regular users with a line such as:

   ```
   galley::10000:mike,rick,terri,maryam
   ```

3. Create the /home/galley directory. Give it proper ownership and permissions with the following commands:

   ```
   # mkdir /home/galley
   # chown nobody.galley
   # chmod 2770 /home/galley
   ```

Lab 4

To make the lab work, first review the various *system-config-** files in the /etc/pam.d directory. Most (except system-config-lvm and system-config-selinux) include the following three directives:

```
auth        include     config-util
account     include     config-util
session     include     config-util
```

They all point to the config-util file in /etc/pam.d directory. Open this file in the text editor of your choice. The first two commands allow users to start this tool automatically:

```
auth    sufficient    pam_rootok.so
auth    sufficient    pam_timestamp.so
```

   The first command checks whether you're the root user. The second command checks to see whether you've opened the given tool recently, based on the conditions of the pam_timestamp module. If you deleted (or commented out) these commands, all users, including the root user, will have to enter the root password when opening this tool. To do so, take the following steps:

1. Open a typical tool such as the Red Hat Security Level Configuration tool in a command line in your GUI. Make sure it opens normally. When it does, close it without making any changes to your current firewall.

2. Back up the current PAM module for config-util to your home directory:

```
# cp /etc/pam.d/config-util ~
```

3. Open the file in /etc/pam.d in the text editor of your choice. Comment out the first two commands in this file.

4. Save the file. If you're not already logged into the GUI as the root user, log out of the GUI. Log back into the GUI as root.

5. Try opening the Red Hat Security Level Configuration tool. What happens?

6. Restore the original configuration. If you don't remember what you did, restore it from the config-util file in your home directory.

7

System Administration Tools

CERTIFICATION OBJECTIVES

7.01   Network Configuration

7.02   The CUPS Printing System

7.03   Automating System Administration: cron and at

7.04   Understanding, Maintaining, and Monitoring System Logs

✓   Two-Minute Drill

Q&A   Self Test

Red Hat Enterprise Linux 5 includes the network configuration tools that have made Linux the operating system backbone of the Internet. To configure your network and troubleshoot any network problems you might encounter during the exam, you need the tools described in this chapter.

Printing is a fundamental service for all operating systems. The default print server for RHEL is CUPS, which has replaced the Line Print Daemon. CUPS supports autoconfiguration of shared network printers and includes a Web-based configuration tool. Red Hat also has a customized graphical configuration tool. Both support connections to printers using other network protocol suites.

A lot of system administration is repetitive. Some of it happens when you want to have a "life," more when you'd rather be asleep. In this chapter, you'll learn how to schedule both one-time and periodic execution of jobs. When troubleshooting, system logging often provides the clues that you need to solve a lot of problems.

You may notice that I diverge slightly from the RH300 course outline in Chapters 5 and 7. To me, it made more sense to include Kickstart with the other package management tools described in Chapter 5.

INSIDE THE EXAM

This chapter directly addresses four items in the Red Hat Exam Prep guide. While the focus is on RHCT requirements, all RHCE candidates need to remember that their exam includes these requirements. The first Red Hat Exam Prep item is associated with the following RHCT Troubleshooting and System Maintenance skill:

- Diagnose and correct misconfigured networking.

This chapter also addresses the following RHCT Installation and Configuration skills:

- Configure the scheduling of tasks using **cron** and **at**.
- Use scripting to automate system maintenance tasks.
- Configure printing.

The final part of this chapter is important for the Troubleshooting and System Maintenance portion of each exam, as log files can help you find the cause of many problems, especially those related to the boot process as well as many services.

If you need to configure SELinux, as defined for the RHCE exam, just about all you can do for the services in this chapter is disable SELinux protection for part or all of each service. However, the SELinux requirements as defined in the Red Hat Exam Prep guide are focused on networking services, which are not covered in this chapter.

CERTIFICATION OBJECTIVE 7.01

Network Configuration

The network is where the power of Red Hat Enterprise Linux really comes alive; however, getting there may not be trivial. As in all other things Linux, it's a learning experience. Many critical network configuration settings are stored in the /etc/sysconfig directory.

In most cases, you'll configure networking when you install RHEL during either exam. However, you may encounter and need to diagnose networking problems, especially during the Troubleshooting portion of either exam.

e x a m

ⓦatch

Learn the configuration files in the /etc/sysconfig/network-scripts/ and /etc/sysconfig/ directories. These are crucial to the configuration of Red Hat Enterprise Linux. If you have a configuration to change or repair, it may involve files in one of these directories. If you have a problem on the troubleshooting exam, you may find the solution in these files. Even if there's an existing well-known configuration file such as httpd.conf, you can find additional configuration options in /etc/sysconfig/httpd. Red Hat has consolidated a number of key configuration files in these directories, so expect them to become even more important in the future.

The configuration file that provides the foundation for others in RHEL 5 networking is /etc/sysconfig/network. It can contain up to six directives, as described in Table 7-1. If you don't see the directives in your /etc/sysconfig/network file, the situation does not apply. For example, if you don't see the **GATEWAYDEV** directive, you probably have only one network card on your computer.

In most cases, /etc/sysconfig/network contains three directives:

```
NETWORKING=yes
NETWORKING_IPV6=yes
HOSTNAME=yourhostname
```

There is no requirement for an NIS domain, and other directives (including the **HOSTNAME**) may be set by the DHCP server.

TABLE 7-1	/etc/sysconfig/network Variables

Variable	Description
NETWORKING	Can be yes or no, to configure or not configure networking.
NETWORKING_IPV6	Can be yes or no, to configure networking under IPv6.
NISDOMAIN	If you're connected to an NIS network, this should be set to the name of the NIS domain.
HOSTNAME	Sets the host name of the local computer. If you don't see this directive, it may be set by a DHCP server.
GATEWAY	Sets the IP address for the gateway for your network. If you don't see this directive, it may be set by a DHCP server.
GATEWAYDEV	Sets the network device, such as eth0, that this computer uses to reach a gateway. You won't see this if you have only one network card on your computer.

The /etc/sysconfig/network-scripts Files

The /etc/sysconfig/network-scripts directory is where Red Hat Enterprise Linux stores and retrieves its networking information. With available Red Hat configuration tools, you don't have to touch these files, but it's good to know they're there. A few representative files are shown in Table 7-2.

on the
Ĵob

Some of the commands in /etc/sysconfig/network-scripts may be hard-linked to files in the /etc/sysconfig/networking/devices and /etc/sysconfig/networking/ profiles/default directories. It's worth your trouble to explore these files as well.

TABLE 7-2	/etc/sysconfig/network-scripts Files

File in /etc/sysconfig/network-scripts	Description
ifcfg-lo	Configures the loopback device, a virtual device that confirms proper installation of TCP/IP.
ifcfg-*	Each installed network adapter, such as eth0, gets its own ifcfg-* script. For example, eth0 gets **ifcfg-eth0**. This file includes the IP address information required to identify this network adapter on a network.
network-functions	This script contains functions used by other network scripts to bring network interfaces up and down.
ifup-* and ifdown-*	These scripts activate and deactivate their assigned protocols. For example, **ifup-ipx** brings up the IPX protocol.

There are several closely related commands in Table 7-3 that can help you manage networking from the command line interface.

Setting Up a Network Interface

There are two ways to configure networking. It's fastest if you can use text commands. And Red Hat also provides an effective GUI Network Configuration utility, which writes changes to various configuration files, such as /etc/sysconfig/ network. You can also use the text mode version of this tool to add, remove, and edit network interfaces. You can start these utilities with the **system-config-network** and **/usr/sbin/system-config-network-tui** commands (**system-config-network-tui** is not available in /usr/bin or in the **PATH** for regular users).

on the
Ö o b

With the system-config-* GUI tools, Red Hat has developed a number of utilities that I believe will encourage Microsoft Windows administrators to make the switch to Linux.

There's one more command, **system-config-network-cmd**, which tells you essentially everything that's configured about your network, in a long list of console directives.

The following exercise illustrates how you can use the Network Configuration utility (see Figure 7-1). It then illustrates how you can monitor and modify your network configuration with various text commands.

TABLE 7-3   Other Network Configuration Commands

Network Script	Description
ifup and **ifdown**	These scripts start and stop a network card such as eth0. **ifup eth0** activates eth0; **ifdown eth0** deactivates this device.
dhclient	**dhclient** activates a connection to a DHCP server for your network. The function of a DHCP server is to lease IP addresses. Normally activated during the boot process through the applicable **ifcfg-*** script in the /etc/sysconfig/network-scripts directory.
ifconfig	The main network interface configuration utility. Can return or set the network parameters on a network device.

FIGURE 7-1

Network
Configuration
utility

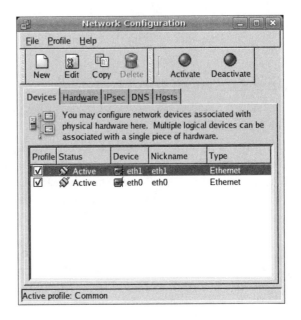

EXERCISE 7-1

Modifying Network Interfaces with system-config-network

1. Start the Network Configuration utility. From a GUI terminal, press ALT-F2, and enter **system-config-network** in the text box that appears. This opens the Network Configuration dialog box.

2. Select the Devices tab if it isn't already active.

3. Select the adapter that you want to modify, and then click Edit. If it is an Ethernet adapter, you'll see an Ethernet Device dialog box similar to the one shown in the next illustration.

4. Pay attention to the Allow All Users To Enable And Disable The Device option. If you activate it, you'll change the **USERCTL** directive in the ifcfg-* script to **yes**. At this point, you should record your current settings for this interface before proceeding.

5. Change the IP value (Address) to **192.168.1.11** and the network mask (Subnet Mask) to **255.255.255.0**.

   Note that if your computer is on the 192.168.1.0 private network, you should use a different private IP address. It should isolate you from all other hosts on the local network. Test this after step 5 by using the **ping** command to try to connect to other hosts on your network.

6. Choose File | Save and wait for the process to complete.

7. At the command prompt, run **ifconfig** from a command line interface to check your new IP settings.

8. Repeat steps 1 to 3 and then reset the values to your previous settings. Run **ifconfig** again to make sure you've restored your original network configuration.

Many values are associated with each network interface. At minimum, each network adapter requires a valid, unique IP address as well as an appropriate network mask. The Network Configuration utility provides five convenient tabs you can use to customize each network adapter; you may need to click New or Edit to make the changes suggested here.

- **Devices**   This tab allows you to add a new network adapter or edit a configured adapter. You can revise the name of the adapter, IP address assignments, static routing, and hardware device information. Different devices are configured in the /etc/sysconfig files described earlier.

- **Hardware**   This tab lets you modify the IRQ port, memory location, I/O address(es), and DMA channel(s) associated with the adapter. Hardware information is documented in different files in the /proc directory.

- **IPsec**   This tab supports virtual private network connections.

- **DNS**   This tab lets you add the addresses of DNS servers available to network adapters on the given network, which is reflected in /etc/resolv.conf.

- **Hosts**   This tab allows you to modify the name, alias, and IP address assigned to the specified adapter, which is shown in /etc/hosts.

on the
job

In the past, Linux has had trouble recognizing second network adapters. If you encounter this problem, you may need to specify hardware addresses such as the IRQ port.

In addition, if you choose Profile | New, you can create different network configurations, which can be useful for flexible configurations, such as a laptop with a wireless card and an office docking port.

ifup/ifdown

Each installed network adapter has a corresponding ifcfg-* file in /etc/sysconfig/
network-scripts. You can activate or deactivate that adapter with the **ifup** and
ifdown commands. Either of the following commands will activate the eth0
network adapter:

```
ifup ifcfg-eth0
ifup eth0
```

ifconfig

The **ifconfig** command is used to configure and display network devices. Here is
some sample output from this command:

```
# ifconfig eth0
eth0      Link encap:Ethernet  HWaddr 00:50:56:40:1E:6A
          inet addr:192.168.30.2  Bcast:192.168.30.255  Mask:255.255.255.0
          inet6 addr: fe80::2e0:4cff:fee3:d106/64 Scope:Link
          UP BROADCAST RUNNING MULTICAST  MTU:1500  Metric:1
          RX packets:11253 errors:0 dropped:0 overruns:0 frame:0
          TX packets:1304 errors:0 dropped:0 overruns:0 carrier:0
          collisions:0 txqueuelen:1000
          RX bytes:2092656 (1.9 Mb)  TX bytes:161329 (157.5 Kb)
          Interrupt:10 Base address:0x10a0
```

The preceding command requests configuration data for the first Ethernet device
on the system, eth0. If you just specify eth0 (or another device), **ifconfig** displays
information about the specified interface only. If you don't specify a device, **ifconfig**
shows all network adapters, including the loopback adapter.

The **ifconfig** command can also be used to configure network interfaces. For example, you can assign a new IP address for eth0 with the following command:

```
# ifconfig eth0 10.11.12.13
```

The first parameter, **eth0**, tells you which interface is being configured. The next argument, **10.11.12.13**, indicates the new IP address being assigned to this interface. To make sure your change worked, issue the **ifconfig** command again (with the name of the adapter device) to view its current settings:

```
# ifconfig eth0
eth0      Link encap:Ethernet  HWaddr 00:50:56:40:1E:6A
          inet addr: 10.11.12.13  Bcast:10.255.255.255  Mask:255.0.0.0
          inet6 addr: fe80::2e0:4cff:fee3:d106/64 Scope:Link
          UP BROADCAST RUNNING MULTICAST  MTU:1500  Metric:1
          RX packets:11253 errors:0 dropped:0 overruns:0 frame:0
          TX packets:1304 errors:0 dropped:0 overruns:0 carrier:0
          collisions:0 txqueuelen:1000
          RX bytes:2092656 (1.9 Mb)  TX bytes:161329 (157.5 Kb)
          Interrupt:10 Base address:0x10a0
```

The output of this command shows that you've successfully changed the IP address on the eth0 interface. But this may not be enough, as you should realize that the broadcast address may not work with this IP address. For example, you may have configured a private network with the 10.11.12.0 network address.

With the right switch, the **ifconfig** command can modify a number of other settings for your network adapter. Some of these switches are shown in Table 7-4.

netstat -r

The **netstat** command is used to display a plethora of network connectivity information. The most commonly used option, **netstat -r**, is used to display local routing tables. Here's a sample **netstat -nr** output:

```
# netstat -nr
Kernel routing table
Destination     Gateway         Genmask         Flags MSS Window  irtt Iface
191.72.1.0      *               255.255.255.0   U     40  0          0 eth0
127.0.0.0       *               255.0.0.0       UH    40  0          0 lo
default         191.72.1.1      255.255.255.0   UG    40  0          0 eth0
```

TABLE 7-4	ifconfig Switches

Parameter	Description
up	Activates the specified adapter.
down	Deactivates the specified adapter.
netmask *address*	Assigns the *address* subnet mask.
broadcast *address*	Assigns the *address* as the broadcast address. Rarely required, since the default broadcast address is standard for most current networks.
metric N	Allows you to set a metric value of N for the routing table associated with the network adapter.
mtu N	Sets the maximum transmission unit as N, in bytes.
-arp	Deactivates the Address Resolution Protocol, which collects network adapter hardware addresses.
promisc	Activates promiscuous mode. This allows the network adapter to read all packets to all hosts on the LAN. Can be used to analyze the network for problems or to try to decipher messages between other users.
-promisc	Deactivates promiscuous mode.
irq *port*	Assigns a specific IRQ *port*.
io_addr *address*	Assigns a specific I/O *address*.

Did you notice the use of the **-n** flag? **-n** tells **netstat** to display addresses as IP addresses, instead of as host names. This makes it a little easier to see what's going on. One equivalent option is the **route -n** command.

In many cases, you'll see 0.0.0.0 instead of *default*; both point to all other network addresses, such as those on the Internet.

The Destination column lists networks by their IP addresses. The *default* destination is associated with all other IP addresses. The Gateway column indicates gateway addresses. If the destination is on the LAN, no gateway is required, so an asterisk (or 0.0.0.0) is shown in this column. The Genmask column lists the network mask. Networks look for a route appropriate to the destination IP address. The IP address is compared against the destination networks, in order. When the IP address is found to be part of one of these networks, it's sent in that direction. If there is a gateway address, it's sent to the computer with that gateway. The Flags column describes how this is done. Flag descriptions are listed in Table 7-5.

arp as a Diagnostic Tool

The Address Resolution Protocol associates the hardware address of a network adapter with an IP address. The **arp** command (in the /sbin directory) displays a table of hardware and IP addresses on the local computer. With **arp**, you can detect

Flag	Description
G	The route uses a gateway.
U	The network adapter (Iface) is up.
H	Only a single host can be reached via this route.
D	This entry was created by an ICMP redirect message.
M	This entry was modified by an ICMP redirect message.

TABLE 7-5

The **netstat** Flag Indicates the Route

problems such as duplicate addresses on the network, or you can manually add **arp** entries as required. Here's a sample **arp** command, showing all **arp** entries in the local database:

```
# arp
Address              HWtype   HWaddress           Flags Mask        Iface
192.168.0.121        ether    52:A5:CB:54:52:A2   C                 eth0
192.168.0.113        ether    00:A0:C5:E2:49:02   C                 eth0
```

If the **arp** table is empty, you haven't made any connections to other computers on your network. The Address column lists known IP addresses, usually on the LAN. The HWtype column shows the hardware type of the adapter, while the HWaddress column shows the hardware address of the adapter.

You can use the **-H** option to limit the output from **arp** to a specific hardware type, such as ax25, ether, or pronet. The default is ether, which is short for Ethernet.

The **arp** command can help you with duplicate IP addresses, which can stop a network completely. To remove the offending machine's **arp** entry from your **arp** table, use the **-d** option:

```
# arp -d bugsy
```

This removes all **arp** information for the host bugsy. To add an **arp** entry, use the **-s** option:

```
# arp -s bugsy 00:00:c0:cf:a1:33
```

This entry will add the host bugsy with the given hardware address to the **arp** table. IP addresses won't work in this case.

DHCP Clients

You can set up your computer as a DHCP client. If the **system-config-network** configuration utility does not work, check the configuration file associated with your network card in the /etc/sysconfig/network-scripts directory. You should not need static IP configuration information, and you should see **BOOTPROTO=dhcp**.

In any case, if you have a working DHCP server on your network, you can connect your computer to it with the **dhclient** command.

CERTIFICATION OBJECTIVE 7.02

The CUPS Printing System

RHEL comes with one print service, the Common Unix Printing System (CUPS). It's the successor to the Line Print Daemon (LPD) and the companion Line Printer Next Generation (LPRng), which is no longer offered with RHEL or Fedora Linux. You can configure printers directly through the CUPS configuration files in the /etc/cups directory. Alternatively, RHEL includes two quality GUI tools that you can use to configure local and remote printers on your network. One is a Web-based interface; Red Hat has a companion printer configuration utility.

CUPS is the Linux/Unix implementation of the Internet Printing Protocol (IPP). I expect IPP to become a fairly universal standard for printer configuration sometime in the future. Microsoft Print servers can now use IPP; Apple systems starting with OS 10.2 use CUPS with IPP.

It doesn't matter how you configure a print server for the Red Hat exams. Whether you use Red Hat's utility or the Web-based tool, or you edit the configuration files directly, all that matters is that you get the result specified on your exam.

Installing and Starting CUPS

CUPS and a number of print databases are installed with the Printing Support package group. It includes 10 RPM packages, some of which appear unrelated. If you haven't already installed this package group during the RHEL installation process, it's likely most efficient to install it using the **yum groupinstall printing** command or the Package Manager described in Chapter 5. If you want to learn to install the packages on your own, you can review the packages and groups as listed in the Package Manager.

It's easy to start and configure CUPS to launch when Linux boots on your computer. The **cups** service script works like most of the other services on RHEL. In other words, you can start it with the following command:

```
# service cups start
```

By substituting **restart**, **stop**, or **reload** for **start**, you can restart or stop the CUPS service or reload the CUPS configuration files. And, as always, you need to make sure the CUPS service starts the next time you (or the person grading your exam) boots your system:

```
# chkconfig cups on
```

CUPS Configuration Files

There are a number of printer configuration files in the /etc/cups directory. Each of these files includes a substantial number of commands and comments. Table 7-6 describes some of these files; I describe some of the commands associated with these files shortly.

While I still believe that it's best in general to edit configuration files directly, the commands associated with CUPS can be difficult to learn. Several of the files in /etc/cups don't include the same quality of comments as seen for other services. And, in my opinion, the Red Hat and the Web-based configuration tools provide an excellent level of functionality.

The Red Hat Printer Configuration Tool

The main Red Hat Printer Configuration tool works well. You can start it with the **system-config-printer** command, which opens the utility shown in Figure 7-2. It is a "front end" that can help you configure the files in the /etc/cups directory.

TABLE 7-6   CUPS Configuration Files

CUPS Configuration File	Description
/etc/cups/classes.conf	Configures groups of printers in a class
/etc/cups/client.conf	Sets the default CUPS server for this computer; it can be local or another remote print server
/etc/cups/cupsd.conf	The main CUPS configuration file
/etc/cups/mime.convs	Includes file format filters, such as images and documents
/etc/cups/mime.types	Sets file types that can be processed through CUPS printers
/etc/cups/pdftops.conf	Specifies additional files for language-specific PDF fonts
/etc/cups/printers.conf	Documents printers configured by the CUPS Web-based tool
/etc/cups/pstoraster.convs	Includes a conversion filter that supports PostScript printers
/etc/cups/snmp.conf	Configures network printer discovery
/etc/printcap	Adds a list of printers for sharing; used by Samba
/etc/cups/ppd/	Includes a directory with customized printer settings
/etc/cups/ssl/	Includes a directory with SSL certificates
/etc/cups/interfaces/	Includes a directory with interface scripts, such as filters

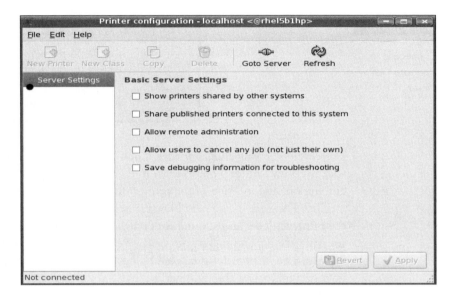

FIGURE 7-2

Red Hat's Printer
Configuration
utility

You can use this tool to manage printers and configure print queues to local ports
or through remote systems:

- Local CUPS serial/parallel ports
- Networked CUPS ports (using the IPP)
- Remote Unix/Linux LPD print services
- Shared Windows printers
- Novell NCP print queues
- HP JetDirect print servers
- Any other printer with a URI

on the
ⓘ o b

*Red Hat no longer includes the text-mode version of the Printer
Configuration tool.*

First, you can use the Printer Configuration tool to configure a printer on a remote
system, assuming it also has the same Printer Configuration tool (and authorized
remote access). In the tool's main window, click Goto Server. In the Connect To
CUPS Server dialog box shown in Figure 7-3, enter the name (or IP address) of
the remote system you want to administer, as well as the authorized username, and
whether encryption is required. You may be prompted for a password. If successful,
you'll see a new Printer Configuration tool with the name of the remote system.

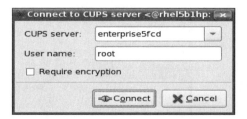

FIGURE 7-3

Connecting to
a remote CUPS
server

Now try defining a local printer. Click New Printer. This should automatically
start the New Printer wizard shown in Figure 7-4, where you can enter the name,
description, and location of the printer similar to what's shown.

Click Forward. In the next New Printer screen, select the type of connection. If
the printer is local and automatically detected, it's shown in this screen. So what you
see will vary, depending on your hardware and attached printers. As shown in Figure
7-5, the detected printer is labeled *HPLaserJet 4L LPT parport0 HPLIP*. Try the other
options, and look at the information that you would need.

The information you need corresponds to Table 7-7. Make any appropriate entries
and click Forward to continue.

Now you can select a printer manufacturer, or enter a driver, as shown in Figure
7-6. If you have a print driver, in .ppd format, you can enter it here. Otherwise,
select a printer manufacturer and click Forward to continue.

FIGURE 7-4

Starting
the printer
configuration
process

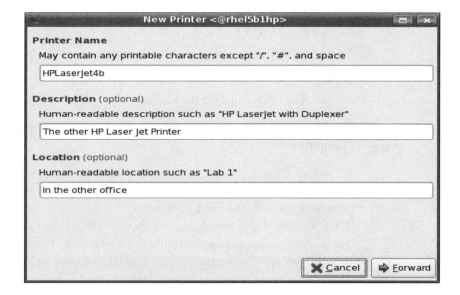

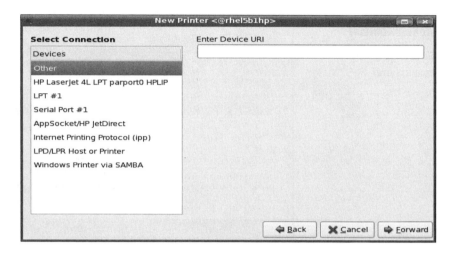

FIGURE 7-5

Selecting a
connection

Next, as shown in Figure 7-7, select the appropriate model. If multiple drivers are
available, select the one most appropriate for your configuration. If you do not want
to choose the default, the comments may be helpful.

Click Forward. Before the Printer Configuration tool creates a print queue, it
documents what it's about to do. If you're satisfied with the configuration, click Apply.
This returns you to the main Printer Configuration window shown in Figure 7-2.

The main Printer Configuration window should now include the name of your
printer. The changes should already be written to the configuration files in the /etc/
cups directory as well as /etc/printcap.

TABLE 7-7   Entries Associated with Different Printer Devices

Device	Required Information
Other	URI (Universal Resource Identifier)
a specific printer	n/a
LPT #1	n/a
Serial Port #1	Baud rate, parity, data bits, flow control
App Socket / HP JetDirect	Host name or IP address and port number (default is 9100)
Internet Printing Protocol (IPP)	Host name, such as ipp://enterprise5.example.net and printer name
LPD/LPR Host or Printer	Host name or IP address and printer name
Windows Printer via SAMBA	Workgroup/Domain; computer and printer name; authentication information

FIGURE 7-6

Selecting a
manufacturer

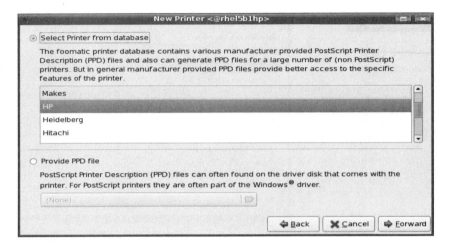

If you have trouble here, you may not have shared the CUPS printer at the
server. To do so at the server, highlight the Server Settings option. Five options
are available, as described in Table 7-8.

Any time you make changes, click Apply to implement them on the local system.

After you have added more than one printer, you may want to create different
classes of printers. A printer class typically includes more than one printer, and the
class can be cited as a printer. When you print to a class, CUPS prints to the first
available printer in that class. All printers in a class are usually located in the same
area or room.

For example, assume you've created a print class named Class1, which consists of
HPLaserJ4La and HPLaserJ4Lb. If you print to a printer named Class1, CUPS prints
to either HPLaserJ4La or HPLaserJ4Lb, whichever is not busy at the time.

FIGURE 7-7

Selecting a printer
and driver

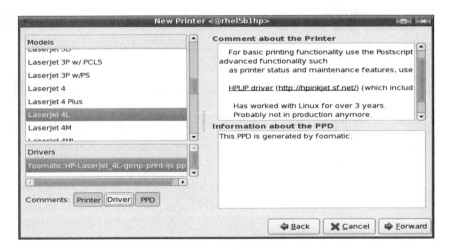

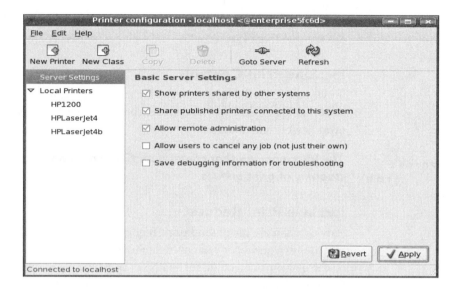

FIGURE 7-8

Sharing a CUPS printer

Creating a print class using the Red Hat Printer Configuration tool is easy. Click New Class, and you'll be able to enter a name, description, and location for the class, similar to Figure 7-4. You can then select the printers to add to that class.

The Line Print Daemon Commands

Even though RHEL uses CUPS, you can still control your print system with LPD commands. Three major commands are associated with the **lpd** service: **lpr**, **lpq**, and **lprm**. They are used to add print requests, list queued print requests, and remove print requests, respectively. One more command can help you administer one or more print queues: **lpc**.

TABLE 7-8   Entries Associated with Different Printer Devices

Server Setting	Description
Show Printers Shared By Other Systems	Searches the network for shared printers, such as through Samba
Share Published Printers Connected To This System	Allows remote CUPS servers to access printers configured on this system
Allow Remote Administration	Allows remote connections to the local CUPS server
Allow Users To Cancel Any Job	Supports the use of **lprm** by any user on any print job
Save Debugging Information For Troubleshooting	Adds more information to the appropriate log file in the /var/log/cups/ directory

There are several more line print commands available, but these are the basics. And I'm not sure that every exam facility includes printers connected to test networks.

lpc: Line Print Control

To view all known queues, run the **lpc status** command; it implements the result shown in Figure 7-9. As you can see, the output helps you easily scan all configured print devices and queues.

on the job *The lpc command that comes with CUPS does not support starting or stopping of print queues.*

lpr: Line Print Request

Any user can use **lpr** to send print requests to any local print queue. You can **lpr** any files to a queue, or you can redirect any output via **lpr**. If you wanted to print to the queue named color, for example, you'd use a command like this: **lpr -Pcolor** *filename*. Note that there is no space between the **-P** switch and the name of the queue (though a space is now allowed in RHEL 5).

lpq: Line Print Query

Now, to examine how the **lpq** command works, you can start by queuing up a new job by issuing these commands:

```
# lpq
WinPrint1 is ready and printing
Rank      Owner    Job  Files                        Total Size
active    root     373  smbprn.000486.6JkBaq         10240 bytes
1st       root     374  smbprn.000487.6JkBaq         10240 bytes
2nd       root     376  smbprn.000488.6JkBaq         10240 bytes
```

FIGURE 7-9

Status of configured printers

```
[root@Enterprise5a ~]# lpc status
HPColor:
        printer is on device 'socket' speed -1
        queuing is enabled
        printing is enabled
        no entries
        daemon present
HPLaserJ4:
        printer is on device 'hp' speed -1
        queuing is enabled
        printing is enabled
        no entries
        daemon present
testclass:
        printer is on device '///dev/null' speed -1
        queuing is enabled
        printing is enabled
        no entries
        daemon present
[root@Enterprise5a ~]#
```

Now you can delete the jobs of your choice. It's simple; just use the **lprm** command with the job number:

```
# lprm 376
```

GUI Front End

RHEL includes a GUI front end for printer management on the GNOME desktop, which allows you to switch default printers. To view the printers that you've configured on the GUI, choose System | Preferences | More Preferences | Default Printer. As shown in Figure 7-10, it allows you to set a different default printer.

The CUPS Web-Based Interface

Another way to configure CUPS is through the Web-based interface. Open up the browser of your choice on the local Linux computer. Direct it to the http://localhost:631 address to get to the main CUPS configuration menu, as shown in Figure 7-11.

There are six virtual tabs atop the main page:

- **Home** Brings you to the introductory page shown in Figure 7-11, which introduces CUPS as a GPL licensed product of Easy Software Products (www.easysw.com).
- **Administration** A basic interface that allows you to add or manage classes of printers, manage print jobs, and add or manage printers. You can also navigate directly to the options from the Home page tab.
- **Classes** Supports viewing and management of installed printer classes.
- **Documentation/Help** Provides extensive documentation.
- **Jobs** Enables you to view and manage active print jobs.
- **Printers** Enables you to manage existing printers.

FIGURE 7-10

GNOME Default
Printer manager

CUPS Web-based
interface

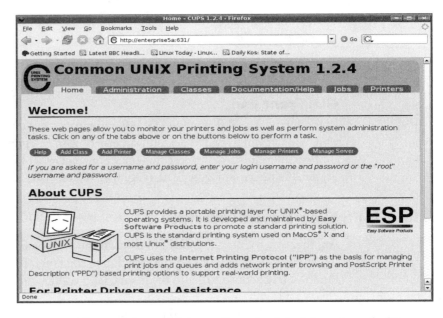

You can manage Classes, Jobs, and Printers from the Administration tab. (You
can read the Documentation/Help section on your own; software upgrades to CUPS
are not covered in this book.) The heart of CUPS is in the Administration tab.
At some point during administrative commands, you're prompted to enter your
administrative root username and password.

Finally, the CUPS Web-based interface supports the same extensive database of
printers that you see in the Red Hat Printer Configuration tool. And with RHEL 5,
the Red Hat tool supports the creation of printer classes and the complete variety of
print protocols supported by CUPS.

CUPS Administration

Select the Administration tab, which brings you to the Administration management
page, shown in Figure 7-12. It includes four sections: The Printers section is where
you add or manage configured printers. In the Classes section, you can configure a
group of printers together. When you use a specific class, CUPS directs your print
job to the first available printer in this class. The Jobs section helps you manage
the print jobs currently in the print queue. In the Servers section, you can edit the
configuration file, view logs, and modify various server settings. Before actually
executing an administrative command, you'll be prompted for administrative
authentication.

As the Red Hat Printer Configuration tool supports a wider variety of printers,
I won't explain the Add Printer dialog box in this book. However, if you want to

FIGURE 7-12

CUPS
Administration
management page

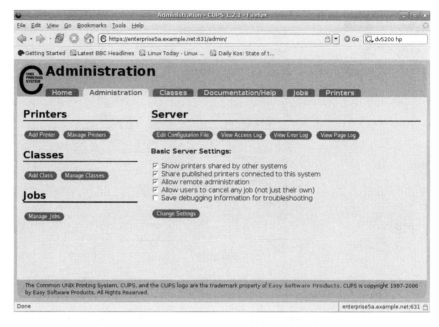

FIGURE 7-12

CUPS
Administration
management page

create a printer class, the CUPS Web-based tool is the easiest way to go. As described earlier, a CUPS printer class allows you to print to a group of printers. CUPS then selects the first available printer in that class when you print to that class.

To proceed, click Add Class. You'll see a dialog box, as shown in Figure 7-13:

■ **Name** The name of the printer class. If you want to print to this printer group, you'll call or connect to this printer class name.

■ **Location** Must be set to the name or IP address of the local print server.

■ **Description** Allows you to add the comment of your choice to help identify the printer class.

After you click Add Class, you'll get to include one or more configured printers in your printer class. If you haven't previously entered administrative authentication for CUPS, you're prompted to do so at this time. The CUPS Web-based tool now creates a print class. Click the Classes tab to see your new print class, as shown in Figure 7-14.

Verifying CUPS Sharing

Once you've configured security for a CUPS printer, you can verify it in three CUPS configuration files in the /etc/cups directory: cupsd.conf, printers.conf, and classes.conf.

FIGURE 7-13

Configuring a
printer class

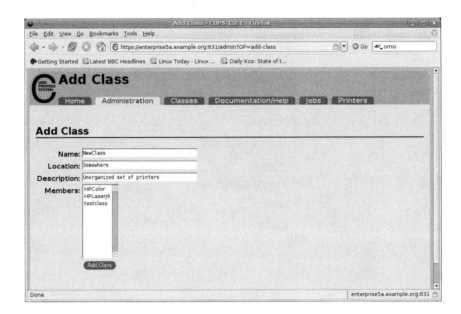

The security commands in this file are fairly straightforward. By default, access to a CUPS printer is limited to the local computer with a directive such as:

```
Browsing Off
```

If you configure a CUPS printer to be shared with the local network, you'll see it replaced with the following commands. The key is **BrowseAddress @LOCAL**,

FIGURE 7-14

The new printer
class

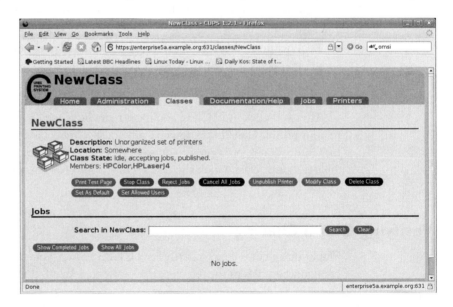

which limits browsing access to the LAN connected directly to the local network card. In contrast, **@ALL** would support access from all connected networks. The **DefaultAuthType Basic** directive uses the /etc/passwd configuration file to search for allowed users.

```
Browsing On
BrowseOrder allow,deny
BrowseAddress @LOCAL
DefaultAuthType Basic
```

For example, printer administrators are as specified in the following cupsd.conf container, which supports basic authentication using /etc/passwd based on users in the @SYSTEM group, also known as *sys* in /etc/group. Remote access to the Web-based tool is supported on the @LOCAL network.

```
<Location /admin/conf>
  AuthType Basic
  Require user @SYSTEM
  # Allow remote access to the configuration files...
  Order allow,deny
  Allow @LOCAL
</Location>
```

You can limit access to specific IP address networks. For example, to support access from the 192.168.30.0 LAN, add the following directive:

```
Allow From 192.168.30.0/255.255.255.0
```

You can also substitute computer or domain names. For example, the following command allows access from the example.com domain:

```
Allow From *.example.com
```

You can't configure these limits using the Red Hat Printer Configuration utility (**system-config-printer**). If you want to set up host-based security in this way, you'll have to edit the cupsd.conf configuration file directly.

However, you can now configure user-based access control per printer in the Printer Configuration utility. Just select the configured printer and click the Access Control tab. You'll be able to add a set of users, and you can limit access to these users (or prohibit access to just those users).

To limit access to a specific printer or print class, add appropriate directives to the printers.conf and classes.conf configuration files.

CUPS and SELinux

If you're configuring SELinux, you can disable SELinux protection for various CUPS services, including:

- **cupsd Backend Server**   Disables protection for CUPS configuration files, per the **cupsd_config_disable_trans** boolean, associated with the now obsolete cups-config-daemon service.
- **cupsd daemon**   Disables protection for the CUPS service, per the **cups_disable_trans** boolean.
- **cups_lpd service**   Disables protection for the **cups-lpd** xinetd service, per the **cupsd_lpd_disable_trans** boolean, which supports communication from LPD printers.
- **CUPS hplip daemon**   Disables protections for the HP Linux Imaging and Printing service, per the **hplip_disable_trans** boolean.

If you want to substitute the LPD daemon for CUPS, you'll also need to activate the Use Lpd Server Instead Of CUPS option, also known as the **use_lpd_server** boolean. These options are available in the SELinux Management Tool, as described in Chapter 15.

CERTIFICATION OBJECTIVE 7.03

Automating System Administration: cron and at

The cron system is essentially a smart alarm clock. When the alarm sounds, Linux runs the commands of your choice automatically. You can set the alarm clock to run at all sorts of regular time intervals. Alternatively, the at system allows you to run the command of your choice, once, at a specified time in the future.

e x a m

ⓦ a t c h   *Because cron always checks for changes, you do not have to restart cron every time you make a change.*

RHEL installs the **cron** daemon (**crond**) by default. It's configured to check the /var/spool/cron directory for jobs by user. It also checks for scheduled jobs for the computer under /etc/crontab and in the /etc/cron.d directory.

The behavior of the Linux **cron** is different from Unix, where the **cron** daemon wakes up only when it needs to launch a program.

The System crontab and Components

The crontab file is set up in a specific format. Each line can be blank, a comment (which begins with #), a variable, or a command. Naturally, blank lines and comments are ignored.

When you run a regular command, the actions of the shell are based on environmental variables. To see the environmental variables, run the **env** command. Some of the standard variables in RHEL include **HOME** as your home directory, **SHELL** as the default shell, and **LOGNAME** as the username.

You can set different variables within the crontab file, or you can set environmental variables with the following syntax:

```
Variable=Value
```

Some variables are already set for you. For example, **MAIL** for me is /var/spool/mail/michael, **LANG** is en_US.UTF-8, and **PATH** is where the shell looks for commands. You can set these variables to different values in your crontab file. For example, the default /etc/crontab file includes the following variables:

```
SHELL=/bin/bash
PATH=/sbin:/bin:/usr/sbin:/usr/bin
MAILTO=root
HOME=/
```

Note that the values of **PATH**, **MAILTO**, and **HOME** are different from those for the standard environment variables.

on the **job**

*The **MAILTO** variable can help you administer several Linux systems. The cron daemon sends output by e-mail. Just add a line such as MAILTO=me@somewhere.com to route all cron messages associated with that file to that e-mail address.*

exam

watch   *Note how the **PATH** variable in a crontab may be different from the **PATH** variable associated with your shell. In fact, the two variables are independent. Therefore, you'll want to*   *know the exact path of every command in your crontab. Specify the absolute path with the command if it isn't in the crontab **PATH**.*

Here is the format of a line in crontab. Each of these columns is explained in more detail in Table 7-9.

```
#minute, hour, day of month, month, day of week, command
*        *      *              *      *               command
```

If you see an asterisk in any column, **cron** runs that command for all possible values of that column. For example, an * in the minute field means that the command is run every minute during the specified hour(s). Consider another example, as shown here:

```
1   5   3   4   *   ls
```

This line runs the **ls** command every April 3 at 5:01 A.M. The asterisk in the day of week column simply means that it does not matter what day of the week it is; crontab still runs the **ls** command at the specified time.

The crontab file is flexible. For example, a 7–10 entry in the hour field would run the specified command at 7:00 A.M., 8:00 A.M., 9:00 A.M., and 10:00 A.M. A list of entries in the minute field such as: 0,5,10,15,20,25,30,35,40,45,50,55 would run the specified command every five minutes. The **cron** daemon also recognizes abbreviations for months and the day of the week.

The actual command is the sixth field. You can set up new lines with a percent (%) symbol. This is useful for formatting standard input. The example of a cron file follows formats input for an e-mail message:

```
# crontab -l
# Sample crontab file
#
# Force /bin/sh to be my shell for all of my scripts.
SHELL=/bin/sh
# Run 15 minutes past Midnight every Saturday
15 0 * * sat    $HOME/scripts/scary.script
# Do routine cleanup on the first of every Month at 4:30 AM
30 4 1 * *      /usr/scripts/removecores >> /tmp/core.tmp 2>>&1
# Mail a message at 10:45 AM every Friday
45 10 * * fri   mail -s "Project Update employees%Can I have a status
update on your project?%%Your Boss.%
# Every other hour check for alert messages
0 */2 * * * /usr/scripts/check.alerts
```

For more examples, review some of the scripts in the /etc/cron.daily directory. Three key scripts include *logrotate*, for rotating log files; *mlocate.cron*, which updates the *locate* file database; and *tmpwatch*, which wipes files from /tmp and /var/tmp after a specific amount of time.

| TABLE 7-9 | Entries in a **crontab** Command Line |

Field	Value
minute	0–59
hour	Based on a 24-hour clock; for example, 23 = 11 P.M.
day of month	1–31
month	1–12, or jan, feb, mar, etc.
day of week	0–7; where 0 and 7 are both Sunday; or sun, mon, tue, etc.
command	The command you want to run

on the **Job** *The only SELinux settings associated with cron disable protection for the daemon and enable access for the fcron scheduler, associated with the cron_disable_trans and fcron_crond booleans.*

Setting Up cron for Users

Each user can use the **crontab** command to create and manage **cron** jobs for their own accounts. There are four switches associated with the **crontab** command:

- **-u** *user*   Allows the root user to edit the crontab of another specific user.
- **-l**   Lists the current entries in the crontab file.
- **-r**   Removes **cron** entries.
- **-e**   Edits an existing **crontab** entry. By default, **crontab** uses vi.

If you want to set up **cron** entries on your own account, start with the **crontab -e** command. It opens the vi editor, where you can add the variables and commands of your choice, similar to what you've seen in /etc/crontab.

EXERCISE 7-2

Creating a cron Job

In this exercise, you will modify the basic Red Hat **cron** job settings to read a text file at 1:05 P.M. every Monday in the month of January. To do so, you'll need to create a directory for yearly **cron** jobs. To do this, use the following steps:

1. Log in as the root user.

2. Create a /etc/cron.yearly directory. Add a file called taxrem, which reads a text file from your home directory. A command such as the following in the taxrem file should suffice:

```
cat ~/reminder
```

Make sure to add appropriate lines to the reminder file in your home directory.

3. Add an appropriate command to your /etc/crontab file. Based on the conditions described, it would read as follows:

```
5 13 * 1 1 root run-parts /etc/cron.yearly
```

4. Save and exit.

Running a Job with the at System

Like **cron**, the **at** daemon supports job processing. However, you can set an **at** job to be run once. Jobs in the **cron** system must be set to run on a regular basis. The **at** daemon works in a way similar to the print process; jobs are spooled in the /var/spool/at directory and run at the specified time.

You can use the **at** daemon to run the command or script of your choice. For the purpose of this section, assume that user michael has created a script named 797 in his home directory to process some airplane sales database to another file in the same directory called sales.

From the command line, you can run the **at** *time* command to start a job to be run at a specified *time*. That *time* can be now; in a specified number of minutes, hours, or days; or at the time of your choice. Several examples are illustrated in Table 7-10.

You can use one of the example commands shown in Table 7-10 to open an **at** job. It opens a different command line interface, where you can specify the command of your choice. For this example, assume you're about to leave work, and want to start the job in an hour. From the conditions specified above, run the following commands:

```
$ at now + 1 hour
at> /home/michael/797 > /home/michael/sales
at> Ctrl-D
```

TABLE 7-10	Examples of the **at** Command

Time Period	Example	Description
Minutes	at now + 10 minutes	Associated jobs will start in 10 minutes.
Hours	at now + 2 hours	Associated jobs will start in 2 hours.
Days	at now + 1 day	Associated jobs will start in 24 hours.
Weeks	at now + 1 week	Associated jobs will start in 7 days.
n/a	at teatime	Associated jobs will start at 4:00 P.M.
n/a	at 3:00 6/13/07	Associated jobs will start on June 13, 2007, at 3:00 A.M.

The CTRL-D command exits the **at** command shell and returns to your original command line interface. To check the status of your jobs, so you can see if it will work, run the following job queue command:

```
$ atq
1         2007-4-12 17:18 a michael
```

If there's a problem with the job, you can remove it with the **atrm** command. For the output shown, you'd remove job number 1 with the following command:

```
$ atrm 1
```

on the job

There is no current SELinux setting associated with the at daemon.

Securing cron and at

You may not want everyone to be able to run a job in the middle of the night. If your system has a security flaw, someone may download important data or worse, and it could be days before you discover the security breach.

As with network firewalls, you can allow or deny users the privilege of using **cron**. You can set up users in /etc/cron.allow and /etc/cron.deny files. If these files don't exist, **cron** usage is not restricted. If users are named in /etc/cron.allow file, all other users won't be able to use **cron**. If there is no /etc/cron.allow file, only users named in /etc/cron.deny can't use **cron**.

These files are formatted as one line per user; if you include the following entries in /etc/cron.deny and no /etc/cron.allow file, users elizabeth and nancy aren't allowed to set up their own **cron** commands:

```
elizabeth
nancy
```

You can secure access to the **at** system in the same way. The corresponding security configuration files are /etc/at.allow and /etc/at.deny.

on the *job*

If you shut down your Linux system at night, the anacron service runs those cron jobs that were scheduled during the down time.

CERTIFICATION OBJECTIVE 7.04

Understanding, Maintaining, and Monitoring System Logs

An important part of maintaining a secure system is keeping track of the activities that take place on the system. If you know what usually happens, such as understanding when users log into your system, you can use log files to spot unusual activity. Red Hat Enterprise Linux comes with several utilities you can use to monitor activity on a system. These utilities can help you identify the culprit if there is a problem.

RHEL comes with two logging daemons. The kernel log daemon service, **klogd**, logs kernel messages and events. The **syslogd** daemon logs all other process activity. You can use the log files that **syslogd** generates to track activities on your system. If you are managing multiple Red Hat Enterprise Linux systems, you can configure the **syslogd** daemon on each system to log messages to a central host system.

Both daemons are typically active by default, and both can be activated by the /etc/init.d/syslog script. Once these daemons start, the **syslogd** daemon examines /etc/syslog.conf to find the logging options that you may have configured.

on the *job*

The only available SELinux options associated with logging services disable protection; they're associated with the klogd_disable_trans and syslogd_ disable_trans booleans.

System Log Configuration File

You can configure what **syslogd** records through the /etc/syslog.conf configuration file. As shown in Figure 7-15, it includes a set of rules for different facilities (if the corresponding packages are installed): authpriv, cron, kern, mail, news, user, and uucp. You may not see everything that's shown in Figure 7-15; for example, if you haven't installed the Internet News Network (INN) service, you won't see the associated directives in this file.

FIGURE 7-15

The syslog.conf
log configuration
file

```
# Log all kernel messages to the console.
# Logging much else clutters up the screen.
#kern.*                                                /dev/console

# Log anything (except mail) of level info or higher.
# Don't log private authentication messages!
*.info;mail.none;news.none;authpriv.none;cron.none         /var/log/message
s

# The authpriv file has restricted access.
authpriv.*                                             /var/log/secure

# Log all the mail messages in one place.
mail.*                                                 -/var/log/maillog

# Log cron stuff
cron.*                                                 /var/log/cron

# Everybody gets emergency messages
*.emerg                                                *

# Save news errors of level crit and higher in a special file.
uucp,news.crit                                         /var/log/spooler

# Save boot messages also to boot.log
local7.*                                               /var/log/boot.log

#
# INN
#
news.=crit                                      /var/log/news/news.crit
news.=err                                       /var/log/news/news.err
news.notice                                     /var/log/news/news.notice
```

Each facility is associated with several different levels of logging, known as the *priority*. In ascending order, log priorities are **debug, info, notice, warn, err, crit, alert, emerg**. There's also a generic **none** priority that logs all messages at all levels.

For each facility and priority, log information is sent to a specific log file. For example, consider the following line from /etc/syslog.conf:

```
*.info;mail.none;news.none;authpriv.none;cron.none /var/log/messages
```

This line sends log information from all of the given facilities to the /var/log/ messages file. This includes:

- All facility messages of info level and higher
- No log messages related to the **mail, news, authpriv** (authentication), and **cron** services

You can use the asterisk as a wildcard in /etc/syslog.conf. For example, a line that starts with ***.*** tells the **syslogd** daemon to log everything. A line that starts with **auth.*** means you want to log all messages from the **authpriv** service.

By default, **syslogd** logs all messages of a given priority or higher. In other words, a **cron.err** line will include all log messages from the **cron** daemon at the **err**, **crit**, **alert**, and **emerg** levels.

Most messages from the **syslogd** daemon are written to files in the /var/log directory. You should scan these logs on a regular basis and look for patterns that could indicate a security breach.

Managing Logs

Logs can easily become very large and difficult to read. By default, the logrotate utility creates a new log file on a weekly basis. You can also configure /etc/logrotate .conf to compress, mail, and remove desired log files. By default, the **cron** daemon runs logrotate on a regular basis, using the configuration files located in the /etc/ logrotate.d directory. As you can see in Figure 7-16, this process works fairly well; up to five weeks of logs are kept for a number of log facilities.

Various log files and their functionality are described in Table 7-11. This is based on the previously described configuration of the /etc/syslog.conf file. All files shown are in the /var/log directory. If you haven't installed or activated the noted service, you may not see the associated log file. For the system depicted in Figure 7-16, I haven't bothered with the INN or PPP services, MySQL databases, or quagga routing messages. You may see a few other log files based on additional services you may have installed.

FIGURE 7-16

A typical set of log files in /var/log

```
[root@Enterprise5a ~]# ls /var/log/
acpid            cron.3     messages      rpmpkgs.1        spooler.3
anaconda.log     cron.4     messages.1    rpmpkgs.2        spooler.4
anaconda.syslog  cups       messages.2    rpmpkgs.3        squid
anaconda.xlog    dmesg      messages.3    rpmpkgs.4        vbox
bittorrent       gdm        messages.4    samba            wtmp
boot.log         httpd      mysqld.log    scrollkeeper.log wtmp.1
boot.log.1       lastlog    mysqld.log.1  secure           xend.log
boot.log.2       mail       mysqld.log.2  secure.1         xferlog
boot.log.3       maillog    mysqld.log.3  secure.2         Xorg.0.log
boot.log.4       maillog.1  mysqld.log.4  secure.3         Xorg.0.log.old
btmp             maillog.2  news          secure.4         Xorg.setup.log
cron             maillog.3  ppp           spooler          yum.log
cron.1           maillog.4  prelink.log   spooler.1        yum.log.1
cron.2           mcelog     rpmpkgs       spooler.2
[root@Enterprise5a ~]#
```

TABLE 7-11	Standard Red Hat Log Files

Log Files	Description
acpid	Specifies events related to the Advanced Control and Power Interface (ACPI) daemon; events indicate ACPI activity
anaconda.*	Three log files: anaconda.log for installation message; anaconda.syslog for the first **dmesg**, and anaconda.xlog for the first start of the GUI server; the anaconda.xlog file won't exist if you install in text mode
audit/	Includes the audit.log file, which collects messages from the kernel 2.6 audit subsystem
boot.log	Associated with services that start and shut down process
btmp	Lists failed login attempts; readable with the **utmpdump btmp** command
conman/	Directory of messages associated with the console management program
cron	Based on scripts run by the **cron** daemon
cups/	Directory of printer access, page, and error logs
dmesg	Basic boot messages
faillog	List of failed login attempts; readable with the **faillog** command
gdm/	Directory of messages associated with starting via the GNOME Display Manager; includes login failures
kdm	Messages associated with starting via the KDE Display Manger; includes login and server failures
httpd/	Directory of log files associated with the Apache Web server
lastlog	Lists login records; readable with the **lastlog** command
mail/	Directory with mail log statistics; readable with the **mailstats** command
maillog	Log messages related to the sendmail and postfix mail servers
messages	Messages from other services as defined in /etc/syslog.conf
ppp/	Directory with Point to Point Protocol statistics; usually associated with telephone modems
prelink.log	Log of prelinked libraries and binaries designed to speed the boot process
rpmpkgs	Current list of installed RPM packages
samba/	Directory of access and service logs for the Samba server
scrollkeeper.log	Log related to GNOME documentation
secure	Lists login and access messages
setroubleshoot	Includes messages associated with the SELinux troubleshooting tool
spooler	Print spool log
squid/	Directory of files related to Squid Proxy Server access, cache, and storage
wtmp	List of logins, in binary format; can be read with the **utmpdump** command
tallylog	Supports pam_tally, which locks out a user after excessive login attempts
up2date	Becoming obsolete; includes access messages associated with updates
vbox/	Directory of logs associated with ISDN utilities
Xorg.0.log	Setup messages for the X Window System; may include configuration problems
yum.log	Logs packages installed, updated, and erased with **yum** or associated front ends such as the Package Updater (Pup)

![EXERCISE 7-3]

Checking Logs

In this exercise, you'll inspect the log files on your computer to try to identify different problems.

1. Restart the Linux computer. Log in as the root user. Use the wrong password once. Log in properly as the root user.

2. In a console, navigate to the /var/log directory and open the file named secure. Navigate to the "FAILED LOGON" message closest to the end of the file. Close the *secure* file.

3. Review other logs in the /var/log directory. Use Table 7-11 for guidance. Look for messages associated with hardware. What log files are they in? Does that make sense?

4. Try some of the logs from the table which require command interpretation, such as **faillog**.

CERTIFICATION SUMMARY

You've read about the configuration files in the /etc/sysconfig hierarchy. Some are important for networking, and others are important for basic parameters such as the system clock, mouse, and keyboard. You also learned about a number of related networking commands, including **ifup**, **ifdown**, **ifconfig**, **netstat**, **arp**, and **dhclient**.

A number of important network client services are associated with Red Hat Enterprise Linux. CUPS supports the configuration of printers locally or over the network. With CUPS, the configuration files are stored primarily in the /etc/cups directory. However, it also includes a list of printers in /etc/printcap to accommodate sharing through Samba. You can edit the CUPS configuration files directly with Red Hat's Printer Configuration tool or the CUPS Web-based interface.

The **cron** and **at** daemons can help you manage when and how services start on your system. Finally, log files can be configured to collect data from any number of services.

TWO-MINUTE DRILL

Here are some of the key points from the certification objectives in Chapter 7.

Network Configuration

❏ Key network configuration files are in the /etc/sysconfig directory: the *network* file, and the networking and network-scripts subdirectories.

❏ You can start the Network Configuration utility with the **system-config-network** command.

❏ To manage network settings on each interface, use **dhclient**, **ifup**, and **ifdown**.

❏ The **ifconfig** command is used to configure and display network devices.

❏ Use **ifup eth0** and **ifdown eth0** to activate and deactivate the eth0 interface.

❏ The **netstat** command is used to display a plethora of network connectivity information; **route -n** is another way to check the current routing table.

❏ The **arp** command is used to view or modify the local hardware address database.

The CUPS Printing System

❏ The Printer Configuration tool, which you can start with the **system-config-printer** command, can be used to configure most popular printers in /etc/cups/cupsd.conf.

❏ CUPS provides a Web-based interface. Once enabled, you can get to this interface in your browser by navigating to http://localhost:631.

Automating System Administration: cron and at

❏ The **cron** system allows any user to schedule jobs so they run at given intervals.

❏ The **at** system allows users to configure jobs to run once at a scheduled time.

❏ The **crontab** command is used to work with cron files. Use **crontab -e** to edit, **crontab -l** to list, or **crontab -d** to delete cron files.

❏ The /etc/cron.allow and /etc/cron.deny files are used to control access to the **cron** job scheduler.

Understanding, Maintaining, and Monitoring System Logs

❏ Red Hat Enterprise Linux includes two logging daemons: **klogd** for kernel messages and **syslogd** for all other process activity. Both are activated by the /etc/init.d/syslog service script.

❏ You can use log files generated by the **syslogd** daemon to track activities on your system.

❏ Most log files are stored in /var/log.

❏ You can configure what is logged through the syslog configuration file, /etc/syslog.conf.

SELF TEST

The following questions will help you measure your understanding of the material presented in this chapter. As no multiple choice questions appear on the Red Hat exams, no multiple choice questions appear in this book. These questions exclusively test your understanding of the chapter. It is okay if you have another way of performing a task. Getting results, not memorizing trivia, is what counts on the Red Hat exams.

Network Configuration

1. What three directives are typically found in the /etc/sysconfig/network file?

   _____

   _____

   _____

2. What command would you use to assign an IP address of 192.168.99.44 to your eth1 network card?

   _____

3. What command returns the current routing table?

   _____

4. What command deactivates the eth0 network device?

   _____

The CUPS Printing System

5. You want to look at your current printer configuration in a GUI desktop interface. What starts the Red Hat GUI Printer Configuration tool?

   _____

6. You want to configure a group of printers as a printer class. Which GUI tool can you use for this purpose?

   _____

7. What is the main CUPS printer configuration file?

   _____

8. What command can you use to remove print job number 12 from the print queue?

   _____

Automating System Administration: cron and at

9. You want to schedule a maintenance job, maintenance.pl, to run from your home directory on the first of every month at 4:00 A.M. You've run the **crontab -e** command to open your personal job file. Assume you've added appropriate **PATH** and **SHELL** directives. What directive would you add to run the specified job at the specified time?

_____

10. If you see the following entry in your /etc/crontab:

```
42 4 1 * * root run-parts /etc/cron.monthly
```

when is the next time Linux will run the jobs in the /etc/cron.monthly directory?

_____

Understanding, Maintaining, and Monitoring System Logs

11. Assume you normally work from a user account called sysadm. What entry might you add to /etc/syslog.conf to notify you whenever there is a serious problem with the kernel?

_____

12. What three log files in /var/log are most relevant to the installation process?

_____

_____

_____

LAB QUESTIONS

Lab 1

In this lab, you'll deliberately misconfigure your network card, observe the results, and see what you can do to restore the original configuration. I assume that you have a computer on a network, as that is a basic requirement of the Red Hat exams. If you have more than one network card, make sure you select the card that you use to connect to outside networks.

This lab assumes a basic understanding of IPv4 network addresses. It also assumes that you have a DHCP server on your system. (For now, it doesn't matter what operating system has the DHCP server; many home routers serve this purpose.) To prepare this lab, take the following steps:

1. Boot your system into a standard runlevel with networking, 3 or 5.

2. Inspect the current configuration of your network card with the **ifconfig** command. Inspect the current routing table, as specified by the **route -n** (or **netstat -nr**) command. If you have several network devices, find the device associated with your gateway.

3. Select the network device that connects to external networks, such as eth0. Change the IP address to a private IPv4 address on a different network. If you have multiple network cards, make sure the new address does not correspond to any existing network.

4. Confirm the change by running **ifconfig** again.

5. Try the **ping** command to the new IP address.

6. Try the **ping** command to an IP address on an external computer. It doesn't matter if the external computer is on a local network or the Internet. What message do you see?

7. Run the **ping** command to a host name of an external computer. It doesn't matter if the external computer is on a local network or the Internet. What message do you see?

8. Run the **route -n** command again. Is there a default route?

9. Assuming the network device you've changed is eth0, run the **dhclient eth0** command. What do you see? Run the **ifconfig** command again. Has the IP address changed?

10. Search through active processes for the **dhclient** command. What did you find?

11. Kill any active **dhclient** command process.

12. Apply the **dhclient** command to the target network device.

13. Redo step 2. What happened to the routing table? What about your network interface?

Lab 2

In this lab, you'll want to use the Red Hat Printer Configuration utility to connect a printer to your Linux system. The printer can be local or remotely connected through your LAN. As you'll want to create a printer class, you'll need more than one printer. (Hint: You can configure the same printer as many times as necessary, as long as you use different names.)

If you have only one physical printer, you can set up multiple print queues with different printer names. CUPS sees each print queue as if it were a separate printer.

Once you've created multiple printers, return to the Printer Configuration tool. Run the **system-config-printer** command in a GUI. Navigate to http://localhost:631. Click Add Class. Follow the prompts to create a printer class with the printers that you've configured.

Once you've created a new printer class, inspect the result in the /etc/cups/classes.conf configuration file. Check the contents of your /etc/printcap and /etc/printers.conf files. What are the names of the printers that you see? Do you see any surprises in the list?

If you have a Microsoft Windows computer on your network, activate the Samba service if required. Check the printer names as shown in the browse list. Do you see any surprises on this list? (For more information on Samba, see Chapter 10.)

Lab 3

As the root user, create jobs that change the login message for users at the text console. To do so, you'll want to change the content of /etc/motd. Make sure that people who log in at different times get appropriate messages:

If users log in between 7 A.M. and 1 P.M., create the login message "Coffee time!"

If users log in between 1 P.M. and 6 P.M., create the login message "Want some ice cream?"

If users log in between 6 P.M. and 7 A.M., create the login message "Shouldn't you be doing something else?"

Lab 4

In this lab, you'll find the value of several different log files. In preparation, use the wrong password to log into a regular account. Then take the following steps:

1. Navigate to /var/log as the root user.

2. Explore the contents of the anaconda.* log files.

3. Run the **utmpdump btmp** command. Do you see the login attempt? Can you tell if it succeeded?

4. Review the contents of the cron log file. Scroll through it. If your computer has been on for a while, most of what you see will be based on the **run-parts /etc/cron.hourly** command. Alternatively, if you reboot on occasion, you'll see messages associated with the **anacron** service.

5. Review the contents of the dmesg log file. Compare the beginning of it with the start of the anaconda.syslog file. Which one includes the currently booted kernel?

6. Navigate toward the bottom of the dmesg file. Can you identify the amount of swap space? What about one or more partitions with the default EXT3 filesystem?

7. Review the maillog log file. Do you see any messages associated with mail messages? If there are a lot of messages associated with the root account, run the **mail** command (to exit from the mail prompt [&], press CTRL-D).

8. Review the secure log file. Navigate to the bottom of the file. Do you see a message associated with the failed login?

9. Finally, review the Xorg.0.log file. Do you see any messages related to the mouse (or other pointing device) near the end of the file? How does that work when you didn't configure a pointing device during the installation process?

SELF TEST ANSWERS

Network Configuration

1. The three directives typically found in the /etc/sysconfig/network file are **NETWORKING**, **NETWORKING_IPV6**, and **HOSTNAME**. If you allow a DHCP server to assign host names, the HOSTNAME directive isn't required.

2. The command that assigns an IP address of 192.168.99.44 to an eth1 network card is

```
# ifconfig eth1 192.168.99.44
```

3. The command that returns the current routing table is

```
# route -n
```

The **netstat -nr** command works as well.

4. The command that deactivates the eth0 network device is

```
# ifconfig eth0 down
```

Alternatives are available, such as **ifdown eth0**.

The CUPS Printing System

5. The command that starts the Red Hat GUI Printer Configuration tool from a GUI command line is **system-config-printer**.

6. To configure a group of printers as a printer class, you can use the CUPS Web-based configuration tool.

7. The main CUPS printer configuration file is /etc/cups/cupsd.conf.

8. The command that removes print job number 12 from the default print queue is

```
# lprm 12
```

Automating System Administration: cron and at

9. The directive that runs the maintenance.pl script from a home directory at the noted time is

```
00 4 1 * * ~/maintenance.pl
```

10. Based on the noted entry in /etc/crontab, the next time Linux will run the jobs in the /etc/cron .monthly directory is on the first of the upcoming month, at 4:42 A.M.

Understanding, Maintaining, and Monitoring System Logs

11. The entry that you might activate in /etc/syslog.conf to notify you whenever a serious problem with the kernel occurs is

```
kern.*       /dev/console
```

12. The log files in /var/log that are most relevant to the installation process are **anaconda.log**, **anaconda.syslog**, and **anaconda.xlog**. If you install in text mode, anaconda.xlog won't be created.

LAB ANSWERS

Lab 1

This set of "answers" explain what you might expect during each step.

1. The standard runlevel for console logins is 3; the standard runlevel for GUI logins is 5. To boot into the runlevel of your choice, press a key when you see "Booting Red Hat Enterprise Linux 5 . . .": press P and enter the GRUB password if required, and press A to modify the kernel arguments. (This works only on a non-Xen kernel option.) You can then specify the boot runlevel by adding it to the end of the kernel command line.

2. If you have several network devices, you can focus by specifying a device with a command such as **ifconfig eth0**. The **route -n** command should collate connected networks with the appropriate network device (**netstat -nr** works just like **route -n**).

3. Make sure the IP address you select is on a different network. It's best if you use private IP addresses. Some address ranges are listed in Chapter 1.

4. When you run **ifconfig** again, you'll see the change you made.

5. When you try the **ping** command to the new IP address, it should work.

6. When you try the **ping** command to an IP address on an external computer, you'll see an error such as:

```
connect: Network is unreachable
```

7. When you run the **ping** command to a host name of an external computer, you'll see a message similar to:

```
ping: unknown host www.yahoo.com
```

8. When you run the **route -n** command again, you'll see that the default router is no longer listed there.

9. When you try the **dhclient eth0** command, you may not see a response. And the IP address won't have changed.

10. To search through active processes for the **dhclient** command, run **ps aux | grep dhclient**. It should identify the process identifier for **dhclient**.

11. To kill an active **dhclient** command process with a PID of 111, use the **kill 111** command.

12. Now you should be able to apply the **dhclient** command to the target network device, and you'll see messages as it finds your DHCP server.

13. Finally, you'll find an appropriate IP address for your network interface and the original routing table.

Lab 2

Starting the Printer Configuration utility is easy. One way in the GUI is to press ALT-F2 and then type **system-config-printer** in the text box that appears. Then you can click the New Printer button to start a configuration wizard. If you like, you can create different print queues for the same printer. Just repeat the same process, using a different printer name.

When you've created two or more printers, click New Class. This starts a similar configuration wizard, where you can collect preconfigured printers of your choice in a print class. As with new printers, a print class requires a name, description, and location.

Click Forward; select more than one computer as members of the printer class. Click Forward; once your new printer class is confirmed, click Apply.

You should now see the printer class and member printers in the /etc/cups/classes.conf file. You'll find a list of printers in /etc/printcap; you'll find the names of any configured printers *and* printer classes in this file. You should also see the list of printers in /etc/printcap in any Microsoft Windows Network Neighborhoods or My Network Places that is connected to the same network. This assumes that you've activated a Samba server on the local print server computer, of course.

Lab 3

To modify the login messages as noted, take the following steps:

1. Log in as the root user.

2. Run the **crontab -e** command.

3. Add appropriate environment variables, at least the following:

```
SHELL=/bin/bash
```

4. Add the following commands to the file to overwrite /etc/motd at the appropriate times:

```
00 7   * * * /bin/echo 'Coffee time!' > /etc/motd
00 13  * * * /bin/echo 'Want some ice cream?' > /etc/motd
00 18  * * * /bin/echo 'Shouldn't you be doing something else?' > /etc/motd
```

Save the file. As long as the **cron** daemon is active (which it is by default), the next user who logs into the console should see the message upon a successful login. If you want to test the result immediately, the **date** command can help. For example, the following command

```
# date 06120659
```

sets a date of June 12, at 6:59 A.M., just before the **cron** daemon should execute the first command in the list. (Of course, you'll want to substitute today's date.)

Lab 4

There are no secret solutions in this lab; the intent is to get you to review the contents of key log files to see what should be there.

When you review the anaconda.* files in /var/log and compare them to other files, you may gain some insight on how to diagnose installation problems. In future chapters, you'll examine some of the log files associated with specific services; many are located in subdirectories such as /var/log/samba/ and /var/log/httpd/.

The failed login should be readily apparent in the /var/log/secure file. You may be able to get hints in the output to the **utmpdump btmp** command.

When you review the /var/log/cron file, you'll see when standard **cron** jobs were run. Most of the file should be filled (by default) by the standard hourly job, **run-parts /etc/cron.hourly**, from the /etc/crontab configuration file. If you've rebooted, you may see the anacron service, and you should be able to search for the job of the same name.

While /var/log/dmesg includes the currently booted kernel, it may be the same kernel as the one associated with /var/log/anaconda.syslog, if you haven't upgraded kernels. At the end of /var/log/dmesg, you can find the filesystems mounted to the EXT3 format, as well as currently mounted swap partitions. For example, the following lists swap partitions that happen to be on two different hard drives:

```
EXT3 FS on sda9, internal journal
EXT3-fs: mounted filesystem with ordered data mode.
Adding 979956k swap on /dev/sda3.  \
Priority:-1 extents:1 across:979956k
Adding 2031608k swap on /dev/VolGroup00/LogVol01. \
 Priority:-2 extents:1 across: 2031608k
```

As you've hopefully discovered, the /var/log/maillog file does not include any information on mail clients, but only servers.

Red Hat used to include a mouse configuration tool. The automatic configuration for pointing devices is now sufficiently reliable; input device information is automatically added to the xorg.conf configuration file and included in the X Window as shown with <default pointer> messages in the /var/log/Xorg.0.log file.

8

Kernel Services and Configuration

CERTIFICATION OBJECTIVES

8.01   The Basics of the Kernel

8.02   New Kernels, the Easy Way

8.03   Kernel Sources

8.04   Recompiling a Kernel

8.05   Advanced Partitioning: Software RAID

8.06   Advanced Partitioning: Logical Volume Management

✓   Two-Minute Drill

Q&A   Self Test

I n this chapter, you'll learn how to upgrade standard kernels as well as configure, compile, and install your own custom kernels. You'll see several different ways to customize and optimize your kernel configuration for size and functionality. Finally, you'll examine recommended techniques for configuring and installing the kernel.

You'll also discover how to manage and modify special partitions associated with RAID arrays and LVM filesystems. While it's most efficient to configure these partitions during the installation process, you may have to modify them during your exam.

In several places in this chapter, I embed a command such as `uname -r` in the name of a directory or file. This command substitutes itself in the name of directory or file. If unsure, run it in your own system.

INSIDE THE EXAM

Managing Kernels

As a competent Linux administrator, you need to know how to install, patch, and recompile kernels. It's easy to install a new kernel from an RPM, which makes it a reasonable requirement on the RHCT and RHCE exams. Early versions of the RHCE Exam Prep guide suggested that you need to know how to recompile the Linux kernel. But that was a long process! However, as the process is now much easier, I would not be surprised to see the requirement return for RHCEs in the near future.

In addition, the current Exam Prep guide suggests that you need to know how to do the following during the Installation and Configuration portion of both exams:

■ Properly update the Kernel package.

■ Use /proc/sys and sysctl to modify and set kernel run-time parameters.

RAID and LVM

The Exam Prep guide also describes skills associated with configuring RAID and LVM after installation. I've included it in this chapter to match the RH300 course outline more closely. While it's easiest (and therefore best) if you can configure RAID and LVM during the installation process, it's not always possible. If you make a mistake during the installation process, you don't need to start over. The Exam Prep guide suggests that during the Troubleshooting and System Maintenance portion of the exam, RHCTs need to know how to

■ Add new partitions, filesystems, and swap to existing systems.

RHCEs need to know how to

■ Add, remove, and resize logical volumes.

Remember, if you're taking the RHCE exam, you also need to meet all RHCT requirements.

CERTIFICATION OBJECTIVE 8.01

The Basics of the Kernel

The kernel is the heart of the operating system. It manages communication with hardware, decides which processes to run, and provides each process with an isolated, virtual address space in which to run. The kernel is what the GRUB boot loader loads into memory. The kernel loads device driver modules. It also allocates hardware resources such as IRQ ports, I/O addresses, and DMA channels. A recompiled kernel can lead to:

- Greatly improved speed at which kernel services operate.
- Direct support for commonly used drivers.
- Dynamic loading of appropriate drivers as modules.
- Lower memory consumption by removing unneeded components.
- Support for high-end hardware, such as memory above 4GB, hardware array controllers, symmetric multiprocessing (multiple CPU) support, and more.

In essence, you can customize the Linux kernel any way you want. The best way to do it is to make it fit every detail of installed hardware. However, you may not need to be so picky. In many cases, all you need to do is install the updated kernel RPM. In other cases, such as compiling third-party drivers, all you need to install is the corresponding kernel-devel RPM.

Best Practices

You should compile your kernel with only the elements you need. The more that is left out, the faster the whole system will run. For example, if there is no sound card, sound card support can be removed from the kernel. By removing unneeded devices, you will:

- Decrease the size of the kernel.

- Provide a modest increase in speed for the devices that are present.
- Make more hardware resources available for other hardware such as network cards, disk controllers, and so on.
- Reduce the risk of hardware limits, such as those that may be based on the size of the compressed kernel.

But don't remove things you don't understand, as those components may be essential to the smooth functioning of the kernel.

Generally, it is a good idea to have device drivers compiled as modules for any equipment that you may add in the near future. For example, if you may use your Linux computer as a router, you'll need a second network card, and you can add support for that card to your kernel. For example, if you have a 3Com 3c595 network card installed but you also have some 3Com 3c905 cards in storage, it may be a good idea to include the 3c905 module. That way, you can simply swap in the new card and let the module load, causing minimum downtime.

Modules are kernel extensions. They are not compiled directly into the kernel but can be plugged in and removed as needed. When configured as a module, a hardware failure such as that of a network card will not cause the whole system to fail.

Kernel Concepts

You will need to understand some basic kernel concepts before you can compile your own kernel. Kernels can be organized as one big unit or as a lot of interconnected pieces. Kernels are called up by boot loaders when you start your system.

Monolithic Versus Modular

A *monolithic* kernel is a kernel in which all the device modules are built directly into the kernel. *Modular* kernels have many of their devices built as separate loadable modules. Monolithic kernels can communicate with devices faster, since the kernels can talk to the hardware only indirectly through a module table. Unfortunately, the typical monolithic kernel is huge, which reduces available RAM. In addition, some systems just can't boot a kernel that's too large.

Linux once had problems loading modular kernels for some hardware. With a monolithic kernel, the drivers are already there and are often more appropriate for certain components such as embedded hardware.

A modular kernel has greater flexibility. You can compile almost all drivers as modules, and then each module can be inserted into the kernel whenever you need it. Modules keep the initial kernel size low, which decreases the boot time and improves overall performance. If Linux has trouble loading a kernel module, you can use the **modprobe** or **insmod** command to load modules as needed, and add those options to the /etc/modprobe.conf file.

Updating the Kernel

Updating the kernel is not as difficult as it looks. You should never overwrite or upgrade an existing kernel, as mistakes happen. New kernels are handled by installing the newly built kernel in /boot and then adding another boot option to your boot loader configuration file (/boot/grub/grub.conf) for the new kernel. GRUB treats the new kernel as if it were an entirely new operating system.

If you install the new kernel directly from a Red Hat configured RPM, it updates the boot loader automatically. Chapter 5 explored this process briefly.

If you do make a drastic mistake and the kernel doesn't boot, you can simply reboot the system and select the old kernel from the GRUB menu. You should also save existing kernel configuration files so that you have a template for newer kernels. This is discussed in more detail later in this chapter.

Other RHEL Kernels

There are a number of different kernels included with the RHEL installation files. You can and should install the kernel best suited to your system. Available RHEL 5 kernels are briefly discussed in Table 8-1. For the real *versionnum*, run the **uname -r** command. To verify your *arch*, or architecture (such as i686), run the **uname -m** command. As described in the table, there are different versions of kernel-devel, kernel-PAE, kernel-xen, and kernel-headers packages for each supported architecture.

I don't list all available RHEL architectures in Table 8-1, and list them just for the basic kernel packages. Remember, the focus of the Red Hat exams is still based on the basic 32-bit Intel/AMD/clone CPU. PPC and s/390 systems are not (yet) supported in RHEL 5.

The table provides just a short list of kernel packages available for RHEL 5. It does not include Xen-related kernels. For more information on RHEL kernels available for multi-CPU or higher-end CPUs, refer to the RHEL documentation available online from www.redhat.com/docs/manuals/enterprise/.

The /boot Partition

The Linux kernel is stored in the partition with the /boot directory. New kernels must also be transferred to this directory. By default, RHEL configures a partition of about 100MB for this directory. This provides enough room for your current kernel plus several additional upgraded kernels.

| TABLE 8-1 | Available Red Hat Enterprise Linux Kernels (and Related Packages) |

Kernel RPM	Description / Architecture
kernel-*versionnum*.i686	Designed for PCs with a single Intel/AMD CPU; also works with dual-core systems
kernel-*versionnum*.ia64	Designed for Itanium2 systems
kernel-devel-*versionnum*	Installs drivers and other information to help compile third-party drivers
kernel-PAE-*versionnum*	If you have more than 4GB of RAM, install the PAE kernel associated with your CPU architecture
kernel-PAE-devel-*versionnum*	If you have more than 4GB of RAM, install the PAE kernel associated with your CPU architecture
kernel-headers-*versionnum*	Includes kernel headers; often sufficient for drivers
kernel-*versionnum*.src.rpm	Includes the source code for the RHEL kernel

The /proc Filesystem

The /proc directory is based on a virtual filesystem; in other words, it does not include any files that are stored on the hard drive. But it is a window into what the kernel sees of your computer. It's a good idea to study the files and directories in /proc, as it can help you diagnose a wide range of problems. Figure 8-1 shows the /proc directory from a typical RHEL computer.

| FIGURE 8-1 |

A Red Hat
Enterprise Linux
/proc directory

```
[michael@enterprise5dl ~]$ \ls /proc/
1     1954  2364  2835  2927  3271  5          ide         partitions
10    1960  2365  2838  2931  329   6          interrupts  schedstat
1024  1981  2381  2839  2936  332   67         iomem       scsi
11    2     2382  2846  2949  3451  7          ioports     self
135   2033  2388  2849  2951  3501  70         irq         slabinfo
136   2058  2393  2851  2957  3505  72         kallsyms    stat
137   2082  2405  2865  2962  3506  acpi       kcore       swaps
138   2106  2455  2870  2964  3509  buddyinfo  keys        sys
1618  2122  2459  2872  2966  3553  bus        key-users   sysrq-trigger
1720  2127  2460  2876  2990  3640  cmdline    kmsg        sysvipc
1737  2144  2463  2878  2992  365   cpuinfo    loadavg     tty
1739  2175  2466  2882  2993  3818  crypto     locks       uptime
1758  2217  2467  2885  3     3861  devices    mdstat      version
1761  2226  2486  2899  3020  3865  diskstats  meminfo     vmcore
1798  2243  2515  290   319   3867  dma        misc        vmstat
1821  2259  2688  2906  3239  3869  driver     modules     zoneinfo
1839  2297  2718  2908  324   399   execdomains mounts
1865  2313  2722  2915  3241  4     fb         mpt
1908  2328  2725  2918  3242  4004  filesystems mtrr
1937  2347  2776  2923  3270  4008  fs         net
[michael@enterprise5dl ~]$ ▇
```

The numbered items are based on process IDs. For example, the process ID of **init** is 1. The files in this directory include the memory segments that make up the active process. The contents of each of these files include the active memory for that process.

The other items in the listing are files and directories that correspond to configuration information for components such as DMA channels or whole subsystems such as memory information.

Take a look at some of these files. For example, the /proc/meminfo file provides excellent information as to the state of memory on the local computer, as shown in Figure 8-2. It can help you determine whether RHEL is having trouble detecting all of the memory on your computer.

It can also help you measure the current memory state of your system. For example, if your system is overloaded, you'll probably find very little free swap space. The **HugePages** settings are associated with systems with over 4GB of RAM.

Now you can examine how Linux looks at your CPU in the /proc/cpuinfo file, as shown in Figure 8-3. In this particular case, the cpu family information is important; the cpu family value of 6 in this figure corresponds to a 686 CPU. If you have a dual-core CPU (and both cores are detected), you'll see two entries, even if you have only one physical CPU.

FIGURE 8-2

Detected
memory
information

```
MemTotal:        513432 kB
MemFree:          46768 kB
Buffers:          21332 kB
Cached:          297780 kB
SwapCached:           0 kB
Active:          215492 kB
Inactive:        207516 kB
HighTotal:            0 kB
HighFree:             0 kB
LowTotal:        513432 kB
LowFree:          46768 kB
SwapTotal:      1048568 kB
SwapFree:       1048568 kB
Dirty:             9504 kB
Writeback:            0 kB
AnonPages:       103644 kB
Mapped:           49080 kB
Slab:             31520 kB
PageTables:        3984 kB
NFS Unstable:         0 kB
Bounce:               0 kB
CommitLimit:    1305284 kB
Committed_AS:    340908 kB
VmallocTotal:    507896 kB
VmallocUsed:       3312 kB
VmallocChunk:    504480 kB
HugePages_Total:      0
HugePages_Free:       0
HugePages_Rsvd:       0
Hugepagesize:      4096 kB
```

FIGURE 8-3

Detected CPU
information

```
processor       : 0
vendor_id       ▌: GenuineIntel
cpu family      : 6
model           : 15
model name      : Intel(R) Core(TM)2 CPU        T7200  @ 2.00GHz
stepping        : 8
cpu MHz         : 1997.358
cache size      : 4096 KB
fdiv_bug        : no
hlt_bug         : no
f00f_bug        : no
coma_bug        : no
fpu             : yes
fpu_exception   : yes
cpuid level     : 10
wp              : yes
flags           : fpu vme de pse tsc msr pae mce cx8 apic mtrr pge mca cmov pat
pse36 clflush dts acpi mmx fxsr sse sse2 ss nx lm constant_tsc pni ds_cpl cx16 l
ahf_lm
bogomips        : 4020.62

processor       : 1
vendor_id       : GenuineIntel
cpu family      : 6
model           : 15
model name      : Intel(R) Core(TM)2 CPU        T7200  @ 2.00GHz
stepping        : 8
cpu MHz         : 1997.358
cache size      : 4096 KB
fdiv_bug        : no
"/proc/cpuinfo" [readonly] 38L, 946C
```

Many programs are available that simply look at the information stored in /proc and interpret it in a more readable format. The **top** utility is a perfect example. It reads the process table, queries RAM and swap usage and the level of CPU use, and presents it all on one screen.

IP Forwarding

More importantly, there are kernel variables that can be altered to change the way the kernel behaves while it's running. Sometimes it's appropriate to configure a Linux computer as a router between networks. By default, it does not forward TCP/IP information. You can confirm this with the following command:

```
# cat /proc/sys/net/ipv4/ip_forward
0
```

If your computer has two or more network cards, you may want to activate IP forwarding with the following command:

```
# echo 1 >> /proc/sys/net/ipv4/ip_forward
# cat /proc/sys/net/ipv4/ip_forward
1
```

Naturally, you'll want to make sure the setting is confirmed the next time you boot by activating the **net.ipv4.ip_forward** directive in the /etc/sysctl.conf file.

Preventing the "Ping of Death"

The following is another useful proc kernel variable (enabled by default), which enables the use of TCP SYN packet cookies. These cookies prevent SYN flood attacks on your system, including the so-called "ping of death." Verify that the tcp_syncookies setting is enabled with the following command:

```
# cat /proc/sys/net/ipv4/tcp_syncookies
1
```

Understanding Kernel Modules

When compiling a kernel, you could set up a monolithic kernel with every driver that you might ever need. Unfortunately, such kernels are large, unwieldy, and take a lot of time to load. Generally, most Linux administrators use kernel modules. As described earlier, a kernel module is not compiled directly into the kernel but instead operates as a pluggable driver that can be loaded and unloaded into the kernel as needed.

To have the kernel dynamically load and unload kernel modules as needed, the kernel module loader is used to control the loading and unloading of modules. For special parameters and options, edit the /etc/modules.conf file.

Most hardware modules are automatically detected. If you've just installed new undetected hardware, you could issue the following command:

```
# depmod -a
```

This will scan through your modules, find different dependencies for all installed modules, and map them out to a file (modules.dep). This command also creates a number of other files in the /lib/modules/`uname -r`/ directory (the version number of the kernel becomes the name of the subdirectory).

Once the **depmod** module scan is complete, you can load additional kernel modules. If that module has dependencies, then all the needed modules will automatically load first.

To load a module, you can use the **modprobe** command with the name of a specific driver, like so:

```
# modprobe ipw2200
```

This command loads the Ethernet module for an Intel Wireless 2200 card common on many laptop systems. This wireless card requires the ieee80211 module to work properly. If **depmod** were run first (and the physical card were detected), then the ieee80211 module would have loaded automatically before the ipw2200 driver. If a dependency in the list fails during loading, then all modules will be automatically unloaded.

Alternatively, you can set up these modules in /etc/modprobe.conf or files in the /etc/modprobe.d/ directory. It should already be configured during the RHEL installation process. Unfortunately, this work can be rather tedious. The following commands are accepted in this file:

- **alias**   Allows you to bind a name to a module.
- **options**   Allows you to specify options for a module.
- **install** *module command*   Use *command* instead of **insmod** on this module.
- **pre-install** *module command*   Run *command* before installing this module.
- **post-install** *module command*   Run *command* after installing this module.
- **remove** *module command*   Use *command* instead of **rmmod** on this module.
- **pre-remove** *module command*   Run *command* before loading this module.
- **post-remove** *module command*   Run *command* after loading this module.

Here are typical excerpts from modprobe.conf:

```
alias eth0 natsemi
alias eth1 ipw2200
alias snd-card-0 snd-ali5451
options snd-card-0 index=0
options snd-ali5451 index=0
remove snd-ali5451 { /usr/sbin/alsactl store 0 >/dev/null 2>&1
|| : ; }; /sbin/modprobe -r --ignore-remove snd-ali5451
```

Here the eth0 device is bound to the natsemi module. To load the network card (if it isn't already loaded), you can then simply type **modprobe eth0** without knowing what card is in the computer. The next directive associates the ipw2200 module to eth1. The lines that follow show the configuration of a **snd-card** module. As suggested by their absence, Red Hat systems don't use most of the available commands for this configuration file.

The /etc/rc.sysinit script loads modules and creates aliases for them if found in this file. To have the sound modules automatically loaded during the Linux boot process, you can simply create an alias for the sound and/or midi modules in the modprobe.conf file.

To see what modules are loaded, you can type either

```
# cat /proc/modules
```

or

```
# lsmod
```

The **lsmod** command returns output that looks something like the following:

```
Module             Size   Used by
nls_utf8           6337   0
radeon           109281   2
drm               72149   3 radeon
autofs4           25029   3
hidp              24001   2
l2cap             31169   5 hidp
bluetooth         57765   2 hidp,l2cap
sunrpc           156925   1
....
```

(Numerous entries omitted.)

```
....
ide_cd            42337   0
cdrom             38497   1 ide_cd
dm_snapshot       22245   0
dm_zero            6337   0
dm_mirror         31889   0
dm_mod            62425   12 dm_snapshot,dm_zero,dm_mirror
ext3             134473   5
jbd               61801   1 ext3
ehci_hcd          35149   0
ohci_hcd          24669   0
uhci_hcd          27213   0
```

The module name is listed on the left, and its size is in the second column. The Used by column shows more detail on how the module is being handled. If a module name, such as ext3, is listed in the right-hand column, then it's a dependency. In this example, jbd depends on the ext3 module.

The /lib/modules/kernel_version/ Directory Structure

All kernel modules are stored in the /lib/modules/*kernel_version*/ directory. As suggested earlier in the chapter, you can substitute `**uname -r**` for *kernel_version*. If you have recently compiled a new *stock* kernel (not from Red Hat source code) and your modules are not loading properly, you've probably forgotten to compile and install the modules. In the source code directory (discussed later in this chapter), run the following commands:

```
# make modules
# make modules_install
```

The first line compiles the modules, while the second places them under the proper directory tree. Be prepared, because these commands can take some time.

In this directory tree, different subdirectories represent different groupings. The following is a sample of a module directory:

```
# ls -l /lib/modules/`uname -r`/kernel/drivers
total 264
drwxr-xr-x  2 root root 4096 Mar 14 09:31 acpi
drwxr-xr-x  2 root root 4096 Mar 14 09:31 atm
drwxr-xr-x  4 root root 4096 Mar 14 09:31 block
drwxr-xr-x  2 root root 4096 Mar 14 09:31 bluetooth
drwxr-xr-x  2 root root 4096 Mar 14 09:31 cdrom
drwxr-xr-x  7 root root 4096 Mar 14 09:31 char
drwxr-xr-x  2 root root 4096 Mar 14 09:31 cpufreq
drwxr-xr-x  2 root root 4096 Mar 14 09:31 crypto
drwxr-xr-x  2 root root 4096 Mar 14 09:31 dma
drwxr-xr-x  2 root root 4096 Mar 14 09:31 edac
drwxr-xr-x  2 root root 4096 Mar 14 09:31 firmware
drwxr-xr-x  2 root root 4096 Mar 14 09:31 hwmon
drwxr-xr-x  5 root root 4096 Mar 14 09:31 i2c
drwxr-xr-x  3 root root 4096 Mar 14 09:31 ide
drwxr-xr-x  6 root root 4096 Mar 14 09:31 infiniband
drwxr-xr-x  8 root root 4096 Mar 14 09:31 input
drwxr-xr-x  8 root root 4096 Mar 14 09:31 isdn
drwxr-xr-x  2 root root 4096 Mar 14 09:31 leds
drwxr-xr-x  2 root root 4096 Mar 14 09:31 md
drwxr-xr-x  5 root root 4096 Mar 14 09:31 media
drwxr-xr-x  4 root root 4096 Mar 14 09:31 message
drwxr-xr-x  3 root root 4096 Mar 14 09:31 misc
drwxr-xr-x  2 root root 4096 Mar 14 09:31 mmc
drwxr-xr-x  6 root root 4096 Mar 14 09:31 mtd
drwxr-xr-x 12 root root 4096 Mar 14 09:31 net
drwxr-xr-x  2 root root 4096 Mar 14 09:31 parport
drwxr-xr-x  3 root root 4096 Mar 14 09:31 pci
drwxr-xr-x  2 root root 4096 Mar 14 09:31 pcmcia
drwxr-xr-x  2 root root 4096 Mar 14 09:31 rtc
drwxr-xr-x 12 root root 4096 Mar 14 09:31 scsi
drwxr-xr-x  3 root root 4096 Mar 14 09:31 serial
drwxr-xr-x 11 root root 4096 Mar 14 09:31 usb
drwxr-xr-x  9 root root 4096 Mar 14 09:31 video
```

Remember that the /lib/modules/`uname -r` directory contains a modules.dep file that lists all the dependencies for all the modules within the directories. Each of these module directories includes a group of kernel modules for a common type of hardware.

You might want to become familiar with where to find certain modules when they're needed. Here are some module types you can find under each subdirectory:

- **block**   Block devices: parallel port IDE drives, network block devices, XT disks, hardware RAID devices
- **cdrom**   Non-ATAPI CD-ROM drivers: Mitsumi, Sony
- **char**   Miscellaneous input and serial devices
- **ide**   Hard disk drivers
- **input**   Input devices (keyboards, mice)
- **md**   RAID devices
- **message**   Specialized I/O adapters
- **net**   Network modules: basic network cards, generic PPP, SLIP
- **parport**   Parallel port devices (not printers)
- **pcmcia**   Drivers used by the PCMCIA **cardmgr** daemon (the actual cards use separate drivers)
- **scsi**   SCSI tape, RAID, hard drive, and video (special video modules for Linux) modules
- **sound**   Sound adapters
- **usb**   Universal Serial Bus hubs and devices
- **video**   Graphics adapters

All module names have the .ko extension (such as prism54.ko). You do not need to specify the full file name, just the first part of the module name (prism54). Once you know the directory structure, you can have the **modprobe** command load all modules for a certain category. For instance, if you are on a PC and you don't know what kind of network card is installed, you can type this:

```
modprobe -lt net
```

This will attempt to load all modules in /lib/modules/*kernel_version*/kernel/drivers/ net, stopping if and when a match is found.

To remove a module such as ipw2200 and all its dependencies, use this command:

```
modprobe -r ipw2200
```

This command removes the modules and all their dependencies, provided they are not in use by another module or not currently active. For example, if your network is active, you can't remove the network ipw2200 driver module. If you want to remove only the module and leave the other dependent drivers, remove the hardware, and then run the **modprobe** command without the **-r** switch.

CERTIFICATION OBJECTIVE 8.02

New Kernels, the Easy Way

On the Red Hat exams, you may expected to upgrade your kernel by installing the latest Red Hat kernel RPM. You may be able to patch an existing kernel.

Before we begin, it's important to understand the way kernels are numbered.

Understanding Kernel Version Numbers

The version number associated with the RHEL kernel may look a little confusing, but it tells you a lot about the history of the kernel. The standard RHEL kernel is a version with a number like 2.6.18-8.el5, formatted in a *majorversion.majorrevision* *.patch-build* format.

The first number (2) is the major version number. These versions provide drastic changes to the kernel. Typically, older version software will *not* work in the newer version when this number changes. Kernel major version numbers are reserved for completely new kernel designs.

The second number (6) actually has two meanings. First, it indicates this is the sixth major revision of major version 2 of the kernel. Second, since it is an even number, it indicates that the kernel release is a stable release. Before version 2.6, an odd second number would indicate a developmental kernel, not suitable for production computers. Now, kernel version 2.7 will also be a production kernel.

on the
Job

To promote stability, Red Hat usually works from a slightly older, and presumably more stable, version of the Linux kernel. This is consistent with the demands of the Red Hat customer base; most business customers want to stay away from the "bleeding edge."

The third number (18) is the patch version number for the kernel. These changes are typically small changes, bug fixes, security fixes, and enhancements. Generally, you can use the **zcat** command to increment one patch at a time. For example, if your current kernel is version 2.6.18, you can use the patch-2.6.19.gz file to upgrade your kernel to version 2.6.19.

The fourth number (-8) is a number added by Red Hat. This is the eighth Red Hat version of Linux kernel 2.6.18, which incorporates features customized for Red Hat Enterprise Linux. In some cases, there will be a fifth and even a sixth number that indicates the build number as created by Red Hat. The final bit may be something like el5 or el5xen.

on the **Job** *Stock kernels use a slightly different four-number system. The first two numbers are identical to the Red Hat system. The third number specifies a major patch; the fourth number specifies a bugfix or security update. If you use a stock kernel, it may overwrite Enterprise-level custom features developed for RHEL 5.*

Upgrading Kernels

During the lifetime of any version of RHEL, you may run across a security advisory that strongly suggests that you upgrade your Linux kernel. In this case, a Red Hat kernel RPM will be available through the Red Hat Network.

e x a m
Watch *You won't have access to the Internet during the Red Hat exams, and therefore, you may not be able to get to the Red Hat Network for updates.*

However, the Exam Prep guide suggests that you may be required to install an upgraded kernel.

Upgrading a kernel from a Red Hat RPM is fairly easy. Basically, all you need to do is install the new kernel with the appropriate **rpm** or **yum** command. When properly configured, the RPM automatically upgrades your default boot loader as well. For example, say you've just downloaded the newest kernel RPM from the Red Hat Network to the /tmp directory.

e x a m
Watch *If you're told to upgrade a new kernel, you'll probably use the rpm -i kernel.rpm command, and not rpm -U kernel.rpm. Installing (and not upgrading)*

newer kernels allows you to boot into the older kernel—in case the new kernel does not work for you.

Be careful. Install (**-i**), don't upgrade (**-U**) your new kernel. Otherwise, if you have a problem, you won't be able to go back to the old working kernel. Installing (**-i**) a new kernel with a command such as

```
# rpm -i /tmp/kernel-2.6.18-2.2.1.i686.rpm
```

installs the kernel, initial RAM disk, System.map, and config files automatically in the /boot directory. In addition, the RPM automatically adds a new stanza to your boot loader configuration file. For GRUB, the file is /boot/grub/grub.conf.

If you're properly connected to an update repository such as the RHN, you may be able to download the new kernel and make updates directly with an even simpler command:

```
# yum install kernel
```

e x a m
🐾 a t c h   *The /boot/grub/grub.conf   /boot/grub/menu.lst. You can open any*
configuration file includes a hard link to   of these file names in the text editor of
/etc/grub.conf as well as a soft link to   your choice.

e x a m
🐾 a t c h   *To change the default   /boot/grub/grub.conf. Similarly, if default=1,*
boot stanza in GRUB, change the default   the default kernel loaded is the second
variable. For example, if default=0, the   stanza in /boot/grub/grub.conf.
default kernel loaded is the first stanza in

Kernel Patches

Sometimes, all you need is a simple patch to a kernel. Patches usually work fairly well if you're upgrading from one patch version to the next higher version, such as from 2.6.21 to 2.6.22.

Kernel patches are easily available from Internet sites such as ftp.kernel.org. For example, if you want to upgrade from kernel version 2.6.21 to kernel version 2.6.22, download the patch-2.6.22.gz file from the Internet. Copy the patch to the /usr/src directory. Move to that directory, and run a command similar to the following to make the upgrade:

```
# zcat patch-2.6.22.gz | patch -p0
```

If it doesn't work, you'll see files with a .rej extension somewhere in your kernel source tree. Use a command such as **find** to check for such files. If you don't find any of these files, you can proceed with the **make clean, make menuconfig,** and **make dep** commands as described later in this chapter.

on the **Job**

Generally, it's a bad idea to use a generic patch on a Red Hat built kernel. Red Hat Enterprise Linux kernels often include "backports," which already includes features found in later kernels.

Updating GRUB

If properly configured, the Red Hat kernel that you install should automatically update your boot loader. But as an RHCT or RHCE, you need to know how to check. If the code described in this chapter has not been added, you'll need to know how to add it.

It is advisable to keep your old kernel in case something goes wrong. So you'll be adding a stanza to /boot/grub/grub.conf. In any case, the changes that you'll make will be as if you're setting up two different operating systems.

Now look at your /boot/grub/grub.conf file. If you have Linux on your system and use GRUB, you should already have a stanza that points to the appropriate locations for your original Linux kernel and initial RAM disk. For example, here is an excerpt from my RHEL 5 /boot/grub/grub.conf file (which includes a dual-boot configuration with Microsoft Windows):

```
title Red Hat Enterprise Linux Server (2.6.18-8.el5)
    root (hd0,0)
    kernel /vmlinuz- 2.6.18-8.el5 ro root=LABEL=/
    initrd /initrd-2.6.18-8.el5.img
title Microsoft Windows
    rootnoverify (hd0,1)
    chainloader +1
```

In Red Hat Enterprise Linux, the **vmlinuz** and **initrd** files are already in the /boot directory. Since you've copied the revised kernels to the same directory, all you need is a second stanza that points to your revised files. If I recompile my kernel, I might change the Makefile in my source code directory to show **EXTRAVERSION=-8.el5custom**.

```
title Red Hat Enterprise Linux Server (2.6.18-8.el5custom)
    root (hd0,0)
    kernel /vmlinuz-2.6.18-8.el5custom ro root=LABEL=/
    initrd /initrd-2.6.18-8.el5custom.img
title Red Hat Enterprise Linux Server (2.6.18-8.el5)
    root (hd0,0)
```

```
    kernel /vmlinuz-2.6.18-8.el5 ro root=LABEL=/
    initrd /initrd-2.6.18-8.el5.img
title DOS
    rootnoverify (hd0,1)
    chainloader +1
```

Since you don't need to load /boot/grub/grub.conf into the MBR, no further action is required. Note how the original kernel is set as the default. If you've watched closely, you'll note that in /boot/grub/grub.conf, the value of **default** was changed from 0 to 1. If you want to set the default to the new kernel, change the value of **default** back to 0, as shown in Figure 8-4.

CERTIFICATION OBJECTIVE 8.03

Kernel Sources

One of the strengths of Linux is the ease with which the kernel can be customized to meet your precise needs. But before starting this process, you need the Linux kernel source code. Kernel modules and associated configuration files are covered in this section.

If you choose to recompile the Linux kernel, you'll need several GB of free space available in the partition or volume that contains the /usr directory.

FIGURE 8-4

GRUB menu
with original
and recompiled
kernels

```
# grub.conf generated by anaconda
#
# Note that you do not have to rerun grub after making changes to this file
# NOTICE:  You have a /boot partition.   This means that
#          all kernel and initrd paths are relative to /boot/, eg.
#          root (hd0,0)
#          kernel /vmlinuz-version ro root=/dev/VolGroup00/LogVol00
#          initrd /initrd-version.img
#boot=/dev/sda
default=1
timeout=5
splashimage=(hd0,0)/grub/splash.xpm.gz
hiddenmenu
title Red Hat Enterprise Linux Server (2.6.18-8.el5custom)
        root (hd0,0)
        kernel /vmlinuz-2.6.18-8.el5custom ro root=/dev/VolGroup00/LogVol00 rhgb
 quiet
        initrd /initrd-2.6.18-8.el5custom.img
title Red Hat Enterprise Linux Server (2.6.18-8.el5)
        root (hd0,0)
        kernel /vmlinuz-2.6.18-8.el5 ro root=/dev/VolGroup00/LogVol00 rhgb quiet
        initrd /initrd-2.6.18-8.el5.img
 ~
```

The Kernel Source Tree and Documentation

When you install the generic kernel source code, it's normally installed in (or linked to) the /usr/src/linux directory. If you install the source code from a Red Hat/Fedora source RPM, the code gets installed in the /usr/src/redhat/BUILD/kernel-2.6.18/ linux-2.6.18.i386/ subdirectory. It can be helpful to link that directory to /usr/src/ linux. Once linked, the /usr/src directory should look similar to the following:

```
# ls -l /usr/src/
total 20
drwxr-xr-x   3 root   root   4096 Mar 14 09:32 kernels
lrwxrwxrwx   1 root   root     54 Mar 14 14:44 linux ->
        /usr/src/redhat/BUILD/kernel-2.6.18/linux-2.6.18.i386/
drwxr-xr-x   7 root   root   4096 Mar 14 09:37 redhat
```

In this case, the actual directory is /usr/src/redhat/BUILD/kernel-2.6.18/linux-2.6.18 .i386/, and there is a soft link from /usr/src/linux that points to this directory. I created this link with the following command:

```
# ln -s /usr/src/redhat/BUILD/kernel-2.6.18/linux-2.6.18.i386/
/usr/src/linux
```

The /usr/src/linux directory on my RHEL 5 system includes the following files and directories:

```
arch        Documentation   ipc         mm              sound
block       drivers         Kbuild      net             usr
configs     fs              kernel      README
COPYING     hdrwarnings.txt lib         REPORTING-BUGS
CREDITS     include         MAINTAINERS scripts
crypto      init            Makefile    security
```

Begin your study of the current kernel with the README file. While the instructions in this chapter work with the current configuration of RHEL 5 on my computer, details can change from kernel to kernel. Also, examine the Documentation directory. It contains everything you need, from information on setting up symmetrical multiprocessors to serial consoles.

The other directories mainly contain source code, and you probably won't need to spend time examining those files (unless, of course, you are a developer). There is also a hidden file, .config, that may be present in this directory. I'll describe this file in more detail later in this chapter.

For the rest of the chapter, I'll refer to the *source code directory* as the directory with source code files, which could be /usr/src/redhat/BUILD/linux-2.6.18/kernel-2.6.18.`uname -m`, or if you've linked it as suggested, /usr/src/linux.

The Kernel RPMs

If you don't see the directories mentioned in the preceding section, then you haven't installed the Linux kernel source code. There are three ways to install the source code. You could access the kernel source RPMs from appropriate download media, directly as a package from the RHN or repository associated with your rebuild distribution, or even from the public ftp.redhat.com server. Remember, in contrast to the past, there is no unique binary kernel-source RPM; you'll need the kernel-`uname -r`.src.rpm package.

Red Hat more than complies with the GPL by posting the source code for its RHEL 5 packages at ftp.redhat.com. You can find them with .src.rpm file name extensions.

Depending on the kernel source, and the actions you take, this process could easily take 3GB of space or more.

When you download the kernel src.rpm package, make sure it corresponds to the current kernel version (or the one you want to compile). Then take the following step to unload the source RPM:

```
# rpm -ivh kernel-`uname -r`.src.rpm
```

You may get warning messages related to users and groups that do not exist. As long as ownership is assigned to the root user, these are of no concern.

Next, navigate to the /usr/src/redhat/SPECS directory. You'll see a kernel-2.6.spec file. Assuming you've installed the rpm-build package, you can now build the source code with the following command. The `**uname -m**` in the command uses the architecture for the current system:

```
# cd /usr/src/redhat/SPECS
# rpmbuild -bp --target=`uname -m` kernel-2.6.spec
```

This command takes a few minutes to load the source code into the /usr/src/redhat/ BUILD/kernel-2.6.18/linux-2.6.18.`uname -m`/ directory. It also loads the "vanilla" version of the given kernel in the /usr/src/redhat/BUILD/kernel-2.6.18/vanilla/ directory.

Sometimes the unpacking stalls with an error like:

```
gpg: WARNING: unsafe permissions on homedir `.
.+++++++++++++......
Not enough random bytes available. Please do some other work to give
the OS a chance to collect more entropy! (Need 258 more bytes)
```

In this case, I opened a second console and ran the /etc/cron.daily/mlocate script. You don't have to run the same script; you just need to create the equivalent amount of activity to help Linux complete the unpacking process. Sometimes a few **df** and **ls** commands are sufficient.

Required Kernel Customization RPMs

To build a kernel from the source code, you need the RPMs not only for the kernel, but also for the tools needed to build the kernel (as well as dependencies). You can check your system to ensure you have the RPM packages described in Table 8-2. Many of these packages have a number of other dependencies, so it's best to use the **yum** command to install them from associated repositories or the RHN.

TABLE 8-2 Kernel Configuration RPMs

Package	Description
glibc-headers	Kernel header files (formerly glibc-kernheaders)
glibc-devel	Required for C libraries
cpp	C language preprocessor
ncurses	Required for menuconfig screen
ncurses-devel	Development libraries for ncurses
binutils	Required binary utilities
gcc	C language compiler
tcl	TCL scripting language—required for xconfig screen
gtk2-devel	TK X Window widgets—required for xconfig screen
qt-devel	QT development libraries required for xconfig screen; requires many additional packages to satisfy dependencies (a good reason to use **yum**)
glib2-devel	Glib2 development header files required for gconfig screen
libglade2-devel	Libglade2 libraries required for gconfig screen; requires several additional packages to satisfy dependencies

The objective is to install these packages with dependencies; for example, to install the gtk2-devel package *with dependencies* from the RHN or a repository, all you need is the **yum install gtk2-devel** command.

The Linux Kernel tar File

Alternatively, you can download the newest kernel from the Linux kernel home page at www.kernel.org. The version numbers are discussed in the next section. Once you have downloaded the kernel source, you will need to install it properly. This example assumes you downloaded linux-2.6.22.tar.gz into the /usr/src/ directory.

```
# cd /usr/src
# tar xzvf linux-2.6.22.tar.gz
# ln -s linux-2.6.22 linux
```

These commands navigate to the /usr/src directory, uncompress the tarball, which creates a linux-2.6.22/ subdirectory, and then link it to the linux/ subdirectory.

Compressed tar files are shown in .tar.gz or .tgz format; they are also known as "tarballs." Some compressed tarballs are compressed in .bz2 format; to uncompress and unpack them, you'd apply the tar xjvf (instead of the tar xzvf) command to the tarball.

CERTIFICATION OBJECTIVE 8.04

Recompiling a Kernel

While references to recompiling the Linux kernel have been removed from the Red Hat exam requirements, RHCEs in the real world are expected to know how to perform high-level tasks such as optimizing and recompiling the Linux kernel.

This section looks at the kernel configuration file and then proceeds with a discussion of the different tools available to edit the kernel configuration. Finally, you'll see the commands needed to compile your new configuration into the kernel, the files added to the /boot directory, and the settings added to the boot loader.

The Kernel Configuration Scripts

After you've configured a kernel once, the configuration information is stored in a hidden file, .config, in the Linux source code directory. It is structured as a listing of variables. Here are some entries from the .config file:

```
CONFIG_NETDEVICES=y
CONFIG_BONDING=m
# CONFIG_EQUALIZER is not set
```

As you can see, there are three main types of variables in this file. The first command compiles in direct support, the second entry compiles support as a module (the **m**), and the third command is commented out and is therefore not compiled into the kernel at all. You should never have to edit this file directly, as there are easier ways to configure your kernel.

Move to the directory with your kernel source files. If you've installed the RHEL kernel source RPM, navigate to the aforementioned source code directory, /usr/src/redhat/BUILD/kernel-2.6.18/linux-2.6.18.`uname -m`. If you've created the link suggested earlier, you can use the /usr/src/linux directory. Four tools can help you configure the kernel configuration file: **make config**, **make menuconfig**, **make xconfig**, and **make gconfig**. The last three of these tools require some of the packages described in Table 8-2.

Back Up Your Configuration

The default configuration for your current Linux kernel is stored in the /boot directory. For the default RHEL system, it's stored in the config-`uname -r` file. Back up this file (and perhaps all contents of /boot) on another location such as a USB key so that you can restore your current kernel configuration if all else fails.

You can use your current configuration as a baseline; the Linux kernel configuration tools will start with these settings. To do so with the current kernel, copy the config-`uname -r` file to the .config file in the source code directory.

Alternatively, there are a number of standard configuration files in the configs/ subdirectory. If you want to start with one of these files, use the configuration file that corresponds most closely to your hardware. You can set that as the starting point for your configuration by copying that to the .config file in the source code directory.

make config

Once you're in the kernel source code directory, you can call a simple script to configure a new kernel with the following command:

```
# make config
```

This script will prompt you through your different options. Figure 8-5 shows an excerpt from the output for this script.

Here the kernel variables are listed in parentheses and the possible answers are in brackets. The default answer is in capital letters. If you type in a **?**, you will see a help page explaining this option. Since several hundred questions are associated with this

FIGURE 8-5

Questions from
the **make config**
utility

```
[root@enterprise5dl linux]# make config
scripts/kconfig/conf arch/i386/Kconfig
*
* Linux Kernel Configuration
*
*
* Code maturity level options
*
Prompt for development and/or incomplete code/drivers (EXPERIMENTAL) [Y/n/?]
*
* General setup
*
Local version - append to kernel release (LOCALVERSION) []
Automatically append version information to the version string (LOCALVERSION_AUT
O) [N/y/?]
Support for paging of anonymous memory (swap) (SWAP) [Y/n/?]
System V IPC (SYSVIPC) [Y/n/?]
POSIX Message Queues (POSIX_MQUEUE) [Y/n/?]
BSD Process Accounting (BSD_PROCESS_ACCT) [Y/n/?]
  BSD Process Accounting version 3 file format (BSD_PROCESS_ACCT_V3) [N/y/?]
Export task/process statistics through netlink (EXPERIMENTAL) (TASKSTATS) [Y/n/?
]
  Enable per-task delay accounting (EXPERIMENTAL) (TASK_DELAY_ACCT) [Y/n/?]
Auditing support (AUDIT) [Y/n/?] ▊
```

script, most administrators use one of the other two scripts to manage their Linux
kernels.

make menuconfig

A nicer way to create the .config file is to use the **make menuconfig** command. This
requires the ncurses RPM package. This opens a text-based menu-driven system
that classifies and organizes the changes that you can make to a kernel. Figure 8-6
illustrates the main menu associated with this command.

The nice thing about **menuconfig** is that it works well over a remote text connection
from other Linux computers (or perhaps that is dangerous!). Also, when you scroll
all the way down, options appear at the bottom of the menu to load or save the
configuration file from a different location.

make xconfig

One graphical way to make changes uses KDE-based libraries. You can generate
a graphical menu system to configure your kernel by running the **make xconfig**
command. Figure 8-7 shows the **xconfig** main menu. You can also use **xconfig** to
load or save the configuration from the file of your choice.

make gconfig

A second graphical way to make changes uses GNOME-based libraries. You can
generate a graphical menu system to configure your kernel by running the **make**

The **make menuconfig** configuration menu

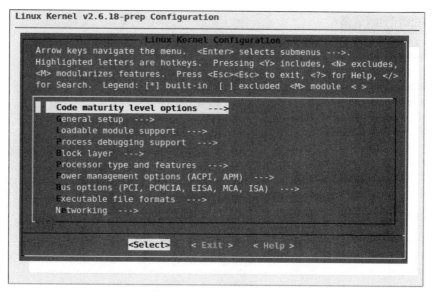

gconfig command. Figure 8-8 shows the **gconfig** main menu. You can also use **gconfig** to load or save the configuration from the file of your choice.

While this menu may look slightly different in other Linux distributions, the principles and basic options remain fairly constant. Each of the Kernel Configuration

The **make xconfig** configuration menu

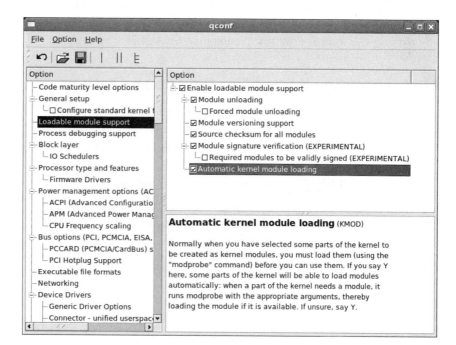

FIGURE 8-8

The **make gconfig** configuration menu

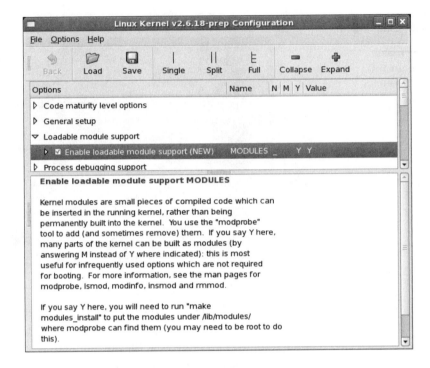

FIGURE 8-8

The **make gconfig** configuration menu

options discussed on the following pages are presented for completeness. It is important for a Linux administrator to have a detailed understanding of the hows and whys of reconfiguring and recompiling the kernel.

Understanding Kernel Configuration Options

To configure a kernel, you need to understand some of the main kernel configuration options. Each of the aforementioned kernel configuration tools includes help menus for just about every available option.

The Basic Kernel Configuration

If you're asked to change a setting such as **CONFIG_EXPERIMENTAL**, you don't have to search through different menus. You can find the governing menu using the information in the /boot/config-`uname -r` configuration file. As you can see in the file,

```
# Code maturity level options
#
CONFIG_EXPERIMENTAL=y
```

the **CONFIG_EXPERIMENTAL** variable can be found under the Code Maturity Level Options menu, described by a Prompt For Development And/Or Incomplete Code/Drivers selection.

The Standard Red Hat Kernel Configuration

The standard RHEL Linux kernel supports a wide variety of hardware and software. Almost every module that could be made is made. This is a big kernel, and numerous modules can be used for it with the standard installation. This is not a problem when you install RHEL, but many administrators prefer a kernel without unwanted modules.

The following sections describe the different kernel configuration menus, section by section. However, since it appears that recompiling the kernel is no longer a requirement on the Red Hat exams, I do not provide any screenshots of additional menus. If you're interested in this level of detail, follow along on your Red Hat computer.

 o n   t h e

This chapter covers only the default configurable kernel options. For a full list in the gconfig or xconfig GUI menus, choose Options | Show All Options.

Code Maturity Level Options

The Code Maturity Level Options menu allows you to incorporate experimental code in the kernel. Common examples include drivers for new hardware, esoteric filesystems, and network protocols. Experimental code is often also known as *alpha level software*. If you have obsolete code that you want to incorporate into your kernel, it also falls in this category, as newer kernels often omit support for older features.

The one option (despite the plural title) relates to the **CONFIG_EXPERIMENTAL** variable. It's enabled by default in RHEL.

General Setup Options

The General Setup Options menu includes some basic hardware and kernel configuration options. Many of these options are self-explanatory, and the defaults are generally acceptable. If you need more information, read the help text associated with a specific kernel option.

General Setup options support memory paging. The System V IPC, POSIX Message Queues, BSD Process Accounting, and Sysctrl support parameters are all standard for current kernels. Other standard settings support netlink-based accounting, auditing, CPUset support, and optimized kernel sizes.

Loadable Module Support Options

The Loadable Module Support options allow you to enable loadable modules. The kernel module loader will automatically load modules for most new hardware, when detected. As discussed earlier, loadable modules allow you to optimize the kernel. If you want to optimize the kernel, keep all of the default options.

Process Debugging Support Options

The Process Debugging Support options enable utrace, an internal Linux kernel interface to track events, which can be useful for tracing user processes, events, and threads.

Block Layer

The Block Layer kernel settings are all enabled by default. Large block devices and files allow support for discs and files greater than 2TB. Related kernel settings allow support for block layer actions. The default I/O scheduler is set to Completely Fair Queuing, known as CFQ.

Processor Type and Features

The Processor Type and Features menu in RHEL supports a wide variety of CPUs, including the latest multicore processors.

Power Management Options

There are three standard categories of power management options related to Advanced Configuration and Power Interface (ACPI), Advanced Power Management (APM), and the CPU frequency scaling that can help conserve power, especially on laptop systems.

Bus Options

On a network, you want networking support. Most computers have PCI cards, and the defaults give you full PCI support, using BIOS detection and documenting the detected cards in the /proc directory. Various types of hot-pluggable devices are now popular, including PCMCIA cards for laptops and PCI hotplug support for removable drives. These settings are available through the Bus Options menu.

Executable File Formats

The Linux kernel includes modular support for binaries in the Executable and Linkable Format (ELF) as well as other miscellaneous formats such as the MS-DOS emulator, Java, and Python. These settings are available through the Executable File Formats menu.

Networking Options

There are many options for networking available in the Linux kernel. The Networking Options menu is extensive. It includes a substantial number of settings for different hardware devices, software settings, and more.

Device Drivers

Relative to previous kernels, several different categories have been organized into a larger Device Drivers category. They include Memory Technology Devices, Parallel Port Support, Plug and Play Support, Block Devices, ATA/ATAPI/MFM/RLL Support, SCSI Device Support, and more. There are many Device Driver subcategories.

Generic Driver Options   Most of the options in this section relate to firmware.

Connector – Unified Userspace – Kernelspace Linker   The Kernelspace includes the memory dedicated to the kernel, extensions, and related drivers. Userspace is the memory allocated to other functions. The linker allows communication between the two.

Memory Technology Devices   The options shown in the Memory Technology Devices menu allow you to set up Linux for basic Flash memory cards, including those that might be installed through a PCMCIA adapter. Unless you're planning to use some of these devices in the future, keep this option disabled.

Parallel Port Support   The options shown in the Parallel Port Support menu are based on hardware that may be connected to your computer through a parallel port. This includes everything from printers through parallel port hard drives. Remember that it is normally best to avoid the Experimental options unless you are a developer working on supporting the associated drivers.

Plug and Play Support   The options shown under the Plug and Play Configuration menu activate basic plug and play support on your Linux computer. While Linux plug and play does not handle all ISA and PCI devices, it does help you configure your computer for Linux.

Block Devices   Under the Block Devices Options menu, you can specify floppy drives and nonstandard hard disks. You can specify support for parallel port ATAPI CD-ROMs, tape drives, and even ATAPI floppy drives. You can also enable loopback support and network block support (which lets you use a physical disk on the network as if it were a local disk). If you have any parallel port devices such as external CD-ROMs or hard drives (different from those connected via USB or IEEE1394), you could enable support for those here. You can also set up support for RAM disks under this menu.

ATA/IDE/MFM/RLL Support The ATA/IDE/MFM/RLL acronyms all relate to various types of regular PC hard disk and CD drive interfaces. Normally, you shouldn't disable this kernel option unless all hard disk storage on your system is based on a SCSI interface. Even then, the flexibility of being able to install IDE devices is usually worth the extra code this adds to the kernel.

SCSI Device Support You can enable SCSI hard disks, tape drivers, and CD-ROM support in this section. If you have a SCSI CD-ROM jukebox, or any other device that requires more than one SCSI Logical Unit Number (LUN), you may have to enable probing of all LUNs.

Near the bottom of the menu, you can configure verbose SCSI error reporting. You can also enable specific low-level SCSI support. Red Hat also includes support for high-end hardware RAID-enabled SCSI host adapters.

Multi-device Support (RAID and LVM) If you're ever going to set up a RAID array of disks to help protect your data, you can enable that option in the Linux kernel under the Multi-device Support (RAID and LVM) menu. If you ever want to put together a volume set, where a directory can span more than one partition on more than one physical hard disk, you can enable that option here as well.

on the job

While there is support for RAID 4 in the Linux kernel, it is not directly supported by RHEL. However, support for RAID 6 is now available.

Fusion MPT Device Support This menu supports modules associated with very high speed SCSI adapters, associated with hardware developed by LSI.

IEEE 1394 (FireWire) Support The IEEE 1394 standard is more popularly known as FireWire or iLink. It's basically a very high speed hot plug and play hardware option, with data transfer speeds in the hundreds of Mbps. Linux support for IEEE 1394 standards is far from complete. However, support for IEEE devices such as external hard drives is readily available and configured as modules by default in RHEL.

I2O Device Support   The I2O specification, also known as Intelligent I/O, supports split drivers that can optimize communication performance between a device and the rest of your computer. Don't enable I2O haphazardly; it requires hardware that supports it.

Network Device Support   Linux supports a wide range of network cards. The Network Device Support menu allows you to enable support for the adapters you may need. Generally, you should enable support only for network devices that you're using now or may use in the future.

ISDN Subsystem   Integrated Services Digital Network (ISDN) lines are still a fairly popular high-speed digital option, especially outside of North America. Adding ISDN support in the ISDN Subsystem menu allows you to use an ISDN card for inbound or outbound dialing connections. The ISDN device has a built-in AT-compatible modem emulator, autodial, channel-bundling, callback, and caller authentication, without the need for an external daemon to be running. The supporting isdn4k-utils RPM is installed by default on RHEL.

Telephony Support   Telephony support on a computer network uses special network cards to convert voice into the type of data that can be sent over a network. This is separate from VoIP projects such as Asterisk; remember that you may not need the full kernel source to compile Asterisk drivers.

Input Device Support   The Input Device Support section configures support for various basic input devices: keyboards, mice, touchscreens, and joysticks. These devices are modular by default, which allows Linux to recognize these basic devices using plug and play detection.

Character Devices   Character devices send their data in byte streams. Typical character devices range from serial ports to virtual consoles. The Character Devices submenu allows you to specify support for a wide variety of devices, including virtual terminals, serial ports, newer AGP video cards, mice, joysticks, non-SCSI tape drives, and more.

I2C Support   I2C devices relate to a serial bus protocol of the same name.

SPI Support   This section allows you to enable support for the Serial Peripheral Interface (SPI).

Dallas's 1-wire Bus   The Dallas's 1-wire Bus section supports modules that enable communication over single pin devices.

Hardware Monitoring Support   The Hardware Monitoring Support section includes modules that help monitor system health, such as temperature monitors, fans, and much more.

Misc Devices   This Misc Devices section includes a module that supports the IBM RSA service processor associated with the eServer.

Multimedia Devices   The Multimedia Devices options support a wide range of video capture and AM/FM radio devices. Select each option (Video for Linux, Radio Adapters) for a list of drivers that you can enable. As always, it is best to keep what you enable to the default or a minimum.

Graphics Support   Linux supports console drivers, which can set up text on most graphics systems, even when Linux doesn't detect the right cards or monitors. The Frame Buffer Support option supports video adapters that store images in frame buffers.

Sound   A wide variety of sound cards are supported by RHEL, normally as modules. They're divided into two categories: the Advanced Linux Sound Architecture and the Open Sound System (which is now deprecated). These cards range from the Ensoniq Audio PCI card to TV card mixers. You can also use these drivers for cards that emulate the appropriate hardware. Check the Sound submenu for the latest list of supported hardware for your kernel. If you have a card that's not named in the list associated with older kernels, try to see if it emulates any card on the list. Many proprietary cards do emulate products from Sound Blaster or offer OPL/2 or OPL/3 compatibility.

USB Support   Linux supports a number of USB mass storage devices, printers, input devices, cameras and scanners, and even modems. Linux support for many USB networking cards is still experimental. Linux support for USB is improving, though some USB drivers that you'll see in the USB support menu are still considered experimental. Unfortunately, this includes support for faster USB 2.0 standard drivers.

MMC/SD Card Support   The multimedia cards associated with digital cameras and other small devices are among the latest in memory cards. The MMC/SD Card Support section allows you to enable the drivers required to detect and read these cards. Keep this in mind as some systems even enable MMC/SD cards as boot devices.

LED Devices   This section controls Light Emitting Diode (LED) devices. These devices are not related to keyboard LEDs.

InfiniBand Support   An InfiniBand device uses a point-to-point bidirectional serial link for very high speed communication, in the GB range.

EDAC – Error Detection and Reporting   The error detection and control (EDAC) system processes hardware-related errors, especially those from RAM with error correction codes (ECCs), and PCI bus parity errors.

Real Time Clock   The real time clock (RTC) kernel settings help the kernel work with the hardware clock.

DMA Engine Support   DMA is direct memory access, associated with certain hardware channels. A DMA engine supports multiple DMA channels.

on the job *If you're interested in virtualization, pay attention to distributions with Kernel 2.6.20, which incorporates Kernel-based Virtual Machine (KVM) support for the first time.*

File Systems

The File Systems subsection is a list of all the different types of filesystems Linux supports. Select the Quota option if you need to support quotas.

Because Linux supports so many different hardware platforms, it includes support for a large number of filesystem types. However, because of the proprietary nature of some filesystems, the degree of support is variable. You'll note that support for a lot of filesystems in this menu is experimental; however, there's always progress. In fact, you can now compile write support over existing files on NTFS partitions.

Instrumentation Support

Instrumentation Support allows you to use the OProfile system to characterize the performance of your system. It is described in more detail at http://oprofile.sourceforge.net.

Kernel Hacking

Kernel Hacking allows you to use the drivers you need to debug driver or related Linux kernel issues.

Security Options

Security Options is a relatively new category that includes modules for authentication tokens, security hooks, IPSec, and of course various options associated with SELinux.

Cryptographic Options

The Cryptographic Options support software associated with strong encryption in Linux.

Library Routines

The Library Routines support compression in Linux.

EXERCISE 8-1

Compiling and Installing a Custom Kernel

This is a very long exercise. For details of the kernel configuration menus, see the previous section. To change and compile a new kernel, take the following steps. It's critical that you do these steps in order: Download and install the kernel source code, as described earlier in this chapter.

1. Run the **cd /usr/src/redhat/BUILD/kernel-2.6.18/linux-2.6.18-`uname -m`** command to reach the source code directory. (If it's linked to /usr/src/linux, just navigate to that directory.) Open the Makefile text file in a text editor. The **EXTRAVERSION** variable is already set to identify a custom kernel. If necessary, change the value of this variable to uniquely identify your kernel. The default value is **-prep**; in this section I use

   ```
   EXTRAVERSION= -mjcustom1
   ```

2. Run the **make mrproper** command to ensure that the source files are in a consistent and clean state.

3. Save the current kernel configuration file. It's stored in the /boot directory, in the config-`uname -r` file. Have it ready with rescue media such as a USB key in case disaster strikes.

   Alternatively, you can start from a standard configuration file in the configs/ subdirectory of the kernel source code directory. A second alternative is to run the **make oldconfig** command.

   If you want to use your current kernel configuration as a baseline, copy it to the .config file in the source code directory.

4. Now you can customize your kernel with one of the following four utilities: The **make config** command runs the text-based configuration script. The **make menuconfig** command runs a low-level graphical configuration script. The **make xconfig** command starts the tool based on KDE libraries; the **make gconfig** command opens the GUI tool based on GNOME libraries.

5. Make any changes as desired. Before you exit from the kernel configuration utility, make sure to save your changes!

   Overall, the process is simpler than it used to be. However, the following commands work only if you're in the actual source code directory, not a linked directory such as /usr/src/linux.

   The **make rpm** command is a front end that runs a series of other commands, including **make clean**; compiles all kernel settings; and creates a custom RPM in the /usr/src/redhat/RPMS/i386 directory. (Although you can customize the Makefile for subarchitectures such as i686, it's not absolutely necessary.)

on the job
The make rpm *process is slow: it took more than an hour on my computer with a 2.4 GHz CPU.*

6. With the kernel now built into a custom RPM, you can install it just like any other kernel RPM. However, it does not do everything that a standard kernel update RPM does. In other words, you still need to create an initial RAM disk and a new stanza in the GRUB configuration file.

7. Verify the changes to the /boot directory. You'll see new kernel configuration and binary files; in this case, the files are named config-2.6.18-mjcustom1 and vmlinuz-2.6.18-mjcustom1.

8. Create an initial RAM disk file in the /boot directory; in this case, you would use the following command:

   ```
   # mkinitrd /boot/initrd-2.6.18-mjcustom1.img 2.6.18-mjcustom1
   ```

9. Add a stanza with the custom kernel files in the GRUB configuration file, /boot/grub/grub.conf. (I usually copy an existing stanza, and change the version numbers of each line.) Reboot your system, open the GRUB menu, and boot from the newly customized kernel!

Building a kernel is an involved process, but it follows a standard pattern. It is very important that you become familiar with kernel construction procedures and troubleshooting. However, this section is already somewhat beyond the scope of this book.

on the job
To see the full range of available options associated with the make command *in the kernel source code directory, run the* make help *command.*

CERTIFICATION OBJECTIVE 8.05

Advanced Partitioning: Software RAID

A Redundant Array of Independent Disks (RAID) is a series of disks that can save your data even if a catastrophic failure occurs on one of the disks. While some versions of RAID make complete copies of your data, others use the so-called parity bit to allow your computer to rebuild the data on lost disks.

Linux RAID has come a long way. A substantial number of hardware RAID products support Linux, especially those from name-brand PC manufacturers. Dedicated RAID hardware can ensure the integrity of your data even if there is a catastrophic *physical* failure on one of the disks. Alternatively, you can configure software-based RAID on multiple partitions on the same physical disk. While this can protect you from a failure on a specific hard drive sector, it does not protect your data if the entire physical hard drive fails.

Depending on definitions, RAID has nine or ten different levels, which can accommodate different levels of data redundancy. Combinations of these levels are possible. Several levels of software RAID are supported directly by RHEL: levels 0, 1, 5, and 6. Hardware RAID uses a RAID controller connected to an array of several hard disks. A driver must be installed to be able to use the controller. Most RAID is hardware based; when properly configured, the failure of one drive for almost all RAID levels (except RAID 0) does not destroy the data in the array.

Linux, meanwhile, offers a software solution to RAID. Once RAID is configured on a sufficient number of partitions, Linux can use those partitions just as it would any other block device. However, to ensure redundancy, it's up to you in real life to make sure that each partition in a Linux software RAID array is configured on a different physical hard disk.

on the job

The RAID md device is a meta device. In other words, it is a composite of two or more other devices such as /dev/hda1 and /dev/hdb1 that might be components of a RAID array.

The following are the basic RAID levels supported on RHEL.

RAID 0

This level of RAID makes it faster to read and write to the hard drives. However, RAID 0 provides no data redundancy. It requires at least two hard disks.

Reads and writes to the hard disks are done in parallel—in other words, to two or more hard disks simultaneously. All hard drives in a RAID 0 array are filled equally.

But since RAID 0 does not provide data redundancy, a failure of any one of the drives will result in total data loss. RAID 0 is also known as *striping without parity*.

RAID 1

This level of RAID mirrors information between two disks (or two sets of disks—see RAID 10). In other words, the same set of information is written to each disk. If one disk is damaged or removed, all of the data is stored on the other hard disk. The disadvantage of RAID 1 is that data has to be written twice, which can reduce performance. You can come close to maintaining the same level of performance if you also use separate hard disk controllers, which prevents the hard disk controller from becoming a bottleneck. RAID 1 is relatively expensive. To support RAID 1, you need an additional hard disk for every hard disk worth of data. RAID 1 is also known as *disk mirroring*.

RAID 4

While this level of RAID is not directly supported by the current Linux distributions associated with Red Hat, it is still supported by the current Linux kernel. RAID 4 requires three or more disks. As with RAID 0, data reads and writes are done in parallel to all disks. One of the disks maintains the parity information, which can be used to reconstruct the data. Reliability is improved, but since parity information is updated with every write operation, the parity disk can be a bottleneck on the system. RAID 4 is known as *disk striping with parity*.

RAID 5

Like RAID 4, RAID 5 requires three or more disks. Unlike RAID 4, RAID 5 distributes, or *stripes*, parity information evenly across all the disks. If one disk fails, the data can be reconstructed from the parity data on the remaining disks. RAID does not stop; all data is still available even after a single disk failure. RAID 5 is the preferred choice in most cases: the performance is good, data integrity is ensured, and only one disk's worth of space is lost to parity data. RAID 5 is also known as *disk striping with parity*.

RAID 6

RAID 6 literally goes one better than RAID 5. In other words, while it requires four or more disks, it has two levels of parity and can survive the failure of two member disks in the array.

RAID 10

I include RAID 10 solely to illustrate one way you can combine RAID levels. RAID 10 is a combination of RAID 0 and RAID 1, which requires a minimum of four disks. First, two sets of disks are organized in RAID 0 arrays, each with their own individual device file, such as /dev/md0 and /dev/md1. These devices are then mirrored. This combines the speed advantages of RAID 0 with the data redundancy associated with mirroring. There are variations: for example, RAID 01 stripes two sets of RAID 1 mirrors. RAID 50 provides a similar combination of RAID 0 and RAID 5.

on the
Job

Hardware RAID systems should be hotswappable. In other words, if one disk fails, the administrator can replace the failed disk while the server is still running. The system will then automatically rebuild the data onto the new disk. Since you can configure different partitions from the same physical disk for a software RAID system, the resulting configuration can easily fail if you use two or more partitions on the same physical disk. Alternatively, you may be able to set up spare disks on your servers; RAID may automatically rebuild data from a lost hard drive on properly configured spare disks.

RAID in Practice

RAID is associated with a substantial amount of data on a server. It's not uncommon to have a couple dozen hard disks working together in a RAID array. That much data can be rather valuable.

INSIDE THE EXAM

Creating RAID Arrays

During the Installation and Configuration portion of the Red Hat exams, it's generally easier to do as much as possible during the installation process. If you're asked to create a RAID array, it's easiest to do so with Disk Druid, which works only during installation. You can create RAID arrays once RHEL is installed, but as you'll see in the following instructions, it is more time consuming and involves a process that is more difficult to remember.

However, if you're required to create a RAID array during your exam and forget to create it during the installation process, not all is lost. You can still use the tools described in this chapter to create and configure RAID arrays during the exam. And the skills you learn here can serve you well throughout your career.

If continued performance through a hardware failure is important, you can assign additional disks for failover, which sets up spare disks for the RAID array. When one disk fails, it is marked as bad. The data is almost immediately reconstructed on the first spare disk, resulting in little or no downtime.

Reviewing an Existing RAID Array

If you created a RAID array during the installation process, you'll see it in the /proc/mdstat file. For example, I see the following on my system:

```
# cat /proc/mdstat
Personalities : [raid6] [raid5] [raid4]
md0 : active raid6 sda13[2] sda12[1] sda10[0] sda9[4] sda8[3]
      312576 blocks level 6, 256k chunk, algorithm 2 [5/5] [UUUUU]
unused devices: <none>
```

Yes, I know, this violates good practice, using RAID partitions from the same hard drive. But my personal resources (and I suspect many exam sites, despite the price) have limits. As you can see, this is a RAID 6 array, associated with device file md0, /dev/md0. You can find out more about this array with the following command:

```
# mdadm --detail /dev/md0
/dev/md0:
          Version : 00.90.03
    Creation Time : Tue Mar 21 04:13:45 2007
       Raid Level : raid6
       Array Size : 312576 (305.30 MiB 320.08 MB)
      Device Size : 104192 (101.77 MiB 106.69 MB)
     Raid Devices : 5
    Total Devices : 5
  Preferred Minor : 0
      Persistence : Superblock is persistent

      Update Time : Wed Dec 20 09:38:43 2006
            State : clean
   Active Devices : 5
  Working Devices : 5
   Failed Devices : 0
    Spare Devices : 0

       Chunk Size : 256K

             UUID : 8d85b38a:0ba072fc:858dfbb2:ba77a998
           Events : 0.4

    Number   Major   Minor   RaidDevice State
       0       3      10        0       active sync /dev/sda10
```

```
     1       3      12      1         active sync /dev/sda12
     2       3      13      2         active sync /dev/sda13
     3       3       8      3         active sync /dev/sda8
     4       3       9      4         active sync /dev/sda9
```

As you can see, this is a RAID 6 array, which requires at least four partitions. It can handle the failure of two partitions. If there were a spare device, the number of **Total Devices** would exceed the number of **Raid Devices**.

Modifying an Existing RAID Array

Modifying an existing RAID array is a straightforward process. You can simulate a failure with the following command. (I suggest that you add **--verbose** to help you get as much information as possible.)

```
# mdadm --verbose /dev/md0 -f /dev/sda13 -r /dev/sda13
mdadm: set /dev/sda13 faulty in /dev/md0
mdadm: hot removed /dev/sda13
```

You can reverse the process; the same command can be used to add the partition of your choice to the array:

```
# mdadm --verbose /dev/md0 -a /dev/sda13
mdadm: re-added /dev/sda13
```

It makes sense to review the results after each command with **cat /proc/mdstat** or **mdadm --detail /dev/md0**.

Creating a New RAID Array

Creating a new RAID array is a straightforward process. The first step is to create RAID partitions. You can do so as described earlier using either **parted** or **fdisk**. In this section, I'll show you how to create a simple RAID 1 array of two partitions. I assume that there are two partitions already available: /dev/sdb1 and /dev/sdb2. Now create a simple array:

```
# mdadm --create --verbose /dev/md1 --level=1 \
--raid-devices=2 /dev/sdb1 /dev/sdb2
mdadm: size set to 97536k
mdadm: array /dev/md1 started.
```

Now it's time to format the new device, presumably to the default ext3 filesystem:

```
# mkfs.ext3 /dev/md1
```

You can now mount the filesystem of your choice on this array. Just remember that if you want to make this permanent, you'll have to add it to your /etc/fstab. For example, to make it work with /tmp, add the following directive to that file:

```
/dev/md1   /tmp   ext3   defaults   0 0
```

watch

Remember that you may not get credit for your work unless your changes survive a reboot.

EXERCISE 8-2

Mirroring the /home Partition with Software RAID

Don't do this exercise on a production computer. If you have a computer with Red Hat Enterprise Linux already installed with several different physical hard drives that you can use for testing, that is best. One alternative is to use virtual machine technology such as VMware or Xen, which can allow you to set up these exercises with minimal risk to a production system. You can also set up several IDE and SCSI hard disks on a VMware machine. When you're ready, use the Linux **parted** or **fdisk** techniques, described in Chapter 4, and add a RAID partition to two different hard drives.

Using the following steps, you can create a mirror of hda5, which stores the /home directory, to the hdb5 partition. (If your partition devices are different, substitute accordingly.)

Assume you haven't created a RAID array before. If you have, check it in the /proc/mdstat file. Make a note of the existing arrays, and take the next device file in sequence. For example, if there's already an /dev/md0 array, plan for a /dev/md1 array in this exercise.

If you're making changes on a production computer, back up the data from the /tmp directory first. Otherwise, all user data in /tmp will be lost.

1. Mark the two partition IDs as type fd using the Linux **fdisk** utility. There are equivalent steps available in **parted**.

```
# fdisk /dev/hda
Command (m for help) : t
Partition number (1-5)
5
```

```
Partition ID (L to list options): fd
Command (m for help) : w
# fdisk /dev/hdb
Command (m for help) : t
Partition number (1-5)
5
Partition ID (L to list options): fd
Command (m for help) : w
```

2. Make sure to write the changes. The **parted** utility does it automatically; if you use **fdisk**, run **partprobe** or reboot.

3. Create a RAID array with the appropriate **mdadm** command. For /dev/hda5 and /dev/hdb5, you can create it with the following:

```
# mdadm --create /dev/md0 --level=1 --raid-devices=2 \
/dev/hda5 /dev/hdb5
```

4. Confirm the changes; run the following commands:

```
# cat /proc/mdstat
# mdadm --verbose /dev/md0
```

5. Now format the newly created RAID device:

```
# mkfs.ext3 /dev/md0
```

6. Now mount it on a test directory; I often create a test/ subdirectory in my home directory for this purpose:

```
# mount /dev/md0 /root/test
```

7. Next, copy all files from the current /home directory. Here's a simple method that copies all files and subdirectories of /home:

```
# cp -ar /home/. /root/test/
```

8. Unmount the test subdirectory:

```
# umount /dev/md0
```

9. Now you should be able to implement this change in /etc/fstab. Remember that during the exam, you may not get full credit for your work unless your Linux system mounts the directory on the RAID device. Based on the parameters described in this exercise, the directive would be

```
/dev/md0    /home    ext3    defaults   0 0
```

10. Now reboot and see what happens. If the /home directory partition contains the files of your users, you've succeeded. Otherwise, remove the directive added in step 9 from /etc/fstab and reboot again.

Advanced Partitioning: Logical Volume Management

Logical Volume Management (LVM) (also known as the Logical Volume Manager) can allow you to manage active partitions. Before LVM, you had no easy way to increase or reduce the size of a partition after Linux was installed. With LVM2, you can even create read-write snapshots; but this is not part of the current exam requirements, so this book won't be addressing that feature.

For example, if you find that you have extra space on the /home directory partition and need more space on your /var directory partition for log files, LVM will let you reallocate the space. Alternatively, if you are managing a server on a growing network, new users will be common. You may reach the point at which you need more room on your /home directory partition. With LVM, you can add a new physical disk and allocate its storage capacity to an existing /home directory partition.

on the **Ö o b**

While LVM can be an important tool to manage partitions, it does not by itself provide redundancy. Do not use it as a substitute for RAID. However, you can use LVM in concert with a properly configured RAID array.

Whenever you change an active PV, LV, or VG, unmount the volume first. If it's an essential filesystem such as the top-level root (/) directory, you may need to use **linux rescue** mode or a third-party bootable Linux such as Knoppix.

In essence, to create a new LVM system, you need to create a new PV, using a command such as **pvcreate**, assign the space to a VG with a command such as **vgcreate**, and allocate the space from some part of available VGs to an LV with a command such as **lvcreate**.

INSIDE THE EXAM

Logical Volume Management

One of the critical decisions during the Installation part of the RHCE and RHCT exams is whether you install in text or graphical mode. Text mode is faster. However, if you're required to create an LVM group during your exam, you can configure custom LVM groups with Disk Druid *only* it if you install RHEL in graphical mode.

I can't give you a concrete time savings between graphical and text mode; it depends on the traffic demands (how many other users) and the hardware available during your exam. I can say that when I installed the standard RHEL server configuration in graphical mode, it took 5 minutes longer than the same process in text mode. If your computer has more than 256MB of RAM (and more than 16MB of video memory), I suspect the difference would decrease.

If you forget to configure LVM during installation or are required to make changes, you can use the techniques I describe in this section to configure LVM groups after installation. Remember that the Red Hat Exam Prep guide suggests that RHCEs, during the Troubleshooting and System Maintenance portion of their exams, need to know how to

■ Add, remove, and resize logical volumes.

To add space to an existing LVM system, you need to add free space from an existing VG with a command such as **lvextend**. If you don't have any existing VG space, you'll need to add to it with unassigned PV space with a command such as **vgextend**. If all of your PVs are taken, you may need to create a new PV from an unassigned partition or hard drive with the **pvcreate** command.

You can also do much of this with the associated Logical Volume Management tool described near the end of this chapter.

Creating a Physical Volume

The first step in creating an LVM is to start with a physical disk. If you have a freshly installed hard disk, you can set up a PV on the entire disk. For example, if that hard disk is attached as the third PATA hard disk (/dev/hdc), and you haven't configured partitions on the drive, you'd run the following command:

```
# pvcreate /dev/hdc
```

Alternatively, you can set up a new PV on a properly formatted partition. For example, assume that you've added a new partition, /dev/hdc2. You could then use **fdisk** or **parted** to set it to the Linux LVM partition type. In **fdisk**, this corresponds to partition type **8e**; in **parted**, it corresponds to **lvm**. The sequence of commands would look similar to the following:

```
# fdisk /dev/hdc
Command (m for help) : t
Partition number (1-4)
2
Partition ID (L to list options): 8e
Command (m for help) : w
```

Once your partition is ready, you can run the following command to create a new PV on that partition (/dev/hdc2) with the following command:

```
# pvcreate /dev/hdc2
```

Creating a Volume Group

Once you have two or more PVs, you can create a volume group (VG). In the following command, substitute the name of your choice for *volumegroup*:

```
# vgcreate volumegroup /dev/hdc2 /dev/hdd2
```

You can add more room to any VG. Assume there's an existing /dev/sda1 partition, using a Linux LVM type, and the **pvcreate** command has been applied to that partition. You can then add that partition to an existing VG with the following command:

```
# vgextend volumegroup /dev/sda1
```

Creating a Logical Volume

However, a new VG doesn't help you unless you can mount a filesystem on it. So you need to create a logical volume (LV) for this purpose. The following command creates an LV. You can add as many chunks of disk space (a.k.a. physical extents, or PEs) as you need.

```
# lvcreate -l number_of_PEs volumegroup -n logvol
```

This creates a device named /dev/*volumegroup*/*logvol*. You can format this device as if it were a regular disk partition, and then mount the directory of your choice on your new logical volume.

But this isn't useful if you don't know how much space is associated with each PE. You could use trial and error, using the **df** command to check the size of the volume after you've mounted a directory on it. Alternatively, you can use the **-L** switch to set a size in MB. For example, the following command creates an LV named flex of 200MB:

```
# lvcreate -L 200M volumegroup -n flex
```

Using a Logical Volume

But that's not the last step. You may not get full credit for your work on the exam unless the directory gets mounted on the LVM group when you reboot your Linux computer. Based on a standard RHEL /etc/fstab configuration file, one option is to add the following line to that file:

```
LABEL=/home/mj   /home/mj    ext3     defaults    1 2
```

Before this line can work, you'll need to set the label for this directory with the following command:

```
# e2label /dev/volumegroup/logvol /home/mj
```

Alternatively, you can just substitute the LVM device file such as /dev/VolGroup00/ LogVol03 for **LABEL=/home/mj**. The /etc/fstab file, including the meaning of the data in each these columns, is described in more detail in Chapter 4.

More LVM Commands

There are a wide variety of LVM commands related to PVs, LVs, and VGs. Generally, they are **pv***, **lv***, and **vg*** in the /usr/sbin directory. Physical volume commands include those listed in Table 8-3.

TABLE 8-3	Available Physical Volume Management Commands

Physical Volume Command	Description
pvchange	Changes attributes of a PV: the **pvchange -x n /dev/sda10** command disables the use of PEs from the /dev/sda10 partition.
pvcreate	Initializes a disk or partition as a PV; the partition should be flagged with the LVM file type.
pvdisplay	Displays currently configured PVs.
pvmove	Moves PVs in a VG from the specified partition to free locations on other partitions; prerequisite to disabling a PE. One example: **pvmove /dev/sda10**.
pvremove	Removes a given PV from a list of recognized volume: for example, **pvremove /dev/sda10**.
pvresize	Changes the amount of a partition allocated to a PV. If you've expanded partition /dev/sda10, **pvresize /dev/sda10** takes advantage of the additional space. Alternatively, **pvresize --setphysicalvolumesize 100M /dev/sda10** reduces the amount of PVs taken from that partition to the noted space.
pvs	Lists configured PVs and the associated VGs, if so assigned.
pvscan	Similar to **pvs**.

As you assign PVs to VGs to LVs, you may need commands to control and configure them. Table 8-4 includes an overview of most related volume group commands. Read the information in the table; while you may need only a few of the commands, you may find use for more in time.

As you assign PVs to VGs to LVs, you may need commands to control and configure them. Table 8-5 includes an overview of related LVM commands. Read over the table; while you may not need to use more than a few of the commands, you may find use for others in time.

Here's an example how this works. Try the **vgscan** command. You can verify configured volume groups (VGs) with the **vgdisplay** command. For example, Figure 8-9 illustrates the configuration of VG VolGroup00.

| TABLE 8-4 | Available Volume Group Commands |

Volume Group Command	Description
vgcfgbackup vgcfgrestore	Backs up and restores the configuration files associated with LVM; by default, they're in the /etc/lvm directory.
vgchange	Similar to **pvchange**, allows you to activate or deactivate a VG. For example, **vgchange -a y** enables all local VGs.
vgconvert	Supports conversions from LVM1 systems to LVM2: **vgconvert -M2 VolGroup00** converts VolGroup00.
vgcreate	Creates a VG, from two or more configured PVs: for example, **vgcreate vgroup00 /dev/sda10 /dev/sda11** creates vgroup00 from PVs as defined on /dev/sda10 and /dev/sda11.
vgdisplay	Displays characteristics of currently configured VGs.
vgexport vgimport	Exports and imports unused VGs from those available for LVs; the **vgexport -a** command exports all inactive VGs.
vgextend	If you've created a new PV: **vgextend vgroup00 /dev/sda11** adds the space from /dev/sda11 to vgroup00.
vgmerge	If you have an unused VG vgroup01, you can merge it into vgroup00 with the following command: **vgmerge vgroup00 vgroup01**.
vgmknodes	Run this command if you have a problem with VG device files.
vgreduce	The **vgreduce vgroup00 /dev/sda11** command removes the /dev/sda11 PV from vgroup00, assuming sufficient free space is available.
vgremove	The **vgremove vgroup00** command removes vgroup00, assuming it is not assigned to any LV.
vgrename	Allows renaming of LVs.
vgs	Displays basic information on configured VGs.
vgscan	Scans and displays basic information on configured VGs.

```
[root@enterprise5dl ~]# vgdisplay
  --- Volume group ---
  VG Name               VolGroup00
  System ID
  Format                lvm2
  Metadata Areas        1
  Metadata Sequence No  3
  VG Access             read/write
  VG Status             resizable
  MAX LV                0
  Cur LV                2
  Open LV               2
  Max PV                0
  Cur PV                1
  Act PV                1
  VG Size               4.88 GB
  PE Size               32.00 MB
  Total PE              156
  Alloc PE / Size       156 / 4.88 GB
  Free  PE / Size       0 / 0
  VG UUID               0j4HjQ-KD45-4iQW-FuPZ-oeoO-sII4-7tXNbJ

[root@enterprise5dl ~]# █
```

TABLE 8-5   Available Logical Volume Commands

Logical Volume Command	Description
lvchange	Similar to **pvchange**, changes the attributes of an LV: for example, the **lvchange -a n vgroup00/lvol00** command disables the use of the LV labeled lvol00.
lvconvert	If there are sufficient available PVs, the **lvconvert -m1 vgroup00/lvol00** command mirrors the LV.
lvcreate	Creates a new LV in an existing VG. For example, **lvcreate -l 200 volume01 -n lvol01** creates lvol01 from 200 extents in the VG named volume01.
lvdisplay	Displays currently configured LVs.
lvextend	Adds space to an LV: the **lvextend -L4G /dev/volume01/lvol01** command extends lvol01 to 4GB, assuming space is available.
lvreduce	Reduces the size of an LV; if there's data in the reduced area, it is lost.
lvremove	Removes an active LV: the **lvremove volume01/lvol01** command removes all lvol01 from VG volume01.
lvrename	Renames an LV.
lvresize	Resizes an LV; can be done by **-L** for size. For example, **lvresize -L 4GB volume01/lvol01** changes the size of lvol01 to 4GB.
lvs	Lists all configured LVs.
lvscan	Scans for all active LVs.

Before logical volumes are useful, you need to know how to add another LV. For example, if you've added more users, and they need more room than you have on the /home directory, you may need to add more LVs for other filesystems or resize the current /home directory LV.

on the
Ĵob

Linux can't read /boot files if they're installed on a Logical Volume. If you feel the need for special provisions for the /boot directory, try a RAID 1 array. However, there have been problems with that configuration as well.

Adding Another Logical Volume

Adding another LV is a straightforward process. For example, if you've just added a fourth SATA hard drive, it's known as device /dev/sdd. If you need more LVs for the /tmp directory, you'd follow these basic steps:

1. Add the new hard drive.
2. Configure the new hard drive with a tool such as **fdisk** or **parted**. Make sure new partitions correspond to the Linux LVM format. It's code **8e** within **fdisk**, or flag **lvm** within **parted**. Alternatively, you can dedicate all space on the new hard drive as a physical volume (PV) with the **pvcreate /dev/sdd** command.
3. If you've created separate partitions, you can dedicate the space of a specific partition to a PV. If you don't already have an empty logical volume, you'll need to create more than one. For example, for the first partition /dev/sdd1, you can do this with the following command:

```
# pvcreate /dev/sdd1
```

4. Next, you'll want to create a volume group (VG) from one or more empty, properly configured partitions (or drives). One way to do this, assuming you have empty /dev/sdc3 and /dev/sdd1 partitions, is with the following command:

```
# vgcreate Volume01 /dev/sdc3 /dev/sdd1
```

5. Before proceeding, you should inspect the VG with the **vgdisplay** command. This was illustrated with an example in Figure 8-9.
6. You should now be able to add another LV with the **lvcreate** command. For example, the following command takes 20 Physical Extents (PEs) for the new LV, LogVol01:

```
# lvcreate -l 20 Volume01 -n LogVol01
```

7. You've added a new LV. Naturally, you'll need to format and mount a directory on this LV before you can use it. For the example shown, you would use the following commands:

```
# mkfs.ext3 /dev/Volume01/LogVol01
# mount /dev/Volume01/LogVol01 /tmp
```

Removing a Logical Volume

Removing an existing LV requires a straightforward command. The basic command is **lvremove**. If you've created an LV in the previous section and want to remove it, the basic steps are simple. However, it will work only from a rescue environment such as the **linux rescue** mode described in Chapter 16, or from a CD/DVD-based system such as Knoppix or the new Fedora Live DVD.

1. Save any data in directories that are mounted on the LV.
2. Unmount any directories associated with the LV. Based on the example in the previous section, you would use the following command:

```
# umount /dev/Volume01/LogVol01
```

3. Apply the **lvremove** command to the LV with a command such as:

```
# lvremove /dev/Volume01/LogVol01
```

4. You should now have the PEs from this LV free for use in other LVs.

Resizing Logical Volumes

If you have an existing LV, you can add a newly created PV to extend the space available on your system. All it takes is appropriate use of the **vgextend** and **lvextend** commands. For example, if you want to add PEs to the VG associated with the aforementioned /home directory, you could take the following basic steps:

1. Back up any data existing on the /home directory.
2. Unmount the /home directory from the current LV.
3. Extend the VG to include the new hard drive or partitions that you've created. For example, if you want to add /dev/sdd1 to the /home VG, you would run the following command:

```
# vgextend Volume00 /dev/sdd1
```

4. Make sure the new partitions are included in the VG with the following command:

```
# vgdisplay Volume00
```

5. Extend the current LV to include the space you need. For example, if you want to extend the LV to 2000MB, you'd run the following command:

```
# lvextend -L 2000M /dev/Volume00/LogVol00
```

The **lvextend** command can help you configure LVs in KB, MB, GB, or even TB. For example, you could get the same result with the following command:

```
# lvextend -L 2G /dev/Volume00/LogVol00
```

6. Reformat and remount the LV, using commands described earlier, so your filesystem can take full advantage of the new space:

```
# mkfs.ext3 /dev/Volume00/LogVol00
# mount /dev/Volume00/LogVol00 /home
```

7. Once remounted, you can restore the information you backed up from the /home directory.

The GUI LVM Management Tool

If this is all confusing, you might try the GUI LVM tool, as shown in Figure 8-10. In the GNOME desktop, you can start it by choosing System | Administration | Logical Volume Management, or running **system-config-lvm** from a GUI command line. In the spirit of the RHCE Troubleshooting and System Maintenance exam requirement, we'll use it to add, remove, and resize logical volumes.

If possible, test the options in these three subsections in one sitting. I assume that the changes you make in the first subsection carry over to the next subsection.

Adding an LV

Assume you've added a new hard drive. For the purpose of this section, I've added a second SCSI drive (can also be a SATA drive), /dev/sdb, and created a new partition of 2500MB, set or flagged to the corresponding partition type, using the **fdisk** utility as described earlier in this chapter. VMware is an excellent option for this purpose.

Remember that if the GUI commands in this tool don't work, you can always use the associated regular text commands described earlier. Based on the tool shown in Figure 8-10, take the following steps:

1. Create a /test directory. (You should already know how to use the **mkdir** command for this purpose.)

2. Open the GUI LVM tool; one method is to run the **system-config-lvm** command inside the GUI.

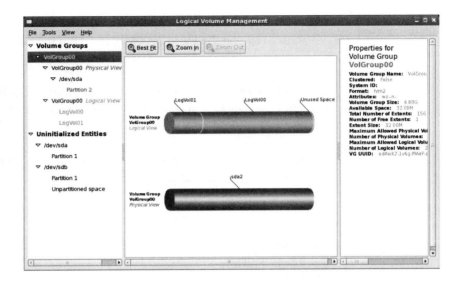

3. Navigate to the Uninitialized Entities associated with the newly created
   SATA or SCSI drive, /dev/sdb.

4. Select the partition previously created; click the Initialize Entity button
   that appears at the bottom of the window. This action applies the **pvcreate**
   command to the new partition. (If you have a command line open, you can
   confirm with the **pvs** command.)

5. You'll see a warning that all data on the partition will be lost. Click Yes.

6. If you haven't seen it before, you'll see an Unallocated Volumes category.
   Select the PV that you've just initialized. You'll see three options:

   ■ The Create New Volume Group option allows you to create a new
   VG for another filesystem, which corresponds to the **vgcreate**
   command.

   ■ Add To Existing Volume Group allows you to increase the space
   associated with the VG of your choice. This corresponds to the
   vgextend command.

   ■ Remove Volume From LVM reverses the process.

   As this section is based on adding a new VG, select Create New Volume
   Group. You'll see the window shown in Figure 8-11, where you can assign a
   name and set the size for the new VG; the default uses all available space. For
   the purpose of this section, I've named the new VG VolGroup01.

FIGURE 8-11

Creating a new
volume group

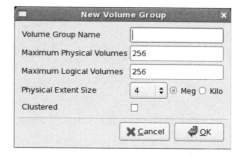

7. You'll see the new VG in the Volume Groups category. Navigate to the name
   of the new VG, in this case, VolGroup01, and select the Logical View for
   this group. Click the Create New Logical Volume button that appears at the
   bottom of the window, which opens the window shown in Figure 8-12.

8. In the Create New Logical Volume window, you can configure the amount
   of space assigned to the LV, the format, and the mount point. In Figure 8-12,
   I've allocated half the space to LogVol02, formatted it to ext3, and set it to be
   mounted on the previously created /test directory.

This new LV is now ready for a new filesystem; you can copy it to the /test
directory, unmount it, and change /etc/fstab to mount it on the desired filesystem.
But for the purpose of this chapter, don't make any of these changes.

FIGURE 8-12

Creating a new
logical volume

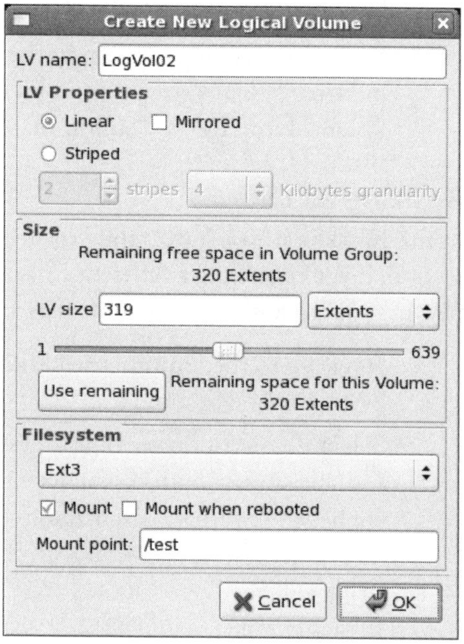

Removing an LV

This section assumes that you've created an LV using the steps described in the previous section. If you're removing a different LV, substitute accordingly.

1. Open the GUI LVM tool.

2. Navigate to LogVol02, under Volume Groups, under the Logical View of VolGroup01. This is the LV assigned to and mounted on the /test directory.

3. Click the Remove Logical Volume button. Naturally, this corresponds to the **lvremove** command.

on the **Job**

Before removing the LV, look at the other options. If you select Create Snapshot, you can mirror the current LV. It works only if there is sufficient unallocated space from available VGs. If you select Edit Properties, you can change the LV settings described in the previous subsection.

You'll see a warning about LogVol02 containing data from directory /test. Any data that you've copied to that directory will be lost if you click Yes. Technically, that's all you need to remove the LV. But you can do more.

4. Move up a bit in the left-hand pane to the Physical View associated with VolGroup01. Navigate down to the partition you created in the previous subsection, and then select Remove Volume From Volume Group, and select Yes when the warning appears.

5. You'll now see the partition in the Unallocated Volumes category, as shown in Figure 8-13. Navigate to and select the subject partition. Click Remove Volume From LVM. Confirm the change when prompted.

Resizing an LV

In this subsection, you'll redo the first steps in adding an LV, as described in an earlier section. If you're resizing a different LV, substitute accordingly. Instead of creating a new LV, you'll add the new space to an existing LV. To do so, take the following steps:

1. Navigate to the Uninitialized Entities associated with the newly created SCSI drive, /dev/sdb.

2. Select the partition previously created, in this case, /dev/sdb1; click the Initialize Entity button that appears at the bottom of the window. This action applies the **pvcreate** command to the new partition. (If you have a command line open, you can confirm with the **pvs** command.)

FIGURE 8-13

Removing a
logical volume

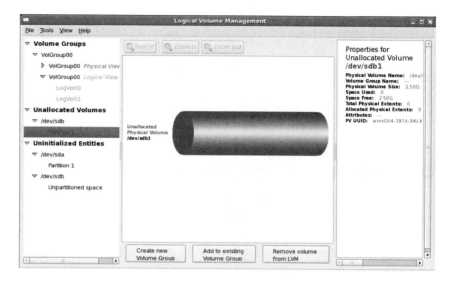

3. If you're resizing a different LV, substitute accordingly. You'll see a warning that all data on the partition will be lost. Click Yes.

4. In the Unallocated Volumes category, select the PV that you've just initialized. In this case, you'll select Add To Existing Volume Group. You'll see the Add Physical Volume To VG window shown in Figure 8-14.

5. Select the existing volume group of your choice and click Add. At this point, you can't do any more with the GUI LVM tool. Click CTRL-Q to exit from this tool.

6. Now you can use the **lvextend** command to take advantage of the new space. For example, the following command extends the volume to 6.3GB of space:

```
# lvextend -L 6.3G /dev/VolGroup00/LogVol00
```

FIGURE 8-14

Adding a physical
volume

7. Finally, you can use the additional space—for a standard ext3 filesystem, that requires the **resize2fs** command. If you don't specify a size, it takes all available space.

```
# resize2fs /dev/VolGroup00/LogVol00
```

Check the result. You should see the additional space when you run the **df** command.

Converting LVM1 Filesystem to LVM2

The conversion process for LVM1 partitions is straightforward; the **vgconvert** command is designed to help. After making sure the associated LV is backed up and unmounted, you can convert an LVM1 filesystem, which might be named VolGroup00, with the following command:

```
# vgconvert -M2 VolGroup00
```

But this is a one-way process; despite what the man page might suggest, it's not possible in most cases with current tools to convert back to LVM1.

CERTIFICATION SUMMARY

Kernels are at the heart of every operating system. The Linux kernel can be customized in a wide variety of ways. Two methods are based on loadable modules and changes to runtime parameters in the /proc directory.

The easiest way to update a kernel is to install (and not upgrade) from a Red Hat RPM, or use the **yum** command to install from your assigned repository. When you do, it automatically updates your boot loader files as needed.

Alternatively, the kernel can be optimized for your particular installation and hardware, and you have detailed control over its configuration. Once customized, it's a lot easier than it used to be to make a modular kernel; the **make rpm** command is all you need to create a customized kernel RPM. It's not perfect, as you still need to create your own initial RAM disk and corresponding stanza in your GRUB configuration file.

While it's best to configure RAID and LVM during the installation process, you may also need to do so after installation. RHEL supports a variety of software RAID types, including RAID 0, RAID 1, RAID 5, and RAID 6. LVM makes it easier to expand the size allocated to an existing filesystem; RHEL includes the GUI LVM tool to help.

TWO-MINUTE DRILL

Here are some of the key points from the certification objectives in Chapter 8.

The Basics of the Kernel

❑ The kernel lies at the heart of the operating system.

❑ Modular kernels, with separate device modules, are more efficient than monolithic kernels, where device drivers are integrated into the kernel.

❑ If you're going to update your kernel, you should keep a copy of your current working kernel.

❑ Linux kernels and related files are stored in the /boot directory.

❑ The /proc directory provides a window to what Linux sees in your computer.

❑ The **lsmod** command lists currently loaded modules; important related commands are **insmod**, **rmmod**, and **modprobe**.

❑ Basic RHEL modules can be loaded from the kernel-devel RPM.

New Kernels, the Easy Way

❑ Kernel version numbers are organized in *major.minor.patch* format. Red Hat adds a build number to the Linux kernels that it builds from source code.

❑ It's fairly easy to install a Red Hat kernel from RPM, as long as you remember to install and not upgrade. This allows you to return to the current working kernel if you have a problem.

❑ Sometimes all you need is a kernel patch, which supports upgrades of one patch version number. Unfortunately, patches are not always the best option for Red Hat built kernels.

❑ When you install a Red Hat kernel from RPM, the process should automatically update your GRUB boot loader.

Kernel Sources

❑ Kernel sources can be loaded from the kernel source RPM or from a Linux kernel tarball downloaded from a site such as ftp.kernel.org.

❑ Installing the Red Hat kernel source RPM requires the **rpmbuild** command.

❑ Once installed, the kernel source tree is available through /usr/src/redhat/ BUILD directory.

Recompiling a Kernel

❑ To optimize the Linux kernel, it is a best practice to compile kernels with only needed elements and configure modules for most hardware.

❑ Your current kernel configuration is stored in the config-`uname -r` file in the /boot directory.

❑ You can modify kernel settings from the kernel source code directory with tools that you can open with one of the following commands: **make config**, **make menuconfig**, **make xconfig**, or **make gconfig**.

❑ Once you've made the proper backups and boot disks and set the **EXTRAVERSION** variable in your Makefile, you're ready to customize your kernel.

❑ Once you've settled on and saved your changes, run the **make rpm** command. It should compile your new kernel and create an RPM in the /usr/src/redhat/RPMS directory, which you can use to install your custom kernel.

Advanced Partitioning: Software RAID

❑ Red Hat supports several levels of software RAID, including RAID 0, RAID 1, RAID 5, and RAID 6.

❑ To make software RAID work, you need to designate the partition specifically as such in **fdisk** or **parted**.

❑ RAID arrays as configured are shown in /proc/mdstat.

❑ RAID arrays can be created and modified with the **mdadm** command.

Advanced Partitioning: Logical Volume Management

❑ LVM is based on physical volumes, logical volumes, and volume groups.

❑ You can create and add LVM systems with a wide variety of commands starting with **pv***, **lv***, and **vg***.

❑ The GUI LVM tool is an alternative for those who don't remember all of the commands required to manage logical volumes.

SELF TEST

The following questions will help you measure your understanding of the material presented in this chapter. As no multiple choice questions appear on the Red Hat exams, no multiple choice questions appear in this book. These questions exclusively test your understanding of the chapter. It is okay if you have another way of performing a task. Getting results, not memorizing trivia, is what counts on the Red Hat exams. There may be more than one answer to many of these questions

The Basics of the Kernel

1. You are troubleshooting someone else's computer and are not sure what network card is inside it. You have checked the output from the **dmesg** command, but no network cards are listed, and even though you have a bunch of compiled network modules, none are currently loaded. What command might load the unknown network device?

_____

2. What directory includes dynamic kernel configuration settings?

_____

New Kernels, the Easy Way

3. When you install a newer kernel from a Red Hat RPM, what else do you need to do before rebooting?

_____

4. What happens if you use the **-U** switch to install a later Red Hat kernel RPM?

_____

Kernel Sources

5. Your kernel is version 2.6.19, and your architecture is x86_64. When you install and build the source code package associated with the Red Hat kernel, you'll find it in what directory?

_____

6. When you install the kernel source code, you'll find kernel-2.6.spec in the /usr/src/redhat/ SPECS directory. What command would you run to unpack the source code?

_____

Recompiling a Kernel

7. Once you've navigated to the directory with the kernel source code, name two commands that would open a menu that can help you configure a custom kernel. Assume all necessary dependencies are also installed.

   _____

   _____

8. You have just compiled and installed a custom kernel from kernel.org. What two other things do you need to do before you restart and boot from that kernel?

   _____

   _____

Advanced Partitioning: Software RAID

9. In what file can you find the current software RAID configuration?

   _____

10. What command can help you build a new RAID array? Just list the basic command; assume that you'll go to the man page for more information.

    _____

Advanced Partitioning: Logical Volume Management

11. Once you've created a new partition and set it to the Logical Volume Management filetype, what command adds it as a PV?

    _____

12. Once you've added more space to an LV, what command would expand the formatted filesystem to fill the new space?

    _____

LAB QUESTIONS

The Red Hat exams are unique based on their reliance on labs and hands-on demonstrations. With these questions, you're practicing the skills you need on both Red Hat exams.

Lab 1

In this lab, you'll install an updated kernel. This requires that an updated kernel be available, and you may not be able to run this lab unless you have such a kernel. However, if an older kernel is available for the distribution, you could add the **--force** switch to the **rpm** command used in this lab to downgrade to the old kernel temporarily.

In most cases, if you have an appropriate connection to the RHN or a rebuild repository (or even the update repositories for Fedora Core 6), you should be able to install the new kernel. List two methods you could use.

Finally, observe what happens to /boot/grub/grub.conf. What changed? What's the default kernel?

Lab 2

In this lab, you'll customize and recompile the kernel. Yes, this is beyond what is listed in the Red Hat Exam Prep guide. However, recent changes to the kernel compilation process leads me to believe that Red Hat may reintroduce this skill into the RHCE exam sometime in the near future.

This lab is more of a detailed kernel building exercise than a typical lab. Even if you don't need to compile a kernel on the Red Hat exams, I predict that you will need to compile a kernel at some point as a Linux system administrator. See the Lab Answers section at the end of this chapter for the exercise.

If you want to try things out for yourself, download and install the kernel src.rpm for the active kernel. Install it, and run the **rpmbuild** command on the associated .spec file. Customize some minor part of the kernel, change the **EXTRAVERSION** directive in the associated Makefile, and run **make rpm** to compile and create an RPM for the custom kernel.

Lab 3

In this lab, you'll add a new RAID array to your system. This is possible if you have free space on the current drive or can add a new drive. That's not as difficult as it appears if you have a VMware-based system. You can even use a USB key for this purpose (assuming you don't need to save any data on that key).

One way to test this lab is to create a separate RAID partition for the /tmp directory. Unless you use it for downloads, it's fairly small; on my system, it has 120KB of data. (If you're using /tmp for downloads, chances are you're using a production system, and that can be dangerous, unless your backups are in order.)

Create a simple RAID 1 mirror. All you need are two partitions. While it's best if the partitions are on different physical drives, it's not required for this lab. Remember to activate the array. Assign and mount it on a new directory. Copy files from your home directory. If the space used by your home directory is greater than available from the RAID array, you don't have to copy everything. Add the information to your /etc/fstab, and test the result.

Lab 4

Lab 4 and Lab 5 are to be run in sequence.

In Lab 4, you'll add a new LV to your system. It doesn't have to be complex; you can use free extents from an available LVM or a single new LVM partition. If possible, you'll want to leave some free extents for Lab 5, or you'll have to create another new LVM partition in that lab.

One way to test this lab is to create a separate LVM for the /tmp directory. Unless you use it for downloads, it's fairly small; on my system, it has 120KB of data. (If you're using /tmp for downloads, chances are you're using a production system, and that can be dangerous, unless your backups are in order.)

Add the information to your /etc/fstab, and run **mount -a** to test the result.

Lab 5

In Lab 5, you'll increase the size of the new LV. First, run the **df** command to review the space taken by the current version of the LV. Unmount it from the directory you've configured. Use available free space from existing LVM partitions, or create a new LVM partition. Remount the newly expanded LV, and test the result. Are the files still there? What is the size of the new LV?

SELF TEST ANSWERS

The Basics of the Kernel

1. Any of these commands might load the unknown network device: **modprobe -lt net**, **modprobe**, and **modprobe eth0**.

2. The directory that includes dynamic kernel configuration settings is **/proc**.

New Kernels, the Easy Way

3. When you install an updated kernel from a Red Hat RPM, you shouldn't have to do anything else. As configured, it should automatically create an initial RAM disk in the /boot directory and add an appropriate stanza to the GRUB configuration file, /boot/grub/grub.conf.

4. If you use the **rpm -U** command, instead of **rpm -i**, you overwrite the currently active kernel. Since you're running from that kernel, you know that the active kernel works. If you overwrite it with a new kernel, and that new kernel doesn't work, you're out of luck.

Kernel Sources

5. If your kernel is some version 2.6.19, and your architecture is x86_64, the kernel source code when installed can be found in the /usr/src/redhat/BUILD/kernel-2.6.19/linux-2.6.19.x86_64 directory.

6. When you install the kernel source code, with the kernel-2.6.spec in the /usr/src/redhat/SPECS directory, you can navigate to that directory and then unpack the code with the **rpmbuild -bb kernel-2.6.spec** command.

Recompiling a Kernel

7. Once you've navigated to the directory with the kernel source code, there are not just two, but four commands available that open a menu that can help you configure a custom kernel: **make config**, **make menuconfig**, **make xconfig**, and **make gconfig**.

8. You have just compiled and installed a custom kernel RPM. The two other things do you need to do before you restart and boot from that kernel is create an initial RAM disk with the **mkinitrd** command and create a new stanza in the GRUB configuration file, /boot/grub/grub.conf.

Advanced Partitioning: Software RAID

9. You can find the current software RAID configuration in /proc/mdstat.

10. The **mdadm** command can help you build a new RAID array.

Advanced Partitioning: Logical Volume Management

11. Once you've created a new partition and set it to the Logical Volume Management filetype, the command that adds it as a PV is **pvcreate**. For example, if the new partition is /dev/hdb2, the command is **pvcreate /dev/hdb2**.

12. Once you've added more space to an LV, the command that would expand the formatted filesystem to fill the new space is **resize2fs**.

LAB ANSWERS

Lab 1

Installing an updated kernel is easy. Assuming it's available from a repository such as the RHN, all you should have to do is run the following command:

```
# yum install kernel
```

However, you can also download and install the kernel RPM. Naturally, if the RPM is readily available, you can install it by applying a command such as **rpm -ivh** to the new kernel RPM. Be sure to avoid *upgrading*; that would overwrite any existing kernel.

As for the GRUB configuration file, you'll see a new stanza associated with the new kernel as well as the associated initial RAM disk. The other parameters should remain the same (except for version numbers) relative to the stanza that boots the existing kernel. The **default** directive in GRUB now points to the existing (and presumably working) kernel. (This is different from previous versions of Red Hat Enterprise Linux.)

Lab 2

Before building a new kernel, you need the correct RPM packages (with dependencies), often associated with the Development Tools package group. As with the rest of this chapter and the Red Hat exams, this assumes that you have a PC with a 32-bit Intel type CPU. The procedures for other CPUs vary and are not, as of this writing, covered on the Red Hat exams.

The following list of RPMs are associated with the source code (version numbers omitted). This does not include dependencies. When possible, use the **yum** command to satisfy and install these dependencies automatically.

```
kernel-`uname -r`.src.rpm
unidef
rpm-build
glibc-headers
glibc-devel
cpp
ncurses
ncurses-devel
binutils
gcc
```

If you want to use a tool such as those you can start with the **make xconfig** or **make gconfig** command, you'll also need the following packages:

```
tcl
gtk2-devel
qt-devel
glib2-devel
libglade2-devel
```

1. When you installed RHEL, if you installed the Development Tools package group, you've probably already installed most of these packages.

2. Install the kernel-`uname -r`.src.rpm. It should install the kernel-2.6.spec file in the /usr/src/ redhat/SPECS directory.

3. Build the kernel; navigate to the SPECS directory, and run the **rpmbuild -bb kernel-2.6.spec** command.

4. Inspect the result in the /usr/src/redhat/BUILD directory. You should see the kernel source code in the kernel-2.6.18/linux-2.6.18.`uname -m` subdirectory. Navigate to that directory. You'll be running the remaining kernel configuration commands there.

5. Set up a unique name for the kernel that you're about to modify. Open the Makefile file in a text editor. Look for the **EXTRAVERSION** variable. Red Hat adds this variable as a suffix to the recompiled kernel. Modify this variable appropriately, perhaps with your initials.

6. Jot down the value of the **EXTRAVERSION** variable here: _____

7. Determine the correct CPU on your hardware. Use the following command:

```
# uname -m
```

8. Jot down the CPU model name here: _____

9. Make sure you're in the kernel source code directory. It is time to configure your kernel, using one of the four major tools:

   - **make config**   A line-by-line tool that gives you a choice with all kernel options.
   - **make menuconfig**   A text-based menu that allows you to select just the changes you want.
   - **make xconfig**   A GUI interface associated with KDE tools.
   - **make gconfig**   A GUI interface associated with GNOME tools.

10. In the kernel configuration menu of your choice, navigate to the General Setup category, and enable the Kernel .config Support option.

11. Save the custom kernel and exit.

12. When you save the new configuration, the kernel configuration tool overwrites the .config file in the local directory.

13. Process the custom kernel with the following command. This will produce a lot of output and may take an hour or more.

```
# make rpm
```

14. Check the /usr/src/redhat/RPMS/`uname -m` subdirectory. You should see a custom RPM that you can now use. Check its name against the **EXTRAVERSION** directive you set earlier in this lab.

15. Install the custom RPM.

16. Create a new initial RAM disk in your /boot directory. For example, if your **EXTRAVERSION=-prep**, create it with the following command:

```
# mkinitrd /boot/initrd-2.6.18-prep 2.6.18-prep
```

17. Create a stanza that points to the kernel and initial RAM disk files. You should be able to use the existing stanza as a model.

18. Congratulations, you have just installed a custom kernel on your new system. As long as you also have your original kernel in your boot loader menu, test it out!

19. Run the **reboot** command. You should see both kernels in the boot loader menu. Try your custom kernel. (If it doesn't work, you can always power cycle your system and boot into the original working kernel.)

Lab 3

This lab assumes that you have some unpartitioned space, either on an existing drive or a new drive that you've just added. A VMware machine is one excellent option that makes adding a new drive relatively easy. For the purpose of this lab, even a USB key will suffice.

To add a new partition, you'll need to use either **fdisk** or **parted**. Allocate no more than half of the available free space to the first partition. Make sure to designate the RAID filetype. If you use **fdisk**, you'll need to either reboot or run **partprobe** to make Linux reread the new partition table. Whatever you do, one simple way to make sure you have a new partition of the RAID filetype is with the following command:

```
# fdisk -l
```

Of course, a RAID 1 mirror requires two different RAID partitions. So if you've created only one RAID partition, you'll have to repeat the process for the second RAID partition.

For the purpose of this lab, I assume the new RAID partitions are associated with /dev/hdb1 and /dev/hdb2, and this is the first RAID array configured on the local system. Just remember this lab is just for practice—you should never configure RAID partitions from the same physical drive. If that drive fails, you'll lose all data on that RAID array.

If your partitions are associated with different devices, substitute accordingly. For example, if this is the second local RAID array, the device is /dev/md1. You can create a RAID 1 mirror with the correct **mdadm** command:

```
# mdadm --create /dev/md0 --level=1 --raid-devices=2 \
/dev/hdb1 /dev/hdb2
```

Now that you've created an array, you'll need to format it. In this case, you can format it to the default ext3 filesystem with the following command:

```
# mkfs.ext3 /dev/md0
```

Assign and mount it on a new directory. I've created a /temp directory for this purpose:

```
# mount /dev/md0 /temp
```

Copy files from the /tmp directory. The dot after /tmp/ makes sure to copy all files and directories, including those that are hidden:

```
# cp -a /tmp/. /temp/
```

Unmount the /temp directory, and mount the RAID array on /tmp:

```
# umount /temp
# mount /dev/md0 /tmp
```

Make sure things are what you expect:

```
# ls -a /tmp
```

Unmount /tmp:

```
# umount /tmp
```

Add the information to your /etc/fstab, and run the following command to test the result. Based on this lab, you'd add the following to /etc/fstab:

```
/dev/md0  /tmp ext3  defaults  0 0
```

Then to test the result, run the following command to mount all filesystems listed in /etc/fstab:

```
# mount -a
```

Lab 4

For this lab, I assume that you've never created an LV before on the local system. The first step is to create (or reallocate) dedicated partitions for this purpose and assign it to the LVM file type. In **fdisk**, that's file type **8e**; to set the first partition to LVM in **parted**, run **set 1 lvm on**. Repeat the process for additional LVM partitions. For the purpose of this lab, I've created a single partition, /dev/sdb1, with 200MB, and assume you're working from the command line. Of course, you can do everything in this lab—after creating a partition—with the GUI Logical Volume Management tool.

Next, create a PV; for example, if the new LVM partition you created is /dev/sdb1, run the following command:

```
# pvcreate /dev/sdb1
```

If you want to confirm the result, run the **pvs** command. Now create a new VG; with the following command, you use the /dev/sdb1 PV to create a VG named vgrp01:

```
# vgcreate vgrp01 /dev/sdb1
```

You can confirm this result with the **vgs** command. Now create a new LV with the **lvcreate** command. The following command creates an LV named lvol01 of 100MB from the previously created VG:

```
# lvcreate -L 100M vgrp01 -n lvol01
```

Confirm this result with the **lvs** command. Next, format the LV you've just created:

```
# mkfs.ext3 /dev/vgrp01/lvol01
```

Now you can mount it on a specific directory. Using the example described in Lab 3, I've created a /test directory and have mounted the LV on it:

```
# mount /dev/vgrp01/lvol01 /test
```

Copy files from the /tmp directory. The dot after /tmp/ makes sure to copy all files and directories, including those that are hidden:

```
# cp -a /tmp/. /temp/
```

Unmount the volume, and remount it on /tmp:

```
# umount /dev/vgrp01/lvol01
# mount /dev/vgrp01/lvol01 /tmp
```

Make sure things are what you expect, that nothing has changed within /tmp:

```
# ls -a /tmp
```

Unmount /tmp:

```
# umount /tmp
```

Add the information to your /etc/fstab, and run the following command to test the result. Based on this lab, add the following to /etc/fstab:

```
/dev/vgrp01/lvol01   /tmp ext3  defaults  0 0
```

Then test the result; the following command mounts all filesystems listed in /etc/fstab:

```
# mount -a
```

Lab 5

In this lab, you'll use free VG space from Lab 4. If you don't have that available, you'll have to repeat the steps described in Lab 4 to create a new PV and VG. To confirm available VG space, run the **vgs** command. In my case, I see the following output from my system:

```
# vgs
  VG         #PV #LV #SN Attr   VSize   Vfree
  vgrp01       1   1   0 wz--n- 192.00M 92.00M
```

As you can see, I have 92MB of free space, which I add to the existing LV with the following command:

```
# lvextend -L +92M /dev/vgrp01/lvol01
```

9
Apache and Squid

CERTIFICATION OBJECTIVES

9.01   The Apache Web Server

9.02   Apache Access Configuration

9.03   Virtual Hosts

9.04   The Squid Web Proxy Cache

✓   Two-Minute Drill

Q&A   Self Test

U nix was developed by AT&T in the late 1960s and early 1970s, and it was freely distributed among a number of major universities during those years. When AT&T started charging for Unix, a number of developers tried to create clones of this operating system. One of these clones, Linux, was developed and released in the early 1990s.

Many of these same universities were also developing the network that evolved into the Internet. With current refinements, this makes Linux perhaps the most Internet-friendly network operating system available. The extensive network services available with Linux are not only the tops in their field, but they create one of the most powerful and useful Internet-ready platforms available today at any price.

Currently, Apache is the most popular Web server on the Internet. According to the Netcraft (www.netcraft.com) survey, which tracks the Web servers associated with virtually every site on the Internet, Apache is currently used by more Internet Web sites than all other Web servers combined. Apache is included with RHEL 5.

RHEL 5 also includes a number of other network services. The service that also focuses on Web access is the Squid Proxy Server, which caches frequently used pages locally.

This chapter deals with the basic concepts surrounding the use of these services and a basic level of configuration. In all cases, the assumption is that your network settings are correct and functioning properly. If you're having problems with your network configuration, read Chapter 7.

As for the RHCE exam, you may have to configure or troubleshoot either Apache or Squid. So as you read this chapter and look through the configuration files and exercises, be willing to experiment. And practice, practice, practice what you learn.

CERTIFICATION OBJECTIVE 9.01

The Apache Web Server

Apache is by far the most popular Web server in use today. Based on the HTTP daemon (**httpd**), Apache provides simple and secure access to all types of content using the regular HTTP protocol as well as its secure cousin, HTTPS.

Apache was developed from the server code created by the National Center for Supercomputing Applications (NCSA). It included so many patches that it became known as "a patchy" server. The Apache Web server continues to advance the art

INSIDE THE EXAM

This chapter directly addresses two items in the Red Hat Exam Prep guide. This is the first chapter to focus on network services, as required of RHCE candidates. Per the latest Exam Prep guide, RHCT candidates do not need to be too concerned with this chapter. As noted in the Exam Prep guide, RHCE candidates "must be capable of configuring the following network services" during the Installation and Configuration portion of that exam:

- HTTP/HTTPS
- Web Proxy

Although you can use a number of different packages to configure HTTP, HTTPS, and Web Proxy services, the publicly available RH300 course outline focuses these services on Apache as a regular and secure Web server, and Squid as the Web Proxy server. The Exam Prep guide also notes that RHCEs should be able to

- Diagnose and correct problems with network services.
- Diagnose and correct networking services problems where SELinux contexts are interfering with proper operation.

This includes those services listed in the Installation and Configuration portion of the RHCE exam. For every network service, you also need to

- Install the packages needed to provide the service.
- Configure SELinux to support the service.
- Configure the service to start when the system is booted.
- Configure the service for basic operation.
- Configure host-based and user-based security for the service.

Installing the required packages is trivial. You'll make sure the service is started when the system is booted with the appropriate **chkconfig** commands. Most of this chapter is dedicated to configuring the service for *basic* operation. Some services support host-based and user-based security in their configuration files; others support it with the tools described in Chapter 15. SELinux is also most easily configured using the SELinux Management tool described in Chapter 15.

of the Web and provides one of the most stable, secure, robust, and reliable Web servers available. This server is under constant development by the Apache Software Foundation (www.apache.org).

While there are numerous other Web servers available, Apache is the only Web service described in the current RH300 course outline.

Apache is a service; basic Apache clients are Web browsers. Therefore, only those concerned with the RHCE need to read this chapter. This provides the briefest of overviews on Apache. For more information, read the documentation online at http://httpd.apache.org/docs-2.2.

Apache 2.2

Red Hat Enterprise Linux includes the latest major release of Apache, which is 2.2.x as of this writing. While there are major differences from previous versions of Apache (1.3.x, 2.0.x), if you're a Web administrator or developer, the differences with respect to the RHCE exam are fairly straightforward. The current version supports virtual hosts and access control, as well as secure (HTTPS) Web services. If you're interested in more, a full list of new features is available from http://httpd .apache.org/docs/2.2/new_features_2_2.html.

The following cites a few of the major changes:

- **New packages** If you're installing Apache from the Red Hat Installation RPMs, all the package names have changed. As you'll see in the following section, most start with *httpd*. Strangely enough, the username associated with Apache services is now *apache*.

- **Modular directive files** Basic directives, such as those based on Perl, PHP, or the Secure Socket Layer, are now configured separately in the /etc/httpd/conf.d directory. They are automatically included in the Apache configuration with the following directive in /etc/httpd/conf/httpd.conf:

```
Include conf.d/*.conf
```

- **Revised directives** Some directives have changed in the httpd.conf configuration file. For example, Apache listens for computers that are looking for Web pages on port 80. You can now change that port with the **Listen** directive.

- **Virtual hosts** Apache configuration is now normally based on virtual hosts, which allows you to host multiple Web sites on the same Apache server, using a single IP address.

- **Larger files** Apache now supports files greater than 2GB.

- **Encryption** Apache now supports encrypted authentication, as well as LDAP.

You may see some of these characteristics if you use Apache 1.3.x, as many of these features have been "backported" from current versions of Apache.

Installation

The RPM packages required by Apache are included in the Web Server package group. If required on the Installation and Configuration portion of the exam, you should install Apache during the installation process. But mistakes happen. Just remember that the simplest way to install Apache after installation is with the following command:

```
# yum install httpd
```

Alternatively, if you need the Red Hat GUI Apache Management tool, run the following command, which also installs the Apache httpd RPM as a dependency:

```
# yum install system-config-httpd
```

Another option is to just install the default packages associated with the entire Web Server package group with the following command:

```
# yum groupinstall web-server
```

If you don't remember the names of available groups, run the **yum grouplist** command. From the output, you should see "Web Server"; in other words, the following command also works:

```
# yum groupinstall "Web Server"
```

If your exam instructions require the installation of other packages such as mod_ssl (required for secure Web sites) and Squid, you can combine their installation in the same command:

```
# yum install mod_ssl squid
```

If in doubt about package names, you can find them in the Web Server package group, as documented on the first installation CD in the Server/repodata/comps-rhel5-server-core.xml file. If you're working with the RHEL 5 desktop, substitute Client for Server (upper- and lowercase). Once you've connected to a repository such as the RHN, the same information should be available in comps.xml in the /var/cache/yum/rhel-i386-server-5 directory. If you're working a different architecture and a client, substitute accordingly.

Starting on Reboot

Once Apache is installed, you'll want to make sure it starts the next time you boot Linux. If it doesn't start when the person who grades your Red Hat exam reboots your computer, you may not get credit for your work on the Apache service.

The most straightforward way to make sure Apache starts the next time you boot
Linux is with the **chkconfig** command. You'll need to set it to start in at least
runlevels 3 and 5, with a command such as:

```
# chkconfig --level 35 httpd on
```

Alternatively, you can configure it to start in all standard runlevels (2, 3, 4, and 5)
with the following command:

```
# chkconfig httpd on
```

To determine whether the **chkconfig** command worked, use the **--list** switch:

```
# chkconfig --list httpd
```

Normally to start services, it's best to use the associated script in the /etc/init.d
directory, which contains an **httpd** script. However, Apache often starts and stops
more gracefully with the following commands:

```
# apachectl stop
# apachectl start
```

W a t c h   *If you see "The 'links'
package is required for this functionality"
error message, you'll need to install the
elinks RPM.*

on the
Job   *If you're administering a currently running Web server, any restart may
disconnect users from the server and make it appear that the server is down
for some period of time. However, a service httpd reload command allows
the server to continue to run, while reading any changes you've made to
the configuration files. With Apache, the control script is apachectl, which
substitutes for service httpd in most control scripts.*

Once you've got Apache running, start a Web browser and enter a URL of **http://
localhost**. If Apache installation is successful, you should see the screen in Figure 9-1.

Read the screen and you will see that RHEL looks for Web page files in the /var/
www/html directory. You can verify this with the **DocumentRoot** directive in the
main Apache configuration file. If you want to create a custom error page, you can
set it in the /etc/httpd/conf.d/welcome.conf file.

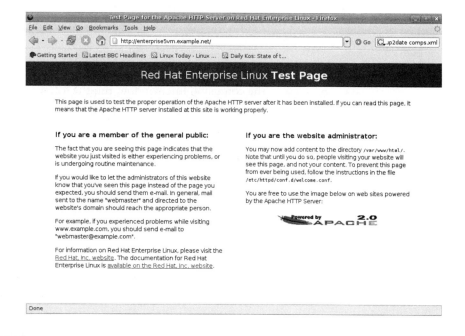

FIGURE 9-1

The default
Apache Web page

EXERCISE 9-1

Installing the Apache Server

In this exercise, you'll be installing all of the packages generally associated with the Apache server. Then you'll test and activate the result so that the Apache daemon, **httpd**, is active the next time you reboot Linux. The twist here is that you'll do it all from the command line interface. This assumes you've already registered with the Red Hat Network; if you haven't done so, you'll do so here as part of the process.

1. If you're in the GUI, open a command line console. Press ALT-F1 and log in as the root user.

2. Review the comps.xml file in the /usr/share/comps/i386 directory, and navigate to the Web Server package group. (If your computer uses another architecture, the directory may vary; however, the Red Hat exams are given on i386 systems.)

3. Make notes on the packages of interest.

4. Run the following command to review available groups. You should see "Web Server" near the end of the list.

```
# yum groupinfo
```

5. You can install all default packages in the "Web Server" package group with the following command:

```
# yum groupinstall "Web Server"
```

6. Back in the command line window, run the following command to see if Apache is already configured to start in any runlevels:

```
# chkconfig --list httpd
```

7. Now use the following command to make sure Apache starts in runlevels 3 and 5 the next time you boot Linux:

```
# chkconfig --level 35 httpd on
```

8. Start the Apache service with the following command:

```
# apachectl start
```

9. Install a text-based Web browser. As you may not have access to the GUI during the Red Hat exams, you need to know how to use text-based browsers. The standard is **elinks**, which you can install with the following command:

```
# yum install elinks
```

10. Now start the **elinks** browser, pointing to the local system, with the following command:

```
# elinks 127.0.0.1
```

11. Review the result. Do you see the Apache test page?

12. Exit from ELinks. Press Q, and when the Exit ELinks text menu appears, confirm that you really want to exit Elinks.

13. Back up the default httpd.conf configuration file; a logical location is your home directory.

The Apache Configuration Files

There are two key configuration files for the Apache Web server: httpd.conf in the /etc/httpd/conf directory and ssl.conf in the /etc/httpd/conf.d directory. The default versions of these files create a generic Web server service you can further customize and optimize, as desired. There are other configuration files in two directories: /etc/httpd/conf and /etc/httpd/conf.d. They're illustrated in Figure 9-2.

Apache
configuration files

```
[root@Enterprise5a ~]# ls /etc/httpd/conf
httpd.conf   magic
[root@Enterprise5a ~]# ls /etc/httpd/conf.d/
manual.conf  proxy_ajp.conf  squid.conf         webalizer.conf
perl.conf    python.conf     squirrelmail.conf  welcome.conf
php.conf     README          ssl.conf
[root@Enterprise5a ~]#
```

on the
job

Previous versions of Apache—1.3.x and earlier—required two other Apache configuration files in the same directory: access.conf and srm.conf. Even though these files were essentially blank in later versions of Apache 1.3.x, they were still required. These files are no longer required in any way in Apache 2.x.

You need to know the httpd.conf file in the /etc/httpd/conf directory well. If you're required to configure a secure Web server during the RHCE exam, you'll also need to configure the ssl.conf configuration file in the /etc/httpd/conf.d directory.

Analyzing the Default Apache Configuration

Apache comes with a well-commented set of default configuration files. In this section, you'll look at the key commands in the httpd.conf configuration file, in the /etc/httpd/conf directory. Browse through this file in your favorite text editor or using a command such as **less**. Before beginning this analysis, keep two things in mind:

■ If you configure Apache with the Red Hat HTTP tool (system-config-httpd), it overwrites any changes that you may have made with a text editor.

■ The main Apache configuration file incorporates the files in the /etc/httpd/conf.d directory with the following directive:

```
Include conf.d/*.conf
```

There are a couple of basic constructs in httpd.conf. First, directories, files, and modules are configured in "containers." The beginning of the container starts with the name of the directory, file, or module to be configured, contained in directional brackets (< >). Examples of this include:

```
<Directory "/var/www/icons">
<Files ~ "^\.ht">
<IfModule mod_mime_magic.c>
```

The end of the container starts with a forward slash (/). For the same examples, the ends of the containers would look like:

```
</Directory>
</Files>
</IfModule>
```

Next, Apache includes a substantial number of directives—commands that Apache can understand that have some resemblance to English. For example, the **ExecCGI** directive allows executable CGI scripts.

As the RHCE course divides the discussion of Apache into different units, I do the same here. However, the following sections, with the exception of secure virtual hosts, are based on the same httpd.conf file in the /etc/httpd/conf/ directory.

While this provides an overview, the devil is often in the details, which are analyzed (briefly) in the next section. For detailed information, see the Apache Web site at http://httpd.apache.org.

Analyzing httpd.conf

This section examines the default Apache configuration file, httpd.conf. If you want to follow along, open it on your system. Only the default active directives in that file are discussed here. Read the comments; they include more information and options.

For detailed information on each directive, see http://httpd.apache.org/docs/2.2/mod/quickreference.html. The default directives are summarized in the following three tables. Table 9-1 specifies directives associated with Section 1: Global Environment.

In all three tables, directives are listed in the order shown in the default version of httpd.conf. If you want to experiment with different values for each directive, save the change and then use **apachectl restart** to restart the Apache daemon. If not defined in these tables, directives are described, later in this chapter, as they appear in the configuration file.

Table 9-2 specifies directives associated with Section 2: Main Server Configuration.

TABLE 9-1	Global Environment Directives

Directive	Description
ServerTokens	Specifies the response code at the bottom of error pages; if you're interested, see what happens when you change the values between OS, Prod, Major, Minor, Min, and Full.
ServerRoot	Sets the default directory; other directives are subdirectories.
PidFile	Names the file with the Process ID (and locks the service).
Timeout	Limits access time for both sent and received messages.
KeepAlive	Supports persistent connections.
MaxKeepAliveRequests	Limits requests during persistent connections (unless set to 0, which is no limit).
KeepAliveTimeout	Sets a time limit, in seconds, before a connection is closed.
StartServers	Adds child Apache processes; normally set to 8, which means 9 Apache processes run upon startup.
MinSpareServers	Specifies a minimum number of idle child servers.
MaxSpareServers	Specifies a maximum number of idle child servers; always at least +1 greater than **MinSpareServers**.
ServerLimit	Sets a limit on configurable processes; cannot exceed 20000.
MaxClients	Limits the number of simultaneous requests; other requests to the server just have to wait.
MaxRequestsPerChild	Limits the requests per child server process.
MinSpareThreads	Specifies the minimum number of spare threads to handle additional requests.
MaxSpareThreads	Specifies the maximum number of available idle threads to handle additional requests.
ThreadsPerChild	Sets the number of threads per child server process.
Listen	Specifies a port and possibly an IP address (for multihomed systems) to listen for requests.
LoadModule	Loads various modular components, such as authentication, user tracking, executable files, and more.
Include	Adds the content of other configuration files.
User	Specifies the username run by Apache on the local system.
Group	Specifies the group name run by Apache on the local system.

| TABLE 9-2 | Main Server Configuration Directives |

Directive	Description
ServerAdmin	Sets the administrative e-mail address; may be shown (or linked to) on default error pages.
UseCanonicalName	Supports the use of **ServerName** as the referenced URL.
DocumentRoot	Assigns the root directory for Web site files.
Options	Specifies features associated with Web directories, such as ExecCGI, FollowSymLinks, Includes, Indexes, MultiViews, and SymLinksIfOwnerMatch.
AllowOverride	Supports overriding of previous directives from .htaccess files.
Order	Sets the sequence for evaluating **Allow** and **Deny** directives.
Allow	Configures host computers that are allowed access.
Deny	Configures host computers that are denied access.
UserDir	Specifies location of user directories; can be set to enable or disable for all or specified users.
DirectoryIndex	Specifies files to look for when navigating to a directory; set to index.html by default.
AccessFileName	Sets a filename within a directory for more directives; normally looks for .htaccess.
TypesConfig	Locates mime.types, which specifies file types associated with extensions.
DefaultType	Sets a default file type if not found in mime.types.
MIMEMagicFile	Normally looks to /etc/httpd/conf/magic to look inside a file for its MIME type.
HostNameLookups	Requires URL lookups for IP addresses; results are logged.
ErrorLog	Locates the error log file, relative to **ServerRoot**.
LogLevel	Specifies the level of log messages.
LogFormat	Sets the information included in log files.
CustomLog	Creates a customized log file, in a different format, with a location relative to **ServerRoot**.
ServerSignature	Adds a list with server version and possibly ServerAdmin e-mail address to error pages and file lists; can be set to **On**, **OFF**, or **EMail**.
Alias	Configures a directory location; similar to a soft link.
DAVLockDB	Specifies the path to the lock file for the WebDAV (Web-based Distributed Authoring and Versioning) database.
ScriptAlias	Similar to **Alias**; for scripts.
IndexOptions	Specifies how files are listed from a **DirectoryIndex**.
AddIconByEncoding	Assigns an icon for a file by MIME encoding.

TABLE 9-2	Main Server Configuration Directives *(continued)*

Directive	Description
AddIconByType	Assigns an icon for a file by MIME type.
AddIcon	Assigns an icon for a file by extension.
DefaultIcon	Sets a default icon for files not otherwise configured.
ReadmeName	Configures a location for a **README** file to go with a directory list.
HeaderName	Configures a location for a **HEADER** file to go with a directory list.
IndexIgnore	Adds files that are not included in a directory list.
AddLanguage	Assigns a language for file name extensions.
LanguagePriority	Sets a priority of languages if not configured in client browsers.
ForceLanguagePriority	Specifies action if a Web page in the preferred language is not found.
AddDefaultCharset	Sets a default character set; you may need to change it for different languages.
AddType	Maps file name extensions to a specified content type.
AddHandler	Maps file name extensions to a specified handler; commonly used for scripts or multiple languages.
AddOutputFilter	Maps file name extensions to a specified filter.
BrowserMatch	Customizes responses to different browser clients.

Table 9-3 specifies directives associated with Section 3: Virtual Hosts. While virtual host directives are disabled by default, I include those directives in the commented example near the end of the default httpd.conf file. While these directives were already used in other sections, you can—and should—customize them for individual virtual hosts to support different Web sites on the same Apache server.

TABLE 9-3	Virtual Host Configuration Directives

Directive	Description
NameVirtualHost	Specifies an IP address for multiple virtual hosts.
ServerAdmin	Assigns an e-mail address for the specified virtual host.
DocumentRoot	Sets a root directory for the virtual host.
ServerName	Names the URL for the virtual host.
ErrorLog	Creates an error log; the location is based on the **DocumentRoot**.
CustomLog	Creates an custom log; the location is based on the **DocumentRoot**.

Basic Apache Configuration for a Simple Web Server

As described earlier, Apache looks for Web pages in the directory specified by the **DocumentRoot** directive. In the default httpd.conf file, this directive points to the /var/www/html directory.

In other words, all you need to get your Web server up and running is to transfer Web pages to the /var/www/html directory.

The default **DirectoryIndex** directive looks for an index.html Web page file in this directory. You can test this for yourself by copying the default Firefox home page file, index.html, from the /usr/share/doc/HTML directory.

The base location of configuration and log files is determined by the **ServerRoot** directive. The default value from httpd.conf is

```
ServerRoot "/etc/httpd"
```

You'll note that the main configuration files are stored in the conf and conf.d subdirectories of the **ServerRoot**. If you run the **ls -l /etc/httpd** command, you'll find that Red Hat links /etc/httpd/logs to the directory with the actual log files, /var/log/httpd.

CERTIFICATION OBJECTIVE 9.02

Apache Access Configuration

There are several parameters associated with security on the Apache Web server. The security of the server is enforced in part by firewalls and SELinux. Internal Apache security measures are associated with the main Apache httpd.conf configuration file.

Now that you've glanced at the configuration file, it's time to analyze it, and its associated directories, with a view toward security.

Basic Apache Security

You can modify the httpd.conf configuration file to secure the entire server or manage security on a directory-by-directory basis. Directory controls secure access by the server, as well as users who connect to the Web sites on the server. To explore the basics of Apache security, start with the first default active line in httpd.conf:

```
ServerTokens OS
```

This line looks deceptively simple; it limits what readers see about your Web server when you browse to a nonexistent page. If you don't use this command, outsiders can see whether you've loaded modules such as Perl, Python, and PHP. Sharing this knowledge can make your system more vulnerable. You can restrict access to the root directory on your Web server as shown here:

```
<Directory />
    Options FollowSymLinks
    AllowOverride None
</Directory>
```

This configures a very restrictive set of permissions. The **Options FollowSymLinks** line supports the use of symbolic links for Web pages. The **AllowOverride None** line disables any .htaccess files. Otherwise, .htaccess can allow others to administer your server, starting from the **DocumentRoot** directory. If .htaccess is in a subdirectory, such as /var/www/html/data/, the additional directives, if permitted by **AllowOverride**, would apply only to that directory.

You can improve this by limiting access to all but explicitly allowed users, such as those within your company, by adding the following commands to the **<Directory>** container:

```
    Order deny,allow
    Deny from all
```

The next excerpt limits access to /var/www/html, which corresponds to the default **DocumentRoot** directive (while these directives are divided by numerous comments, they are all in the same stanza):

```
<Directory /var/www/html>
    Options Indexes FollowSymLinks
    AllowOverride None
    Order allow,deny
    Allow from all
</Directory>
```

You'll note that the **Options** directive has changed; the **Indexes** setting allows readers to see a list of files on your Web server if no index.html file is present in the directory as defined by **DocumentRoot**. The **Order** and **Allow** lines allow all users to access the Web pages on this server.

Finally, the **Listen** directive defines the IP address and TCP/IP port for this server. For example, the default shown next means that this server will work with every computer that requests a Web page from any of the IP addresses for your computer on the standard TCP/IP port, 80:

```
Listen 80
```

If you have more than one IP address on your computer, you can use this directive to limit this Web server to one specific IP address. For example, if you've set up an intranet on this Web server, you could use the IP address that connects to your private network here.

If you're also setting up secure Web services, there's a second **Listen** directive in the ssl.conf file in the /etc/httpd/conf.d directory. The data from this file is automatically incorporated into your Apache configuration. It includes the following directive, which points to the default secure HTTP (HTTPS) port for TCP/IP, 443:

```
Listen 443
```

<table>
<tr><td>**watch**</td><td>*The Red Hat Exam Prep guide suggests that you need to be ready*</td><td>*to configure a regular HTTP and a secure HTTPS Web site.*</td></tr>
</table>

Apache and Security Arrangements

If you have an **iptables** firewall on your computer, you'll need to disable it at least for TCP/IP port 80. If you're configuring a secure Web site, you'll also need to disable **iptables** for port 443. If you've enabled SELinux, you'll need to change the Access Control List (ACL) security contexts of key directories. Chapter 15 describes these processes in detail. For now, just take the following two steps:

1. Run **system-config-securitylevel**, allow incoming WWW (HTTP) and Secure WWW (HTTPS) connections as "Trusted Services," and exit normally.

2. Run the **ls -Z /var/www** command. Note the ACL settings. If you configure other directories for Web services, you'll need to change their ACL settings. For example, if you create and then use the /www directory, run the following commands:

```
# chcon -R -u system_u /www/
# chcon -R -t httpd_sys_content_t /www/
```

EXERCISE 9-2

Creating a List of Files

In this exercise, you'll be setting up a list of files to share with others who access your Web server. The process is fairly simple; you'll configure an appropriate firewall, create a subdirectory of **DocumentRoot**, fill it with the files of your choice, set up appropriate security contexts, and activate Apache. This assumes you've installed the ELinks RPM as described in Exercise 9-1.

1. Make sure the firewall does not block access to port 80. One way to do so is with the Red Hat Security Configuration tool, which you can start with the **system-config-securitylevel** command. If you're required to activate a firewall (on your exam), make sure to allow incoming WWW (HTTP) connections (and any others required on your exam).

2. Create a subdirectory of **DocumentRoot**. In the default /etc/httpd/conf/httpd.conf file, it's /var/www/html. For this exercise, I've created the /var/www/html/sharing/ directory.

3. Add the files of your choice to this directory; I've copied the files from the /etc/httpd/conf.d directory:

```
# cp -ar /var/www/manual/* /var/www/html/sharing/
```

4. Activate the Apache service with the following command:

```
# apachectl start
```

5. Make sure Apache starts the next time you boot:

```
# chkconfig httpd on
```

6. Use the **ls -Z /var/www/html** and **ls -Z /var/www/html/sharing** commands to review the security contexts for the /var/www/html/sharing directory and copied files. If it doesn't already correspond to the contexts shown here, set them up with the following commands:

```
# chcon -R -u system_u /var/www/html/sharing/
# chcon -R -t httpd_sys_content_t /var/www/html/sharing/
```

7. Try starting the elinks browser on the local server, pointing to the sharing subdirectory:

```
# elinks 127.0.0.1/sharing
```

8. Go to a remote system and try accessing the same Web directory. For example, if the IP address of the local system is 192.168.0.50, navigate to http://192.168.0.50/sharing. If possible, try this a second time from a conventional GUI browser.

Host-Based Security

You can add the **Order, allow,** and **deny** directives to regulate access based on host names or IP addresses. This basic command allows access by default. It reads the **deny** directive first:

```
Order deny,allow
```

You can **deny** or **allow** from various forms of host names or IP addresses. For example, the following directive denies access from all computers in the osborne .com domain:

```
Deny from osborne.com
```

It's preferable to use IP addresses, so communication with a DNS server does not slow down your Web server. The following example directives use a single IP address; alternatively, you can set up the 192.168.30.0 subnet in partial, netmask, or CIDR (Classless InterDomain Routing) notation, as shown here:

```
Deny from 192.168.30.66
Allow from 192.168.30
Deny from 192.168.30.0/255.255.255.0
Allow from 192.168.30.0/24
```

User-Based Security

You can limit access to your Web sites to authorized users with passwords. As describe shortly, these passwords can be different from the regular password database on your Linux computer.

If you want to configure user-based security for the virtual Web site described earlier, you'll need to set up a **<Directory>** container for the selected directory, in this case, it's /var/www/html/test. You'll want several commands in the **<Directory>** container:

- To set up basic authentication, you'll need an **AuthType Basic** directive.
- To describe the site to requesting users, you can include an **AuthName** *"some comment"* directive.

- To refer to a Web server password database named /etc/httpd/testpass, you'll need a **AuthUserFile /etc/httpd/testpass** directive.
- To limit the site to a single user named engineer1, you could add a **Require user engineer1** directive.
- Alternatively, to limit the site to a group as defined in /etc/httpd/webgroups, you'd add the **AuthGroupFile /etc/httpd/webgroups** directive. You would also need a directive such as **Require group *Design***, where *Design* is the name of the group specified in webgroups.

Here's an example of code that I've added after the **<Virtual Host>** container:

```
<Directory "/var/www/html/test">
    AuthType Basic
    AuthName "Password Protected Test"
    AuthUserFile /etc/httpd/testpass
    Require user engineer1
</Directory>
```

When properly configured, the next time you try accessing the http://enterprise5a.example.net/test Web site directory in the Firefox browser, you're prompted for a username and password, as shown in Figure 9-3.

FIGURE 9-3

A password-protected Web site

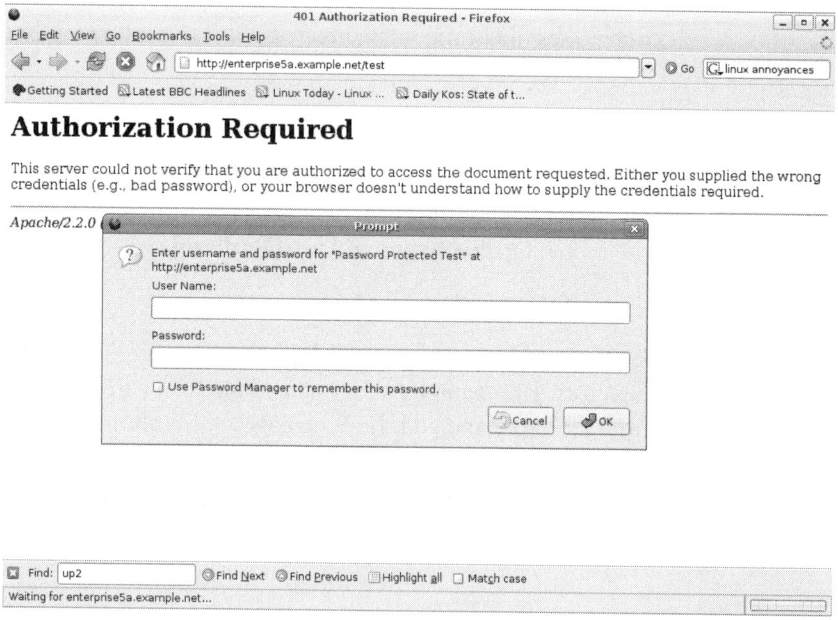

Configuring Web Passwords

To configure passwords for a Web site on your server, you need to create a separate database of usernames and passwords. As the **useradd** and **passwd** commands are used for regular users, the **htpasswd** command is used to set up usernames and passwords for your Web server.

For example, if you want to create a database file named webpass in the /etc/httpd directory, you'd start with the following command:

```
# htpasswd -c /etc/httpd/webpass engineer1
```

The **-c** switch creates the specified file, and the first user is engineer1. You're prompted to enter a password for engineer1. Users in the webpass database do not need to have a regular account on your Linux computer. Note how I set up the file in the **ServerRoot** directory when I configure virtual hosts later in this chapter. The permissions limit access to specific users and override any settings that use the default **DocumentRoot** /var/www/html directory.

Once you've created the database file, you can add to it without the **-c** switch; for example, the following command prompts you for a password for drafter1 before adding it to your testpass database:

```
# htpasswd /etc/httpd/testpass drafter1
```

To set up access for more than one user, you'll also need a group file. For the example described earlier in the "User-Based Security" section, you can set up the webgroups file in the same directory with the following line of users:

```
Design: engineer1 drafter1 lead1
```

Web Access to Home Directories

One useful option through Apache is access to a user's home directory. If you change the following directive from **UserDir disable** to

```
UserDir public_html
```

anyone will have access to Web pages that a user puts in his or her ~/public_html directory. For example, a user named michael can create a /home/michael/public_html directory and add the Web pages of his choice.

However, this requires a bit of a security compromise; you need to make michael's home directory executable for all users. This is also known as *701 permissions*, which you can configure with the following command:

```
# chmod 701 /home/michael
```

You'll also need to make the public_html subdirectory readable and executable by all users, also known as *705 permissions*:

```
# chmod 705 /home/michael/public_html
```

As this is a Web server, you will need to add at least an index.html file to this directory. It can be a text file for test purposes. The commented stanza that follows is one excellent way to help keep home directories so shared a bit more secure. For more information, see the Apache documents available from http://httpd.apache .org, or those you may have copied to the /var/www/html/sharing directory as described in Exercise 9-2. In that case, they'll be available locally as http://localhost/ sharing, as long as you haven't activated "Virtual Hosts" as described later in the section of the same name.

```
#<Directory /home/*/public_html>
#    AllowOverride FileInfo AuthConfig Limit
#    Options MultiViews Indexes SymLinksIfOwnerMatch IncludesNoExec
#    <Limit GET POST OPTIONS>
#        Order allow,deny
#        Allow from all
#    </Limit>
#    <LimitExcept GET POST OPTIONS>
#        Order deny,allow
#        Deny from all
#    </LimitExcept>
#</Directory>
```

Of course, you need to configure firewalls and allow SELinux access in appropriate ways. Firewalls must allow access to the standard HTTP port, 80. SELinux must be configured to "Allow HTTPD To Read Home Directories." (Alternatively, activate the httpd_ enable_homedirs boolean with the **setsebool -P htttpd.enable.homedirs 1** command.) Finally, the ACL must be revised accordingly. Once the following command is run

```
# chcon -R -t httpd_sys_content_t /home/michael/public_html
```

and **apachectl reload** is executed, you can finally access the files in the public_html/ subdirectory. For example, if I've made these changes on the Enteprise5a system, I'd point my browser to http://Enteprise5a/~michael URL.

Control Through .htaccess

There is a way to override inherited permissions in any subdirectory. If you're willing to set the following command in the **<Directory>** containers of your choice,

```
AllowOverride Options
```

you can configure .htaccess files to override previously set permissions. In this way, you can customize permissions on different virtual hosts. For example, you can configure an intranet site that's limited to your employees and an Internet site for general access on the same Apache server.

You can store an .htaccess file in any Web directory. While you can configure all types of Apache directives in this file, the Red Hat Exam Prep guide suggests that all you need to do is configure host-based and user-based security for the service.

Options and .htaccess

There are many ways to activate the **Options** directive. The simplest two are **Options None** and **Options All**. They would do the following:

- **None** For no custom options in force.
- **All** Allows all options except **MultiViews**.

You can also set finer options with keywords. Some examples include:

- **ExecCGI** Permits Web pages to run CGI scripts.
- **FollowSymLinks** Permits symbolic links to directories outside of **DocumentRoot**.
- **Includes** Allows server-side includes.
- **Indexes** Permits FTP-style directory indexing; this directive controls directory indexing, which is the name for file lists that are generated automatically by Apache.

EXERCISE 9-3

Password Protection for a Web Directory

In this exercise, you'll configure password-protection for your regular user account on a subdirectory of **DocumentRoot**. This involves use of the **AuthType Basic**, **AuthName**, and **AuthUserFile** directives. This will be done with the standard Apache Web site; virtual hosts are covered in the next major section.

1. Open the main configuration file, httpd.conf from the /etc/httpd/conf directory, in a text editor.
2. Navigate below the stanza **<Directory "/var/www/html">**.

3. Create your own stanza for a **DocumentRoot** subdirectory. Assuming you've kept the defaults (and haven't yet created this subdirectory), make it the /var/www/html/test directory. In the default version of httpd.conf, it's just before the commented options for the **UserDir** directive. The first and last directives in the stanza would look like:

```
<Directory "/var/www/html/test">
</Directory>
```

4. Add the following directives: **AuthType Basic** to set up basic authentication, the **AuthName "Password Protected Test"** directive to configure a comment that you should see shortly, and the **AuthUserFile /etc/httpd/ testpass** directive to point to a password file. Substitute your regular username for *testuser* in **Require user *testuser***.

```
<Directory "/var/www/html/test">
    AuthType Basic
    AuthName "Password Protected Test"
    AuthUserFile /etc/httpd/testpass
    Require user testuser
</Directory>
```

5. Check the syntax of your changes with either of the following commands.

```
# httpd -t
# httpd -S
```

6. Assuming the syntax checks out, make Apache reread the configuration files:

```
# apachectl restart
```

If you're concerned about currently connected users, make Apache reread the configuration file, without disconnections, with the **service httpd reload** command.

7. Add an appropriate index.html file to the /var/www/html/test/ directory. It's okay to use a text editor to enter a simple line such as "test was successful". No HTML coding is required.

8. Create the /etc/httpd/testpass file with an appropriate password. On my system, I created a web password for user michael in the noted file with the following command:

```
# htpasswd -c /etc/httpd/testpass michael
```

Additional users can be added without the **-c** switch.

9. Test the result, preferably from another system. For example, if your Apache server is configured on enterprise5a.example.net, navigate to http://enterprise5a.example.net/test.

10. You should now see a request for a username and password, with the comment associated with your **AuthName** directive. Enter the username and password you just added to /etc/httpd/testpass and observe the result.

11. Close your browser, and restore any earlier configuration.

CERTIFICATION OBJECTIVE 9.03

Virtual Hosts

Another useful feature of Apache 2.2 is its ability to manage Web sites using a single IP address. You can do so by creating multiple virtual hosts on the same Web server. You can configure virtual hosts for regular Web sites in the main Apache configuration file, /etc/httpd/conf/httpd.conf. In that way, you can link multiple domain names such as www.example.com and www.mommabears.com to the same IP address on the same Apache server.

on the job

The example.com, example.org, and example.net domain names cannot be registered and are officially reserved by the Internet society for documentation.

You can also create multiple secure Web sites that conform to the HTTPS protocol by configuring virtual hosts in the /etc/httpd/conf.d/ssl.conf configuration file. While the details vary, the basic directives that you'd use in this file are the same.

exam

watch

While truly secure HTTPS sites include server certificates, there is no cited requirement in the Red Hat Exam *Prep guide or associated RH300 course to create such certificates.*

Virtual Hosts

As described earlier, Section 3 of the default httpd.conf includes sample commands that you might use to create one or more virtual hosts. To activate the virtual host feature, you'll first want to activate this directive:

```
#NameVirtualHost *:80
```

If you're using a name-based host, leave the asterisk after this directive. Otherwise, set the IP address for your interface. It's often more reliable to substitute the IP address, as it avoids the delays sometimes associated with name resolution through a DNS server. However, you may need to create multiple name-based virtual hosts as well.

---

exam

⍟atch　　*If you're required to create a virtual host for a secure Web site, you'll need a second* **NameVirtualHost** *directive for the HTTPS port, 443. The other commands come from /etc/httpd/conf.d/*

ssl.conf and are incorporated through the **Include conf.d/*.conf** *directive. If you prefer, you can include* **NameVirtualHost *:443** *in ssl.conf.*

You should already know that TCP/IP port 80 is the default for serving Web pages. If you want to direct all requests on this server via IP address 192.168.30.2 on port 80, you can substitute **<VirtualHost 192.168.30.2:80>** for the first line. But this defeats the purpose of virtual hosts, as you would need different IP addresses for any additional virtual host Web sites.

```
#<VirtualHost *:80>
#      ServerAdmin webmaster@dummy-host.example.com
#      DocumentRoot /www/docs/dummy-host.example.com
#      ServerName dummy-host.example.com
#      ErrorLog logs/dummy-host.example.com-error_log
#      CustomLog logs/dummy-host.example.com-access_log common
#</VirtualHost>
```

Don't forget to uncomment the commands shown by removing the **#** in front of each line. As you can see, this includes a number of directives from the main part of the configuration file. Here are the highlights of this container:

■ Error messages are sent to the e-mail address defined by **ServerAdmin**.

- The Web pages can be stored in the **DocumentRoot** directory. Check the SELinux security contexts of the **DocumentRoot** directory you create, as described earlier in the "Apache and Security Arrangements" section. Apply the **chcon** command as required to make the security contexts match
- Clients can call this Web site through the **ServerName**.
- The **ErrorLog** and **CustomLog** directives use the *relative* log directory, relative to the **ServerRoot**. Unless you've created a different **ServerRoot** for this virtual host, you can find these files in the /etc/httpd/logs directory. As noted earlier, this directory is linked to /var/logs/httpd.

It's easy to create your own virtual host site. Substitute the IP domain names, directories, files, and e-mail addresses of your choice. Create the **DocumentRoot** directory if required. You can test the syntax of what you've done with the following command:

```
# httpd -t
```

Apache will verify your configuration or identify specific problems. When you run this command on the default configuration, you'll get the following message:

```
Syntax OK
```

If you've created multiple virtual hosts, you can check them as well with the following command:

```
# httpd -D DUMP_VHOSTS
```

The output should list the default and individual virtual hosts. For example, I see the following output from one of my RHEL 5 systems:

```
[Fri Dec 16 13:38:14 2007] [warn] _default_ VirtualHost overlap on
port 80, the first has precedence
VirtualHost configuration:
wildcard NameVirtualHosts and _default_ servers:
_default_:443   Enterprise5a.example.net (/etc/httpd/conf.d/ssl.conf:81)
*:80            site1.example.net (/etc/httpd/conf/httpd.conf:999)
*:80            site2.example.net (/etc/httpd/conf/httpd.conf:1006)
Syntax OK
```

If you still get a "using 127.0.0.1 for ServerName" error, you haven't assigned a value for the **ServerName** directive.

Secure Virtual Hosts

If you're configuring a secure Web server that conforms to the HTTPS protocol, Red Hat provides a different configuration file for this purpose: ssl.conf in the /etc/httpd/

conf.d directory. If you don't see this file, you need to install the mod_ssl RPM. Before you begin editing this file, make sure the following **Listen** directive is active:

```
Listen 443
```

Later in this file, pay attention to the **<VirtualHost _default_:443>** container. Make a comparison to the **<VirtualHost>** container in httpd.conf. You'll need to address at least the same directives as shown in httpd.conf. If you accidentally leave out some of these commands, you'll end up with a nonworking Web server. You can replace _default_ in the **VirtualHost** container with an asterisk (*).

Follow the same guidelines described earlier for the regular virtual host. Ideally, you should configure a **DocumentRoot** in a directory other than the default for the Web server—or the virtual host. You'll also need to add an index.html file to this directory. One possible option for **DocumentRoot** is

```
DocumentRoot /www/secure/dummy-host.example.com
```

You'll also need to add a **ServerName** directive, pointing to the secure HTTP port, 443. For the previously noted virtual host domain, that would lead to the following directive:

```
ServerName dummy-host.example.com:443
```

Add desired error logs. The default options are usually appropriate and should be configured to write to files that are different from the logs for a regular virtual host Web site:

```
ErrorLog logs/ssl_error_log
TransferLog logs/ssl_access_log
LogLevel warn
CustomLog logs/ssl_request_log \
          "%t %h %{SSL_PROTOCOL}x %{SSL_CIPHER}x \"%r\" %b"
```

A Basic Web Page

You may need to create some index.html files during your exam. Fortunately, the Red Hat exams don't test knowledge of HTML. You could use Apache's default Web page. You can change this or any other Web page with a text- or HTML-specific editor.

You can even save a simple text file as index.html. For example, you might save the following line in the text editor of your choice as *index.html*. You could then copy it to the appropriate **DocumentRoot** directory.

```
This is a simple Web page
```

To see the effect for yourself, create your own index.html file with the text of your choice. Open the file in any browser to see what happens.

Checking Syntax

You can check the work that you've done to create virtual hosts with the following command:

```
# httpd -S
```

Assuming no problems are found, you should be able to start your Web server and connect to your local service with a browser request.

The beauty of **VirtualHost** containers is that you can copy virtually the same stanza to create as many Web sites on your Apache server as your computer can handle. All you require is one IP address. When you set up the next **VirtualHost** container, make sure that you revise at least the **ServerName**, the locations of the log files, and the **DocumentRoot**.

Be prepared to create multiple Web sites on an Apache Web server using virtual hosts. If you're required to do so on your exam, create a separate VirtualHost container for this purpose.

Executable Files in Apache

You can set up Apache resources in many different ways. Some might be available in different languages, different media types, or other variations. When you set up multiple resources, Apache can select the file that is opened based on the browser-supplied preferences for media type, languages, character set, and encoding.

You can use the **ScriptAlias** directive for directories with executable CGI files. Various **Alias** directives link files or directories, similar to the **ln -s** command. The following **ScriptAlias** directive links the default cgi-bin directory to /var/www/cgi-bin. You can set up CGI scripts in a directory other than /var/www/cgi-bin and change the reference accordingly.

```
ScriptAlias /cgi-bin/ "/var/www/cgi-bin"

<Directory /var/www/cgi-bin>
    AllowOverride None
    Options None
    Order allow,deny
    Allow from all
</Directory>
```

This excerpt from the default httpd.conf file first identifies the directory with server scripts. Permissions for those other than root are adjusted through the **<Directory /var/www/cgi-bin>** container. The **AllowOverride None** command prevents regular users from changing permissions/settings in that directory. Otherwise, smarter users could read the CGI files in your directory, potentially compromising the security of your Web server. The **Options None** line prevents other users from running CGI scripts in the given directory. The **Order allow,deny** command sets up authorization checks; **Allow from all** lets all users run scripts in this directory.

The **Alias /icons/ "/var/www/icons"** directive identifies a directory for icons on your Web site. If the **DocumentRoot** is /www.example.com, you can set up the icons in HTML code on your page in the /www.example.com/icons directory. You can then store the icons on your computer in the /var/www/icons directory.

Finally, you can add access control for any other directories available via your Web interface. Just wrap the directory you want to control in a **<Directory /path/ to/dir>. . . </Directory>** container and set the access restrictions you need. The following stanza limits access based first on the **Deny** directive:

```
<Directory /path/to/your/directory/goes/here/>
    Options Indexes FollowSymLinks
    Order deny,allow
    Deny from .evil.crackers.net
    Allow from .yourdomain.net
</Directory>
```

Apache Log Files

As described earlier, the log files in httpd.conf are configured in the /etc/httpd/logs directory. It's linked to /var/log/httpd. Access to your Web server is logged in the access_log file; errors are recorded in the error_log file. If you want more details about your Web site for tuning or statistical reasons, you can have the Web server generate more information, generate separate log files for each virtual Web site, and create new log files at different frequencies (such as daily, weekly, or monthly).

There are standard Apache log file formats. For more information, take a look at the **LogFormat** directive in Figure 9-4. Four different formats are shown: combined, common, the referrer (the Web page with the link used to get to your site), and the agent (the user's Web browser). The first two **LogFormat** lines include a number of percent signs followed by lowercase letters. These directives determine what goes into the log.

You then use the **CustomLog** directive to select a location for the log file (for example, logs/access_log) and which log file format you want to use (for example, common). For more information on log files and formats, refer to http://httpd .apache.org/docs-2.2/logs.html.

FIGURE 9-4

Customized
Apache logs

```
# alert, emerg.
#
LogLevel warn

#
# The following directives define some format nicknames for use with
# a CustomLog directive (see below).
#
LogFormat "%h %l %u %t \"%r\" %>s %b \"%{Referer}i\" \"%{User-Agent}i\"" combine
d
LogFormat "%h %l %u %t \"%r\" %>s %b" common
LogFormat "%{Referer}i -> %U" referer
LogFormat "%{User-agent}i" agent

# "combinedio" includes actual counts of actual bytes received (%I) and sent (%O
); this
# requires the mod_logio module to be loaded.
#LogFormat "%h %l %u %t \"%r\" %>s %b \"%{Referer}i\" \"%{User-Agent}i\" %I %O"
combinedio

#
# The location and format of the access logfile (Common Logfile Format).
# If you do not define any access logfiles within a <VirtualHost>
```

on the

Some Web log analyzers have specific requirements for log file formats. For example, the popular open source tool awstats (advanced Web Stats) requires the combined log format. It will fail to run if you leave the default common format. Awstats is a great tool for graphically displaying site activity. You can download it from a site such as www.sourceforge.net.

Apache Troubleshooting

When you install the right Apache packages, the default configuration normally creates a running system. But if you're setting up a real Web site, you probably want more than just the test page. Before you start changing the configuration, back up the httpd.conf Apache configuration file. If something goes wrong, you can always start over.

Some Apache errors fall into the following categories:

- **Error message about an inability to bind to an address**   Another network process may already be using the default http port (80). Alternatively, your computer is running httpd as a normal user (not the user apache) with a port below 1024.

- **Network addressing or routing errors**   Double-check your network settings. For more information on configuring your computer for networking, see Chapter 9.

■ **Apache isn't running**   Check the error message when you use the **apachectl** command to start or restart the Apache server. Check the error_log in the /var/log/httpd directory.

■ **Apache isn't running after a reboot**   Run **chkconfig --list httpd**. Make sure Apache (httpd) is set to start at appropriate runlevels during the boot process with the command

```
# chkconfig httpd on
```

■ **You need to stop Apache**   Send the parent process a **TERM** signal, based on its PID. By default, this is located in /var/run/httpd.pid. You kill Apache with a command such as

```
#kill -TERM `cat /var/run/httpd.pid`
```

■ Alternatively, you can use the **apachectl stop** command.

EXERCISE 9-4

Updating a Home Page

In this exercise, you'll update the home page associated with your Web site on the Apache server. You can use these techniques to copy the actual HTML formatted pages for your Web site.

1. Start the Apache Web server with the default configuration. (If you've previously created virtual hosts, comment out those directives. If you've saved the default verison of httpd.conf as suggested in Exercise 9-1, restore it from your home directory.)

2. Copy an HTML file such as /var/www/error/noindex.html to /var/www/html/index.html.

3. Edit the file /var/www/html/index.html.

4. Change the title of the page to reflect your personal or corporate name; save the changes.

5. Use a Web browser such as Firefox to connect to localhost (or 127.0.0.1).

6. Close the Web browser.

on the **job**

Apache administration is a necessary skill for any Linux system administrator. You should develop the ability to install, configure, and troubleshoot Apache quickly. You should also be able to set up and customize virtual Web sites, which will make you a more effective Webmaster. You can test your skills using the Exercise and Labs that follow.

EXERCISE 9-5

Setting Up a Virtual Web Server

In this exercise, you'll set up a Web server with a virtual Web site. You can use this technique with different directories to set up additional virtual Web sites on the same Apache server.

1. Back up your httpd.conf file.

2. Add a virtual Web site for the fictional company LuvLinex, with a URL of www.example.net. Don't forget to modify the **Name Virtual Host** directive. Use the sample comments at the end of the httpd.conf file for hints as needed.

3. Assign the **DocumentRoot** directive to the /luvlinex directory. (Don't forget to create this directory on your system as well.)

4. Open the /luvlinex/index.html file in your text editor. Add a simple line in text format such as:

```
This is the placeholder for the LuvLinex Web site.
```

5. Save this file.

6. If you've enabled SELinux on this system, you'll have to apply the **chcon** command to this directory:

```
# chcon -R -u system_u /luvlinex/
# chcon -R -t httpd_sys_content_t /luvlinex/
```

7. If you've created a DNS service, as discussed in Chapter 11, update the associated database. Otherwise, update /etc/hosts with www.example.net and the appropriate IP address.

8. If you want to check the syntax, run the **httpd -t** and **httpd -D DUMP_VHOSTS** commands.

9. Remember to restart the Apache service; the proper way is with the **apachectl restart** command.

10. Open the browser of your choice. Test access the configured Web site (www. example.net) and the Web site on the localhost computer.

11. Go to a remote system and repeat steps 7 and 10. When pointing a browser to the Web server's system, use its host name or IP address. Update the remote /etc/hosts if appropriate.

12. Close the browsers on both systems. Restore the original httpd.conf configuration file.

The Red Hat httpd Configuration Tool

Red Hat has its own graphical configuration tool for Apache, **system-config-httpd**, which you can install from the RPM of the same name. Before using this tool, back up your current /etc/httpd/conf/httpd.conf configuration file. Any changes that you make with this tool overwrite this file.

You will find that **system-config-httpd** is a straightforward tool, with four different tabs that can help you configure the httpd.conf configuration file. You can also open this tool in the GNOME desktop with the System | Administration | Server Settings | HTTP command (substitute Main Menu for System if you're using KDE). However, as it cannot be used to edit the ssl.conf configuration file, therefore you should not use it to create a secure (HTTPS) Web server.

---

e x a m

ⓦatch   *I recommend that you do not use the Red Hat GUI HTTPD configuration tool, system-config-httpd, during the Red Hat exams. In my opinion,* *it is faster to edit the Apache configuration files from the command line interface, using the techniques described earlier in this chapter.*

However, it may be useful to practice creating virtual hosts with this utility, so I'll described the tabs shown in Figure 9-5.

■ **Main**   The Main tab allows you to set basic parameters for your Apache server, including the Server Name, the Webmaster e-mail address, and the **Listen** directive.

■ **Virtual Hosts**   The Virtual Hosts tab permits you to set the properties for different Web sites that you host on your Apache server. This includes the **DocumentRoot**, basic HTML file names and locations, SSL support, basic log file configuration, CGI script directives, and default directories.

FIGURE 9-5

The Apache
configuration
tool, Main tab

- **Server** The Server tab enables you to set the basic lock and PID files, as well as the user and group associated with the httpd service. In most cases, you should not have to change these settings.

- **Performance Tuning** The Performance Tuning tab allows you to set basic connection parameters.

Even if you do master this tool for configuring a regular Web server, you'll need to manually edit the ssl.conf file (in the /etc/httpd/conf.d/ directory) to create a secure Web server. And I believe that it's easier to learn and faster to edit the Apache configuration file, /etc/httpd/conf/httpd.conf, directly in a text editor. Remember that time may be of the essence when you take the RHCE exam.

CERTIFICATION OBJECTIVE 9.04

The Squid Web Proxy Cache

Squid is a high-performance HTTP and FTP caching proxy server. It is also known as a Web proxy cache. It can make your network connections more efficient. As it stores data from frequently used Web pages and files, it can often give your users the data they need without their systems having to look to the Internet.

Studies on very busy networks suggest that a Squid server can reduce the size, or bandwidth, of your Internet connection by 10 to 20 percent. That can lead to considerable savings for larger offices.

Squid uses the Inter-Cache Protocol (ICP) for transfers between participating peer and parent/child cache servers. It can be used either as a traditional caching proxy or as a front-end accelerator for a traditional Web server. Squid accepts only HTTP requests but speaks FTP on the server side when FTP objects are requested. For more information, see www.squid-cache.org. One book dedicated to this service is Duane Wessels's *Squid: The Definitive Guide*, published by O'Reilly.

Key Squid Files and Directories

The Squid RPM package is installed by default when you install the Web Server package group. So if you've installed Apache and have not tinkered with the defaults, the Squid RPM should also be installed on your computer. This RPM package installs a substantial number of files and scripts; some of the key files include the following:

- **/etc/rc.d/init.d/squid** Start/stop script
- **/etc/squid/** Configuration directory
- **/etc/sysconfig/squid** Other configurable options
- **/usr/share/doc/squid-*versionnumber*** Documentation, mostly in HTML format
- **/usr/lib/squid/** Support files and internationalized error messages
- **/usr/sbin/squid** Main Squid daemon
- **/usr/share/squid** Various squid configuration add-ons
- **/var/log/squid/** Log directory
- **/var/spool/squid/** Cache directory (once Squid is active, this directory includes hundreds of MBs, and maybe more, in hashed directories)

Starting Squid on Reboot

The Squid Web Proxy is not started by default. To do so, you'll want to activate it using a command such as **chkconfig** or the Service Configuration utility described in Chapter 3. The easiest way to set Squid to start the next time you boot Linux is with the following command:

```
# chkconfig squid on
```

When the Squid proxy server starts for the first time, the /etc/init.d/squid start script starts the **squid** daemon. Squid runs as a caching proxy server on port 3128. You can then set up Web browsers on your LAN to point your computer to Squid on port 3128 instead of an external network such as the Internet. In that way, Squid would get the first chance at serving the needs of users on your network.

Basic Squid Configuration

You can configure and customize the way Squid operates through its configuration file, /etc/squid/squid.conf. The default version of this file includes a large number of comments that can help you tune and secure Squid. Since it has more than 4000 lines, this isn't the easiest file to review.

/etc/sysconfig/squid

Squid also works through its /etc/sysconfig/squid file, which specifies switches for the **squid** daemon when it starts. By default, it disables DNS checking with the -D option, as described by the following directive:

```
SQUID_OPTS="-D"
```

It also specifies a shutdown timeout in seconds with the following directive:

```
SQUID_SHUTDOWN_TIMEOUT=100
```

You can add more options to the **SQUID_OPTS** directive as specified in the man page for the **squid** command; other directives are used by the /etc/rc.d/init.d/squid script.

/etc/squid/squid.conf

Now we'll examine the defaults in the main Squid configuration file, squid.conf in the /etc/squid/ directory. Although there are over 4000 lines in this file, only a few are active by default. Most of this file is filled with comments that describe most directives and associated options. You may note a squid.conf.default file, which serves as an effective backup to the original configuration file.

If you're following on your own system, note that several of these directives are split by several dozen lines of comments. In other words, you may need to scroll through the squid.conf configuration file to see the different directives as described in this section.

First, the default port is shown with the following directive:

```
http_port 3128
```

The **hierarchy_stoplist** directive specifies conditions where Squid doesn't look in its cache and forwards requests directly to the server. In this case, URLs with *cgi-bin* and

? are not stored and are directly forwarded. The directive is used with the following two commands, which never caches URLs with the same characters and then denies caching to said searches:

```
hierarchy_stoplist cgi-bin ?
acl QUERY urlpath_regex cgi-bin \?
cache deny QUERY
```

More than 1000 lines later, the **refresh_pattern** directive specifies when data *from* a specified server is considered "fresh"; in other words, data that fits in these parameters is taken from the local Squid cache. The following directives specify that FTP data is fresh for at least 1440 minutes. If there's no explicit "freshness" life, as defined by the remote server, and the file was last modified 10 hours ago, 20% means that the data will be considered fresh for another 2 hours. The maximum "freshness" date for FTP data in a Squid cache based on the first directive is 10080 minutes.

```
refresh_pattern ^ftp:        1440    20%    10080
refresh_pattern ^gopher:     1440    0%     1440
refresh_pattern .            0       20%    4320
```

Next, Squid continues to configure ACLs with the **acl** directive (this is unrelated to the Access Control Lists described in Chapter 14). First, it allows management access from all IP addresses (which we'll limit shortly), using the **cache_object** protocol. It specifies the **localhost** variable as a source and the **to_localhost** variable as a destination address:

```
acl all src 0.0.0.0/0.0.0.0
acl manager proto cache_object
acl localhost src 127.0.0.1/255.255.255.255
acl to_localhost dst 127.0.0.0/8
```

The following **acl** directives specify ports through which traffic is cached. The port numbers are all TCP/IP ports, which can be verified in /etc/services:

```
acl SSL_ports port 443 563
acl Safe_ports port 80
acl Safe_ports port 21
acl Safe_ports port 443
acl Safe_ports port 70
acl Safe_ports port 210
acl Safe_ports port 1025-65535
acl Safe_ports port 280
acl Safe_ports port 488
acl Safe_ports port 591
acl Safe_ports port 777
```

Squid as a proxy service can also help protect your network. The following **http_access** directives support access from the local computer, deny them from all others, and deny requests (with the **!**, also known as a "bang") that use anything but the aforementioned **Safe_ports** and **SSL_ports** variables.

```
http_access allow manager localhost
http_access deny manager
http_access deny !Safe_ports
http_access deny CONNECT !SSL_ports
```

After this group of default directives, you can configure access to local networks. If active, the following allows access to the two noted private IP networks:

```
#acl our_networks src 192.168.1.0/24 192.168.2.0/24
#http_access allow our_networks
```

The following directives also allow access from the local computer and deny access to all other computers:

```
http_access allow localhost
http_access deny all
```

But communication goes in both directions. If access is allowed, the following directive supports replies:

```
http_reply_access allow all
```

Of course, the Squid Web Proxy follows the InterCache Protocol (ICP), so all queries that follow ICP are allowed:

```
icp_access allow all
```

As you've seen, there are a substantial number of other options shown in comments in the file. It's not possible to cover even a fraction of the available options here. Fortunately, you don't need to know them for the Red Hat exams.

Configuration Options

You need to add three lines to the squid.conf file in the /etc/squid/ directory before activating Squid. For example, if the name of the local computer is Enterprise5a, you'd add the following line:

```
visible_hostname Enterprise5a
```

Make sure you add the line near the associated comment in the file.

Next, to support regular Web (HTTP) access, you'll need to set the **http_access** directive to allow some arbitrary name. As described earlier, the appropriate location and sample commands are included in the default squid.conf file:

```
#acl our_networks src 192.168.1.0/24 192.168.2.0/24
#http_access allow our_networks
```

In my case, I use the 192.168.0.0/24 network, so I include the following access control list directive:

```
acl local_net src 192.168.0.0/24
```

Next, you'll need to add your local network to the Squid Access Control List. This particular command line uses the **local_net** variable that I just created and adds the IP addresses of a private network that I've used:

```
http_access allow local_net
```

Now you can save your changes and exit the squid.conf configuration file. You can then create the basic cache directories in /var/spool/squid with the following command:

```
# squid -z
```

Finally, start the Squid service for the first time with the appropriate **service** command:

```
# service squid start
```

While you're unlikely to have a chance to configure more than one computer with Squid, its power is in connecting the cache from multiple servers. You can configure this with the **cache_peer** directives, which specify parent and sibling Squid cache servers. If your Linux computer is part of a group of Squid servers, these lines allow your Squid servers to check these other Squid servers before going to the Internet.

Squid first checks its own cache and then queries its siblings and parents for the desired object such as a Web page. If neither the cache host nor its siblings have the object, it asks one of its parents to fetch it from the source. If no parent servers are available, it fetches the object itself.

on the
job

Squid can greatly improve the performance of a corporate intranet. If your company has many employees who surf the Net, a Squid server can reduce your network connection costs by decreasing the bandwidth you need for your Internet connection.

Security Options

When you configure Squid on your system, you need to allow access through appropriate ports and SELinux settings. The simplest approach with respect to Squid configuration assumes that all clients use the default Squid port 3128, using TCP, where traffic is allowed through that port. Alternatively, you can redirect requests to the standard Web server port (80) to Squid port 3128, using an appropriate **iptables** command.

You can configure the RHEL firewall in these two ways through that port using the techniques described in Chapter 15. Briefly, you can open TCP port 3128 in the firewall using the Security Level Configuration tool; the technique is elementary. If you want to add an **iptables** command to forward TCP port 80 traffic to TCP port 3128, you would use the following:

```
# iptables -t nat -A PREROUTING -i eth0 -p tcp --dport 80 -j REDIRECT \
--to-ports 3128
```

a t c h   *As described by the Red*
Hat Exam Prep guide, RHCEs must be   *able to use* **iptables** *to implement packet*
filtering and/or NAT.

As for SELinux, you'll at least want to use the Security Level Configuration tool to activate the Allow Squid Daemon To Connect To The Network option, also known as the **squid_connect_any** boolean. Alternatively, you can activate this boolean with the following command:

```
# setsebool -P squid_connect_any 1
```

EXERCISE 9-6

Configuring Squid to Act as a Proxy Server

This exercise assumes you have a LAN. One of the computers on the LAN is also a server that is connected to the Internet, with Squid properly installed. Then you can configure Squid to act as a proxy for Web and FTP services for your LAN.

1. Open the Squid configuration file, /etc/squid/squid.conf, in a text editor.
2. Add the name of your computer to this file. Add the following command near the comments associated with **visible_hostname**:

```
visible_hostname computername
```

3. Add an **http_access** command to allow access from your local network. You can set an arbitrary name of your choice for the network, but you'll need to use it in the command afterward. Locate the command near the other **http_access** commands in this file:

```
http_access allow lan_net
```

4. Configure access from your LAN to Squid with an appropriate **acl** command. The following command allows access from your **lan_net** with an IP network address of 172.168.30.0:

```
acl lan_net src 172.168.30.0/24
```

5. Save your changes and exit.

6. Stop the Squid service if it isn't already running with the **service squid stop** command.

7. Create Squid swap directories with the **squid -z** command.

8. Start the Squid service with the **service squid start** command.

9. Configure a test client such as a Web browser to use your Squid service.

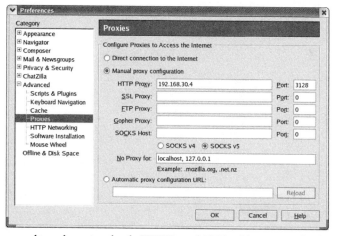

10. Test your client by using both HTTP and FTP addresses in the browser address field. Use it to retrieve files from various sites on the Internet, such as www.redhat.com and ftp.kernel.org.

11. If problems occur from external systems, you may have configured a firewall and/or SELinux protection that you don't want. Open the Security Level Configuration tool. If you want a firewall, make sure to disable the firewall for TCP port 3128. If you want an active version of SELinux, make sure to activate the **squid_connect_any** boolean.

CERTIFICATION SUMMARY

You can configure a number of network sharing services on your RHEL computer. Apache is the most important Web server on the Internet. Squid allows you to save bandwidth.

Apache was developed from the NCSA Web server. Once the appropriate packages are installed, you can access a structure and sample Web pages in the /var/www/html directory, based on the /etc/httpd/conf/httpd.conf configuration file. The httpd.conf file is organized in containers. You can create virtual hosts for multiple Web sites on your computer, even if you have only one IP address.

Squid is a proxy server that allows a network to filter its HTTP and FTP traffic through a cache. Requests are taken from the cache when possible. This reduces the load between the LAN and the Internet, reducing your network costs. When users access cached files, they get better performance from the external network.

As the RHCE is a performance-based exam, it is important to practice all the skills discussed in this chapter. You may need to use these skills on the exam!

TWO-MINUTE DRILL

Here are some of the key points from the certification objectives in Chapter 9.

The Apache Web Server

❑ Red Hat Enterprise Linux includes the Apache Web server, which is currently used by more than twice as many Internet Web sites as all other Web servers combined.

❑ Web services are an easy way to provide simple, secure access to many types of documents. The Apache Web server provides both normal and secure Web services using the HTTP and HTTPS protocols.

Apache Access Configuration

❑ Apache supports security by specifying active ports through the **Listen** and **NameVirtualHost** directives.

❑ Apache supports host-based security by IP address or domain name.

❑ Apache supports user-based security by password, with the help of the **htpasswd** command.

Virtual Hosts

❑ With Apache 2.2, you can configure multiple Web sites on your server, even if you have only one IP address. This is possible through the use of virtual hosts.

❑ The RHEL configuration supports the configuration of virtual hosts for regular Web sites at the end of the /etc/httpd/conf/httpd.conf file.

❑ The RHEL configuration supports the configuration of secure virtual hosts for regular Web sites at the end of the /etc/httpd/conf.d/ssl.conf file.

The Squid Web Proxy Cache

❑ Squid is a high-performance HTTP and FTP caching proxy server.

❑ The main Squid configuration file is long, but all you need to do in /etc/squid/squid.conf is configure the following parameters: **visible_hostname**, **http_access**, and **acl**.

❑ Squid can refer requests to sibling and parent proxy servers. If the request still isn't available, a parent proxy server refers the request to the Internet.

❑ Once Squid is configured, you can set each computer on the LAN to browse Web pages to the proxy server on port 3128, or redirect requests with the help of an appropriate **iptables** routing command.

SELF TEST

The following questions will help you measure your understanding of the material presented in this chapter. As no multiple choice questions appear on the Red Hat exams, no multiple choice questions appear in this book. These questions exclusively test your understanding of the chapter. It is okay if you have another way of performing a task. Getting results, not memorizing trivia, is what counts on the Red Hat exams. There may be more than one answer to many of these questions.

The Apache Web Server

1. What is the Apache directive that specifies the base directory for configuration and log files?

   _____

2. Once you've modified httpd.conf, what command should you use to reread this file?

   _____

3. What directive specifies the TCP/IP port associated with Apache?

   _____

Apache Access Configuration

4. What command creates the /etc/httpd/passwords file and configures a password for user elizabeth? _____

5. If you see the following directives limiting access within the stanza for a virtual host, what computers are allowed access?

   ```
   Order Allow,Deny
   Allow from 192.168.0.0/24
   ```

   _____

6. What standard ports do you need to open in a firewall to allow access to a regular and secure Web site? _____

Virtual Hosts

7. What file does RHEL provide to help you configure a virtual host as a secure server?

   _____

8. If you're creating an IP address–based virtual host, how many IP addresses would you need for three virtual servers? _____

9. If you want to check your configuration of virtual hosts, what switch can you use with the **httpd** command? _____

The Squid Web Proxy Cache

10. Which directive in squid.conf is used to point to the network IP address served by Squid?

_____

11. What command configures the Squid cache directories and is required before you start this service for the first time? _____

12. What port and protocol are the defaults for Squid communication? _____

LAB QUESTIONS

Lab 1

In this first lab, you'll install and configure Apache to start and run automatically the next time you boot your computer. You'll also configure the default home page for the local distribution as the default home page for the local computer.

Lab 2

In this lab, you'll configure two Web sites on the local Apache server. Call them big.example.big and small.example.small. Don't forget to create the directories that you need and set up these Web sites on your DNS server or /etc/hosts file. Make sure your Web sites are accessible to users from remote computers on your network. Add an appropriate index.html file to the **DocumentRoot** for each Web site. Simple Web pages, such as a single line of text, are acceptable (no HTML coding is necessary). Don't forget that SELinux settings need to be compatible with what you configure.

Part 3

Continuing on with Apache, now configure secure versions for each of your two Web sites. Make sure that appropriate directories are available for each secure Web site.

Lab 4

Set up a Squid Proxy Server on your computer. Set up access to your LAN on the 10.11.12.0/ 255.255.255.0 network. Assign appropriate values to **acl**, **http_access**, and **visible_hostname**. Set up the cache directories for Squid. Make sure it starts now and automatically the next time you reboot your computer. If there are problems, make sure the SELinux settings are compatible.

SELF TEST ANSWERS

The Apache Web Server

1. The **ServerRoot** directive sets the default directory for the Apache server. Any files and directories not otherwise configured—or configured as a relative directory—are set relative to **ServerRoot**.

2. There are two basic ways to make Apache reread the configuration file. You can restart the service with a command such as **apachectl restart**, or you can keep Apache running and make it reread the file with **service httpd reload**.

3. The **Listen** directive specifies the TCP port associated with Apache.

Apache Access Configuration

4. The command that creates the /etc/httpd/passwords file and configures a password for user elizabeth is **htpasswd -c /etc/httpd/passwords elizabeth**. If /etc/httpd/passwords already exists, all that's required is **htpasswd elizabeth**.

5. As described in the chapter, the **Order Allow,Deny** directive denies access to all systems by default, except those explicitly allowed access. So access is limited to computers on the 192.168.0.0/24 network.

6. The standard ports you need to open in a firewall to allow access to a regular and secure Web sites are 80 and 443.

Virtual Hosts

7. The file associated with secure servers for virtual hosts is ssl.conf in the /etc/httpd/conf.d/ directory.

8. Three IP addresses are needed for three virtual servers. IP address-based virtual hosts each require their own IP addresses. If you want to configure multiple virtual hosts, you need name-based virtual hosts, typically starting with the **NameVirtualHost *:80** directive.

9. To check your configuration of virtual hosts, you can use two switches with the **httpd** command: **httpd -S** checks the configuration file, including virtual host settings. Alternatively, **httpd -D DUMP_VHOSTS** focuses on the virtual host configuration.

The Squid Web Proxy Cache

10. The **acl** and **http_access allow** directives in squid.conf can be used to specify the network to be served by Squid. For example, the following directives support access from the 192.168.0.0/24 network:

```
acl local_net src 192.168.0.0/24
http_access allow local_net
```

11. The **squid -z** command sets up the directories for the Squid cache, which is required before you start the Squid service for the first time.

12. The default port for Squid communication is 3128; the default protocol is ICP (InterCache Protocol).

LAB ANSWERS

Lab 1

First, make sure the Apache Web server is installed. If an **rpm -q httpd** command tells you that it is missing, you haven't installed the Web Server package group. The most efficient way to do so is with the **yum install "Web Server"** command. (To find appropriate package group names, see the comps-rhel5-server-core.xml file in the Server/repodata subdirectory on the first installation CD, or run the **yum groupinfo** command.) This assumes a proper connection to a repository; if you're using RHEL 5, this requires a properly enabled subscription to the Red Hat Network. Other update options are covered in Chapter 5.

To configure Apache to start, run the **apachectl start** command. To make sure it starts the next time you boot your computer, run the **chkconfig httpd on** command.

Once Apache is installed, you should be able to access it by opening a browser and navigating to http://localhost. You can see in the default Apache configuration file that the **DocumentRoot** is located in /var/www/html. The default home page is located at /usr/share/doc/HTML/index.html. You can copy that index.html file to the /var/www/html directory and test the result by navigating once again to http://localhost. If you did not copy the other files associated with the default home page, you'll be missing some icons.

Lab 2

This lab requires that you create two virtual hosts in the main Apache configuration file, /etc/httpd/conf/httpd.conf. To make this happen, you should take the following steps:

1. The **ServerRoot** directive sets the default directory for the Apache server. Any files and directories not otherwise configured—or configured as a relative directory—are set relative to **ServerRoot**. Don't change this unless you're ready to adjust the SELinux contexts of the new directory accordingly.

2. Set the **NameVirtualHost** directive to the port (80) serving your intended network audience. Don't assign any IP addresses.

3. Add a **VirtualHost** container with the same IP address.

4. Assign the **ServerAdmin** to the e-mail address of this Web site's administrator.

5. Configure a unique **DocumentRoot** directory.

6. Set the first **ServerName** to big.example.big.

7. Add **ErrorLog** and **CustomLog** directives, and set them to unique file names in the /etc/httpd/ logs directory. With the default **ServerRoot**, you can use a relative logs directory, such as this:

```
ErrorLog logs/big.example.big-error_log
```

8. Make sure to close the **VirtualHost** container (with a **</VirtualHost>** directive at the end of the stanza).

9. Repeat the process for the second Web site, making sure to set the second **ServerName** to **small.example.small**.

10. Close and save the httpd.conf file with your changes.

11. Create any new directories that you configured with the **DocumentRoot** directives.

12. Create index.html text files in each directory defined by your new **DocumentRoot** directives. Don't worry about HTML code; a text file is fine for the purpose of this lab.

13. Make sure these domain names are configured in your DNS server or in /etc/hosts. For example, you could add the following lines to /etc/hosts:

```
192.168.30.2 big.example.big
192.168.30.2 small.example.small
```

14. Use the Security Level Configuration tool (**system-config-securitylevel**) utility to allow HTTP data through your firewall; see Chapter 15 for more information on this process.

15. Assuming you've enabled SELinux (and the Red Hat Exam Prep guide suggests that you need to do so for the RHCE exam), you'll need to configure appropriate ACLs on the directory associated with the **DocumentRoot**. For example, if that directory is /virt1, run the following commands:

```
# chcon -R -u system_u /virt1/
# chcon -R -t httpd_sys_content_t /virt1
```

Alternatively, disable SELinux if you're allowed to do so. For more information, see Chapter 15.

16. Finally, make sure to run the **apachectl restart** command to reread the httpd.conf configuration file, so Apache reads your changes. (While the **service httpd reload** command works as well, **apachectl** is preferred.)

17. Now you can test the results in the browser of your choice. If it works, the big.example.big and small.example.small domain names should direct you to the index.html files that you created for each Web site.

Lab 3

The basics of this lab are straightforward. You'll need to repeat the same basic steps that you performed in Lab 2; you're just editing the /etc/httpd/conf.d/ssl.conf configuration file. However, you should be concerned about the following:

1. Make sure that the top **VirtualHost** directive points to the IP address that you're using for your Web server.

2. Set up the **DocumentRoot** in a directory different from a regular Web server.

3. Configure the **ErrorLog** and **CustomLog** separately; select names to associate these log files with the name of the secure Web site.

4. Continuing on with Apache, now configure secure versions for each of your two Web sites. Make sure that appropriate directories are available for each secure Web site.

Lab 4

Squid is installed by default when you install the Web Server package group. To configure a Squid Proxy Server for your network, you'll need to configure /etc/squid/squid.conf. Assume the name of your computer is myproxy, and you're arbitrarily assigning mylan as the name for your LAN. If your network IP address is not 10.11.12.0, substitute accordingly. In this file, you'll need to add directives similar to:

```
visible_hostname=myproxy
acl mylan src 10.11.12.0/255.255.255.0
http_access allow mylan
```

Next, set up the Squid directories with the following command:

```
# squid -z
```

Finally, to configure Squid to start, run the **service squid start** command. To make sure it starts the next time you boot your computer, run the **chkconfig squid on** command.

But you'll also need to activate proxy server access in client applications such as Web browsers. Remember that you can do so by pointing your browsers to port 3128.

10

Network File-
Sharing Services

CERTIFICATION OBJECTIVES

10.01   Configuring a Network File System
        (NFS) Server

10.02   Client-Side NFS

10.03   The File Transfer Protocol and vsFTP

10.04   Samba Services

✓   Two-Minute Drill

Q&A   Self Test

L inux is designed for networking, and there are three major protocols associated with sharing files on a network: NFS, FTP, and Samba. While some excellent GUI tools are available, I recommend that you learn to configure these services from the command line. If you know these services, you can do more in less time by directly editing key configuration files.

This chapter starts with a description of the Network File System (NFS), a powerful and versatile way of sharing filesystems between servers and workstations. NFS clients are installed with a default installation of RHEL 5 and support connections to NFS servers. RHEL includes an excellent GUI-based configuration tool.

The chapter continues with the Very Secure FTP (vsFTP) daemon, which provides both basic and secure FTP server services. With vsFTP, you can secure users, directories, subdirectories, and files with various levels of access control.

This chapter finishes with a detailed analysis of networking with the various Microsoft Windows operating systems. Microsoft networking is based on the Common Internet File System (CIFS), which was developed from the Server Message Block (SMB) protocol. Samba was developed as a freely available SMB server for all Unix-related operating systems, including Linux, and has been upgraded to support CIFS.

Samba interacts with CIFS so transparently that Microsoft clients cannot tell your Linux server from a genuine Windows NT/2000/XP/2003/Vista server, and with Samba on Linux there are no server, client, or client access licenses to purchase. If you can learn to edit the main Samba configuration file from the command line interface, you can configure Samba quickly. RHEL includes a GUI alternative—the Samba Server Configuration utility. There's even a Samba Web Administration Tool, which we won't discuss in this book.

As you learn about these network services, you're learning about the services that you might configure and/or troubleshoot on the Red Hat exams. Take the time you need to understand the configuration files associated with each of these services, and practice making them work on your Linux computer. In some cases, two computers running Linux will be useful to practice what you learn in this chapter.

CERTIFICATION OBJECTIVE 10.01

Configuring a Network File System (NFS) Server

The NFS is the standard for sharing files and printers on a directory with Linux and Unix computers. It was originally developed by Sun Microsystems in the mid-

INSIDE THE EXAM

More Network Services

The Red Hat Exam Prep guide suggests that you can expect to configure NFS, FTP, and Samba servers during the Installation and Configuration portion of the RHCE exam. As described in the Red Hat Exam Prep guide, for each of these services, RHCEs must be able to do the following:

- Install the packages needed to provide the service.
- Configure SELinux to support the service.
- Configure the service to start when the system is booted.
- Configure the service for basic operation.

- Configure host-based and user-based security for the service.

It also suggests that you need to know how to "diagnose and correct problems with (these) network services" as well as SELinux-related network issues during the Troubleshooting and System Maintenance portion of this exam.

In this chapter, the NFS service should be installed automatically with RHEL 5. vsFTP and Samba are important server options for many administrators, and it's very possible that you'll install them during the RHCE exam. For each service, remember to use a command such as **chkconfig** to make sure it starts the next time you boot Linux. It also will help you get full credit for the work you do on the Red Hat exams.

1980s. Linux has supported NFS (both as a client and a server) for years, and NFS continues to be popular in organizations with Unix- or Linux-based networks.

You can create shared NFS directories directly by editing the /etc/exports configuration file, or with Red Hat's NFS Configuration tool. As NFS servers come first, that's what this chapter covers first.

exam
watch

I believe even beginning Linux administrators should know how to connect to a shared NFS directory. While the Red Hat Exam Prep guide does not explicitly require RHCT candidates to have this knowledge, it is consistent with the spirit of that exam. The Red Hat Exam Prep guide does explicitly require that RHCE candidates know how to configure and troubleshoot an NFS server.

NFS Server Configuration and Operation

NFS servers are relatively easy to configure. All you need to do is export a filesystem, either generally or to a specific host, and then mount that filesystem from a remote client. In Chapter 2, you configured an NFS server to install RHEL over a network. This chapter goes further into the basics of NFS server configuration and operation.

Required Packages

Two RPM packages are closely associated with NFS: portmap and nfs-utils. They should be installed by default. Just in case, you can use the **rpm -q** *packagename* command to make sure these packages are installed. The **rpm -ql** *packagename* command provides a list of files installed from that package. The nfs-utils package includes a number of key files. The following is not a complete list:

- **/etc/rc.d/init.d/nfs** Control script for NFS, hard linked to /etc/init.d/nfs
- **/etc/rc.d/init.d/nfslock** Control script for lockd and statd, which locks files currently in use, hard linked to /etc/init.d/nfslock
- **/usr/share/doc/nfs-utils-*versionnumber*** Documentation, mostly in HTML format
- **Server daemons in /usr/sbin** rpc.mountd, rpc.nfsd, rpc.rquotad
- **Server daemons in /sbin** rpc.lockd, rpc.statd
- **Control programs in /usr/sbin** exportfs, nfsstat, nhfsgraph, nhfsnums, nhfsrun, nhfsstone, showmount
- **Status files in /var/lib/nfs** etab, rmtab, statd, state, xtab

The portmap RPM package includes the following key files (also not a complete list):

- **/etc/rc.d/init.d/portmap** Control script, hard linked to /etc/init.d/portmap
- **/usr/share/doc/portmap-4.0** Documentation
- **Server daemon in /sbin** portmap
- **Control programs in /usr/sbin** pmap_dump, pmap_set

Configuring NFS to Start

Once configured, NFS can be set up to start during the Linux boot process or can be started with the **service nfs start** command. NFS also depends on the portmap package, which helps secure NFS directories that are shared through /etc/exports. Because of this dependency, you need to make sure to start the portmap daemon before starting NFS, and don't stop it until after stopping NFS.

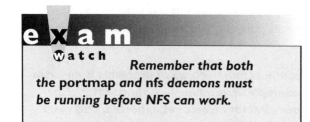

The **nfs** service script starts the following processes:

- **rpc.mountd**   Handles mount requests
- **nfsd**   Starts an nfsd kernel process for each shared directory
- **rpc.rquotad**   Reports disk quota statistics to clients

If any of these processes is not running, NFS won't work. Fortunately, it's easy to check for these processes by running the **rpcinfo -p** command. As with other service scripts, if you want it to start when RHEL boots, you'll need to run a command such as this:

```
# chkconfig nfs on
```

This command makes sure NFS starts the next time you boot into runlevels 2, 3, 4, or 5. Alternatively, you can use the Red Hat Service Management utility described in Chapter 3 to make sure NFS starts the next time you boot RHEL.

Configuring NFS for Basic Operation

NFS is fairly simple. The only major NFS configuration file is /etc/exports. Once configured, you can export these directories with the **exportfs -a** command. Each line in this file lists the directory to be exported, the hosts to which it will be exported, and the options that apply to this export. You can export a particular directory only once. Take the following examples from an /etc/exports file:

```
/pub        (ro,insecure,sync) one.example.net(rw,insecure,sync)
/home       *.example.net(rw,insecure,sync)
/tftpboot   nodisk.example.net(rw,insecure,no_root_squash,sync)
```

In this example, the /pub directory is exported to all users as read-only. It is also exported to one specific computer with read/write privileges. The /home directory is exported, with read/write privileges, to any computer on the .example.net network. Finally, the /tftpboot directory is exported with full read/write privileges (even for root users) to the nodisk.example.net computer.

All of these options include the **sync** flag. This requires all changes to be written to disk before a command such as a file copy is complete. They also include the

insecure flag, which allows access on ports above 1024. If you want to run NFS through a firewall, you'll need to specify ports for NFS communication, as described later in this chapter.

on the
job

Be very careful with /etc/exports; one common cause of problems is an extra space between expressions. For example, if you type in a space after either comma in (ro,insecure,sync), your directory won't get exported, and you'll get an error message.

Wildcards and Globbing

In Linux network configuration files, you can specify a group of computers with the right wildcard, which in Linux is also known as *globbing*. What you do for a wildcard depends on the configuration file. The NFS /etc/exports file uses "conventional" wildcards: for example, *.example.net specifies all computers within the example .net domain. In contrast, /etc/hosts.deny is less conventional; .example.net, with the leading dot, specifies all computers in that same domain.

For IPv4 networks, wildcards often require some form of the subnet mask. For example, 192.168.0.0/255.255.255.0 specifies the 192.168.0.0 network of computers with IP addresses that range from 192.168.0.1 to 192.168.0.254. Some services support the use of CIDR (Classless InterDomain Routing) notation. In CIDR, since 255.255.255.0 masks 24 bits, CIDR represents this with the number *24*. If you're configuring a network in CIDR notation, you can represent this network as 192.168.0.0/24. For details, see the discussion for each applicable service in Chapter 7 and Chapters 9 through 15.

Activating the List of Exports

Once you've modified /etc/exports, you need to do more. First, this file is simply the default set of exported directories. You need to activate them with the **exportfs -a** command. The next time you boot RHEL, if you've activated **nfs** at the appropriate runlevels, the nfs start script (/etc/init.d/nfs) automatically runs the **exportfs -r** command, which synchronizes exported directories.

When you add a share to /etc/exports, the **exportfs -r** command adds the new directories. However, if you're modifying, moving, or deleting a share, it is safest to temporarily unexport all filesystems first with the **exportfs -ua** command before reexporting the shares with the **exportfs -a** command.

Once exports are active, they're easy to check. Just run the **showmount -e** command on the server. If you're looking for the export list for a remote NFS server, just add the name of the NFS server. For example, the **showmount -e enterprise5** command looks for the list of exported NFS directories from the enterprise5 computer. If this command doesn't work, you may have blocked NFS messages with a firewall.

NFS Server Configuration Tool

It's easy to configure /etc/exports, and the Red Hat NFS Server Configuration tool is also easy to use and is reliable. To start this tool, type the **system-config-nfs** command in a GUI terminal, or choose System (or KDE Main Menu) | Administration | Server Settings | NFS. This opens the NFS Server Configuration window shown in Figure 10-1. After you go through these steps, you'll see how much simpler it is to add a line to /etc/exports.

To add a shared NFS directory, take the following steps:

1. Click Add or choose File | Add Share. This opens the Add NFS Share window shown in Figure 10-2.
2. Under the Basic tab, add the directory that you want to share. If you want to limit access to a specific host or domain, add the appropriate names or IP addresses to the Host(s) text box. If you want to allow access to all hosts, enter an asterisk (*). Set read-only or read/write permissions as desired. Click the General Options tab.
3. Under the General Options tab, you can set several parameters for this share, as described in Table 10-1. Note that **sync** and **hide** options are active by default. The default is sufficient unless you receive specific instructions for an NFS share on your exam. If you want to activate NFS through a firewall, activate the Allow Connections From Port 1024 And Higher (**insecure**) option. (But this isn't sufficient.) Click the User Access tab.

FIGURE 10-1

NFS Server Configuration

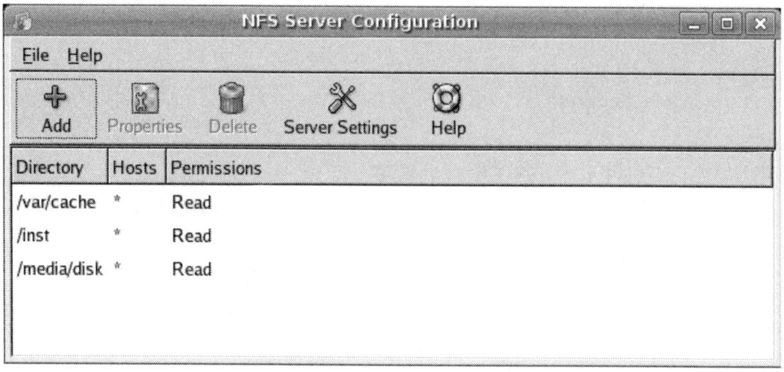

FIGURE 10-2

The Add NFS
Share window

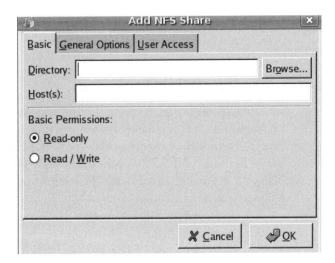

4. Under the User Access tab, you can set different parameters for remote users, as defined in Table 10-2.

5. Once you've finished configuring your shared NFS directory, click OK. The directory is automatically exported with the **exportfs -r** command, and, as long as you aren't blocking access with firewalls, it should now be ready for use.

TABLE 10-1   NFS Tool General Options

Parameter	Corresponding /etc/exports Command and Explanation
Allow connections from ports 1024 or higher	**insecure** This supports NFS messages above ports 1024.
Allow insecure file locking	**insecure_locks** If you have an older NFS client, this does not check user permissions to a file.
Disable subtree checking	**no_subtree_check** If you export a subdirectory such as /mnt/inst, this feature disables checks of higher level directories for permissions.
Sync write operations on request	**sync** Data is written upon request. Active by default.
Force sync of write operations immediately	**no_wdelay** Data is written to the share immediately.
Hide filesystems beneath	**hide** If you export a directory and subdirectory such as /mnt and /mnt/inst, shares to /mnt/inst must be explicitly mounted.
Export only if mounted	**mp** Requires the export point to also be a mount point on the client.
Optional mount point	Specifies a mount directory for **mp**; must be used by the client.
Set explicit filesystem ID	**fsid** Specifies a numeric identifier for the exported filesystem.

TABLE 10-2   NFS Tool User Access Options

Parameter	Corresponding /etc/exports Command and Explanation
Treat remote root user as local root	**no_root_squash** Remote root users get root privileges on the shared directory.
Treat all client users as anonymous users	**all_squash** All remote users are mapped as an anonymous user. In RHEL 3, that user is nfsnobody, which you can see in /etc/passwd.
Specify local user ID for anonymous users	**anonuid=*userid*** Allows you to map remote users to a specific user ID such as pcguest.
Specify local group ID for anonymous users	**anongid=*groupid*** Allows you to map remote groups to a specific group ID such as pcguest.

6. If you have problems, check for firewalls. Check for limitations in /etc/hosts .allow and /etc/hosts.deny. For more information on firewall management, read Chapter 15. If necessary, use the **service nfs stop** and **service nfs start** commands to restart the NFS service. If problems continue, you may find more information in your /var/log/messages file.

Unfortunately, the NFS Server Configuration tool does not activate NFS at the appropriate runlevels for the next time you boot Linux.

If you need to run NFS through a firewall, return to the NFS Server Configuration tool. Click File | Server Settings. Set unused ports for the noted services:

- rpc.lockd (TCP)
- rpc.lockd (UDP)
- rpc.mountd (TCP)
- rpc.statd (TCP)

In Linux documentation, common ports for these services are 32764, 32765, 32766, and 32767. But these ports are cited only because they're unused in /etc/ services. You'll also need to designate a port for the rpc.rquotad service in /etc/ services. If rpc.rquotad is running, you'll have to stop and restart the daemon.

Whatever ports you choose, you'll need to make sure that these ports (as well as TCP and UDP ports 111 for the **portmap** daemon) are allowed through any configured firewall. For more information, see Chapter 15.

Making NFS Work with SELinux

There are four directives associated with making NFS work with SELinux in targeted mode:

- **allow_gssd_read_tmp** supports the reading of temporary directories by the General Security Services daemon, **gssd**, which helps protect NFS using Kerberos 5.
- **allow_nfsd_anon_write** supports NFS servers when they modify files on public file transfer services.
- **nfs_export_all_ro** supports read-only access to shared NFS directories.
- **nfs_export_all_rw** supports read-write access to shared NFS directories.

To set these directives, use the **setsebool** command. For example, to activate read-write access, run the following command:

```
# setsebool -P nfs_export_all_rw 1
```

Quirks and Limitations of NFS

NFS does have its problems. Any administrator who controls shared NFS directories would be wise to take note of these limitations.

Statelessness

NFS is a "stateless" protocol. In other words, you don't need to log in separately to access a shared NFS directory. Instead, the NFS client normally contacts rpc.mountd on the server. The **rpc.mounted** daemon handles mount requests. It checks the request against currently exported filesystems. If the request is valid, **rpc.mounted** provides an *NFS file handle* (a "magic cookie"), which is then used for further client/server communication for this share.

The stateless protocol allows the NFS client to wait if the NFS server ever has to be rebooted. The software waits, and waits, and waits. This can cause the NFS client to hang.

This can also lead to problems with insecure single-user clients. When a file is opened through a share, it may be "locked out" from other users. When an NFS server is rebooted, handling the locked file can be difficult. The security problems can be so severe that NFS communication is blocked even by the default Red Hat Enterprise Linux firewall.

In theory, the recent change to NFS, setting up sync as the default for file transfers, should help address this problem. In theory, locked-out users should not lose any data that they've written with the appropriate commands.

Absolute and Relative Symbolic Links

If you have any symbolic links on an exported directory, be careful. The client interprets a symbolically linked file with respect to its own local filesystem. Unless the mount point and filesystem structures are identical, the linked file can point to an unexpected location, which may lead to unpredictable consequences.

You have a couple of ways to address this issue. You can take care to limit the use of symbolic links within an exported directory. Alternatively, NFS offers a server-side export option (**link_relative**) that converts absolute links to relative links; however, this can have counterintuitive results if the client mounts a subdirectory of the exported directory.

Root Squash

By default, NFS is set up to **root_squash**, which prevents root users on an NFS client from gaining root access to a share on an NFS server. Specifically, the root user on a client (with a user ID of 0) is mapped to the *nfsnobody* unprivileged account (yes, this user exists if you've installed the right packages—check your /etc/passwd file).

This behavior can be disabled via the **no_root_squash** server export option in /etc/exports. For exported directories so disabled, remote root users can use their root privileges on the shared NFS directory.

NFS Hangs

Because NFS is stateless, NFS clients may wait up to several minutes for a server. In some cases, an NFS client may wait indefinitely if a server goes down. During the wait, any process that looks for a file on the mounted NFS share will hang. Once this happens, it is generally difficult or impossible to unmount the offending filesystems. You can do several things to reduce the impact of this problem:

- Take great care to ensure the reliability of NFS servers and the network.
- Avoid mounting many different NFS servers at once. If several computers mount each other's NFS directories, this could cause problems throughout the network.

- Mount infrequently used NFS exports only when needed. NFS clients should unmount these clients after use.
- Set up NFS shares with the **sync** option, which should at least reduce the incidence of lost files.
- Don't configure a mission-critical computer as an NFS client, if at all possible.
- Keep NFS mounted directories out of the search path for users, especially that of root.
- Keep NFS mounted directories out of the root (/) directory; instead, segregate them to a less frequently used filesystem, if possible, on a separate partition.

Inverse DNS Pointers

An NFS server daemon checks mount requests. First, it looks at the current list of exports, based on /etc/exports. Then it looks up the client's IP address to find its host name. This requires a reverse DNS lookup.

This host name is then finally checked against the list of exports. If NFS can't find a host name, **rpc.mountd** will deny access to that client. For security reasons, it also adds a "request from unknown host" entry in /var/log/messages.

File Locking

Multiple NFS clients can be set up to mount the same exported directory from the same server. It's quite possible that people on different computers end up trying to use the same shared file. This is addressed by the file-locking daemon service.

NFS has historically had serious problems making file locking work. If you have an application that depends on file locking over NFS, test it thoroughly before putting it into production.

on the
job

There may still be "file-locking" issues with other applications; for example, file locking was only recently incorporated in the OpenOffice.org suite, which prevents different users from editing the same file simultaneously.

Performance Tips

You can do several things to keep NFS running in a stable and reliable manner. As you gain experience with NFS, you might monitor or even experiment with the following factors:

- Eight kernel NFS daemons, which is the default, is generally sufficient for good performance, even under fairly heavy loads. If your NFS server is busy, you may want to add additional NFS daemons through the **RPCNFSDCOUNT** directive in the /etc/init.d/nfs script. Just keep in mind that the extra kernel processes consume valuable kernel resources.

■ NFS write performance can be extremely slow, particularly with NFS v2 clients, as the client waits for each block of data to be written to disk.

■ You may try specialized hardware with nonvolatile RAM. Data that is stored on such RAM isn't lost if you have trouble with network connectivity or a power failure.

■ In applications where data loss is not a big concern, you may try the **async** option. This makes NFS faster because **async** NFS mounts do not write files to disk until other operations are complete. However, a loss of power or network connectivity can result in a loss of data.

■ Host name lookups are performed frequently by the NFS server; you can start the Name Switch Cache Daemon (**nscd**) to speed lookup performance.

on the Job

NFS is a powerful file-sharing system. But there are risks associated with NFS. If an NFS server is down, it could affect your entire network. It's also not sufficiently secure to use on the Internet. NFS is primarily used on secure networks.

NFS Security

NFS includes a number of serious security problems and should never be used in hostile environments (such as on a server directly exposed to the Internet), at least not without strong precautions.

Shortcomings and Risks

NFS is an easy-to-use yet powerful file-sharing system. However, it is not without its problems. The following are a few security issues to keep in mind:

■ **Authentication**   NFS relies on the host to report user and group IDs. However, this can expose your files if root users on other computers access your NFS shares. In other words, data that is accessible via NFS to *any user* can potentially be accessed by *any other* user.

■ **Privacy**   Not even "secure" NFS encrypts its network traffic.

■ **portmap infrastructure**   Both the NFS client and server depend on the RPC portmap daemon. The portmap daemon has historically had a number of serious security holes. For this reason, portmap is not recommended for use on computers that are directly connected to the Internet or other potentially hostile networks.

Security Tips

If NFS *must* be used in or near a hostile environment, you can reduce the security risks:

- Educate yourself in detail about NFS security. If you do not clearly understand the risks, you should restrict your NFS use to friendly, internal networks behind a good firewall.

- Export as little data as possible, and export filesystems as read-only if possible.

- Use the **root_squash** option to prevent clients from having root access to exported filesystems.

- If an NFS client has a direct connection to the Internet, use separate network adapters for the Internet connection and the LAN.

- Use appropriate firewall settings to deny access to the portmapper and nfsd ports, except from explicitly trusted hosts or networks. For more information, see Chapter 15. The known ports are

  ```
  111      TCP/UDP      portmapper      (server and client)
  2049     TCP/UDP      nfsd            (server)
  ```

- Fix the port associated with NFS; it's possible in /etc/sysconfig/nfs with the following directives (which are read by the /etc/init.d/nfs script). You can choose a different port number; it should be unused in /etc/services and remembered when a firewall is configured:

  ```
  LOCKD_TCPPORT=32765
  LOCKD_UDPPORT=32765
  MOUNTD_PORT=32767
  STATD_PORT=32766
  ```

- Create a port for **rquotad** in /etc/services, stop, and restart the **rpc.quotad** daemon.

- Use a port scanner to verify that these ports are blocked for untrusted network(s).

exam
ⓦatch   *While some may find it easier to learn with GUI tools, these tools are usually more time consuming and less flexible than direct action from the command line. As time is often short on the RHCE exam, I recommend that you learn how to configure and activate NFS and other services from the command line.*

EXERCISE 10-1

NFS

This exercise requires two computers: one set up as an NFS server, the other as an NFS client. For this exercise, disable any currently active firewall and SELinux protection. Then, on the NFS server, take the following steps:

1. Set up a group named IT for the Information Technology group in /etc/group.

2. Create the /MIS directory. Assign ownership to the MIS group with the **chgrp** command.

3. Set the SGID bit on this directory to enforce group ownership.

4. Update /etc/exports file to allow read and write for your local network. Run the following command to set it up under NFS:

   ```
   # exportfs -a
   ```

5. Restart the NFS service.

   Then, on an NFS client, take the following steps:

6. Create a directory for the server share called /mnt/MIS.

7. Mount the shared NFS directory on /mnt/MIS.

8. List all exported shares from the server and save this output as /mnt/MIS/shares.list.

9. Make this service a permanent connection in the /etc/fstab file. Assume that the connection might be troublesome and add the appropriate options, such as soft mounting.

10. Run the **mount -a** command to reread /etc/fstab. (This is quicker than rebooting the client computer.) Check to see if the share is properly remounted.

11. Test the NFS connection. Stop the service on the server, and then try copying a file to the /mnt/MIS directory. While the attempt to copy will fail, it should not hang the client.

12. Restart the NFS server.

13. Edit /etc/fstab again. This time, assume that NFS is reliable, and remove the special options that you added in step 9.

14. Now test what happens when you shut down the server. The mounted NFS directory on the client should hang when you try to access the service.

15. The client computer will probably lock. If so, reboot the client computer; you may need to boot into single-user mode, as described in Chapter 3, to boot without being locked by an NFS problem. Restore the original configuration.

Remember that one of the tasks during the Troubleshooting and System Maintenance portion of the RHCE exam is to diagnose and correct problems *with network services, including NFS. This exercise illustrates one potential problem with NFS.*

EXERCISE 10-2

Using the NFS Server Configuration Tool

In this exercise, you'll use the options associated with the NFS Server Configuration tool to experiment with creating a shared directory in /etc/exports. While it's best and usually fastest to edit a Linux configuration file directly, Red Hat GUI configuration tools such as the NFS Server Configuration tool can help you learn about different options for Linux services.

1. Open a GUI on an RHEL computer. Log in using the graphical login menu; or, from a text menu, use the **startx** command.

2. Start the NFS Server Configuration tool. You can run **system-config-nfs** from a command line interface, or choose GNOME's System (or KDE Main Menu) | Administration | Server Settings | NFS.

3. In the NFS Server Configuration tool, click Add. This opens the Add NFS Share window with the Basic tab. Set up a share for your home directory. Share it with one specific host on your LAN, with read-only permissions.

4. Click the General Options tab. Select the options of your choice. It does not matter what you select; the purpose of this lab is to demonstrate the effect of the NFS Server Configuration tool on the /etc/exports file.

5. Click the User Access tab. Select the options of your choice.

6. Click OK. The settings you chose are saved in /etc/exports.

7. Open a command line window. Right-click the desktop, and select New Terminal from the pop-up menu that appears.

8. Open the /etc/exports file in the text editor of your choice. What is the relationship between the options you selected in the NFS Server Configuration tool and the command options associated with your home directory in /etc/exports? Close the /etc/exports file.

9. Back in the NFS Server Configuration tool, highlight the line associated with your home directory, and then click Properties. This opens the Edit NFS Share window with the settings that you just created.

10. Make additional changes under the three tabs in this window. After you click OK, check the results in /etc/exports. What happened?

11. If you don't actually want to export your home directory, highlight the appropriate line in the NFS Server Configuration tool and click Delete. What happens to /etc/exports?

12. Click the Server Settings button, which opens the NFS Server Settings window. Assign otherwise unused ports above 1024 (and below 65535) to the given daemons. To see if a port is used, check /etc/services. To make sure the port you select is unused, check /etc/exports. Click OK and check the result in /etc/sysconfig/nfs. Review the directives, and look at their impact on /etc/init.d/nfs.

    Open up /etc/services, and set TCP and UDP ports for the **rquotad** service. Stop and start the **rpc.rquotad** daemon, and make sure the new ports are actually being used with the **rpcinfo -p** command.

    When you fix ports for NFS, you can set up a firewall that allows traffic through the ports you set in /etc/sysconfig/nfs. For more information, see Chapter 15.

13. Exit from the NFS Server Configuration tool.

CERTIFICATION OBJECTIVE 10.02

Client-Side NFS

Now you can mount a shared NFS directory from a client computer. The commands and configuration files are similar to those used for any local filesystem. In the previous section, you configured an NFS server; for the moment, stay where you are, because computers that serve as NFS servers are also NFS clients.

Mounting an NFS Directory from the Command Line

Before doing anything elaborate, you should test the shared NFS directory from a Linux or Unix client computer. But first, you should check for the list of shared NFS directories. If you're on an NFS server and want to check the local list, the command is easy:

```
# showmount -e
```

If you don't see a list of shared directories, review the steps described earlier in this chapter. Make sure you've configured your /etc/exports file properly. Remember to export the shared directories. And your NFS server can't work if you haven't started the NFS daemon on your computer.

If you're on a remote NFS client computer and want to see the list of shared directories from the enterprise5 computer, run the following command:

```
# showmount -e enterprise5
```

If it doesn't work, there are three more things to check: firewalls, your /etc/hosts or DNS server, and SELinux settings. If you have a problem with your /etc/hosts or DNS server, you can substitute the IP address of the NFS server. You'll see output similar to the following:

```
Export list for enterprise5
/mnt/inst *
```

Now if you want to mount this directory locally, you'll need an empty local directory. Create a directory such as /mnt/remote if required. You can then mount the shared directory from the enterprise5 computer with the following command:

```
# mount -t nfs enterprise5:/mnt/inst /mnt/remote
```

This command mounts the /mnt/inst directory from the computer named enterprise5. This command specifies the use of the NFS protocol (**-t nfs**), and mounts the share on the local /mnt/remote directory. Depending on traffic on your network, this command may take a few seconds, so be patient! When it works, you'll be able to access files on /mnt/inst as if it were a local directory.

Client-Side Helper Processes

When you start NFS as a client, it adds a few new system processes, including these:

- **rpc.statd** Tracks the status of servers, for use by rpc.lockd in recovering locks after a server crash
- **rpc.lockd** Manages the client side of file locking; the current RHEL 5

NFS and /etc/fstab

You can also configure an NFS client to mount a remote NFS directory during the boot process, as defined in /etc/fstab. For example, the following entry in a client /etc/fstab mounts the /homenfs share from the computer named nfsserv, on the local /nfs/home directory:

```
## Server: Directory    Mount Point   Type   Mount Options      Dump Fsckorder
nfsserv:/homenfs         /nfs/home     nfs    soft,timeout=100   0    0
```

Alternatively, an automounter, such as autofs or amd, can be used to mount NFS filesystems dynamically as required by the client computer. The automounter can also unmount these remote filesystems after a period of inactivity. For more information, see Chapter 4.

Without a timeout, NFS mounts through /etc/fstab can be troublesome. For example, if the network or the NFS server is down, the lack of a timeout can hang the client. (I discussed this issue in more detail earlier in this chapter.) A hang is a big problem if it happens during the boot process, because the boot may never complete, and you would have to restore your system by booting into some runlevel where networking is not started, such as 1, single, or emergency.

Diskless Clients

NFS supports diskless clients, which are computers that do not store the operating system locally. A diskless client may use a boot floppy or a boot PROM to get started. Then embedded commands can mount the appropriate root (/) directory, swap space, set the /usr directory as read-only, and configure other shared directories such as /home in read/write mode. If your computer uses a boot PROM, you'll also need access to DHCP and TFTP servers for network and kernel information.

Red Hat Enterprise Linux includes features that support diskless clients. While not listed as part of the current Red Hat exam requirements or related course outlines, I would not be surprised to see such requirements in the future. Red Hat is working on a new tool on this subject. For more information, see the Cobbler project at http://cobbler.et.redhat.com/.

Soft Mounting

Consider using the **soft** option when mounting NFS filesystems. When an NFS server fails, a soft-mounted NFS filesystem will fail rather than hang. However, this risks the failure of long-running processes due to temporary network outages.

In addition, you can use the **timeo** option to set a timeout interval, in tenths of a second. For example, the following command would mount /nfs/home with a timeout of 30 seconds (**timeo** uses tenths of a second):

```
# mount -o soft,timeo=300 myserver:/home /nfs/home
```

CERTIFICATION OBJECTIVE 10.03

The File Transfer Protocol and vsFTPd

The File Transfer Protocol is one of the original network applications developed with the TCP/IP protocol suite. It follows the standard model for network services, as FTP requires a client and a server. The FTP client is installed by default on most operating systems, including Red Hat Enterprise Linux. If you've installed the FTP Server package group, you've installed the default Red Hat FTP Server, the very secure FTP (vsFTP) daemon.

In this section, you'll look solely at the vsFTP server. The **lftp** client was examined in Chapter 1, and other FTP servers are not supported on RHEL 5.

Installing the Very Secure FTP Server

The only FTP server included with RHEL is vsFTP. If it isn't already installed, you could use a GUI tool to install it. But the simplest method, based on a proper connection to the Red Hat Network or a rebuild repository, is with the following command:

```
# yum install vsftpd
```

In the following sections, I'll show you how to start the vsFTP service the next time you reboot your computer, how it's already configured by default, and how to secure it by user. If you want to limit access to vsFTP by computer or network, you can use the tcp_wrappers system (which works even though vsFTP is not an inetd service), a firewall, or even SELinux, as described in Chapter 15.

Configuring SELinux Support for vsFTP

There are five directives associated with making a vsFTP server work with SELinux in targeted mode:

- **allow_ftpd_anon_write** supports the writing of files to directories configured with the **public_content_rw_t** SELinux setting.

- **allow_ftpd_use_cifs** allows the use of files shared via CIFS on an FTP server.
- **allow_ftpd_use_nfs** allows the use of files shared via NFS on an FTP server.
- **ftp_is_daemon is** required for a stand-alone FTP server daemon (as opposed to an xinetd service).
- **ftp_home_directory** supports FTP read/write access to user home directories.

To set these directives, use the **setsebool** command. For example, to activate read-write access from FTP on user home directories, run the following command:

```
# setsebool -P ftp_home_directory 1
```

Starting on Reboot

Once vsFTP is installed, make sure it starts the next time you boot Linux. If it doesn't start when the person who grades your Red Hat exam reboots your computer, you may not get credit for your work configuring an FTP server.

The most straightforward way to make sure the FTP server starts the next time you boot Linux is with the **chkconfig** command. You'll need to set it to start in at least runlevels 3 and 5, with a command such as this:

```
# chkconfig vsftpd on
```

To see if the **chkconfig** command worked, use the **--list** switch:

```
# chkconfig --list vsftpd
```

If you want to start the vsFTP server, just start the service script with the following command:

```
# service vsftpd start
```

vsFTP Server Security

Despite its name, if you configure vsFTP incorrectly, you could end up providing access to the top-level root directory, with regular accounts. To start securing your system you can configure vsFTP to disable logins from regular users. You can configure vsFTP through the vsftpd.conf configuration file, in the /etc/vsftpd directory.

The commands in this file are straightforward. I urge you to read the file for yourself; the comments make many of the commands self-explanatory. You can examine a few of these commands in Table 10-3. I focus here on those commands that you might change to enhance the security of your system. The commands in the default vsftpd.conf file are just a small fraction of the commands that you can use. You can review the RHEL Deployment Guide available online at www.redhat .com/ docs/manuals/enterprise for detailed information.

| TABLE 10-3 | Some vsFTP Server Configuration Commands |

Command	Description
anonymous_enable=YES	If you don't want anonymous access, you'll have to set this to **NO**.
local_enable=YES	If you don't want regular users to log in, comment this out by adding a pound (#) character at the beginning of the line.
write_enable=YES	If you don't want remote users writing to your directories, comment out this command.
#chroot_list_enable=YES	If you set **chroot_local_user=YES** (see the discussion that follows), you can configure users who are allowed to roam through your directories by activating this command.
pam_service_name=vsftpd	Configures Pluggable Authentication Modules (PAM) security. For more information, see Chapter 6.
userlist_enable=YES	Don't change this! This keeps users such as root from logging into your system.
tcp_wrappers=YES	Supports the use of security commands in /etc/hosts.allow and /etc/hosts .deny. See Chapter 15.

By default, vsFTP is configured to disable logins from sensitive users such as root, bin, and mail. The **userlist_enable=YES** command points to a list of disabled users in /etc/vsftpd/user_list. As vsFTP also uses Pluggable Authentication Modules (PAM) for security, it also disables the users in /etc/vsftpd/ftpusers. The lists of users in the default versions of these files are identical.

If you want regular users to log into your FTP server, you should add the **chroot_ local_user=YES** directive. This helps secure your system by keeping regular users from navigating to your top-level root directory (/).

on the **Job**

If you set chroot_local_user=YES, be careful. Red Hat documentation suggests security issues related to users who can upload to the server; one risk is loading scripts that allow root-level access.

A couple of useful features for users help welcome them to your server. The following command provides a message for users who are logging into your system:

```
ftpd_banner=Welcome to blah FTP service
```

This next message looks for a .message file in each directory and sends it to the client:

```
dirmessage_enable=YES
```

Unfortunately, these messages don't work for users who log into your system using a client such as **lftp**.

Access by root and many service users is disabled by default. If you try to log in as root using **lftp**, it will look like you're connected. But when you try to do something as root, you'll see messages delaying your commands "before reconnect."

EXERCISE 10-3

Configuring a Basic vsFTP Server

In this exercise, you'll install and activate a basic vsFTP server on your RHEL system. Ideally, you should also have a second computer, but this isn't absolutely necessary here. This exercise assumes that you've at least configured FTP access through any existing firewall. If you've enabled SELinux, and want to support an FTP server just for downloads, you'll also need to modify SELinux policies to "Allow Ftpd To Run Directly Without Inetd" and "Allow Ftpd To Read/Write Files In The User Home Directories", which corresponds to the boolean **ftp_is_daemon** and **ftp_home_dir** options described earlier. For more information on using the SELinux Management Tool, see Chapter 15.

1. Check your system to determine whether the vsFTP server is installed. The easiest way is with the following command:

   ```
   # rpm -q vsftpd
   ```

2. If it isn't already installed, use the techniques discussed earlier to install the vsFTP RPM package.

3. Activate the vsFTP server with the **service vsftpd start** command.

4. Make sure this server is automatically activated the next time you boot Linux with the following command:

   ```
   # chkconfig vsftpd on
   ```

5. Log into the vsFTP server as a regular user. You should preferably log in from a remote computer.

6. Once you're logged in, run the **cd ..** command twice (remember the space between the command and the two dots). Explore the local directory. You should see a danger here, as this is the root directory for the FTP server computer.

7. Close the FTP client session.

8. If you're concerned about the security issues, deactivate the vsFTP server. The best way to secure your system from FTP-based attacks is to uninstall the vsFTP server. However, if you need a vsFTP server, work with the lab at the end of the chapter.

CERTIFICATION OBJECTIVE 10.04

Samba Services

Microsoft's CIFS was built on the Server Message Block (SMB) protocol. SMB was developed in the 1980s by IBM, Microsoft, and Intel as a way to share files and printers over a network.

As Microsoft has developed SMB into CIFS, the Samba developers have upgraded Samba accordingly. Samba services provide a stable, reliable, fast, and highly compatible file and print sharing service that allows your computer to act as a client, a member server, or even a Primary Domain Controller (PDC) or a member of an Active Directory (AD) service on Microsoft-based networks. While Samba does not include every feature built into the latest Microsoft networks, I have confidence that it will in the near future.

on the
job

I look forward to the release of Samba 4.0, which will make it possible for Linux to act as an AD controller on a Microsoft-based network. However, I don't believe you will see Samba 4.0 in Red Hat distributions until RHEL 6 is released.

SMB network communication over a Microsoft-based network is also known as NetBIOS over TCP/IP. Through the collective works of Andrew Tridgell and the Samba team, Linux systems provide transparent and reliable SMB support over TCP/IP via a package known as Samba. You can do four basic things with Samba:

- Share a Linux directory tree with Windows and Linux/Unix computers
- Share a Windows directory with Linux/Unix computers
- Share a Linux printer with Windows and Linux/Unix computers
- Share a Windows printer with Linux/Unix computers

Samba emulates many of the advanced network features and functions associated with the Win9x/Me and NT/2000/XP/2003/Vista operating systems through the SMB protocol. Complete information can be found at the official Samba Web site at www.samba.org. It is easy to configure Samba to do a number of things on a Microsoft-based network. Here are some examples:

- Participate in a Microsoft Windows 9x–style workgroup or an NT/2000/XP/2003 domain as a client, member server, or even a PDC.Share user home directories.

- Act as a WINS (Windows Internet Name Service) client or server.
- Link to or manage a workgroup browse service.
- Act as a master browser.
- Provide user/password and share security databases locally, from another Samba server or from a Microsoft NT 4 PDC.
- Configure local directories as shared SMB filesystems.
- Synchronize passwords between Windows and Linux systems.
- Support Microsoft Access Control Lists.

Samba can do more, but you get the idea. Samba features are configured through one very big file, smb.conf, in the /etc/samba directory. As this file may intimidate some users, Red Hat's Samba Server Configuration tool (**system-config-samba**) provides an easier interface. RHEL 5 does not include the Samba Web Administration Tool, so don't expect it to be available on the Red Hat exams.

exam
Watch

I believe that Red Hat's Samba Server Configuration utility is an effective tool. But if you know how to edit the /etc/samba/smb.conf configuration file in a text editor, you're more likely to have time to configure the other elements you need to pass the exam. But don't be afraid to use the method that is fastest for you.

Installing Samba Services

If you selected the Windows File Server package group when you installed RHEL 5, the Samba RPM packages should already be installed. These are the four Samba RPM packages that you need:

- The samba RPM package includes the basic SMB server software for sharing files and printers.
- The samba-client RPM package provides the utilities needed to connect to shares from Microsoft computers.
- The system-config-samba package installs the Red Hat Samba Server Configuration utility.
- The samba-common RPM package contains common Samba configuration files.

It's easy to start the Samba Server Configuration tool. You can do so from a command line interface in the GUI with the **system-config-samba** command. Alternatively, you can choose System (or KDE Main Menu) | Administration | Server Settings | Samba. Either command opens the utility shown in Figure 10-3.

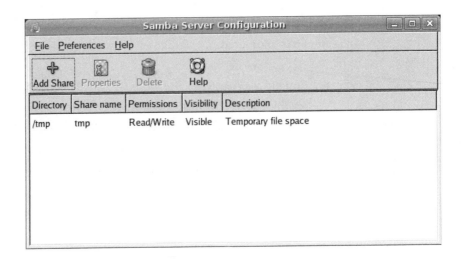

Configuring SELinux Support for Samba

There are four directives associated with making a Samba server work with SELinux in targeted mode:

- **allow_smb_anon_write** supports the writing of files to directories configured with the **public_content_rw_t** SELinux setting.
- **samba_enable_home_dirs** allows Samba to share users' home directories.
- **samba_share_nfs** allows Samba to share directories already shared via NFS.
- **use_samba_home_dirs** supports remote access to local home directories using Samba.

To set these directives, use the **setsebool** command. For example, to allow Samba to share local home directories with others on the network, run the following command:

```
# setsebool -P samba_enable_home_dirs 1
```

Configuring Samba to Start

Configuring Samba to start when Linux boots is a straightforward process. Configure Samba to start in at least runlevels 3 and 5, and then start the Samba server. The following two commands activate Samba in runlevels 2, 3, 4, and 5, and start the service:

```
# chkconfig smb on
# service smb start
```

Some Samba Background

Samba services provide interoperability between Microsoft Windows and Linux/Unix computers. Before you begin configuring Samba, you need a basic understanding of how Microsoft Windows networking works with TCP/IP.

The original Microsoft Windows networks were configured with computer host names, known as NetBIOS names, limited to 15 characters. These unique host names provided a simple, flat host name system for the computers on a LAN. All computer identification requests were made through broadcasts. This overall network transport system is known as NetBEUI, which is not "routable." In other words, it does not allow communication between two different LANs. As a result, the original Microsoft-based PC networks were limited in size to 255 nodes.

While Microsoft networks could use the Novell IPX/SPX protocol stack to route messages between networks, that was not enough. As the Internet grew, so did the dominance of TCP/IP. Microsoft adapted its NetBIOS system to TCP/IP with SMB. Since Microsoft published SMB as an industry-wide standard, anyone could set up their own service to work with SMB. As Microsoft has moved toward CIFS, Samba developers have adapted well. But some fairly recent changes have affected the configuration file as well as the main command line client **mount** command.

One of the nice features of Windows networks is the browser service. All computers register their NetBIOS names with one "elected" master browser, the keeper of the database of network-wide services. In fact, a browse database is maintained by some elected host for every protocol running on the network. For instance, if the NetBEUI, IPX/SPX, and TCP/IP protocols were installed on a host, then three duplicate browse databases were required—one per protocol—as the services available may differ between protocols.

Name Resolution: WINS

WINS was designed as a dynamic, centralized, and robust service. It was supposed to become a viable alternative to DNS. Each WINS server maintained a central database with multiple records for all machines. On a large network, this was a big datafile.

WINS needs about three to ten data records for each computer. Naturally, this is cumbersome for larger networks. This is another reason why Microsoft is phasing out WINS.

What About Samba?

This is where Samba fits in. Samba on Linux provides all the Windows networking services available on any Windows TCP/IP client or server. To configure Samba, you simply need to know the name of your NT/2000/XP/2003/Vista domain or workgroup and configure the parameters accordingly for your Linux workstation or server to match the settings on the local Microsoft network.

Fortunately, Samba comes with extensive online documentation (with examples) available in the smb.conf configuration file. The following lists some of the key Samba commands and files:

```
/usr/sbin/smbd        - main SMB service daemon
/usr/sbin/nmbd        - NetBIOS name service daemon
/etc/samba/smb.conf   - SAMBA's primary configuration file
/usr/bin/smbclient    - connects to SMB shares, ftp-like syntax
/sbin/mount.cifs      - mounts SMB shares on a designated directory
/sbin/umount.cifs     - unmounts a SMB shared directory
/usr/bin/testparm     - tests validity of /etc/samba/smb.conf file
/etc/init.d/smb       - daemon start and stop control script
cifs                  - file system extension to mount SMB shares on
                        directories; use with the mount -t command.
/usr/bin/smbprint     - a script to print to a printer on an SMB host
/usr/bin/smbstatus    - lists current SMB connections for the local host
```

Samba Has Two Daemons

You need two daemons to run Samba: **smbd** and **nmbd**, both located in /usr/sbin. Both are configured through the /etc/samba/smb.conf configuration file. It's easy to check the syntax of this large configuration file with the **testparm** command. If problems arise, this program produces error messages to help you correct them.

Configuring Samba as a Client

You can configure two types of clients through Samba. One connects to directories shared from Microsoft Windows servers or Samba servers on Linux/Unix. The second connects to shared printers from one of the same two types of servers.

When you have installed the samba-client RPM package, you've installed the Samba client commands that you need to find browse lists and mount shared directories locally.

Checking Samba File and Print Services

If you want to browse shared directories from a Linux computer, you should know how to use **smbclient**. This can help you test connectivity to any SMB host on a Windows- or Samba-based Linux/Unix computer. You can use **smbclient** to check the shared directories and printers from remote computers on your network. For example, the **smbclient** command shown in Figure 10-4 checks shared directories and printers from a remote Linux-based Samba PDC.

FIGURE 10-4

List of shared
directories and
printers from a
remote PDC

```
[michael@enterprise5fc6d ~]$ smbclient -L enterprise5fc6d -U michael
Password:
Domain=[ENTERPRISE5FC6D] OS=[Unix] Server=[Samba 3.0.23c-2]

        Sharename      Type      Comment
        ---------      ----      -------
        IPC$           IPC       IPC Service (Samba PDC Server)
        backups        Disk      Laptop Backups
        OfficeSpace    Disk      Office Space Files
        tmp            Disk      Temporary file space
        HPLaserJet4b   Printer   The other HP Laser Jet Printer
        HPLaserJet4    Printer   Printer in the Office
        HP1200         Printer   Color Printer Downstairs
        michael        Disk      Home Directories
Domain=[ENTERPRISE5FC6D] OS=[Unix] Server=[Samba 3.0.23c-2]

        Server                   Comment
        ---------                -------

        Workgroup                Master
        ---------                -------
        THEDOMAIN                ENTERPRISE5FC6D
        WORKGROUP                POOHBEAR
[michael@enterprise5fc6d ~]$ █
```

As you can see in the figure, I've specified two arguments with the **smbclient** command: **-L** allows you to specify the name of the Samba server, and **-U** allows you to specify a username on the remote computer. When the command reaches the Samba server, you're prompted for the appropriate password.

Alternatively, you can browse shared Samba directories using the graphical Nautilus client. In the GNOME desktop, choose Places | Home Folder. This opens the Nautilus file manager with a list of files in your home directory. Press CTRL-L and then, in the Location text box, enter **smb:///**.

If you're connected to a network with Windows and/or Samba-enabled Linux computers, you'll see an icon associated with connected workgroups and/or domains. Click the workgroup or domain of your choice. You should see a list of Windows and Samba-enabled Linux computers on that workgroup or domain.

Select the computer of your choice. You'll be prompted for a username and password on the remote computer. Once entered, you'll see a list of shared directories, as shown in Figure 10-5.

Mounting Shared Samba Directories During Login

You can also configure automated mounting during the login process. Earlier in this chapter, you saw how to configure connections to shared NFS directories. You can use the same process with shared Samba directories.

There's one drawback: unless you're willing to add the shared directory to your /etc/fstab file, or you're limiting yourself to the root user, you can't use the **mount**

FIGURE 10-5

Browsing remote
shared directories

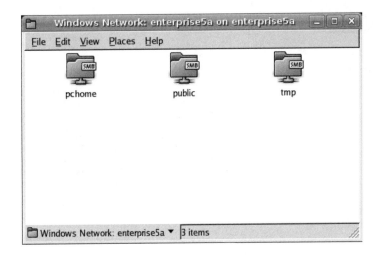

command. There are other options: the **mount.cifs** and **umount.cifs** commands. Once you've set them up to be executable with the following commands, you can add them to each individual user's .bashrc and .bash_logout files:

```
# chmod u+s /sbin/mount.cifs
# chmod u+s /sbin/umount.cifs
```

on the **Ĵob**

The smbmount and smbumount commands are not available for RHEL 5; they have been replaced by mount.cifs and umount.cifs.

These commands set the SUID bit, which is described briefly in Chapter 1 and used in Chapter 4. Once the SUID bit is set, regular users mount shared Samba directories. For example, if you want to mount and unmount a share named tmp from a computer named enterprise5a on the test directory, you can do so with the following commands:

```
$ /sbin/mount.cifs //enterprise5a/tmp test -o username=michael
$ /sbin/umount.cifs test
```

With the first command, you're prompted for a password for user michael on the computer named enterprise5a. Alternatively, if user michael's password is a2b3c4d5, you could use the following command:

```
$ /sbin/mount.cifs //enterprise5a/tmp  test -o username=michael%a2b3c4d5
```

Once you've verified that the selected **mount.cifs** and **umount.cifs** commands work, you can add these commands to the user's .bashrc and .bash_logout files.

Alternatively, if your users log in through GNOME, you can set up the same **mount** command through the Sessions utility. As discussed in Chapter 14, you can start this utility by choosing System | Preferences | More Preferences | Sessions. Figure 10-6 illustrates the preceding command, with a password, added to the graphical startup programs list for the root user. Obviously, clear text passwords are not secure.

Client Configuration for Print Services

There is a simple option line in the /etc/samba/smb.conf file that shares all local printer systems as if this were another Windows host.

In /etc/samba/smb.conf, printer configurations start with the section heading **[printers]**. Using the same share options used for directories, Samba can create a shared print service for each installed print queue. These print shares are available to Microsoft clients when users install network printers. (For more information on the **[printers]** share, see the next section.)

Once the printers are shared, you can use a service such as CUPS to connect to them. In fact, you learned how this was done with the Red Hat Printer Configuration utility in Chapter 7.

Configuring a Samba Server

If you want to configure a Samba server, you'll need to edit the main Samba configuration file, /etc/samba/smb.conf. This file is long and includes a number of commands that require a good understanding of Microsoft Windows networking. Fortunately, the default version of this file also includes helpful documentation with suggestions and example configurations that you can use.

FIGURE 10-6

Using Startup Programs to connect to a shared Samba directory

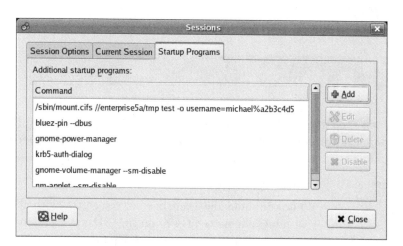

You can edit this file directly, or create directory shares using Red Hat's Samba Server Configuration utility. It's useful to study the original /etc/samba/smb.conf file. Once you see how the file is structured, back it up. Try editing the file directly. Try changing the file with the Samba Server Configuration utility (described in the next section). Test the result by restarting the Samba server with the following command:

```
# service smb restart
```

To help you with this process, I'll analyze the RHEL 5 version of this file. The code shown next is essentially a complete view of this file. I've replaced the comments in the file with my own explanations. You might want to browse your own /etc/samba/smb.conf file as well.

The smb.conf file includes two types of comment lines. The hash symbol (#) is used for a general text comment. This is typically verbiage that describes a feature. The second comment symbol is the semicolon (;), used to comment out Samba directives (which you may later wish to uncomment to enable the disabled feature).

(Note that the physical dimensions of this book limit the lengths of lines of code. In a few cases, I've modified the code lines slightly to meet this limitation, without changing the intent of any command in this configuration file. Some comments I've left out with a **<comments deleted>** label.)

```
# This is the main Samba configuration file. You should read the
# smb.conf(5) manual page in order to understand the options listed
# here. Samba has a huge number of configurable options (perhaps
# too many!) most of which are not shown in this example.
#
# <comments deleted>
# NOTE: Whenever you modify this file you should run the command
# "testparm" to check that you have not made any basic syntactic
# errors.
```

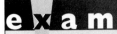

exam

Watch *As stated in the Red Hat Exam Prep guide, RHCEs must be able to configure various services, including Samba,* *for basic operation. I go into detail on the smb.conf file that, in my opinion, goes beyond basic operation.*

Global Settings

While you should be aware of what you can do with all the different global settings, you should change as little as possible. The less you change, the less can go wrong. Perfect configuration files are not required. Configuration files that meet the specific requirements of your exam are.

In smb.conf, the global settings, which define the overall attributes of your server, follow the first set of comments. This section starts with the following two lines:

```
#======================= Global Settings ============================
[global]
```

Now examine the critical global settings. First, with respect to the **workgroup** variable, this Samba server will become a member of that Microsoft workgroup or domain. The default Samba **workgroup** is **WORKGROUP**. If you know Microsoft Windows, you'll recognize it as the old name of the default peer-to-peer workgroup. The same variable is used if you're joining this computer to a Microsoft-style domain.

```
# workgroup = NT-Domain-Name or Workgroup-Name, eg: MIDEARTH
    workgroup = MYGROUP
```

While not included in the default version of smb.conf, it's a good idea to add a NetBIOS name for your computer to this file. This becomes what other clients see in network browse lists such as those shown from Network Neighborhood/My Network Places and the **smbclient** command. The command that follows becomes the comment shown with the browse list:

```
# local computer NetBIOS name
    netbios name = enterprise5a
# server string is the equivalent of the NT Description field
    server string = Samba Server
```

The **security** command may be a bit confusing. This command means that connections check the local password database. It is appropriate if you're configuring this computer as a Domain Controller (DC), specifically a PDC.

```
security = user
```

If you want to configure this computer as a member server on a domain, use a password database from a DC. Strangely enough, in that case, you would substitute the following command:

```
security = domain
```

on the
job

If you want to set up this computer as a workstation that happens to share directories on a Microsoft domain, you'll need to set up the computer as a member server on that domain.

If you're configuring this system as a member server on an Active Directory domain, you'd substitute the following command:

```
security = ads
```

Alternatively, if you just want to use a database from another computer that is not a DC, you'd substitute the following command:

```
security = server
```

Finally, if you're configuring this computer on a peer-to-peer workgroup, you want to substitute the following command:

```
security = share
```

To summarize, there are five basic authentication options: **share**, **user**, **server**, **domain**, and **ads**.

Now, refocus this directive on the authentication database. The default is **security = user**; in this case, make sure the Samba usernames and passwords that you create match those on individual Windows NT/2000/XP/Vista systems on your network.

If you use the **server** authentication option, you can name another Samba server to carry the database of usernames and passwords.

If you use the **domain** authentication option, you can name an NT/2000/2003/ Vista domain controller. You can set up a Samba server as a domain controller as well, emulating the functionality of a Windows domain controller.

on the Job

*With Samba version 3.x, you can configure a Samba-enabled Linux computer as a member server on an Active Directory network. If that's what you want, set up **security = ads**.*

If you activate the **hosts allow** directive, you can limit access to the specified network. The following default would limit access to the networks with the 192.168.1.0 and 192.168.2.0 network IP addresses, as well as the local computer (127.):

```
;   hosts allow = 192.168.1. 192.168.2. 127.
```

These default printer settings are required to share printers from this Samba server, loading printers as defined by **printcap name = /etc/printcap**. If you've configured an LPD-based print server, consider the **printcap name = lpstat** directive. You shouldn't need to activate the **printing = cups** directive. The **cups options = raw** directive means that print jobs are already processed by the CUPS service.

```
    load printers = yes
    printcap name = /etc/printcap
;   printing = cups
cups options = raw
```

If you want to configure a special guest account, you can activate this command, as long as you add a pcguest user with the **useradd** command described in Chapter 6.

```
;   guest account = pcguest
```

The next command sets up separate log files for every computer that connects to this Samba server. For example, if a computer named allaccess connects to this Samba server, you can find a log of its access problems in /var/log/samba/allaccess .log. By default, the log file is limited to 50Kb.

```
log file = /var/log/samba/%m.log
max log size = 50
```

If you've set up **security = domain** or **share**, you'll also want to activate the following directive and add the name of the password server (replace with a * to have Samba search for the password server):

```
;    password server = <NT-Server-Name>
```

If you've set up **security = ads**, you'll also want to activate the following directive to specify the Active Directory (AD) realm, substituting your actual AD realm for **MY_REALM**:

```
;    realm = MY_REALM
```

For a local password database, there are three options for the **passdb backend** directive. The default is still the smbpasswd file in /etc/samba, which is discussed later in this section, and is what Samba looks for unless you activate the following directive. Options include the so-called Trivial Database (tdbsam), and a LDAP database (ldapsam).

```
;  passdb backend = tdbsam
```

You can customize the local Samba configuration by the computer (machine) client that connects by activating the following command. Configuring these computer-specific command files is complex and I suspect beyond configuring "the service for basic operation." The file suggested in the comment does not exist; I suggest /etc/samba/smb.conf.%m instead.

```
;    include = /usr/local/samba/lib/smb.conf.%m
```

If your computer is connected to more than one network, you can specify the networks served by your Samba server here:

```
;    interfaces = 192.168.12.2/24 192.168.13.2/24
```

Unless you specifically designate this computer to be a local browse master, Samba participates in browser elections like any other Microsoft Windows computer, using the **os level** that you designate. Alternatively, if you don't already have a Domain Controller acting as a browse master, you can give the responsibility to the Samba server. Or, if you just want to make it easier for the local computer to win the browser election, activate the **preferred master** command:

```
;    local master = no
;    os level = 33
```

```
;       domain master = yes
;       preferred master = yes
```

If you have Windows 95 computers on your network, activate the following command, as many Windows 95 computers (pre-OSR2) can't handle encryption:

```
;       domain logons = yes
```

The following commands set up Microsoft command line batch files by computer and user. The command afterward stores Microsoft user profiles on the local Samba server. That means these commands can't be tested on the Red Hat exams unless you have access to a Microsoft Windows computer. Since I can't tell you what's on the Red Hat exams, I can only ask you whether Red Hat would want separate Microsoft Windows computers available during their exams.

```
;       logon script = %m.bat
;       logon script = %U.bat
;       logon path = \\%L\Profiles\%U
```

If you activate the following command, Samba activates a WINS server on the local computer:

```
;       wins support = yes
```

Alternatively, you can point the local computer to a remote WINS server on the network; of course, you'd have to substitute the IP address for *w.x.y.z.*

```
;       wins server = w.x.y.z
```

If non-WINS–capable computers are on the network, such as Linux computers without the Samba server software, you can activate this command:

```
;       wins proxy = yes
```

on the
() o b

Adding Linux to a Microsoft Windows NT/2000/2003/Vista network can be made easier by configuring the Samba service to look like another Windows host on the network. You can configure the Samba server to act as a WINS client of the WINS server, share files and printers just like all the other Windows hosts, and participate in the browser service.

If you change this setting to **yes**, name searches can go through available DNS databases:

```
dns proxy = no
```

The remaining commands are fairly self-explanatory, as scripts which add and delete users, groups, and machine accounts.

```
;    add user script = /usr/sbin/useradd %u
;    add group script = /usr/sbin/groupadd %g
;    add machine script = /usr/sbin/adduser -n -g \
       machines -c Machine -d /dev/null -s /bin/false %u
;    delete user script = /usr/sbin/userdel %u
;    delete user from group script = /usr/sbin/deluser %u %g
;    delete group script = /usr/sbin/groupdel %g
```

on the
job

If you want to set up a Samba server to use a Microsoft Windows database of usernames and passwords, you'll need to activate the winbindd daemon. With the appropriate commands in smb.conf, you can also set up Microsoft users and groups with the UIDs and GIDs of your choice on your Linux system.

Share Settings

Share settings are organized into *stanzas*, which are groups of commands associated with a share name. (*Stanza* doesn't seem like a technical term, but some believe that well-constructed configuration code is like good poetry.) The first four lines in this section define the **[homes]** share, which automatically shares the home directory of the logged-in user. Every user gets access to their own home directory; the **browseable = no** command keeps users away from each other's home directory.

There is no default /homes directory. It's just a label. You don't need to supply a home directory, because Samba will read the user's account record in /etc/passwd to determine the directory to be shared.

By default, this does not allow access to unknown users (**guest ok = no**). If you prefer, you can limit the systems that can use this share (**hosts allow = ?**, and **hosts deny = ?**). The effects of the **hosts allow** and **hosts deny** directives are as described earlier but are limited to the stanza where they are used.

```
#============================= Share Definitions =============
[homes]
    comment = Home Directories
    browseable = no
    writable = yes
```

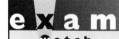

exam

Watch   *If you forget the meaning of a specific Samba variable, you can find information in the Samba man page; just run the man smb.conf command.*

If you activate the commands in the following stanza, you can set up a **[netlogon]** share for Microsoft Windows workstations. As there are no **[netlogon]** shares even for Samba-enabled Linux workstations, this section requires a Microsoft Windows computer to verify functionality. If you believe that you'll have access to a Microsoft Windows computer during the Red Hat exams, you should study this section carefully.

```
# Un-comment the following and create the netlogon directory for
# Domain Logons
; [netlogon]
;    comment = Network Logon Service
;    path = /usr/local/samba/lib/netlogon
;    guest ok = yes
;    writable = no
;    share modes = no
```

This next stanza configures profiles for Microsoft Windows workstations. As these profiles become a part of a Microsoft Windows registry when you log on to one of those workstations, you're unlikely to configure this section in a network of Linux-only computers. Make your own judgment on whether you might have to configure this section during the RHCE exam.

```
# Un-comment the following to provide a specific roving profile
# share; the default is to use the user's home directory
;[Profiles]
;    path = /usr/local/samba/profiles
;    browseable = no
;    guest ok = yes
```

The **[printers]** stanza normally works as is, to allow access by all users with accounts on your computer or domain. If you want to limit access to specific users, review the **[fredsprn]** stanza later in this default file. While the spool directory (/usr/spool/samba) is not browsable, the associated printers are browsable by their NetBIOS names. In fact, the spool directory doesn't even exist; you should change it to /var/spool/samba. When you configure a printer later in this chapter, the name you designate automatically becomes the NetBIOS name.

```
# NOTE: If you have a BSD-style print system there is no need to
# specifically define each individual printer
[printers]
    comment = All Printers
    path = /usr/spool/samba
    browseable = no
# Set public = yes to allow user 'guest account' to print
    guest ok = no
    writable = no
    printable = yes
```

If you activate the **[tmp]** share, it's a standard location for people to download and share files; all users get write access to this share.

```
# This one is useful for people to share files
;[tmp]
;    comment = Temporary file space
;    path = /tmp
;    read only = no
;    public = yes
```

The following stanza, as suggested by the comment, configures the /home/samba directory to be shared by the group named staff. You can configure this group in /etc/group or through the Network Information Service (Chapter 6). And you need to configure special ownership and permissions for /home/samba, as described in the User Private Group model, also in Chapter 6.

```
# A publicly accessible directory, but read only, except for
# people in the "staff" group
;[public]
;    comment = Public Stuff
;    path = /home/samba
;    public = yes
;    writable = yes
;    printable = no
;    write list = @staff
```

If you activate the following stanza, it would configure a printer exclusively for one user. The default smb.conf file has an error; it lists the path to Fred's home directory as /homes/fred. (Of course, it should be /home/fred.)

```
# A private printer, usable only by fred. Spool data will be
# placed in fred's home directory. Note that fred must have
# write access to the spool directory,
# wherever it is.
;[fredsprn]
;    comment = Fred's Printer
;    valid users = fred
;    path = /homes/fred
;    printer = freds_printer
;    public = no
;    writable = no
;    printable = yes
```

This stanza configures a directory for Fred's exclusive use. If you need to limit printer use to specific users, these directives can help. A better location for the **path**, which you need to create, is within the /home directory.

```
# A private directory, usable only by fred. Note that fred
# requires write access to the directory.
```

```
; [fredsdir]
;    comment = Fred's Service
;    path = /usr/somewhere/private
;    valid users = fred
;    public = no
;    writable = yes
;    printable = no
```

You can also set up directories by workstation; the **%m** variable is replaced by the name of the computer (machine) that connects to the Samba server. In my opinion, a better location for the path is the /home/pc/%m directory.

```
# The %m gets replaced with the machine name that is connecting.
; [pchome]
;    comment = PC Directories
;    path = /usr/pc/%m
;    public = no
;    writable = yes
```

The following stanza is slightly different from the **[tmp]** share. Once connected, the only user that connects is a guest. Unless you've configured a guest user, this defaults to the user named nobody.

```
# A publicly accessible directory, read/write to all users. Note
# that all files created in the directory by users will be owned
# by the default user, so any user with access can delete any
# other user's files. Obviously this directory must be writable
# by the default user. Another user could of course be specified,
# in which case all files would be owned by that user instead.
; [public]
;    path = /usr/somewhere/else/public
;    public = yes
;    only guest = yes
;    writable = yes
;    printable = no
```

Finally, this is another variation on the User Private Group scheme, which creates a group directory. Unlike the **[public]** stanza, this share is private.

```
# The following two entries demonstrate how to share a directory so
# that two users can place files there that will be owned by the
# specific users. In this setup, the directory should be writable
# by both users and should have the sticky bit set on it to prevent
# abuse. Obviously this could be extended to as many users as required.
; [myshare]
;    comment = Mary's and Fred's stuff
;    path = /usr/somewhere/shared
```

```
;    valid users = mary fred
;    public = no
;    writable = yes
;    printable = no
;    create mask = 0765
```

To summarize, the settings for each shared directory start with a section name, such as **[tmp]**. This section name contains the name that will be seen by Microsoft clients only if the service is set to be browsable (**browseable = yes**).

*There are a number of variables in smb.conf that are not spelled correctly, such as **browseable**. In many cases, the correct spelling (browsable) also works. They are still accepted Samba variables and generally should be spelled per the Samba defaults, not standard written English.*

Joining a Domain

If you've configured a Samba server, and it's not the DC for your network, you'll need to set it to join the domain. Essentially, you're configuring an account on the DC for the network. As long as there's one domain on this network, it's easy to do with the following command:

```
# net rpc join -U root
```

(If you have more than one domain, substitute the name of the controller for *DC* in the **net rpc join -S DC -U root** command.) This assumes that root is the administrative user on the DC; if you're joining a domain governed by a Microsoft Windows computer, the administrative user is *administrator*. If successful, you're prompted for the root password on the remote DC. An account for the local computer is added to the DC's user database in /etc/passwd.

Configuring Samba Users

You could set up identical usernames and passwords for your Microsoft Windows and Samba-enabled Linux computers. However, this is not always possible, especially when there are preexisting databases. In that case, set up a database of Samba users and passwords that correspond to current Microsoft usernames and passwords on your network. A template is available in /etc/samba/smbusers.

If you're comfortable with the command line interface, the quickest way to set up Samba users is with the **smbpasswd** command. Remember that you can create a new Samba user only from valid accounts on your Linux computer.

Managing Samba Users

You can set up Samba users on a list independent from your Linux users who have accounts on your Linux system. The Samba development team chose to do this for the following reasons:

- There is no reason to grant Samba access to all Linux users.
- You may wish to manage user access via some form of Microsoft Windows, so Linux wouldn't necessarily even know about your Samba users.
- Samba user authentication may involve clear text passwords (for compatibility with Windows 95 and Windows 3.1). This could potentially compromise your Linux system.

To support these features, you can set up separate user accounts in the /etc/samba directory, in the smbusers and smbpasswd files. Two steps are required to make and enable a new Samba user:

1. Create a Samba user entry by name and add a password for the user. Samba users can be created only from the current users on your Linux system.

2. Enable Samba access for the new user.

If the username that you want does not yet exist, create it with the **useradd** *username* command. Then you can set that user up as a Samba user with the **smbpasswd** command. Use the following command; you're prompted to enter a password. That password can be different from the password used to log in directly to that Linux computer.

```
# smbpasswd -a newUser
New SMB password:
Retype SMB password:
#
```

Changes made by **smbpasswd** are passed to the Samba server to be copied to the system with the username and password database for your network.

If you've configured Samba as a DC for your network, the /etc/passwd file should govern the basic usernames and passwords for your system. You can use the **mksmbpasswd.sh** script in the /user/bin/ directory to add all passwords to the /etc/samba/smbpasswd configuration file.

The **smbpasswd** command is powerful; it includes a number of switches that you should learn, as described in Table 10-4.

TABLE 10-4 Various **smbpasswd** Commands

smbpasswd Switch	Description
-a *username*	Adds the specified *username* to /etc/samba/smbpasswd.
-d *username*	Disables the specified *username*; thus disables that password from Microsoft networking.
-e *username*	Enables the specified *username*; opposite of **-d**.
-r *computername*	Allows you to change your Windows or Samba password on a remote computer. Normally goes with **-U**.
-U *username*	Normally changes the *username* on a remote computer, if specified with the **-r** switch.
-x *username*	Deletes the specified *username* from /etc/samba/smbpasswd.

If you need to configure different usernames and passwords for your Linux and Microsoft computers, you'll need to edit them directly into the /etc/samba/smbusers file—or you can use the Samba Server Configuration utility.

EXERCISE 10-4

Using Home Directories

In this exercise, you'll learn about the basic home directory share. You'll need at least two computers, one of which should be a Samba server. The other can be a Linux or Microsoft Windows workstation. You'll connect to the Samba server from the workstation and access the files in your home directory on the Samba server.

1. Install and configure Samba to start using the methods described earlier in this chapter.

2. Open the /etc/samba/smb.conf configuration file. Look for the current value of **workgroup**.

3. Make sure that the computers on your network have the same value for **workgroup**. If your computer is on a domain, set **workgroup** to the name of the domain. If you don't already have a WINS server on this network, you'll also want to activate the **wins support = yes** command.

4. Test the syntax of your Samba configuration file with the **testparm** command (I'll describe how this works shortly).

5. Read and address any problems that you might see in the output from the **testparm** command. Fix any syntax problems with your smb.conf configuration file.

6. Set up the root user on the server in the Samba database with the following command (enter an appropriate password when prompted):

   ```
   # smbpasswd -a root
   ```

7. Make Samba reread the smb.conf file with the following command:

   ```
   # service smb reload
   ```

8. Now go to a remote Linux or Microsoft Windows workstation on the same domain or workgroup.

9. If you can browse the list of computers from the Samba server with the following command, browsing and probably WINS is working properly. (Alternatively, from a Microsoft Windows computer, you should see a list of computers in the Network Neighborhood or My Network Places window.) Substitute the name of the configured computer for *sambaserver*.

   ```
   # smbclient -L sambaserver -U root
   ```

10. Enter the root username on the remote Samba server.

11. If you're on a Linux computer, use the **/sbin/mount.cifs** or **mount** command (depending on whether you're regular or a root user) to configure the remote [homes] directory share on an empty local directory. For example, as the root user, you could mount on the local /share directory (create it if required) with the following command:

    ```
    # mount -o username=root "//sambaserver/homes" /share
    ```

12. Test the result. Can you browse your home directory on the remote computer?

Think about this a bit. Do you really want to allow access to the administrative account over the network via Samba? What happens when you disable the administrative password in /etc/samba/smbpasswd? Look up the **invalid users** directive in the man page for smb.conf; could that help?

The Red Hat Samba Server Configuration Utility

RHEL includes Red Hat's graphical configuration tool for Samba, **system-config-samba**, which you can install from the RPM of the same name. Before you use this tool to modify your configuration, back up the files in your /etc/samba directory.

Also known as the Samba Server Configuration utility, you can use this tool to set basic global parameters and configure shared directories. You can start it from a GUI command line with the **system-config-samba** command, or you can choose System (or KDE Main Menu) | Administration | Server Settings | Samba. You saw the basic tool back in Figure 10-3.

This tool is straightforward. You can configure general Samba directives such as **security level** and **workgroup** through the Preferences | Server Settings command. The Add button enables you to set up a new share.

You can also use this tool to configure Samba usernames and passwords. In other words, you can use this tool to configure your smb.conf file as well as Samba usernames and passwords through the smbusers and smbpasswd files in the /etc/samba directory.

There are drawbacks to the Samba Server Configuration utility. For example, you can't use it to edit all global parameters or share printers. You can't use it to set a Samba member server to join a domain.

Global Settings

To see what the Samba Server Configuration utility can do to the global settings in the smb.conf configuration file, choose Preferences | Server Settings. As you can probably guess from Figure 10-7, the basic settings set the **workgroup** and **server string** directives.

When you use this utility and assign default variables, it erases the variable from your smb.conf file. For example, if you set the **workgroup** name to **WORKGROUP**, this utility erases the **workgroup** command line from smb.conf. Therefore, it's an excellent idea to back up smb.conf before using the Samba Server Configuration utility.

In contrast, the Security tab supports a few more settings, as you can see in Figure 10-8. The entries are fairly straightforward. If you want more information on these variables, refer to the discussion on smb.conf earlier in this chapter:

■ Authentication Mode sets the **security** value in /etc/samba/smb.conf. The default is **user**.

FIGURE 10-7

Samba Server
basic settings

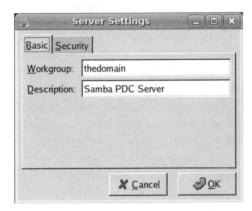

- Authentication Server sets up the location of the **password server**. There is no default.
- The Kerberos Realm is associated with an Active Directory user/password database and can be assigned only if **security = ads**.
- Encrypt Passwords is associated with the variable of the same name. The default is **yes**.
- Guest Account is associated with the variable of the same name. The default is **nobody**.

If you've selected a default, you may still see the variable in the smb.conf file in comments. Alternatively, you may see the variable in an unexpected location relative to the default comments.

FIGURE 10-8

Samba Server
security settings

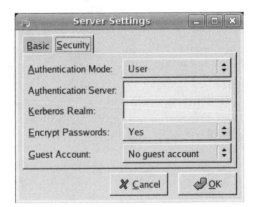

Share Settings

Click the Add Share button. This opens the Create Samba Share window shown in Figure 10-9. The Basic tab helps you define the basic parameters associated with the share:

- Directory defines the directory that you want to share, using the **path** variable.
- By default, the Share Name is taken from the last part of the directory name. For example, if you're sharing the /usr/share/to/path1, Samba designates [**path1**] as the share name. You can also assign your own share name.
- Description allows you to define the comment that users can see in the browse list.
- Basic permissions lets you set **writable** as yes or no; read only (**writable=no**) is the default. (This is another case where two spellings for the same variable are acceptable; *writeable* is also an acceptable spelling in smb.conf.) The **visible** option, if activated, makes the share browsable.

The Access tab is simpler; it allows you to limit access to specific users from the smbpasswd configuration file. In other words, you can only limit access to users from the Samba password database. Once you've clicked OK, the Samba Server Configuration tool automatically updates the smb.conf configuration file.

Samba Users

The Samba Server Configuration tool also allows you to configure Samba users, based on the users already present in your /etc/passwd configuration file. Unfortunately, it can use only local password databases as of this writing. However, that's good enough to configure Microsoft usernames on this computer. To add Samba users from the

FIGURE 10-9

Basic components of Create Samba Share

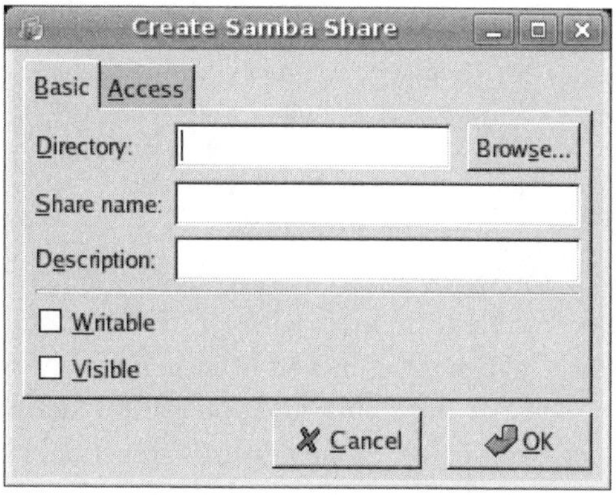

Samba Server Configuration tool, choose Preferences | Samba Users. This opens the Samba Users window shown in Figure 10-10.

As you can see, this window includes a list of currently configured Samba users. Click Add User. This opens the Create New Samba User window shown in Figure 10-11, where you can:

- Select an existing username from /etc/passwd.
- Enter the corresponding Microsoft Windows username.
- Set up a password for that Samba user. It can be different from that user's Linux password.

Click OK when you're done. Naturally, you can also change the Windows username and password for each Samba user, or even delete Samba users with the Edit User and Delete User buttons in the Samba Users window. Click OK to exit from the Samba Users window.

Creating a Public Share

Now you can create a public access share for use with the entire network. For the purpose of this chapter, create the /home/PublicShare directory. From the mail Samba Server Configuration screen, click Add Share to open the Create Samba Share window.

Enter the directory that you want to share, **/home/PublicShare**, in the Directory text box. Enter an appropriate Description, and select Writable and Visible. In the Access tab, select the Allow Access To Everyone option. Click OK, and exit from the Samba Server Configuration tool with the File | Quit command.

Now you'll have to finish the task directly from the text editor. The instructions so far add the following commands in the /etc/samba/smb.conf configuration file:

```
[PublicShare]
    comment= Shared Public Directory
    path = /home/PublicShare
    writeable = yes
    browseable = yes
    guest ok = yes
```

You may want to modify these commands. Assume the **[PublicShare]** should be accessible to all users with a Linux account on your computer. It should also deny access to guest users and others. You want to provide access to anyone in your domain (.myCompany.com), and you want to deny access to a suspect computer (say, evil .crackers.com). Finally, your shares should be browsable to valid users.

To make this happen, change the last command in this stanza. As **guest ok = no** is the default, you can just erase the **guest ok = yes** directive command or change

FIGURE 10-10

Current Samba
users

the value appropriately. To provide access to all users in the given domain, add the
following command:

```
hosts allow = .myCompany.com
```

If you wanted to deny access to one specific computer on that network, you could
add **EXCEPT evil.crackers.com** to the end of this command. Alternatively, if this
domain is on the 192.168.99.0 network, you could use one of the following commands:

```
hosts allow = 192.168.99.
hosts allow = 192.168.99.0/255.255.255.0
```

You could specifically deny access to computers with a command such as the following:

```
hosts deny = evil.crackers.com
```

Or you could substitute IP addresses in the same format as with the **hosts allow**
directive. You've defined the share attributes in the Samba smb.conf configuration
file. But you need to modify the directory associated with the share with the
following command:

```
# chmod 1777 /home/PublicShare
```

FIGURE 10-11

Creating a New
Samba User

The digit 1 in front of the 777 directory permission string is known as the "sticky bit." By enabling the sticky bit, you are saying that anyone can do anything in the directory (because of the 777 permission value) but only to files they create! Otherwise, any user could delete or rename any file in the /home/PublicShare directory, regardless of the file's owner.

Testing Changes to /etc/samba/smb.conf

After making any changes to /etc/samba/smb.conf, you should always test your system before putting it into production. You can do a simple syntax check on the Samba configuration file with the **testparm** test utility, as shown in Figure 10-12. This does not actually check to determine whether the service is running or functioning correctly; it checks only basic text syntax and command stanzas.

FIGURE 10-12

Testing smb.conf syntax

```
[root@Enterprise5a ~]# testparm | more
Load smb config files from /etc/samba/smb.conf
Processing section "[homes]"
Processing section "[printers]"
Processing section "[tmp]"
Processing section "[public]"
Processing section "[pchome]"
Loaded services file OK.
WARNING: passdb expand explicit = yes is deprecated
Server role: ROLE_STANDALONE
Press enter to see a dump of your service definitions
[global]
        workgroup = THEDOMAIN
        server string = Samba PDC Server
        log file = /var/log/samba/%m.log
        max log size = 50
        socket options = TCP_NODELAY SO_RCVBUF=8192 SO_SNDBUF=8192
        printcap name = /etc/printcap
        os level = 64
        preferred master = Yes
        domain master = Yes
        dns proxy = No
        cups options = raw

[homes]
        comment = Home Directories
        read only = No
        browseable = No

[printers]
        comment = All Printers
        path = /var/spool/samba
        printable = Yes
        browseable = No

--More--
```

EXERCISE 10-5

Configuring Samba with Shares

In this exercise, you'll configure Samba to do something useful: sharing a directory and any configured printers. For this purpose, you can't use the Samba Server Configuration tool; therefore, you'll need to edit the /etc/samba/smb.conf file directly in a text editor.

1. Install the Samba RPMs as described earlier in this chapter.

2. Create a /home/ftp/public directory. Change ownership to the ftp user and group, with full permissions (770).

3. Open the /etc/samba/smb.conf file in a text editor.

4. Configure Samba to share all installed print queues to all users. Normally the default [printers] stanza in smb.conf should suffice. But there's an error in the path directive (there is no /user/spool/samba.directory), corrected in bold. And, as you're about to create a guest account, add the last command shown here:

```
[printers]
     comment = All printers
     path = /var/spool/samba
     browseable = no
     printable = yes
     guest ok = yes
```

5. Configure Samba to share as public, in read-only mode, the /home/ftp/pub directory tree. In the Share Definitions section, you could add the following commands:

```
[pub]
     comment = shared FTP directory
     path = /home/ftp/pub
```

6. Allow guest access to all public shares. In smb.conf, this means adding the following line to the **[pub]** stanza:

```
     guest ok = yes
```

7. Since you're about to create a guest account, you'll need to activate the following command in smb.conf:

```
; guest account = pcguest
```

8. Create a guest account for pcguest, associate it with an unused UID and GID 600. (If you already have a user with this ID, substitute an unused ID number.) Set the password to be "anonymous." While you can do this with the Red Hat User Manager discussed in Chapter 6, the quickest way to do this is with the following commands:

```
# useradd pcguest -u 600
# passwd pcguest
```

9. Create separate log files for each computer host that connects. This is already active by default with the following command:

```
log file = /var/log/samba/%m.log
```

10. If you have a WINS server configured, authorize Samba to participate as a WINS client. Use the IP of that WINS server. While you don't want to enable the **wins support** command, you do want to point the **wins server** command to the IP address of your WINS server (substitute for 10.11.12.13):

```
wins server = 10.11.12.13
```

11. Write and save your changes to the smb.conf file.

12. You can see if Samba is already running with the **service smb status** command. If it's stopped, you can start it with the **service smb start** command. If it's running, you can make Samba reread your configuration file with the following command:

```
# service smb reload
```

This final option allows you to change your Samba configuration without disconnecting users from your Samba server.

CERTIFICATION SUMMARY

Networking services are an integral part of Red Hat Enterprise Linux. NFS, vsFTP, and Samba are a few of the services that you can configure for this operating system.

NFS allows you to share filesystems between Linux and Unix computers. This is a powerful method of controlling data and distributing I/O load, but there are many security concerns involved with its use. Be careful when setting up an NFS share on an unprotected network.

Red Hat includes one FTP server, the very secure FTP service. You can configure it in detail through the /etc/vsftpd/vsftpd.conf configuration file.

Samba allows a Linux computer to appear like any other Microsoft computer on a Microsoft Windows–based network. Samba is based on the Server Message Block protocol, which allows Microsoft computers to communicate on a TCP/IP network. It has evolved as Microsoft has adapted SMB to the Common Internet File System.

The main Samba configuration file, /etc/samba/smb.conf, includes separate sections for global settings and share definitions. The Red Hat Samba Server Configuration tool is a GUI tool that makes it easier to configure smb.conf. Changes to smb.conf can be easily tested with the **testparm** utility.

TWO-MINUTE DRILL

Here are some of the key points from the certification objectives in Chapter 10.

Configuring a Network File System (NFS) Server

❑ NFS is the standard for sharing files and printers between Linux and Unix computers.

❑ Key NFS processes are **rpc.mountd** for mount requests, **rpc.rquotad** for quota requests, and **nfsd** for each network share.

❑ NFS shares are configured in /etc/exports and activated with the **exportfs -a** command.

Client-Side NFS

❑ Clients can make permanent connections for NFS shares through /etc/fstab.

❑ If an NFS server fails, it can "hang" an NFS client. When possible, avoid using NFS on mission-critical computers.

❑ NFS and portmap have security problems. Limit their use when possible to secure internal networks protected by an appropriate firewall.

The File Transfer Protocol and vsFTPd

❑ RHEL includes the vsFTP server. The default configuration allows anonymous and real user access.

❑ You can customize vsFTP through the /etc/vsftpd/vsftpd.conf configuration file. It also uses authentication files in the /etc/vsftpd/ directory: ftpusers, user_list, and chroot_list.

Samba Services

❑ Samba allows Microsoft Windows computers to share files and printers across networks, using the Server Message Block (SMB) protocol on the TCP/IP protocol stack.

❑ Samba includes a client and a server. Variations on the **mount -t cifs** or **/sbin/mount.cifs** commands allow you to connect to a Microsoft Windows shared directory.

❏ The main Samba configuration file is /etc/samba/smb.conf. You can configure it in a text editor or a GUI tool such as the Samba Server Configuration tool.

❏ Samba allows you to configure your Linux computer as a member of a Microsoft Windows 9x–style workgroup.

❏ Samba allows you to configure your Linux computer as a Microsoft Windows server. It can also provide Microsoft browsing, WINS, and Domain Controller services, even on an Active Directory network.

SELF TEST

The following questions will help you measure your understanding of the material presented in this chapter. As no multiple choice questions appear on the Red Hat exams, no multiple choice questions appear in this book. These questions exclusively test your understanding of the chapter. It is okay if you have another way of performing a task. Getting results, not memorizing trivia, is what counts on the Red Hat exams. There may be more than one answer to many of these questions.

Configuring a Network File System (NFS) Server

1. In the /etc/exports file, if you want to export the /data directory as read-only to all hosts and grant read and write permission to the host superv in domain.com, what directive would you enter in that file?

   _____

2. Once you've configured /etc/exports, what command exports these shares?

   _____

3. Your company has just suffered an external security breach. As a result, the security group in your department has tightened the screws on all the servers, routers, and firewalls (but not SELinux). Up until this point, all user data had been mounted over NFS, but now nothing works. What's the most likely cause?

   _____

Client-Side NFS

4. You're experiencing problems with NFS clients for various reasons, including frequent downtime on the NFS server and network outages between NFS clients and servers. What type of mounting can prevent problems on NFS clients?

   _____

The File Transfer Protocol and vsFTPd

5. What default directive in /etc/vsftpd/vsftpd.conf should you disable if you don't want users logging into their accounts through the vsFTP server?

   _____

6. What directive should you enable if you want to keep regular users from getting to the top-level root directory (/) on your computer?

   _____

7. Based on the default RHEL 5 configuration, what file includes a list of users not allowed to log into the vsFTP server?

_____

8. What additional directives do you need to add to the default vsFTP configuration file to allow security using PAM and TCP wrappers?

_____

Samba Services

9. A group that prefers Microsoft servers has set up a Windows 2000 server to handle file and print sharing services. This server correctly refers to a WINS server on 192.168.55.3 for name resolution and configures all user logins through the PDC on 192.168.55.8. If you're configuring the local Linux system as a PDC, what directive, at minimum, do you have to configure in the local Samba configuration file?

_____

10. What command can be used to mount remotely shared Microsoft directories?

_____

11. You made a couple of quick changes to your Samba configuration file and you need to test it quickly for syntax errors. What command tests smb.conf for syntax errors?

_____

12. You've recently revised the Samba configuration file and do not want to disconnect any current users. What command forces the Samba service to reread the configuration file—without having to disconnect your Microsoft users or restarting the service?

_____

LAB QUESTIONS

Lab 1

You'll need two Linux computers for this lab: one as an NFS server, and a second as an NFS client. Call these computers nfssvr.example.com and nfsclient.example.com. On the server, share the /home directories and provide write permissions to the client computer. On the client, set up the /home directory from the NFS server to be mounted the next time you boot that client computer.

Lab 2

Configure an FTP server for your computer. Make sure to allow only anonymous access. Don't allow anonymous users to upload to your server. Enable messages when users access your /var/ftp and /var/ftp/pub directories. Add an appropriate one-line message to each directory. Test the result, preferably from a remote computer. Start the vsFTP server and see that it starts automatically the next time you reboot your computer.

Lab 3: Configuring Samba

This is a multi-part lab.

Part 1: Installing and Starting Samba

1. Ensure that all four components of the Samba service are correctly installed. What RPMs did you install and how did you install them?

2. Use one of the available service management tools to ensure that the Samba services are configured to start correctly when you boot Linux. What tool did you use?

3. Start Samba services now. You can use either the service management script located directly in /etc/rc.d/init.d or the "service" startup tool. How did you start your Samba service?

4. Verify that Samba services are running. How did you do this?

Part 2: Configuring Samba's Global Settings

1. You'll use Red Hat's Samba Server Configuration tool to configure your Samba service. Start this tool. If you didn't log in as the root user, did something happen before the tool started?

2. Configure the Samba global settings. You will provide workgroup services to your users. Set the workgroup name to something appropriate for your company.

3. Can you limit access to your company's domain name (such as example.com) through this tool? If you have to edit the Samba configuration file directly, what do you have to do?

4. Can you prevent access to evil.cracker.com through this tool? If you have to edit the Samba configuration file directly, what do you have to do?

5. Commit your changes. What do you need to do to make Samba reread the configuration file?

Part 3: Configuring File Shares

1. Open the main Samba configuration file.

2. Navigate to the predefined [homes] share.

3. Ensure that the [homes] share is available only to hosts on your example.com network.

4. Ensure that the share is writable to authenticated users but not available to guest users.

5. Commit your changes.

6. Create a new share called [public].

7. Change the path to the public share to /home/public.

8. Configure the public share so anyone in your domain can access the share.

9. Create the /home/public directory as required. Change the permissions to this directory to 1777.

10. Why do you set permissions to 1777?

11. Commit your changes.

Part 4: Setting Up Printer Shares

1. Your Linux server has many printers defined. You want to offer access to them to your desktop client users. Enable access to the generic printers share now.

2. Again, restrict access to your print shares to members of your example.com domain.

3. Commit your changes.

Part 5: Verifying the smb.conf File

1. You want to verify your changes. Start a terminal window. Run the syntax tester tool on your Samba configuration tool. What program did you use?

2. Review the /etc/samba/smb.conf file. Look over each section including the **[global]** section. Ensure that all updates are correct and reflect the requirements previously stated. Go back and make changes, if necessary. Commit all changes.

Again, go back and make revisions if the test program indicates problems with the smb.conf file.

Part 6: Starting the Samba Servers

1. Navigate to a command line interface.

2. Start the Samba server. Which daemons does it start?

3. If possible, go to a Microsoft Windows computer on your network. Use a Microsoft browsing tool such as Network Neighborhood or My Network Places in Windows Explorer. See if you can connect to the Samba public share. Alternatively, you can go to another Linux computer, and browse Nautilus by navigating to smb:///.

Congratulations! You have just configured your Samba server to share files with your local workgroup.

Part 7: Persistency Check   It is important for your server (and critical to pass the RHCE exam) that any changes you make to your server should be persistent. This means that changes should be active when you reboot Linux. Perform an orderly reboot of your server now and verify that Samba starts when you boot Linux.

1. How did you make your changes persistent?

2. What command did you use to perform an orderly shutdown?

SELF TEST ANSWERS

Configuring a Network File System (NFS) Server

1. The following entry in /etc/exports would export the /data directory as read-only to all hosts and grant read and write permission to the host superv in domain.com:

   ```
   /data(ro,sync)  superv.domain.com(rw,sync)
   ```

2. Once you've revised /etc/exports, the **exportfs -a** command exports all filesystems. Yes, you can re-export filesystems with the **exportfs-r** command. But there's no indication that NFS shares have yet been exported.

3. The most likely cause of NFS problems after security is boosted is an overzealous firewall.

Client-Side NFS

4. Soft mounting can prevent problems such as lockups with NFS clients.

The File Transfer Protocol and vsFTPd

5. The default directive in /etc/vsftpd/vsftpd.conf that you should disable if you don't want users logging into their accounts through the vsFTP server is **local_enable=YES**.

6. The directive you should add if you want to keep regular users from getting to the top-level root directory (/) on your computer is **chroot_user=YES**.

7. Based on the default RHEL 5 configuration, both ftpusers and user_list in the /etc/vsftpd directory include a list of users not allowed to log into the vsFTP server.

8. The additional directives you need to add to the default vsFTP configuration file to allow security using PAM and TCP wrappers are **pam_service_name=vsftpd** and **tcp_wrappers=YES**.

Samba Services

9. At minimum, to configure a Linux system as a PDC, you need to configure the **security = user** directive.

10. The command that can be used to mount remotely shared Microsoft directories is **mount.cifs**.

11. The command that tests smb.conf for syntax errors is **testparm**.

12. The command that forces the Samba service to reread the configuration file—without having to disconnect your Microsoft users or restarting the service—is **service smb reload**.

LAB ANSWERS

Lab 1

This lab is the first step toward creating a single /home directory for your network. Once you get it working on a single client/server combination, you can set it up on all clients and servers. You can then use the NIS server described in Chapter 6 for a single Linux/Unix database of usernames and passwords for your network. On the NFS server, take the following steps:

1. Set up some users and special files that you'll remember in some of the users' home directories on the server. The details are not important—just make a note of what you've done.

2. Share the /home directory in /etc/exports with the nfsclient.example.com client. You can do this in this file with the following command:

    ```
    /home nfsclient(rw,sync)
    ```

3. Export this directory with the following command:

    ```
    # exportfs -a
    ```

4. Restart the NFS service:

    ```
    # service NFS stop
    # service NFS start
    ```

5. Make sure that the exported /home directory shows in the export list. On the local server, you can do this with the following command:

    ```
    # showmount -e
    ```

6. If you have problems with any step in this process, make sure you don't have extra spaces in /etc/exports and that the NFS service is actually running with the **service nfs status** command. You may also want to check your firewall and make sure the appropriate services described in this chapter are running with the **rpcinfo -p** command.

7. Remember to make sure that the NFS server starts automatically the next time you boot that computer. One way to do so is with the following command:

    ```
    # chkconfig nfs on
    ```

    Now on the NFS client, take the following steps to connect to the shared /home directory:

8. First, make sure that you can see the shared /home directory. If your DNS server is not working in any of these commands, you can substitute the IP address of the appropriate computer:

    ```
    # showmount -e nfssvr.example.com
    ```

9. Now **mount** the share that is offered on the local /home directory:

   ```
   # mount -t nfs nfssvr.example.com:/home /home
   ```

10. Check to see that the mounting has worked. If it did, you'll see the NFS mount in the output to the **mount** command.

11. Now look through the mounted /home directory for the special files that you created in step 1. If you find them from the NFS client, you've succeeded in creating and connecting to the /home directory share.

12. To make the mount permanent, add it to your /etc/fstab file. Once you've added a command such as the following to that file, the Linux client automatically mounts the shared /home directory from the NFS server.

    ```
    nfssvr.example.com:/home   /home   nfs   soft,timeout=100  0  0
    ```

Lab 2

The vsFTP server is part of a simple package group. So if you have not installed this server during the installation process, the quickest thing to do is to connect to your installation source (CD or network) and install it from that location. For example, if the source is mounted on /mnt/source, you'd install it with the following command:

```
# rpm --Uvh /mnt/source/Server/vsftpd-*
```

This also installs configuration files in the /etc and /etc/vsftpd directories. The main configuration file is /etc/vsftpd/vsftpd.conf. Based on the RHEL default version of this file, you can make the following changes. To allow only anonymous access, comment out the following line:

```
local_enable=yes
```

Anonymous users are already prevented from uploading files to your server. You could enable it by activating the **anon_upload_enable=yes** command. By default, messages are already enabled for directory access on an FTP server, courtesy of the following command:

```
dirmessage_enable=yes
```

Actually configuring a message is a matter of creating a text file and saving it as .message in the desired directories, /var/ftp and /var/ftp/pub. You could add a simple line such as "root directory for the FTP server" or "main download directory."

Finally, to configure the Red Hat FTP server to start, run the **service vsftpd start** command. To make sure it starts the next time you boot your computer, run the **chkconfig vsftpd on** command.

Lab 3

The chapter lab on Samba is designed to be easy to follow. However, you'll need explicit Linux knowledge to complete some specific steps. Answers to these steps can be found in the following:

Part 1

1. You've installed the Windows File Manager package group, which includes the samba-client, samba, and system-config-samba RPMs. These RPMs depend on the samba-common RPM, which you'll also need to install.

2. You can use the **chkconfig smb on** command or the Service Configuration utility described in Chapter 3 to make sure Samba starts the next time you boot Linux.

3. Use the **service smb start** command to begin the Samba service.

4. One way to verify Samba is to look for the existence of the **smbd** and **nmbd** processes in the process table. Use **ps aux | grep mbd** to see if these processes are present. Another way is with a service command such as **service smb status**.

Part 2

1. To use the Samba Server Configuration tool, you'll need the root password.

2. Many administrators stick with the standard Microsoft Windows **workgroup** name of **WORKGROUP**. You can find it in the output from the **smbclient -L //clientname** command.

3. If you want to limit access to your Samba server, you can't do it through the Samba Server Configuration tool. Set up the **hosts allow** command in /etc/samba/smb.conf.

4. If you want to restrict access from a specific computer to your Samba server, you can't do it through the Samba Server Configuration tool. Set up the **hosts deny = evil crackers.com** command in /etc/samba/smb.conf.

5. When you exit the Samba Server Configuration tool or save the smb.conf file, you can make Samba read the changes with the **service smb reload** command. But before committing the changes, you should test them with the **testparm** command.

Part 3

1. Open the main Samba configuration file, /etc/samba/smb.conf, in a text editor.

2. Navigate to the **[homes]** share in the last part of this file.

   Unless there is a limitation in the [global] section in this file, you can limit the **[homes]** share with the **hosts allow = example.com**. Commit your changes. Restart or reload the Samba daemon, **smb**, under the Status menu or with the appropriate **service** command.

3. Add a **guest ok = no** to the **[homes]** stanza.

4. Save the changes you've made so far.

5. At the end of the file, start a **[public]** stanza. Add an appropriate comment for the stanza.

6. Set **path = /home/public**. Save your changes to the smb.conf file.

7. Make sure to set **hosts allow = example.com**.

8. Set permissions for the public share with the following commands:

```
# mkdir /home/public
# chmod 1777 /home/public
```

Create a new directory, /home/public; configure that share and call it public. Set the **hosts allow** setting, and list the domain associated with your network. Deny access to all other systems.

The *777* setting for permissions grants read, write, and execute/search permissions to all users (root, root's group, and everyone else). The *1* at the beginning of the permission value sets the sticky bit. This bit, when set on directories, keeps users from deleting or renaming files they don't own.

9. Commit your changes with the **service smb reload** command.

Part 4

1. Open your /etc/samba/smb.conf configuration file. Navigate to the **[printers]** stanza. The default version of this stanza should already enable access to all users who connect.

2. In this stanza, use the **hosts allow** command as before.

3. Commit your changes by closing and saving the smb.conf file and then running the **service smb reload** command.

Part 5

1. You can use the Samba syntax checker, **testparm**, to make sure no glaring problems exist in your Samba configuration file.

2. This is more of an exercise; if you don't have any problems, you might want to add some deliberately to your smb.conf file and rerun **testparm**. It's helpful to be familiar with different kinds of Samba syntax issues. Don't forget to restore a working version of the smb.conf file!

Part 6

1. Again, this is more of an exercise than a lab. The steps are generally self-explanatory. If your Samba configuration is successful, you should be able to review browsable shares from a Microsoft Windows computer on the same LAN.

Part 7

1. To complete many Linux configuration changes, you need to make sure that the service will start automatically when you reboot your computer. In general, the key command is **chkconfig**. In this case, the **chkconfig smb on** command sets up the **smbd** daemon to become active when you boot Linux in a standard runlevel.

2. You can use various commands to perform an orderly shutdown, such as **shutdown, halt, init 0,** and more.

11

Domain Name Service

CERTIFICATION OBJECTIVES

11.01   Understanding DNS: Zones, Domains, and Delegation

11.02   The Berkeley Internet Name Domain (BIND)

11.03   BIND Utilities

✓   Two-Minute Drill

Q&A   Self Test

T his chapter focuses on the Domain Name System (DNS), a service that translates human-readable domain names such as www.mommabears.com to IP addresses such as 10.245.43.5, and vice versa. DNS is a distributed database; each server has its own delegated zone of authority for one or more domains.

The DNS service associated with RHEL is the Berkeley Internet Name Domain (BIND). In this chapter, you'll learn how to edit and modify BIND configuration files to create authoritative DNS servers as well as slave and caching servers.

Once configured, there are a number of BIND utilities that can help find the systems on the local network as well as those on any other connected network, including the Internet.

on the Job

If you're interested in Dynamic DNS and Linux, one place to start is the Secure Dynamic DNS HOWTO from the Internet Engineering Task Force, at http://ops.ietf.org/dns/dynupd/secure-ddns-howto.html.

INSIDE THE EXAM

More Network Services

Both Red Hat exams require that you configure a Linux workstation as a client on a network. On a network with Linux computers, that naturally includes using DNS clients and servers.

This chapter may be related to two different items on the Troubleshooting and System Maintenance portion of the RHCT exam:

- Diagnose and correct misconfigured networking.
- Diagnose and correct host name resolution problems.

It's also related to the following item on the Troubleshooting and System Maintenance portion of the RHCE exam:

- Diagnose and correct problems with network services.

This naturally includes DNS. As noted in the Installation and Configuration

requirements associated with the RHCE exam, this means being able to

- Configure DNS as a caching and a slave name service.

The omission of DNS as a master server in the Red Hat Exam Prep requirements is conspicuous by its absence. As always, Red Hat can change its requirements at any time (even halfway through the RHEL 5 release), so check the Red Hat Exam Prep Web site for the latest information (https://www.redhat .com/training/rhce/examprep.html).

But as the only SELinux targeted setting relates to the overwriting of master zone files, there are very few SELinux issues addressed in this chapter.

Nevertheless, this chapter includes basic instructions for configuring a master DNS server.

Understanding DNS: Zones, Domains, and Delegation

DNS, the Domain Name System, maintains a database that can help your computer translate domain names such as www.redhat.com to IP addresses such as 209.132.177.50. As no individual DNS server is large enough to keep a database for the entire Internet, each server is configured by default to refer requests to other DNS servers.

Basic Parameters

DNS on RHEL 5 is based on the **named** daemon, which is built on the BIND package developed through the Internet Software Consortium. (More information is available from the BIND home page at www.isc.org/products/BIND.) RHEL 5 includes BIND version 9.3. While this version of BIND supports the use of the /usr/sbin/rndc configuration interface, RHEL 5 still includes sample files based on the older /etc/named.conf configuration file. However, you can use the **rndc** command to manage DNS operation, in the same way that you used **apachectl** to manage the Apache server.

Packages

If you're configuring your Linux computer solely as a DNS client, you can skip this section. The basic DNS client configuration files are automatically installed with even a minimal installation of RHEL 5.

On the other hand, if you're configuring your Linux computer as a DNS server, you'll need to install the packages associated with the DNS Name Server package group. You can do so with the package management tools described in Chapter 5. However, there are nine RPM packages associated with DNS:

- **bind**   Includes the basic name server software, including /usr/sbin/named.
- **bind-chroot**   Includes directories that isolate BIND in a so-called "chroot jail," which limits access if DNS is compromised.
- **bind-devel**   Includes development libraries for BIND.
- **bind-libbind-devel**   Contains the libbind BIND resolver library.
- **bind-libs**   Adds library files used by the bind and bind-utils RPMs.
- **bind-sdb**   Supports alternative databases, such as LDAP. Per the Red Hat Exam Prep guide and course outlines, I see no evidence that such relationships are covered on the Red Hat exams.

- **bind-utils** Contains tools such as **dig** and **host** that provide information about a specific Internet host. It should already be installed in any minimum installation of RHEL.
- **caching-nameserver** Includes files associated with a caching nameserver.
- **system-config-bind** A GUI configuration tool useful for adding host and reverse address lookup data. It's not officially a part of the DNS Name Server package group.

These tools are easy to install from any Red Hat network installation source that you may have created in Chapter 2. Different options and commands for installing RPMs from a remote installation source are described in Chapter 5.

A DNS Client

There are two client configuration files associated with DNS: /etc/hosts and /etc/resolv.conf. They are fairly straightforward, as described in the next section.

When your computer looks for another computer on a TCP/IP network such as the Internet, it typically looks in two places: /etc/hosts and any DNS servers that you've set up for your network. The order is determined by a single line in /etc/nsswitch.conf:

```
hosts: files,dns
```

When your computer searches for another computer, this line tells your computer to search first through the /etc/hosts database. The following line in my /etc/hosts drives a Web browser address to my local IP address:

```
127.0.0.1    Enterprise5    localhost.localdomain    localhost
```

While you could theoretically also configure every computer on the Internet in your /etc/hosts configuration file, it's not realistic. However, if your LAN is small, you could add the IP address and host name of each computer on your network on /etc/hosts. You could then duplicate this file on each computer on your LAN. Then you could use an external DNS server, provided by your ISP, for Internet access.

It's easy to configure a Linux computer as a DNS client. You may have already done so during the RHEL installation process. If you have a working DHCP server, it probably provided the settings you need as a DNS client. Alternatively, you can configure your computer as a DNS client with the Network Configuration utility described in Chapter 7. You can even configure your computer directly through your /etc/resolv.conf file. It's easy to do; the following version of this file lists two DNS servers on the Internet:

```
nameserver 207.217.120.83
nameserver 207.217.126.81
```

If you want to add or change the DNS servers for your computer, you can open this file directly in the text editor of your choice.

In the following section, you'll get a chance to learn about DNS nameserver configuration files from the ground up. Many of the lessons associated with a caching-only name server apply to slave and master DNS servers.

on the **Job**

As with a number of directives on other Linux services, name server *and* nameserver *are both in common use with respect to servers that conform to Domain Name Service (DNS), and I use both variations throughout the book.*

CERTIFICATION OBJECTIVE 11.02

The Berkeley Internet Name Domain (BIND)

You can configure a DNS server by directly editing the DNS configuration files. Alternatively, you can configure a DNS server using the Red Hat Domain Name Service configuration tool. Careful use of both tools can help you learn more about DNS.

You can set up four different types of DNS servers:

- A master DNS server for your domain(s), which stores authoritative records for your domain.
- A slave DNS server, which relies on a master DNS server for data.
- A caching-only DNS server, which stores recent requests like a proxy server. It otherwise refers to other DNS servers.
- A forwarding-only DNS server, which refers all requests to other DNS servers.

on the **Job**

system-config-bind *is the successor to* **bindconf.** *Red Hat Enterprise Linux includes a link from* **bindconf** *to* **system-config-bind.**

The DNS Configuration Files

DNS configuration files are required to configure your Linux computer as a client and as a server. The client configuration was described earlier in this section. There are a number of additional configuration files that support the use of DNS as a server, as described in Table 11-1. You may have to create some of these files as you configure DNS. If you've installed the bind-chroot package, you'll find the real copy of these files in the /var/named/chroot/var/named directory, linked to /var/named.

As noted in the default copy of /etc/sysconfig/named, the **ROOTDIR** directive points to /var/named/chroot/ as the root directory for all other DNS server configuration files. We assume that you've installed bind-chroot, in which case, all files in Table 11-1 are in that directory unless otherwise noted. Some may be linked to that directory. For example, once created, /etc/named.conf is actually a soft link to /var/named/chroot/etc/named.conf.

In many cases, you do not have to use the file names listed in Table 11-1. All you need to do is make sure the file is properly cited in the main named.conf configuration file. Remember that if you've installed the bind-chroot RPM, these files will be linked to files in the /var/named/chroot/ directory.

Many of these files include templates in the DNS documentation directory, /usr/share/doc/bind-*versionnum*/sample.

In the following sections, you'll see how to configure the files that you need for a working DNS server. But first, you should know how to configure your computer as a DNS client. One thing to remember is that all of the files in /var/named include a

TABLE 11-1   DNS Server Configuration Files

DNS Configuration File	Description
/etc/sysconfig/named	Set up different configuration and data file directories through this file.
/etc/named.conf	The main DNS configuration file. Incorporates data from other files with the **include** directive.
/etc/named-caching-nameserver.conf	A template DNS configuration file for a caching DNS server.
/etc/named.rfc1912.zones	Adds appropriate zones for localhost names and addresses.
/var/named/chroot/etc/rndc.key	The authentication key required to support requests to the DNS server.
/var/named/my.internal.zone.db	The zone file for the local network.
/var/named/slaves/my.slave.internal.zone.db	The zone file for a slave DNS server.
/var/named/slaves/my.ddns.internal.zone.db	The zone file for a dynamic DNS server.
/var/named/localdomain.zone	The zone file for the localhost's domain.
/var/named/localhost.zone	The zone file for the localhost computer.
/var/named/named.broadcast	A broadcast record for the localhost.
/var/named/named.ca	A list of root DNS servers on the Internet.
/var/named/named.local	A reverse zone record for the localhost.
/var/named/named.ip6.local	An IPv6 version of named.local.
/var/named/named.zero	Defaults to the broadcast record for the localhost.
/var/named/data/named.stats.txt	Statistics from your DNS server, only available after DNS is active.

dot at the end of each domain name. For example, /var/named/named.local lists the local computer as:

```
localhost.
```

In contrast, the domain names in /etc/named.conf and /etc/named.rfc1912.zones do not have dots at the end of their domain names.

A Caching-Only Name Server

When you request a Web page such as www.osborne.com, your network asks the configured DNS server for the associated IP address. This is usually known as a *name query*. If the DNS server is outside your network, this request can take time. If you have a caching-only name server, these queries are stored locally, which can save significant time while you or others on your network are browsing the same sites on the Internet.

When configuring a caching-only name server, the first step is to look at the /etc/named .caching-nameserver.conf configuration file. The directives in the default version of this file are shown in Figure 11-1.

The current version of the Red Hat Exam Prep guide suggests that you need to know how to configure a caching-only DNS server for the RHCE exam.

FIGURE 11-1

/etc/named
.caching-
nameserver.conf

```
options {
        listen-on port 53 { 127.0.0.1; };
        listen-on-v6 port 53 { ::1; };
        directory       "/var/named";
        dump-file       "/var/named/data/cache_dump.db";
        statistics-file "/var/named/data/named_stats.txt";
        memstatistics-file "/var/named/data/named_mem_stats.txt";
        query-source    port 53;
        query-source-v6 port 53;
        allow-query     { localhost; };
};
logging {
        channel default_debug {
                file "data/named.run";
                severity dynamic;
        };
};
view localhost_resolver {
        match-clients       { localhost; };
        match-destinations { localhost; };
        recursion yes;
        include "/etc/named.rfc1912.zones";
};
```

- The **options** directive encompasses several basic DNS directives, including the following:
  - The **listen-on port** (and **listen-on-v6 port**) directives—as well as the **query-source port** (and **query-source-v6 port**) directives—specify the TCP/IP port number (for IPv4 and IPv6).

    If you're extending this to your local network, you'll need to include the IP address of the local network card. For example, if it's 192.168.0.15, the directive would be (don't forget the semicolon after each IP address)

    ```
    listen-on port 53 { 127.0.0.1; 192.168.0.15; }
    ```

  - The **directory** directive tells your DNS server where to look for data files. Remember that if you've installed the bind-chroot RPM, these files will be linked to /var/named/chroot/ subdirectories.
  - The **dump-file** specifies the cache for the current DNS database and the output from the **rndc dumpdb** command.
  - The **statistics-file** specifies the cache for the current DNS database and the output from the **rndc stats** command.
  - The **memstatistics-file** specifies the location for memory usage statistics.
  - The **allow-query** lists the IP addresses allowed to get information from this server. If you want to extend this to the 192.168.0.0 network, you could change this directive to this:

    ```
    allow-query { 127.0.0.1; 192.168.0.0/24; }
    ```

- The **logging** directive specifies several more parameters; the **channel** directive specifies output methods, in this case to **default_debug**, activated in the data/ named.run subdirectory, logging only **dynamic** issues.
- The **view localhost_resolver** directive identifies this caching nameserver as the client and destination for the localhost computer, with the settings described in /etc/named.rfc1912.zones.

on the
Job

If you have an older hardware firewall, it might expect DNS communication on TCP/IP port 53. If it does, you'll want to activate the query-source address * port 53 command.

Now, to create a caching DNS server, all you need to do is copy the /var/named/chroot/ etc/named.caching-nameserver.conf file to /var/named/chroot/etc/named.conf, and make the changes suggested in this section. As described in the comments to this file, changes are overwritten if you use the Red Hat BIND configuration tool, but if the changes you need to make are so simple, why bother?

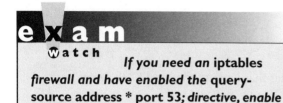

ⓦatch *If you need an iptables firewall and have enabled the query-source address * port 53; directive, enable UDP communication through port 53.*

A Slave Name Server

Note that there is no period at the end of any address in /etc/named.conf. If you want to create a slave server, the information that you'd enter is similar:

```
zone "example.org" IN {
    type slave;
    file "slaves/example.com.org";
    masters {
            192.168.30.5
                };
};
```

The task for a slave server is easier; it periodically checks with the master DNS server, in this case the computer with an IP address of 192.168.30.5. When it does, it automatically reads the master DNS server data and creates the slave.example.com. zone file in the /var/named/chroot/var/named/slaves directory.

A Forwarding-Only Name Server

This type of DNS server is simple. It requires a single command in the /etc/named .conf configuration file (remember that it's linked to /var/named/chroot/etc/named .conf). As you can see, it's straightforward; I've set it to refer to the DNS servers that I had configured as a client:

```
options {
    directory "/var/named";
    forward only;
    forwarders {
```

```
                    207.217.120.83;
                    207.217.126.81;
            };
        };
```

With this configuration, any computer that looks to the local DNS server is forwarded to the IP addresses shown.

If the data can't be found in those DNS servers, it's up to those servers to ask others for the information. The alternative is to used the /var/named/named.ca file described later in this chapter.

named.ca

If your DNS servers don't have the IP address for a domain name in the database, that server can refer to other databases. By default, the DNS server refers to the /var/named/named.ca file, which is a list of the root DNS servers for the Internet. (This file is normally linked to /var/named/chroot/var/named/named.ca.) An excerpt is shown in Figure 11-2.

The root DNS servers are stored in named.ca.

```
;      This file holds the information on root name servers needed to
;      initialize cache of Internet domain name servers
;      (e.g. reference this file in the "cache  .  <file>"
;      configuration file of BIND domain name servers).
;
;      This file is made available by InterNIC
;      under anonymous FTP as
;          file                /domain/named.cache
;          on server           FTP.INTERNIC.NET
;      -OR-                     RS.INTERNIC.NET
;
;      last update:   Jan 29, 2004
;      related version of root zone:   2004012900
;
;
; formerly NS.INTERNIC.NET
;
.                         3600000  IN  NS   A.ROOT-SERVERS.NET.
A.ROOT-SERVERS.NET.       3600000      A    198.41.0.4
;
; formerly NS1.ISI.EDU
;
.                         3600000      NS   B.ROOT-SERVERS.NET.
B.ROOT-SERVERS.NET.       3600000      A    192.228.79.201
;
; formerly C.PSI.NET
;
.                         3600000      NS   C.ROOT-SERVERS.NET.
C.ROOT-SERVERS.NET.       3600000      A    192.33.4.12
;
; formerly TERP.UMD.EDU
;
.                         3600000      NS   D.ROOT-SERVERS.NET.
D.ROOT-SERVERS.NET.       3600000      A    128.8.10.90
;
; formerly NS.NASA.GOV
;
.                         3600000      NS   E.ROOT-SERVERS.NET.
E.ROOT-SERVERS.NET.       3600000      A    192.203.230.10
```

localhost.zone

The default /var/named/localhost.zone file is shown in Figure 11-3. (Remember, it's linked to /var/named/chroot/var/named/localhost.zone.) It incorporates a basic DNS entry for the local computer, which you can use as a template for other computers on your network.

Reverse Lookups with named.local

The /var/named/named.local file provides a reverse-lookup record for your computer, as localhost. (Remember, it's linked to /var/named/chroot/var/named/localhost.zone.) As shown in Figure 11-4, the PTR record (on the last line in the file) is *1*, which associates the loopback address, 127.0.0.1, with your computer.

Configuring a Simple Domain

Review the /etc/named.rfc1912.zones configuration template file. With what we know about DNS configuration files, we can use it to create a master DNS server. Assume that you've defined a simple domain for the computers on your network; call it example.org.

on the **Job** *The example.com, example.net, and example.org domains are generic domain names that can't be assigned on the Internet. You can therefore use any of these domain names on your private network.*

exam
Watch *The current version of the Red Hat Exam Prep guide suggests that you need to know how to configure only a slave and caching DNS name server for* *the RHCE exam. However, understanding how to create a master DNS name server is an important skill for Linux system administrators.*

FIGURE 11-3

The localhost.zone
DNS datafile

```
$TTL      86400
@                    IN SOA  @       root (
                                       42           ; serial (d. adams)
                                       3H           ; refresh
                                       15M          ; retry
                                       1W           ; expiry
                                       1D )         ; minimum

              IN NS          @
              IN A           127.0.0.1
              IN AAAA        ::1

~
~
"/var/named/localhost.zone" 12L, 195C
```

FIGURE 11-4

The named.local
reverse DNS file

```
$TTL    86400
@       IN      SOA     localhost. root.localhost. (
                                      1997022700 ; Serial
                                      28800      ; Refresh
                                      14400      ; Retry
                                      3600000    ; Expire
                                      86400 )    ; Minimum
        IN      NS      localhost.
1       IN      PTR     localhost.
~
~
~
~
~
"/var/named/named.local" 9L, 426C
```

Before you continue, activate the **named_write_master_zones** SELinux setting.
You can do so from the SELinux Management Tool, or by running the following
command:

```
# setsebool -P named_write_master_zones 1
```

Now return to the named.conf file. Look at the **zone "0.0.127.in-addr.arpa" IN**
line near the middle of this file. This says that the **zone 0.0.127.in-addr.arpa** will be
defined, that the **localhost** is the master server (**type master**) for that zone, associated
data is stored in a **file** called **named.local**, and no other DNS server is allowed to
"update" or change the IP address associated with **localhost (allow-update { none; })**.

on the
job

*Not all characters are allowed in host names. DNS can read only regular
letters, numbers, and the hyphen (-) character. Unlike Linux, DNS does not
distinguish between upper- and lowercase characters; for example, Mail
.Example.Com is equivalent to mail.example.com.*

Copy the named.rfc1912.zones file to /etc/named.conf. *But wait*—remember that
it's based on links to the /var/named/chroot/etc/ directory. So to preserve the links,
make the change with commands such as these:

```
# cd /var/named/chroot/etc
# cp named.rfc1912.zones named.conf
```

But that's not enough. You need to tell DNS where to look, and more. The simplest
solution is to open the file in a text editor and then add the **options** stanza described
earlier for the caching nameserver:

```
options {
        listen-on port 53 { 127.0.0.1; 192.168.0.15; };
        listen-on-v6 port 53 { ::1; };
        directory       "/var/named";
```

```
dump-file        "/var/named/data/cache_dump.db";
statistics-file "/var/named/data/named_stats.txt";
memstatistics-file "/var/named/data/named_mem_stats.txt";
query-source     port 53;
query-source-v6 port 53;
allow-query      { localhost; 192.168.0.0/24; };
};
```

This isn't the default **options** directive from /etc/named.caching-nameserver.conf. Notice how I added the IP address for my network card to the **listen-on port 53** directive (**192.168.0.15**) and the network address to the **allow-query** directive.

Now you can add your network to your DNS server. Start by inserting new forward and reverse zone sections in the /etc/named.conf file, followed by the **include "/etc/rndc.key";** directive. (I assume that you're not going to overwrite these changes with the Red Hat GUI Domain Name Service tool.) The following is based on my example.org domain, on the 192.168.0.0/24 network:

```
zone "example.org" IN {
    type master;
    file "example.org.zone";
};

zone "0.168.192.in-addr.arpa" IN {
    type master;
    file "example.org.rr.zone";
};

include "/etc/rndc.key";
```

For further guidance, see the named.conf file in the /usr/share/doc/bind-9.3.3/ sample/etc/ directory.

Creating an RNDC Key

Now you need to create an RNDC (Remote Name Daemon Control) key and configuration file in the /etc/ directory, linked to actual locations in the /var/named/ chroot/etc directory. The simplest method is with the **rndc-confgen** command, which sets up entries for the aforementioned files:

```
# rndc-confgen

# Start of rndc.conf
key "rndckey" {
        algorithm hmac-md5;
        secret "jRqhTi7E4pjZcvjJ/GdT0g==";
};
```

```
options {
        default-key "rndckey";
        default-server 127.0.0.1;
        default-port 953;
};
# End of rndc.conf

# Use with the following in named.conf, adjusting the allow list as needed:
# key "rndckey" {
#       algorithm hmac-md5;
#       secret "jRqhTi7E4pjZcvjJ/GdT0g==";
# };
#
# controls {
#       inet 127.0.0.1 port 953
#               allow { 127.0.0.1; } keys { "rndckey"; };
# };
# End of named.conf
```

While you could substitute entries as noted, that would override expected directives in RHEL's /etc/rndc.key. Fortunately, there's an easier way, which automatically includes a key in /etc/rndc.key (which is linked to /var/named/chroot/etc/rndc.key). The **-b 512** switch includes a 512 bit encryption key:

```
# rndc-confgen -a -b 512
```

And the following entry in /etc/named.conf refers to the rndc.key file:

```
include "/etc/rndc.key";
```

Creating a Zone File

If you're creating a master DNS server, you'll need to create a zone file. Based on the configuration so far, this will be an example.org.zone file in the /var/named directory (linked to /var/named/chroot/var/named/example.org.zone). I've created one for my own network, as shown in Figure 11-5.

Now let's decipher some of the language in this file.

$TTL 86400 means that the default Time To Live (TTL) for data on this DNS server is three days. It's also common to have a **TTL** of **3D**, which corresponds to three days. You can specify individual TTLs for each entry in this file.

The **SOA** (Start Of Authority) record is the preamble to all zone files. It describes the zone where it comes from (a computer called enterprise5vm.example.org), the

FIGURE 11-5

An example.org
.zone file

```
$TTL    86400
@       IN      SOA Enterprise5vm.example.org. root.Enterprise5vm.example.org. (
                                2007022700 ; Serial
                                28800      ; Refresh
                                14400      ; Retry
                                3600000    ; Expire
                                86400 )    ; Minimum
                IN      NS      enterprise5vm
                IN      MX 10   enterprise5vm
drakelaptop     IN  A   192.168.0.17
drakeoffice     IN  A   192.168.0.13
enterprise5vm   IN  A   192.168.0.15
enterprise5a    IN  A   192.168.0.50
www1            IN  CNAME enterprise5a
~
~
~
~
```

administrator e-mail for this DNS server (**root@Enterprise5vm.example.org**). The **SOA** record command line also specifies a number of other parameters:

- Serial number is based on the date and version number. Based on the one shown in Figure 11-5, this database file is the first one created for this server on February 27, 2007.

- The refresh frequency determines how long the local DNS slave server waits before checking for updates from any master DNS servers.

- The retry frequency specifies how often the local DNS slave server retries contacting the master server.

- If there is no response from a DNS master server before the end of the expiration period, the local server stops accepting requests for the given domain.

- The TTL is the minimum amount of time other DNS servers should keep the local zone information in their remote cache.

The **NS** is the name server resource record, which refers to the name of the DNS server computer—in this case, **enterprise5vm.example.org**.

The **MX** is the Mail Exchange record, which directs e-mail information to a particular computer—in this case it's also **enterprise5vm.example.org**. Some number such as what's shown (**10**) is required with any **MX** record. If you have multiple mail servers, the number specifies the priority (lower numbers are served first).

In my example.org.zone file shown in Figure 11-5, I also have entries for three computers in this DNS zone. Each is associated with an **A** (address) record, its IP address. The final three entries specify canonical names (**CNAME**) for specific computers. For this zone file, www1.example.org is also known as enterprise5a.example.org.

CNAME allows you to assign several names to each computer. In this case, **www1** is an alias for the enterprise5a computer. You can use additional **CNAME** directives to specify the same address for an FTP or even an rsync server. However, a **CNAME** is not a legal host name for an e-mail address. For example, admin@www1 .example.org won't work based on the example.org.zone file shown in the figure.

If you have more than one mail server, you can add a number before the name of each MX computer. For example, based on these directives,

```
IN      MX      10      mail.example.org.
IN      MX      20      mail2.example.org.
```

any e-mail directed to this domain is first sent to mail.example.com.

Save this file, and reread the configuration files with the **rndc reload** command.

The Reverse Zone

Now programs can convert the names in your-domain.com to real IP addresses. You're ready for the next step: a *reverse zone* file, which allows a DNS server to convert backward, from an IP address to a host name. Reverse zone lookups are used by many servers of different kinds (FTP, IRC, WWW, and others) to decide if they even want to talk to a computer asking for information. It's a common way for a mail server to check whether an e-mail has come from a valid domain. Therefore, for full access to all Internet services, you need a reverse zone. Start by adding another zone to the /etc/named.conf configuration file:

```
zone "0.168.192.in-addr.arpa" IN {
        type master;
        file "example.com.rr.zone";
};
```

This is similar to the 0.0.127.in-addr.arpa zone described in /etc/named.conf. I've created an example.com.rr.zone file in the /var/named directory for the computers on my network, as shown in Figure 11-6.

Once again, restart **named** and examine the output of **host -l your-domain.com**. If the results do not look similar to the actual zone file, look for error messages in /var/log/messages.

on the Job

Reverse zones can be used by several different services, such as sendmail and Apache. The reverse zone DNS database allows a server to verify if the name of a requesting computer matches its IP address, which can keep crackers from trying to "spoof" your system.

FIGURE 11-6

A reverse DNS
zone file

```
$TTL    86400
@       IN      SOA Enterprise5vm.example.org. root.Enterprise5vm.example.org.  (
                               2007022700 ; Serial
                               28800      ; Refresh
                               14400      ; Retry
                               3600000    ; Expire
                               86400 )    ; Minimum
                IN      NS      enterprise5vm.example.org.
        15      IN      PTR     enterprise5vm.example.org.
        17      IN      PTR     drakelaptop.example.org.
        13      IN      PTR     drakeoffice.example.org.
        15      IN      PTR     enterprise5vm.example.org.
        50      IN      PTR     enterprise5a.example.org.
~
~
~
~
"/var/named/example.org.rr.zone" 13L, 726C
```

Starting named

Make sure your computer is connected to a network. Now you can start your DNS
server through the **named** daemon with the **rndc start** command. View the syslog
message file (usually called /var/log/messages) with the **tail -f /var/log/messages**
command. If there are problems, you'll see error messages here.

If there are any error messages, the **named** daemon will display the file with
the error. Stop the service with the **rndc stop** command and check the applicable
configuration files.

Once you're satisfied with your configuration, you'll want to make sure that DNS
starts the next time you reboot Linux. Naturally, that may be the only way that you
would get full credit for your work on the RHCE exam. The following command
makes sure that the **named** daemon starts the next time you boot Linux in the
standard login runlevels:

```
# chkconfig named on
```

Common DNS Pitfalls

DNS is an Internet-wide database of domain names and IP addresses. If you want your
DNS server to participate, make sure the information that goes into the database is
up to date and properly formatted. Many network outages can be traced to poorly
administered DNS servers. A few examples of common DNS errors are described in
the following sections.

Timing

Sometimes, all you need to do is wait a while. Whenever a change is made in a DNS
database, it takes some time before the change is noted (a.k.a. propagated) to other
DNS servers on the Internet. When I change web hosts, I'm told to wait up to 48

hours until propagation is complete. Therefore, whenever you change something such as the IP address associated with a Web server, it's advisable to keep the old IP address available for that Web server until the new IP address has time to propagate.

The Serial Number Wasn't Incremented

The single most common DNS error occurs when an administrator makes updates to a zone file, restarts DNS, and notices that no one else on the Internet knows about the updates. If another DNS server doesn't detect a new serial number on a zone file, the server assumes the file is the same and sticks with its cache. No data is taken from the update, and other DNS servers don't get the revised information.

When you update a zone file, don't forget to update the serial number. It's best done with the current date in the format shown in the examples (four-digit year, two-digit month, and two-digit date, followed by a one-digit increment number). If you've updated the DNS more than once today, increment the last number as well.

The Reverse Zone Isn't Delegated

Not all network administrators have control over their DNS servers. Some administrators contract with an ISP for this service.

Now assume you're that ISP administrator. You'll need to assign this customer a range of IP addresses for a domain name. Then you'll need to assign the domain name and IP addresses to a specific DNS "zone of authority."

Next, you'll also need to set up the reverse zone. For example, if you assign the 192.168.1. network (192.168.1. is short for the IPv4 network address of 192.168.1.0), you'll need to add NS records in the forward zone, and PTR records in the reverse zone.

on the Job

From an end-user perspective, DNS might be considered the glue that holds the Internet together. Pay special attention to the nuances of the configuration files, to avoid network-wide problems.

CERTIFICATION OBJECTIVE 11.03

BIND Utilities

Once you've configured BIND as a DNS server, there are a number of commands you can use to keep it working. Red Hat even has its own GUI configuration tool for BIND. While I describe the Red Hat tool briefly, it's somewhat complex. Red

Hat didn't even include a GUI tool for RHEL 4, so its reliability in RHEL 5 may not have been fully tested in production.

BIND Commands

There are three commands associated with the BIND service: **rndc**, **host**, and **dig**. The **rndc** command is a better way to control the service. The **rndc** and **host** commands are successors to **nslookup**.

The **rndc** commands are straightforward. When you run **rndc** by itself, the output guides you through the available options. The options I use are straightforward: **rndc stop** and **rndc start** don't require explanation. The **rndc reload** command rereads any changes you've made to the configuration or DNS database files. The **rndc status** command confirms that DNS is running, along with information on the DNS database.

While you can still use commands such as **service named start** and **service named reload**, the **rndc** command can do more. Because the current Red Hat Exam Prep guide suggests that you need only know how to create a caching and slave nameserver, the details are not important for this book.

After you configure DNS and make it reread your configuration files with the **rndc reload** command, examine the results with the **host -l example.com** command. I've shown the results from my zone file in Figure 11-7.

Now test the setup. Use the **dig** command to examine your work. For example, if you use **dig** to look up the address of www.redhat.com, you'll see something like the output shown in Figure 11-8.

The dig command asks your DNS server to look for the www.redhat.com server. Assuming IP address information for www.redhat.com isn't stored locally, it then contacts one of the name server computers listed in /etc/resolv.conf. If that doesn't work, it goes to one of the name servers listed in the named.ca file and makes its requests from there. The request may be passed on to other DNS servers. Therefore, it can take some time before you see an answer.

on the **job**

The nslookup *command is now deprecated, and you may not even be able to use it in a future release of Red Hat Enterprise Linux.*

FIGURE 11-7

Listing a working DNS zone

```
[root@Enterprise5vm ~]# host -l example.org
example.org name server enterprise5vm.
drakelaptop.example.org has address 192.168.0.17
drakeoffice.example.org has address 192.168.0.13
enterprise5a.example.org has address 192.168.0.50
Enterprise5vm.example.org has address 192.168.0.15
[root@Enterprise5vm ~]# ▉
```

FIGURE 11-8

DNS query
using dig

```
[root@Enterprise5vm ~]# dig www.redhat.com

; <<>> DiG 9.3.2 <<>> www.redhat.com
;; global options:  printcmd
;; Got answer:
;; ->>HEADER<<- opcode: QUERY, status: SERVFAIL, id: 14785
;; flags: qr rd ra; QUERY: 1, ANSWER: 0, AUTHORITY: 0, ADDITIONAL: 0

;; QUESTION SECTION:
;www.redhat.com.                         IN      A

;; Query time: 101 msec
;; SERVER: 192.168.0.15#53(192.168.0.15)
;; WHEN: Tue Jul 25 12:35:51 2006
;; MSG SIZE  rcvd: 32

[root@Enterprise5vm ~]# 
```

The DNS Configuration Tool

Red Hat has created a number of excellent GUI configuration tools. They are "front ends" that can help many administrators create the configuration files that they need. While the Red Hat Domain Name Service tool is promising, it was just introduced for RHEL 5. Red Hat did not even include a GUI configuration tool for BIND in RHEL 4.

In any case, it is best if you learn how to configure Linux services, including DNS, directly from the configuration files. As a Linux systems administrator, you may not always have access to the GUI. You may need to administer servers remotely, which makes GUI configuration difficult at best.

If you want to try the Red Hat Domain Name Service configuration tool, back up your DNS configuration files first: /etc/named.conf, as well as the files in the /var/named directory (subdirectories, and links actual files in other directories).

EXERCISE 11-1

Setting Up Your Own DNS Server

Following the example files shown previously, set up your own DNS server. Set it up to serve the domain called rhce.test. As long as your domain is private, it doesn't matter that rhce.test does not match the standard domain name types such as .com or .net.

1. Edit the /etc/named.conf file to reflect the configuration files that you plan to use. Name the zone file rhce.test.zone and set it to be a master domain.

2. Edit the file /var/named/rhce.test.zone and place the proper zone information in it. Start by adding in the header with the serial number and expiration information.

3. Add the SOA resource record (RR) with a proper administrative e-mail address contact.

4. Add NS and MX RRs for the domain. Use the 192.168.0.0/24 address range. If you're configuring an actual TCP/IP network with static IP addresses, feel free to use the assigned IP addresses on your network.

5. Add several hosts to the zone file. Use WWW, FTP, and mail for a few.

6. Save the zone file and then restart **named** with the **rndc reload** command.

7. Use the **dig** command to check the rhce.test domain. If it works, you have a working DNS server.

CERTIFICATION SUMMARY

DNS provides a database of domain names and IP addresses that help Web browsers and more find sites on the Internet. The default DNS server for RHEL uses the Berkeley Internet Name Domain (BIND). It's a distributed database for which each administrator is responsible for his or her own zone of authority.

DNS can be controlled with various **rndc** commands. The diagnostic tool for DNS is now **dig**. You can also use the more traditional **nslookup** command, but it has been deprecated in RHEL 5.

TWO-MINUTE DRILL

Here are some of the key points from the certification objectives in Chapter 11.

Understanding DNS: Zones, Domains, and Delegation

❏ DNS is based on the Berkeley Internet Name Domain (BIND), using the **named** daemon.

❏ Key packages include bind-chroot, which adds security by supporting DNS in a chroot jail.

The Berkeley Internet Name Domain (BIND)

❏ Critical DNS configuration files include /etc/named.conf and the files in the /var/named directory.

❏ Caching-only DNS servers store requests and their associated IP addresses on a computer.

❏ Slave DNS servers need to point to a master DNS server, with the appropriate **masters** directive in /etc/named.conf.

❏ Every time you change DNS, remember to update the serial number in your zone file. Otherwise, other DNS servers don't realize that you've changed anything.

BIND Utilities

❏ There are a number of BIND utilities that can help you manage the service, including **rndc** and **rndc-confgen**. Others can help you check the database, including **dig** and **host**.

SELF TEST

The following questions will help you measure your understanding of the material presented in this chapter. As no multiple choice questions appear on the Red Hat exams, no multiple choice questions appear in this book. These questions exclusively test your understanding of the chapter. It is okay if you have another way of performing a task. Getting results, not memorizing trivia, is what counts on the Red Hat exams. There may be more than one answer to many of these questions.

Understanding DNS: Zones, Domains, and Delegation

1. If you're configuring a connection from a client to a DNS server, what file would you use?

   _____

2. If your ISP has a DNS server address of 10.11.12.13, what directive would you add to the DNS client configuration file used in question 1?

   _____

The Berkeley Internet Name Domain (BIND)

3. If you configure DNS communication on port 53, what changes would you make to a firewall to support access by other clients to the local DNS server?

   _____

4. What file includes a basic template for a DNS caching nameserver?

   _____

5. What file includes a basic template for a master DNS server?

   _____

6. If you've installed the bind-chroot RPM, where will you find the actual DNS server configuration files?

   _____

7. If you've installed the bind-chroot RPM, where will you find links to the actual DNS server configuration files?

   _____

8. Why would you configure a reverse DNS zone database?

   _____

9. If there are errors when you start the DNS service, where are error messages available by default?

_____

10. What command makes sure that the DNS service starts the next time you boot Linux?

_____

BIND Utilities

11. What command lists the data associated with the example.net domain on a properly configured DNS server?

_____

12. After you revise the DNS database files, what command most appropriately rereads the database, without restarting the service?

_____

LAB QUESTIONS

Lab 1

In this lab, you'll set up a caching DNS nameserver on your network. Use the /etc/named.caching-nameserver.conf file, modify appropriate files on the clients on your network, and make sure the appropriate daemon is active and starts the next time you boot Linux.

Lab 2

Your internal network is growing, and you're having trouble keeping up with the different workstations that are being added on a regular basis. You use the good.example.com subdomain for your internal network, and you've named your computers for your departments, such as engr1 through engr10.good .example.com.

Your mail server is named postal, your Web server is named www, your FTP server is named ftp. You want to configure a DNS server on the computer named names. What do you need to do?

While you may not have enough information in this lab to create a complete and working file, you should be able to determine an outline of what you need to do, with the possible exception of specific IP addresses.

SELF TEST ANSWERS

Understanding DNS: Zones, Domains, and Delegation

1. If you want to configure a connection from a client to a DNS server, you would use /etc/resolv.conf.

2. If your ISP has a DNS server address of 10.11.12.13, you would add the following directive to the /etc/resolv.conf file:

```
nameserver 10.11.12.13
```

The Berkeley Internet Name Domain (BIND)

3. To support access by other clients to the local DNS server, make sure TCP and UDP traffic is supported through the firewall on port 53.

4. The /etc/named.caching-nameserver.conf file includes a basic template for a DNS caching nameserver. Alternatively, named.conf in the /usr/share/system-config-bind/profiles/default directory also includes a default caching nameserver template.

5. The /etc/named.rfc1912.zones file includes a basic template for a master DNS server. Sample files are also available in the /usr/share/doc/bind-*versionnum*/sample/ directory.

6. If you've installed the bind-chroot RPM, the actual DNS server configuration files can be found in the /var/named/chroot/etc and /var/named/chroot/var/named directories.

7. If you've installed the bind-chroot RPM, you can find links to the actual DNS server configuration files in the /etc and /var/named directories.

8. You would configure a reverse DNS zone database to help other services such as sendmail verify the domain names associated with IP addresses.

9. If there are errors when you start the DNS service, error messages are available by default in /var/log/messages.

10. The command that makes sure that the DNS service starts the next time you boot Linux is

```
# chkconfig named on
```

BIND Utilities

11. The command that lists the data associated with the example.net domain on a properly configured DNS server is

```
# host -l example.net
```

12. After you revise the DNS database files, the command that most appropriately rereads the database, without restarting the service, is

```
# rndc reload
```

LAB ANSWERS

Lab I

In this lab, you have the benefit of the /etc/named.caching-nameserver.conf configuration file. All you need to do is:

1. Copy the template configuration file to /etc/named.conf.

2. Modify the **listen-on port 53** directive to include the local IP address; for example, if your IP address is 10.11.12.13, the directive will look like:

   ```
   listen-on port 53 { 127.0.0.1; 10.11.12.13; };
   ```

3. Modify the **allow-query** directive to include the local IP address; for example, if your network IP address is 10.11.12.0/24, the directive will look like:

   ```
   allow-query { localhost; 10.11.12.0/24; };
   ```

4. Save your changes to /etc/named.conf.

5. Start the **named** service using the remote **named** daemon control facility, also known as the **rndc** command.

   ```
   # rndc start
   ```

6. Change the local client to point to the local DNS caching name server; replace any **nameserver** directives in /etc/resolv.conf with the IP address of the local system. For example, if the local computer is on 10.11.12.13, the directive is

   ```
   nameserver 10.11.12.13
   ```

7. Now test it out. Try commands such as **dig www.yahoo.com**. You should see the following near the end of the output:

   ```
   ;; SERVER: 10.11.12.13#53(10.11.12.13)
   ```

8. This comes from Chapter 7; to make sure the local system (and any other systems you reconfigure) points to the DNS server, add the aforementioned **nameserver** directive to /etc/resolv.conf:

   ```
   nameserver 10.11.12.13
   ```

   Then make sure **PEERDNS=no** in the appropriate network card configuration file, such as ifcfg-eth0 in the /etc/sysconfig/network-scripts/ directory.

9. To make sure the DNS service starts the next time you boot Linux, run the following command:

   ```
   # chkconfig named on
   ```

Lab 2

While you could subcontract out the task to an ISP, it's easy to create a DNS server for your internal network. The basic files are already available in RHEL 5. All you need to do is modify these files and add appropriate zone files to your /var/named/chroot/var/named directory. I'll describe the basics on how you can set up a DNS server by directly editing the appropriate configuration files. Assume that you're using the 10.11.12.0/255.255.255.0 network addresses for your LAN.

First, you'll need to modify the default /etc/named.conf configuration file. It's best to start by backing up this file. You'll need to add stanzas that refer to a zone and a reverse zone file. The stanzas are straightforward:

```
zone "good.example.com" IN {
     type master;
     file "good.example.com.zone";
};

zone "12.11.10.in-addr.apra" IN {
     type master;
     file "good.example.com.rr.zone";
     allow-update { none; }
};
```

Next, you can create the good.example.com.zone and good.example.com.rr.zone files in the /var/named/chroot/var/named and link them to the /var/named directory. These files will contain a database of local and reverse local computer names and IP addresses for your LAN.

In the good.example.com.zone file, you'll want to create the forward database for your DNS server. It will contain the records for your domain as well as the administrator e-mail address. There's not enough information in the problem to set up a full file, but the following principles apply:

1. You need to start the zone file with a general Time To Live (**TTL**) variable; for example, the following command sets a standard **TTL** (4 days) for data on this DNS server:

   ```
   $TTL 4D
   ```

2. You'll need a Start Of Authority (**SOA**) record with the name of the DNS server and your administrative e-mail address. The format of the e-mail address is a little strange; the following line sets an e-mail address of admin@good.example.com. It also sets a serial number based on the date (which you should change to reflect the current date), a refresh (16 hours) and a retry frequency (4 hours), an expatriation period (2 weeks), as well as a **TTL** (4 days). Do note the dot at the end of each name:

   ```
   @    IN    SOA    names.good.example.com. admin.good.example.com. (
                     200402121
                     16H
                     4H
                     2W
                     4D
   ```

3. Now you can specify the computers associated with the DNS and mail servers:

```
IN   NS      names.good.example.com.
IN   MX      10 postal.good.example.com.
```

4. Then you can specify the different computers on your network. While no specific IP addresses are given, you know that you have computers with the following names in the good.example .com.zone file. I've added arbitrary IP addresses on the given IPv4 network. You'll have to find the proper IP addresses for yourself with **ifconfig** commands on each computer:

```
engr1    IN   A    10.11.12.1
engr2    IN   A    10.11.12.2
engr3    IN   A    10.11.12.3
engr4    IN   A    10.11.12.4
engr5    IN   A    10.11.12.5
engr6    IN   A    10.11.12.6
engr7    IN   A    10.11.12.7
engr8    IN   A    10.11.12.8
engr9    IN   A    10.11.12.9
engr10   IN   A    10.11.12.10
ftp      IN   A    10.11.12.11
www      IN   A    10.11.12.12
postal   IN   A    10.11.12.13
```

5. Finally, to make sure that the DNS server works the next time you boot this Linux computer, you'll want to set it to run at the appropriate runlevels with a command such as the following:

```
# chkconfig named on
```

12
Electronic Mail

CERTIFICATION OBJECTIVES

12.01	Mail Transport Agents, Mail Delivery Agents, and Mail User Agents	12.04	Configuring and Activating Postfix
12.02	Reception with Dovecot	12.05	Selecting an E-mail System
12.03	sendmail Configuration	✓	Two-Minute Drill
		Q&A	Self Test

Linux offers a number of alternative methods for handling incoming and outgoing e-mail. Red Hat Enterprise Linux includes sendmail, Postfix, and Dovecot for this purpose. (Yes, it includes exim and squirrelmail as well, but sendmail, Postfix, and Dovecot are what's listed in the RH300 course outline, and Dovecot is the new default for incoming e-mail.)

Perhaps the most common server for outgoing e-mail is sendmail, which may already be installed on your RHEL system. Once it is installed and configured, you can set up sendmail as your own personal mail server (subject to the limitations of your ISP). RHEL includes the open-source version of sendmail; the commercial version is known as Sendmail (with the capital S). One alternative to sendmail that is installed on RHEL is known as Postfix.

RHEL includes Dovecot for standard incoming e-mail protocols. It's relatively easy to configure these protocols, including POP3 (Post Office Protocol), POP3S (the secure version), IMAP (Internet Message Access Protocol), and IMAPS (the secure version).

exam

watch

A number of alternatives to sendmail are not covered in this book; they include procmail, mail.local, exim, Cyrus IMAP, and uucp. Only sendmail, Postfix, and Dovecot are currently part of Red Hat's public RH300 course outline.

INSIDE THE EXAM

More Network Services

This chapter is focused on the RHCE exam. While the ability to configure an e-mail client is a prerequisite skill for both exams, the Red Hat Exam Prep guide suggests that RHCE candidates must know how to configure the following network services:

■ SMTP

■ IMAP, IMAPS, and POP3

While sendmail and Postfix are not specified in the Exam Prep guide, the RHCE course, RH300, includes coverage of Dovecot, sendmail, and Postfix. Dovecot is one RHEL 5 service that can handle IMAP, IMAPS, and POP3.

This chapter is related to the following items on the Troubleshooting and System Maintenance portion of the RHCE exam:

■ Diagnose and correct problems with network services, including whatever mail related services that you've configured.

There's also the related Troubleshooting and System Maintenance requirement to

■ Diagnose and correct networking services problems where SELinux contexts are interfering with proper operation.

But the only e-mail related option is to disable SELinux protection for Postfix (and fetchmail).

You may need to install, configure, and secure these services during the Installation and Configuration portion of the exam. And don't forget to make sure any required services are active when you reboot, or you may not get credit for your work.

As for the RHCE exam, you may have to configure or troubleshoot the e-mail services discussed in this chapter. So as you read this chapter and look through the configuration files and exercises, be willing to experiment. And practice, practice, practice what you learn.

CERTIFICATION OBJECTIVE 12.01

Mail Transport Agents, Mail Delivery Agents, and Mail User Agents

When you install sendmail, Postfix, and/or Dovecot, you also get huge and difficult-to-read configuration files. Do not be intimidated, as it's likely that you'll have to change only a few entries in each file.

Definitions

A mail server has three major components, as described in Table 12-1. You need all three components to have a fully functional mail system. Fortunately, as the other components are already installed, you should have to install only the MTAs that you need on a standard RHEL system.

On any Linux computer, you can configure some mail transfer agents (sendmail or Postfix) for various outbound services, such as forwarding, relaying, method of transport (such as TCP or UDP), lists of computers with other MTAs, optional aliases, and spooling directories. Others, such as Dovecot, are designed to handle only incoming e-mail services.

E-mail systems are heavily dependent on name resolution. While you could handle name resolution through /etc/hosts on a small network, any mail system that requires Internet access needs access to a fully functional DNS server.

The sendmail and Postfix systems use SMTP to send e-mail. But that is only one end of the mail system. You also need to use a service such as Dovecot to enable POP3 and/or IMAP (or the secure cousins, POP3s and IMAPS) to receive e-mail.

TABLE 12-1 Mail Server Components

Abbreviation	Meaning	Examples
MTA	Mail transfer agent	sendmail, Postfix, Dovecot
MUA	Mail user agent	mail, Evolution, elm
MDA	Mail delivery agent	procmail, maildrop

While this chapter refers to the IMAP and IMAPS protocols, rest assured that these options support the current versions of these protocols, IMAP4 and IMAP4S.

SMTP, the Simple Mail Transfer Protocol, has become one of the most important service protocols of the modern era. Much of the Internet-connected world lives and dies by e-mail and relies on SMTP to deliver it. Like POP3 and IMAP, SMTP is a *protocol*, a set of rules for transferring data used by various mail transfer agents.

Installing Mail Server Packages

The RPM packages associated with sendmail and Postfix are both part of the Mail Server package group. Key packages are listed in Table 12-2. You can install them with the **rpm** or **yum** command. Just remember that you may not need to install everything in this table.

When you install the default Mail Server package group, you're installing the sendmail and Dovecot packages. Since you may not need all of these packages, it may be faster to install these with the **rpm** or **yum** command, especially if you're configuring your Linux computer from the text console. It takes time to start the GUI.

TABLE 12-2   Key Mail Server RPMs

RPM Package	Description
cyrus-imapd*	Installs the Cyrus IMAP enterprise e-mail system (several packages); may require perl-Cyrus
cyrus-sasl	Adds the Cyrus implementation of the Simple Authentication and Security Layer (SASL)
dovecot	Supports both the IMAP and the POP incoming e-mail protocols
exim	Adds another MTA; another alternative to sendmail and Postfix
mailman	Supports e-mail discussion lists
postfix	Includes an alternative to sendmail
sendmail	Installs the most popular mail server of the same name
sendmail-cf	Adds a number of templates that you can use to generate your sendmail configuration file
spamassassin	Includes the spam fighting package of the same name
squirrelmail	Installs a Web-based e-mail server
system-switch-mail system-switch-mail-gnome	Adds a GUI method for switching between sendmail and Postfix

You can find a list of RPMs associated with each package group on the first installation CD in the /Server/repodata directory in the comps-rhel5-server-core.xml file. If you're running the RHEL 5 desktop, substitute "Client" for "Server."

CERTIFICATION OBJECTIVE 12.02

Reception with Dovecot

Once you've installed the Dovecot package, it's easy to configure. All you need to do is add the appropriate directive in the Dovecot configuration file and make sure it starts the next time you start Linux. If you use a secure incoming e-mail protocol such as POP3S or IMAPS, you'll want to configure an appropriate certificate as well.

The process has changed significantly relative to RHEL 4. But first, let's review the POP3 and IMAP protocols.

POP

The Post Office Protocol (POP) is one of the major mail delivery protocols. It includes some basic commands that allow you or an e-mail client to send and retrieve messages. A mail service can be configured to be a central depository for incoming mail messages from any other MTA service. Client applications then download the mail messages from the POP server for processing at the local host.

The current version of POP is known as POP3.

You can configure user accounts that are designed to service only POP user accounts, where users log in and receive mail only and no interactive service is provided. Just set up the appropriate mail client in the login configuration sequence for a given user.

IMAP

The IMAP (Internet Message Access Protocol) is the other major mail delivery protocol. While POP downloads all e-mail to the client, an IMAP server maintains all mail messages on the server, as a database. IMAP is commonly used by businesses that service users who log in from different locations. It's also the most common mail delivery protocol for Web-based mail services.

The current version of IMAP is known as IMAP4.

Configuration File

Now that you've reviewed the protocols, let's start configuring Dovecot. The main configuration file, /etc/dovecot.conf, is well commented. As the file is nearly 1000 lines long, this section focuses on a few key directives. The first thing to note is this comment:

```
# Default values are shown after each value, it's not required to
# uncomment any of the lines.
```

The protocols you select depend on what's specified during your exam. As suggested earlier, IMAPS and POP3S are secure versions of IMAP and POP3. Normally, you should not activate a protocol unless you intend to use it; otherwise, you're opening up a potential security hole:

```
#protocols = imap imaps pop3 pop3s
```

If you have multiple network cards (or multiple IP addresses on your network card), you'll want to specify an IP address where the server listens for connections. You can do so by activating the following directives with appropriate IP addresses. If you use nonstandard ports, you can specify them here as well. Here are two examples:

```
#listen = 192.168.0.22:10110
#ssl listen = 192.168.0.23:10943
```

If you want POP3S or IMAP4S support, you'll want to retain this directive (pay attention—it's a double-negative; in other words, this directive tells Dovecot that it should not disable SSL protocols):

```
#ssl_disable = no
```

For secure support, you'll also need certificates and keys. The default locations are shown as commented. I'll describe how you can create your own certificate shortly:

```
#ssl_cert_file = /etc/pki/dovecot/certs/dovecot.pem
#ssl_key_file = /etc/pki/dovecot/private/dovecot.pem
```

Part of the way down the file, you can specify the location where e-mail is stored, with the **mail_location** directive (this is the successor to the old **default_mail_env** setting). You should specify a location; otherwise Dovecot will have problems with users who don't yet have a dedicated directory. Some suggestions are listed in the comments of the configuration file. Naturally, this depends on the default mail directories associated with your users' preferred e-mail programs.

Activating Dovecot

Activating Dovecot is a straightforward process and should already be familiar to you. I repeat it here because you probably won't get credit for your work if your system does not activate Dovecot (or any other required service) when you boot Linux. The commands should be familiar; while alternatives are available, the following commands start Dovecot and make sure that it starts when you reboot Linux into four different runlevels (2, 3, 4, and 5):

```
# service dovecot on
# chkconfig dovecot on
```

And to make sure that you didn't make a mistake, you can confirm that Dovecot is active and will boot in desired runlevels with the following commands:

```
# service dovecot status
# chkconfig --list dovecot
```

Dovecot Secure Certificates

There have been changes in the way Dovecot certificates are created. As shown in the configuration file, certificates are now stored in two /etc/pki/dovecot subdirectories. To create your own certificate, you'll need to modify the dovecot-openssl.cnf file in /etc/pki/dovecot. As described in Table 12-3, the directives are straightforward and are normally set to defaults that you would not want to use. Everything you need to activate is in the **[req_dn]** stanza.

You'll have to delete (or move) the default certificates, both named dovecot.pem, in the following directories:

```
/etc/pki/dovecot/certs
/etc/pki/dovecot/private
```

Make sure the associated script, mkcert.sh, in the /usr/share/doc/dovecot-*versionnum*/ examples/ directory is executable, and then run it:

```
# /usr/share/doc/dovecot-versionnum/examples/mkcert.sh
```

TABLE 12-3 Directives in dovecot-openssl.cnf for Your Own SSL Certificate

Directive	Description
C	Country code; use the standard two-letter code for your country as defined
ST	State or province name; if you're in the USA, use the two-letter postal code for your state
L	Name of your locality (city or town)
O	Name of your organization or company
OU	Name of the group within your organization
CN	Common or FQDN of your IMAP server
emailAddress	Administrative e-mail address for the server
nsCertType	Normally specifies a server

CERTIFICATION OBJECTIVE 12.03

sendmail Configuration

The sendmail daemon is configured from a directory of files in /etc/mail and a directory of configuration files in /usr/share/sendmail-cf. There are two basic configuration files: sendmail.cf for incoming mail and submit.cf for outgoing mail. I describe the key configuration files in /etc/mail in a bit of detail here.

- **sendmail.cf**   The main sendmail configuration file.
- **sendmail.mc**   A macro that's easier to edit, which can be used to generate a new sendmail.cf file.
- **access**   Supports outgoing access control to your sendmail server. The default version of this file supports access from the local computer. You can add host names or networks to this list, with a message to **REJECT** with an error message, **DISCARD** without an error message, or **RELAY** to accept and send the e-mail.
- **domaintable**   Allows you to map different domains. For example, if you've changed your domain name from Osborne.com to Mcgraw-hill.com, people might still send e-mails to addresses such as michael@Osborne.com. The following line would forward that e-mail to michael@Mcgraw-hill.com.

  ```
  Osborne.com   Mcgraw-hill.com
  ```

- **helpfile**   Supports help commands when you manage your mail server from the sendmail prompt, which you can access with the **telnet localhost 25** command.
- **local-host-names**   Allows you to add host names or aliases for your computer as a sendmail server. Enter one alias per line in this file.
- **mailertable**   Rarely used.
- **Makefile**   Supports compiling the sendmail.mc file.
- **spamassassin/**   A directory that includes configuration files that can help you minimize spam. If you want to configure it on locally received e-mail, add the following line to /etc/procmailrc:

  ```
  INCLUDERC=/etc/mail/spamassassin/spamassassin-default.rc
  ```

on the **job**

If you forget this detail, run the **rpm -qi spamassassin** *command. You'll see it in the description.*

- **statistic**   Collects statistics on sendmail usage in binary format. You can read it with the **mailstats** command. Does not exist until the sendmail service starts processing mail.
- **submit.cf**   The main outgoing sendmail configuration file.
- **submit.mc**   A macro that you can edit and then generate a new submit.cf file.
- **trusted-users**   Lists special users that can send e-mail without warnings. For example, you saw e-mail addresses in the Apache configuration file; if you include the apache user in this list, it can send messages to your Web server administrators without generating sendmail warning messages.
- **virtusertable**   Supports e-mail forwarding; if some users outside your network use your sendmail server, you can enter individual e-mail addresses or domains for allowed users.

If you don't see some of these files or directories, you may not have both sendmail RPM packages installed: sendmail and sendmail-cf. Use the **rpm -q** *packagename* command to determine whether these packages are installed and install them as required.

You'll also need to make sure the file is properly cited in sendmail.mc. For example, the following directive incorporates /etc/mail/virtusertable in your sendmail.mc configuration file:

```
FEATURE(`virtusertable',`hash -o /etc/mail/virtusertable.db')dnl
```

You may notice several versions of these files with .db extensions. These are the database files used by sendmail. When you make changes to the base files, the **make -C /etc/mail** command, described shortly, processes these files into the .db databases.

There's one more important file, /etc/aliases, described later in this chapter. This file allows you to create forwarders on the same domain. For example, if user mary leaves the company, you can use this file to have her mail forwarded to user cindy.

Configuring sendmail for Basic Operation

When sendmail starts, it reads the /etc/mail/sendmail.cf and /etc/mail/submit.cf files. The sendmail.cf file is a long (around 1800 lines) file that may seem difficult to decipher but includes a wealth of helpful comments. The submit.cf file is nearly as long. This file provides detailed rules (organized into rulesets) on how sendmail should process e-mail addresses, filter spam, talk to other mail servers, and more.

This file is extremely complex and uses cryptic syntax. Fortunately, most of the directives included in this file are standards that you don't need to change. Many are required by various Internet agreements relating to e-mail address, mail transfer agents, and so on.

Red Hat simplifies this process with a smaller file, /etc/mail/sendmail.mc, which contains only the most relevant configuration directives. It is composed entirely of macros that define key sendmail.cf settings. Once you've configured this file, you can use the **make** command to compile a new, custom sendmail.cf file. However, the default RHEL version of this file is still around 200 lines long. Remember that the Red Hat Exam Prep guide requires only that you know how to configure the service for *basic* operation. Therefore, I'll highlight those directives that you may want to change or modify for that purpose.

The sendmail.mc file is made up of directives (macros) used to create content for sendmail.cf. (Other related .mc files follow the same criteria and use many of the same commands). These macros do the following:

- Add comments to aid in comprehension
- Define key variables and values
- Enable or disable features
- Create variables with specific settings

The most basic macro is **dnl**, which tells **m4** to delete from this point through to the end of the line. It is used to comment out descriptive text or disable a feature that would otherwise be included.

The **include** directive instructs the **make** command to read the contents of the named file and insert it at the current location in the output. This is how additional configuration information (needed by sendmail but not relevant to mail configuration) is kept separately from settings you may wish to change.

The **define** directive sets files or enables features that you want to use. Some examples in sendmail.mc allow you to set the path to your administrative e-mail name in the **ALIAS_FILE** (/etc/aliases), identify where procmail lives (**PROCMAIL_MAILER_ PATH**), and provide the path for the official database of e-mail users—in this case, in virtualusertable.db.

The **FEATURE** directive enables specific features. For example, one **FEATURE** directive allows sendmail to **accept_unresolvable_domains**. This allows sendmail to accept mail even if it can't figure out the domain of the user who sent the e-mail. Specifically, a domain is regarded as unresolvable when a reverse IP address lookup does not find the associated domain name. If you don't have reliable DNS access, you may need this feature, or else your sendmail configuration may refuse a lot of valid e-mail.

DAEMON_OPTIONS directly controls the SMTP daemon. The default active **DAEMON_OPTIONS** directive does not accept any mail from outside the local system, as defined by the localhost address:

```
DAEMON_OPTIONS(`Port=smtp,Addr=127.0.0.1, Name=MTA')dnl
```

You'll notice unusual quote characters in most of these lines. The command inside parenthesis starts with a back quote (`` ` ``) and ends with a single quote (').

Configuring and Securing sendmail

In this section, you'll modify the sendmail.mc configuration file. Back it up first! You need to make only a couple of adjustments to get your system ready for use on the Internet. By default, the following line limits sendmail access to the local computer:

```
DAEMON_OPTIONS(`Port=smtp,Addr=127.0.0.1, Name=MTA')dnl
```

You can allow other computers to use your sendmail server by commenting out this line. As described earlier, this requires a **dnl** directive, as shown:

```
dnl DAEMON_OPTIONS(`Port=smtp,Addr=127.0.0.1, Name=MTA')dnl
```

Next, if you have reliable DNS access, comment out the **FEATURE** directive that allows you to **accept_unresolvable_domains**. This blocks spammers who use just an IP address or spammers who fake their domain name to hide themselves:

```
FEATURE(`accept_unresolvable_domains')dnl
```

But that's not enough. If you want to allow remote computers or networks access to your sendmail server, you'll need to add their names or addresses to the /etc/mail/ access file. For example, if you wanted to allow access to the 192.168.30.0 domain, you'd add the following line to that file:

```
192.168.30          RELAY
```

Watch the notation; unlike other services, there is no dot (.) at the end of the address. It covers all computers on the 192.168.30.0 network. Alternatively, you could designate the example.com domain or a specific computer name or IP address.

Back up the current sendmail.cf file. Then you can generate a new sendmail .cf file, process the other files in /etc/mail, and restart sendmail services with the following command:

```
# make -C /etc/mail/
```

Now you can reconfigure e-mail clients such as Novell Evolution or even Microsoft Outlook Express to send outgoing e-mail through your sendmail server. You'll need to set your sendmail computer domain name or IP address as the SMTP outgoing mail server.

*In previous versions of sendmail, all you needed to do was process sendmail .mc; it was therefore sufficient to use the m4 macro command. But you may be processing more files. The **make -C /etc/mail** command shown processes all files in the /etc/mail directory.*

Configuring sendmail to Start at Reboot

Now start or restart sendmail to make sure it reads your new sendmail.cf configuration file:

```
# chkconfig sendmail on
# service sendmail restart
```

Your sendmail (SMTP) service should now be up and running and ready to accept mail from any (valid) source. To check the result, the following commands show that sendmail is currently running and starts in the desired runlevels:

```
# service sendmail status
# chkconfig --list sendmail
```

Troubleshooting sendmail

When name resolution is not working on your network, sendmail doesn't know where to send your outbound e-mail. These messages are placed in a queue that tries to resend your e-mail at regular intervals. Other mail forwarders and relay hosts on the Internet provide the same functionality if a network segment is not working. As an administrator, you need to monitor this queue. If it gets overloaded, you may wish to reconfigure messages for that network to be sent at more irregular times. See the following code for an example of a problem message (yes, this is old software from 1993, but is still a dependable part of RHEL). The prompt in this utility is the ampersand (&):

```
# mail
Mail version 8.1 6/6/93.  Type ? for help.
```

```
"/var/spool/mail/root" 1 messages 1 new
>N  1 MAILER-DAEMON@enterp  Wed Dec 3 08:55  60/1914  "Returned mail: see tr"
```

Press ENTER to see each message, or the message number at the prompt (**&**):

```
Message 1:
From MAILER-DAEMON@localhost.localdomain  Wed Dec  6 08:55:39 2006
Date: Wed, 6 Dec 2006 08:55:39 -0500
From: Mail Delivery Subsystem <MAILER-DAEMON@enterprise5a.example.org>
To:   root@ enterprise5a.example.org
MIME-Version: 1.0
Content-Type: multipart/report; report-type=delivery-status;
        boundary="DAA03153.938948139/enterprise5a.example.org"
Subject: Returned mail: see transcript for details
Auto-Submitted: auto-generated (failure)
This is a MIME-encapsulated message
--DAA03153.938948139/enterprise5a.example.org
The original message was received at Wed, 6 Dec 2006 08:55:39 -0500
from root@enterprise5a.example.org


—- The following addresses had transient non-fatal errors —-
<michael@mommabears.cob>
    (reason: 550 Host unknown)
  —- Transcript of session follows —-
550 5.1.2 <michael@mommabears.cob>... Host unknown
(Name server: mommabears.cob: host not found)
..
(additional details deleted)
..
```

Now the **d** command deletes the current message, and the **q** command exits from the mail utility.

In the preceding example, the destination name server (mommabears.cob) could not be resolved (it is actually mommabears.com). Consequently, sendmail notifies the sender (root@localhost.localdomain) that the mail could not be delivered.

In this case, the problem is straightforward: you've specified an nonstandard domain. However, you may get a similar error for any of the following reasons:

- No DNS server available, if so required in sendmail.mc.
- Access from a computer not listed or specifically denied in the /etc/mail/ access configuration file.
- Some firewall blocking access. You can configure a firewall to allow incoming e-mail through TCP/IP port 25. You can find more information about this in Chapter 15.

CERTIFICATION OBJECTIVE 12.04

Configuring and Activating Postfix

You can configure the Postfix mail server as a substitute for sendmail. The configuration files are stored in the /etc/postfix directory. The main configuration file, main.cf, is somewhat simpler than sendmail.cf, as it includes over 600 lines. Back up this file and open it in a text editor. There are several things that you should configure in this file to get it working—and limit access to your system and network:

- Activate and modify the following **myhostname** directive to point to the name of your computer:

```
#myhostname = host.domain.tld
```

- Activate and modify the following **mydomain** directive to reflect the domain name or IP network address of your system (if you substitute your IP network address, use the same format as illustrated for the sendmail.mc file):

```
#mydomain = domain.tld
```

- Activate and modify the following **myorigin** directive, assuming you've activated the aforementioned **myhostname** directive.

```
#myorigin = $mydomain
```

- The following two commands set Postfix to listen to only the local computer. Activate and deactivate the following commands to remove that limitation:

```
#inet_interfaces = all
inet_interfaces = localhost
```

- Activate and modify the following **mynetworks** command to point to the IP network address that you want to serve.

```
#mynetworks = 168.100.189.0/28, 127.0.0.0/8
```

Configuring Postfix to Start at Reboot

Now start or restart Postfix to make sure it reads your new /etc/postfix/main.cf configuration file:

```
# chkconfig postfix on
# service postfix restart
```

Your Postfix service should now be up and running and ready to accept mail from any (valid) source, as specified by the preceding directives.

Selecting an E-mail System

If you have installed and configured both sendmail and Postfix, be careful. Don't activate both. There are two simple commands that can help you select the default e-mail server: **alternatives** and **system-switch-mail**.

Once you select a system, you need to know how to test the system. Sure, you can set up Thunderbird or Evolution, but that takes time. It's easiest to use the **mail** utility to send a quick e-mail. When you do so from a remote system, you can make sure the active server does what you want, and does not accept mail from other systems.

Using alternatives to Select an E-mail System

The **alternatives** command is straightforward. Try the following:

```
# alternatives --config mta
```

You'll see this output, which allows you to choose from installed e-mail servers:

```
There are 2 programs which provide 'mta'.

  Selection    Command
-----------------------------------------------
*+ 1           /usr/sbin/sendmail.sendmail
   2           /usr/sbin/sendmail.postfix

Enter to keep the current selection[+], or type selection number:
```

When you select sendmail or Postfix, **alternatives** changes the appropriate runlevel scripts, which you can confirm with the following commands:

```
# chkconfig --list sendmail
# chkconfig --list postfix
```

For example, if you've previously activated Postfix and select sendmail, **alternatives** stops Postfix and starts sendmail. However, if neither service is started, you'll have to do it yourself with *one* of the following commands:

```
# service sendmail on
# service postfix on
```

Don't activate both sendmail and Postfix on the same system.

Switching with system-switch-mail

If you can't remember how to use **alternatives**, you can use the **system-switch-mail** command. If you use it, it opens a simple console tool, as shown in Figure 12-1. As you can see, all you need to do is use your keyboard to select between installed e-mail servers.

The disadvantage of **system-switch-mail** is that it's not installed by default; you may have to install the **system-switch-mail** RPM to use the associated command.

E-mail Clients

One of the prerequisite skills for the Red Hat exams is to configure an e-mail client. This should be easy for anyone who has used Linux for any length of time. In fact, the process for graphical Linux clients such as Evolution or Thunderbird is quite similar to the process for various Microsoft e-mail clients. But as you've seen earlier in this section, there are text-based mail clients as well.

Command Line Mail

To test your mail system, you can use the built-in command line **mail** utility, a simple text-based interface. The system keeps each user's mail in a system directory. Once users read a message, they can reply, forward, or delete it. If they do not delete the message before quitting the **mail** utility, the system stores the message in the /var/ mail directory in a file named after the applicable username.

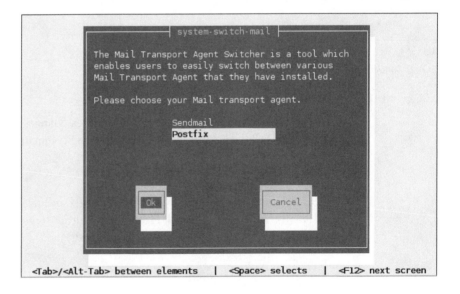

FIGURE 12-1

system-switch-mail

You can certainly use any of the other mail readers, such as mutt or the e-mail managers associated with different GUI Web browsers, to test your system. Other mail readers store messages in different directories. For example, pine would create and store messages for user mj in the /home/mj/mail directory.

To send mail to another user, you can use the **mail** command line utility. There are two basic methods for using **mail**. First, you can enter the subject and then the text of your message. When you're done, press CTRL-D and then enter another addressee in the Cc: line, if desired. When you press ENTER, the message is sent and the **mail** utility stops and sends you back to the command line.

```
$ mail Michael
Subject: Test Message
Sent and received
Cc: mjang@example.com
$
```

But even that takes time. Alternatively, you can redirect a file as the text of an e-mail to another user. For example, the following command sends a copy of /etc/hosts to the root user, with the subject name of *hosts file*:

```
$ mail root@enterprise5a.example.net -s "hosts file" < /etc/hosts
```

Here's one more example, which sends an e-mail containing the words *test message* under a subject name of *test subject*.

```
$ echo "test message" | mail -s "test subject" root@enterprise5a.example.net
```

e x a m

ⓦatch　　　**You may want to test mail servers with a simple command line client such as mail. It's certainly faster** **than configuring a client such as mutt or Evolution.**

Reading Mail Messages

By default, the mail system doesn't open unless you actually have e-mail in your inbox. Once the mail system is open, you'll see a list of new and already read messages. To read a specific message, enter the number of the message and press ENTER. If you press ENTER with no argument, the mail utility assumes you want to read the next unread message. To delete a mail message, use the **d** command after reading the message, or use **d#** to delete the message numbered #.

Mail Group "Alias" Lists

If you have a distribution list of people for the same e-mail, you can set it up in the /etc/aliases file. By default, it's set up to forward e-mail from pseudo-accounts such as system and apache to root. You can change it by adding a group list similar to the following:

```
groupname:  user01, user02, othergroupname
```

Alternatively, you can forward e-mail from one employee to another. For example, you can add the following line to forward e-mail from oldemployee@yourdomain.abc to newemployee@yourdomain.abc:

```
oldemployee: newemployee
```

You can then run the **newaliases** command to compile this database. Then all you need to do is name the group of users as addressees for your e-mail.

Testing the Results

If you have to install an e-mail server during the RHCE exam, you'll want to be able to test the results. You could configure familiar GUI e-mail clients, but that takes time. The easiest method uses the **mail** command, which is part of the default **mailx** package. Once you've configured sendmail or Postfix and Dovecot to run on your system, you can try it out at least from the local computer.

EXERCISE 12-1

Testing E-mail Services

If you haven't started an e-mail server such as sendmail or Postfix, this exercise won't work. If necessary, configure one of these servers as described earlier in this chapter. This exercise also assumes you have a working DNS server. If you do not, make sure you configure host names and IP addresses in /etc/hosts.

1. Activate the Dovecot service on the local computer. If you haven't already done so, configure it as described earlier in this chapter.

2. If you have problems activating Dovecot, make sure SELinux protection for this service is disabled.

3. Open /etc/aliases, and have e-mail forwarded from one user to another. For the purpose of this exercise, I have e-mail forwarded from user nancy to user

michael. User nancy does not have an account on my system. I've added the following entry to /etc/aliases:

```
nancy:   michael
```

4. Run the **newaliases** command to process the alias.

5. Inspect the result in /var/log/maillog. What do you see?

6. Go to another system. It's acceptable to do so with a remote service such as SSH (described in Chapter 13).

7. Send an e-mail to the user on your original system. In my case, I'm sending it to user nancy.

8. Check the result in the mail spool and log files. If everything works, you'll see the message in /var/spool/mail/michael (substitute your target username for michael). You'll also see a message in the remote system's (the computer from where you sent the e-mail) /var/log/maillog file. If there's a problem, you'll see a message in /var/log/maillog similar to this:

```
connection refused by:
```

CERTIFICATION SUMMARY

Red Hat uses the Dovecot service for incoming e-mail. It can be configured for use with both the POP3 and IMAP protocols, as well as their secure cousins (POP3S and IMAPS). If you want to handle secure incoming e-mail, you'll want to set up SSL certificates in the /etc/pki/dovecot/certs and /etc/pki/dovecot/private directories. The mkcert.sh script is designed to help create custom certificates, using settings you add to the /etc/pki/dovecot/dovecot-openssl.cnf file.

Red Hat includes two servers for outgoing e-mail: sendmail and Postfix. Both rely on SMTP to send e-mail. The sendmail service includes difficult-to-read configuration files: sendmail.cf and submit.cf, both in the /etc/mail directory. Fortunately, you can configure these files through easier-to-read macro files, sendmail.mc and submit.mc. Postfix is somewhat easier to configure directly through its own configuration file, /etc/postfix/main.cf. Red Hat also provides a variety of e-mail clients, including **mail**, mutt, and the mail clients that come with the various Web browsers that are also available for Linux. These clients use either POP or IMAP protocols to receive e-mail.

Because RHCE is a performance-based exam, just like life, it is important to practice all the skills discussed in this chapter. You may need to use these skills on the exam!

TWO-MINUTE DRILL

Here are some of the key points from the certification objectives in Chapter 12.

Mail Transport Agents, Mail Delivery Agents, and Mail User Agents

❑ Mail transport agents (MTA) are servers that carry e-mail to and from users.

❑ Three MTAs include sendmail, Postfix, and Dovecot.

❑ Mail user agents (MUA) are e-mail clients such as mail and Evolution.

❑ Mail delivery agents (MDA) are used with MTAs to transmit e-mail.

Reception with Dovecot

❑ The Dovecot service supports receipt of both POP3 and IMAP4 e-mail.

❑ Dovecot supports secure SSL versions of POP3 and IMAP4; you'll need to create SSL certificates in appropriate /etc/pki/dovecot directories.

sendmail Configuration

❑ The main sendmail configuration file is /etc/mail/sendmail.cf. It's easier to configure sendmail through its macro file, /etc/mail/sendmail.mc.

❑ You can customize the computers allowed to access your sendmail server through the access and virtusertable files in the /etc/mail directory.

❑ The **make -C /etc/mail** command processes all files in that directory, to configure sendmail completely.

Configuring and Activating Postfix

❑ The Postfix server is easier to configure through configuration files in the /etc/postfix directory. In fact, you can configure the main.cf file directly.

❑ Postfix also uses /etc/aliases to map and forward e-mail from old to new addresses.

Selecting an E-mail System

❑ RHEL 5 allows you to select between sendmail and Postfix. Don't activate both.

❑ Available tools for selecting a service are **alternatives** and **system-switch-mail**.

❑ Different mail clients can receive e-mail using the POP or IMAP protocols. Mail clients such as **mail** and mutt are available at the command line. GUI mail clients such as Thunderbird and Evolution are also available.

SELF TEST

The following questions will help you measure your understanding of the material presented in this chapter. As no multiple choice questions appear on the Red Hat exams, no multiple choice questions appear in this book. These questions exclusively test your understanding of the chapter. It is okay if you have another way of performing a task. Getting results, not memorizing trivia, is what counts on the Red Hat exams. There may be more than one answer to many of the questions.

Mail Transport Agents, Mail Delivery Agents, and Mail User Agents

1. What package described in this chapter can be configured for incoming POP3 and IMAP4 e-mail? _____

Reception with Dovecot

2. If you don't want to allow secure incoming e-mail, what would you do with the following directive in /etc/dovecot.conf?

    ```
    #protocols = imap imaps pop3 pop3s
    ```

    _____

3. What script should you use to configure an SSL certificate for Dovecot?

    _____

4. What certificate files do you need to move or delete before creating a customized SSL certificate?

    _____

sendmail Configuration

5. In what file would you store forwarding e-mail addresses?

    _____

6. Why would you want to comment out the following directive in sendmail.mc?

    ```
    DAEMON_OPTIONS(`Port=smtp,Addr=127.0.0.1, Name=MTA')dnl
    ```

    _____

7. What do you need if you want to comment out the following directive in sendmail.mc?

    ```
    FEATURE(`accept_unresolvable_domains')dnl
    ```

    _____

8. What command processes all files in /etc/mail?

_____

Configuring and Activating Postfix

9. How would you change the following directive in /etc/postfix/main.cf to open Postfix to all systems?

   ```
   inet_interfaces = localhost
   ```

_____

10. If you use /etc/aliases for forwarding e-mail, what command processes these files into an appropriate database file for Postfix?

_____

Selecting an E-mail System

11. What command allows you to select between the Postfix and sendmail servers?

_____

12. What command line e-mail client can you use to test a server?

_____

   Extra Credit: What can you run directly from the command line to send a simple test e-mail?

_____

LAB QUESTIONS

Lab 1

Configure Thunderbird or Evolution to read your e-mail. You can set it up to read e-mail without downloading it from the server (even if it's a POP3 server).

Run the **mail** command as the root user. Browse through available e-mails. Normally, you should have more than a few based on issues such as bad logins and logwatch jobs.

Review the appropriate mail server spool and log files. Current Postfix mail log messages can also be found in /var/log/maillog.

Lab 2

Configure a Dovecot server with support for regular and secure POP3 and IMAP4 services. Create appropriate SSL certificates in default directories, based on your location.

Lab 3

Set up a sendmail mail server for your network. First, make sure to disable local-only access in the /etc/mail/sendmail.mc file. Add your network to the /etc/mail/access file. Test the results, preferably from a remote computer on your network.

Set up two users on your system. You can use existing users. For the purpose of this lab, assume these users are linus and bill. Make sure e-mail is forwarded from bill to linus.

Make sure to start the sendmail server now, and see that it starts automatically the next time you reboot your computer.

Lab 4

Set up a Postfix mail server for your network. Test the results, preferably from a remote computer on your network. Retain the forwarding from Lab 2, where e-mail addressed to user bill is forwarded to user linus. Connect to a remote system, and send e-mail to user bill.

SELF TEST ANSWERS

Mail Transport Agents, Mail Delivery Agents, and Mail User Agents

1. The package that can be configured to receive POP3 and IMAP4 e-mail is Dovecot.

Reception with Dovecot

2. If you don't want to allow secure incoming e-mail (for whatever reason), you need to activate and change the **protocols** directive to specify only the nonsecure e-mail protocols:

   ```
   protocols = imap pop3
   ```

3. The script that helps configure an SSL certificate for Dovecot is mkcert.sh, in the /usr/share/doc/dovecot-1.0/examples directory.

4. The certificate files that you need to move or delete before creating a customized SSL certificate are both named dovecot.pem, in the /etc/pki/dovecot/certs and /etc/pki/dovecot/private directories.

sendmail Configuration

5. Forwarding e-mail addresses for both sendmail and Postfix are normally stored in /etc/aliases. If you're forwarding e-mail for entire domains, the appropriate file is /etc/mail/domaintable. Make sure to process these files into appropriate databases; for /etc/aliases, the database is updated with the **newaliases** command. For /etc/mail/domaintable, the database is updated with the next **make -C /etc/mail** command.

6. The noted directive limits sendmail server access to the localhost computer, IP address 127.0.0.1.

7. If you don't want to accept unresolvable domains, say to minimize spam on your system, you'll need reliable DNS service. Otherwise, reverse DNS searches may fail, and your system may not accept even legitimate e-mail.

8. The **make -C /etc/mail** command processes all files in /etc/mail, including sendmail.mc, submit.mc, and the database files in that directory. It does not process any forwarding aliases in /etc/aliases; if you make a change to this file, you need to use the **newaliases** command.

Configuring and Activating Postfix

9. The simplest solution is to change the directive to

   ```
   inet_interfaces = all
   ```

10. Forwarding e-mail addresses for both sendmail and Postfix are normally stored in /etc/aliases. Make sure to process these files into appropriate databases; for /etc/aliases, the database is updated with the **newaliases** command.

Selecting an E-mail System

11. There are a wide variety of solutions to this problem. The simplest solutions are fastest and best. Two simple commands can help you switch between Postfix and sendmail: **alternatives --config mta** and **system-switch-mail**.

12. Several command-line e-mail clients are available for RHEL, including mutt and **mail**.

Extra Credit: One simple way to send a message with the **mail** client is with the following command (variations are acceptable, as the point is to check the e-mail server quickly from a remote location). The e-mail subject in this case is *test subject* and the message is *hello kitty*.

```
# echo "hello kitty" | mail -s "test subject" michael@enterprise5a
```

Once the message is sent, you can confirm in the mail spool for the user and the log file for the server.

LAB ANSWERS

Lab 1

This should be a trivial lab for most users. Anyone who is preparing for the RHCE exam should already know how to configure GUI e-mail clients such as Thunderbird and Evolution. This part of the lab is designed to get you to think about what these e-mail clients do and how you can configure e-mail clients.

But there is more. The **mail** command opens the e-mail client of the same name. It's already linked to mails in the local account, collected in /var/spool/mail/*USERNAME*.

When you review log messages in /var/log/maillog, you may see some errors. For example, if you see something similar to this,

```
fatal: bind 0.0.0.0 port 25: Address already in use
```

both sendmail and Postfix may be running on the same system. Note messages that direct e-mails to specific addresses.

Lab 2

This lab assumes you haven't protected access with a firewall, tcp_wrappers, or SELinux, as described in Chapter 15. One way to perform this lab is with the following steps:

1. Make sure the dovecot RPM is installed. Open /etc/dovecot.conf, and activate the following directive:

```
protocols = imap imaps pop3 pop3s
```

As this is the default, activating this directive isn't absolutely necessary. However, it's a good practice, as you never know when defaults change.

2. Move or rename the default Dovecot security certificates, both named dovecot.pem, from the /etc/pki/dovecot/certs and /etc/pki/dovecot/private directories.

3. Configure the Dovecot SSL configuration file, dovecot-openssl.cnf, in the /etc/pki/dovecot directory.

4. Back up the default dovecot.pem files from the /etc/pki/dovecot/certs and /etc/pki/dovecot/private directories.

5. Make sure the associated script, **mkcert.sh** in the /usr/share/doc/dovecot-*versionnum*/examples/ directory, is executable, and then run it:

```
# /usr/share/doc/dovecot-versionnum/examples/mkcert.sh
```

6. Make sure your new certificates are available in the previously noted directories, /etc/pki/dovecot/certs and /etc/pki/dovecot/private.

7. Activate the Dovecot service, and make sure it runs the next time you reboot:

```
# service dovecot start
# chkconfig dovecot on
```

Lab 3

In sendmail, to disable local-only access in the /etc/mail/sendmail.mc file, comment out the following line. Unlike most Linux configuration files, the comment code is a **dnl** at the start of this line:

```
DAEMON_OPTIONS(`Port=smtp,Addr=127.0.0.1, Name=MTA')dnl
```

The **dnl** at the end of the line does not affect the command to its left.

Next, you'll want to enable support through /etc/mail/access. If you want to support your LAN with this server, and its network address is 10.11.12.0, you'd add the following command line to /etc/mail/access:

```
10.11.12                    RELAY
```

Make sure sendmail is active (and any alternative mail servers such as Postfix are not).

You can test the results from the e-mail client of your choice. It's quickest to use a client such as mail. This assumes you've already configured Dovecot as described in Lab 2.

Alternatively, if you're configuring a GUI client, you'll need to know the name of your incoming mail server, whether it conforms to the POP3 or IMAP4 protocols, and the name (and password) of your account. You presumably already know the name of the outgoing mail server, the name of the computer with the mail server that you just configured.

To check incoming e-mails, look at /var/log/maillog. If all is well, you should see an entry sending your message to linus@yourcomputer. You should also see an update to user linus's mail spool, in /var/spool/mail. Unless user linus has already checked his e-mail, you should be able to read it yourself in /var/spool/mail/linus.

Lab 4

In Postfix, to disable local-only access in the /etc/postfix/main.cf file, change the **inet_interfaces** directive to accept **all** connections:

```
inet_interfaces = all
```

Make sure Postfix is active (and any alternative mail servers such as sendmail are not).

You can test the results from the e-mail client of your choice. It's quickest to use a client such as mail. This assumes you've already configured Dovecot as described in Lab 2.

The process of checking incoming e-mails is the same as that for the previous lab. Look at /var/log/maillog. If all is well, you should see an entry sending your message to linus@yourcomputer. You should also see an update to user linus's mail spool, in /var/spool/mail. Unless user linus has already checked his e-mail, you should be able to read it yourself in /var/spool/mail/linus.

13

Other Networking Services

CERTIFICATION OBJECTIVES

13.01   The Extended Internet Services Daemon
        (xinetd)

13.02   The Secure Shell Package

13.03   Dynamic Host Configuration Protocol
        (DHCP)

13.04   The Network Time Protocol (NTP)

✓   Two-Minute Drill

Q&A   Self Test

This chapter starts with a description of the Extended Internet Services Daemon (xinetd), also known as the "Internet Super Server." It governs a lot of services that do not have their own individual daemons. The techniques required to configure and control xinetd services are subtly different from regular services.

This chapter continues with a discussion of the Secure Shell package, which allows you to connect remotely to the systems you need to administer. While it already encrypts what you type over a network, you can configure it with more levels of security. It's also one way to configure remote connections to GUI applications.

DHCP allows a Linux computer to serve dynamic IP addresses. You can configure a range of IP addresses, reserve a specific IP address for the hardware address associated with a client's network card, and assign more information such as the gateway and DNS IP address to every system that requests an IP address.

Finally, the Network Time Protocol (NTP) can help keep the computers on a network running on the same time. That can be important for logs and for keeping backup servers in sync, which can be especially important for financial transactions.

CERTIFICATION OBJECTIVE 13.01

The Extended Internet Services Daemon (xinetd)

Linux typically supports network communication between clients and servers. For example, you can use Telnet to connect to a remote system. The Telnet client on your computer makes a connection with a Telnet server daemon on the remote system. This section assumes that you've installed the default RHEL krb5-workstation RPM package, which includes a more secure version of Telnet.

While the focus in this section is on the Kerberos-secured Telnet, other xinetd packages of note include rsync, which is popular for backups; cvs, popular for software development version control; and gssftp, which is a Kerberos-secured FTP service. As no xinetd service is explicitly cited in the RHCE Exam Prep guide, I keep the coverage of xinetd services to a minimum.

INSIDE THE EXAM

More Network Services

Both Red Hat exams require that you configure a Linux workstation as a client on a network. However, the secure shell is not included in the current version of the RHCT portion of the Exam Prep guide. And client configuration with a DHCP server was covered in Chapter 7. So this chapter focuses on the needs of RHCE candidates.

The Red Hat Exam Prep guide suggests that you can expect to configure SSH services during the exam. It also suggests that you need to know how to configure host- and user-based security for each service. While much of that is discussed in Chapter 15, some security configuration options are available for SSH.

While neither DHCP servers nor xinetd services are listed in the Red Hat Exam Prep guide, they are listed in the RH300 course outline, the prep course for the RHCE. And remember that changes can be made to the Red Hat Exam Prep guide at any time.

As of this writing, Red Hat has just added the Network Time Protocol (NTP) to the list of services required for the RHCE. As with other network services, per the RHCE section

of the Red Hat Exam Prep guide, RHCEs must be able to do the following:

- Install the packages needed to provide the service.
- Configure SELinux to support the service.
- Configure the service to start when the system is booted.
- Configure the service for basic operation.
- Configure host-based and user-based security for the service.

It also suggests that you need to know how to "diagnose and correct problems with (these) network services" as well as SELinux-related network issues during the Troubleshooting and System Maintenance portion of this exam. As of this writing, the only available SELinux option related to NTP and DHCP is to disable protection for this service. Some additional protections may be available for individual xinetd services such as rsync and cvs; however, as of this writing, no individual xinetd service is listed in either the Red Hat Exam Prep guide or curriculum for RH133 and RH300.

To establish the connection on a TCP/IP network, a client application needs the IP address of the server and the *port number* associated with the server daemon. All common TCP/IP applications have a standard port number; some examples are shown in Table 13-1.

	Port Number	Service
TABLE 13-1 Typical TCP/IP Port Numbers	21	FTP
	22	SSH
	23	Telnet
	25	SMTP (outgoing mail)
	80	HTTP
	443	HTTPS (secure HTTP)
	631	Internet Printing Protocol (CUPS configuration)

If you don't specify the port number, TCP/IP assumes that you're using the default port for the specified service. Clients can't connect unless the corresponding server is running on the remote system. If you are managing a server, you may have a number of server daemons to start when Linux is booted.

The **xinetd** (which stands for the Extended Internet Services Daemon) service can start a number of these server daemons simultaneously. The **xinetd** service listens for connection requests for all of the *active* servers with scripts in the /etc/xinetd.d directory. There's a generic configuration file for xinetd services, /etc/xinetd.conf. The scripts in the /etc/xinetd.d directory function as service-specific configuration files.

Generic xinetd Configuration

The generic configuration for xinetd services is stored in the /etc/xinetd.conf file. As RHCE candidates need to configure services only for "basic operation," this chapter analyzes only the active directives in this file. First, a number of default settings are enabled with the following command:

```
defaults
```

This allows services such as rsync to retain their default TCP/IP ports (873) within the xinetd service.

This is followed by

```
log_type SYSLOG daemon info
```

which specifies logging through the syslog daemon as described in Chapter 7, as configured in /etc/syslog.conf.

This is followed by

```
log_on_failure HOST
```

which specifies the logging information when a login through an xinetd-controlled service fails. Naturally, this specifies the host name (or IP address) of the client host. It might help to add USERID to the list, which lists the UID number associated with the failed login. This can help you identify compromised accounts.

This line,

```
log_on_success PID HOST DURATION EXIT
```

specifies the logging information associated with a successful connection. For example, once I logged off a Telnet connection from a remote system, and this led to the following entry in /var/log/messages:

```
Jul 25 17:54:31 Enterprise5vm xinetd[4618]: EXIT: telnet status=1
pid=4667 duration=472(sec)
```

The effect from /etc/xinetd.conf is straightforward. The next active line is

```
cps = 50 10
```

The **cps** command prevents attempts to "flood" any xinetd service; this line limits connections to 50 per second. If this limit is exceeded, xinetd waits 10 seconds before allowing a remote user to try again.

The next line,

```
instances = 50
```

limits the number of active services for a particular service; in this case, no more than 50 users can be logged into your Kerberos Telnet server simultaneously (less if other xinetd services are running).

This is followed by a related directive:

```
per_source = 10
```

This limits the number of connections from each IP address.

The next active directive is almost self-explanatory:

```
v6only = no
```

If you changed this to **yes**, access would be limited to systems with IPv6 addresses.

A couple of environment directives

```
groups = yes
umask = 002
```

allow execution with the xinetd group, or one defined with the **group** directive (singular).

Finally, the last line supports the use of the other configuration files specified in the /etc/xinetd.d directory:

```
includedir /etc/xinetd.d
```

Sample xinetd Configuration

Each file in the /etc/xinetd.d directory specifies a particular service you want to allow xinetd to manage. By default, scripts in this directory are disabled. The following code shows a sample of the /etc/xinetd.d/krb5-telnet configuration file, with this service disabled:

```
# default: off
# description: The kerberized telnet server accepts normal telnet
#              sessions, but can also use Kerberos 5 authentication.
service telnet
{
        flags           = REUSE
        socket_type     = stream
        wait            = no
        user            = root
        server          = /usr/kerberos/sbin/telnetd
        log_on_failure  += USERID
        disable         = yes
}
```

This is a typical /etc/xinetd.d configuration file. The variables (and a few additional variables that you can use) are described in Table 13-2. This is a versatile configuration file; other fields are described in the man pages for xinetd.conf. Read this man page; the **only_from** and **no_access** directives may be of particular interest—as per the Exam Prep guide, they can help you "configure host-based and user-based security for the service."

You can enable any xinetd service by changing **disable = yes** to **disable = no**.

CIDR notation is based on Classless InterDomain Routing. Under CIDR, all you need are the number of bits associated with the subnet; for example, 192.168.0.0/255.255.255.0 is 192.168.0.0/24 in CIDR notation. It also works with IPv6; for example, a single IPv6 IP address would have a /128 mask, in CIDR notation.

TABLE 13-2   Standard Parameters for xinetd Configuration Files

Field	Description of Field Entry
flags	Supports different parameters for the service; **REUSE** is a default that supports continuous use of the service. Options include IPv6 to set this as a service for those types of networks.
socket_type	Specifies the communication stream.
wait	Set to **yes** for single-threaded applications or **no** for multithreaded applications.
user	Account under which the server should run.
group	Group under which the server should run.
server	The server program.
only_from	Host name or IP address allowed to use the server. CIDR notation (such as 192.168.0.0/24) is okay.
no_access	Host name or IP address not allowed to use the server. CIDR notation is okay.
log_on_failure	If there's a failed login attempt, this specifies the information sent to a log file.
disable	By default, set to **yes**, which disables the service.

You can activate a service in two ways. You can edit the configuration file directly by changing the **disable** field from **no** to **yes**. Then make the xinetd daemon reread the configuration files with the **service xinetd reload** command.

Alternatively, you can use the **chkconfig *servicename* on** command, which automatically makes this change and makes xinetd reread the configuration file.

e x a m

ⓦ a t c h   *Always remember to make sure that a service will be active after a reboot. The chkconfig servicename on command is one way to do this for xinetd services. Otherwise, anything you configure may not work after your computer is rebooted—and you may not get credit for how you configured that service on your exam.*

Configuring xinetd

In this exercise, you will enable the Telnet service using xinetd. Attempt to establish a Telnet session using the command **telnet localhost**. If you're successful, Telnet is already enabled; disable it first with the **chkconfig krb5-telnet off** command.

1. Edit /etc/xinetd.d/krb5-telnet and change the value of **disable** from **yes** to **no**.

2. Tell xinetd to reread its configuration file using this command:

```
# service xinetd reload
```

3. Try the **telnet localhost** command again. It should work.

4. Try to log in with a bad username or password.

5. Log into another terminal. What do you see when you run **utmpdump /var/log/wtmp**?

6. Now log in with a good username and password.

7. What do you see in /var/log/messages?

8. Log out of the Telnet session. What do you see now in /var/log/messages?

9. Use the **chkconfig** command to disable Telnet. (Remember that the name of the service is krb5-telnet.) Try connecting to the Telnet server again. Do you have to restart or reload xinetd?

10. What happens when you use **chkconfig** to disable Telnet? Does it change the /etc/xinted.d/krb5-telnet configuration file?

The Secure Shell Package

Red Hat Enterprise Linux installs the Secure Shell (SSH) packages by default, using the openssh-server, openssh-clients, openssh-askpass, and openssh RPMs. The Secure Shell and Secure Copy programs, **ssh** and **scp**, are replacements for the **rsh**, **telnet**, and **rcp** programs. They encrypt communication between different computers. The secure daemon, **sshd**, listens for all inbound traffic on TCP port 22. The SSH configuration files are located in the /etc/ssh directory.

The Secure Shell daemon works because it encrypts messages. RHEL incorporates SSH version 2, which includes an enhanced key exchange algorithm.

Basic Encrypted Communication

Basic encryption in computer networking normally requires a private key and a public key. You keep the private key and send the public key to others. When they want to send data to you through SSH, their messages are encrypted with the public key. Your computer can descramble the message with the private key.

Encryption keys are based on random numbers. The numbers are so large (typically 512 bits or more) that the chance that someone will break into your system, at least with a PC, is quite small in the foreseeable future. Private and public encryption keys are based on a matched set of these random numbers.

Private Keys

Your private key (essentially a file with your special number) must be secure. When you enable an application, it can attach the key to your messages. Anything you send—say, from your e-mail account—can then be digitally signed and encrypted. The public key is added to the end as part of your signature. Only the recipient will be able to decrypt the message.

Public Keys

Your public key value is just that, publicly available. A central authority such as VeriSign, GlobalSign, or Thawte provides public access to public keys they have created. If they generate a private key for you, they'll keep a secure copy on their system. You can just attach your public key to the e-mail, or the end users can publicly retrieve it from the Web site associated with the central authority.

The example shown in Figure 13-1 lists the directories and files associated with SSH usage as well as a public key that has been added to your "keyring."

This key is like a password used to encrypt your data. Imagine trying to remember the 1024-bit number expressed in hexadecimal value as shown here.

```
3081 8902 8181 00D4 596E 01DE A012 3CAD 51B7
7835 05A4 DEFC C70B 4382 A733 5D62 A51B B9D6
29EA 860B EC2B 7AB8 2E96 3A4C 71A2 D087 11D0
E149 4DD5 1E20 8382 FA58 C7DA D9B0 3865 FF6E
88C7 B672 51F5 5094 3B35 D8AA BC68 BBEB BFE3
9063 AE75 8B57 09F9 DCF8 FFA4 E32C A17F 82E9
7A4C 0E10 E62D 8A97 0845 007B 169A 0676 E7CF
5713 1423 96E0 8E6C 9502 0301 0001
```

FIGURE 13-1

A public key

```
[root@Enterprise5vm ~]# ls .ssh/
id_dsa  id_dsa.pub  identity  identity.pub  known_hosts
[root@Enterprise5vm ~]# cat .ssh/id_dsa.pub
ssh-dss AAAAB3NzaC1kc3MAAACBAJQ+84NL84wuw3SP6iUcE3/Mr8hqYoOFbv3uinYns3EzjWuraYhN
X3bS7zuz7AkGBCQm5PD27GpbEUzSBqDOqPhVraysUXcqAWi/TUOfotFbo6Q4/H8RKLjSy3421G9sRgZk
9YGuk+f5mTw3O5w8kG5HmoqHhpeT2hTd2Q2DbAs1AAAAFQDnyLg13u5FYRgmqEBHi7XfEvnQNwAAAIAM
RhxF9P6pEr4XTKG6SYHW/G17Vm93Pmq7S/q2bVFMRWwy5kP76EI33L2FMB1O2Um3mvMc76WuLiACpXiq
zkK6Mhxg1HrBwsc/gCrg3R5fUmq3LJDcamn79snf2Q0aZGzAa5S25NQFps28fsLphIB1Lp1XwwgxWE1g
ehqBo5RAYQAAAIA2VU/JYrHR01bOJS46xbkhnldP3/ZcfcudXA33UVV1rV6Q0xC3beFEQrdQbMxtni4n
jwwXndepqsSxbvssHVjernRduwjrC5RpjF1UPxsGGq/p53xBTchZyQBnAXubOv2KOjiDNgkgrqfd5NGD
4baWLbRxnIhiKXcqMDhayc8z7w== root@Enterprise5vm.example.net
[root@Enterprise5vm ~]# cat .ssh/identity.pub
2048 35 2470907289825797424224903924025794796866500975589060891137182033024031960
10941502943452722772064198913632484009738517664553501719331970612078641419844002
44006402884428565618822985741070015788630858056091963698205782347945631228960485
76527831918397945832561992086979541126968887793387929595350448875194975181978556
73017731928054286680687659142284977951692328784617438994392115975722472018296427
82319694036519760311255917338246468305003783508803958661948122833399320459049430
40289127772450120471755565921648576287690336873438044015232177483932487091798374
51362499821852820027960484395879058878449660244164320700076200271 root@Enterpris
e5vm.example.net
[root@Enterprise5vm ~]#
```

That is why the applications save this value for you, on a "public keyring." You can add as many public keys from other users, sites, and services as you wish.

Your private key is similar, *but you must keep it private,* or this whole system fails. Keeping it private means no one should have access to your PC. If your PC is public, secure your system with a passphrase (password), as shown in Figure 13-2, to use this key. Don't forget the passphrase, or you'll have to remove and reinstall the Secure Shell.

FIGURE 13-2

Generating
encryption keys

```
[root@Enterprise5vm ~]# ssh-keygen -t dsa
Generating public/private dsa key pair.
Enter file in which to save the key (/root/.ssh/id_dsa):
Created directory '/root/.ssh'.
Enter passphrase (empty for no passphrase):
Enter same passphrase again:
Your identification has been saved in /root/.ssh/id_dsa.
Your public key has been saved in /root/.ssh/id_dsa.pub.
The key fingerprint is:
ea:e2:49:bf:e6:b2:1a:40:1f:ed:c9:22:0f:31:cc:62 root@Enterprise5vm.example.net
[root@Enterprise5vm ~]# ssh-keygen -t rsa1
Generating public/private rsa1 key pair.
Enter file in which to save the key (/root/.ssh/identity):
Enter passphrase (empty for no passphrase):
Enter same passphrase again:
Your identification has been saved in /root/.ssh/identity.
Your public key has been saved in /root/.ssh/identity.pub.
The key fingerprint is:
d8:cb:f2:f3:f0:2e:99:d9:32:d7:c3:7f:81:90:50:bc root@Enterprise5vm.example.net
[root@Enterprise5vm ~]#
```

How to Generate Your Keys

There are a few SSH-oriented utilities you need to know about:

- **sshd**   The daemon service; this must be running for inbound Secure Shell client requests.

- **ssh-agent**   A program to hold private keys used for RSA authentication. The idea is that the **ssh-agent** command is started in the beginning of an X session or a login session, and all other windows or programs are started as clients to the **ssh-agent** program.

- **ssh-add**   Adds RSA identities to the authentication agent, **ssh-agent**.

- **ssh**   The Secure Shell command, **ssh**, is a secure way to log in to a remote machine, similar to Telnet or **rlogin**. To make this work, you need a private key on the server and a public key on the client. Take the public key file, identity.pub or id_dsa.pub, created later in this section. Copy it to the client. Place it in the home directory of an authorized user, in the ~/.ssh/authorized_ keys or ~/.ssh/authorized_keys2 file.

- **ssh-keygen**   A utility that will create your keys for you. The **ssh-keygen -t** *keytype* command will create the keys you desire. The *keytype* can be DSA (Digital Secure Algorithm) or RSA1 (RSA Security). The command works as shown in Figure 13-2.

All you need to do is transfer the public key, with the .pub extension, to an authorized user. It's important to add a passphrase to protect that digital signature. In the worst case, a cracker could use the passphrase to steal your identity.

While encryption keys are important, remember that the Red Hat exams require that you configure services for basic operation. So if you're not already familiar with SSH, stay focused on getting it working, as described in the rest of this section.

Why Use SSH?

The Internet is a public network. If you're connected to the Internet, anyone in the world could conceivably access your computer through this public network. All that is needed is Internet access from an anonymous location. In other words, a skilled cracker may be able to capture your passwords from a computer in a public library.

In contrast, private networks are used for security applications. Merchants who dial into a central server to check authorized credit card numbers are connecting to a private network. Access to such private networks can be expensive.

Unix and the network that became the Internet started in an educational setting, where there is a premium on the free exchange of information. While the resulting openness of the Internet is good, it can present security challenges. The original Unix tools developed for networks were not designed with security in mind.

These tools include **telnet**, **ftp**, and the "r" (remote) commands (**rlogin, rcp, rsh**). These utilities pass all information, including login names and passwords, across the network in clear text format. Anyone with a simple protocol analyzer such as Ethereal can find your password in this way. The Wireshark (successor to Ethereal) output shown in Figure 13-3 highlights one of the letters in a Telnet password on my private LAN (it's an *e*). The other Telnet packets contain the other letters and/or numbers of the password.

on the **Ø**ob
To take full advantage of Kerberos-based Telnet, you'll need to set up Kerberos keys for each member of your network. For more information, see the Kerberos Infrastructure HOWTO at www.tldp.org.

on the **Ø**ob
I do not in any way endorse the cracking of passwords. However, as a system administrator, you do need to know your vulnerabilities. If you can trace clear text passwords on your own network, you are at risk.

FIGURE 13-3   It's easy to decipher a clear text password.

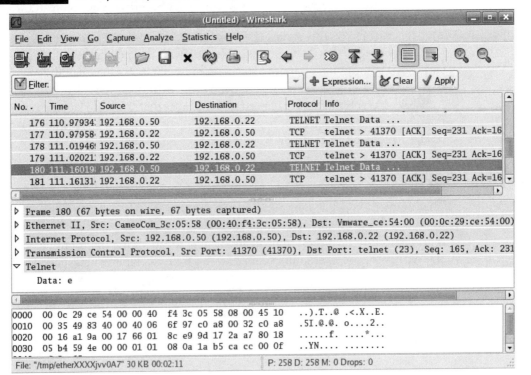

The Secure Shell utilities were an answer to this problem, using high encryption standards. The Secure Shell tools replaced their insecure brethren and provided full encryption of all data between the hosts that is very hard to break, even by the brute force method.

Configuring an SSH Server

You don't have to do much to configure an SSH server for basic operation. Install the packages described earlier, activate the service, make sure it's active the next time you reboot your system, and open the appropriate port in any firewalls that you've configured. Then all you need to add is host- or user-based security for the service.

The SSH server configuration file is /etc/ssh/sshd_config. The first directive (**Protocol 2**) configures SSH version 2, which is more secure. By default, it also includes the following directives.

```
SyslogFacility AUTHPRIV
```

The first directive sends all logging attempts, successful and otherwise, to the appropriate log file; in this case, /var/log/secure.

The next directive authorizes password authentication, based on local user passwords:

```
PasswordAuthentication = yes
```

The next directive disables PAM authentication, despite the **UsePAM=yes** later in this file.

```
ChallengeResponseAuthentication = no
```

This is followed by a directive that supports authentication using the Generic Security Services Application Programming Interface for client-server authentication:

```
GSSAPIAuthentication = yes
```

The next directives allow the client to set several environmental variables. The details are normally trivial between two Red Hat Enterprise Linux systems:

```
AcceptEnv LANG LC_CTYPE LC_NUMERIC LC_TIME LC_COLLATE LC_MONETARY LC_MESSAGES
AcceptEnv LC_PAPER LC_NAME LC_ADDRESS LC_TELEPHONE LC_MEASUREMENT
AcceptEnv LC_IDENTIFICATION LC_ALL
```

The following directive is important for anyone who needs remote access to a GUI tool:

```
X11Forwarding yes
```

For example, when I'm working from my patio, I can connect to and open GUI tools from Red Hat systems in my office when I use SSH to connect with the following command:

```
# ssh -X michael@enterprise5a
```

The final directive supports the use of SSH encryption for secure FTP file transfers:

```
Subsystem  sftp   /usr/libexec/openssh/sftp-server
```

I like to add two directives that promote security by user and host. For example, logins by the root user are allowed. By adding the following directive,

```
PermitRootLogin no
```

I keep administrative users from logging in with SSH. They can still use the **su** or **sudo** command (as authorized) to the administrative account once connected. This reduces the risk of crackers identifying the administrative password at the beginning of an SSH session.

I also like to limit the users allowed to access a system via SSH. The key is the **AllowUsers** directive. You can limit by user with a directive such as:

```
AllowUsers michael donna
```

Alternatively, you can limit access by each user to certain hosts with a directive such as:

```
AllowUsers michael@enterprise5vm donna@poohbear
```

Configuring an SSH Client

Configuring an SSH client is a simpler process. The standard configuration file for a client system is /etc/ssh/ssh_config. Individual users can have custom SSH client configurations in their ~/.ssh/config files. There are four directives included by default:

```
Host *
GSSAPIAuthentication yes
ForwardX11Trusted yes
SendEnv LANG LC_CTYPE LC_NUMERIC LC_TIME LC_COLLATE LC_MONETARY
SendEnv LC_MESSAGES LC_PAPER LC_NAME LC_ADDRESS LC_TELEPHONE
SendEnv LC_MEASUREMENT LC_IDENTIFICATION LC_ALL
```

The **Host *** directive applies the other directives to all connections. The other directives match the same directives described earlier under /etc/ssh/sshd_config.

on the job *Many of us still have to administer Microsoft Windows computers. You can still take advantage of SSH security from these systems. All you need is an SSH service such as OpenSSH from http://sshwindows.sourceforge.net, and you can use SSH to administer your Linux systems even from a Microsoft Windows system. I have not tested this option from Microsoft Windows Vista.*

Dynamic Host Configuration Protocol (DHCP)

There are two protocols that allow a client computer to get network configuration information from a server: DHCP (Dynamic Host Configuration Protocol) and BOOTP. DHCP works if you have a DHCP server on the local network. The BOOTP protocol is required if you're getting information from a DHCP server on another network.

DHCP servers can simplify and centralize network administration if you're administering more than a few computers on a network. They are especially convenient for networks with a significant number of mobile users. The BOOTP protocol is essentially just a way to access a DHCP server on a remote network.

As of this writing, Red Hat does not include any GUI tool to configure a DHCP server. You'll have to do your work in this section from the command line interface.

---

e x a m

w a t c h   *While DHCP knowledge is not explicitly listed in the current Red Hat Exam Prep guide, it is a part of the associated curriculum. Based on their outlines, the RHCT course, RH133, examines the configuration of a DHCP client. The RHCE course, RH300, addresses*   *DHCP servers. It is important for any network administrator to know DHCP. However, it's not in the Red Hat Exam Prep guide; you'll have to make your own decision about whether to learn how to create a DHCP server for your RHCE exam.*

Installing DHCP Packages

As with most network services, DHCP has a client and a server. These are based on the dhcp and dhclient RPM packages. The dhclient RPM package should be installed by default; if you're using a service such as NetworkManager, you'll also need the dhcdbd package. If you're working with IPv6, you'll need the dhcpv6_client. On the server side, the dhcp RPM package is installed by default with the Network Server package group.

on the

job   *Red Hat seems to change the commands and packages related to the DHCP client frequently. Older versions of Red Hat have used dhcpcd and pump as DHCP client commands. Just be aware of this if you're working with an older version of Red Hat.*

DHCP Server Configuration

A DHCP server sends messages to multiple computers on a LAN. This is also known as a multicast. It should be enabled by default. You can confirm this with the **ifconfig** command. The output should resemble Figure 13-4, which includes a **MULTICAST** setting for the active network card.

If you don't see **MULTICAST** associated with your network card, someone has compiled this feature out of your kernel. For more information on the kernel management process, see Chapter 8.

Now configure the DHCP server daemon, **dhcpd**, by creating or editing the /etc/dhcpd.conf configuration file. Normally, this file allows the DHCP server to assign IP addresses randomly from a specific range. But the default version of this file is blank. You can start with the dhcpd.conf.sample file in the /usr/share/doc/dhcp-*versionnum* directory. The lines that start with a hash mark (**#**) are comments in the file. Let's analyze this sample file in detail:

- **ddns-update-style interim**   With this command, the RHEL DHCP server conforms as closely as possible to the current Dynamic DNS standard, where the DNS database is updated when the DNS server renews its DHCP lease. It is "interim" because the standards for DDNS are not complete as of this writing.

- **ignore client-updates**   A good setting if you don't want to allow users on client computers to change their host names.

- **subnet 192.168.0.0 netmask 255.255.255.0**   Describes a network with an address of 192.168.0.0 and a subnet mask of 255.255.255.0. This allows

```
[root@Enterprise5vm ~]# ifconfig
eth0      Link encap:Ethernet  HWaddr 00:0C:29:CE:54:00
          inet addr:192.168.0.22  Bcast:192.168.0.255  Mask:255.255.255.0
          inet6 addr: fe80::20c:29ff:fece:5400/64 Scope:Link
          UP BROADCAST RUNNING MULTICAST  MTU:1492  Metric:1
          RX packets:13668 errors:0 dropped:0 overruns:0 frame:0
          TX packets:5209 errors:0 dropped:0 overruns:0 carrier:0
          collisions:0 txqueuelen:1000
          RX bytes:12235808 (11.6 MiB)  TX bytes:879604 (858.9 KiB)
          Interrupt:177 Base address:0x1080

lo        Link encap:Local Loopback
          inet addr:127.0.0.1  Mask:255.0.0.0
          inet6 addr: ::1/128 Scope:Host
          UP LOOPBACK RUNNING  MTU:16436  Metric:1
          RX packets:8716 errors:0 dropped:0 overruns:0 frame:0
          TX packets:8716 errors:0 dropped:0 overruns:0 carrier:0
          collisions:0 txqueuelen:0
          RX bytes:6047214 (5.7 MiB)  TX bytes:6047214 (5.7 MiB)

[root@Enterprise5vm ~]#
```

the local DHCP server to assign addresses in the range 192.168.0.1 to 192.168.0.254 to different computers on this network. If you've configured a different network IP address, you'll want to change these settings accordingly.

- **option routers**   Lists the default router. You can use more than one **option routers** directive if you have more than one connection to an outside network. This information is passed to DHCP clients as the default gateway, which supports access to outside networks such as the Internet. You'll want this command to reflect the IP address for the gateway for your network.

- **option subnet-mask**   Specifies the subnet mask for the local network.

- **option nis-domain**   Notes the server that provides the NIS shared authorization database. If you've configured NIS on your network, you'll want to substitute the name of your NIS domain for *domain.org*. Otherwise, you should comment out this command.

- **option domain-name**   Adds the domain name for your network. Substitute the IP address for the DNS servers you want your clients to use.

- **option domain-name-servers**   Notes the IP address for the DNS server for your network. You can add more commands of this type to specify additional DNS servers.

- **option time-offset**   Lists the difference from Greenwich Mean Time, also known as UTC (a French acronym), in seconds.

- **option ntp-servers**   Notes any Network Time Protocol (NTP) servers for keeping the time on the local computer in sync with UTC. I describe NTP later in this chapter.

- **option netbios-name-servers**   Adds the location of any Windows Internet Naming Service (WINS) servers for your network. As this is a Microsoft service, I refer to it briefly in the description of Samba in Chapter 10.

- **option netbios-node-type 2**   Peer-to-peer node searches, associated with WINS.

- **range dynamic-bootp 192.168.0.128 192.168.0.254**   Specifies the assignable IP addresses to *remote* networks, using the BOOTP protocol.

- **default-lease-time**   Specifies the lease time for IP address information, in seconds.

- **max-lease-time**   Specifies the maximum lease time for IP address information, in seconds.

- **next-server**   Notes the boot server for network computers. If you don't have any network computers, you can comment out this entire stanza.

You can also assign a specific IP address to a computer based on a client's Ethernet address. Just add an entry similar to the following to /etc/dhcpd.conf:

```
host mommabears {
        hardware ethernet 08:00:12:23:4d:3f;
        fixed-address 192.168.0.201;
    }
```

This specifies what the DHCP server does when a network card with a hardware address of 08:00:12:23:4d:3f tries to connect via Ethernet. In this case, the IP address 192.168.0.201 is assigned to a client named mommabears.

Naturally, you'll want to modify this file accordingly for your particular network. For example, if you've configured computers on the example.org network described earlier in this book, you'll want to substitute example.org and the associated IP addresses in your /etc/dhcpd.conf file. I've done this for my network in Figure 13-5.

on the *j* o b

To assign an IP address to a specific network card on a specific computer, you need the hardware address, which can be found next to the HWaddr in the output to the ifconfig command.

FIGURE 13-5

Sample DHCP configuration file

```
ddns-update-style interim;
ignore client-updates;

subnet 192.168.0.0 netmask 255.255.255.0 {

# --- default gateway
        option routers                  192.168.0.1;
        option subnet-mask              255.255.255.0;

        option domain-name              "example.org";
        option domain-name-servers      192.168.0.1;

        option time-offset              -18000; # Eastern Standard Time
        option ntp-servers              192.168.0.30;
#       option netbios-name-servers     192.168.1.1;
# --- Selects point-to-point node (default is hybrid). Don't change this unless
# -- you understand Netbios very well
#       option netbios-node-type 2;

        range dynamic-bootp 192.168.0.128 192.168.0.254;
        default-lease-time 21600;
        max-lease-time 43200;

        # we want the nameserver to appear at a fixed address
        host ns {
                hardware ethernet 00:0D:9D:86:36:A0;
                fixed-address 192.168.0.30;
        }
}
~
```

DHCP can be customized for individual computers. You can set up static IP addresses for servers. Once you're ready, start the dhcpd service with the following command:

```
# service dhcpd start
```

By default, this starts a DHCP server, which listens for requests on the eth0 network card. Alternatively, to have a DHCP server listen on the eth1 network interface, run the following command:

```
# service dhcpd start eth1
```

If these commands don't get a response, you probably haven't created a /etc/dhcpd .conf configuration file.

You can watch the DHCP server in action. Stop the DHCP server with the **service dhcpd stop** command. You can then restart it in the foreground with standard error descriptors with the following command:

```
# /usr/sbin/dhcpd -d -f
```

Start another Linux/Unix client. Make it look for another DHCP lease with the **dhclient -r** and **dhclient** commands, and then watch the console of the server. You'll see a number of DHCP communication messages on the server that illustrates the process of leasing an IP address to a client.

on the job

A second way to get the MAC address for a given client is to watch the DHCP server messages, normally sent to /var/log/messages.

Once you've configured your DHCP server to your satisfaction, remember to activate it at the appropriate runlevels with a command such as:

```
# chkconfig dhcpd on
```

DHCP and Microsoft Windows

In order for the DHCP server to work correctly with picky DHCP clients such as Microsoft Windows 9x, the server needs to send data to the broadcast address: 255.255.255.255. Unfortunately, Linux insists on changing 255.255.255.255 into the local subnet broadcast address. The mixed message results in a DHCP protocol violation, and while Linux DHCP clients don't notice the problem, Microsoft DHCP clients do. Normally, such clients can't see DHCPOFFER messages and therefore don't know when to take an IP address offered from the DHCP server. If you're configuring a DHCP server for a network with Microsoft Windows computers, run the following command,

```
# route add --host 255.255.255.255 dev eth0
```

where **eth0** is the name of the NIC that connects the server to the network.

Client Configuration

You can set up DHCP as a client using the **dhclient** command, or you can use the Red Hat Network Configuration tool (which you can also start with the System | Administration | Network command). Alternatively, configuring a DHCP client at the command line is not difficult (and is faster on the Red Hat exams). Make sure that the /etc/sysconfig/network configuration file includes the following line:

```
NETWORKING=yes
```

Next, make sure that the /etc/sysconfig/network-scripts/ifcfg-eth0 script contains the following lines (if you're using a different network device, modify the appropriate file in /etc/sysconfig/network-scripts directory):

```
BOOTPROTO='dhcp'
ONBOOT='yes'
```

If you don't want the DHCP server to assign a DNS server in the client's /etc/resolv.conf, add the following directive:

```
PEERDNS=no
```

The next time you reboot, your network configuration should look for DHCP address information automatically from the DHCP server for your network.

Alternatively, you can use the Network Configuration tool from a GUI to configure DHCP. You can also start it from a GUI terminal console with the **system-config-network** command. When the tool opens, select your network card and click Edit. You should see a window similar to what is shown in Figure 13-6.

If you want to use DHCP on this computer, select the Automatically Obtain IP Address Settings With option. You'll then get to choose between getting IP address information from a DHCP server on your local network, using BOOTP to get IP address information from a remote network, or going through a dial-up connection, such as to an ISP. Once you've activated the changes, restart the network daemon with the **service network restart** command. Your network card will then look for IP address information from a DHCP server.

DHCP Client Troubleshooting

If the DHCP client configuration instructions in this chapter are not working, there may be a problem with the way the network is set up on your Linux computer. For example,

- The NIC is not configured properly. See Chapter 7 for information on reconfiguring your network card.
- If the computer is still having problems finding a DHCP server, check your firewall. If port 67 or 68 is blocked, your computer won't be able to get a message to the server.

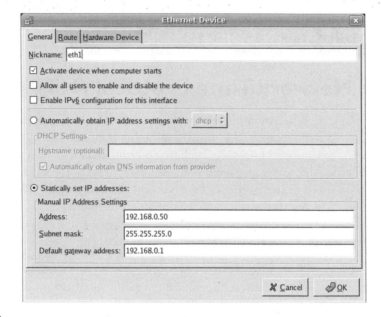

FIGURE 13-6

Configuring your
network card

EXERCISE 13-3

Configuring DHCP

To run this exercise, you'll need two different computers: a DHCP server and a
DHCP client on the same LAN. The IP addresses listed in this exercise are just
examples; substitute IP addresses appropriate for your network.

1. Open /etc/dhcpd.conf. Configure the server with an IP address range of
   192.168.11.11–192.168.11.15 and with a network mask of 255.255.255.0.

2. Configure the client computer to use DHCP. Restart the network service on
   the client and record the IP address that it gets.

3. Add gateway and DNS server options with IP addresses of 192.168.11.254
   and 12.34.45.56, respectively. If you already have a gateway and a DNS server,
   substitute the appropriate IP addresses. Restart the DHCP service. Restart
   networking on the client to make it renew the lease on the IP address.

4. Check the settings on the client. The **ifconfig** command should list your
   network card (usually eth0) with an IP address within the range described in
   step 1. The /etc/resolv.conf should show the DNS server address, unless the
   file listed in step 5 includes **PEERDNS=no**.

5. The /etc/sysconfig/networking/devices/ifcfg-eth0 configuration file should list
   the gateway address defined in step 3.

CERTIFICATION OBJECTIVE 13.04

The Network Time Protocol (NTP)

When multiple servers are being used for the same purpose, it's important to keep their time clocks in sync. Whether it be a database, timestamped entries for an online business, or backup servers used for load balancing, consistent times are important for smooth operation. This section provides instructions on how to create and configure your own Network Time Protocol (NTP) server for *basic* operation. But first, you'll need to configure a client.

NTP Client Configuration

I'll show you how to configure a client using the GUI. This is one of the few services where client configuration is actually more awkward from the command line. Open the Date/Time Properties tool; one way is to run **system-config-date** from a command line console in the GUI.

I assume the information defined in the Date & Time and Time Zone tabs is already correct. (The information in the tabs should at least be close; the NTP client may have trouble if your clock is off by more than 1000 seconds.) Select the Network Time Protocol tab, as shown in Figure 13-7.

Make sure the Enable Network Time Protocol option is active. Your administrator (or possibly exam proctor) may tell you to use a different NTP server, which can be changed in the NTP Servers text box. If you want to find a public NTP server other than the defaults shown, refer to http://ntp.isc.org/bin/view/Servers/WebHome. Generally, you should only connect to a "Stratum Two" time server. Even then, you'll generally need to ask permission of the NTP server administrator before connecting your time server. Too many connections to an NTP server can degrade performance, leading to delays. And delays are never good for a time server.

on the
job

One option to Stratum Two servers is available from the Public NTP Time Server project, available at www.pool.ntp.org. Red Hat's default time servers for RHEL 5 are part of this project.

Once you configure a local NTP time server, you can set other NTP clients to synchronize with that server.

Under the Advanced options, unless there are problems with the initial network connection, you should select Synchronize System Clock Before Starting Service. On the other hand, this option can slow the boot process, which can be a problem during an exam.

FIGURE 13-7

Configuring the
Network Time
Protocol

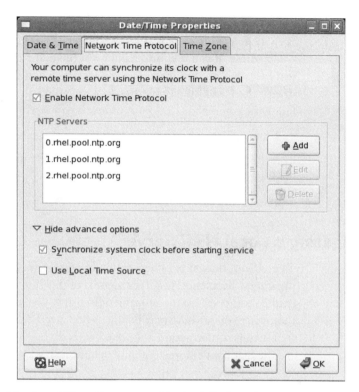

If you select Use Local Time Source, it adds the following directive to /etc/ntp.conf:

```
server 127.127.1.0
```

This is an arbitrary address—yes, it's in the "loopback" IP address network, but don't confuse it with the standard loopback address of 127.0.0.1.

Basic Configuration

As defined in the Red Hat Exam Prep guide, you need to make sure the package for a service is installed. Fortunately, NTP is installed by default. If necessary, you can install or update the ntp RPM package, using the techniques described for other services in other chapters.

If there are problems with SELinux, all that is possible as of this writing is to disable SELinux protection for the NTP service. The simplest way to do so is from the command line with the **setsebool** command, specifically:

```
# setsebool -P ntpd_disable_trans 1
```

This command is also available in the SELinux Management Tool, under Booleans, in the SELinux Service Protection category, as "Disable SELinux Protection for ntpd daemon."

To make NTP work with a firewall, you'll need to open access in port 123, for both TCP and UDP packets. See Chapter 15 for basic instructions on this process.

Of course, if you're running NTP (or have to configure it on your exam, or in real life), you need to make sure NTP starts when Linux boots. If you've activated it with the Date/Time Properties tool, it should already be active. To make sure, the following command checks all runlevels to see when NTP is active:

```
# chkconfig --list ntpd
```

If the active runlevels aren't satisfactory, the following command activates the NTP service in runlevels 2, 3, 4, and 5:

```
# chkconfig ntpd on
```

Configuring a Local NTP Server

To configure a local NTP server, you'll need to modify the configuration file, /etc/ntp.conf. I'll examine just a few details of this file; remember, all that's needed is to configure the service for *basic* operation. If you've run the Date/Time Configuration tool, what you see here may be different. Specifically, the Date/Time Configuration tool removes information associated with IPv6.

The first active lines configure default restrictions for IPv4 and IPv6:

```
restrict default kod nomodify notrap nopeer noquery
restrict -6 default kod nomodify notrap nopeer noquery
```

The **kod** prevents so-called "Kiss of Death" packets from bringing down the server. The **nomodify** option prevents other NTP servers from modifying this one; the **notrap** option denies the message trap service. These options should not be changed.

But to configure a local NTP server, you don't need the **nopeer** and **noquery** options to enable others to synchronize and request information. If you believe that nobody on your LAN will attack your system with the "Kiss of Death," leave out the **kod** option. So to enable access to the 10.11.12.0 network with the noted subnet mask, you could add the following IPv4 directive:

```
restrict 10.11.12.0 mask 255.255.255.0 nomodify notrap
```

You can add more **restrict** directives, as needed for other networks that you administer. The IPv6 version of this directive would be similar on the noted subnet:

```
restrict -6 0011:838:0:1:: mask ffff:ffff:ffff:ffff:: kod nomodify notrap
```

The following default **restrict** directives limit administrative access to the local system for the IPv4 and IPv6 loopback addresses:

```
restrict 127.0.0.1
restrict -6 ::1
```

If you want to add a remote administrative interface, specify its IP address with another directive:

```
restrict 10.11.12.13
```

The **server** directives that follow specify the remote NTP servers. The defaults shown here are based on what RHEL uses on the Public NTP Server project:

```
server 0.rhel.pool.ntp.org
server 1.rhel.pool.ntp.org
server 2.rhel.pool.ntp.org
```

That's all you absolutely have to change to configure a local NTP server for *basic* operation. Of course, after saving these changes, you should activate the NTP server with a command like:

```
# service ntpd start
```

CERTIFICATION SUMMARY

Networking services are an integral part of Red Hat Enterprise Linux. While most network services have been covered in other chapters, a few just don't fit neatly into other categories. Some are controlled through the xinetd daemon. SSH and DHCP are two other network services.

The Extended Internet Services Daemon, xinetd, governs the services configured though the /etc/xinetd.d directory. It controls services such as rsync, gssftp, and krb5-telnet, when installed.

Any network that is connected to an insecure network such as the Internet is vulnerable. Older protocols such as Telnet allowed passwords in clear text, which can be easily captured with tools such as Wireshark. The OpenSSH server can help you set up encrypted communication between computers.

DHCP allows a network administrator to manage IP address assignments of the computers on a LAN from a centralized server. DHCP requires some specialized setup on both the client and the server; however, it is easy to maintain once it is configured.

NTP services support time synchronization, which can keep changes such as moving to backup servers, load balancing, logs, and more, seamless to the end user. Clients can be configured with the Date/Time configuration tool or in /etc/ntp.conf. Configuring an NTP server requires specialized settings in /etc/ntp.conf.

TWO-MINUTE DRILL

Here are some of the key points from the certification objectives in Chapter 13.

The Extended Internet Services Daemon (xinetd)

❑ xinetd acts as a "super-server" for a number of other network services, such as the Kerberos secured versions of Telnet and rsync.

❑ Individual services have their own management scripts in the /etc/xinetd.d directory.

❑ Most xinetd services are disabled by default.

❑ You can activate an xinetd service with the appropriate **chkconfig** command or by directly editing its xinetd script.

❑ xinetd listens for connection requests from client applications.

❑ When xinetd receives a connection request, it starts the server associated with the TCP/IP port and then waits for other connection requests.

The Secure Shell Package

❑ The OpenSSH command utilities—**sshd, ssh, ssh-keygen, ssh-add**, and **ssh-agent**—provide secure remote services over any network connections.

❑ Encryption is based on private and public keys.

❑ Public keys are shared with others, so that they can communicate with you through SSH.

❑ As it is easy to decipher traffic, even passwords, from **telnet, ftp**, and the "r" commands, it is best to use SSH on any publicly accessible network.

Dynamic Host Configuration Protocol (DHCP)

❑ DHCP allows a client computer to obtain network information (such as an IP number) from a server.

❑ The BOOTP protocol allows a client computer to access a DHCP server on a remote network.

❑ DHCP servers are configured through /etc/dhcpd.conf.

❑ The DHCP server daemon is **dhcpd**; the DHCP client daemon is **dhclient**.

The Network Time Protocol (NTP)

❑ NTP servers can help synchronize the systems on a network.

❑ NTP clients can be configured with the Date/Time Configuration tool, which can be started with the **system-config-date** command. Alternatively, clients can also be configured in /etc/ntp.conf.

❑ NTP clients can be synchronized with Stratum Two servers with the permission of their administrators; one alternative is the Public Time Server project at pool.ntp.org.

❑ To configure an NTP client as a server, the /etc/ntp.conf file needs to be configured to allow access to the desired networks.

SELF TEST

The following questions will help you measure your understanding of the material presented in this chapter. As no multiple choice questions appear on the Red Hat exams, no multiple choice questions appear in this book. These questions exclusively test your understanding of the chapter. It is okay if you have another way of performing a task. Getting results, not memorizing trivia, is what counts on the Red Hat exams. There may be more than one answer for many of these questions.

The Extended Internet Services Daemon (xinetd)

1. You are using the xinetd program to start services. What command makes sure the Kerberos version of Telnet, as configured in /etc/xinetd.d/krb5-telnet, starts the next time you boot Linux? Assume the xinetd service is active.

   _____

2. What command rereads any configuration changes you've made to a file in the /etc/xinetd.d directory?

   _____

The Secure Shell Package

3. Once configured, what do you have to do to an existing firewall to allow Secure Shell (SSH) access?

   _____

4. You've started the SSH service and have a local account under username troosevelt. The local computer name is conservation. How would you log into that account from a remote computer?

   _____

5. Where are SSH keys stored for user michael? Assume a standard home directory.

   _____

6. When configuring an SSH server, what directive prohibits SSH logins by the root user?

   _____

7. When configuring an SSH server, what directive supports access to remote GUI applications?

   _____

8. If you've configured access to remote GUI applications, how would you log into the account described in question 4?

   _____

Dynamic Host Configuration Protocol (DHCP)

9. What would you add to the /etc/dhcpd.conf configuration file if the DNS server you want your clients to use has an IP address of 10.11.12.1?

_____

10. You add a new workstation to your /etc/dhcpd.conf file. You're in a hurry to finish, so you save and go to lunch. When you return, your phone mail is full of user complaints that they can't access the Internet, but the local network is fine. You surmise that you accidentally changed something in the dhcpd.conf file. What directive should you look at first in dhcpd.conf?

_____

The Network Time Protocol

11. From the /etc/ntp.conf file, there's the following directive:

```
restrict default kod nomodify notrap nopeer noquery
```

What directive would you add to open access to the 192.168.0.0/24 network?

_____

12. What Web site is associated with the public NTP server project?

_____

LAB QUESTIONS

Lab 1

Your company bought another competitor on the opposite coast recently, just as the new corporate application was being deployed everywhere, so you sent the app to them, too. They use a Unix host for this application on their network. You need to be able to connect to this host *securely* for maintenance purposes on the new system-wide application you deployed. Both networks have Internet access.

What do you do?

Lab 2

You'll also need two Linux computers for this lab: one as a DHCP server and a second as a DHCP client. Using the DHCP server created earlier in this chapter, set up a static IP address for the computer of your choice. You'll want to assign a specific name for that server, precious.example.com, and a special IP address on the 10.11.12.0 network, 10.11.12.13. Assume that you've already set up the example.com network as well as an appropriately configured DNS server.

Lab 3

To do this lab, you'll need the help of a partner. Have him or her set up your system as described in the answer to this lab in the next section. The intent of this lab is to help improve your troubleshooting skills for the Troubleshooting and System Maintenance section of the RHCE exam.

Lab 4

This lab includes a matching scenario to Lab 3 for your partner. Refer to the "Lab Answers" section for what you need to configure.

Lab 5

This lab requires two Red Hat–capable systems, or at least a second system that you know how to configure as an NTP client. Configure the RHEL system as an NTP server. Allow access on your local IP address subnet. Make sure the service is started and will start the next time you boot Linux.

SELF TEST ANSWERS

The Extended Internet Services Daemon (xinetd)

1. The command that makes sure that the Kerberos version of Telnet starts the next time you boot Linux is **chkconfig krb5-telnet on**. This assumes the xinetd service is active when you boot. Naturally, you can edit /etc/xinetd.d/krb5-telnet directly for the same result.

2. The command that rereads any configuration changes you've made to a file in the /etc/xinetd.d directory is **service xinetd reload**.

The Secure Shell Package

3. Once configured, you need to open TCP port 22 to allow Secure Shell (SSH) access. It's easy to do with the Red Hat Security Level configuration tool described in Chapter 15.

4. To log into the troosevelt account from a remote computer, use the **ssh troosevelt@conservation** command.

5. SSH keys for user michael are stored in the /home/michael/.ssh/ directory.

6. When configuring an SSH server, the directive that prohibits SSH logins by the root user is **PermitRootLogin no**.

7. When configuring an SSH server, the directive that supports access to remote GUI applications is **X11Forwarding yes**.

8. If you've configured access to remote GUI applications, you would use the **ssh -X troosevelt@conservation** command to log into the account described in question 5. You can then access GUI applications such as Firefox and OpenOffice.org writer through the SSH connection.

Dynamic Host Configuration Protocol (DHCP)

9. If the DNS server you want your clients to use has an IP address of 10.11.12.1, add the **domain-name-servers 10.11.12.1;** directive to your /etc/dhcpd.conf configuration file.

10. A missing **routers** directive in /etc/dhcpd.conf would keep your hosts from getting the gateway address, which is required to access the Internet from an internal network.

The Network Time Protocol

11. The appropriate directive that limits access to the 192.168.0.0/24 network is

```
restrict 192.168.0.0 mask 255.255.255.0 nomodify notrap
```

12. Pool.ntp.org is the Web site associated with the Public Time Server project. If you've used the Date/Time Properties tool, you should be familiar with this from the Red Hat defaults.

LAB ANSWERS

Lab 1

If you need access now, and both systems are connected to the Internet, you can set up SSH for secure communications. If the other network does not already have it installed, have the administrator in the remote location download and install it, and then create an account for you.

The basic steps outlined here may vary with the version of Unix used on the other network. If it's Red Hat Enterprise Linux, all you need are the SSH packages described in this chapter, but you may not have that luxury.

Download the source code for OpenSSH and put it into a specific directory. Assuming your version of Unix can't handle RPMs, you'll need to unpack a tarball. You can then unpackage the files in the tarball and use the files in the resulting directory to compile and configure a Secure Shell server. Once it is configured, you have the option to set up private and public keys.

If you don't need immediate access, you could, alternatively, configure a computer with Red Hat Enterprise Linux and a Secure Shell server. Send the computer to the administrator of the remote Unix network. Have the admin add it to his or her network, and you can check the problem from your site securely. The application is running on the Linux computer that you sent. (Alternatively, you can set up OpenSSH on Microsoft Windows, as described earlier in this chapter.)

Lab 2

Assuming you've read the chapter, you've seen the template in the dhcpd.conf.sample configuration file for a static IP address:

```
host ns {
    next-server marvin.redhat.com
    hardware ethernet 12:34:56:78:AB:CD;
    fixed-address 207.175.42.254;
}
```

As described in the chapter, the **next-server** command is associated with the boot server for this computer; since there is no boot server mentioned, you won't need this command. To set up the DHCP server, take the following steps:

1. On the DHCP server computer, open the /etc/dhcpd.conf file. If this file doesn't exist, you haven't yet created a DHCP server on this computer.

2. Set up a new host in the DHCP configuration file:

   ```
   host precious {
   ```

3. On the DHCP client, run the **ifconfig** command to find the hardware address associated with that computer's Ethernet network card. For the purpose of this exercise, substitute the hardware address of your own card for AB:CD:EF:12:34:56 in the following command line:

   ```
   hardware ethernet AB:CD:EF:12:34:56
   ```

4. Finally, you can complete this line by setting up the static IP address that you want to assign to the DHCP client computer:

```
        fixed-address 10.11.12.13
    }
```

5. Save your changes to the /etc/dhcpd.conf configuration file. Restart the DHCP server daemon with the following command:

```
    # service dhcpd restart
```

6. Now proceed to the DHCP client, the precious.example.com computer. You can release any current DHCP client with the following command:

```
    # dhclient -r
```

7. Finally, you can see whether the DHCP client actually takes the static IP address from the DHCP server with the following commands:

```
    # dhclient
    # ifconfig
```

Lab 3: Part I

You're going to set up this lab for your partner (I've set up these "answers" in a different order, first the setup of the lab, to help discourage "shoulder surfing"), using the following steps:

1. Make sure your system supports the SSH service, is active, and includes an account for your partner's username and password. If the password is secret, let your partner enter the password.

2. Take over your partner's RHEL system. Make sure there's a connection between your computers.

3. Configure the SSH service as described in this chapter. If you have a firewall configured on this system, make sure to open port 22 to allow communication to the local SSH service. You can use the Red Hat Security Level configuration tool described in Chapter 15 to help.

4. Modify the SSH server configuration file to allow users, not including the regular username for your partner. As described in this chapter, this involves the **AllowUsers** directive in the /etc/ssh/sshd_config file.

5. Don't forget to make the sshd service reread the configuration file with a command such as **service sshd reload**.

6. Pass your partner's system back to him or her. Instructions for your partner can be found in Part 2 of Lab 3.

Lab 4: Part I

1. Make sure your system supports the SSH service, is active, and includes an account for your partner's username and password. If the password is secret, let your partner enter the password.

2. Take over your partner's RHEL system. Make sure there's a connection between your computers.

3. Configure the SSH service as described in this chapter. If you have a firewall configured on this system, make sure to open port 22 to allow communication to the local SSH service. You can use the Red Hat Security Level configuration tool described in Chapter 15 to help.

4. Modify the SSH server configuration file to prohibit logins by the root user. As described in this chapter, this involves the **PermitRootLogin no** directive in the /etc/ssh/sshd_config file.

5. Don't forget to make the sshd service reread the configuration file with a command such as **service sshd reload.**

6. Pass your partner's system back to him or her. Instructions for your partner can be found in Part 2 of Lab 4.

Lab 3: Part 2

1. Take your system back from your partner. Log in as a regular user. Use the **ssh** command to log into your partner's system under your username. Repeat the process to log back into your own system. What happens?

2. Return to your own system. Analyze the logs. What do you see? Is there anything special in /var/log/secure?

Lab 4: Part 2

1. Take your system back from your partner. Log in as a regular user. Use the **ssh** command to log into your partner's system as the root user. Repeat the process to log back into your own system. What happens?

2. Return to your own system. Analyze the logs. What do you see? Is there anything special in /var/log/secure?

Lab 5

Before configuring a system as an NTP server, you have to first configure it as a client. The simplest method for doing so is to use the Date/Time Configuration tool, which can be started in the GUI with the **system-config-date** command.

Once configured as a client, make sure the NTP service is running and set to start the next time Linux is booted on the local system. The simplest method involves the following commands, which should be familiar if you've configured other services on Red Hat systems:

```
# chkconfig ntpd on
# service ntpd start
```

Open the NTP configuration file, /etc/ntp.conf. Add an appropriate **restrict** directive to open access to other systems. One example suitable for the 192.168.1.0 network is shown in the comments to the file:

```
# restrict 192.168.1.0 mask 255.255.255.0 nomodify notrap
```

If your LAN uses a different network address and subnet mask, substitute accordingly. If it's an IPv6 network, the directive is **restrict -6**. After saving the changes, the following command makes NTP reread the service configuration file:

```
# service ntpd reload
```

Now you can go to the second system and configure its client to connect to the local NTP server that you just created. If you have the Date/Time Configuration tool on that second server, the simplest method is to start it with the **system-config-date** command and point to the domain name or IP address of the NTP server you just created.

14

The X Window System

CERTIFICATION OBJECTIVES

14.01   X with Clients and Servers

14.02   The X.org Server Configuration

14.03   Tools for X.org Configuration

14.04   Running Remote X Applications

14.05   Desktops and Window Managers

✓   Two-Minute Drill

Q&A   Self Test

O
ne of the most important aspects of getting a Linux system up and running is configuring the user interface. As RHCEs and RHCTs are expected to configure computers for non-administrative users, the Red Hat exams test your ability to configure the X Window System, which is the foundation of the Linux graphical user interface (GUI). While the GUI plays an integral part of other operating systems such as Microsoft Windows, the X Window System on Linux is essentially just another application.

Many administrators don't even bother with the GUI; the command line interface is enough for most administrative purposes. However, regular users on a Linux workstation are more productive using the GUI and the multitude of X Window–based applications. If you are helping users migrate from Microsoft Windows to Linux, the X Window System allows you to provide a less intimidating environment.

Not all Linux computers require the X Window System. For example, computers that are used as dedicated DHCP, DNS, or NFS servers generally don't serve as workstations for anyone and therefore don't need any sort of GUI. Many Linux gurus are biased against the GUI. While Red Hat and others have developed some helpful GUI tools, they are almost always "front ends," or programs that customize one or more commands at the command line interface.

But if you're administering a network of Linux computers for regular users, you'll need to know how to administer the X Window System, a skill that requires a basic understanding of the available desktops and graphical applications.

Most Linux distributions (including RHEL) have converted display software from the XFree86 to the X.org system. While the names of the configuration files and some of the commands have changed, the basic settings and tools have not. If you learned to configure the X Window using XFree86, you should have no trouble configuring the X.org system.

This chapter starts with the X server, as configured on the local computer. It continues with X clients, as generic applications that you can run from the local or a remote network computer. Once everything is configured, you're ready to take a step back to the start process for the X Window. The chapter moves on to the two major Linux graphical desktops, and finally covers a very few of the available graphical applications.

INSIDE THE EXAM

The Linux Graphical User Interface

The Red Hat Exam Prep guide suggests that you need to know how to configure the X Window, presumably for non-administrative users. Remember that RHCE candidates must successfully complete *all* RHCT Troubleshooting and System Maintenance requirements, including configuring the X Window System and a desktop environment. You also need to know how to configure the X Window on a local computer. There are a number of reasons why the X Window may fail.

The X configuration files can be difficult to learn. It may be more efficient to use the Red Hat GUI X Window Display Settings configuration tool, which you can start with the **system-config-display** command. While Linux geeks generally shy away from GUI tools, you need to use the system that works most quickly for you.

The X Window System can work over a network. Once properly configured, you can run GUI applications from a remote computer. To make this work, you need to understand modularity of the X server and X clients, as well as the way X Window security is managed on your network.

exam

watch   *I use the Red Hat Display Settings tool and system-config-display command interchangeably; the command is the fastest way to start the tool.*

CERTIFICATION OBJECTIVE 14.01

X with Clients and Servers

The X Window System is designed as a flexible and powerful client/server-based system. To configure and troubleshoot the X Window interface, you need to understand the client/server nature of the X Window System.

As you might have guessed from the terms *client* and *server*, the X Window System is designed to work in a networked environment. The client and server can both reside on your own computer or on separate computers on the network. In other words, not only can you run X applications on your system, you can run X applications on other computers on your network. The graphical displays from those remote applications are sent to your monitor.

In fact, X Window applications handle this task so well that, providing the network is fast enough, you really can't tell from a performance point of view which applications are running locally and which applications are running remotely.

When you configure the X server, I'll show you the modularity of the system. In brief, components such as keyboards, mice, and monitors are configured separately and all become modular components of the X server. While one X server process controls the display, you can run as many X clients as your hardware resources, primarily RAM, will support. If your Linux system is part of a network, you can also start X clients on other systems on the network and have those clients send their displays to your X server.

X clients exist for almost every basic application—word processing, spreadsheets, games, and more. The Red Hat GUI configuration tools were developed as X clients. There are even X client versions of popular utilities such as the emacs editor.

Different Meanings for Client and Server

Normally on a network, the local computer is the client and the remote computer acts as the server. X Window clients and servers work on a different paradigm. The X server controls the graphics on the local computer. The X server draws images on your screen and takes input from *your* keyboard and mouse. In contrast, X clients are local or remote applications such as **xclock** that you can run on the local X server.

You can run an X client locally or remotely. Local X clients run on your workstation; remote X clients run on the local X server. When you run a remote X Window client application, you start the program on a different computer and send its output to use the X server on your local computer. Figure 14-1 illustrates a local X server with one local and one remote X client.

Before reading more about running X client applications, you need to first configure an X server. While RHEL normally configures most hardware configurations during the installation process, you need to know how to edit the X Window configuration file, directly in a text editor or with the Red Hat Display Settings tool (**system-config-display**).

FIGURE 14-1

Running X
Window clients
from remote or
local computers

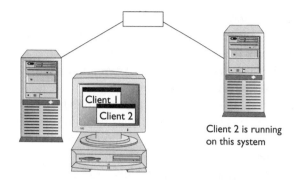

Your workstation running X-server
and one X-client (Client 1)

Client 2 is running
on this system

Both X-client applications get their input
from the keyboard and mouse attached to
your workstation

on the
jOb

If you're in the GNOME (GNU Network Object Model Environment) or KDE (K Desktop Environment) desktops, you can also start the Red Hat Display Settings tool with the GNOME System (or KDE Main Menu) | Administration | Display command.

Supported Hardware

If a Linux installation program does not successfully configure the X Window System, it can be difficult to configure the GUI on a Linux workstation. Fortunately, RHEL comes with tools and drivers that make this job relatively painless and easy.

But it all depends on the hardware. Linux may not always work with the latest and greatest video card or monitor. Many video cards and monitors include proprietary software; it may take some time before Linux developers are able to "reverse-engineer" these components. For the latest official information, check the Linux Video and DVD Project at www.linuxvideo.org, the Linux Hardware Compatibility List at www.tldp.org/HOWTO/Hardware-HOWTO/, and the Red Hat Hardware Catalog at https://hardware.redhat.com/hwcert/.

on the
jOb

Linux provides world-class support for graphics. The list of movie studios that use Linux to create feature films is impressive (including Disney, DreamWorks, Industrial Light and Magic, Paramount, and so on). If you need motion picture–quality graphics support, you may want to consider commercial alternatives to the X.org server, such as Accelerated-X from X_i Graphics (www.xinside.com).

The X Window server shipped with RHEL 5 is an open-source X server program from X.org. This server supports hundreds of video cards and monitors. The best places to check to determine whether your video card and monitor are supported are the hardware lists described earlier. Alternatively, navigate to the X.org Web site to find the latest support information.

The latest version of X.org includes modules for different video servers. Hardware support for most video servers is already there. If you learn of updates, changes are easy. Just add the module, and then point to it in the /etc/X11/xorg.conf configuration file.

If you are using an unsupported video card, support is also included for generic VGA and VESA devices. Most video cards and monitors will work with these X servers.

Default X Clients

When you configure a workstation for most users, you'll be configuring their GUI. You may need to specify a default desktop such as GNOME or KDE. I'll describe these desktops later in this chapter. You may want to set up specific icons for that user's desktop. Settings for default X clients are stored in each user's home directory, in various hidden directories. In RHEL, KDE configuration files are stored in each user's ~/.kde directory (where the tilde, ~, represents a Linux home directory). GNOME configuration files are stored in hidden directories such as ~/.gconf, ~/.gnome, and ~/.gnome2.

EXERCISE 14-1

Starting X Server

In this exercise, you will start your X server without a window manager. You'll then start an X client application known as **xterm**. Some of the commands used in this exercise are covered later in the chapter. If the X Window System is not running, you can skip steps 1 and 3.

1. If the X Window System is running, change to a text console by pressing CTRL-ALT-F1.
2. If you see a login prompt, log in at the text console as the root user. Otherwise, press CTRL-C to stop the X Window.

3. When you log in as root at the text console, stop the current X Window server with the following command (**telinit 3** works as well):

   ```
   # init 3
   ```

4. Now log in as a regular user. You can log out and log back in, or you can log in more directly. For example, I access my own account with the following command:

   ```
   # su - michael
   ```

5. Start the X.org server by typing this command:

   ```
   # X &
   ```

   Your X server will start, but all you will see is a blank gray screen, with an "x" that represents your mouse cursor.

6. Switch back to your text console session by pressing CTRL-ALT-F1.

7. Type the following command:

   ```
   # xterm -display localhost:0.0  &
   ```

   (Note: there is only one hyphen before the display switch.)

8. Switch back to your X Window display by pressing ALT-F7.

You should now have an **xterm** terminal window. Select the window and enter commands at the **xterm** command line. Check out the contents of the /usr/X11R6/bin directory. Try starting other X client applications such as **xclipboard** and **xminicom** from the **xterm** command line. Reboot your system to return things to normal.

One last keystroke hint for X: pressing the CTRL-ALT-BACKSPACE keys sends a termination signal to the X server. In some situations, the Linux GUI crashes and it's not possible to start a text console session by pressing CTRL-ALT-F1. In this case, the CTRL-ALT-BACKSPACE key combination can keep you from having to reboot your computer.

X Clients and Command Line Options

Starting an X client is very easy. When you start the X Window System for the first time, it puts X client icons on the desktop by default. You can start additional X clients by selecting a program from a menu, or you can start an X client from a command line terminal screen. Later, I'll show you how to set up default X clients when you start the Linux GUI.

It's almost as easy to start running X clients from remote servers. All you need to do is configure a remote server to provide X clients using the Secure Shell, SSH. Just log in with the **-X** or **-Y** switch. For more information, see Chapter 13.

X clients are standard Linux applications, which you can start with commands such as **xclock**, **xeyes**, **xterm**, **xclipboard**, and so on. If you choose to start an X client from a command line, you can follow the command name with any number of options. Most X clients understand a common set of options. These options are used to control such things as the size and location of the X client's window, the font the application uses to display the text, and even the display on which the application should display its output. Table 14-1 lists some of the more useful options you can supply when you start an X client from the command line.

The **-geometry** option is used to specify both the size and location of the window in which the X client starts up. Notice that the first two numbers, the *XSIZE* and the *YSIZE*, are separated by a lowercase *x*. These two numbers specify the size of the client window in either pixels or characters, depending on the application. For example, if you are opening an **xterm** window, the size represents a terminal screen with *XSIZE* columns and *YSIZE* lines. If you are starting an **xclock**, the size represents a window *XSIZE*×*YSIZE* in pixels.

The next two numbers specify where you want the client window to appear on your display. The numbers are relative to the upper-left and lower-right corners of the desktop: **+0+0** represents the upper-left corner, **-0-0** represents the lower-right corner. These specs are shown in Table 14-2.

TABLE 14-1   Common X Client Command Line Options

Option	Example	Result
-geometry XSIZE×YSIZE+XOFF+YOFF	-geometry 100×100+10+20	Specify the size and location of the window. In this case, we want a window 100×100 pixels in size, offset from the upper-left corner by 10 pixels horizontally and 20 pixels vertically.
-font *fontname*	-font lucidasans-14	Display text for this client using a specific font.
-background *color*	-background blue	Set the window background to blue.
-foreground *color*	-foreground white	Set the window foreground to white.
-title *string*	-title "My Window"	Place a title on the client window's title bar.
-bordercolor *color*	-bordercolor green	Make the window border green.
-borderwidth *pixels*	-borderwidth 5	Make the window border 5 pixels wide.

XSIZE×YSIZE	Description
-0-0	Lower-right corner
-0+0	Upper-right corner
+0-0	Lower-left corner
+0+0	Upper-left corner

TABLE 14-2

X Client
Geometrical
Positioning

Therefore, for *XOFF+YOFF*, if you specify **+10+10**, the client is positioned 10 pixels from the left edge of the screen and 10 pixels from the top of the screen. Alternatively, **-10-10** positions the client 10 pixels from the right edge of the screen and 10 pixels up from the bottom of the screen.

The **-font** option specifies the font that the X client should use to display text. The X Window System comes with a wide variety of both fixed and proportionally spaced fonts. The default list is located in the /usr/share/X11/fonts directory. This directory contains a number of subdirectories, each of which contains font files for the various types of fonts installed on your system.

Many of the X client command line options enable you to specify colors for different parts of the client window. You can specify a simple color such as red, green, white, and black. Alternatively, you can specify a color by indicating the red, green, and blue components of the color:

```
# xclock -background RGB:FF/00/FF
```

xterm

One of the most useful X clients is a program called **xterm**. As its name implies, **xterm** is a client that creates a terminal window on your X display. So, after all the hard work you've gone through to get a nice windowing display, you're right back where you started, with a command line interface.

The difference is that now you can start up as many of these command line interfaces as you like, and you can switch between them with the click of a mouse. Since **xterm** is an X client, you can even open terminal windows on other computers on your network and have them display to your desktop. You can start **xterm** either from a menu or from a command line prompt.

Red Hat has configured **gnome-terminal** as the default command line interface within the default GNOME desktop, which you can start by choosing Applications | Accessories | Terminal. Alternatively, the KDE Konsole is accessible by choosing Main Menu | System | Terminal.

The X.org Server Configuration

Most configuration files associated with the X.org server can be found in the /etc/X11 directory. While the focus is on the xorg.conf file, there are other files in that directory. The way the X.org server is designed, you can start the X Window in multiple terminals. You can boot directly into the X Window in your choice of display managers or use **startx** to start it from a command line console.

X.org Server Configuration Files

A wide variety of X Window configuration files are located in the /etc/X11 directory. Many are discussed in other parts of this chapter. While I don't cover these files in detail, the Red Hat Exam Prep guide doesn't say much about configuring the X Window in detail.

Therefore, I focus here on the primary X Window configuration file, xorg.conf. It's instructive to read the associated man page carefully. It is well documented and includes a number of commented sample commands that can help you configure your system in a number of special ways. For example, it includes tips on how you can

- Configure different keyboards.
- Set up multiple monitors, in what is known as a "multi-head" configuration.
- Disable switching from the GUI to other virtual terminals with the following command:

```
Option "DontVTSwitch" "on"
```

- Disable the CTRL-ALT-BACKSPACE key sequence, which normally exits from the GUI with the following command:

```
Option "DontZap" "on"
```

This is just a small sample of the things you can do with your X Window configuration—and the kinds of problems that you may have to troubleshoot in real life. And remember that the Red Hat exam is supposed to reflect problems that you may encounter in real life.

Starting the X Window

The default server is linked to the **X** command. X is called up by the **startx** command. Both of these commands are located in the /usr/bin directory. Examine the long listing for the **X** command. You'll see that it's linked to the **Xorg** command:

```
# ls -l /usr/bin/X
lrwxrwxrwx    1 root   root    4 Jul 30 07:33 /usr/bin/X -> Xorg
```

The Display Settings tool normally writes its changes to /etc/X11/xorg.conf. When the X.org server starts, it reads this file.

EXERCISE 14-2

Starting Multiple X Servers

In this exercise, you will start two different X servers. If the X Window System is not running, you can skip steps 1 and 3.

1. If the X Window System is running, change to a text console by pressing CTRL-ALT-F1.

2. If you see a login prompt, log in at the text console as root. Otherwise, press CTRL-C to stop the X Window.

3. If you logged in at the graphical console, stop the current X Window server by typing this:

   ```
   init 3
   ```

4. Start the X.org server by typing this command:

   ```
   # startx &
   ```

   The default GUI will start.

5. Switch back to your text console session by pressing CTRL-ALT-F1. Return to your GUI by pressing ALT-F7. Switch back again to your text console session. (If these commands do not work, check for a DontVTSwitch option in your /etc/X11/xorg.conf file.)

6. Type the following command:

   ```
   # startx -- :1  &
   ```

7. You should now have two different GUIs. Switch to the first GUI by pressing CTRL-ALT-F7. Return to the second GUI by pressing CTRL-ALT-F8.

8. Log out from both GUIs. If no logout menu option is available, press CTRL-ALT-BACKSPACE.

xorg.conf in Detail

As you learn the intricacies of configuring the Linux X Window Server, it's worth some trouble to examine the /etc/X11/xorg.conf file in detail. It's interesting to note that this file is very similar to previous /etc/X11/XF86Config files on the older RHEL 3 system. The available directives are the same. The configuration file is quite a bit simpler; for example, there are no longer default sections for modules or fonts.

The first line is a comment that indicates whether your X Window System was last configured by the Red Hat installation program or the Display Settings tool. The two options are

```
# Xorg configuration created by pyxf86config
# Xorg configuration created by system-config-display
```

The first section binds the other sections together. In other words, you'll see sections later in this file, each associated with an **Identifier** variable: **Screen0**, **Keyboard0**, and **Synaptics**.

```
Section "ServerLayout"
    Identifier      "single head configuration"
    Screen      0   "Screen0" 0 0
    InputDevice     "Keyboard0" "CoreKeyboard"
    InputDevice     "Synaptics" "CorePointer"
EndSection
```

e x a m

ⓦ a t c h   *RHEL 5 can handle multiple monitors. If so configured, you'll see a different value for Identifier, such as "dual head configuration". However, as two monitors per workstation would be* *rather expensive (especially in a classroom with a dozen or more systems), I don't believe you need to worry about this on your exam. But as they say, your mileage may vary.*

Next, take a look at a couple of different sections, both labeled **InputDevice**. The first configures your keyboard as a regular US keyboard with 105 keys. The second configures a PS/2 mouse. The **Emulate3Buttons** option, when active, configures the X server to activate middle mouse button functionality when you click the left and right mouse buttons simultaneously.

```
Section "InputDevice"
    Identifier  "Keyboard0"
    Driver      "kbd"
    Option      "XkbModel" "pc105"
    Option      "XkbLayout" "us"
EndSection

Section "InputDevice"
    Identifier  "Synaptics"
    Driver      "synaptics"
    Option      "Device" "/dev/input/mice"
    Option      "protocol" "auto-dev"
    Option      "Emulate3Buttons" "yes"
EndSection
```

The following **Monitor, Device,** and **Screen** sections are associated with the monitor detected during the installation process or configured with the **system-config-display** command:

```
Section "Monitor"
        Identifier   "Monitor0"
        ModelName    "LCD Panel 1440x900"
        HorizSync    31.5 - 100.0
        VertRefresh  59.0 - 75.0
        Option       "dpms"
EndSection

Section "Device"
        Identifier   "Videocard0"
        Driver       "radeon"
EndSection

Section "Screen"
        Identifier "Screen0"
        Device     "Videocard0"
        Monitor    "Monitor0"
        DefaultDepth   24
        SubSection "Display"
                Viewport   0 0
```

```
                       Depth       24
             EndSubSection
     EndSection
```

As you can see, the **Screen** section associates the **Device** and **Monitor** as identified by **Monitor0**, **Videocard0**, and **Screen0**. If the Red Hat installation program or the Display Settings tool gives you the wrong **DefaultDepth** or inappropriate screen sizes (**Modes**), you can add or modify them here. I've added the matching sections from a different system for your reference.

```
     Section "Monitor"
             Identifier    "Monitor0"
             ModelName     "LCD Panel 1024x768"
             HorizSync     31.5 - 48.5
             VertRefresh   40.0 - 70.0
             Option        "dpms"
     EndSection

     Section "Device"
             Identifier    "Videocard0"
             Driver        "vesa"
     EndSection

     Section "Screen"
             Identifier "Screen0"
             Device     "Videocard0"
             Monitor    "Monitor0"
             DefaultDepth    24
             SubSection "Display"
                     Viewport   0 0
                     Depth      24
                     Modes      "800x600" "640x480"
             EndSubSection
     EndSection
```

Text or Graphical GUI Access

RHEL now configures the X Window interface to start automatically when your system boots, by setting the **id** directive to runlevel 5 in /etc/inittab. If you set **id** to runlevel 3, you can choose to start the X Window System manually. In this case, the Linux GUI can be started with the **startx** command. If you select a graphical login, you can also select the graphical login manager of your choice.

Text Login Mode

To access a Linux system, you need to log in. In other words, you identify yourself to the system with a username and a password, using a login program. When you log into Linux at a regular command line interface, the **mingetty** command calls up a login program that prompts you for your username and password. Six **mingetty** terminals are configured through /etc/inittab.

There are six active runlevels in Linux. The two of concern here are runlevels 3 and 5. If you start Linux in runlevel 3, you get a text login. If you start Linux in runlevel 5, you get a graphical login screen.

It's easy to change the default boot mode from the X Window to the command line. Just edit the /etc/inittab file. Go to the line with the **initdefault** variable. To make Linux start a text console (with no GUI) automatically, use your favorite text editor and change the line in /etc/inittab that reads

```
id:5:initdefault:
```

to

```
id:3:initdefault:
```

Of course, you can reverse this process. This change does not take effect until you reboot. If you are running as the root user, you can also use the **init** (or **telninit**) command to switch between runlevel 5 and runlevel 3. Running this command,

```
# init 3
```

switches your display from X Window back to text terminal mode; whereas,

```
# init 5
```

switches you from text terminal mode to X Window, specifically the default graphical login screen, as started by the display manager. You can find more information on different runlevels and /etc/inittab in Chapter 3.

Display Managers: gdm and kdm

When you configure Linux to start from runlevel 5, you can log in through a special X client, the *display manager*. The display manager is a fairly simple program; it simply displays a dialog box on the screen asking for your username and password. You can use any of three major display managers. The default display manager is the GNOME Display Manager, or **gdm**. To change your display manager, edit the **prefdm** shell script in the /etc/X11 directory, as shown in Figure 14-2.

Take the **preferred** directive and set it to **kdm** or **gdm** for the KDE Display Manager or GNOME Display Manager, respectively, as shown on line 14. Alternatively, set the DISPLAYMANAGER directive to GNOME or KDE in etc/sysconfig/desktop.

on the **job**

Even though the code in /etc/X11/prefdm suggests otherwise, the X Display Manager, xdm, is not included with RHEL 5.

FIGURE 14-2

Set your
preferred display
manager in /etc/
X11/prefdm.

```
 1 #!/bin/sh
 2 █
 3 PATH=/sbin:/usr/sbin:/bin:/usr/bin
 4
 5 # shut down any graphical boot that might exist
 6 if [ -x /usr/bin/rhgb-client ]; then
 7    /usr/bin/rhgb-client --quit
 8 fi
 9
10 # We need to source this so that the login screens get translated
11 [ -f /etc/sysconfig/i18n ] && . /etc/sysconfig/i18n
12
13 # Run preferred X display manager
14 preferred=kdm
15 if [ -f /etc/sysconfig/desktop ]; then
16         . /etc/sysconfig/desktop
17         if [ "$DISPLAYMANAGER" = GNOME ]; then
18                 preferred=/usr/sbin/gdm
19         elif [ "$DISPLAYMANAGER" = KDE ]; then
20                 preferred=/usr/bin/kdm
21         elif [ "$DISPLAYMANAGER" = XDM ]; then
22                 preferred=/usr/bin/xdm
23         elif [ -n "$DISPLAYMANAGER" ]; then
24                 preferred=$DISPLAYMANAGER
25         fi
26 fi
:set nu
```

How you start the X Window System affects its behavior. Assume you start X Window through one of the graphical display managers. When you exit an X Window session, you're returned to the same display manager. To continue, you would need to log in again.

The default behavior for the **gdm** window manager launches a GNOME session. The **kdm** window manager by default launches a KDE session. However, you can start GNOME or KDE from either login manager.

Both the GNOME and KDE environments use their own startup files. Through the use of option buttons, both the GNOME and KDE display managers allow you to choose the desktop environment that you want to start. From the GNOME Display Manager, click the Session button. This starts a window where you can select from several desktop options, as shown in Figure 14-3.

From the KDE Display Manager shown in Figure 14-4, press ALT-T. You can then select from the available desktop environments.

If you log in using a display manager, X Window starts somewhat differently when compared to using **startx**. When you run **startx**, the X Window runs as a child process of your text-based login shell. Even though the X Window System is running, Linux is still at runlevel 3. After you exit the X Window System, you still have to log out of this shell to terminate your login session.

The GNOME
Display Manager,
gdm

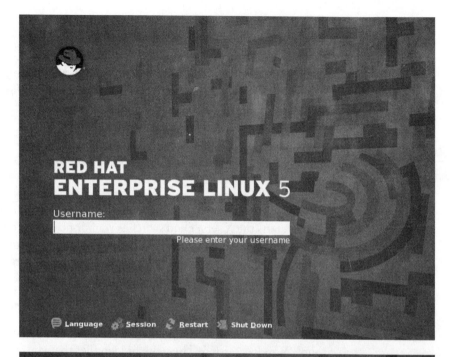

The KDE Display
Manager, **kdm**

Analyzing startx

You've already seen that you can start the Linux GUI with the **startx** command. This command starts the X server and switches your display into graphics mode. It also runs through a series of configuration files that prompt Linux to start your selected desktop and other desired applications. The start of this script is illustrated in Figure 14-5.

on the !job *The startx command is actually a shell script that serves as a front end to the xinit command. The default location for both startx and xinit is /usr/bin.*

There are a number of configuration files that can help you customize the behavior of your X Window session. These are hidden files that you can install into users' home directories. If **startx** doesn't find a particular configuration file in a home directory, it uses a default version of the same file.

Take a look at two of the first lines in the **startx** script:

```
userclientrc=$HOME/.xinitrc
sysclientrc=/etc/X11/xinit/xinitrc
```

FIGURE 14-5

The **startx** script

```
#!/bin/sh

# $Xorg: startx.cpp,v 1.3 2000/08/17 19:54:29 cpqbld Exp $
#
# This is just a sample implementation of a slightly less primitive
# interface than xinit. It looks for user .xinitrc and .xserverrc
# files, then system xinitrc and xserverrc files, else lets xinit choose
# its default. The system xinitrc should probably do things like check
# for .Xresources files and merge them in, startup up a window manager,
# and pop a clock and serveral xterms.
#
# Site administrators are STRONGLY urged to write nicer versions.
#
# $XFree86: xc/programs/xinit/startx.cpp,v 3.16tsi Exp $
userclientrc=$HOME/.xinitrc
sysclientrc=/etc/X11/xinit/xinitrc


userserverrc=$HOME/.xserverrc
sysserverrc=/etc/X11/xinit/xserverrc
defaultclient=xterm
defaultserver=/usr/bin/X
defaultclientargs=""
"/usr/bin/startx" [readonly] 171L, 3836C
```

When you start the X Window System with the **startx** command, the **userclientrc** directive looks for a file to run named .xinitrc in your home directory. It then reads the /etc/X11/xinit/xinitrc configuration script. This file, in turn, runs either the file **$HOME** /.Xclients, or, if that file doesn't exist, /etc/X11/xinit/Xclients.

A typical ~/.xinitrc file includes commands that start various X clients. (Remember that the tilde represents the home directory.)

on the job *You can also configure X clients to start when you start the GNOME desktop through the Sessions utility. Settings are stored in each user's home directory in the ~/.gnome2/session-manual file.*

e x a m
watch
There is more than one way to do many things in Linux, including the setup of default X clients. Knowing *these options can help you troubleshoot problems during the Red Hat exams.*

The following is an illustration of a simple ~/.xinitrc file:

```
#!/bin/bash
xterm &
xclock -geometry 200x200-20+20 &
xclipboard -geometry 300x300-20-20 &
exec twm
```

The first line sets **bash** as the shell for this script. The next line starts an **xterm** terminal client. The following line starts **xclock** with a specific size and location. The line after that brings up an X Window clipboard, also with a specific size and location. Notice that the first three command lines end with an ampersand (**&**). This is important; it tells the shell to run each command line and return control to the shell for this script. The final line uses the **exec** command to start the **twm** window manager. I illustrate the result in Figure 14-6; this supersedes any default desktop and X clients that you may have otherwise configured.

You can start other desktops through this file; for example, substitute one of the following commands for **exec twm** in the previous example of an .xinitrc configuration file.

```
exec gnome-session
exec startkde
```

You can create an ~/.xinitrc file with a text editor of your choice. Once you've saved the file, **startx** executes the commands in this file, with the results shown in Figure 14-6.

A GUI as custom configured through ~/.xinitrc

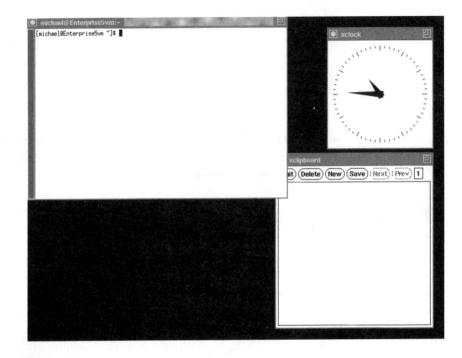

EXERCISE 14-3

Customizing the startx Process

In this exercise, configure the X Window System to use a customized .xinitrc file.

1. If the X Window System is running, change to a text console by pressing CTRL-ALT-F1.

2. If you see a login prompt, log in at the text console as root. Otherwise, press CTRL-C to stop the current X Window session.

3. If you logged in from the GUI (using a window manager such as **gdm**), stop the current X Window server with the following command:

   ```
   # init 3
   ```

4. Make sure you're in your home directory, logged in under your account. I access my home account from root with the **su – michael** command. Use your favorite text editor to create a .xinitrc file. If you're not sure what to do, use the sample file shown in the preceding section.

5. Start the X Window System with the following command:

```
# startx
```

Your X Window session should automatically start the applications in your .xinitrc file.

6. Assuming you used the sample .xinitrc file described earlier, exit from the twm desktop. To do so, left-click the desktop to bring up the twm main menu and click Exit.

7. If you want to restore your original desktop settings, to allow you to start GNOME or KDE with the **startx** command, remove the .xinitrc file from your home directory.

Now that you have seen how X Window clients and the X Window server work together, refer to the following Scenario & Solution for some common situations you may encounter, along with their solutions.

SCENARIO & SOLUTION

I'm having problems getting X.org to run on my hardware.	Check the Red Hat hardware support site. Run **system-config-display**.
I want to use a different desktop environment.	Use the **switchdesk** command to change your desktop environment.
I want to stop the X Window System without rebooting Linux. When I try logging out, all I see is a graphical login manager.	Use the **init 3** (or **telinit 3**) command to change the system runlevel to runlevel 3.
I'm having problems starting an X client.	Check that the **DISPLAY** variable is properly set with the following command: **# export DISPLAY=localhost:0.0** Check for underlying network problems. Check X security problems.
My X Window display is acting strangely and I can't log in.	Switch to a virtual console and log in. Check the error logs. See if your X Font Server (**xfs**) is running. If it isn't, check for errors in ~/.xsession-errors and /var/log/messages. Make sure your /tmp and /home directory partitions are not full. As a last resort, rerun **system-config-display** or **Xorg -configure**.

CERTIFICATION OBJECTIVE 14.03

Tools for X.org Configuration

If you want to configure your X Window System, there are three options: Direct configuration of the X Window configuration file, the Red Hat Display Settings tool (**system-config-display**), or automatic installation and configuration of the X Window during the installation process.

Even if you didn't install any graphics software when you installed RHEL, you can still use the **system-config-display** command. It starts its own default graphics mode if it detects a graphics driver.

Red Hat Display Settings Tool

The Red Hat Display Settings tool is a stand-alone program that you can run at any time from the command line. The basic routines that start with the **system-config-display** command are also used by the Red Hat installation program if you choose to install and configure the X Window System at that time.

The **system-config-display** program is a character-based menu-driven interface that helps you configure your video hardware. If you're starting from a text console, it automatically probes your video card and selects the appropriate X server image. If **system-config-display** cannot detect your graphics card, it allows you to select it from the list of supported video cards.

It's easy to start the Red Hat Display Settings tool. Just type **system-config-display** at a command line interface. It provides a simple GUI, even if you start it from a regular text console. It starts the Display Settings window similar to that shown in Figure 14-7.

You can set the default resolution and color depth under the Settings tab. If the Display Settings tool successfully identifies your hardware, you'll see it listed under the Hardware tab. In this case, it detected a VMware graphics driver with a LCD monitor. You can change these settings by clicking the associated button. If your hardware supports it, you can configure:

- Monitor resolutions between 640×480 and 1920×1440.
- A color depth of thousands or millions of colors. Thousands corresponds to 16-bit color, and millions corresponds to 24- or 32-bit color, depending on the capability of your hardware.

But if you want to select a different hardware component, you can select it from a list. Click the Hardware tab, shown in Figure 14-8.

FIGURE 14-7

The Display
Settings tool,
started from the
text console

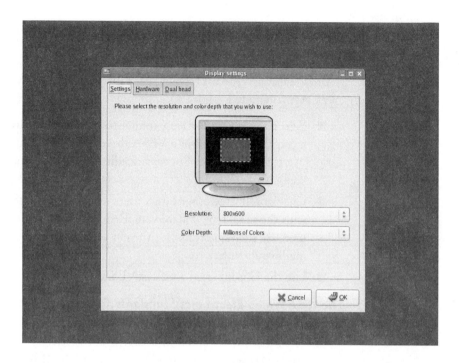

FIGURE 14-8

Display settings

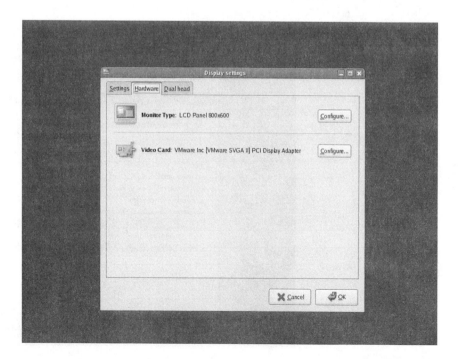

You'll see options to configure your monitor and video card. Click the Configure button in the Video Card section. This should bring up the Video Card dialog box shown in Figure 14-9.

Browse through the list of video cards. If you do not see your graphics card here, it may not be supported. In this case, there are several options:

■ Select a video card at least similar to your model. Alternatively, you may find a generic server such as a VESA driver (generic) that is compatible with your video card. Test and if necessary edit the /etc/X11/xorg.conf file to complete your changes.

■ Check online for other Linux users who are running the X Window System with the same type of hardware. Red Hat maintains mailing lists where many users ask such questions; for the current set of lists, see www.redhat.com/mailman/listinfo.

■ Use the Unsupported VGA or VESA compatible X Window Server.

The VESA (Video Electronics Standards Association) driver is also known as SVGA (Super Video Graphics Array).

■ Go to www.X.org and download the latest drivers. You'll need to edit the /etc/X11/xorg.conf file directly to point to this driver.

FIGURE 14-9

Selecting a
graphics card

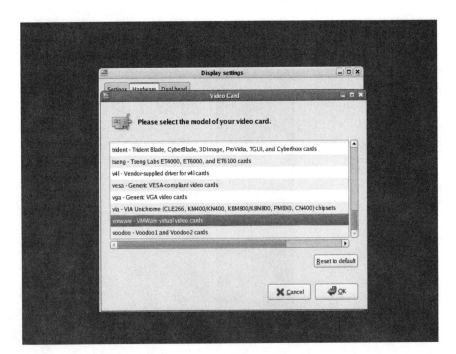

Once your selections are complete, click OK. This returns you to the Hardware tab. If your video card is so capable, you'll be able to activate the Enable Hardware 3D Acceleration option. (Otherwise, you won't even see the option in the menu.) Next, configure the Monitor. Click the Configure button in the Monitor Type section of the Hardware tab to open the dialog box shown in Figure 14-10.

Configuring the X Window System to run on a laptop can create challenges. If you are planning to install Red Hat Enterprise Linux on a laptop, a good source for tips and additional information is the Linux on Laptops Web site at www.linux-laptop.net. When all else failed during a recent installation, I was able to run system-config-display remotely, over an SSH connection.

Other Available Tools

There are a number of ways to configure the X Window with command line tools. If you have problems with the X Window, the first thing to do is check the log file, in /var/log/Xorg.0.log. More information is available in the "Troubleshooting" section later in this chapter.

For a quicker look at the start process, move to runlevel 3 with the **init 3** command. Simulate the GUI start process with the following command:

```
# Xorg -probeonly
```

Some problems may keep the **system-config-display** command from working. In that case, you can use a command line option to probe your hardware and create a local xorg.conf configuration file:

```
# Xorg -configure
```

You can then back up the existing /etc/X11/xorg.conf and copy the new xorg.conf to that directory.

FIGURE 14-10

Selecting a monitor

on the **job**   *Xorg -configure **may not work for all hardware configurations, such as RHEL 5 within VMware.***

X Font Server Issues

Assuming your X server is properly configured, you should be able to start a GUI with the **startx** command. One thing that can go wrong is the X Font Server. The X Window System needs fonts. Linux manages fonts through the X Font Server. RHEL manages the X Font Server with the **xfs** service script. Many different fonts are normally available in the /usr/share/X11/fonts directory.

The X Font Server can be an Achilles' heel for X Window. If you can't start the X Window, check the status of the X Font Server with the following command:

```
# service xfs status
```

If the X Font Server is not running, you'll want to go through the following troubleshooting list:

- The **xfs** service could be stopped or dead. In this case, you may need to try restarting **xfs**.
- The **xfs** service might not be set to start in your current runlevel; you can inspect and change this with the appropriate **chkconfig** command.
- The filesystems with /tmp or /home could be full. The **xfs** service can't start if either of these filesystems is full. There may also be problems if /tmp is on a different physical hard disk from other X Window files.
- Fonts could be missing from the default /usr/share/X11/fonts directory. For example, missing 100 dpi or 75 dpi fonts could cause applications in a Linux GUI to look strange.
- The font configuration file, /etc/X11/fs/config, could be flawed. The simplest solution is to replace it from the associated RPM package, xorg-x11-xfs.

on the **job**   *If you want to use an existing RPM to restore a missing configuration (or other) file, install it with the --force switch. For example, if the /etc/X11/fs/ config file is missing, you can replace it from the original RPM with the rpm -ivh --force xorg-x11-xfs-1*.rpm command.*

Any of these problems could make trouble for the Linux X Window. While RHEL 5 is more resiliant to X Font Server problems, you still need to know how to fix them.

on the **job**   *Do not confuse the X Font Server service script, xfs, with the filesystem with the same initials, which was developed for very large files and partitions by Silicon Graphics.*

Running Remote X Applications

One of the most powerful features of the X Window System is its networking support. The X Window System was designed to run in a networked environment. If you are a system administrator responsible for a number of RHEL systems, you don't have to run to the server room every time you want to run a GUI administration tool. With the X Window System, you can connect to any number of systems and redirect the output from X clients running on those systems back to the X server running on your desktop.

One method for running remote X applications was described in Chapter 13. It required appropriate configuration of SSH on the remote X client system, permission on the firewall, and appropriate login (with the **ssh -X** or **ssh -Y** command, followed by *login@remotepc*).

EXERCISE 14-4

Starting a Display from a Remote Client

In this exercise, examine the steps required to run a display from a remote client. This assumes a basic knowledge of the Secure Shell and its associated command, **ssh**. For more information on running the **ssh** command, see Chapter 13. You'll need two computers running Linux. While RHEL is not required on both computers, you will need the Secure Shell installed on both. The Secure Shell service, **sshd**, should be running on the remote computer. You'll also need the root password for both computers. In my example, the local computer is named Enterprise, and the remote computer is named cosmicc (which is short for Cosmic Charlie, my favorite Grateful Dead teddy bear). Substitute the names (or IP addresses) of your computers accordingly.

1. On the Enterprise computer, start the X Window. If it isn't already open, use the **startx** command.

2. When the Linux GUI is open, access a new terminal. In GNOME, click Applications | Accessories | Terminal. (In KDE, click Main Menu | System | Terminal.)

3. Log into the remote computer using the Secure Shell. To log in as root, use the following command. Enter the root password on the remote computer when prompted. If you're asked if you want to set up a encryption key, type **yes**. This should log you into the remote computer.

   ```
   # ssh -X root@cosmicc
   root@cosmicc's password:
   ```

4. Now you can start the GUI applications of your choice. Start with some easy X clients, such as **xterm**, **xclock**, and **xeyes**. Where do you see these clients displayed? If you have the GUI open on the remote computer, you can walk over there and check the other computer for yourself. Close whatever X clients you open.

5. You should be able to run most of the Red Hat GUI utilities from the remote computer. Try some with commands such as **system-config-network**, **system-config-samba**, and **system-config-securitylevel**. You can now edit the configuration on the remote computer. Remember to close the GUI utilities that you open.

6. If you run any remote GUI configuration utilities, check the results in the appropriate configuration file.

Troubleshooting

The X Window System is very robust and stable, but occasionally problems can arise. You can try several things when you troubleshoot X Window problems:

- Session managers create log files in your home directory such as ~/.xsession-errors. Check these log files as well as /var/log/messages and /var/log/Xorg.0.log for error messages from your X server.

- Check the **DISPLAY** environment variable to make sure it is set correctly. If you are running X clients locally, they still use this variable. You can set it with one of the following commands:

```
export DISPLAY=localhost:0.0
```

or

```
export DISPLAY=:0.0
```

- Check for underlying system problems or network problems that could be causing problems with the X Window System.

- Even if your X server is not responding or you can't read the display, don't forget that you can switch to a text console to gain access to the system.

- If you are troubleshooting X server problems on a remote system, try starting an X client from your workstation using the remote X server's display. Note that you will need to have logged into the remote system with the **ssh -X** *username@remotesys* command.

Desktops and Window Managers

Part of the Linux GUI is a special type of X client known as a *window manager*. Earlier in this chapter in Exercise 14-1, you started the X.org server with the **X** command (which is linked to /usr/bin/Xorg). It turned your display into a blank electronic canvas. This is the default desktop display for the X.org server, which is an uninteresting textured gray background. The default mouse pointer for the X Window display is a graphic representation of an X.

Once the X.org server starts and this canvas is on your screen, the X server is ready to start serving X clients.

Still, you don't have any of the useful features that you've come to expect in a GUI, such as borders, title bars, menu bars, and minimize/maximize buttons. For this purpose, you need a window manager. A window manager is a special type of X client that can run only with an X server. The window manager controls how other X clients appear on your display. This includes everything from placing title bars and drawing borders around the window for each X client application you start, to determining the size of your desktop. In a nutshell, the window manager controls the look and feel of your GUI.

As is usually the case with all things Linux, you have multiple ways to do the same thing. RHEL can be installed with several different window managers and desktops. The GNOME and KDE desktops include their own window managers. Your choice of window manager and desktop will drive the look, feel, and functionality of the Linux X Window System.

The GNOME and KDE Desktops

Two powerful virtual desktop environments that come with RHEL are the GNOME Desktop Environment and KDE Desktop Environment. The GNOME desktop, shown in Figure 14-11, is the default desktop for RHEL that you first see after installing the X Window System. The KDE desktop, shown in Figure 14-12, is the main alternate desktop system. KDE is the default for several other Linux distributions.

FIGURE 14-11

The GNOME
desktop

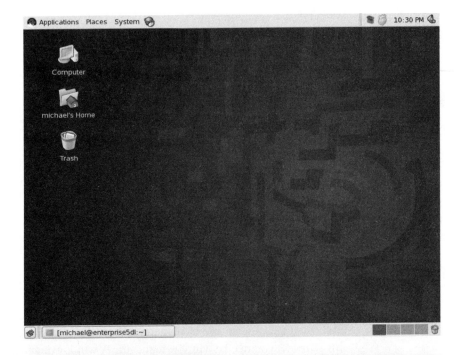

FIGURE 14-12

The KDE desktop

GNOME Features

The GNOME desktop includes support for the GTK+ (GIMP) toolkit, which allows GNOME software components written in any language and running on different systems to work together. In addition, GNOME includes support from a number of other projects, including GConf, ORBIT, and more.

Using GNOME

Many of the features of the GNOME interface will be familiar to you from other desktop environments. On the left side of the screen are icons representing files and applications that you can be open by double-clicking them with the mouse. The GNOME Desktop Environment also provides several virtual desktops. Next to the application buttons on the right side of the panel is a pager you can use to move from one area of the desktop to another.

One of the key features of GNOME are the *panels*, which you can see at the top and bottom of the screen in Figure 14-11. These panels are the control centers for most of your activities while you use GNOME. The button at the far left of the top panel with the imprint of a red hat is the Applications button. Click this button, and you will see a list of menus and submenus that start applications. The button associated with the System menu launches a similar submenu; The System | Administration submenu opens a number of interesting administrative applications.

GNOME includes a number of applications, including graphics tools and an office suite, GNOME Office. As the default Red Hat desktop is GNOME, the remainder of this book will be based on this desktop environment. Nevertheless, the Red Hat exam requirements do not specify a preferred desktop; you should have no problems using KDE or the command line console to do everything that is required for the exam. You may be asked to configure either desktop on the Red Hat exams.

If you configure the default GNOME desktop for your users, you may want to configure GNOME in a special way. Normally, GNOME opens with a number of icons and possibly default applications such as nautilus. You can add more default applications such as a new terminal window or applets such as the **xminicom** modem manager with the Sessions tool, which you can access via the System | Preferences | More Preferences | Sessions command.

KDE Features

The KDE desktop is built on the Qt C++ cross-platform GUI toolkit. This is another versatile way to create GUI applications for Linux.

Many of the features of KDE should also be familiar to you from other desktop environments. In fact, you can configure KDE to a look and feel that is quite similar to Windows 9x/2000/XP/Vista. As shown in Figure 14-12, it includes a Main Menu button, represented by the Red Hat in the lower-left corner of the desktop. Like GNOME, it can include pagers and buttons representing the open programs on the desktop. However, the default version of the KDE desktop is pretty empty, which does not illustrate the capabilities of KDE, and I'm guessing displeases most KDE loyalists.

Default Desktop

Once you've configured the X Window, it's easy to start a Linux GUI. If it isn't already configured to start automatically, run the **startx** command. This command, in the /usr/bin directory, calls configuration files from your home directory. If these files don't exist, they are taken from the default directory for GUI configuration, /etc/X11.

To manage the default desktop, use the **switchdesk** command. It's also known as the Desktop Switching Tool; as they're not installed by default, you may need to first install at least the switchdesk RPM—and if you want to use the GUI version, the switchdesk-gui RPM packages. For example, the following commands set the default desktop to KDE and GNOME, respectively:

```
# switchdesk KDE
# switchdesk GNOME
```

The **switchdesk** program creates two hidden files in your home directory, ~/.Xclients and ~/.Xclients-default, that are used to start your alternate desktop. You don't need to use **switchdesk**; once you have an ~/.Xclients-default file, you can edit it directly. It is a simple file with one key line:

```
WM="startkde"
```

If your default desktop is GNOME, this file has a different line:

```
WM="gnome-session"
```

Alternatively, you can use **switchdesk** to set up twm, known as Tom's Window Manager. The version of twm in RHEL includes a textured blue screen similar to the undefined gray screen that you saw earlier with the **X** command. The ~/.Xclients-default file would include the following line:

```
WM="twm"
```

If you have other desktops or window managers installed, you can use those instead. When run from the command line, the **switchdesk** command can also let you set FVWM, Enlightenment, or WindowMaker as the default window manager. You'll see the new default the next time you run the **startx** command from a console command line interface.

EXERCISE 14-5

Exploring Desktops

In this exercise, use the **switchdesk** command to explore the various desktops available in RHEL.

1. The easiest way to make this work is if you've disabled any automatic login through the GUI. To do so, open a terminal window and run the **init 3** command.

2. Now enter the GUI with the **startx** command.

3. Open a terminal window in a GUI and choose GNOME System | Preferences | More Preferences (or KDE Main Menu | Settings) | Desktop Switching Tool. You can also open it from a GUI command line with the **switchdesk** command.

4. Your current desktop (probably GNOME) is selected. Try one of the other desktops (such as KDE).

5. Log out of your current session with the GNOME System (or KDE Main Menu) | Log Out command.

6. Log back in again. This time you should see the other desktop environment.

7. Repeat step 3.

8. In the Desktop Switching Tool, try switching to twm.

9. Log out of KDE, and run the **startx** command again. You should see that twm is a much more basic window manager. You'll need to log out again for your changes to take effect.

10. To exit from twm, left-click the desktop. In the pop-up menu that appears, click Exit.

11. Run **switchdesk** from the command line. Select your favorite desktop. For example, if you want to make GNOME your default desktop again, run the **switchdesk gnome** command.

CERTIFICATION SUMMARY

The X Window System provides a state-of-the-art graphical user interface and offers features not found in other GUI environments. Although the X Window System can be complicated, you should be able to configure it during the RHEL installation process. Alternatively, the Red Hat Display Settings tool simplifies the setup or reconfiguration process.

One of the key parts of the X Window System is the X Font Server. If it isn't running, or the /tmp or /home directory partitions are full, you can't run the Linux GUI.

The X Window System works as client and server. X clients and X servers can be located on different computers on a network. With an appropriate firewall configuration, you can take advantage of it with the Secure Shell.

The look and feel of the X Window interface is determined by your choice of desktop. RHEL comes with several desktop environments, including GNOME, KDE, and twm; the default is GNOME.

You can customize the GUI start process in a number of ways. You can configure a default login manager. With an appropriate .xinitrc file, you can set up X clients to start when you run the **startx** command. Plus, you can configure a default desktop with the **switchdesk** command, which defined it in the local .Xclients-default file. Alternatively, you can run the Sessions utility to configure X clients in the GNOME desktop.

TWO-MINUTE DRILL

Here are some of the key points from the certification objectives in Chapter 14.

X with Clients and Servers

❑ The X server software manages the graphics display on the local computer, which includes your monitor/graphics adapter, keyboard, and mouse.

❑ You can configure the X server during the installation process. You can also configure or modify the configuration using the Red Hat Display Settings tool.

❑ The X server configuration is stored in the /etc/X11/xorg.conf file.

The X.org Server Configuration

❑ There are a variety of X.org server configuration files in the /etc/X11 directory.

❑ You can start X servers in multiple consoles.

❑ You can configure the X Window to boot directly into a GUI login manager, or start it from a text console.

❑ When you start the X Window, you can customize the process.

Tools for X.org Configuration

❑ The main X.org Server Configuration utility is the Red Hat Display Settings tool, which you can start in either the GUI or a text console with the **system-config-display** command.

❑ Other X.org command line tools are available, such as **Xorg -configure** and **Xorg -probeonly**.

Running Remote X Applications

❑ By default, X clients sends display output to the local computer.

❑ You can log into the remote client using the Secure Shell; if you log in with the **-X** or **-Y** switch, you can send remote X clients back to your local system.

Desktops and Window Managers

❑ The X Window System gives you a blank electronic canvas. The look and feel of a GUI is provided by the window manager and desktop.

❑ The two main desktop environments are GNOME and KDE.

❑ You can use **switchdesk** from a terminal window or the command line interface console to select your default desktop.

SELF TEST

The following questions will help you measure your understanding of the material presented in this chapter. As no multiple choice questions appear on the Red Hat exams, no multiple choice questions appear in this book. These questions exclusively test your understanding of the chapter. It is okay if you have another way of performing a task. Getting results, not memorizing trivia, is what counts on the Red Hat exams. There may be more than one answer to many of these questions.

X with Clients and Servers

1. If you're running a GUI tool from a remote system, where is the X client?

   _____

2. What is the main X configuration file? In what directory?

   _____

3. What command starts a GUI with a blank screen?

   _____

The X.org Server Configuration

4. What directive in xorg.conf is associated with keyboards and mice?

   _____

5. What command is a text script that starts the GUI from a command line console?

   _____

6. What configuration file in /etc/X11 can you use to specify a default GUI login manager?

   _____

Tools for X.org Configuration

7. What command tests the X.org start sequence, without actually starting the X Window?

   _____

8. If you've logged into the command line console in runlevel 3, what command allows you to start the graphical X configuration tool?

   _____

9. If you've logged into the command line console in runlevel 3 and can't start the graphical X configuration tool, what command creates a local xorg.conf file?

   _____

Running Remote X Applications

10. You've configured the Secure Shell on both systems. If you're logging into the cosmicc.example .net system as user michael, what command would you use to gain access to X applications on the remote system?

_____

Desktops and Window Managers

11. What command switches the default desktop environment to KDE?

_____

12. In the future, you want to boot Linux directly into the GUI. How would you make this happen in /etc/inittab?

_____

LAB QUESTIONS

Lab 1

You want to upgrade the video card in your Linux system. Your old video card is slow and doesn't have enough display memory to provide you with the resolution and color depth you require. You have obtained a new ATI 32MB Radeon card (I'm using this product for example purposes only). What steps might you follow to replace your old card with your new card?

Lab 2

You want to see what happens when there are problems starting the Linux GUI. With RHEL 5, the X.org server is configured by default. The configuration of the X server is stored in the /etc/X11/xorg .conf configuration file. Before Linux starts the X server, it reads this file. To do this lab, you'll want to back up your current /etc/X11/xorg.conf file, delete a line in the file, and then reboot your computer into runlevel 5. You can restore it after the lab is complete.

Lab 3

For this lab, you'll need two Linux computers connected over a network and a shared NFS directory from the local computer. You can use the same directory that you may have used in Chapter 2 to share the RHEL installation files. Start a Secure Shell connection between the two computers. Start the GUI on the local computer, and use the Secure Shell to log in remotely to the other computer.

Once you log in, run the Red Hat root password program from the remote computer. Make changes to the password. When you log out and try to log back into the remote computer, you should be able to confirm that the root password on the remote computer has changed.

Lab 4

In this lab, you'll set up a GUI workstation. It'll start with the **kdm** login manager and automatically start GNOME, open the Firefox Web browser, and start a gnome-terminal session when you boot this Linux computer.

SELF TEST ANSWERS

X with Clients and Servers

1. If you're running a GUI tool from a remote system, the X client comes from the remote system. The X server is local and manages the hardware.

2. The main X.org configuration file is xorg.conf, in the /etc/X11 directory.

3. The main command that starts the GUI with a blank screen is **X**; as it's linked to the **Xorg** command, you can use it as well. Yes, with appropriate changes to configuration files, you can start the GUI in a blank screen with other commands, most easily in twm.

The X.org Server Configuration

4. The directive in xorg.conf associated with keyboards and mice is **InputDevice**.

5. The text script command that starts the GUI from a command line console is **startx**. You can edit it directly in the /usr/bin/ directory.

6. The configuration file in the /etc/X11 directory that you can use to specify a default GUI login manager is prefdm; the key directive in this file is **preferred**.

Tools for X.org Configuration

7. The command that tests the X.org start sequence, without actually starting the X Window, is **Xorg -probeonly**. (As you can confirm in the Xorg man page, only one dash is required for **Xorg** command switches.)

8. If you've logged into the command line console in runlevel 3, the command that allows you to start the graphical X configuration tool is **system-config-display**.

9. If you've logged into the command line console in runlevel 3 and can't start the graphical X configuration tool, you can create a local xorg.conf file with the **Xorg -configure** command.

Running Remote X Applications

10. You've configured the Secure Shell on both systems. To log into the cosmicc.example .net system as user michael, with access to GUI applications, run either the **ssh -X michael@cosmicc.example.net** or **ssh -Y michael@cosmicc.example.net** command.

Desktops and Window Managers

11. The command that sets the default desktop to KDE is **switchdesk kde**.

12. In the future, to boot Linux directly into the GUI, make sure /etc/inittab includes the following directive, which boots Linux into runlevel 5:

```
id:5:initdefault
```

LAB ANSWERS

Lab 1

1. Before you stop Linux on your computer, you should configure it so it no longer attempts to start the X server when Linux boots. This is controlled by the **initdefault** line in the /etc/inittab file. Edit this file and change the second field from **5** (Multi-User With X Support) to **3** (Multi-User With No X Support). You could use vi, joe, emacs, or any other suitable text editor to do this job.

2. Perform an orderly shutdown on your system at a safe time. Use the **shutdown -h now** command.

3. Now that the system is off, replace your video card.

4. Start your computer and boot into RHEL. During the boot process, the Red Hat **hal** hardware detection system or the **kudzu** command automatically probes for new hardware. If this probe finds your new video card, you can configure it when prompted.

5. If the automated **hal** or **kudzu** tools fail to find your new hardware, you should use the root account to run the Red Hat Display Settings tool.

6. The Red Hat Display Settings tool should correctly identify your new hardware. You should select the correct amount of display memory (32MB) and the graphics resolutions and color depths you desire. Otherwise, you can configure it manually using the available settings.

7. Test the result. Run the **startx** or **init 5** command to start the Linux GUI.

Lab 2

1. Back up /etc/X11/xorg.conf to a safe location such as your home directory.

2. As the root user, delete any active line in the /etc/X11/xorg.conf file.

3. Open /etc/inittab in your favorite text editor. Look at the line with **initdefault**. Change the number right before this variable from a **3** to a **5** if required.

4. When you reboot your computer, observe what happens when Linux tries to find the default login display manager. Review the Xorg.0.log file.

5. Restore your original settings.

If you are interested in more experiments, try deleting other lines in xorg.conf. Alternatively, try changing ownership of the .Xauthority file for a specific user to root. Log in as that user, run startx, and observe what happens.

Lab 3

For this lab, you'll need two Linux computers connected over a network and a shared NFS directory from the local computer. You can use the same directory that you may have used in Chapter 2 to share the RHEL installation files. You'll start a Secure Shell connection between the two computers. You'll start the GUI on the local computer, and use the Secure Shell to log in remotely to the other computer, with the **-X** or **-Y** switch. You can then see what happens when you start X clients from the remote computer.

Once you do, run the Red Hat GUI firewall program from the remote computer. Make changes to the firewall, and see what happens. Finally,

1. On the local computer, start the GUI. If you're currently at the text interface, you can do so with the **startx** command.

2. Open a command line interface. Assuming you're using the default GNOME desktop, right-click the desktop and click New Terminal from the pop-up menu.

3. In the new terminal, confirm any currently exported directories with the **showmount -e** command. Based on /etc/exports, select a directory that is set as writable. Use the techniques described in Chapter 10 if required to make it so. You'll be connecting back to one of these directories from your remote computer.

4. Authorize access from the remote computer. Open the Security Level Configuration tool and allow access through SSH.

5. Connect to the remote computer using the Secure Shell. Assuming the remote computer is named desktop2, run the following command:

   ```
   # ssh -X root@desktop2
   ```

   (If you have a problem making the connection, you may need to go to the remote computer and activate the Secure Shell service with the **service sshd start** command. You can also substitute the IP address for the computer name.)

6. Enter the root password on the remote computer when prompted.

7. Now try running the **system-config-rootpassword** command. If successful, you'll be changing the root password on the remote computer. (If this command is not available, you'll have to install the RPM package of the same name.)

8. Log out of the remote computer. Log back in using the **ssh** command from step 5. Did the root password change?

9. Restore the original root password on the remote computer.

   Think about this a bit. Do you really want to allow root logins through the SSH service? Using what you learned from Chapter 13, change the /etc/ssh/sshd_config file to disable root logins. If in doubt on how to do this, review the associated man page and the **PermitRootLogin** directive.

Lab 4

1. Since you're setting up this workstation for a user, you'll want it to start automatically in the GUI. To do so, open the /etc/inittab file in a text editor, and make sure the **initdefault** variable is set to runlevel 5 as follows:

```
id:5:initdefault
```

2. Make sure you don't have other settings defined in the local home directory, in the ~/.xinitrc file.

3. As you want to start with the kdm login manager, you'll want to set it as the preferred login manager in the /etc/X11/prefdm file. You can do it by setting the **preferred** variable as shown:

```
preferred=kdm
```

4. Make sure that GNOME is the default desktop. If you see an .Xclients-default file, it should contain the following line:

```
WM="gnome-session"
```

5. If you don't see this line, or the file does not exist, you can set it up and make GNOME the default desktop with the following command (you may need to install the **switchdesk** RPM):

```
# switchdesk gnome
```

6. Now reboot your computer. From the command line, you can run the **reboot** command. Alternatively, if you're already in GNOME, click System | Log Out and select the Reboot option.

7. If you've taken the steps described, you should now see the xdm login manager. Log in through that interface.

8. Now in GNOME, click System | Preferences | More Preferences | Sessions. This opens the Sessions utility.

9. Click the Startup Programs tab. Click Add. This opens the Add A New Session window.

10. Enter the **gnome-terminal** command and click OK.

11. Repeat step 9.

12. Enter the **firefox** command in Add A New Session window and click OK.

13. Click Close in the Session window.

14. Log out of GNOME, and log back in.

15. You should now see the GNOME desktop with the **gnome-terminal** command line interface and the Firefox Web browser.

15

Securing Services

CERTIFICATION OBJECTIVES

15.01   Using tcp_wrappers to Secure Services

15.02   Firewalls and Packet Filtering Using netfilter

15.03   Network Address Translation

15.04   Security Enhanced Linux

✓   Two-Minute Drill

Q&A   Self Test

As a Red Hat Enterprise Linux systems manager, you probably wear several hats, one of which is that of security manager. This is especially true if you work for a small company. Even if you work for a large organization with a dedicated network or systems security staff, most of the administrators are probably responsible for other operating systems. You're probably responsible for security policies on your Linux systems.

You may spend very little time thinking about Linux security, or it may turn out to be a full-time job. The level of security you choose to configure depends on many factors, including the purpose of the system and the overall security policies of your company or organization, as well as the size and number of computers in the company.

For example, a Red Hat Enterprise Linux workstation at home does not require as much security as a secure Red Hat Enterprise Linux server that is being used to process credit card orders for a Web site.

Red Hat Enterprise Linux comes with a large and varied assortment of tools for handling security. This includes tools for managing the security on individual Linux computers and tools for managing security for an entire network of systems, both Linux and otherwise. In this chapter, you'll examine some of the tools provided by RHEL for managing security. You'll start out by looking at tools for controlling access to individual Linux host systems, then you'll explore tools for securing networks, and finally, you'll examine the basics of Security Enhanced Linux (SELinux).

INSIDE THE EXAM

This chapter is focused on RHCE requirements. As described in the Red Hat Exam Prep guide, RHCEs must be able to

- Configure host-based and user-based security for the service
- Configure SELinux to support the service

for the network services described in the Installation and Configuration portion of the RHCE exam.

These services include HTTP/HTTPS, Samba, NFS, FTP, Web proxy, SMTP, IMAP, IMAPS, POP3, SSH, DNS, and NTP. We've described some security settings in earlier chapters. This chapter looks at several generic security tools that you can use for these services. (For a discussion of Pluggable Authentication Modules, see Chapter 6.)

You'll need to know how to protect your computer and network. Sometimes this means you'll turn off, deactivate, or even uninstall a service. Other times, you'll set specific levels of security for different users. You can even regulate the type of traffic coming in, going out, and being transferred through your computer.

CERTIFICATION OBJECTIVE 15.01

Using tcp_wrappers to Secure Services

A network is only as secure as the most open system in that network. Although no system can be 100-percent secure, there are certain basic host measures to enhance the security on any given system and, consequently, your network. When devising security measures, you should plan for two types of security violations: user accidents and break-ins.

Accidents happen because users lack adequate training or are unwilling to follow procedures. If security is too burdensome, productivity may suffer, and your users will try to get around your rules. Password rules are sometimes so rigorous, users end up writing their passwords on their desks.

When a cracker breaks in to your system, he or she may be looking for secrets such as credit card information. Others may just want to bring down your system. You can do several things to keep your network secure. Monitor Red Hat errata for the latest issues. Using **yum**, you can keep your Red Hat system updated with the latest packages.

Red Hat is moving away from up2date to yum. RHEL 5 still includes the Red Hat Network registration and management tools such as rhn_register and rhn_check. If you use Fedora Core 6 or a rebuild such as CentOS to prepare for the RHCE exam, the Red Hat Network is not available to you. Fortunately, knowledge of the Red Hat Network is not part of the publicly listed Red Hat exam requirements.

As you'll see later in this chapter, you can manage your computer's response to certain requests through the /etc/hosts.allow and /etc/hosts.deny files. You can set up protection within the kernel through firewalls based on **iptables** or **ipchains**. One simple way to promote security is to uninstall as many network access programs as possible.

Security by User or Host

The best way to prevent a cracker from using a service is to remove it completely from your Linux system. However, you may want to keep a service loaded because you're planning to use it in the near future.

You can achieve some measure of security by disabling or removing unused services in the /etc/xinetd.d and /etc/init.d directories. With the services you need, you can block access to specific users, computers, or even networks through the hosts.allow or hosts.deny files in the /etc directory. This system is known as tcp_wrappers, which is enabled by default, and is focused on protecting xinetd services described in Chapter 13.

When a system receives a network request for a service, it passes the request on to tcp_wrappers. This system logs the request and then checks its access rules. If there are no limits on the particular host or IP address, tcp_wrappers passes control back to the service.

The key files are hosts.allow and hosts.deny. The philosophy is fairly straightforward: users and clients listed in hosts.allow are allowed access; users and clients listed in hosts.deny are denied access. As users and/or clients may be listed in both files, the tcp_wrappers system takes the following steps:

1. It searches /etc/hosts.allow. If tcp_wrappers finds a match, it grants access. No additional searches are required.

2. It searches /etc/hosts.deny. If tcp_wrappers finds a match, it denies access.

3. If the host isn't found in either file, access is automatically granted to the client.

You use the same access control language in both /etc/hosts.allow and /etc/hosts .deny to tell tcp_wrappers which clients to allow or deny. The basic format for commands in each file is as follows:

```
daemon_list : client_list
```

The simplest version of this format is

```
ALL : ALL
```

This specifies all services and makes the rule applicable to all hosts on all IP addresses. If you set this line in /etc/hosts.deny, access is prohibited to all services. However, you can create finer filters. For example, the following line in /etc/hosts .allow allows the client with an IP address of 192.168.1.5 to connect to your system through Telnet:

```
telnetd : 192.168.1.5
```

The same line in /etc/hosts.deny would prevent the computer with that IP address from using Telnet to connect to your system. You can specify clients a number of different ways, as shown in Table 15-1.

As you can see in Table 15-1, there are two different types of wildcards. **ALL** can be used to represent any client or service, and the dot (**.**) specifies all hosts with the specified domain name or IP network address.

You can set up multiple services and addresses with commas. Exceptions are easy to make with the **EXCEPT** operator. Review the following example excerpt from a /etc/hosts.allow file:

```
#hosts.allow
ALL : .example.com
telnetd : 192.168.25.0/255.255.255.0 EXCEPT 192.168.25.73
sshd, in.tftpd : 192.168.1.10
```

The first line in this file is simply a comment. The next line opens **ALL** services to all computers in the example.com domain. The following line opens the Telnet service to any computer on the 192.168.25.0 network, except the one with an IP address of 192.168.25.73. Then the SSH and TFTP services are opened to the computer with an IP address of 192.168.1.10.

The code that follows contains a hosts.deny file to see how lists can be built to control access:

```
#hosts.deny
ALL EXCEPT in.tftpd : .example.org

telnetd : ALL EXCEPT 192.168.1.10
ALL:ALL
```

TABLE 15-1   Sample Commands in /etc/hosts.allow and /etc/hosts.deny

Client	Description
.example.com	Domain name. Since this domain name begins with a dot, it specifies all clients on the example.com domain.
172.16.	IP address. Since this address ends with a dot, it specifies all clients with an IP address of 172.16.x.y.
172.16.72.0/255.255.254.0	IP network address with subnet mask. CIDR notation not recognized.
ALL	Any client, any daemon.
user@linux1.example.com	Applies to the specific user on the given computer.

TABLE 15-2   tcp_wrappers Operators

Field	Description	Field	Description
%a	Client address	%h	Client host name
%A	Host address	%H	Server host name
%c	Client information	%p	Process ID
%d	Process name	%s	Server information

The first line in the hosts.deny file is a comment. The second line denies all services except TFTP to computers in the example.org domain. The third line states that the only computer allowed to access our Telnet server has an IP address of 192.168.1.10. Finally, the last line is a blanket denial; all other computers are denied access to all services controlled by tcp_wrappers.

You can also use the **twist** or **spawn** command in /etc/hosts.allow or /etc/hosts.deny to access shell commands; they're primarily intended to send messages, track access, and log problems. For example, take the following line in a /etc/hosts.deny file:

```
telnetd : .crack.org : twist /bin/echo Sorry %c, access denied
```

This sends a customized error message for Telnet users on the crack.org domain. Different operators such as **%c** are described in Table 15-2. Some of these operators may be able to help you track the intruder.

EXERCISE 15-1

Configuring tcp_wrappers

In this exercise, you will use tcp_wrappers to control access to network resources. Since tcp_wrappers is enabled by default, you shouldn't have to make any modifications to installed services.

1. Verify that you can telnet to the system using the address localhost. You may need to do several things first:

   A. Install the Kerberos Telnet service, from the krb5-workstation RPM.

   B. Activate the service with the **chkconfig krb5-telnet on** command.

   C. Allow telnet through any active firewall and SELinux service.

D. Add the following line to /etc/hosts (substitute your computer's host name for rhel511).

```
127.0.0.1   rhel511   localhost.localdomain   localhost
```

E. Recognize that the Telnet service included with RHEL 5 does not allow root logins by default.

2. Edit /etc/hosts.deny and add the following line (don't forget to write the file):

```
ALL : ALL
```

3. What happens when you try to telnet to the address localhost?
4. Edit /etc/hosts.allow and add the following line:

```
telnetd : 127.0.0.1
```

5. Now what happens when you try to telnet to the address localhost?
6. If you have other systems available to you, try restricting access to the Telnet service using some of the other tcp_wrappers rules.
7. Undo your changes when finished.

Firewalls and Packet Filtering Using netfilter

A firewall sits between your company's internal LAN and an outside network. A firewall can be configured to examine every network packet that passes into or out of your LAN. When configured with appropriate rules, it can filter out those packets that may pose a security risk to your system.

To understand how *packet filtering* works, you have to understand a little bit about how information is sent across networks.

Before you send a message over a network, the message is broken down into smaller units called *packets*. Administrative information, including the type of data, the source address, and destination address, is added to each packet. The packets are reassembled when they reach the destination computer. A firewall examines these administrative fields in each packet to determine whether to allow the packet to pass.

Red Hat Enterprise Linux comes with everything you need to configure a system to be a firewall, including the **iptables** command.

on the
job

RHEL 5 also includes a firewall command for IPv6 networks, ip6tables.

Configuring iptables

The philosophy behind **iptables** is based on "chains." These are sets of rules applied to each network packet. Each rule does two things: it specifies the conditions a packet must meet to match the rule, and it specifies the action if the packet matches.

The **iptables** command uses the following basic format:

```
iptables -t tabletype <action direction> <packet pattern> -j <what to do>
```

Now analyze this command, step by step. First is the **-t** *tabletype* switch. There are two basic *tabletype* options for **iptables**:

■ **filter**   Sets a rule for filtering packets.

■ **nat**   Configures Network Address Translation, also known as masquerading, discussed later in this chapter.

The default is **filter**; if you don't specify a **-t** *tabletype*, the **iptables** command assumes that you're trying to affect a filtering rule.

Next is the **<*action direction*>**. There are four basic actions associated with **iptables** rules:

■ **-A (--append)**   Appends a rule to the end of a chain.

■ **-D (--delete)**   Deletes a rule from a chain. Specify the rule by the number or the packet pattern.

■ **-L (--list)**   Lists the currently configured rules in the chain.

■ **-F (--flush)**   Flushes all of the rules in the current **iptables** chain.

If you're appending to (**-A**) or deleting from (**-D**) a chain, you'll want to apply it to network data traveling in one of three directions:

■ **INPUT**   All incoming packets are checked against the rules in this chain.

■ **OUTPUT**   All outgoing packets are checked against the rules in this chain.

■ **FORWARD**   All packets being sent to another computer are checked against the rules in this chain.

Next, you need to configure a <*packet pattern*>. All iptables firewalls check every packet against this pattern. The simplest pattern is by IP address:

- **-s ip_address**   All packets are checked for a specific source IP address.
- **-d ip_address**   All packets are checked for a specific destination IP address.

Packet patterns can be more complex. In TCP/IP, packets are transported using the TCP, UDP, or ICMP protocol. You can specify the protocol with the **-p** switch, followed by the destination port (**--dport**). For example, the **-p tcp --dport 80** extension affects users outside your network who are trying to use an HTTP connection.

Once the **iptables** command finds a packet pattern match, it needs to know what to do with that packet, which leads to the last part of the command, **-j <*what to do*>**. There are three basic options:

- **DROP**   The packet is dropped. No message is sent to the requesting computer.
- **REJECT**   The packet is dropped. An error message is sent to the requesting computer.
- **ACCEPT**   The packet is allowed to proceed as specified with the **-A** action: **INPUT**, **OUTPUT**, or **FORWARD**.

Take a look at some examples of how you can use **iptables** commands to configure a firewall. The first step is always to see what is currently configured, with the following command:

```
# iptables -L
```

If **iptables** is properly configured, it should return chain rules in three different categories: **INPUT**, **FORWARD**, and **OUTPUT**.

The following command defines a rule that rejects all traffic from the 192.168.75.0 subnet, and it sends a "destination unreachable" error message back to any client that tried to connect:

```
# iptables -A INPUT -s 192.168.75.0/24 -j REJECT
```

This rule stops users from the computer with an IP address of 192.168.25.200 from "pinging" your system (remember that the **ping** command uses the ICMP protocol):

```
# iptables -A INPUT -s 192.168.25.200 -p icmp -j DROP
```

The following command guards against TCP SYN attacks from outside your network. Assume that your network IP address is 192.168.1.0. The exclamation point (!) inverts the meaning; in this case, the command applies to all IP addresses except those with a 192.168.1.0 network address (and a 255.255.255.0 subnet mask).

```
# iptables -A INPUT -s !192.168.1.0/24 -p tcp -j DROP
```

Then, if you want to delete the rule related to the **ping** command in this list, use the following command:

```
# iptables -D INPUT -s 192.168.25.200 -p icmp -j DROP
```

The default rule for **INPUT**, **OUTPUT**, and **FORWARD** is to **ACCEPT** all packets. One way to stop packet forwarding is to add the following rule:

```
# iptables -A FORWARD -j DROP
```

Maintaining Netfilter Rules

Once you've added the **iptables** commands of your choice, the following command saves your new firewall configuration to a file:

```
# service iptables save
```

This saves your chains in the /etc/sysconfig/iptables configuration file. The **iptables** service script then reads this file, if it is active for the appropriate runlevel when you start Linux. You can configure **iptables** so that it is active for all network runlevels (2, 3, 4, and 5) with the **chkconfig** command, as follows:

```
# chkconfig iptables on
# chkconfig --list iptables
iptables        0:off   1:off   2:on    3:on    4:on    5:on    6:off
```

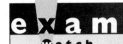

watch   *Knowing how to secure a Red Hat Enterprise Linux system against unauthorized access is critical. Be sure you*   *understand the concepts and commands discussed in this chapter.*

The Red Hat Firewall Configurator

You can automate the process of configuring a firewall. RHEL includes the Security Level Configuration tool. You can start it with the **system-config-securitylevel** command or by clicking System | Administration | Security Level. This is a straightforward tool, as shown in Figure 15-1.

If you've installed RHEL before, this menu should look familiar; the choices are identical to those shown during the standard RHEL First Boot process. There is a similar text-based version of this tool, which can be started with the **system-config-securitylevel-tui** command.

Red Hat has changed this tool for RHEL 5; as you'll see toward the end of this chapter, it can now only set SELinux to run in Enforcing, Permissive, or Disabled mode. (SELinux configuration is now the province of the SELinux Management Tool.) It also supports easy configuration of other ports; just click Add, specify the port number in the text box that appears, set the protocol to TCP or UDP, and click

FIGURE 15-1

The Security Level Configuration tool

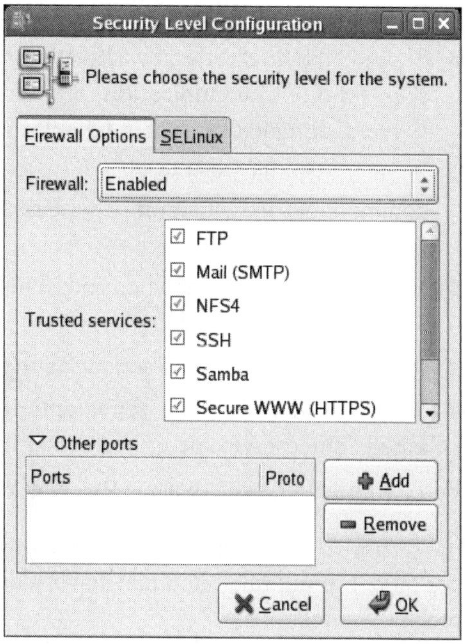

OK. The Security Level Configuration tool automatically adds the port to what's allowed through the firewall.

■ The default RHEL firewall allows external users to apply the **ping** command, access to external e-mail and DNS servers, and support of the Internet Printer Protocol (IPP). If you want to secure your firewall from these services, you'll have to modify the /etc/sysconfig/iptables file after closing the Security Level Configuration tool.

■ The default RHEL firewall blocks all inbound request traffic unless requested from within the network. For example, DNS replies are allowed.

As shown in Figure 15-1, you can allow incoming traffic to a number of services. For example, if you select WWW (HTTP), others can connect to a Web server on your computer. With the available settings, you can also allow incoming connections to:

■ An FTP server such as the vsFTP service, by activating the FTP option.

■ Mail services through the sendmail or Postfix services described in Chapter 12, by activating the Mail (SMTP) option.

■ Shared NFS directories, by activating the NFS4 option. This assumes fixed ports for NFS communication, as described in the discussion on the NFS Server Configuration tool in Chapter 10.

■ A Secure Shell (SSH) service, by activating the SSH option. This is a common method for administering remote Linux computers, as described in Chapter 13.

■ Shared directories over Microsoft Windows–based networks, using the Samba option.

■ A Secure Web server, by activating the Secure WWW (HTTPS) option.

■ Telnet, by activating the Telnet option. This also works with the Kerberos-based Telnet service described earlier in this chapter.

■ A Web server, by activating the WWW (HTTP) option.

The settings that you create are documented in /etc/sysconfig/iptables. But there may be more firewall rules. You may have added some firewall chains with an **iptables** command.

As you can see in Figure 15-2, you can use the Port(s) text box to allow data to come through using other incoming TCP/IP ports.

FIGURE 15-2

Customizing
using the Red Hat
Security Level
Configuration
tool

For example, if you wanted to allow access to a proxy server through your firewall, you could enter port 3128, using the TCP protocol, in the Add Port dialog box. As noted in /etc/services (and /etc/squid/squid.conf), this opens communication through the TCP/IP port associated with the Squid Web proxy server, and is equivalent to the following **iptables** command:

```
# iptables -A INPUT -p tcp --dport 3128 -j ACCEPT
```

CERTIFICATION OBJECTIVE 15.03

Network Address Translation

Network Address Translation (NAT) lets you hide the IP address of the computers on your network that make a connection to the Internet. NAT replaces the source address with the IP address of the firewall computer, which also serves as a gateway between your network and the Internet. The source address is cached on the gateway, so it knows which computer made the request.

When the firewall receives data such as a Web page, the process is reversed. As the packets pass through the firewall, the originating computer is identified in the cache. The header of each packet is modified accordingly before the packets are sent on their way.

This approach is useful for several reasons. Disguising your internal IP addresses makes it harder for someone to break into your network. NAT allows you to connect computers to the Internet without having to have an official IP address for each computer. This allows you to use the private IP addresses discussed in Chapter 1 on your internal LAN. In the Linux world, this process is known as *IP masquerading*.

IP Masquerading

Red Hat Enterprise Linux supports a variation of NAT called *IP masquerading*. IP masquerading allows you to provide Internet access to multiple computers with a single officially assigned IP address. IP masquerading lets you map multiple internal IP addresses to a single valid external IP address.

Connecting multiple systems to the Internet using IP masquerading is a fairly straightforward process. Your firewall computer will need one network card to connect to your LAN and a second network card for the Internet. This second network card can be a telephone modem, or it can be connected to a cable modem or DSL adapter. This configuration requires the following steps:

1. Assign your official IP address to the network card that is directly connected to the Internet.
2. Assign computers on your LAN one of the private IP addresses described in Chapter 1.
3. Reserve one private IP address for the network card on your firewall that is connected to the LAN.
4. Use **iptables** to set up IP masquerading.
5. Enable IP forwarding on the firewall computer.
6. Configure the computers on your LAN with the IP address of your firewall computer as their Internet gateway.

Take a careful look at when a message comes from a computer on a LAN, through a firewall, to the Internet. When a computer on your LAN wants a Web page on the Internet, it sends packets to the firewall. The firewall replaces the source IP address on each packet with the firewall's official IP address. It then assigns a new port number to the packet. The firewall caches the original source IP address and port number.

When a packet comes in from the Internet to the firewall, it should include a port number. If your firewall can match it with the port number assigned to a specific outgoing packet, the process is reversed. The firewall replaces the destination IP address and port number with the internal computer's private IP address and then forwards the packet back to the original client on the LAN.

The next step in the process is to use **iptables** to enable masquerading. The following command assumes that eth1 represents the network card that is directly connected to the Internet, and that your LAN has a network address of 192.168.0.0/24:

```
# iptables -t nat -A POSTROUTING -s 192.168.0.0/24 -o eth1 -j MASQUERADE
```

The following command enables FTP connection tracking through your firewall:

```
# modprobe -a ip_conntrack_ftp ip_nat_ftp
```

If you've installed the kernel source code, similar modules are available in your kernel directory, in the following subdirectory:

```
/usr/src/redhat/BUILD/kernel-2.6.18/linux-2.6.18.i386/net/ipv4/netfilter
```

But there is one more thing. IP masquerading does not work unless you've enabled IP forwarding, as described in the next section.

IP Forwarding

IP forwarding is more commonly referred to as *routing*. Routing is critical to the operation of the Internet or any IP network. Routers connect and facilitate communication between multiple networks. When you set up a computer to find a site on an outside network, you need a gateway address. This corresponds to the IP address of your router on your LAN.

A router looks at the destination IP address of each packet. If the IP address is on one of its LANs, it routes the packet directly to the proper computer. Otherwise, it sends the packet to another gateway closer to its final destination. To use a Red Hat Enterprise Linux system as a router, you must enable IP forwarding in the /etc/sysctl .conf configuration file by changing

```
net.ipv4.ip_forward = 0
```

to

```
net.ipv4.ip_forward = 1
```

These settings take effect the next time you reboot your system. Until you reboot, you can enable forwarding directly in your kernel with the following command:

```
echo 1 > /proc/sys/net/ipv4/ip_forward
```

Now that you have seen some of the security capabilities of Red Hat Enterprise Linux, refer to the following Scenario & Solution for some possible scenario questions and their answers. It does not matter what you do, as long as it solves the problem.

SCENARIO & SOLUTION

You have only one official IP address, but you need to provide Internet access to all of the systems on your LAN. Each computer on the LAN has its own private IP address.	Use **iptables** to implement IP masquerading. Make sure IP forwarding is active.
You have installed an e-mail server on your corporate network, and you want to restrict access to certain departments. Each department has its own subnet.	Use the /etc/hosts.deny file in the tcp_wrappers package to block e-mail access (**dovecot**) to the unwanted subnets.
You have a LAN of Linux and Unix computers and want to implement a single authentication database of usernames and passwords for the network.	Implement NFS file sharing on the network. Set up an NIS server. Set up the other computers on your LAN as NIS clients.
You want to modify the commands associated with halting and rebooting your computer so they're accessible only to the root user.	Set up the appropriate Pluggable Authentication Module configuration files in /etc/pam.d to use the **system-auth** module.

CERTIFICATION OBJECTIVE 15.04

Security Enhanced Linux

Security Enhanced Linux (SELinux) provides one more layer of security. Developed by the US National Security Agency, SELinux makes it more difficult for crackers to use or access any file or service if they break in. SELinux assigns different contexts to each file, known as *subjects*, *objects*, and *actions*.

To see the context of a particular file, run the **ls -Z** command. As an example, review what this command does in Figure 15-3, as it displays security contexts in my /root directory.

For this purpose, we'll examine basic configuration tools for SELinux, including the SELinux Management Tool and the Setroubleshoot Browser.

Most SELinux settings are boolean—in other words, they're activated and deactivated by setting them to 1 or 0. Naturally, the booleans are stored in the /selinux/booleans directory. One simple example is **user_ping**, which is normally set to 1, which allows users to run the **ping** command. For a fuller description, see the NSA Guide to Security Policy Configuration using SELinux at www.nsa.gov/selinux/papers/policy/node1.html.

FIGURE 15-3

ls -Z output

```
[root@Enterprise5vm ~]# \ls -Z
-rw-------  root root root:object_r:user_home_t      anaconda-ks.cfg
drwxr-xr-x  root root root:object_r:user_home_t      Desktop
-rw-r--r--  root root root:object_r:user_home_t      f1501.tif
-rw-r--r--  root root root:object_r:user_home_t      f1502.tif
-rw-r--r--  root root root:object_r:user_home_t      f1504.tif
-rw-r--r--  root root root:object_r:user_home_t      install.log
-rw-r--r--  root root root:object_r:user_home_t      install.log.syslog
drwxr-xr-x  root root root:object_r:user_home_t      test
[root@Enterprise5vm ~]# _
```

on the **Job**

If you just want to experiment with SELinux, configure it in Permissive mode. It'll log any violations without stopping anything. It's easy to set up with the Security Level Configuration tool, or you can set **SELINUX=permissive** *in /etc/sysconfig/selinux.*

SELinux Status

There are three possible statuses for SELinux: **enforcing**, **permissive**, and **disabled**. **enforcing** and **disabled** are self-explanatory. **permissive** means that any SELinux rules that are violated are logged; however, permissive SELinux doesn't stop anything.

If SELinux is active, it protects systems in two ways: in **targeted** or in **strict** mode. The default is **targeted**, and that is what I recommend that you use; it allows you to customize what it protects, and how.

As you'll see shortly, SELinux is easy to configure with the GUI SELinux Management Tool. However, the basics can be easily configured in the /etc/sysconfig/selinux configuration file. There are three directives in this file, as described in Table 15-3.

If you want to change the basic status of SELinux, change the **SELINUX** directive. The next time you reboot, the changes are applied to your system.

TABLE 15-3   Sample Commands in /etc/sysconfig/selinux

Directive	Description
SELINUX	Basic SELinux status; may be set to **enforcing**, **permissive**, or **disabled**.
SELINUXTYPE	Specifies the level of protection; set to **targeted** by default, where protection is limited to daemons. The alternative is **strict**, which is associated with full SELinux protection.
SETLOCALDEFS	Supports the configuration of local SELinux policies. Set to **0** (disabled) by default.

If you have to configure SELinux during your exam, it's no longer possible to do so during the installation process (except to specify enforcing, permissive, or disabled). If you have to configure SELinux and have to reboot, the process of applying SELinux policies can take several minutes. You won't be able to log in or do anything else during your exam. So plan ahead!

Configuring Manually

SELinux is still relatively new. If you don't understand it well, it may be more efficient to use the SELinux Management Tool to configure SELinux settings. And it's much improved from the GUI SELinux functionality that was part of the Security Level Configuration tool. You can even set SELinux contexts for individual directories from the new tool.

However, as this tool is new, many will believe it's unproven, perhaps until RHEL 6 is released. In Chapter 9, I described how you can set SELinux contexts manually for Apache virtual hosts.

To this end, there are some essential SELinux commands. If you've enabled SELinux, the **ls -Z** command displays the current contexts, as described earlier in Figure 15-3. To see the current status of SELinux, run the **getenforce** command; it returns one of three self-explanatory options: **enforcing**, **permissive**, or **disabled**.

You can change the current SELinux status with the **setenforce** command; the options are straightforward:

```
# setenforce enforcing
# setenforce permissive
```

This changes the /selinux/enforce boolean. Naturally, you can also change the boolean directly with a command such as:

```
# cat "1" > /selinux/enforce
```

If you want to change the settings of a file or directory, you can use the **chcon** command. For example, if you wanted to configure a non-standard directory for an FTP server, you'll want to make sure the context matches the default FTP directory. As you can see from the following command:

```
# ls -Z /var/ftp/
drwxr-xr-x  root     root     system_u:object_r:public_content_t pub
```

The contexts are the system user (**system_u**) and system objects (**object_r**), for type sharing with others (**public_content_t**). If you create another directory for FTP service, you'll need to assign the same security contexts to that directory. For example, if you create an /ftp directory as the root user and run the **ls -Z /** command, you'll see the contexts associated with the /ftp directory as shown:

```
drwxr-xr-x   root      root      user_u:object_r:root_t          ftp
```

To change the context, use the **chcon** command. If there are subdirectories, you'll want to make sure changes are made recursively with the **-R** switch. In this case, to change the user and type contexts to match /var/ftp, run the following command:

```
# chcon -R -u user_u -t public_content_t /ftp
```

If you want to support uploads to your FTP server, you'll have to assign a different type context, specifically **public_content_rw_t**. That corresponds to the following command:

```
# chcon -R -u user_u -t public_content_rw_t /ftp
```

Default contexts are configured in /etc/selinux/targeted/contexts/files/file_contexts. If you make a mistake and want to restore the original SELinux settings for a file, the **restorecon** command restores those settings based on the file_contexts configuration file. However, the defaults in a directory are not necessarily the same as the contexts you created. For example, the following command leads to a different set of contexts for the /ftp directory:

```
# restorecon -F /ftp
# ls -Z /
drwxr-xr-x  root      root      system_u:object_r:default_t      ftp
```

Configuring with the SELinux Management Tool

This section assumes you've enabled SELinux in **enforcing** or **permissive** mode, using one of the methods described earlier. The easiest way to change SELinux settings is with the SELinux Management Tool, which you can start with the **system-config-selinux** command. If you haven't enabled it, you won't even be able to start the tool as shown in Figure 15-4, at least until bug 232544 is addressed. Enable SELinux, at least in **permissive** mode, and reboot, before continuing with this chapter. If you have to use SELinux during the RHCE exam, you'll probably have to configure SELinux in **enforcing** mode.

The SELinux Management Tool is much more capable than the previous utility that was part of the Security Level Configuration tool. As you can see, there are options for Default and Current enforcing modes, which you can set to Enabled,

FIGURE 15-4

SELinux
Management Tool

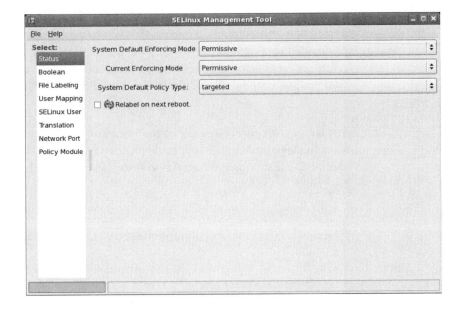

Permissive, or Disabled. As of this writing, this tool supports only a targeted system default policy type. Generally, you don't need to activate the Relabel On Next Reboot option unless you've changed the default policy type.

There are a number of categories shown in the left pane of the SELinux Management Tool window which are described in the following sections. Most of the focus here will be in the Boolean category, where most of SELinux policies are customized.

SELinux Boolean Settings

As you can see, SELinux policy can be modified in a number of different categories, some related to administrative functions, others to specific services. Some of these options are shown in Figure 15-5. Any changes you make are reflected in boolean variables in the /selinux/booleans directory. You may not see these variables in /selinux/booleans until you make those changes.

As the Security Level Configuration tool is updated regularly, the detailed information in this section of the book may not be completely up to date. You may even see more categories and options than what I describe in this section, depending on the services and packages you have installed.

I do not cover every option. Don't get lost in these options, even though Red Hat has just added SELinux as a requirement for the RHCE and RHCT exams.

FIGURE 15-5

SELinux Boolean
options

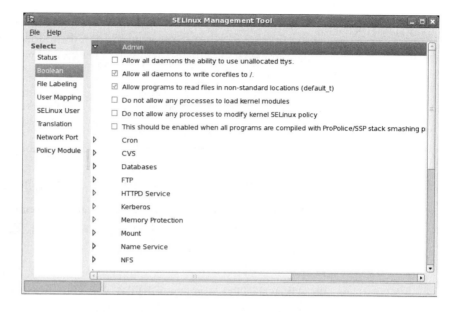

Admin   Under the Admin category, you can allow systems to use unallocated
terminals (ttys), allow writing to the top-level root (/) directory, read files from
non-standard locations, prevent any process from loading kernel modules, prevent
any modifications to SELinux policy, and enable support for the ProPolice SSP stack
smashing protector.

Cron   In this section, you can enable extra rules to support the **fcron** command
scheduler as well as disable SELinux protection for the cron daemon.

CVS   If you use the CVS revision control system, you may want to allow it to read
shadow passwords.

Databases   If you install the MySQL or PostgreSQL database systems, you can
disable SELinux protection for such.

FTP   There are six configuration options in this section. By default, RHEL 5's SELinux
configuration allows FTP services to run as individual services, separate from the xinetd
super server described in Chapter 13. One supports the running of vsftpd as a regular
service, not connected to inetd, or the Red Hat version of the service, xinetd. Others
allow uploads to directories configured with the **public_content_rw_t** directive discussed
earlier. You can also support the use of CIFS and NFS for file transfer, allow reads and
writes to user home directories, or even disable SELinux protection for FTP services.

HTTPD Service There are a number of SELinux directives available to help secure the Apache Web server, as summarized in the following bullet points. Most are straightforward and self-explanatory. In a few cases, I've added additional explanation in parentheses.

- Allow Apache to use **mod_auth_pam** (Pluggable Authentication Modules)
- Allow HTTPD cgi support (for CGI scripts)
- Allow httpd daemon to write files in directories labeled **public_content_rw_t** (similar to FTP)
- Allow HTTPD scripts and modules to connect to the network
- Allow HTTPD scripts and modules to network connect to databases
- Allow HTTPD scripts to write files in directories labeled **public_content_rw_t** (similar to FTP)
- Allow HTTPD to read home directories
- Allow HTTPD to run as an FTP server
- Allow HTTPD to run SSI executables in the same domain as system CGI scripts
- Allow HTTPD to support built-in scripting
- Disable SELinux protection for httpd daemon
- Disable SELinux protection for httpd suexec (executable files run by the HTTPD service)
- Unify HTTPD handling of all content files
- Unify HTTPD to communicate with the terminal; needed for handling certificates

Kerberos There are three options in this section. One allows other daemons to use Kerberos files (enabled by default). The other two options disable protection for the Kerberos administrative daemon (**kadmind**) and the Kerberos key control daemon (**krb5kdc**).

Memory Protection The memory protection options are not related to any services or systems cited in the current version of the Red Hat Exam Prep guide.

Mount The settings in this category relate to the automount service; you can configure it to allow the automounter to mount any directory or file, as well as disable SELinux protection for this service.

Name Service   The Name Service daemon (**named**) is the RHEL DNS service. If you maintain a zone, you'll probably want to allow the **named** daemon to overwrite master zone files. You can also disable SELinux protection for **named** as well as the name services cache daemon (**ncsd**).

NFS   Before using NFS with SELinux, you'll want to enable at least the reading of NFS file systems. If you're sharing with NFS, you'll also want to enable read/write/create on an NFS file system. If you configure home directories on a server and share them with NFS, you'll also want to support NFS home directories. There's also support for the General Security Services daemon, **gssd**.

NIS   If you want to run NIS on a SELinux system, you'll want to allow daemons to run with NIS. You can disable SELinux protection for the NIS password and NIS transfer daemons. If all else fails, you can disable SELinux protection for the associated daemon, **ypbind**.

Other   These miscellaneous options can allow full file access via FTP and unlabeled packets. They can also disable SELinux protection for PC Card readers and specialized time zone data.

Polyinstatiation   Polyinstatiation is a mouthful; it means different users may see different things when looking at the same directory, such as /tmp. You can enable this support in the SELinux tool.

pppd   The **pppd** daemon governs communication primarily over telephone modems. You can allow **pppd** to insert modules in the kernel, which supports communication, or disable SELinux protection for this daemon.

Printing   This section allows you to disable SELinux protection for the different CUPS-related daemons, including the CUPS back-end server, the **cupsd** daemon, the **cupsd-lpd** service, and the HP imaging (**hplip**) daemon. You can even enable the use of LPD instead of CUPS.

rsync   The rsync section allows you to configure writes to directories where the **public_content_rw_t** type context is assigned, as described earlier in the chapter. You can also disable SELinux protection for this daemon.

Samba   There are several ways you can modify SELinux protections for Samba. The options are straightforward:

■   Allow Samba to share nfs directories.

- Allow Samba to share users' home directories.
- Allow Samba to write files in directories labeled **public_content_rw_t**.
- Allow users to log in with CIFS home directories.
- Disable SELinux protection for **nmbd** daemon (the NetBIOS daemon).
- Disable SELinux protection for **smbd** daemon (the Samba daemon).
- Disable SELinux protection for **winbind** daemon (the WINS server daemon).

SASL Authentication Server   The simple authentication and security layer (SASL) server is another authentication method; with the Security Level Configuration tool, you can allow it access to your /etc/shadow authentication database, and disable SELinux protection for the related daemon.

on the **Job**   *As of this writing, there are categories for the "sasl authentication server" and "sasl authentications server." This is a mistake related to bug 231868 documented at https://bugzilla.redhat.com.*

SELinux Service Protection   The SELinux Service Protection category allows you to disable SELinux protection for a wide variety of daemons, from amanda to zebra. These services are not already configured in other categories.

Spam Protection   The Spam Protection category works with the SpamAssassin service. Access to home directories is required for regular users. Of course, you can also disable SELinux protection for this service.

SQUID   If you want to set up the Squid Web Proxy cache, discussed in Chapter 9, you'll want to allow it to access the network. And you can disable SELinux protection for this service.

Universal SSL Tunnel   If you configure a secure tunnel for network communication, you can configure additional protection with SELinux. You can use this tool to allow stunnel to run as a stand-alone service and disable SELinux protection.

Zebra   You can use this tool to let the Zebra routing service write to routing tables.

File Labeling

You can change the default labels associated with files, some of which are described earlier in this chapter (and in other chapters discussing SELinux contexts). Some of the options are shown in Figure 15-6.

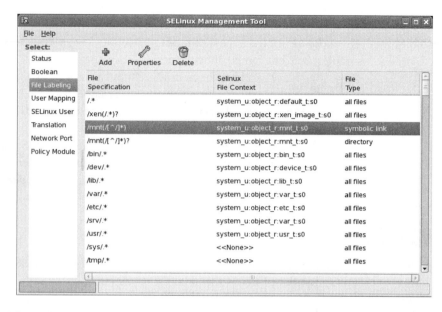

SELinux
Management File
Labeling

User Mapping

The User Mapping section allows you to go beyond the defaults for regular and administrative users.

SELinux User

The SELinux User section allows you to specify default roles for standard users, such as regular users (**user_u**), system users (**system_u**), and the administrative root user.

Translation

The Translation section allows you to customize sensitivity levels.

Network Port

The Network Port section associates standard ports to services.

Policy Module

The Policy Module section specifies the SELinux policy version number applied to each module.

The Setroubleshoot Browser

If you have problems with SELinux, it may not be obvious. For example, if you have a problem with Samba, you may not even see an error message; if you do, it may not be clear whether you've forgotten to add the right password to the Samba authentication database or if SELinux is blocking access. You could analyze the log files, but that can be difficult for those newer to SELinux.

Red Hat has added the Setroubleshoot Browser shown in Figure 15-7. It provides tips and advice on any problems that you may encounter, in a language more Linux administrators can understand, often including commands that you can run and that will address the subject problem.

To start the Setroubleshoot Browser from the GNOME desktop, click System | Administration | SELinux Troubleshooter; or run **sealert -b** from a GUI-based command line. There are other options associated with **sealert**, which you can review by running the **sealert -h** command.

| FIGURE 15-7 | SELinux Setroubleshoot Browser |

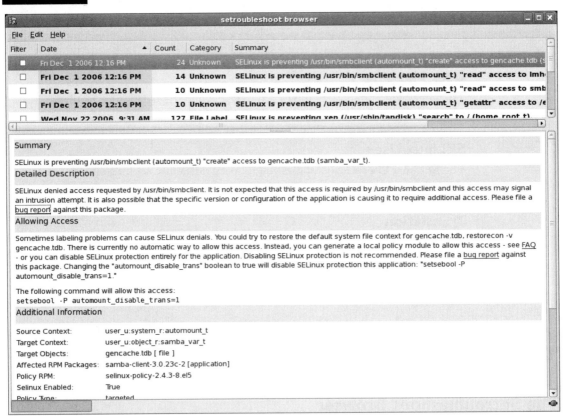

CERTIFICATION SUMMARY

One of the basic functions of a Red Hat Enterprise Linux system administrator is to protect a Linux computer and a network from inside and outside attacks. RHEL includes a variety of tools that can help you establish a secure computing environment.

RHEL includes powerful tools for securing networks from outside attacks. As these tools work in different ways, they provide layers of security. The tcp_wrappers tools use /etc/hosts.allow and /etc/hosts.deny to secure services by host and user. With **iptables** at your disposal, you can create a firewall that can further protect your RHEL system. The firewall can include IP masquerading to hide the IP addresses of the computers inside your LAN. SELinux uses Access Control Lists to secure individual services in different ways.

The Security Level Configuration tool supports fine-grained configuration of host and network security using **iptables**. The SELinux Management Tool supports fine-grained control of SELinux targeted policies. The Setroubleshoot Browser can help diagnose SELinux-related problems and even suggest solutions.

TWO-MINUTE DRILL

The following are some of the key points from the certification objectives in Chapter 15.

Using tcp_wrappers to Secure Services

❑ Red Hat Enterprise Linux comes with a package known as tcp_wrappers. This package, which is enabled by default, allows you to limit access to various services.

❑ You configure the access rules for tcp_wrappers through the /etc/hosts.allow and /etc/hosts.deny configuration files.

❑ Clients listed in /etc/hosts.allow are allowed access; clients listed in /etc/hosts.deny are denied access.

❑ Services can also be configured in /etc/hosts.allow and /etc/hosts.deny. Remember to use the actual executable name of the daemon, normally in /usr/sbin, such as **in.tftpd**.

Firewalls and Packet Filtering Using netfilter

❑ Firewalls can secure an internal network as a packet filter that controls the information that comes in, goes out, and is forwarded through the internal network.

❑ The current firewall configuration utility is **iptables**.

❑ The **iptables** directives are sets of rules, chained together, that are compared and then applied to each network packet.

❑ Each rule sets conditions required to match the rule and then specifies the action taken if the packet matches the rule.

❑ Use the **service iptables save** command to save any chains that you configure in the /etc/sysconfig/iptables configuration file.

Network Address Translation

❑ NAT modifies the header in packets coming from a LAN. It replaces the source address with the public address of the firewall computer, with a random port number.

❏ Linux supports a variation of NAT called IP masquerading.

❏ IP masquerading allows you to provide Internet access to multiple computers with a single officially assigned IP address.

❏ To enable IP forwarding immediately, type the **echo 1 > /proc/sys/net/ipv4/ip_forward** command. To enable it upon reboot, set **net.ipv4.ip_forward = 0** in /etc/sysctl.conf.

Security Enhanced Linux

❏ Security Enhanced Linux (SELinux) provides a different level of security. Basic settings are shown in the /etc/sysconfig/selinux file.

❏ If you're just experimenting with SELinux, configure it in permissive mode.

❏ SELinux is relatively easy to configure with the SELinux Management Tool.

❏ Any changes you make with the SELinux Management Tool are reflected in boolean settings in the /selinux/booleans/ directory.

❏ The Setroubleshoot Browser can help you decipher related errors.

SELF TEST

The following questions will help you measure your understanding of the material presented in this chapter. As no multiple choice questions appear on the Red Hat exams, no multiple choice questions appear in this book. These questions exclusively test your understanding of the chapter. It is okay if you have another way of performing a task. Getting results, not memorizing trivia, is what counts on the Red Hat exams. There may be more than one answer to many of these questions.

Using tcp_wrappers to Secure Services

1. What happens to a service if you allow the service in /etc/hosts.allow and prohibit it in /etc/hosts.deny?

_____

2. You are using the xinetd program to start services. How could you limit Telnet access to clients on the 192.168.170.0 network? Hint: The telnet daemon, when installed, is in /usr/kerberos/sbin/telnetd.

_____

Firewalls and Packet Filtering Using netfilter

3. You have recently connected your organization's network to the Internet, and you are a little worried because nothing other than your router is standing between your network and the Internet. You have a spare 400 MHz PC with 256MB of RAM that just happens to have two Ethernet cards. You also have a mixture of systems on your network that includes Macintosh, Windows 2000, and Linux. You also want your system to reject unwanted packets. What might you do to alleviate your concerns?

_____

_____

4. Consider the following command:

```
# iptables -A INPUT -s 192.168.77.77 -j REJECT
```

Once saved to your firewall, what effect will this have when the client with an IP of 192.168.77.77 tries to connect to your system?

_____

5. What command saves **iptables** rules?

_____

6. Where are **iptables** rules stored?

_____

Network Address Translation

7. You are setting up a small office and would like to provide Internet access to a small number of users, but you don't want to pay for a dedicated IP address for each system on the network. What can you do?

_____

_____

8. What **iptables** command switch sets up masquerading?

_____

Security Enhanced Linux

9. What directive activates Security Enhanced Linux in /etc/sysconfig/selinux?

_____

10. If you want to let SELinux allow vsFTP service for user home directories, what would you do?

_____

11. Where are standard SELinux boolean directives stored?

_____

12. If you want to disable SELinux, what would you do?

_____

_____

LAB QUESTIONS

Lab 1

You want to set up an RHEL computer as a secure Web server. To keep that system secure, you'll want to configure an appropriate firewall and disable any services that you don't need. What should you do?

Lab 2

You want to set up Telnet service on your internal LAN, accessible only to one specific IP address. You want to block access from outside the LAN. Assume that your LAN's network address is 192.168.1.0, and the IP address of the computer that should get access is 192.168.1.33. For the purpose of this lab, feel free to substitute the IP address of a second Linux computer on your network. What do you do?

Lab 3

You want to set up a secure Web server on your corporate LAN that supports inbound requests from your LAN and the Internet, but you do not want any of these requests from the Internet to get into your intranet. What can you do?

There are three scenarios in this lab. First, assume cost is no object, and there are three computers available—two for firewalls and one for the Web server. Second, assume a cost-conscious situation where you need to configure the firewalls and Web server on the same system. Third, repeat scenarios one and two, with SELinux in **enforcing** mode.

Lab 4

You want to work with SELinux, but you are unsure about how it will affect the dozen services that you run from your system. What can you do and what should you monitor to try out SELinux, without affecting any services that are currently running? How can you monitor the process? Test all configured services, and use Setroubleshoot Browser suggestions to configure your system. When you're confident that everything will work, activate SELinux in **enforcing** mode.

SELF TEST ANSWERS

Using tcp_wrappers to Secure Services

1. If you allow a service in /etc/hosts.allow and prohibit it in /etc/hosts.deny, the service is allowed.

2. You are using the xinetd program to start services. To limit Telnet access to clients on the 192.168.170.0 network, you'd allow access to the network in /etc/hosts.allow and deny it to all others in /etc/hosts.deny. As /usr/kerberos/sbin is in the root user path, you can cite **telnetd** directly and add the following directive to /etc/hosts.allow (remember, CIDR notation doesn't work in these files):

```
telnetd : 192.168.0.170/255.255.255.0
```

Then add the following to /etc/hosts.deny:

```
telnetd : ALL
```

Firewalls and Packet Filtering Using netfilter

3. It's best to create a firewall using the **iptables** command. The standard Red Hat Security Level Configuration tool creates **iptables** commands that **REJECT** unwanted packets by default. You can now even support access to the network that can communicate natively with Microsoft and modern Macintosh systems, Samba. All you need is to allow access using the tool.

4. Based on the given command, any connection attempt (including pings) from the 192.168.77.77 system is rejected.

5. The command that saves **iptables** rules is **iptables-save**.

6. Rules associated with **iptables** rules are stored in /etc/sysconfig/iptables.

Network Address Translation

7. To set up a small office while providing Internet access to a small number of users, all you need is one dedicated IP address. The other addresses can be on a private network. Masquerading makes this possible.

8. The **iptables** command switch that sets up masquerading is **-t nat**.

Security Enhanced Linux

9. The directive in /etc/sysconfig/selinux that activates Security Enhanced Linux is **SELINUX=enabled**.

10. If you want SELinux to allow reading of home directories via an FTP server, activate the Allow Ftp To Read/Write Files In The User Home Directories option. Alternatively, run the **setsebool -P ftp_home_dir 1** command. Additional configuration is required in the vsFTP configuration file, as defined in Chapter 10.

11. Standard SELinux boolean directives are stored in the /selinux/booleans directory.

12. You can disable SELinux in a number of ways. You can do so directly in /etc/sysconfig/selinux by setting **SELINUX=disabled**. You can use the Security Level Configuration tool or even the SELinux Management Tool. You can even add the **selinux=0** directive to the kernel configuration line in your GRUB bootloader. I can even visualize a situation where all these options are used, which would make it more difficult for an RHCE candidate to enable SELinux during an exam.

LAB ANSWERS

Lab 1

If you want to set up an RHEL computer as a secure Web server, it's a straightforward process. You'll want to set up a firewall to block all but the most essential ports. This should include TCP/IP ports 80 and 443, which allow outside computers to access your regular and secure Web services.

The easiest way to set this up is with the Red Hat Security Level Configuration tool, which you can start with the **system-config-securitylevel** command. Once you're in the Red Hat tool, take the following steps:

1. Enable the firewall. This configures a basic set of firewall rules that prohibits access except for requests that come from inside the firewall.

2. Scroll down the Trusted Services window. (If you're in the text-based tool, click Customize to open the Firewall Configuration – Customize window.) Activate the WWW (HTTP) option. This allows access from outside the local computer to your regular Web site. Activate the Secure WWW (HTTPS) services as well.

3. Click OK to exit from the Security Level Configuration tool.

4. Enter the following command to check your resulting firewall.

```
# iptables -L
```

5. Once you've configured a Web service as described in Chapter 9, you'll be able to access both the regular and secure Web servers from remote computers, while retaining a firewall that protects the other services on your system.

Lab 2

Several steps are required to set up any xinetd service such as Telnet. You'll need to modify the xinetd Telnet configuration file and set up filtering in one of three ways: in the /etc/xinetd.d/krb5-telnet configuration file, through tcp_wrappers, or with the appropriate firewall commands.

1. First, you want to enable Telnet. Make sure that the krb5-telnet RPM is installed.

2. Activate Telnet. Use the **chkconfig krb5-telnet on** command to revise the /etc/xinetd.d/krb5-telnet configuration script.

3. Edit the /etc/xinetd.d/krb5-telnet configuration file. Add the **only_from = 192.168.1.33** line. (If you have another computer on your network with a private IP address, substitute accordingly in all steps in this lab.)

4. Save the configuration file and reload the xinetd service script with the **service xinetd reload** command. Try accessing Telnet from the local computer. What happens?

5. Try accessing Telnet from the computer with the IP address of 192.168.1.33. What happens? Try again from a different computer on your LAN.

6. Restore the previous /etc/xinetd.d/krb5-telnet configuration file. Don't forget to reload the xinetd service script with the **service xinetd reload** command.

7. Edit /etc/hosts.deny. Add the **telnetd : ALL EXCEPT 192.168.1.33** line.

8. Try accessing Telnet from the computer with the IP address of 192.168.1.33. What happens? Try again from a different computer on your LAN.

9. Restore the previous /etc/hosts.deny file.

10. Save any existing **iptables** chains. Back up /etc/sysconfig/iptables, if that file currently exists to ~/bak.iptables.

11. Flush current firewall rules with the **iptables -F** command.

12. Block the Telnet port, 23, for all IP addresses except 192.168.1.33 with the **iptables -A INPUT -s ! 192.168.1.33 -p tcp --dport 23 -j DROP** command.

13. Try accessing the Telnet server from the computer with the IP address of 192.168.1.33. What happens? Try again from a different computer on your LAN.

14. Flush current firewall rules with the **iptables -F** command.

15. Restore any previous firewall rules with the **iptables-restore < ~/bak.iptables** command.

16. Bonus: Repeat these commands for other services and networks.

Lab 3

Scenario 1: Cost is not an object. This means you can build a DMZ using two firewalls and a separate Web server, all running Linux. You should have the Web server dedicated only to the Web. You configure two more Linux hosts, each with two network cards, and essentially isolate the intranet behind one firewall. You then put the Web server in the middle, placing the second firewall between the Web server and the Internet. You configure the firewall on the intranet with IP masquerading to ensure anonymity for all your intranet hosts.

    Scenario 2: You have one old computer available, and the Web server is a separate computer. Use your one computer as the firewall between you and the Internet and only forward HTTP packets to the Web server IP address directly; use NAT for all intranet requests going out to the Internet for HTTP and FTP. Disallow all other services.

    Scenario 3: Repeat scenarios 1 and 2; configure SELinux in **enforcing** mode and activate the appropriate booleans for the scenarios.

Lab 4

The simplest way to experiment with SELinux is to set it to permissive mode. All violations of SELinux are logged in /var/log/messages with the avc label. You can set SELinux to permissive mode with the SELinux Management Tool or by setting **SELINUX=permissive** in /etc/sysconfig/selinux. Open the Setroubleshoot Browser, and try out various services—locally and remotely. Follow any suggestions made by the browser. When you're confident that your configured network services will work with SELinux, set **SELinux=enforcing** in /etc/sysconfig/selinux, reboot, and test configured network services again.

16

Troubleshooting

CERTIFICATION OBJECTIVES

16.01   Troubleshooting Strategies

16.02   Required RHCT Troubleshooting Skills

16.03   Required RHCE Troubleshooting Skills

✓   Two-Minute Drill

Q&A   Self Test

W hile you've read about many troubleshooting scenarios throughout this book, it's the troubleshooting part of the Red Hat exams that I believe causes the most "fear and loathing" among Red Hat certification candidates.

Troubleshooting is a mindset based on experience and a systematic way of thinking. Troubleshooting strategies on the Red Hat exams are based on the simplest problems that you can check quickly, moving to more complex problems.

Red Hat has done excellent work addressing some problems that formerly led to unbootable systems. For example, flaws in the /etc/fstab file used to lead to an unbootable system. Now most users would hardly know the difference if this file is missing.

The most important troubleshooting tool is the **linux rescue** environment, which can bypass boot problems, from a missing GRUB boot loader to a missing kernel. In most cases, the first installation CD, booted into the **linux rescue** environment, can detect and mount even damaged installations of RHEL.

This chapter focuses on the Troubleshooting and System Maintenance section of the RHCT and RHCE exams, as defined in the Inside The Exam sidebar. It further focuses on troubleshooting skills, as they evoke more concern than regular system maintenance.

This chapter includes a number of exercises for which you'll need the help of a partner. When you start an exercise, let your partner have your computer and wait until your system begins to reboot. This chapter includes enough exercises to allow you and your partner to take turns working with the system.

CERTIFICATION OBJECTIVE 16.01

Troubleshooting Strategies

When you encounter problems, proceed calmly. If you've read this book thoroughly, have the requisite experience, and *do not panic*, you'll usually be able to identify the cause of a problem fairly quickly.

If you can't identify the cause right away, try the simplest solutions first. They take less time and are less likely to sabotage your system.

If you have to go into more detail, remember the seven basic steps of the scientific method (as defined in Wikipedia). They can be applied to the Troubleshooting and System Maintenance portion of your Red Hat exam. If you have experience, you may be able to jump to a solution at any of these steps.

INSIDE THE EXAM

Troubleshooting and System Maintenance

As described in the Red Hat Exam Prep guide (www.redhat.com/training/rhce/examprep .html), there are Troubleshooting and System Maintenance requirements for both the RHCT and RHCE exams. To qualify as an RHCE, you need to complete all RHCT requirements during the first hour of the exam. These requirements can fall into the following categories:

- Boot systems into different runlevels for troubleshooting and system maintenance.
- Diagnose and correct misconfigured networking.
- Diagnose and correct hostname resolution problems.
- Configure the X Window System and a desktop environment.
- Add new partitions, filesystems, and swap to existing systems.
- Use standard command line tools to analyze problems and configure system.

To qualify as an RHCE, you also need to complete enough of the RHCE requirements

for an overall score of 80%, which can fall in the following categories:

- Use the rescue environment provided by first installation CD.
- Diagnose and correct boot failures arising from boot loader, module, and filesystem errors.
- Diagnose and correct problems with network services (see Installation and Configuration below for a list of these services). (The reference is to the Installation and Configuration section of the RHCE exam.)
- Add, remove, and resize logical volumes.
- Diagnose and correct networking services problems where SELinux contexts are interfering with proper operation.

For example, if there are five RHCT problems and five RHCE problems, you'll have to answer all five RHCT problems and three RHCE problems correctly to qualify as an RHCE on this part of the exam.

The network service issues you may encounter may include one or more of the services described throughout this book, including Apache, Samba, NFS, FTP, Squid, sendmail, Postfix, Dovecot, SSH, DNS, and NTP.

1. Define the question.

   Understand what happened. Take the error messages you see. If possible, analyze log files for other messages. If you've read this book and run the labs, you may recognize the problem and cause immediately.

2. Gather information and resources.

   Analyze your system. This may require that you check the relevant configuration files to make sure that appropriate services are running and that security or other characteristics of your system are working as they should. If you have experience, you'll often recognize the problem and cause when you see something wrong in these areas.

3. Form a hypothesis.

   If you're still not sure what's wrong, make your best guess. Remember that time is severely limited during the Red Hat exams, so if you can afford it, consider skipping a problem. (To qualify for either the RHCT or RHCE, you're required to solve *all* RHCT-level Troubleshooting and System Maintenance issues.)

4. Perform experiments and collect data.

   Before performing any experiments, back up anything you might change. For example, if you think the problem is with your Samba configuration file, back up your /etc/samba/smb.conf file, in case your hypothesis makes things worse.

5. Analyze data.

   This is essentially identical to step 1. If what you do doesn't solve the problem, you'll need to analyze what went wrong, using error messages and log files as appropriate.

6. Interpret data and draw conclusions that serve as a starting point for new hypotheses.

   In many cases, you'll want to restore what you did from the backup in step 4, repeat steps 2 through 4, and try again.

7. Publish the results.

   Once you've solved the problem, you'll want to make sure the problem remains solved after rebooting your system. For example, if you've addressed a Samba problem, you'll want to "publish" by making sure the Samba daemon starts the next time your Linux system boots.

Two places where you are likely to make errors that result in an unbootable system are in the boot loader and init configuration files, /boot/grub/grub.conf and /etc/ inittab. For example, identifying the wrong partition as the root partition (/) can lead to a kernel panic. Other configuration errors in /boot/grub/grub.conf can also cause

As a Red Hat Enterprise Linux administrator, you will be expected to know how to fix improperly configured files related to the boot process. For this

reason, a substantial portion of the exam is devoted to testing your troubleshooting and analysis skills.

a kernel panic when you boot Linux. Whenever you make changes to these files, the only way to fully test them out is to reboot Linux.

The following scenarios and solutions list some possible problems and solutions that you can have during the boot process, and possible associated solutions. It is far from comprehensive. The solutions that I've listed work on my computer, as I've configured it. There may be (and often is) more than one possible cause. *These solutions may not work for you on your computer or on the Red Hat exams. To know what else to try, use your experience.*

To get the equivalent of more experience, try additional scenarios (remember: never do these things on a production computer). Once you're familiar with the **linux rescue** environment, test these scenarios. These scenarios worked as shown when I tested them on RHEL 5. However, they lead to different errors on RHEL 4 and RHEL 3.

For the first scenario shown, change the name of the grub.conf file so it can't be loaded. Reboot and see what it does on your system. Use the **linux rescue** environment to boot into RHEL and use the noted solution to fix your system.

For the second scenario shown, overwrite the MBR; on a SATA/SCSI drive, you can do so with the following command (substitute **hda** for **sda** if your system uses an IDE/PATA drive):

```
# dd if=/dev/zero of=/dev/sda bs=446 count=1
```

The third scenario is misleading; it's what happened when I overwrote my **/bin/ mount** command with **/sbin/mount.nfs** and rebooted.

The fourth scenario is what happened when I overwrote my /bin/init command.

The fifth scenario is based on a missing /etc/inittab; I suspect it's much more likely that you'll see some major error (such as a key command, commented out) in that file.

The sixth scenario results in the messages shown in Figure 16-1, which happened when I set the default runlevel to 3 and commented out the commands with the **mingetty** directives in /etc/inittab.

The seventh scenario is based on a typo in the **root** directive in /boot/grub/grub. conf, which results in the messages shown in Figure 16-2.

Sometimes, you may run into a problem with the default runlevel. But you're not stuck. There are two ways to boot into different runlevels. You can boot directly from the GRUB configuration menu, or you can boot into the **linux rescue** environment from the first RHEL installation CD.

SCENARIO & SOLUTION

When you boot, you see a **grub>** prompt.	You may have a problem that prevents the boot loader from reading the GRUB configuration file, grub.conf. The file may be missing or corrupt. For hints on creating a new grub.conf, see menu.1st in the /usr/ share/doc/grub-*versionnum* directory.
When you boot your computer, you see a message such as "Missing operating system" or "Operating System Not Found."	Your master boot record (MBR) has been erased, and you'll need to reload GRUB on the MBR using **grub-install**. (It's possible that everything has been erased, which I believe is beyond the scope of this part of the exam.)
During the boot process, you see the "Could not start the X server (graphical environment) due to some internal error" message.	You could have problems with a full or unmounted /tmp or /home directory. If these directories are not mounted, the **mount** command may be corrupt. In that case, you'll need to reload it from the mount RPM.
You see an "exec of init (/sbin/init) failed!!!" error.	Your **init** command may be corrupt. Try reloading it from the SysVinit RPM.
You see the "INIT: No inittab file found" message.	This is straightforward—there is something wrong with your /etc/inittab file. RHEL 5 prompts you to "Enter runlevel"; as of this writing, if /etc/inittab is missing, enter **s** to see a **bash** prompt.
You see a message such as what's shown in Figure 16-1.	You may not have anything starting a text or GUI console in the active runlevel; trace it starting with /etc/inittab.
You see a message such as what's shown in Figure 16-2. Take careful note of the last file cited in the message.	RHEL has encountered some problems when reading the grub.conf configuration file. Start the **linux rescue** environment and check this file as well as the referenced files in the /boot directory.

```
Starting hpssd:                                            [  OK  ]
Starting cups:                                             [  OK  ]
Starting sshd:                                             [  OK  ]
Starting xinetd:                                           [  OK  ]
Starting NFS services:                                     [  OK  ]
Starting NFS quotas:                                       [  OK  ]
Starting NFS daemon: NFSD: Using /var/lib/nfs/v4recovery as the NFSv4 state reco
very directory
NFSD: starting 90-second grace period
                                                           [  OK  ]
Starting NFS mountd:                                       [  OK  ]
Starting sendmail:                                         [  OK  ]
Starting sm-client:                                        [  OK  ]
Starting console mouse services:                           [  OK  ]
Starting crond:                                            [  OK  ]
Starting xfs:                                              [  OK  ]
Starting anacron:                                          [  OK  ]
Starting atd:                                              [  OK  ]
Starting Red Hat Network Daemon:                           [  OK  ]
Starting yum-updatesd:                                     [  OK  ]
Starting Avahi daemon...                                   [  OK  ]
Starting HAL daemon:                                       [  OK  ]
Starting smartd:                                           [  OK  ]
INIT: no more processes left in this runlevel
_
```

Booting Into Different Runlevels

In brief, you can boot into the runlevel of your choice from the GRUB configuration
menu. This is one of the RHCT Troubleshooting and System Maintenance skills
and also an essential skill for all Linux administrators. Specifically, you can boot into
the runlevels described in Table 16-1.

The Red Hat Exam Prep guide states that "RHCTs should be able to boot
systems into different run levels for troubleshooting and system maintenance."
This is straightforward; at the boot loader prompt, you can start Linux at a different
runlevel. This may be useful for two purposes. If your default runlevel in /etc/inittab
is 5, your system normally boots into the GUI. If you're having problems booting
into the GUI, you can start RHEL into the standard text mode, runlevel 3.

```
     Booting command-list

root (hd1,0)
 Filesystem type unknown, partition type 0xfd
kernel /vmlinuz-2.6.18-8.1.1.el5 ro root=/dev/VolGroup00/LogVol00 rhgb quiet

Error 17: Cannot mount selected partition

Press any key to continue..._
```

TABLE 16-1	Linux Runlevels

Runlevel	Description
0	Halts the system
1	Activates SELinux; runs /etc/rc.sysinit, which checks and mounts filesystems; executes all scripts in the /etc/rc1.d directory
s or single	Single-user mode; activates SELinux; runs /etc/rc.sysinit, which checks and mounts filesystems
emergency	Emergency boot mode; activates SELinux; mounts only the root (/) filesystem
init=/bin/sh	Emergency boot mode; mounts only the root (/) filesystem
2	Multiuser mode with some networking; does not include some NFS functions, the automounter, or CUPS
3	Multiuser mode with networking; boots into a text login console
4	Generally unused; however, the defaults support near-identical settings to runlevel 3
5	Multiuser mode with the X Window; boots into an X-based login screen
6	Reboots the system

One other option to help rescue a damaged Linux system is *single-user mode*. This is appropriate if your system can find at least the root filesystem (/). Your system may not have problems finding its root partition and starting the boot process, but it may encounter problems such as damaged configuration files or an inability to boot into one of the higher runlevels. When you boot into single-user mode, options are similar to those of the standard **linux rescue** environment described later in this chapter. Other runlevels shown in Table 16-1 may be useful in specialized circumstances.

To boot into a different runlevel, first assume that you're using the default RHEL boot loader, GRUB. In that case, press (lowercase) **p** to enter the GRUB password if required. Type (lowercase) **a** to modify the kernel arguments. When you see a line similar to

```
grub append> ro root=LABEL=/ rhgb quiet
```

add one of the following commands (shown in boldface) to the end of that line:

```
grub append> ro root=LABEL=/ single
grub append> ro root=LABEL=/ init=/bin/sh
grub append> ro root=LABEL=/ emergency
grub append> ro root=LABEL=/ 1
```

You can use the same technique to boot into another runlevel. For example, to boot from the GRUB boot loader into runlevel 3, navigate to where you can modify the kernel arguments, and add the following command to the end of the following line:

```
grub append> ro root=LABEL=/ 3
```

The terms boot loader and bootloader are used interchangeably. In this book, I've normally used the term boot loader, as that seems to be the direction of the Red Hat documentation. However, the term bootloader is still common even in Red Hat documentation.

```
grub append> ro root=LABEL=/ 3
```

When you boot into runlevel 1, no password is required to access the system. As you'll see later in this chapter, running your system in this runlevel is somewhat similar to running a system booted in rescue mode. Many of the commands and utilities you normally use are unavailable. You may have to mount additional drives or partitions and specify the full pathname when running some commands.

When you have corrected the problem, you can reboot the system. Alternatively, you can type the **exit** command to boot into the default runlevel as defined in /etc/ inittab, probably runlevel 3 or 5.

on the **()ob** *In runlevel 1, any user can change the root password. You do not want people rebooting your computer to go into this runlevel to change your root password. Therefore, it's important to keep your server in a secure location. You can also password-protect GRUB (see Chapter 3) or even the BIOS menu to keep anyone with physical access to your computer from booting it in single-user mode.*

The linux rescue Environment

In brief, you can boot even an unbootable system using the **linux rescue** environment. Using the first RHEL installation CD, type **linux rescue** at the **boot:** prompt. The first couple of steps are the same as those for installing RHEL 5. If the **linux rescue** environment detects your system, it may mount the standard directories in /mnt/ sysimage subdirectories in read-write or in read-only mode. If your filesystems are not mountable, you can open a command prompt and continue with your troubleshooting.

When you type **linux rescue** at the installation boot prompt and go through the steps, the installation discs install a compact version of a root filesystem. To boot into **linux rescue** mode, first boot your system using the first installation CD in a bootable CD-ROM drive, as shown in Figure 16-3.

exam

ⓦatch *The RHCE portion of the Red Hat Exam Prep guide explicitly states that you need to know how to use the rescue environment provided by the first RHEL installation CD.*

FIGURE 16-3

Booting into
linux rescue
mode

```
RED HAT
ENTERPRISE LINUX 5

 -  To install or upgrade in graphical mode, press the          key.

 -  To install or upgrade in text mode, type:              .

 -  Use the function keys listed below for more information.

[F1-Main] [F2-Options] [F3-General] [F4-Kernel] [F5-Rescue]
boot: linux rescue_
```

Now take the following steps:

1. Boot your system from the first RHEL 5 installation CD.

2. Type **linux rescue** at the **boot:** prompt as shown in Figure 16-3. Your system boots a basic Linux system from the first installation CD.

3. Select an appropriate language when prompted.

4. Select an appropriate keyboard type when prompted.

5. You'll see the following message, briefly:

```
Running anaconda, the Red Hat Enterprise Linux rescue mode - please wait...
```

6. You'll be asked whether you want to set up the network interfaces on the local system, as shown in Figure 16-4. Select Yes if you need to connect to a network installation source to install other packages; otherwise, select No and skip to step 8.

7. You'll see a network configuration window for the local network card, similar to what's shown in Figure 16-5. If directed by your instructor or exam proctor to set up a static IP address, follow the instructions carefully; otherwise, try to configure this interface using a local network DHCP server. If you set up a static IP address, you'll see another screen where you're prompted to enter a gateway, a primary DNS, and a secondary DNS IP address.

FIGURE 16-4

Networking interface options in **linux rescue** mode

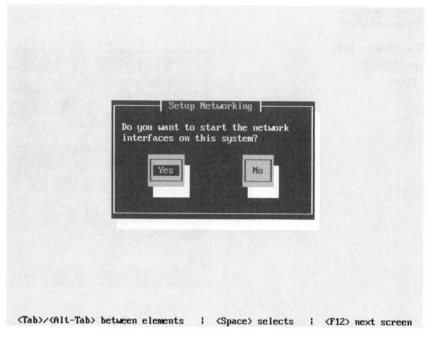

8. Select one of the three options for the rescue environment, as shown in Figure 16-6. Generally, you should try the Continue option first, followed by Read-Only. Continue mounts your RHEL filesystems in read-write mode. Read-Only mounts RHEL file systems in read-only mode. Skip does not mount any of your RHEL filesystems. I address each of these three options in detail in the following sections.

FIGURE 16-5

Networking interface configuration in **linux rescue** mode

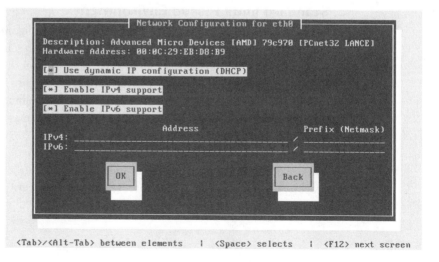

FIGURE 16-6

The **linux rescue**
environment
options

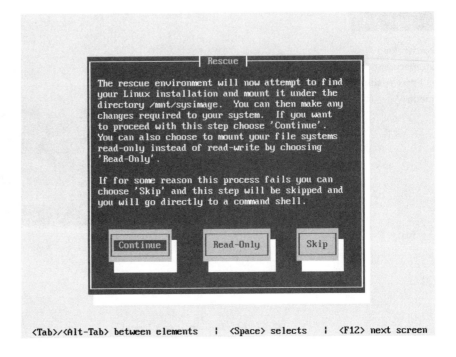

9. When successful, you'll see a message to the effect that your system has been mounted under /mnt/sysimage. When you select OK (the only option), you'll see the following prompt, where you have root privileges.

```
sh-3.1#
```

Standard linux rescue Environment

When you select Continue from the screen shown in Figure 16-6, you're taken through the standard **linux rescue** environment. The rescue files search for your root directory (/) filesystem. If found, your standard root directory (/) is mounted on /mnt/sysimage. All of your other regular filesystems are subdirectories of root; for example, your /boot directory will be found on /mnt/sysimage/boot.

Not all of your filesystems may mount properly. You may see error messages such as:

```
An error occurred trying to mount some or all of your filesystem
```

This suggests that at least one of the filesystems listed in /etc/fstab isn't mounting properly for some reason. If the **linux rescue** environment has no problems, you'll see a message noting that your system has been mounted, as shown in Figure 16-7.

FIGURE 16-7

The **linux rescue** environment has found your root directory (/).

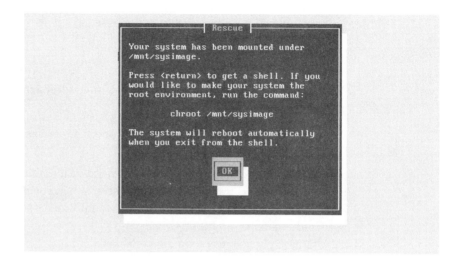

Select OK. You should see the following prompt messages:

```
Your system is mounted under the /mnt/sysimage directory.
When finished please exit from the shell and your system will reboot.

sh-3.1#
```

You'll use the **chroot /mnt/sysimage** command shortly. Now you can work on repairing any files or filesystems that might be damaged. First, check for unmounted filesystems. Run a **df** command. The output should look similar to Figure 16-8.

Compare the result to the /mnt/sysimage/etc/fstab configuration file. If some filesystem is not mounted, it may be configured incorrectly in the fstab file. Alternatively, the label associated with a partition may not match the filesystem shown in your fstab file. For example, to find the label associated with /dev/sda1, run the following command:

```
# e2label /dev/sda1
```

This should return the name of a filesystem to be mounted on that partition such as /boot.

FIGURE 16-8

Labels, filesystems, and partitions

```
sh-3.1# df
Filesystem                1K-blocks      Used Available Use% Mounted on
/dev                         135188         0    135188   0% /dev
/tmp/loop0                    75776     75776         0 100% /mnt/runtime
/dev/VolGroup00/LogVol00
                            4380240   2705380   1448764  66% /mnt/sysimage
/dev/hda1                    101086     15437     80430  17% /mnt/sysimage/boot
/dev                         135188         0    135188   0% /mnt/sysimage/dev
sh-3.1# _
```

Sometimes an unmounted filesystem just needs a little cleaning; remember, a command such as the following cleans the /dev/sdb1 partition:

```
# fsck /dev/sdb1
```

The **fsck** command works only on an unmounted filesystem. For example, if you get a message such as:

```
WARNING!!! Running e2fsck on a mounted filesystem may cause
SEVERE filesystem damage.
```

unmount the subject filesystem with a command such as **umount /mnt/sysimage/boot**. If that doesn't work, restart the rescue process. When you get to the screen shown in Figure 16-6, select Skip and read the "No Mount **linux rescue** Environment" section later in this chapter.

Alternatively, you may see a message like:

```
fsck.ext2: Device or resource busy while trying to open /dev/hda2
filesystem mounted or opened exclusively by another program?
```

This is presented when the partition, in this case /dev/hda2, is part of a Logical Volume Manager (LVM) array as described in Chapter 8. In that case, you'll need to review your /mnt/sysimage/etc/fstab file for the appropriate logical volume (and unmount it), before trying to apply the **fsck** command to it.

 on the job

Don't let messages associated with the ext2 filesystem bother you; they'll appear even if your filesystems are mounted to ext3.

Remember the message in Figure 16-7? It includes an important clue. All you need to do to restore the original filesystem structure is to run the following command:

```
# chroot /mnt/sysimage
```

When you use the rescue disc, your standard root directory (/) is actually mounted on the /mnt/sysimage directory. This command resets your standard root directory (/), so you don't have to go to the /mnt/sysimage subdirectory.

When you've made your changes, run the **sync** command to make sure any changes you've made are written to disk. Type the **exit** command, twice. Linux *should* automatically run the **sync** command again when you exit, making sure any changes are written to disk. Then it stops, allowing you to reboot or restart your computer.

 on the job

Normally it should not be necessary to run the sync command. However, running it does make sure that any pending data is actually written to your hard disks.

Read-Only linux rescue Environment

When you select the Read-Only option shown in Figure 16-6, you'll get the same basic prompt. There is little difference between regular and read-only rescue mode. The rescue system attempts to do everything that it would under regular mode, except all partitions associated with your standard system are mounted read-only. (Some of the rescue system filesystems are still mounted as read-write.)

This is appropriate if you have a large number of mounted filesystems; it can help you cull through what is and isn't working with less risk of overwriting key configuration files.

No Mount linux rescue Environment

When you select the Skip option shown in Figure 16-6, the rescue environment doesn't even search for a Linux installation. A minimal root image is loaded into a RAM disk created by the kernel, and you're taken to a root shell prompt (#), as shown:

```
When finished, please exit from the shell and your system will reboot.
sh-3.1#
```

At this point, you have access to a basic set of commands. You can mount filesystems, create directories, move files, and use editors such as vi. As nothing from your physical drives is mounted, you can apply the **fdisk** and **fsck** commands to various hard disks and partitions. A few other basic commands are also available.

The great difficulty in operating from the rescue environment is that you are working with a minimal version of the Linux operating system. Many of the commands you are accustomed to having at your disposal are not available at this level. If your root partition has not been completely destroyed, you may be able to mount this partition to your temporary root directory in memory and access commands from there.

But you may need a little help identifying the partitions on your system. As I'll show you shortly, the **fdisk -l /dev/hda** command lists the configured partitions on the first IDE hard drive. You can create a new directory such as /mnt/sysimage, mount a partition such as /dev/hda2 on that directory, and check the result with the following commands:

```
# mkdir /mnt/sysimage
# mount /dev/hda2 /mnt/sysimage
# ls /mnt/sysimage
```

If you can verify that you've mounted the standard root directory (/) filesystem on the /mnt/sysimage directory, you can run the **chroot /mnt/sysimage** command. You can then have full access to the commands and configuration files available under that mounted partition.

If you mount partitions from your hard drive in rescue mode and then make changes to files on those partitions, remember to use the sync command. This writes your files to disk so the information isn't lost if you hit the power button on your computer. Alternatively, a umount command applied to any partition also writes data to disk.

CERTIFICATION OBJECTIVE 16.02

Required RHCT Troubleshooting Skills

As described in the "Inside the Exam" section at the start of the chapter, the Red Hat Exam Prep guide lists six RHCT-level troubleshooting and system maintenance skills. If you're studying for the RHCE, you must complete all RHCT requirements within the first hour on this part of the exam. You've already read about techniques for booting systems into different runlevels. Now you'll learn about the other RHCT-level items as described in the Red Hat Exam Prep guide.

All the items described in this section have been covered in other chapters. This chapter summarizes important files and commands from those chapters to help focus your thoughts as you move your way through the RHCT-related Troubleshooting and System Maintenance issues.

There are several exercises in this section. Most require the assistance of a partner. Before you perform these exercises, you should have a backup, or a snapshot, of your system, such as that available on a VMware server.

Diagnosing and Correcting Network Problems

To diagnose misconfigured networking, you need to use the commands and analyze the files described in Chapter 7. To check your current network settings, you'll want to run commands such as:

- **ifconfig** to find the settings of your network card(s)
- **ping** to confirm connectivity to other systems
- **route** to confirm the current routing table

You'll also want to check key files, such as:

- /etc/sysconfig/network to confirm that **NETWORKING=yes**

- ▪ /etc/sysconfig/network-scripts/ifcfg-eth0 to confirm defaults for your network card (assuming the default eth0 device for the network card)
- ▪ /etc/resolv.conf to confirm connections to DNS servers (which is associated with **PEERDNS=yes** in the aforementioned ifcfg-eth0 configuration file)

Refer to Chapter 7 for more information on these commands and files. There are a lot of details; if you forget something, it may be easier to use a Red Hat utility such as the GUI-based Network Configuration tool. Remember, as long as you don't cheat, it doesn't matter how you solve a problem during the Red Hat exams.

EXERCISE 16-1

Diagnosing and Correcting Network Problems

For this exercise, you'll need a partner. Have that partner make changes to your system. Let that partner work privately on your system, until told that the computer is rebooting. Don't look at this lab, until you've solved the problem as created by your partner.

1. Run the **ifconfig** command and review your current network settings.

2. Back up the configuration file associated with the network card, usually ifcfg-eth0 in the /etc/sysconfig/network-scripts directory. Make sure to back up this file to a non-standard location, in case your partner also backs up any files before changing them.

3. Open up the ifcfg-eth0 file in a text editor.

4. Set **BOOTPROTO=none** if it isn't already done.

5. Set or add an **IPADDR** directive. Make it just a little different from the IP Address setting you saw in the output from **ifconfig**. Make sure the new address is on a different network; for example, if the original IP Address and network mask was 192.168.0.50 and 255.255.255.0, set **IPADDR=192.168.1.50** and **NETMASK=255.255.255.0**.

6. Reboot your system, and let your partner back at the computer. Tell him or her to try connecting to another system on your network.

7. Tell your partner to back up any files that he or she might change to the home directory.

8. If your partner gives up, restore the original ifcfg-eth0 configuration file to the /etc/sysconfig/network-scripts directory.

Diagnosing and Correcting Hostname Resolution Problems

Hostname resolution is based on the relationship between hostnames such as enterprise5a.example.org and IP addresses such as 192.168.44.66. First, the default hostname is defined in /etc/sysconfig/network, based on the **HOSTNAME** directive. Hostnames are associated with IP addresses in /etc/hosts. If you use a DNS service, you need to make sure that the DNS server's IP address is identified in /etc/resolv.conf. If you use DHCP to get your IP address, it overwrites the DNS server addresses /etc/ resolv.conf, unless **PEERDNS=no** before the **BOOTPROTO=dhcp** directive in /etc/ sysconfig/network-scripts/ifcfg-eth0. Then a command like **dhclient eth0** will acquire the DNS server address(es) from the DHCP server and place them in /etc/resolv.conf.

When there's appropriate routing information, as shown by the **route** command, along with DNS information in /etc/resolv.conf, you can apply the **ping** command to confirm connectivity to the external host of your choice.

EXERCISE 16-2

Diagnosing and Correcting Hostname Resolution Problems

For this exercise, you'll need a partner. Have your partner make changes to your system. As your partner works to create a network problem for you to solve on your computer, look away until the computer is rebooting.

1. Back up the configuration file associated with the DNS server, /etc/resolv .conf. Back up the /etc/hosts configuration file. Back up the /etc/host.conf configuration file. Make sure to back up these files to a non-standard location, in case your partner also backs up any files before changing them.

2. Open the /etc/host.conf configuration file in a text editor. If it isn't already as shown, change the directive in this file to:

```
order hosts,bind
```

3. Open the /etc/hosts configuration file. Set the name of another computer on your network (which supports SSH access) to an incorrect IP address.

4. Reboot your system, and let your partner back at the computer. Tell him or her to try connecting to another system on your network (the one you've set to the wrong IP address).

5. Make sure to tell your partner to back up any files that he or she might change to the appropriate home directory.

6. If your partner gives up, restore the original /etc/hosts configuration file (and anything else your partner might have changed).

Configuring the X Window System

There are a number of issues associated with the smooth operation of the X Window System. If there are problems with the X configuration file, you may be able to fix it directly using a text editor, create a new file using the Red Hat Display tool (**system-config-display**), or use a command line tool such as **Xorg -configure**.

And as discussed in Chapter 14, the X Window may not work under certain conditions. Naturally, Linux doesn't boot into an X login window unless the default runlevel in /etc/inittab is set to 5. The X Window can't run without the X Font Server. And it can't start if the partitions associated with certain directories are full or have inappropriate permissions.

EXERCISE 16-3

Configuring the X Window System

For this exercise, you'll need a partner. Have your partner make changes to your system. As your partner works to create a network problem for you to solve on your computer, look away until the computer is rebooting.

1. Back up the configuration file associated with the X Window System, /etc/X11/xorg.conf. Make sure to back up this file to a non-standard location, in case your partner also backs up any files before changing them.

2. Open the /etc/X11/xorg.conf configuration file in a text editor. Near the end of the file, you'll see the following directive:

```
Section "Screen"
```

3. Change the directive to:

```
Section "Scree"
```

4. Configure the system to start in runlevel 3, in /etc/inittab.

5. Reboot the system, and let your partner back at the computer. Tell him or her to try starting the GUI.

6. Make sure to tell your partner to back up any files that he or she might change to the appropriate home directory.

7. If your partner gives up, restore the original /etc/X11/xorg.conf configuration file.

Configuring a Desktop Environment

Configuring a desktop environment is a slightly different process than configuring the X Window. As discussed in Chapter 14, the default login manager is configured in /etc/X11/prefdm. The default desktop environment can be changed with the **switchdesk** command. Standard applications can be started with the desktop environment using settings in /etc/X11/xinit/xinitrc and files in the /etc/X11/xinit/xinitrc.d directory.

You can also customize a desktop environment based on hidden files in each user's home directory. These files are read first by the key scripts that start the X Window.

EXERCISE 16-4

Configuring a Desktop Environment

For this exercise, you'll need a partner. Have your partner make changes to your system. As your partner works to create a network problem for you to solve on your computer, look away until the computer is rebooting.

1. Back up the configuration file associated with the display manager, /etc/X11/prefdm. Make sure to back up this file to a non-standard location, in case your partner also backs up any files before changing them.

2. Open the /etc/X11/prefdm configuration file in a text editor. Near the beginning of the file, you'll see the following directive:

```
# Run preferred X display manager
preferred=
```

3. Change the directive to:

```
preferred=kdm
```

4. Make sure the default runlevel in /etc/inittab is set to 5.

5. Reboot the system, and let your partner back at the computer. Tell him or her to configure the system to boot into the GNOME Display Manager.

6. Make sure to tell your partner to back up any files that he or she might change to the appropriate home directory.

7. Whatever happens, restore the original /etc/X11/prefdm configuration file when your partner is finished with this exercise.

Adding New Partitions, Filesystems, and Swap

Reading the Red Hat Exam Prep guide carefully, this skill states that RHCTs should be able to *add new partitions, filesystems, and swap to existing systems* (I've added the boldface to provide emphasis on this particular Exam Prep requirement). This implies that space is available on the hard drive(s) that you are using during your exam.

You need to know how to add new partitions, which suggests that you need to know how to use the **fdisk** and **parted** utilities described in Chapter 4. When you create a new partition, make sure the partition type is associated with what you're creating; there are different partition types for standard Linux and swap partitions.

EXERCISE 16-5

Adding a New Partition

This is one exercise that does not require a partner. However, it assumes that you've installed RHEL with extra available space on any existing hard drives. If you don't have any additional space, you can substitute a spare USB key.

This exercise assumes you'll be creating a partition on a second SATA or SCSI hard drive. If you're using a different drive and partition, substitute device file names accordingly.

1. If you've configured a VMware machine to practice for the Red Hat exam, take a snapshot of your current configuration (unless you're willing to keep the changes made during this exercise).

2. Run the **fdisk -l** command to display configured partitions. The cylinders will tell you if space is available. For example, the following output suggests that 5000 cylinders are free:

```
Disk /dev/sdb: 160.0 GB, 160041885696 bytes
255 heads, 63 sectors/track, 19457 cylinders
Units = cylinders of 16065 * 512 = 8225280 bytes

    Device Boot      Start         End      Blocks   Id  System
/dev/sdb1   *            1        9205    73939131   83  Linux
/dev/sdb2              9206       14457    42349190   83  Linux
```

3. Add a new partition of 500MB. It doesn't have to be exact. Make sure that the partition type is associated with Linux. I don't specify exact steps, as you can use either **fdisk** or **parted** to create the new partition.

4. Write the changes to disk, and use the **partprobe** command or reboot the system.

5. Format the new partition. For example, if the new partition device is /dev/sdb3, you can do so with the **mkfs.ext3 /dev/sdb3** command.

6. Assign the partition to user michael's home directory in /etc/fstab. (Create user michael if needed.) For example, if the partition device is /dev/sdb3, you can do so with the following directive in that file:

```
/dev/sdb3      /home/michael      ext3      defaults      1 2
```

7. Mount /dev/sdb3 on the /home/michael directory. Reboot your system to make sure your system recognizes the changes and mounts the new partition.

8. Run the **fdisk -l, mount,** and **df** commands to verify the new partition.

9. If you took a VMware snapshot, press the Revert button in the VMware window to revert to the snapshot.

Important Command Line Tools

The Red Hat Exam Prep guide states that RHCTs should be able to *use standard command-line tools to analyze problems and configure system*. There are a number of standard command line tools that you can use to analyze problems and configure your system, as described throughout this book.

CERTIFICATION OBJECTIVE 16.03

Required RHCE Troubleshooting Skills

At some point in your career as a Red Hat Enterprise Linux administrator, maybe even on the Red Hat exams, you're going to be faced with a system that will not boot. It will be up to you to determine the cause of the problem and implement a fix. Sometimes, the problem may be due to hardware failure: the system in question has a bad power supply or has experienced a hard disk crash.

Quite often, however, the failure of a system to boot can be traced back to the actions of a user: you, the system administrator! When you are editing certain system configuration files, typographical errors can render your system unbootable.

Any time you plan to make any substantial modifications to your system or change key configuration files, back them up first. Then, after making changes, you should actually reboot your system rather than assume that it will boot up the next time you need a reboot. It's much better to encounter problems while you can still remember exactly which changes you made. It is even better if you can go back to a working configuration file.

As described earlier in this chapter, the main tool is the **linux rescue** environment provided by the first installation CD. Per the Exam Prep guide, you also need to know how to *diagnose and correct boot failures arising from bootloader, module, and filesystem errors*; It's broken down into three sections. In addition, some of the key tools to *diagnose and correct problems with network services*, as described in previous chapters, are summarized here. Key tools are discussed that allow you to *add, remove, and resize logical volumes*. And finally to diagnose and correct networking services problems where SELinux contexts are interfering with proper operation, use the Setroubleshoot browser described in Chapter 15.

Troubleshooting the Boot Loader

The boot loader associated with Red Hat Enterprise Linux 5 is GRUB. For an extensive discussion, see Chapter 3. It can help you to know how to:

- Associate the **root** directive with the partition with the /boot directory.
- Boot into the desired, non-default runlevel.
- Access the GRUB command line.
- Test different GRUB commands.
- Use command completion to find and use the exact names of your kernel and initial RAM disk.

While it isn't necessary to know all these skills, they can help you diagnose problems more quickly during your exam.

EXERCISE 16-6

Troubleshooting the Boot Loader

For this exercise, you'll need a partner. Have your partner make changes to your system. As your partner works to create a network problem for you to solve on your computer, look away until the computer is rebooting.

It's most helpful if you have a VMware snapshot of your RHEL system. Problems like those created in this exercise have caused administrators to mess up their systems in other ways. You'll also need the first RHEL installation CD.

1. Back up the configuration file associated with the boot loader, /boot/grub/ grub.conf. Make sure to back up this file to a non-standard location, in case your partner also backs up any files before changing them.

2. Open the /boot/grub/grub.conf configuration file in a text editor. Focus on the **kernel** command line, which might look like one of the following:

   ```
   kernel /vmlinuz-2.6.18-8.el5 ro root=/dev/VolGroup00/LogVol00
   ```

   or

   ```
   kernel /vmlinuz-2.6.18-8.el5 ro root=LABEL=/
   ```

3. Introduce a typographical error in the **root** directive in the **kernel** command line.

4. Reboot the system, and let your partner back at the computer. Tell him or her to address the error message shown. Give your partner the first RHEL 5 installation CD.

5. Make sure to tell your partner to back up any files that he or she might change to the appropriate home directory.

6. Whatever happens, restore the original /boot/grub/grub.conf configuration file when your partner is finished with this exercise. (Alternatively, you can restore the configuration from a VMware snapshot.)

Module Errors

Most kernels are compiled with loadable modules. Current Linux distributions, including RHEL, configure modules in the initial RAM disk, which is compiled into a initrd-* file in the /boot directory. As you can see in the GRUB configuration file, the initial RAM disk is normally associated with the last line in a GRUB configuration stanza. As described in Chapter 8, you can create a new initial RAM disk configuration file with the **mkinitrd** command. But errors are also possible, as you'll see in the following exercise.

EXERCISE 16-7

Troubleshooting Boot Loader Modules

For this exercise, you'll need a partner. Have your partner make changes to your system. As your partner works to create a network problem for you to solve on your computer, look away until the computer is rebooting.

It's most helpful if you have a VMware snapshot of your RHEL system. Problems like those created in this exercise have caused administrators to mess up their systems in other ways. You'll also need the first RHEL installation CD.

1. Back up the configuration file associated with the boot loader, /boot/grub/ grub.conf. Make sure to back up this file to a non-standard location, in case your partner also backs up any files before changing them.

2. Open the /boot/grub/grub.conf configuration file in a text editor. Focus on the **initrd** command line, which might look like the following:

```
initrd /initrd-2.6.18-8.el5.img
```

3. Misspell both **initrd** words in this line.

4. Reboot the system, and let your partner back at the computer. Tell him or her to address the error message shown. Give your partner the first RHEL 5 installation CD.

5. Make sure to tell your partner to back up any files that he or she might change to the appropriate home directory.

6. Whatever happens, restore the original /boot/grub/grub.conf configuration file when your partner is finished with this exercise. (Alternatively, you can restore the configuration from a VMware snapshot.)

Filesystem Corruption and Checking

Although there are potentially many things that will prevent a system from booting, these problems can be generally categorized as either hardware problems or software and configuration problems. The most common hardware-related problem you will probably encounter is a bad hard drive; like all mechanical devices with moving parts, these have a finite lifetime and will eventually fail. Fortunately, the Red Hat exams do not require you to address hardware failures.

Software and configuration problems, however, can be a little more difficult. At first glance, they can look just like regular hardware problems.

In addition to knowing how to mount disk partitions, edit files, and manipulate files, you will need to know how to use several other commands to fix problems from rescue mode or single-user mode. The most useful of these are the **df**, **fdisk**, and the **fsck** commands. To diagnose a problem, you need to know how these commands work at least at a rudimentary level.

df

The Linux **df** command was covered briefly in Chapter 4. When you use **df**, you can find mounted directories, the capacity of each partition, and the percentage of each partition that's filled with files. The result shown back in Figure 16-8 illustrates the result in kilobytes. There are a couple of simple variations; the following commands provide output in megabytes and inodes:

```
# df -m
# df -i
```

fdisk and parted

The Linux **fdisk** and **parted** utilities were covered briefly in Chapter 4. When you use **fdisk** or **parted**, you can find the partitions you have available for mounting. For example, the **fdisk -l /dev/hda** (or **parted /dev/hda print**) command lists available partitions on the first IDE hard disk:

```
# fdisk -l /dev/hda

Disk /dev/hda: 15.0GB, 15020457984 bytes
240 heads, 63 sectors/track, 1940 cylinders
Units = cylinders of 15120 * 512 = 7741440 bytes
   Device  Boot   Start      End      Blocks     Id  System
/dev/hda1    *       1        949     7174408+    b  Win95 FAT32
/dev/hda2          950        963      105840     83  Linux
/dev/hda3          964       1871     6864480     83  Linux
/dev/hda4         1872       1940      521640      f  Win95 Ext'd (LBA)
/dev/hda5         1872       1940      521608+    82  Linux swap
```

Looking at the output from **fdisk**, it's easy to identify the partitions configured with a Linux format, /dev/hda2, /dev/hda3, and /dev/hda5. Given the size of each partition, it is reasonable to conclude that /dev/hda2 is associated with /boot, and /dev/hda3 is associated with root (/). Here's a fairly complex output from **parted**:

```
# parted /dev/sda print

Model: ATA HDS728080PLA380 (scsi)
Disk /dev/sda: 82.3GB
Sector size (logical/physical): 512B/512B
Partition Table: msdos

Number Start    End     Size     Type      File system  Flags
   1   32.3kB  197MB   197MB    primary   ext3         boot
   2   197MB   15.2GB  15.0GB   primary   ext3
   3   15.2GB  16.2GB  1003MB   primary   linux-swap
   4   16.2GB  82.3GB  66.1GB   extended
   5   16.2GB  16.3GB  107MB    logical   ext3
   6   16.3GB  26.8GB  10.5GB   logical   ext3
   7   26.8GB  41.8GB  15.0GB   logical   fat32        lba
   8   41.8GB  51.8GB  10.0GB   logical   ext3
   9   51.8GB  82.3GB  30.5GB   logical   ext3

Information: Don't forget to update /etc/fstab, if necessary.
```

In this example, it's easy to identify the Linux swap partition. Since /boot partitions are small and normally configured toward the front of a drive (with a boot flag), it's reasonable to associate it with /dev/sda1.

For simple partitioning schemes, this is easy. It gets far more complicated when you have lots of partitions. You should always have some documentation available that clearly identifies your partition layout within your filesystem:

```
# fdisk -l /dev/hda
Disk /dev/hda: 26.8 GB, 26843545600
255 heads, 63 sectors/track, 3263 cylinders
Units = cylinders of 16065 * 512 = 8225280 bytes

   Device Boot    Start     End     Blocks      Id  System
/dev/hda1    *     1        13      104391      83  Linux
/dev/hda2          14       268     2048287+    b   Win95 FAT32
/dev/hda3          269      396     1028160     83  Linux
/dev/hda4          397      3263    23029177+   f   Win95 Ext'd (LBA)
/dev/hda5          397      1097    5630751     83  Linux
/dev/hda6          1098     1734    5116671     83  Linux
/dev/hda7          1735     1989    2048256     83  Linux
/dev/hda8          1990     2244    2048256     83  Linux
/dev/hda9          2245     2372    1028218+    83  Linux
/dev/hda10         2373     2499    1020096     82  Linux swap
/dev/hda11         2500     2626    1020096     83  Linux
/dev/hda12         2627     2753    1020096     83  Linux
/dev/hda13         2754     2880    1020096     83  Linux
/dev/hda14         2881     3007    1020096     83  Linux
/dev/hda15         3008     3134    1020096     83  Linux
/dev/hda16         3135     3236    1020096     83  Linux
```

In this example, it's easy to identify the Linux swap partition. Since /boot partitions are small and normally configured toward the front of a drive, it's reasonable to associate it with /dev/hda1.

However, that is just a guess; some trial and error may be required. For example, after mounting /dev/hda2 on an empty directory, you would want to check the contents of that directory for the typical contents of /boot.

e2label

Based on the previous output from **fdisk -l**, you could probably use a little help to identify the filesystems associated with the other partitions. The **e2label** command can help. When you set up a new filesystem, the associated partition is normally marked with a label. For example, the following command tells you that the /usr filesystem is normally mounted on /dev/hda5.

```
# e2label
Usage: e2label device [newlabel]
```

```
# e2label /dev/hda5
/usr
```

dumpe2fs

You can get a lot more information on each partition with the **dumpe2fs** command, as shown in Figure 16-9.

The **dumpe2fs** command not only does the job of **e2label** but also tells you about the format, whether it has a journal, and the block size. Proceed further through the output, and you'll find the locations for backup superblocks, which can help you use the **fsck** or **e2fsck** command to select the appropriate superblock for your Linux partition.

on the
Job

fsck is a "front end" for e2fsck, which is used to check partitions formatted to the ext2 and ext3 filesystems.

Filesystem Check—fsck

You should also know how to use the **fsck** command. This command is a front end for most of the filesystem formats available in Linux, such as ext2, ext3, reiserfs, vfat, and more. This command is used to check the filesystem on a partition for consistency. In order to use the **fsck** command effectively, you need to understand something about how filesystems are laid out on disk partitions.

FIGURE 16-9	

The **dumpe2fs** command provides a lot of information.

```
[root@Enterprise5a ~]# dumpe2fs /dev/sda1 | more
dumpe2fs 1.38 (30-Jun-2005)
Filesystem volume name:   <none>
Last mounted on:          <not available>
Filesystem UUID:          ee834073-da53-4872-9b80-cbf39d5b1801
Filesystem magic number:  0xEF53
Filesystem revision #:    1 (dynamic)
Filesystem features:      has_journal filetype sparse_super
Default mount options:    (none)
Filesystem state:         clean
Errors behavior:          Continue
Filesystem OS type:       Linux
Inode count:              96384
Block count:              192748
Reserved block count:     9637
Free blocks:              165969
Free inodes:              96355
First block:              1
Block size:               1024
Fragment size:            1024
Blocks per group:         8192
Fragments per group:      8192
Inodes per group:         4016
Inode blocks per group:   502
Last mount time:          Tue Aug  8 12:49:30 2006
Last write time:          Tue Aug  8 12:49:30 2006
Mount count:              9
Maximum mount count:      30
Last checked:             Wed Dec 31 16:00:00 1969
Check interval:           0 (<none>)
--More--
```

When you format a disk partition under Linux using the **mkfs** command, it sets aside a certain portion of the disk to use for storing *inodes*, which are data structures that contain the actual disk block addresses that point to file data on a disk. The **mkfs** command also stores information about the size of the filesystem, the filesystem label, and the number of inodes in a special location at the start of the partition called the *superblock*. If the superblock is corrupted or destroyed, the remaining information on the disk is unreadable. Because the superblock is so vital to the integrity of the data on a partition, the **mkfs** command makes duplicate copies of the superblock at fixed intervals on the partition, which you can find with the **dumpe2fs** command described earlier.

The **fsck** command checks for and corrects problems with filesystem consistency by looking for things such as disk blocks that are marked as free but are actually in use (and vice versa), inodes that don't have a corresponding directory entry, inodes with incorrect link counts, and a number of other problems. The **fsck** command will also fix a corrupted superblock. If **fsck** fails due to a corrupt superblock, you can use the **fsck** command with the **-b** option to specify an alternative superblock. For example, the following command performs a consistency check on the filesystem on disk partition /dev/hda5, using the superblock located at disk block 8193:

```
#   fsck -b 8193 /dev/hda5
```

File Corruption

You may find corruption in some key files or commands such as **bash** or **init**. If you do, one option is to reload the files from the original RPMs. For example, if the **init** command were to be corrupted or erased, you can reload it from the SysVinit RPM.

When you boot your system into the **linux rescue** environment, you'll still need to connect to the network source associated with the installation RPMs. So you should set up networking as described earlier when you boot into the **linux rescue** environment. Assume the **/bin/bash** command is corrupt or missing and has to be replaced. With that in mind, take the following steps:

1. Run the **df** command. You should see how the **linux rescue** environment mounted your partitions.

2. If possible, mount the network source. If it's an NFS share in the /inst directory on the server.example.com system, you can do so on the /mnt/ source directory (create /mnt/source if required) with the following command:

```
# mount -t nfs server.example.com:/inst /mnt/source
```

3. Copy the bash RPM from the /mnt/source directory. It isn't necessary, but can help if your connection is dropped. Use the following command:

```
# cp /mnt/source/Server/bash-*.rpm .
```

4. Install the bash RPM, forcing installation over current files:

```
# rpm -Uvh --force --root=/mnt/sysimage bash-*.rpm
```

5. Run the following **chroot** command to move into the standard directory tree:

```
# chroot /mnt/sysimage
```

6. Check the status of the **bash** command.

```
# rpm -Vf /bin/bash
```

If you see no output, you'll know that there is no longer a problem with the **bash** command. (You can also use this command at the start of the process to see if there is a problem.) You should now be able to run the **exit** command twice to reboot your computer—and at least this problem should be solved.

Network Service Issues

The Red Hat Exam Prep guide says that you may have to *diagnose and correct problems with network services* during the Troubleshooting and System Maintenance portion of the RHCE exam. These are the same network services that you may need to configure during the Installation and Configuration portion of the same exam. Example scenarios and solutions are shown as follows. Needless to say, the solutions are far from complete: for example, firewalls and network configuration issues can prevent communication to any network service.

Add, Remove, and Resize Logical Volumes

You may need to add, remove, and/or resize a logical volume (LV) during the Troubleshooting and System Maintenance portion of the RHCE exam. As you'll recall from Chapter 8, LVs involve commands that manage physical volumes (PVs),

SCENARIO & SOLUTION

A connection to a local Web server results in a 404 file not found error.	Make sure there is an appropriate index.html in the **DocumentRoot** directory, and the SELinux permissions for index.html match what you see from a **ls -Z/var/www/html** command.
You're unable to connect to your Samba home directory on a remote system.	Check the **[homes]** share in /etc/samba/smb.conf. Use **testparm** to check that configuration file for errors.
You have trouble connecting to a remote NFS share.	Make sure the directory is shared properly in /etc/exports, the directory has been exported, is visible from a **showmount -e hostname** command, and appropriate services are running.
You're unable to log into the remote FTP server anonymously.	Make sure anonymous access is enabled in /etc/vsftpd/vsftpd.conf.
You can't connect through the Web proxy server.	Make sure appropriate access is enabled to the right network in /etc/squid/squid.conf.
You're unable to send outgoing e-mail through a local network server.	Make sure one outgoing mail server (sendmail or Postfix) is active and properly configured.
You're unable to receive secure POP3 e-mail through a local network server.	Make sure the Dovecot service is properly configured in /etc/dovecot.conf. If you use an alternative service, configure its configuration file instead.
You want to limit SSH access to specific users.	Use the **AllowUsers** directive in /etc/ssh/sshd_config.

LVs, and volume groups (VGs). You can manage this process from the command line or the LVM Configuration Tool. For detailed information on each process, see Chapter 8. In this section, we'll review the basics. (If you're not already familiar with logical volumes, reread Chapter 8. Otherwise, this section will probably confuse you to no end.)

First, to check the current status of your LVs, PVs, and VGs, the **lvdisplay**, **pvdisplay**, and **vgdisplay** commands can help. Those commands work with the **mount** command and the contents of /etc/fstab to confirm your configuration and the currently mounted LVs.

Adding a Logical Volume

If you need to add an LV, and you don't have sufficient free space in your PVs/VGs, you'll need to create a new partition, configured to the appropriate partition type in a tool such as **fdisk** or **parted**. This section examines the process of creating a new LV. If you have room in existing PVs or VGs, you can skip ahead and add an LV more quickly.

To create a new PV from a properly configured partition, you can use the **pvcreate** command. For example, if you've just created /dev/hda9 and /dev/hda10 for this purpose, use the following command:

```
# pvcreate /dev/hda9 /dev/hda10
```

You can reverse the process with the **pvremove** command—in this case:

```
# pvremove /dev/hda9 /dev/hda10
```

If you've already assigned space from the noted partitions to an LV, the **pvremove** command will give you an error message.

To create a new VG from one or more unused PVs, use the **vgcreate** command. For example, if you wanted to create a VG named myvg from the aforementioned PVs, use the following command:

```
# vgcreate myvg /dev/hda9 /dev/hda10
```

If this command works, you'll find a VG device in /dev/myvg.

To create a new LV from an available VG, the **lvcreate** command can help. For example, if you wanted to create a new LV of 1000MB from the VG named myvg, run the following command:

```
# lvcreate -L 1000 myvg
```

You'll see the name of the new LV in the output; normally it'll be something like lvol0. In this case, the LV device is /dev/myvg/lvol0.

Expanding a Logical Volume

Expanding the space available from an LV is a two-step process. First, you'll extend the LV in available free space, perhaps from a PV that you've just created. Then you'll expand the filesystem to fill the LV with the **resize2fs** command.

To expand an existing LV, use the **lvextend** command. You'll need an existing PV partition with available free space, such as /dev/sda2. For example, if you're increasing the size of the aforementioned LV by 500MB, use the following command:

```
# lvextend -L +500 /dev/myvg/lvol0 /dev/sda2
```

You can then resize ext2 or ext3 formatted filesystems with the **resize2fs** command. For the noted device, the command would be

```
# resize2fs /dev/myvg/lvol0
```

If you're decreasing the size of an LV, the process is more complex. There is no command similar to **resize2fs** that reduces the size of a formatted filesystem. You'll need to unmount the LV, and then apply the **resize2fs** command to the LV device file, with the desired smaller size at the end of the command.

Removing a Logical Volume

Removing an LV is easy; as long as the data in the LV has been saved, the **lvremove** command works well. For example, if you've created a second LV in the same VG, you might use the following command:

```
# lvremove /dev/myvg/lvol1
```

Diagnosing SELinux-related Network Service Issues

The final Troubleshooting and System Maintenance item in the RHCE part of the Exam Prep guide is the ability to *diagnose and correct networking services problems where SELinux contexts are interfering with proper operation.*

In most cases, this is simpler than it looks. SELinux log messages are stored in /var/log/messages with an **avc** label. But even better, the Setroubleshoot browser can identify SELinux issues, describe causes, and even suggest solutions. Watch it for suggested commands such as **chcon** to change SELinux contexts and **sesetbool** to set SELinux booleans. All you need to do is open the browser in a GUI with the **sealert -b** command, and browse the most recent errors. For more information, see Chapter 15.

CERTIFICATION SUMMARY

One of the most valuable skills as a systems administrator is knowing how to troubleshoot a system. Understanding the scientific method is the first skill. Knowing how to boot into different runlevels and how to use the **linux rescue** mode from the first installation CD are other key skills.

The Troubleshooting and System Maintenance portion of the Red Hat exams includes RHCT and RHCE skills. If you're taking the RHCE exam, you'll need to pass both sections to qualify for the RHCE. The RHCT section requires that you know how to diagnose and correct misconfigured networking, diagnose and correct hostname resolution problems, configure the X Window System and a desktop environment, add new partitions and filesystems, and swap to existing systems. You also need to know how to use standard command line tools and configure your system. All of these skills were covered in this book and are summarized in this chapter.

RHCE candidates also have their own set of challenges during the Troubleshooting and System Maintenance portion of that exam. You'll need to know how to diagnose and correct boot failures arising from boot loader, module, and filesystem errors, as well as add, remove, and resize logical volumes. You'll also need to know how to diagnose and correct problems with any of the network services described throughout the book as well as related issues where SELinux is interfering with proper operation of these services.

TWO-MINUTE DRILL

Here are some of the key points from the certification objectives in Chapter 16.

Troubleshooting Strategies

❑ During the Troubleshooting and System Maintenance exam, use your experience. You may have seen the problem before.

❑ If you aren't sure about a problem, try the simplest solution first.

❑ If all else fails, use the scientific method.

❑ Know how to boot Linux into different runlevels; it can help you bypass many problems and boot a system.

❑ RHCE candidates should also know how to boot Linux from the first installation CD, using **linux rescue** mode.

Required RHCT Troubleshooting Skills

❑ Misconfigured networking can be diagnosed with key commands such as **ifconfig** and **ping**. It can be corrected in related configuration files or with the Red Hat Network Configuration tool.

❑ Misconfigured hostname resolution problems relate to connections to /etc/ hosts or DNS servers.

❑ Configure the X Window System using the Red Hat Display Configuration tool, commands such as **Xorg -configure**, or by directly editing /etc/X11/xorg.conf.

❑ Configure a desktop environment and login manager with key configuration files such as /etc/X11/prefdm and /etc/X11/xinit/xinitrc.

Required RHCE Troubleshooting Skills

❑ Knowing how to diagnose and correct boot failures means knowing the GRUB configuration file and command line.

❑ Understand how to manage boot modules with the correct initial RAM disk.

❑ If there are filesystem errors, they may show up during the boot process and require that you use commands such as **fsck** to diagnose and solve them.

❑ Adding, removing, and resizing LVs require skills described in detail in Chapter 8.

❑ Know how to diagnose and solve service issues as described throughout this book.

❑ Use the Setroubleshoot browser to diagnose network service problems related to SELinux.

SELF TEST

The following questions will help you measure your understanding of the material presented in this chapter. As no multiple choice questions appear on the Red Hat exams, no multiple choice questions appear in this book. These questions exclusively test your understanding of the chapter. It is okay if you have another way of performing a task. Getting results, not memorizing trivia, is what counts on the Red Hat exams. There may be more than one answer for many of these questions.

As this chapter contains references to many other chapters in this book, some of the questions here require knowledge from reading other chapters.

Troubleshooting Strategies

1. What runlevel options are there if you do not want to boot into runlevels 0, 2, 3, 4, 5, or 6?

_____

_____

_____

2. If **linux rescue** mode successfully finds an existing RHEL installation, where is it mounted?

_____

Required RHCT Troubleshooting Skills

3. If you want to set network card eth0 to acquire IP address information from a DHCP server, what directive would you use in /etc/sysconfig/network-scripts/ifcfg-eth0?

_____

4. What files are associated with hostname configuration during the boot process?

_____

_____

5. If you want to start from scratch and create a new xorg.conf configuration file, what command would you use?

_____

6. If you want to set up a default application in the X Window that will work for both GNOME and KDE, what file or directory would you change?

_____

7. What command formats /dev/sda5 to the ext3 filesystem?

_____

Required RHCE Troubleshooting Skills

8. Other than possibly the version number of the kernel, what's wrong with the following line from /boot/grub/grub.conf?

```
kernel vmlinuz-2.6.18-8.el5 ro root=LABEL=/dev/hda2 rghb quiet
```

_____

9. What's wrong with the following line from /boot/grub/grub.conf?

```
initrd /initrd 2.6.18-8.el5
```

_____

10. If you have a problem with the Samba configuration file and suspect a syntax error, what command would you use?

_____

11. If you have a problem with the Apache configuration file and suspect a syntax error with virtual hosts, what command would you use?

_____

12. What command increases the size of an existing LV, /dev/thisvg/lvol1, by 1000MB, using space available from a properly configured /dev/sda10 device?

_____

LAB QUESTIONS

Lab I

For this lab, you'll need a partner. The first steps will set up the lab for that person. To prepare this lab, take the following steps:

1. Log in as the root user.

2. Open /etc/inittab in a text editor.

3. Change the default runlevel to 0.

4. Save your changes.

5. Power down the computer. Pass the system to your partner. Tell your partner that the problem should appear when the computer boots into Linux.

****

6. Now that your partner has set up this system for you, power on the computer and boot into Linux. What happens? What do you see? What can you do?

Lab 2

For this lab, let your partner set up your computer for you.

****

Now you'll set up this system for your partner using the following steps.

1. If you've configured your RHEL system on VMware, make sure you have a current snapshot. It's invaluable if your partner is unable to solve this problem.

2. Boot into your partner's system normally.

3. Open the /etc/fstab configuration file. There should be a line associated with the /boot directory, similar to:

```
LABEL=/boot    /boot    ext3    defaults    1 2
```

4. Change the line, introducing a typo, as shown:

```
LABEL=boot    /boot    ext3    defaults    1 2
```

5. Power down the system, and tell your partner to boot the system.

****

6. Now that your partner has set up this system for you, power on the computer and boot into Linux. What happens? What do you see? What can you do?

Lab 3

For this exercise, use a test computer. Do not use a production computer. Do not use a computer with any data might be important to you. If something goes wrong, and you are unable to restore from a backup, you may need to reinstall Linux. This exercise assumes that you're using the default Red Hat Enterprise Linux boot loader, GRUB.

Navigate to the /boot directory. Change the name of the initrd-*versionnumber*.img file. Make sure it's something easy to remember such as initrd-*versionnumber*.bak. Reboot Linux. As GRUB goes through the boot sequence, it will probably stop when it can't find your initial RAM Disk (initrd) file, with a file not found message.

Now that your boot loader isn't working, what do you do? Can you try to start Linux in single-user mode?

Lab 4

In this lab, you'll create new PEs and use them to increase the size of a configured LV. You're doing this for the LV used by the /var directory. Because of the increasing demands of your Web site, you need more room for the /var directory for your Web site data. Assume your /etc/fstab configuration file includes the following line:

```
/dev/Volume00/LogVol00    /var    ext3    defaults    1 2
```

You've created PEs from the /dev/sde and /dev/sdf hard drives, and have just added another SCSI hard drive, /dev/sdg. Assume you've backed up the data that you need from the /var directory.

SELF TEST ANSWERS

Troubleshooting Strategies

1. If you do not want to boot into runlevels 0, 2, 3, 4, 5, or 6, you can boot into runlevels 1, s, or emergency; you can also boot with the **init=/bin/sh** command appended to the end of the kernel command line.

2. If **linux rescue** mode successfully finds an existing RHEL installation, it is mounted on the /mnt/sysimage directory.

Required RHCT Troubleshooting Skills

3. If you want to set network card eth0 to acquire IP address information from a DHCP server, you would use the **BOOTPROTO=dhcp** directive in /etc/sysconfig/network-scripts/ifcfg-eth0.

4. The files that determine the hostname when you boot Linux are /etc/hosts and /etc/sysconfig/ network.

5. If you want to start from scratch and create a new xorg.conf configuration file, you could use the **system-config-display** command to create it in the appropriate /etc/X11 directory. Alternatively, if you use the **Xorg -configure** command, you'll have to copy xorg.conf from the local directory to /etc/X11.

6. If you want to set up a default application in the X Window that will work for both GNOME and KDE, you would change /etc/X11/xinit/xinitrc or files in the /etc/X11/xinit/xinitrc.d/ directory.

7. The command that formats /dev/sda5 to the ext3 filesystem is **mkfs.ext3 /dev/sda5**.

Required RHCE Troubleshooting Skills

8. The line from /boot/grub/grub.conf is missing the forward slash in front of /vmlinuz-2.6.18-8.el5; it's the /boot directory as defined by the **root(hd0,0)** (or similar) directive. It should read as follows:

```
kernel /vmlinuz-2.6.18-8.el5 ro root=LABEL=/dev/hda2 rghb quiet
```

9. The line from /boot/grub/grub.conf is missing the .img extension at the end of the initial RAM disk file; it should read as follows:

```
initrd /initrd 2.6.18-8.el5.img
```

10. If you have a problem with the Samba configuration file and suspect a syntax error, you would use the **testparm** command.

11. If you have a problem with the Apache configuration file and suspect a syntax error with virtual hosts, you could use either of the following commands:

```
# httpd -S
# httpd -t -D DUMP_VHOSTS
```

12. The command that increases the size of an existing LV, /dev/thisvg/lvol1, by 1000MB, using space available from a properly configured /dev/sda10 device, is shown here:

```
# lvextend -L +1000 /dev/thisvg/lvol1 /dev/sda10
```

LAB ANSWERS

Lab 1

To solve this problem, you need to observe what happens when you boot this system. While not required, the first step you should take is to use the GRUB boot menu to boot into a specific runlevel. If you have any experience with Linux, you should know that an immediate shutdown after Linux goes through the boot process is associated with runlevel 0.

Lab 2

In this lab, you should know almost immediately that there's a problem with the **LABEL** associated with the /boot directory, with an error message similar to:

```
fsck.ext3: Unable to resolve 'LABEL=boot'
```

During your exam, this may be a bit tricky. If you're very familiar with the contents of /etc/fstab, you may be able to recognize this problem right away.

Otherwise, you can verify the **LABEL** associated with each partition on your hard drive with the **e2label** command. For example, if you're checking the /dev/hda1 partition, the command would be

```
# e2label /dev/hda1
```

Some trial and error may be required, but you'll eventually see the **LABEL** you need in the output. For example, I see the following output from this command on my VMware-based RHEL system:

```
/boot
```

This provides the hint I need to know how to repair my /etc/fstab configuration file.

Lab 3

As you practice learning about Linux for the RHCE exam, it's important to know how GRUB works. By default, it requires an initial RAM disk file, initrd-*versionnumber*.img. If GRUB can't find this file, it'll give you a file not found error. Since your computer does not boot, you'll need to boot with a rescue disc before you can fix the initrd file. Remember to make sure that the filename matches the name shown in /boot/grub/grub.conf *exactly*.

You can repeat this process with the vmlinuz file or the root directive in grub.conf. Make sure to have backups of key files so you can restore your original configuration. When you repeat this process, what happens after you select a kernel from the GRUB menu? Do you see a different error? Is it associated with a different file?

Understanding these answers can help you learn to use GRUB messages to more precisely diagnose specific problems with Linux.

Lab 4

If you've just added the new hard drive, you'll need to set up partitions or use the entire hard drive for PEs. Based on the premises of the lab, you have the entire SCSI /dev/sdg hard drive available, so you can just allocate this entire hard drive as PEs with the following command:

```
# pvcreate /dev/sdg
```

The next step is to extend the VG, **Volume00**, to include the newly configured PEs. You can do so with the following command:

```
# vgextend Volume00 /dev/sdg
```

With the additional PEs at your disposal, you can increase the size of the LV allocated to the /var directory. For example, if you wanted to increase the size to 2GB, you could run the following command:

```
# lvextend -L2G /dev/Volume00/LogVol00
```

A

Sample Exam 1

T

he following questions will help you measure your understanding of the material presented in this book.

As discussed in the introduction, the RHCE exam consists of two different, equally weighted sections: Troubleshooting and System Maintenance (2.5 hours) and Installation and Configuration (3.0 hours). There are RHCE and RHCT components to each section. To earn the RHCE, you need to meet all of the following requirements. To earn the RHCT, you need to meet the noted RHCT requirements.

On the Troubleshooting and System Maintenance section:

- Successfully complete all five RHCT-level problems within the first hour.
- Answer enough RHCE requirements (three of five) to earn an overall section score of 80 (of 100).

On the Installation and Configuration section:

- Earn a score of 70 or higher on the RHCT components.
- Address enough issues correctly to get a grade of 70 on the RHCE components.

Both exams are "closed book." However, you are allowed to use any documentation, such as man pages, that you can find on the Red Hat Enterprise Linux computer. You are allowed a pen or pencil and paper to make any notes that you might need.

If you pass the RHCT components of both sections, you'll qualify as a Red Hat Certified Technician. If you pass the RHCT and RHCE components of both exams, you will also become a Red Hat Certified Engineer.

In most cases, there is no one solution, no single method to solve a problem or install a service. There are a nearly infinite number of options with Linux, so I can't cover all possible scenarios.

Troubleshooting and System Maintenance

For this sample section, you need a computer that you're willing to dedicate for experimental purposes. Actual troubleshooting questions require the installation of the latest version of Red Hat Enterprise Linux, configured with a specific problem. The exam conditions would delete any and all data that you have on that computer. One option is a virtual machine solution such as that provided by VMware; as of this writing, no-cost subscriptions for VMware Server are available at www.vmware.com. I used VMware, using the tips that I describe in "Studying with a Virtual Machine" in the Online Learning Center (http://highered.mhhe.com/sites/0072264543), to write much of this book. Another alternative is Xen, also described in "Studying with a Virtual Machine."

If possible, get a friend, fellow student, or colleague to help set up the exercises for this exam. That's the best way to simulate real-world conditions. As shown in the RHCE and RHCT Exam Prep guide at www.redhat.com/training/rhce/examprep.html, you may have to boot into different runlevels, solve networking and host name problems, configure the GUI, add partitions of various types, and use standard command line tools to analyze and configure your system. You can use any documentation that you can find on your Red Hat Enterprise Linux computer; however, you're not allowed to reinstall Linux to address these problems.

You can't pass either exam unless you solve all of the RHCT-level troubleshooting problems. On the other hand, you need to budget your time judiciously; if you can't solve one RHCE-level problem, you may want to give up and move on to the next problem. But you may not be able to go back. You may be able to debug the next problem in just a few minutes. Even if you have time left over at the end of the section, you may not be able to go back and will not get any credit for any problems that you abandon.

These are not actual questions, but exercises consistent with the guidelines in the Red Hat Exam Prep guide. As exercises, they have no answers per se; however, they include a lot of information that can help you as a Linux administrator. However, I've set them up in a format that can allow someone else to set up exercises similar to what I'm guessing you *might* see on the Red Hat exams.

Even for these exercises, *do not use a production computer.* Some or all of these exercises are designed to make Linux unbootable. If you're unable to recover from the steps documented in these exercises, you may need to reinstall Red Hat Enterprise Linux. Saving any data that you have on your computer at that point may not be possible.

Troubleshooting and System Maintenance Exercise: RHCT Components

There are five problems on the RHCT part of this section. You have to reconfigure your computer to address all five problems appropriately, within the first hour of your exam. In this exercise, you'll set up five different problems on the same computer or virtual machine.

Ideally, you'll have a friend or classmate who can help you prepare your computer. Assume that you have a network server with the RHEL installation files. When your friend or classmate installs RHEL on this text computer, assume that you're on a network with an IP address of 10.20.30.0 (you can substitute a different network IP address if you want). Include the GNOME Desktop Environment in the installation. Then have your friend or classmate take the following steps:

1. Configure an RHEL system with some empty space on a hard drive. For the purpose of this section, I'll assume that you've configured a system with at least 5000MB of free space.

2. If you have a DHCP server on your network, disconnect or deactivate it.

3. Configure an IP address for your network card of 10.20.30.40, with a network mask of 255.255.255.0. You can use a tool such as **system-config-network**. Once saved, assign an IP address in /etc/hosts of 10.20.30.50 to the local host name; for example, on my /etc/hosts, I've configured:

```
127.0.0.1   localhost.localdomain   localhost
10.20.30.50 enterprise5
```

4. If necessary, configure this system to start in runlevel 3 by changing the appropriate command in /etc/inittab to:

```
id:3:initdefault
```

5. Make the system start with the KDE Display Manager for a login screen; open /etc/X11/prefdm, and a few lines inside the file, set:

```
preferred=kdm
```

6. Deactivate the **named** (DNS) services, and make sure it isn't active on reboot. The simplest way is with the following command:

```
# chkconfig named off
```

7. Back up and then edit /etc/X11/xorg.conf; delete the first **EndSection** directive.

8. Make sure SELinux is disabled the next time this system is booted. The quickest way is to set **SELINUX=disabled** in /etc/sysconfig/selinux.

9. Run the **poweroff** command. It is now ready for this part of the exam.

10. Now have the person taking the exam start the computer. Do not tell the candidate about the steps you took to prepare this computer. Tell him or her that there are problems with the configuration of the local network card (suggest that the candidate try pinging the local host name on the LAN) and an error associated with logging into the GUI. This computer should be configured to start the GUI automatically when Linux is booted, with a GDM login screen. Finally, the candidate should dedicate the remaining free space on the hard drive as a swap partition. Tell the candidate that you'll check his or her work after a reboot.

Troubleshooting and System Maintenance: RHCE Components

You have to solve three of these five simulated RHCE-level problems correctly. Your time starts after you've answered *all* of the simulated RHCT problems correctly; thus, you'll have at least 1.5 hours for this part of the exam. It's best if a friend or classmate helps you prepare your computer. Assume that you have access to a network server with the RHEL installation files.

You may want to have your friend or classmate prepare additional questions. Some boot exercises can be easily created from the Scenario & Solution list in Chapter 16. Other exercises on network services can be created based on what you've learned in Chapters 7 and 9–15. Exercises related to adding, removing, and resizing logical volumes can be developed from the information in Chapter 8.

In these exercises, you'll be working with an RHEL computer with an error in a key file created by a friend or classmate. Assume that you have a network server with the RHEL installation files. This should be on a system with some free unpartitioned space on the hard drive. Assuming you've run the RHCT exercise, you can use the swap partition created then; delete the associated entry from your /etc/fstab, and delete the partition using **fdisk** or **parted**. (Just don't remove both swap partitions.)

You'll also need a computer on which you can boot directly from your CD drive, so you can use the first Red Hat installation CD. (If you can boot from the USB, you can substitute a specially prepared boot USB drive described in Chapter 2.) Then have the person preparing your exam take the following steps:

1. If there are problems with the solutions in the RHCT troubleshooting section, you may need to reinstall or restore from a VMware snapshot.

2. Make sure to enable SELinux. Do not make any changes to the SELinux defaults.

3. Enable the firewall, and do not enable SMTP as a trusted service.

4. Open the /boot/grub/grub.conf configuration file, and create a typo in the boot stanza. For this exercise, change the **initrd** directive by removing the .*img* from the end of the file name; in other words for example, you might change

   ```
   initrd /initrd-2.6.18-8.el5.img
   ```

   to

   ```
   initrd /initrd-2.6.18-8.el5
   ```

5. Install sendmail if needed; make sure the sendmail.mc file is in the original configuration, including the following directive:

   ```
   DAEMON_OPTIONS(`Port=smtp,Addr=127.0.0.1, Name=MTA')dnl
   ```

6. In /etc/fstab, change the directive associated with the top-level root directory. Introduce a typo. For example, you might change

   ```
   /dev/VolGroup00/LogVol00 /   ext3   defaults   1 1
   ```

   to

   ```
   /dev/VolGroup00/LogVol0 /   ext3   defaults   1 1
   ```

7. Define a standard root password, which you'll tell your partner or candidate.

8. Make sure you have a boot disc or USB key that can serve as a rescue disc. As the Red Hat Exam Prep guide requires the use of the first RHEL

installation CD as a rescue disc, make sure that your computer can boot from this CD.

9. Have the person taking the exam start the computer. Do not tell the person about the steps you took to prepare this computer. Make sure the first RHEL installation CD is available. Advise that there may be a boot problem, that a mail server needs to be configured for more than just the local system, and provide the root user password that you created. Note that there is a firewall that can't be disabled for most services. Finally, advise the candidate to create a new swap partition of 100MB based on a logical volume created from existing free space.

Troubleshooting and System Maintenance Discussion

You shouldn't read this discussion until you've had a chance to try out the problems. I describe one possible solution to each problem. The solutions that you come up with can vary. The method you use doesn't matter; the results are what count. As of this writing, in the Troubleshooting and System Maintenance section, you can't reinstall RHEL on the target computer, and you can't go to the Internet for help during the exam.

Troubleshooting and System Maintenance Exam: RHCT-Level Problems

To pass either exam, you need to solve all five RHCT-level Troubleshooting and System Maintenance problems. In this simulation, you'll need to:

- Find any problems with the configuration of the local network card; try pinging the local host name.
- Make sure the computer is configured to start the GUI automatically when Linux is booted.
- Solve the errors that keep you from logging into the GUI.
- When booting into the GUI, make sure it boots into a GDM login screen.
- Dedicate the remaining free space on the hard drive as a swap partition.

To accomplish this, take the following steps (there may be other ways of solving these problems):

1. When you first start this computer, watch the start messages carefully. Make a note of anything unusual.
2. Try pinging the local host name. What happens? What are sources for local host names? Is DNS active? If not, where does the **ping** command search?

Make any needed changes to /etc/hosts, and make sure it corresponds to what you see when you run **ifconfig** on the local network card.

3. To make sure the system boots directly into the GUI, you need to make sure the default runlevel in /etc/inittab is appropriate (runlevel 5). The system may offer you the chance to run the Display Configuration tool. It might work. If there are still problems, it's possible that some needed services aren't active in runlevel 5, or perhaps there are problems with a key configuration file, such as /etc/X11/xorg.conf.

4. When you move into runlevel 5, perhaps by reboot or with the **init 5** command, what happens? Based on what you know from the book, what could be the cause? Check the space available in partitions associated with the /home and /tmp directories, or even some sort of error related to the X Window configuration files, including xorg.conf and xinitrc. If it's service related, make sure that service starts the next time you boot this system.

5. If that all works, you'll see an X login screen when you start or boot in runlevel 5. But remember that you need to make sure you're booted into the GDM screen.

6. Now to dedicate the remaining free space as a swap partition, open **fdisk** or **parted**, and create a new partition with the available free space. Make sure it's associated with the Linux swap file type, and format it with the **mkswap** command.

   Once created, you'll then want to add it to /etc/fstab, as a swap partition. For example, if the new freshly formatted partition is /dev/hda10, you could add the following directive to /etc/fstab:

   ```
   /dev/hda10   swap   swap   defaults   0 0
   ```

7. Reboot your computer to make sure your changes work.

8. Show your partner or instructor what you did.

Troubleshooting and System Maintenance: RHCE-Level Problems

You'll see what's wrong when you boot RHEL. Be prepared to use the first RHEL installation CD to rescue this system. If you get instructions for a network source for the RHEL installation files, take careful notes. You've been told that:

- There may be a boot problem.
- A mail server needs to be configured for more than just the local system.
- You know the root user password created by your partner or instructor.

- You need to create a new swap partition of 100MB based on a logical volume created from existing free space.
- There may also be related issues associated with a firewall.

1. When you see your boot loader, select your current version of RHEL.

2. Watch the messages as they scroll across the screen. You'll probably see a message similar to:

```
Error 15: File Not Found
```

3. Chances are, this is related to the last message you've seen, probably something like this:

```
initrd /initrd-2.6.18-8.el5
```

4. If you're paying attention, you'll realize that this file name isn't right. You can confirm this from the GRUB command line; reboot and press **e** (unless there's password protection) to see the commands associated with the stanza. Make a note of the directives, then press **c** for a **grub>** prompt.

5. At the **grub>** prompt, type the root directive, probably something like:

```
grub> root (hd0,0)
```

6. Assuming you get a proper response, you should be able to follow up with the other commands associated with the stanza, as you saw in step 4. The error was "file not found." Use command completion to make sure the files cited actually exist.

7. After entering the noted commands, enter the **boot** command. If it's correct, Linux will boot normally and you won't even need the first Red Hat installation CD.

8. Well, Linux isn't booting normally yet. You'll see an error message like:

```
fsck.ext3: No such file or directory while trying to open
/dev/VolGroup00/LogVol0
```

followed by the following prompt; enter the root password (as defined by your proctor or instructor).

```
Give root password for maintenance
(or type Control-D to continue):
```

9. Run the **mount** command to see mounted filesystems. You should see a message like this:

```
/dev/mapper/VolGroup00-LogVol00 on / type ext3 (rw)
```

This should give you a hint to the problem. You should be able to confirm that there is no /dev/VolGroup00/LogVol0 device, but /dev/VolGroup00/LogVol00 and /dev/VolGroup00/LogVol01.

10. But even though the output suggests that files in this volume are writable, it's not so. To make it writable, run the following command:

    ```
    # mount -o remount /dev/VolGroup00/LogVol00 /
    ```

11. Now you should be able to modify your /etc/fstab. You should see the typo now. Change

    ```
    /dev/VolGroup00/LogVol0 on / type ext3 (rw)
    ```

    to (change is bolded)

    ```
    /dev/VolGroup00/LogVol00 on / type ext3 (rw)
    ```

12. You should also be able to mount the /boot directory; if /etc/fstab is in sufficient order, simply run

    ```
    # mount /boot
    ```

13. You can now open the GRUB configuration file, /boot/grub/grub.conf, where you can correct the typo that caused the original "file not found" problem.

14. Reboot to make sure you've solved the boot problems.

15. Install the mail server of your choice, sendmail or postfix. If it's sendmail, comment out the following directive by adding a **dnl** in front:

    ```
    DAEMON_OPTIONS(`Port=smtp,Addr=127.0.0.1, Name=MTA')dnl
    ```

16. Make sure to activate the sendmail service and use **chkconfig** to activate it the next time you boot:

    ```
    # service sendmail start
    # chkconfig sendmail on
    ```

    Of course, similar actions are possible if you install postfix, but that's another option left for the candidate.

17. Don't forget to make sure that mail (SMTP) services are allowed through any existing firewall; it's easiest with the Security Level Configuration tool.

18. Check the current space allocated to swap with the **top** command.

19. Finally, you can create the new swap volume of 100MB from existing free space. All you need for a logical volume is one partition, created to the Linux LVM file type. You can use **fdisk** or **parted** for this purpose. Remember, if you use **fdisk**, run **partprobe** to reread the partition table. Then create a PV,

assign the space to a VG, and allocate it to an LV. You can use commands such as **pvcreate**, **vgcreate**, and **lvcreate**, or the Logical Volume Management GUI tool. For example, if you've created an LVM partition on /dev/hda10, run the following commands:

```
# pvcreate /dev/hda10
# vgcreate vgrp1 /dev/hda10
# lvcreate --size=100M vgrp1 /dev/hda10
```

You'll see the following message from the **lvcreate** command:

```
Logical volume "lvol0" created
```

This should create a new device, /dev/vgrp1/lvol0; you can confirm the new volume with the **lvs** command.

20. Now format the new device:

```
# mkswap /dev/vgrp1/lvol0
```

21. Add the new swap device to your /etc/fstab, to make sure it's read the next time you boot Linux. On my system, I did that with the following directive:

```
/dev/vgrp1/lvol0   swap    swap    defaults   0 0
```

22. You can activate the new device with the **swapon /dev/vgrp1/lvol0** command, check active LVs with the **lvs** command, and see the new space allocated to swap with the **top** command.

23. If there are SELinux-related issues, review the Setroubleshooter, which can be started in the GUI with the **sealert -b** command. Follow any recent recommendations, especially since your test system was last booted.

24. Reboot the system, and make sure the changes you've made are implemented.

Installation and Configuration

The Installation and Configuration section is the second part of the Red Hat exam. If you're taking the RHCT, you're allowed 2.0 hours; if you're taking the RHCE, you're allowed 3.0 hours to install and configure Red Hat Enterprise Linux. You may get partial credit on some of these problems. You have access to the Red Hat Enterprise Linux installation files through a network server (the Exam Prep guide specifies a network installation). Once Red Hat Enterprise Linux is installed, you also have access to the man pages as well as any other documentation that you may have installed.

If you're studying for the RHCT, you can limit your focus to the RHCT-level skills; if you're studying for the RHCE, you'll need to complete all RHCT- and RHCE-level skills, in the time allotted.

No specific techniques or commands are required. Any reasonable technique is allowed if it gets you to the objective. For example, if you need to limit access to a specific service, you can use **iptables**, /etc/hosts.deny, or even SELinux. As long as it does the job, the configuration can get you full credit for that part of the exam.

You may need to limit access to network servers to specific users or other computers. However, this is a certification exam. Do not expect to have *physical* access to any other computer to test your settings. You will not have access to any outside networks such as the Internet.

If you're going for your RHCT, you'll need a grade of at least 70 percent in the RHCE-level skills. If you're going for your RHCE, you'll need a score of 70 percent on both sections.

e x a m

ⓦ a t c h

Read the entire Installation and Configuration exam before you finish installing RHEL. It's easier to configure RAID and logical volumes during the installation process. It can save time to install required servers during the installation process. And remember, you can start configuring RHEL through the CTRL-ALT-F2 console even while packages are being installed.

If you're preparing for the RHCT exam, you can ignore the RHCE issues. If you're preparing for the RHCE exam, you'll want to address *all* requirements in this section. Remember, the RHCE is inclusive of the RHCT.

Server Installation Problem: RHCT-Level Skills

Install Red Hat Enterprise Linux. The following conditions specify a network server, configured with some very specific partitions. You'll also need to limit access to some or all of your network servers to specific users, computers, entire networks, or more.

Install Linux over a network connection with the partitions shown in Table A-1. The sizes shown are minimums. Use a reasonable size for the swap partition.

TABLE A-1	Filesystem	Size
Available Red Hat Enterprise Linux Kernels (and Related Packages)	/boot	100MB
	/	4000MB
	/home	1000MB
	/var	1000MB

You'll want a RAID 6 array for the /home directory where your users can store at least 1000MB of data. Assume this computer has an IP address of 10.11.12.13 on the 10.11.12.0/255.255.255.0 network.

Configure the following users for RHEL: nancy, randy, donna, and mike. Make nancy and randy part of a group named angels. Create a /home/angels directory and allow them to share files without having to change permissions or ownership on any file they put in this directory. Do not give donna or mike read privileges on this directory. Configure quotas for donna and mike to limit the space available in their home directories to 100MB.

Set up Access Control Lists on the /home directory partition. Set up a project .test file in user mike's home directory. Configure ACLs on project.test to allow user donna to read this file.

Make **kdm** the default window manager. Make sure users are directed to the graphical login interface when RHEL starts on this computer. Configure a connection to an LDAP client, on the vtc.com domain, on IP address 10.11.12.15.

Set up a job to delete all of the regular files in the /home/mike directory on the second day of every month at 3:50 A.M. Configure the automounter to connect to the NFS installation source on the /var/ftp/pub directory from IP address 192.168.0.50 (substitute the directory and IP address from your own network accordingly). Connect to and configure a remote CUPS printer; make it the default for this computer.

Install The GIMP after installation. Install the later version of the kernel that's available from the network installation source. Set up another GRUB stanza to boot your system in runlevel 1.

Finally, allow the local system to accept source routing. While normally disabled, it's often associated with systems configured as routers.

Server Installation Problem: RHCE-Level Skills

In this part of the exam, you'll configure a number of different servers on the RHEL computer.

When you install, configure a logical volume, dedicated to the /var directory. Enable ssh logins, and limit access to the local network. Configure Samba to share the /home/angels directory with the users specified earlier. Configure a vsFTP server. Limit access to computers on the LAN. Support access from users over FTP from one other system on the LAN to their home directories. Set up a local NTP server, accessible to other workstations on the LAN.

Configure an NFS server to share the files in /tmp only with users on the LAN. Configure Apache to serve a homepage.html page from within the /var/www/html directory. Do not limit access to the computers on the LAN. Add a secure.html page for connections to a secure Web server. Set up a proxy server that can be used by other computers on your LAN. Make sure SELinux settings allow these options.

Set up a Kickstart file, ready to use with a boot CD. Copy it to a USB key in that system's top-level directory. Configure a local caching nameserver. Add a non-secure POP3 server for the local network; do not support IMAP or secure protocols on that server.

When you reboot your computer, all of the services that you've created and settings that you've made should be enabled automatically.

Installation Discussion

Since there is no one way to set up a Red Hat Enterprise Linux configuration, there is no one right answer for the listed requirements. But there are some general things to remember. You need to make sure your changes work after a reboot. If you're going for the RHCE, you'll need to make sure that the services that you set up are active at the appropriate runlevels. For example, if you're configuring Apache, it should be active for at least runlevels 3 and 5.

First, examine the RHCT-level skills. You can set up the required partitions through Disk Druid during the RHEL installation process, or with the **fdisk** or **parted** utilities after RHEL is installed. Remember, you need (at least) four partitions for a RAID 6 array. If you're creating the array after installation, use the **mdadm** command.

Remember your CIDR notation; 10.11.12.0/24 specifies a subnet mask of 255.255.255.0. Use the SGID bit and assign 770 permissions on /home/angels, and make sure to assign group ownership of that directory to angels. Before you can configure quotas, you'll need to remount /home with at least the **usrquota** setting, and add it to /etc/fstab. Create appropriate quota configuration files with **quotacheck -cuvm** (or reboot); and then activate quotas with **quotaon**; configure quotas for users donna and mike, using the **edquota** command.

Before configuring ACLs, you need to set up the applicable partition with **acl** settings. You should do so in /etc/fstab. To make it work before a reboot, remount the /home directory partition with the **mount -o remount,acl /dev/partitionnumber /home** command. If it works, you'll be able to confirm with the **mount** command by itself.

Make your default window manager through the /etc/X11/prefdm file; in this case, you can set **preferred=kdm**. Remember, the GUI login is associated with runlevel 5 in /etc/inittab. Setting up a connection to an LDAP server means understanding the distinguished names associated with the vtc.com domain, where **dc=vtc** and **dc=com**, and the LDAP server is on IP address 10.11.12.15.

Setting up a job to delete files in any specific directory on a periodic basis is a job for the **cron** daemon. You can create your own job with **crontab**, or you can set it up through a script similar to **/etc/cron.daily/tmpwatch**. For example, I ran **crontab -e** as user michael and added the following:

```
SHELL=/bin/bash
PATH=/sbin:/bin:/usr/sbin:/usr/bin
```

```
MAILTO=michael
HOME=/home/michael

50 3 * * * rm /home/mike/*
```

To configure the automounter to point to the network installation source, you
need to activate the **autofs** service. Assume the server properly shares NFS from
the 192.168.0.50, and you should be able to access the share with the following
command:

```
# ls /net/192.168.0.50/var/ftp/pub
```

It's easiest to install a new printer with the Printer Configuration tool. If it's a remote
printer, you'll need the data associated with the source, such as the computer and
share names.

To install The GIMP and any new Linux kernel, you can even access the
installation server directory associated with the automounter.

When you need to update a Linux kernel, make sure to *install*, and not upgrade,
the kernel. This allows you to go back to the old working kernel, and it automatically
adds the option to the boot loader menu. To add a runlevel 1 option in the default
GRUB boot loader file, copy an existing stanza and add **1** to the end of the kernel
directive. It's advisable to add a label such as "single user mode" to the new stanza.

To enable source routing after the next reboot, set the following in /etc/sysctl.conf:

```
net.ipv4.conf.default.accept_source_route = 1
```

If you need source routing enabled immediately, you could run the following:

```
# echo "1" > /proc/sys/net/ipv4/conf/default/accept_source_route
```

Now let's examine the RHCE issues in this section.

It's easiest to install logical volumes during the installation process. Don't forget
to do so while using Disk Druid. Remember, it's 1000MB on the /var directory.
Sharing /home/angels through Samba for specified users means adding them to the
Samba authentication list with the **smbpasswd** command. Limiting vsFTP access
to the LAN can be done using appropriate commands in the /etc/hosts.deny file.
Remember to allow users access to their home directories in /etc/vsftpd/vsftpd.conf.

Sharing /tmp through NFS means configuring this directory in /etc/exports
(where you can also limit access to the local network), and applying **exportfs -a**.
Make sure that the appropriate NFS daemons are active, including **portmap** and
rpc.mountd. If you have problems, it may be related to SELinux. Change the
DirectoryIndex in the default httpd.conf to make Apache read the default Web
page from homepage.html. Add a **DirectoryIndex secure.html** directive to ssl.conf
in the /etc/httpd/conf.d/ directory.

Configuring a Squid Proxy Server is straightforward; all you need are three lines associated with **visible_hostname**, **acl** for the local network, and **http_access allow** to limit access to that network. Examples are embedded in the default Squid configuration file, /etc/squid/squid.conf.

Make sure the SELinux booleans are compatible with these settings. If you use non-standard directories, you may have to apply the **chcon** command to make sure these directories have the same SELinux labels as the default directories.

Before the ks.cfg file is ready, you'll need to make sure the appropriate partition commands are active. You can then copy it as ks.cfg to the desired USB key, which you can call from the installation boot prompt with the **linux ks=hd:sdb:/ks.cfg** command (you may need to substitute another device name for **sdb**).

Configuring a local caching nameserver is straightforward; just install the caching-nameserver RPM and activate the **named** daemon. Adding a non-secure POP3 server means installing the Dovecot service and making sure to list only **pop3** with the **protocols** directive. Making an NTP server work is a two-step process; first you need to configure it as a client. During this exercise, it's okay to do so with a connection to the default servers, based on the Red Hat Date/Time Configuration tool. During the exam, you may not have Internet access, so follow the instructions from your proctor as closely as possible. Edit the /etc/ntp.conf file; there's a commented model for a local network, which you can customize for your LAN's network address.

B

Sample Exam 2

T he following questions will help you measure your understanding of the material presented in this book.

As discussed in the introduction, the RHCE exam consists of two different, equally weighted exams: Troubleshooting and System Maintenance (2.5 hours) and Installation and Configuration (3.0 hours). There are RHCE and RHCT components on each exam. To earn the RHCE, you need to meet the following requirements.

On the Troubleshooting and System Maintenance exam, you need to

- Successfully complete all five RHCT-level problems within the first hour.
- Answer enough RHCE requirements (three of five) to earn an overall section score of 80 (of 100).

On the Installation and Configuration section, you need to

- Earn a score of 70 or higher on the RHCT components.
- Address enough issues correctly to get a grade of 70 on the RHCE components.

Both exams are "closed book." However, you are allowed to use any documentation that you can find on the Red Hat Enterprise Linux computer, such as man pages. You are allowed a pen or pencil and paper to make any notes that you might need.

If you pass the RHCT components of both exams, you'll qualify as a Red Hat Certified Technician. If you pass the RHCT and RHCE components of both exams, you will also become a Red Hat Certified Engineer.

In most cases, there is no one solution, no single method to solve a problem or install a service. There are a nearly infinite number of options with Linux, so I can't cover all possible scenarios.

Troubleshooting and System Maintenance

For this sample section, you need a computer that you're willing to dedicate for experimental purposes. Actual troubleshooting questions require the installation of the latest version of Red Hat Enterprise Linux, configured with a specific problem. The exam conditions would delete any and all data that you have on that computer. One option is a virtual machine solution such as that provided by VMware; as of this writing, no-cost subscriptions for VMware Server are available at www.vmware.com. I used VMware, using the tips that I describe in "Studying with a Virtual Machine" in the Online Learning Center (http://highered.mhhe.com/sites/0072264543), to write much of this book. Another alternative is Xen, also described in "Studying with a Virtual Machine."

If possible, get a friend, fellow student, or colleague to help set up the exercises for this exam. That's the best way to simulate real-world conditions. As shown in the RHCE Exam Prep guide at www.redhat.com/training/rhce/examprep.html, you may have to boot into different runlevels, solve networking and host name problems, configure the GUI, add partitions of various types, and use standard command line tools to analyze and configure your system. You can use any documentation that you can find on your Red Hat Enterprise Linux computer; however, you're not allowed to reinstall Linux to address these problems.

You can't pass either exam unless you solve all of the RHCT-level troubleshooting problems within the first hour. On the other hand, you need to budget your time judiciously; if you can't solve one RHCE-level problem, you may want to give up and move on to the next problem. But you may not be able to go back. You may be able to debug the next problem in just a few minutes, but even if you have time left over at the end of the section, you may not be able to go back to skipped problems and will not get any credit for the problems that you have abandoned.

These are not actual questions, but exercises consistent with the guidelines in the Red Hat Exam Prep guide. As exercises, they have no answers per se; however, they include a lot of information that can help you as a Linux administrator. However, I've set them up in a format that can allow someone else to set up exercises similar to what I'm guessing you *might* see on the Red Hat exams.

Even for these exercises, *do not use a production computer*. Some or all of these exercises are designed to make Linux unbootable. If you're unable to recover from the steps documented in these exercises, you may need to reinstall Red Hat Enterprise Linux. Saving any data that you have on your computer at that point may not be possible.

Troubleshooting and System Maintenance Exam: RHCT Components

There are five problems on the RHCT part of this section. You have to reconfigure your computer to address all five problems appropriately, within the first hour of your exam. In this exercise, you'll set up five different problems on the same computer or virtual machine.

Ideally, you'll have a friend or classmate who can help you prepare your computer. Assume that you have a network server with the RHEL installation files. When you install RHEL on this text computer, assume that you're on a network with an IP address of 172.16.32.0 (you can substitute a different network IP address if you desire). Include the K Desktop Environment in the installation. Then have your colleague take the following steps:

1. Install RHEL with at least 256MB of space that is unallocated to any partition. Create a /data directory on a logical volume.

2. Make sure RHEL boots from the command line, by setting the **id** directive in /etc/inittab to runlevel 1.

3. Set up Firefox to open automatically in the default GNOME Desktop Environment, using the Sessions manager (which you can open with the **gnome-session-properties** command in the GUI). Remember, this is user dependent, so you'll have to specify the user whose GUI the candidate is to configure.

4. Open /etc/X11/xorg.conf; create a typo in the **Screen** directive as defined in the first stanza. In my configuration, I changed

   ```
   Screen   0   "Screen0" 0 0
   ```

   to

   ```
   Screen   0   "Screen" 0 0
   ```

5. In the /etc/sysconfig/network file, make sure that **NETWORKING=no** and **HOSTNAME=localhost**.

6. Disable SELinux; the simplest method, since you'll soon reboot, is to set SELinux=disabled **in /etc/sysconfig/selinux**.

7. In /etc/hosts, make sure the directive associated with the localhost IPv4 address is shown as:

   ```
   127.0.0.1   localhost.localdomain   localhost   localhost
   ```

8. Run the **poweroff** command on the computer. It is now ready for this part of the exam.

9. Have the person taking the exam start the computer. Do not tell the candidate about the steps you took to prepare this computer. Tell him or her to

   - Allocate half of the free space on the current drive to a partition dedicated to the /test directory.
   - Make Linux boot into the GUI.
   - Address any problems you see the next time you boot Linux.
   - Configure the GNOME desktop to open a command line window for the selected user when you boot.
   - Assign a host name of enterprise5 to this system, and configure the network card to connect with DHCP.

Troubleshooting and System Maintenance: RHCE Components

You have to solve three of the five simulated RHCE-level problems correctly. Your time starts after you've answered *all* of the simulated RHCT problems correctly; thus, you'll have at least 1.5 hours for this part of the exam. Ideally, you'll have a friend or classmate help you prepare your computer. Assume that you have access to a network server with the RHEL installation files.

You may want to have your friend or classmate prepare additional questions. Some boot exercises can be easily created from the Scenario and Solution list in Chapter 16. Other exercises on network services can be created based on what you've learned in Chapters 7 and 9–15. Exercises related to adding, removing, and resizing logical volumes can be developed from the information in Chapter 8.

In these exercises, you'll be working with an RHEL computer with some key files messed up. Ideally, you'll have a friend or classmate help you prepare your computer. Assume that you have a network server with the RHEL installation files. This should be on a system with some free unpartitioned space on the hard drive, and one filesystem, /tmp, on a logical volume.

You'll also need a computer on which you can boot directly from your CD drive, so you can use the first Red Hat installation CD. (If you can boot from the USB, you can substitute a specially prepared boot USB drive described in Chapter 2.) Then walk away, and have the colleague who is preparing the exam take the following steps:

1. Copy and back up the /etc/inittab configuration file. One possible name is /etc/bak.inittab.

2. Open /etc/inittab file in a text editor.

3. Change the *x* in the **id:x:initdefault** line to 4.

4. Comment out the **l4:4:wait:/etc/rc.d/rc 4** line in /etc/inittab. Save your changes.

5. Activate SELinux in enforcing mode.

6. Change the kernel directive in the GRUB configuration file (/boot/grub/grub .conf), to point the root directive as shown:

   ```
   root=LABEL=/boot
   ```

7. Open /etc/fstab, and comment out the directive associated with the /boot directory filesystem; the result should be similar to:

   ```
   LABEL=/boot    /boot    ext3    defaults   1 2
   ```

8. Make sure that the Apache, NFS, sendmail, and vsFTP services aren't set to start in runlevel 4, but are set to start in other standard runlevels (2, 3, and 5). To make this work, you can use commands such as:

   ```
   # chkconfig httpd on
   # chkconfig httpd --level 4 off
   ```

9. Disable SELinux protection for the Apache, NFS, and vsFTP server daemons. Use the SELinux Management Tool.

10. Set up a regular standard firewall with the **system-config-securitylevel** command. Don't allow in any special traffic.

11. Check your /etc/hosts.allow and /etc/hosts.deny files. If there are rules related to **ftpd** or **ALL** services in either file, comment them out.

12. Open the Samba configuration file, and comment out the **[homes]** stanza. If required, in the SELinux Management tool, disable the Allow Samba To Share Users Home Directories option.

13. Make sure you have a boot disc or USB key that can serve as a rescue disc. As the Red Hat Exam Prep guide requires the use of the first RHEL installation CD as a rescue disc, make sure your computer can boot from this CD.

14. Use the **poweroff** command to stop Linux.

15. Tell the RHCE candidate that he or she will face a challenge during the boot process, will need to make sure /boot is properly mounted, and will need to reduce the space available to the /tmp filesystem on a logical volume. Ask the candidate to make sure the NFS, sendmail, Apache, and vsFTP services are working and available to other systems. Suggest that if SELinux is deactivated, everything else has to be done perfectly.

Troubleshooting and System Maintenance Discussion

You shouldn't read this discussion until you've had a chance to try out the problems. I describe one possible solution to each problem. The solutions that you come up with can vary. The method you use doesn't matter; the result is what counts. As of this writing, in the Troubleshooting and System Maintenance section, you can't reinstall RHEL on the target computer and you can't go to the Internet for help during the exam.

Troubleshooting and System Maintenance Exam: RHCT-Level Problems

To pass either exam, you need to solve all five RHCT-level Troubleshooting and System Maintenance problems. In this simulation, you'll need to

- Allocate half of the free space on the current drive to a partition dedicated to the /test directory.
- Make Linux boot into the GUI.
- Address any problems you see the next time you boot Linux.
- Configure the GNOME desktop to open a command line window for the selected user when you boot.
- Assign a host name of enterprise5 to this system, and configure the network card to connect with DHCP.

Address the problems that you've been given. In most cases, there are other ways to solve these problems. When you boot this system, the first thing you'll see is this:

```
sh-3.1#
```

You may already recognize this as the root prompt associated with runlevel 1. But you need to make Linux boot into the GUI, which means you need to make Linux boot into runlevel 5. And this is controlled in /etc/inittab, with the following directive:

```
id:5:initdefault:
```

Now you can reboot, or just run **init 5** to move to that runlevel. But when you do, you'll see error messages related to the X Window, and are prompted for the root password to try to "fix" the problem. There's a key hint after you enter the password:

```
Data incomplete in file /etc/X11/xorg.conf
Undefined Screen "Screen" referenced by ServerLayout "Default Layout"
```

This suggests an error in the **ServerLayout** stanza in /etc/X11/xorg.conf. You could solve the problem here, but you're taken to the Display Settings Configuration tool, which is probably the quickest way to solve the problem. If successful, you'll see the GUI login screen.

When you log in, you'll see the Firefox Web browser. You could remove that from the applications that are automatically opened; all you need to do is make sure that a command line terminal is open. User applications in the GNOME desktop are driven by the GNOME Sessions tool and any existing .xinitrc file in that user's home directory. Add the command line terminal of your choice; the default for GNOME is **gnome-session**; **xterm** and **konsole**, if installed, are acceptable alternatives.

The simplest way to configure a host name and set networking to get address information from a DHCP server is with the GUI Network Configuration tool. You can also do this in /etc/sysconfig/network, /etc/hosts, and associated ifcfg-eth0 scripts.

Finally, to allocate free space to a new partition, you'll need to use the **fdisk** or **parted** utilities to create the partition, make sure it's the appropriate Linux file type, format it with a command such as **mkfs.ext3**, **mount** it to make sure it works, and add an appropriate directive to /etc/fstab to make sure it's mounted on /test the next time you boot Linux.

Troubleshooting and System Maintenance: RHCE-Level Problems

You'll see what's wrong when you try to log into RHEL. Be prepared to use the first RHEL installation CD to rescue this system. If you get instructions for a network source for the RHEL installation files, take careful notes. You've been told the following:

- You will face a challenge during the boot process.

- You'll want to make sure /boot is properly mounted.
- You'll need to reduce the space available to the /tmp filesystem on a logical volume.
- Make sure the NFS, sendmail, Apache, and vsFTP services are working and available to other systems.

(Yes, I know that's more than five problems.)

1. When you see your boot loader, probably GRUB, select your current version of RHEL.

2. Boot your RHEL computer. Watch the start messages carefully. In this case, you'll see the following messages, which could intimidate most Linux administrators:

```
setuproot: moving /dev failed: No such file or directory
setuproot: error mounting /proc: No such file or directory
setuproot: error mounting /sys: No such file or directory

Kernel panic - not syncing: Attempted to kill init!
```

3. Look at these messages carefully. If you're experienced with Linux, you'll recognize that RHEL experienced a kernel panic because it had trouble finding key directories. That suggests problems with the root directive in the GRUB configuration file.

4. Restart your computer. Insert the first RHEL installation CD, and set your computer to boot from this disk. At the installation prompt, type **linux rescue**. This assumes you have access to your installation source, just in case you need to reinstall the Linux kernel.

5. Proceed as if you're installing RHEL. Set up networking when prompted, as you may need access to some of the installation RPMs.

6. When you see the Rescue screen, click Continue. If it doesn't work, all that means is that Linux is having trouble mounting your system in read-write mode. In that case, you can select one of the other two options.

7. If successful, you'll see a note that your system has been mounted under /mnt/sysimage. Click OK, and then run the **chroot /mnt/sysimage** command at the prompt.

8. Look for the /boot directory. You won't see anything there, which suggests that it wasn't mounted. So use a command like **fdisk -l** to review configured partitions, to find a logical candidate for /boot, and **mount** it. Just as one example, I show the result from my VMware system—your output is likely to be quite different:

```
Disk /dev/sda: 5368 MB, 5368709120 bytes
255 heads, 63 sectors/track, 652 cylinders
Units = cylinders of 16065 * 512 = 8225280 bytes

   Device Boot    Start    End    Blocks   Id  System
/dev/sda1    *        1     14    104391   83  Linux
/dev/sda2          2677    652   5132767+  8e  Linux LVM
```

In this case, as the /boot directory can't be mounted on a logical volume, the only partition that could include the /boot directory files is /dev/sda1. So I follow up with this command (of course, if your system is different, substitute accordingly; if there are multiple possible /boot partitions, some trial and error may be required):

```
# mount /dev/sda1 /boot
```

9. Now you should be able to find the GRUB configuration file. As suggested earlier, there's a problem with the **root** directive:

```
root=LABEL=/boot
```

If you're as familiar as you should be with the GRUB configuration file, you'll see the error right away. The **root** directive in this line should point to the device associated with the top-level root directory. You'll find it in /etc/fstab:

```
/dev/VolGroup00/LogVol00  /  ext3  defaults 1 1
```

This tells me what should be associated with the **root** directive:

```
root=/dev/VolGroup00/LogVol00
```

If the **root** directive in the GRUB configuration file is associated with a partition device, you might see something like **LABEL=/** in /etc/fstab. In that case, you'd substitute the following:

```
root=LABEL=/
```

Alternatively, if you can't figure out the **LABEL** (with a command like **e2label /dev/hda1**), and the top-level root (/) directory is not on a logical volume, a **LABEL** may not have been assigned; just substitute the appropriate partition name:

```
root=/dev/sda2
```

10. Yes, you could also test this from the GRUB command line, as described in Chapter 3. But for this exercise, just reboot and see what happens. In rescue mode, type **exit** to get out of the **chroot** command, and then type the **exit** command again to reboot.

11. If you reboot, you'll note that the /boot directory still doesn't get mounted. Remember how mounting works—it depends on /etc/fstab. If you're observant, you'll see the directive associated with the /boot directory commented out. When you activate the command, /boot is mounted the next time you start this system. Alternatively, you can mount everything in /etc/fstab with the **mount -a** command.

12. At this time, make sure the noted services are active with a command like this:

```
# /etc/init.d/nfs status
```

When you see that NFS, vsFTP, Apache, and sendmail are not active, you could activate them and try rebooting. But if you're observant, you'll run a command like this:

```
# chkconfig --list httpd
httpd   0:off  1:off  2:on  3:on  4:on  5:on  6:off
```

You'll see that it's supposed to be on. This suggests another problem. If you know how the boot process works, you'll trace your way through /etc/inittab, and find the following problem directives:

```
id:4:initdefault:
```

```
#14:4:wait:/etc/rc.d/rc 4
```

These suggest that this configuration uses a non-standard runlevel, and since the script that starts services is commented out, no services in that runlevel are started. So all you absolutely need to do is change the default runlevel.

13. Modify /etc/inittab to reflect an appropriate default runlevel, such as 5, and reboot. You'll see the desired services running now.

14. To make sure the noted services are available, run commands such as this:

```
# service httpd status
```

15. Make sure the noted services are available to others. Make sure SELinux is active, and open up access through a firewall. It's easiest to do both with the Security Level Configuration tool, which now allows you to create access to all the noted services.

    If there are SELinux-related problems, they'll be shown with the SELinux troubleshooter, which can be started in the GUI with the **sealert -b** command. When there are problems, this tool often suggests solutions.

If you have access to a remote system, say via SSH, it's best to log into the remote system. Then you can make sure you (and others on the network) have remote access to the noted services.

16. Finally, to reduce the amount of space available to a volume, you'll first need to back up the information in that volume. The **ext2online** command has been replaced with **resize2fs**, which can reduce the size of a volume. Alternatively, you can also back up the information on /tmp, unmount that directory, reduce the number of LV extents on the associated volume, remount /tmp, and restore the information. The key command is **lvreduce**; for example, the following command reduces the allocation for the noted volume to (approximately) 50MB:

```
# lvreduce -L 50M /dev/vgrp0/lvol0/
```

Installation and Configuration

The Installation and Configuration section is the second part of the Red Hat exam. If you're taking the RHCT, you're allowed 2.0 hours; if you're taking the RHCE, you're allowed 3.0 hours to install and configure Red Hat Enterprise Linux. You may get partial credit on some of these problems. You'll have access to the Red Hat Enterprise Linux installation files through a network server (the Exam Prep guide specifies a network installation). Once Red Hat Enterprise Linux is installed, you'll also have access to the man pages as well as any other documentation that you may have installed.

If you're studying for the RHCT, you can limit your focus to the RHCT-level skills; if you're studying for the RHCE, you'll need to complete all RHCT- and RHCE-level skills, in the time allotted.

No specific techniques or commands are required. Any reasonable technique is allowed if it gets you to the objective. For example, if you need to limit access to a specific service, you can use **iptables**, /etc/hosts.deny, or even SELinux. As long as it does the job, the configuration can get you full credit for that part of the exam.

You may need to limit access to network servers to specific users or other computers. However, this is a certification exam. Do not expect to have *physical* access to any other computer to test your settings. You will not have access to any outside networks such as the Internet.

If you're going for your RHCT, you'll need a grade of at least 70 percent in the RHCT-level skills. If you're going for your RHCE, you'll need a score of 70 percent on both sections.

exam
ⓦatch

Read the entire Installation and Configuration exam before you finish installing RHEL. It's easier to configure RAID and logical volumes during the installation process. It can save time *to install required servers during the installation process. And remember that you can start configuring RHEL through the CTRL-ALT-F2 console even while packages are being installed.*

Most of you will find it difficult to complete this exercise within 3 hours. I've deliberately added extra difficulty to this second sample exam, which will hopefully ease your required effort during the actual RHCE exam. I've also split up this sample exam into RHCT- and RHCE-level skills for your convenience; it may not represent what you'll actually see on the exam. (I'm not allowed to tell you about it.)

If you're preparing for the RHCT exam, you can ignore the RHCE issues. If you're preparing for the RHCE exam, you'll have to meet *all* requirements in this section. Remember that the RHCE is inclusive of the RHCT.

Once you've mastered the skills in this book, try other variations. Practice with different scenarios until you become comfortable with the scenarios described in this book, as well as in the Red Hat Exam Prep guide.

Server Installation Problem: RHCT-Level Skills

Install Red Hat Enterprise Linux. The following conditions specify a connection to network servers, configured with some very specific partitions. Assume this computer gets its IP addressing information from a DHCP server. Let users start at a virtual console.

Install Linux with the partitions shown in Table B-1. The sizes shown are minimums. Make sure that the /home directory is configured in a RAID 5 software array with no spare partitions. Leave 1000MB of free, unallocated space on the hard drive. If your system has less available hard drive space, some adjustments may be possible, such as reducing the amount of space allocated to / and /usr to 2000MB each.

TABLE B-1	Filesystem	Size
	/boot	100MB
Required Partitions	/	4000MB
	/home	1000MB
	/var	1000MB
	/usr	4000MB

Once RHEL is installed, you'll also want to configure the following:

- A connection to a local printer
- Active networking only during working hours (8:00 A.M to 5:00 P.M.)
- An NIS client, on the biglan NIS domain
- The automounter, configured to read the CD on the /misc/cd directory
- Support for IP forwarding, as this computer may be a router in the future
- Installation of the system-config-boot RPM
- A Linux kernel, upgraded to the latest requirements

Configure a cross-functional group of users: avionics, vendor, seats, and galleys. Set them up as a group named pcplane. Create a /home/pcplane directory and allow them to share files without having to change permissions or ownership on any file they put in this directory. Do not give vendor read privileges on this directory. Limit each of these users to 100MB of files in this directory. Make it possible to create ACLs on the /home directory partition. Configure secret.doc (with a user and group owner of galleys) in /home/galleys with ACLs that allow user michael read-write access.

Set up appropriate partitions as a RAID 1 array (with one spare partition), dedicated to the /home/pcplane directory. While you could do this during the installation process, do so after installation, for the purpose of this exercise.

Server Installation Problem: RHCE-Level Skills

In this part of the exam, you'll configure a number of different servers on the RHEL system. Assume this computer is on a gateway between your LAN and an external network such as the Internet. Based on the configuration shown in Table B-1, set up /var on an LVM array.

Set up both a regular and a secure Web server. Make sure the home pages for each server are different. Limit access to within the LAN only, and to the users avionics, seats, and galleys. Create and activate a Web proxy server. Configure a Samba server that allows users to access their home directories from remote computers on the LAN. Create an NFS share, with full privileges, on your /tmp directory. Make sure SELinux settings support access to this share.

Set up an FTP server that supports only anonymous access, even from outside your LAN. Configure sendmail to support access from within the LAN; do not require address confirmation from a DNS server. Configure an incoming e-mail service that supports regular, non-secure IMAP4 connections. Activate the Secure Shell service, and allow access from inside and outside the LAN. Do not allow direct root logins through the Secure Shell connection.

Edit the Kickstart file that is created; set it up to be usable for other computers with an identical hardware configuration. The Kickstart file should also support the creation of the same partitions.

Installation Discussion

Since you can set up a Red Hat Enterprise Linux configuration in several ways, there is no one right answer for the listed requirements. But you should remember a few general concepts. It's normally fastest to include packages during the installation process. It's easiest (and generally faster) to set up RAID arrays and LVM groups during the installation process. Make sure that the services you set up are active at the appropriate runlevels.

You can set up DHCP addressing through the Red Hat installation program or in /etc/sysconfig/network. You'll also want to allow incoming connections to your SSH and FTP servers. You can do this with the Security Level Configuration tool, commands in /etc/hosts.allow and /etc/hosts.deny, directives in service-level configuration files, or even with appropriate **iptables** commands.

You can connect to a local printer by editing the files in /etc/cups or using the Printer Configuration utility. You can limit networking to working hours using appropriate **cron** jobs, stored in the /etc/cron.daily directory. Setting up an NIS client means activating the **ypbind** daemon and using **domainname** to designate the biglan NIS domain, or you can use the Authentication Configuration tool. Also, activate the SELinux **allow_ypbind** (Allow Daemons To Run With NIS) setting. Before the automounter works, you have to activate the **autofs** service as well as the appropriate commands in /etc/auto.master and /etc/auto.misc.

To support IP forwarding, you'll need to set the **net.ipv4.ip_forward** variable in /etc/sysctl.conf and activate it in the /proc/sys/net/ipv4/ip_forward file. You can install the RPMs of your choice, including system-config-boot, with the appropriate **rpm -ivh** *packagename* command; if there are dependencies, and you're connected to an appropriate repository, you can use the **yum install** *packagename* command. When you upgrade the Linux kernel, however, you should install it with **rpm -i** just in case the new kernel doesn't work. When you set up users in a special directory, don't forget to set up the directory with the SGID bit.

To make the /home directory work with quotas and ACL, you'll need to add the **usrquota** and **acl** options to the associated directive in /etc/fstab. Before you can configure quotas, you'll need to remount /home with at least the **usrquota** and **acl** settings. To give user michael read-write permissions to secret.doc in /home/galleys, set appropriate permissions to /home/galleys:

```
# chmod 701 /home/galleys/
```

and set appropriate permissions on /home/galleys/secret.doc:

```
# setfacl -m user:michael:rw- /home/galleys/secret.doc
```

Now that quotas are set, create appropriate quota configuration files with **quotacheck -cuvm** (or reboot); and then activate quotas with **quotaon**. You can then add quotas on a *username* with the **edquota** *username* command.

If you're setting up a RAID array after installation, you'll first need to configure appropriate partitions using **fdisk** or **parted**, and then collect them into an array with the right **mdadm** command. Remember that a RAID 1 array requires two partitions, and one spare is specified in the exam requirements (for a total of three RAID partitions). To make sure the configuration takes after you reboot, you'll need to configure the RAID array device, such as /dev/md0, with the specified directory, /home/pcplane, in the /etc/fstab configuration file.

Remember to set up a regular Web server in /etc/httpd/conf/httpd.conf and a secure Web server in /etc/httpd/conf.d/ssl.conf. You can set up index.html home pages in the appropriate **DocumentRoot** directories; plain text in these files is sufficient. To limit access to specific users, you'll want to set up a group with the **htpasswd** command and add the group name to the appropriate configuration file with the **AuthUserFile** command.

The Squid Web Proxy server is straightforward; it requires configuration of three commands in your /etc/squid/squid.conf file: **visible_hostname**, **http_access**, and **acl**. The default Samba server configuration already allows user access to their home directories, but you'll need to add passwords with the **smbpasswd -a** *username* command. But this won't work until you enable the Allow Samba To Share Users Home Directories option using the SELinux Management tool (or the corresponding **setsebool -P samba_enable_home_dirs 1** command). You can set up an NFS share through /etc/exports or the NFS Server Configuration tool and the appropriate commands.

The vsFTP server already allows only anonymous access by default. To configure sendmail to support access within the LAN, you need to comment out the command in sendmail.mc that limits access to the local computer; it's well commented. Similarly, the command that allows connections to domain names unverified by DNS is active by default and need not be changed. The standard e-mail service for RHEL 5 that supports incoming connections is Dovecot. You can configure it in /etc/dovecot.conf. If you want to limit the protocols to IMAP4 connections, use the **protocols** directive; a helpful sample is included in the default version of this file. To activate the Secure Shell service (**sshd**), as well as the others, use the **service** command (or run the script from the /etc/init.d directory). For a hint on how to limit access to non-root users, look up the **PermitRootLogin** directive in the man page for sshd_config.

Make sure the SELinux booleans are compatible with these settings. If you use non-standard directories, you may have to apply the **chcon** command to make sure these directories have the same SELinux labels as the default directories. The SELinux Management Tool can help give access to appropriate services, as well as options such as home directory access

A default, partially disabled Kickstart file is available in the /root/anaconda-ks.cfg file. Once you've activated the partition command and saved it as ks.cfg, you can use it to install RHEL on other computers with a nearly identical hardware configuration. If you've saved it on a floppy, you can cite it at the installation boot prompt with the **linux ks=hd:fd0:/ks.cfg** command or on the local CD with the **linux ks=cdrom:/ks.cfg** command.

Glossary

A s the Red Hat exams are an advanced challenge, I limit this glossary to what you would see beyond the prerequisites; don't expect to see most basic terms from Chapter 1 here.

Access Control Lists (ACLs)   Access Control Lists (ACLs) provide an additional layer of access control to files and directories; associated with the **setfacl** and **getfacl** commands.

Address Resolution Protocol (ARP)   A protocol that maps an IP address to the hardware address on a network card.

anacron   The anacron service is designed to run **cron** jobs that could not run while a server was powered down.

Apache Web server   The Apache Web server provides both normal and secure Web services, controlled by the **httpd** daemon.

apachectl   The **apachectl** command is the preferred method to start and stop an Apache server.

arp (Address Resolution Protocol)   The **arp** command is used to view or modify the kernel's ARP table. Using **arp**, you can detect problems such as duplicate addresses on the network. Alternatively, you can use **arp** to add the required entries from your LAN.

at   The **at** command is similar to **cron**, but it allows you to run a job on a one-time basis.

authentication   The way Linux checks the login rights of a user. Linux and Unix users are normally authenticated through use of a username and password, checked against /etc/passwd and related files.

automounter   The automounter can be configured to mount local and network directories on an as-needed basis. It's configured in /etc/auto.master, /etc/auto.misc, /etc/auto.smb, and /etc/auto.net.

BIND (Berkeley Internet Name Domain)   BIND is the Unix/Linux software that is used to set up a Domain Name System (DNS) service. The associated daemon is **named**.

BIOS   The BIOS is the Basic Input/Output System that runs basic commands when you power up your computer. The BIOS menu allows you to customize many options, including the sequence of boot media.

/boot   The directory with the main files required to boot Linux, including the Linux kernel and initial RAM disk. By default, /boot is mounted on a separate partition.

BOOTP   A TCP/IP protocol that sends IP address information from a remote DHCP server.

caching-only name server   A caching-only name server that performs many of the functions of a DNS server. It stores the IP address associated with recent name searches, for use by other computers on your LAN.

chage   The **chage** command manages the expiration date of a password.

chattr   The **chattr** command allows you to change file attributes.

chgrp   The **chgrp** command changes the group that owns a file.

chkconfig   The **chkconfig** command manages runlevel service information. It can activate or deactivate services. It can also customize services at specific runlevels.

chmod   The **chmod** command changes the permissions on a file.

chown   The **chown** command changes ownership on a file.

CIFS (Common Internet File System)   CIFS is the Microsoft name for advances in its networking software. It's also covered by the latest version of Samba, 3.0, which is included with RHEL.

client   A client is a computer that accesses information or resources from a server.

CNAME (canonical name)   The CNAME is a way to assign several different names to a computer in a DNS database. For example, you can set up *www* as an alias for the computer with your Web server. CNAME records cannot be assigned to a mail server (MX) or a Start of Authority (SOA) record.

cron   A service that runs jobs on a periodic basis. It's configured in /etc/crontab; by default, it executes jobs in the /etc/cron.hourly, /etc/cron.daily, /etc/cron.weekly, and /etc/cron.monthly directories.

crontab   Individual users can run the **crontab** command to configure jobs that are run periodically.

CUPS (Common Unix Printing System)   CUPS is the default print service for RHEL.

daemon   A process such as the Web service (**httpd**) or X Font Server (**xfs**) that runs in the background and executes as required.

/dev   The directory with device files, used to represent hardware and software components.

DHCP (Dynamic Host Configuration Protocol)   DHCP clients lease IP addresses for a fixed period of time from a DHCP server on a local network. The BOOTP protocol allows DHCP clients to get IP address information from a remote DHCP server. The DHCP server daemon is **dhcpd**; the DHCP client daemon is **dhclient**.

Disk Druid   Anaconda's hard disk management program. While the functionality is similar to **fdisk** and **parted**, Disk Druid is easier to use. However, it is available only during the Linux installation process.

display manager   A Linux display manager includes a dialog box for your username and password. Two major display managers are used in RHEL: **gdm** (GNOME) and **kdm** (KDE).

dmesg The **dmesg** command lists the kernel ring buffer and the initial boot messages. If your system successfully boots, /var/log/dmesg is one place to look for messages if you think you have boot problems.

DNS (Domain Name System) The DNS service maintains a database of fully qualified domain names such as www.redhat.com and IP addresses such as 206.132.41.202. If the domain name is not in the local database, DNS is normally configured to look to other, more authoritative, DNS servers. The associated daemon is **named**.

Dovecot The Dovecot service is associated with POP and IMAP e-mail.

dual-core / multi-core A dual-core CPU is one type of multiple-core CPU in which one physical integrated circuit includes two or more CPUs.

dumpe2fs The **dumpe2fs** command provides a lot of information about the format of a partition.

e2label The **e2label** command associates a device with a label, typically a filesystem directory.

edquota The **edquota** command edits the quota for a user or a group.

emacs The emacs editor is a popular text editor that can be run from a text console.

environment Each user's environment specifies default settings such as login prompts, terminals, the PATH, mail directories, and more.

/etc/fstab The/etc/fstab configuration file defines default mounted directories.

/etc/inittab The /etc/inittab configuration file sets the default runlevel and starts key processes such as terminal gettys.

/etc/X11/prefdm The /etc/X11/prefdm configuration file specifies the preferred GUI display manager.

exportfs   The **exportfs** command allows shared NFS directories to be shared with a network.

ExpressCard   An ExpressCard is the successor to the PC Card/PCMCIA standard. The two standards are not compatible, and PCMCIA cards do not fit into ExpressCard slots.

fdisk   A standard disk partition command utility that allows you to modify the physical and logical disk partition layout.

Fedora Linux   The successor to the freely available version of Red Hat Linux; more information on this Linux distribution is available online at www. fedoraproject.org. Formerly known as Fedora Core Linux, starting with Fedora 7, it includes all former Core and Extras packages.

filesystem   Filesystem has multiple meanings in Linux. It refers to mounted directories; the root directory (/) filesystem is formatted on its own partition. It also refers to file formats; Linux partitions are typically formatted to the ext3 filesystem.

Filesystem Hierarchy Standard   The Filesystem Hierarchy Standard is the official way to organize files in Unix and Linux directories. The top-level directory is known as the root directory (/); users' home directories are configured in /home.

find   The **find** command searches for a desired file through a given directory and its subdirectories.

fips   The First Interactive Partition Splitter, **fips**, allows you to split existing VFAT partitions.

firewall   A hardware or software system that prevents unauthorized access over a network. Normally used to protect a private LAN from attacks through the Internet.

firstboot   The process that starts when you've configured RHEL during installation to boot into the GUI (runlevel 5); also known as First Boot.

fsck   The **fsck** command checks the filesystem on a Linux partition for consistency.

FTP (File Transfer Protocol)   The FTP protocol is a TCP/IP protocol designed to optimize file transfer between computers.

gateway   A gateway is a route from a computer to another network. A default gateway address is the IP address of a computer or router that connects a LAN with another network such as the Internet.

getfacl   The **getfacl** command lets you read Access Control Lists (ACLs) on files and directories.

getty   A getty is a terminal program that includes prompts for a login and a password. Virtual console gettys are configured through the **mingetty** program via /etc/inittab.

GNOME (GNU Network Object Model Environment)   GNOME is the default GUI desktop for Red Hat Enterprise Linux.

GPG (GNU Privacy Guard)   GPG is an implementation of the OpenPGP standard included with Red Hat Enterprise Linux.

group ID   Every Linux group has a group ID, as defined in /etc/group.

GRUB (Grand Unified Bootloader)   The default boot loader for RHEL.

grub-install   The **grub-install** command makes your BIOS look for your GRUB boot loader.

hard limits   Associated with user quotas. Specifies the permanent maximum amount of space a user can have on a partition, independent of grace periods.

home directory   The home directory is the login directory for Linux users. Normally, this is /home/*user*, where *user* is the user's login name. It's also represented by the tilde (~) in any Linux command.

htpasswd   The **htpasswd** command helps create passwords for accessing a local Web site.

ICMP (Internet Control Message Protocol)   A protocol for sending online error control messages. Associated with the **ping** command.

ifconfig   The **ifconfig** command is used to configure and display network devices.

init   The **init** process is the first Linux process called by the kernel. This process starts other processes that compose a working Linux system, including the shell.

Initial RAM Disk   RHEL uses an initial RAM disk in the boot process; it's stored as an initrd-`uname -r`.img file in the /boot directory. You can create your own from the currently booted kernel with the **mkinitrd initrd-`uname -r`.img `uname -r`** command.

Internet Print Protocol (IPP)   The Internet Print Protocol (IPP) is the evolving standard for printers shared over networks. It's being adapted by all major operating systems; the Linux implementation is CUPS.

IP forwarding   IP forwarding is when data is forwarded between computers or networks through your computer.

iptables   The **iptables** command is the basic command for firewalls and masquerading.

IPv4, IPv6   IPv4 and IPv6 are different systems of IP addressing. Version 4 is what we use today and is based on 32-bit addresses; version 6 is coming on line and is based on 128-bit addresses.

iSCSI (Internet *SCSI*)   Internet SCSI is a network protocol standard, associated with SCSI-3 specifications on network storage devices.

KDE   A GUI for Linux and Unix computers. Also known as the K Desktop Environment.

Kdump   The Kdump service allows you to configure what happens in the event of a kernel crash. You can dedicate a specific amount of RAM to the process, which is then unavailable for other processes.

kernel   The kernel is the heart of any operating system. It loads device drivers. You can recompile a Linux kernel for additional drivers, for faster loading and to minimize the required memory.

kernel module   Kernel modules are pluggable drivers that can be loaded and unloaded into the kernel as needed. Some loaded kernel modules are shown with the **lsmod** command.

Kickstart   Kickstart is the Red Hat automated installation system that allows you to supply the answers required during the installation process. When properly configured, a kickstart floppy can allow you to start your computer and install RHEL automatically from a network source.

LDP (Linux Documentation Project)   The LDP is a global effort to produce reliable documentation for all aspects of the Linux operating system. Its work is available online at www.tldp.org.

lftp   The **lftp** command starts a slightly more flexible FTP command line client.

Lightweight Directory Access Protocol (LDAP)   The Lightweight Directory Access Protocol allows you to keep authentication information on a central server on your network.

locate   The **locate** command searches through a default database of files and directories. The database is refreshed daily with the mlocate.cron script in the /etc/cron.daily/ directory.

logrotate   The **logrotate** command utility allows you to maintain log files. By default, RHEL uses the **cron** daemon to rotate, compress, and remove various log files.

lpc   You can use the **lpc** command to scan all configured print devices and queues.

lpq   You can use the **lpq** command to view print jobs still in progress.

lpr   You can use the **lpr** command to send print requests.

lprm   You can use the **lprm** command to remove print jobs from the queue.

logical extent (LE)   A logical extent (LE) chunk of disk space that corresponds to a physical extent (PE).

logical volume (LV)   A logical volume (LV) is composed of a group of logical extents (LEs).

Logical Volume Management (LVM)   Logical Volume Management (LVM) allows you to set up a filesystem on multiple partitions. Also known as the Logical Volume Manager.

lsattr   The **lsattr** command lists file attributes.

lvcreate   The **lvcreate** command creates a logical volume (LV) from a specified number of available physical extents (PEs).

lvdisplay   The **lvdisplay** command specifies current configuration information for logical volumes (LVs).

lvextend   The **lvextend** command allows you to increase the physical volume (PV) area allocated to a logical volume (LV).

lvremove   Functionally opposite to the **lvcreate** command.

masquerading   Masquerading enables you to provide Internet access to all of the computers on a LAN with a single public IP address.

MBR (Master Boot Record)   The first sector of a bootable disk. Once the BIOS cycle is complete, it looks for a pointer on the boot disk's MBR, which then looks at a boot loader configuration file such as grub.conf to see how to start an operating system.

mdadm   The **mdadm** command can help you view and configure RAID arrays.

mkbootdisk   The **mkbootdisk** command can create a boot disk, customized for your system.

mkfs   The **mkfs** command can help you format a newly configured partition. Variations are available including **mkfs.ext3**, which formats to the default ext3 filesystem.

modprobe   You can use the **modprobe** command to control device modules to be installed.

mount   You can use the **mount** command to specify mounted partitions, or attach local or network partitions to specified directories.

mount.cifs and umount.cifs   The **mount.cifs** and **umount.cifs** commands, when properly configured, allow regular users to mount directories shared over a Microsoft Windows network through Samba.

NAT (Network Address Translation)   NAT is a feature associated with firewall commands such as **iptables,** which connects computers inside your LAN to the Internet while disguising their true IP addresses. NAT modifies IP packet headers. The process is reversed for return messages. Closely related to masquerading.

netstat   The **netstat** command displays connectivity information for your network cards. For example, the **netstat -r** command is used to display the routing tables as stored in your kernel.

Network Time Protocol (NTP)   The Network Time Protocol allows you to synchronize your computer with a central timeserver. You can do this on RHEL with the Date/Time Configuration tool or by editing /etc/ntpd.conf and activating the ntpd service.

NFS (Network File System)   NFS is a file-sharing protocol originally developed by Sun Microsystems; it is the networked filesystem most commonly used for networks of Linux and Unix computers.

NIC (Network Interface Card)   A NIC connects your computer to a network. A NIC can be anything from a Gigabit Ethernet adapter to a telephone modem.

NIS (Network Information System)   NIS allows you to share one centrally managed authorization database for the Linux and Unix systems on your network.

PAM (Pluggable Authentication Module)   PAM separates the authentication process from individual applications. PAM consists of a set of dynamically loadable library modules that configures how an application verifies its users before allowing access.

parted   parted is a standard disk partition command utility that allows you to modify the physical and logical disk partition layout. Be careful when using it, as changes are immediately written to the partition table.

partprobe   You can use the **partprobe** command to reread a recently changed partition table without rebooting.

PATH   A shell variable that specifies the directories (and in what order) the shell automatically searches for input commands and files.

PGP (Pretty Good Privacy)   A technique for encrypting messages, often used for e-mail. It includes a secure private- and public-key system similar to RSA. The Linux version of PGP is known as GPG (GNU Privacy Guard).

physical extent (PE)   A chunk of disk space created from a physical volume (PV) for Logical Volume Manager (LVM).

physical volume (PV)   An area of space for Logical Volume Manager (LVM) that usually corresponds to a partition or a hard drive.

Pirut   Pirut is the name of the RHEL package management tool.

Primary ATA (PATA)   Primary ATA is the media standard associated with older IDE drives, also known as ATA (Advanced Technology Attachment).

Primary Domain Controller (PDC)   A PDC is the governing server on a Microsoft Windows NT 4 network. You can configure RHEL with Samba to function as a PDC or as a member server on more current Microsoft networks.

/proc   /proc is the Linux *virtual* filesystem. *Virtual* means that it doesn't occupy real disk space. /proc files are used to provide information on kernel configuration and device status.

public/private key   Encryption standards such as PGP, GPG, or RSA are based on public/private key pairs. The private key is kept on the local computer; others can decrypt it with the public key.

Pup   Pup is short for the Package Updater, which monitors the Red Hat Network (RHN) for packages available for update.

pvcreate   The **pvcreate** command allows you to configure physical extents (PEs) from a properly configured partition.

pvdisplay   The **pvdisplay** command specifies current configuration information for physical volumes (PVs).

quota   In Linux, a quota can limit users and/or groups by number of inodes or disk space. Quotas can include hard and soft limits.

quotacheck   The **quotacheck** command scans and creates user and group quota files.

quotaon   The **quotaon** command activates configured quotas.

RAID (Redundant Array of Independent Disks)   RHEL supports software RAID. You can use Anaconda to set up software RAID 0, 1, 5, and 6 arrays. You can also set up RAID arrays using the **fdisk** or **parted** command with **mdadm**. Also known as Redundant Array of Inexpensive Disks.

RAID 0   A RAID 0 array requires two or more partitions or hard drives. Reads and writes are done in parallel, increasing performance, filling up all partitions or hard drives equally. RAID 0 includes no redundancy; if any partition or hard drive in the array fails, all data in the array is lost.

RAID 1   A RAID 1 array requires two or more partitions or hard drives. RAID 1 is also known as mirroring, because the same information is written to both partitions. If one disk is damaged, all data will still be intact and accessible from the other disk.

RAID 5   A RAID 5 array requires three or more partitions. Parity information is striped across all partitions. If one partition fails, the data can be rebuilt. It can be automatically written to a spare disk.

RAID 6   A RAID 6 array requires four or more partitions. Parity information is striped twice across all partitions. If one or two partitions fail, the data can be rebuilt. It can be automatically written to a spare disk.

Red Hat Certified Engineer (RHCE)   Perhaps the elite certification available for Linux systems administrators. Designed to qualify Linux administrators with significant experience in configuring Linux LANs with Red Hat Enterprise Linux.

Red Hat Certified Technician (RHCT)   Another elite certification for newer Linux administrators. Designed to qualify Linux administrators with significant experience in configuring Linux workstations with RHEL. RHCEs must also meet all RHCT requirements.

Red Hat Hardware Compatibility List   The Red Hat Hardware Compatibility List (HCL) specifies all hardware that has been tested on systems running the various Red Hat operating systems. Red Hat provides installation support for any hardware that is listed as "support" on their HCL.

Red Hat Network (RHN)   The Red Hat Network (RHN) supports remote control and administration of systems with RHN subscriptions.

Red Hat Package Manager (RPM)   The Red Hat Package Manager is a system that sets up software in discrete packages. The associated **rpm** command allows you to add, remove, and upgrade packages.

refresh rate   The refresh rate regulates the rate at which the image you see on your screen is redrawn, in hertz (Hz).

repquota   The **repquota** command reports disk consumption.

resize2fs   The **resize2fs** command allows you to change the size of a filesystem, often used after increasing the space associated with an LVM.

reverse (inverse) zone   A DNS reverse (inverse) zone can be required by some servers, such as Apache and sendmail, to make sure an IP address points to a real computer. If the reverse zone host name does not match the IP address, the server might not respond.

rndc   The **rndc** command is used to manage the operation of a DNS server; it's preferred over commands such as **service named start**.

root   This word has multiple meanings in Linux. The root user is the default administrative user. The root directory (/) is the top-level directory in Linux. The root user's home directory, /root, is a subdirectory of the root directory (/).

router   A computer that transfers messages between LANs. Computers that are connected to multiple networks often serve as routers.

rpmbuild   The **rpmbuild** command allows you to build source code based on information in a .spec file.

runlevel   RHEL includes six available runlevels, as defined in /etc/inittab. Key runlevels include 1, single-user mode; 3, text login; and 5, GUI login.

Samba   The Linux and Unix implementation of the Server Message Block protocol and the Common Internet File System (CIFS). Allows computers that run Linux and Unix to communicate with computers that run Microsoft Windows operating systems. I expect Samba 4.0, when released, to provide nearly full functionality as a Microsoft Active Directory Domain Controller.

secure virtual hosts   You can configure multiple secure virtual hosts on a single Apache server using the secure configuration file, /etc/httpd/conf.d/ssl.conf.

Security Enhanced Linux (SELinux)   An implementation of mandatory access control integrated into the Linux kernel; in essence, a different way of layering security within Linux.

sendmail   A standard e-mail server application used by most Internet e-mail.

Serial ATA (SATA)   The new standard on hard drives that makes it easier to chain hard drives in a series inside a physical system. SATA drives have device file labels similar to SCSI; for example, the first SATA drive is known as /dev/sda.

server   A computer that controls centralized resources such as files and printers. Servers can share these resources with client computers on a network.

setfacl   The **setfacl** command lets you control Access Control Lists (ACLs) on files and directories.

SGID   The SGID bit sets common group ID permissions on a file or directory.

Shadow Password Suite   The Shadow Password Suite creates an additional layer of protection for Linux users and groups in the /etc/shadow and /etc/gshadow files.

showmount   The **showmount** command lists the shared directories from an NFS server.

single-user mode   When you start RHEL in single-user mode, you're automatically logged in as the root user, without networking or most services. If your Linux system has boot problems, single-user mode may allow enough access to fix the problem.

smbpasswd   The **smbpasswd** command helps you create usernames and passwords for a Samba (Microsoft Windows) network.

SMTP (Simple Mail Transfer Protocol)   SMTP is a TCP/IP protocol for sending mail; used by sendmail.

SOA (Start of Authority)   In a DNS database, the SOA record is the preamble to all zone files. It describes the zone, the DNS server computer (such as ns.*your-domain*.com), the responsible administrator (such as hostmaster@your-domain.com), the serial number associated with this file, and other information related to caching and secondary DNS servers.

soft limit   Associated with user quotas. Specifies the maximum amount of space a user can have on a partition. Soft limits can be configured with grace periods.

spec file   Spec files are associated with source RPMs (SRPMS). You can modify an SRPM spec file to change the way an RPM package is built.

Squid   Squid is a high-performance HTTP and FTP caching proxy server.

SRPM (source RPM)   SRPMs include the source code required to build a binary RPM package. SRPMs are installed with the **rpm -i** command, which installs SRPM files within the /usr/src/redhat directory. You can then use the **rpmbuild** command to create a binary RPM.

Structured Query Language (SQL)   The basis for several database systems that can be run on Linux, including MySQL and PostgreSQL.

SUID   The SUID bit sets common user ID permissions on a file or directory.

superuser   The superuser represents a regular user who has taken root user privileges. Closely associated with the **su** and **sudo** commands.

swap space   Linux uses swap space for less frequently used data that would otherwise be stored in RAM. It is normally configured in Linux in a swap partition.

system-config-*   Red Hat has created a series of GUI configuration tools to help configure a number of different systems and services. You can start them with a number of different commands that start with **system-config-***. While it's usually faster to configure a configuration file directly, not every experienced administrator knows every detail of every major configuration file.

TCP/IP (Transmission Control Protocol/Internet Protocol)   TCP/IP is a suite of communications protocols for internetwork communication. It is primarily used as the communication system for the Internet.

Telnet   A terminal emulation program that allows you to connect to remote computers. RHEL includes the Kerberos version of the Telnet server, as configured through the /etc/xinetd.d/krb5-telnet configuration file.

tmpwatch   The **tmpwatch** command removes files that have not been accessed in a specified number of hours. The default daily **tmpwatch** script checks files in the /tmp and /var/tmp directories.

umask   The **umask** command defines default permissions for newly created files.

user ID (UID)   Every Linux user has a user ID, as defined in /etc/passwd.

usermod   The **usermod** command modifies different settings in /etc/passwd, such as expiration date and additional groups.

Very Secure FTP (vsFTP)   The Very Secure FTP service is the default FTP server for RHEL.

vgcreate   The **vgcreate** command creates a volume group (VG) from one or more physical volumes (PVs) for Logical Volume Manager (LVM).

vgdisplay   The **vgdisplay** command specifies current configuration information for volume groups (VGs).

vgextend   The **vgextend** command allows you to increase the extents or space allocated to a volume group (VG).

vi   The vi editor is a basic Linux text editor. While other editors are more popular, vi may be the only editor you have available in certain rescue environments.

virtual hosts   You can configure multiple Web sites on a single Apache server by configuring a number of virtual hosts in your /etc/httpd/conf/httpd.conf configuration file.

virtualization   Virtualization is an abstraction of computer resources; most often associated with platform virtualization, in which you can include one or more virtual machines on a physical system. Two options for virtualization are VMware and Xen.

VMware   VMware is a proprietary system with virtualization products freely available to all. With snapshots, it can help you test a system with less risk. I've written much of this book with RHEL installed on a VMware Server.

volume group (VG)   A collection of physical volumes (PVs) in Logical Volume Manager (LVM).

window manager   The window manager is a special type of X client that controls how other X clients appear on your display.

WINS (Windows Internet Name Service)   WINS provides name resolution on Microsoft networks; it can be activated on Samba.

X client   An X client is an application that uses the X server services to display output.

X Display   The X Display is a console and a virtual window. By default, there are six virtual text consoles configured with Linux; the X Display is associated with virtual console number seven.

X server   The X server is the part of the X Window System that runs on your desktop. The X server draws images on your screen, takes input from your keyboard and mouse, and controls access to your display.

X Window System   The GUI for Linux is also known as the X Window. Unlike other applications, the X Window System is a layered application.

Xen   Xen is the native virtualization technology to RHEL. It requires the use of a custom Xen kernel and can support virtual machines in paravirtualized and fully hardware virtualized modes.

xhost   The **xhost** command can be used to allow other hosts to access your X server. In other words, you can configure remote X clients to send their display to the local X server.

xinetd daemon   The **xinetd** "super-server" daemon controls connections to servers in the /etc/xinetd.d directory such as the **rsync** and Kerberos Telnet servers.

X.org   The X.org server is the default X server for RHEL.

ypbind   The NIS client service is **ypbind**.

ypserv   The NIS server service is **ypserv**.

yum   The **yum** command allows you to update and install RPMs from remote sources, including dependencies. On RHEL 5, **yum** has replaced **up2date** for updates.

INDEX

SYMBOLS

(pound sign)
    root shell prompt, 741
    text comments indicated
        with, 524
& (ampersand), 596, 597
' (single quote), 595
* wildcard, 25
. (dot)
    hosts.allow and hosts.deny
        wildcard, 695
    indicating hidden files, 286
/ (forward slash)
    Apache container end indicated
        with, 452
    root directory indicated by, 12
< > (directional brackets), 451
> (redirection arrows), 29, 30
? wildcard, 25
[ ] wildcard, 25
\ (backslash), 305
` (back quote), 595
~ (tilde), 20

A

absolute paths, 20
Accelerated-X, 653
access
    overriding inherited permissions,
        463–464
    setting Apache host-based, 460
    using Apache Web server pages
        from home directory, 462–463
access control lists. See ACLs
access.conf file, 451
ACLs (access control lists)
    configuring filesystem for, 208
    defined, 800
    managing, 209
    setting permissions for, 208
    using with tcp_wrappers, 694
ACPI (Advanced Configuration and
    Power Interface), 74
activating
    automounter, 206
    Dovecot, 590–591
Active Directory, 525–527

Add NFS Share dialog (NFS Server
    Configuration tool), 500
Add Physical Volume to VG dialog
    (GUI LVM Management tool),
    429, 430
Add Port dialog (Security Level
    Configuration tool), 701–703
adding logical volumes, 423–424,
    757–758
Address Resolution Protocol
    (ARP), 800
addresses. See also IP addresses
    I/O, 6
    assignable ranges for IP, 39
    DMA, 6
administration. See administrators;
    system administration tools; user
    administration
Administration tab (CUPS interface),
    350–351
administrative commands, 24–25
administrators. See also Red
    Hat Package Manager; user
    administration
    backing up and restoring data,
        36–38
    controlling network services with
        daemons, 35
    knowledge required for, 34–38,
        58–59
    managing system log files, 38
    prerequisites required for, 3
    RPM package management,
        222–223
    running yum from root
        account, 239
    superuser privileges, 34
    tips for managing user accounts,
        280–281
    uses for cron daemon, 36
    using /etc/skel for home
        directories, 35
    working with other Unix-style
        operating systems, 255
Advanced Configuration and Power
    Interface (ACPI), 74
Advanced Power Management
    (APM), 74

alternatives command, 599
ampersand (&), 596, 597
Anaconda
    about, 70
    configuring TCP/IP on network
        card during installation, 87, 88
    creating kickstart configuration
        file with, 245
    installing from files located by, 92
    listing packages installed
        with, 127
anacron, 360, 800
answers. See lab questions and answers;
    self test and answers
Apache, 444–476. See also Apache
    Web servers
    administering, 474
    changes in version 2.2, 446
    checking virtual host container
        syntax, 470
    configuration directives for virtual
        hosts, 452, 455
    configuration files for, 450–451
    creating list of files to share,
        458–459
    default configuration for, 451–452
    defined, 800
    executable files for virtual
        hosts, 470
    firewall and port configurations
        for, 458
    global environment directives for
        httpd.conf, 452, 453
    host-based security, 460
    HTTPD Service options in
        SELinux Management
        Tool, 711
    installation of, 447
    lab questions and answers, 487,
        489–491
    log files for, 471–472
    main server configuration
        directives in httpd.conf, 452,
        454–455
    overriding inherited permissions,
        463–464
    popularity of, 444
    prerequisite skills for, 46–47

Red Hat httpd Configuration tool
for, 475–476
secure virtual hosts, 468–469
security for, 456–458
self test and answers, 486–487,
488–489
server installation, 449–450
starting on reboot, 447–449
summarized, 484
troubleshooting errors, 472–473
two-minute drill, 485
updating home page on Apache
server, 473
used-based security, 460–461
virtual hosts, 466–468
Apache Web servers, 456–466
access to pages on home directory,
462–463
configuring, 456
configuring Web passwords, 462
creating list of files to share,
458–459
firewall and port configurations
for, 458
host-based security, 460
password protecting Web directory,
464–466
security for, 456–458
setting up virtual, 474–475
updating home page on, 473
used-based security, 460–461
apachectl command, 448, 800
APM (Advanced Power
Management), 74
applications
applications package groups,
113–114
remote X, 675–677
architecture
exams historically based on x86, 75
kernel types and, 379, 380
knowledge required of, 5
ARP (Address Resolution
Protocol), 800
arp command, 339–340, 800
at command, 358, 359, 800
at daemon
running job with, 358–359
securing, 359–360

authentication. *See also* LDAP;
NIS; PAM
authorizing users with PAM,
305–313
configuring client, 316–317
defined, 800
Kickstart Configurator protocols
for, 259
NFS, 505
NIS and LDAP for network,
313–317
Samba server, 537–538
setting up for halting and
rebooting computer, 706
Authentication Configuration
dialog, 317
autofs daemon, 206
automatic dependency resolution for
RPM updates, 237
automating
firewall configuration, 701–703
package installation, 244–260
quota settings, 298
system administration, 354–360
automounter, 203–207
activating, 206
configuring, 206–207
defined, 800
/etc/auto.master file with, 204
/etc/auto.misc file with, 204–205
mounting USB key or floppy drive
with, 207
reviewing and reading shared NFS
directories, 205–206
using, 203–204
awk command, 24
awstats (advanced Web Stats) tool, 472

B

back quote (`` ` ``), 595
backslash (\), 305
backups
about, 36–37
DVD/CD, 37
editing configuration files after
making, 293–294
gzip and bzip2 commands for,
37–38
hard drive (RAID), 37

kernel configuration, 397
making sendmail configuration
file, 595, 596
tape, 37
tar command for, 38
using mkfs command after
making, 17
Base System package group, 118–120
bash (Bourne Again Shell) shell
default Linux shell for exams, 290
default shell, 27
installation, 118
Basic Configuration screen (Kickstart
Configurator), 256, 257
Basic tab (Samba Server Configuration
utility), 537, 538
BIND (Berkeley Internet Name
Domain), 561–577
about, 558
caching-only DNS name servers,
561, 563–565
configuration files for DNS servers,
561–563
configuring simple domains,
567–569
creating RNDC key, 569–570
defined, 801
forwarding-only name servers, 561,
565–566
lab questions and answers, 580,
582–584
localhost.zone file, 567
named daemon, 559
required packages for DNS servers,
559–560
reverse lookups with named.local
file, 567, 568
reverse zone, 572–573, 574, 813
searching named.ca for root DNS
servers on Internet, 566
self test and answers, 579–580, 581
serial number errors in DNS, 574
shortcomings of DNS, 573–574
slave name servers, 561, 565
starting named daemon, 573
two-minute drill, 578
types of DNS servers, 561
utilities for, 574–577
zone files for master DNS server,
570–572

BIND utilities, 574–577
    overview, 574–575
    Red Hat Domain Name Service
        configuration tool, 576
    rndc, host, and dig commands,
        575–576
BIOS (Basic Input/Output System)
    basics of, 145
    defined, 801
    effect of multiple controllers on
        older, 105
    need to know initialization
        sequence, 144–145
    password-protecting menus, 735
    starting boot loader, 146
    troubleshooting USB ports or PCI
        card from menu, 5
    working from BIOS menu,
        145–146
books
    helpful for exams, 2
    reference guides to RPM
        system, 232
Boolean operations in SELinux
    Management Tool, 710–714
boot loaders. *See also* GRUB
    booting into different runlevels,
        733–735
    configuring, 106–107
    GRUB, 147–157
    Kickstart Configurator options for,
        257–258
    LILO, 147
    module errors in, 750–751
    starting, 146
    terminology for, 735
    troubleshooting, 749–750
/boot directory, 801
/boot files on logical volumes, 423
/boot partition with stored kernels, 379
booting, 144–182. *See also* First Boot
    process; linux rescue environment
    BIOS initialization sequence,
        144–146
    from boot floppy, 90
    configuring boot loader, 106–107
    configuring Samba to start on, 518
    controlling services, 167–169
    from first CD/DVD, 89
    First process and /etc/inittab,
        159–160

GRUB loader, 147–157
    handling disk quotas during, 293
    initial RAM disk for, 806
    into different runlevels, 144,
        164–167, 733–735
    kernel initialization and First
        process, 157–158
    lab questions and answers,
        176–179, 181–182
    likely errors configuring, 730–731
    linux rescue environment for,
        735–738
    multiple controllers with older
        BIOS may affect, 105
    options for exam, 88–89
    runlevels and, 161–167
    self test and answers, 175–176,
        180–181
    setting up boot USB using
        kickstart, 245–246
    summarized, 172
    system configuration files, 169–172
    two-minute drill, 173–174
    using installation boot CD or USB
        key, 90, 91–92
BOOTP protocol, 627, 801
Bourne Again Shell. *See* bash
browsers
    accessing URLs with text or
        graphical, 50–51
    Apache clients as Web, 446
    configuring CUPS via Web-based
        interface, 349–350
bzip2 command, 37–38

C

caching-only DNS name servers, 561,
    563–565, 801
canonical names (CNAME), 802
case insensitivity of DNS, 568
cat command, 21, 29
cd command, 20
CDs/DVDs
    avoiding exam installation from
        CDs, 89
    booting from installation, 91–92
    creating installation, 89–90
    initial booting from, 89
    using linux rescue environment
        from installation, 735, 736–738

certificates
    Dovecot secure, 591
    server, 466
chage command, 283–284, 801
chattr command, 801
chcon command, 709
chgrp command, 801
chkconfig command, 167, 169, 619, 801
chmod command, 30–31, 801
chown command, 801
chroot_local_user=YES command, 514
CIDR (Classless Inter-Domain Routing)
    notation, 618
CIFS (Common Internet File System),
    494, 519, 801
classes
    adding CUPS printer, 351, 352
    IP address, 39, 40
Classless Inter-Domain Routing (CIDR)
    notation, 618
clients. *See also* DNS clients; e-mail
    clients; NFS clients; Samba clients
        Apache, 446
        configuring with Red Hat
            Authentication Configuration
            tool, 316–317
        defined, 802
        DHCP, 340, 627, 631, 632–633
        e-mail, 600–602
        finding MAC addresses for
            DHCP, 631
        LDAP for configuring, 314–315
        NIS for configuring, 314
        NTP, 634–635
        Samba, 520–523
        sharing NFS directories with,
            509–512
        SSH, 626
        starting display from remote,
            675–676
        troubleshooting NFS hangs,
            503–504
        working with symbolically linked
            files, 503
        X Window System, 651–653,
            655–657, 667, 669, 817
CNAME (canonical name), 802
command line
    adding users from, 276, 277
    backslash in, 305
    configuring LVM in text mode, 418

controlling services from, 167
DHCP configuration from, 627
editing Apache configuration files
    from, 475
GRUB, 155–157
managing users from, 283–284
mounting NFS directory from
    client with, 510
network configuration from, 333
NFS configurations from, 506
NTP configuration not
    recommended from, 634
registering for Red Hat Network
    from, 235–236
Samba global setting
    configurations from, 537
setting disk quotas from, 291
testing mail system from, 600–601
tools for user administration using,
    274–277
troubleshooting skills from, 748
using mail utility at, 49–50,
    600–601
virtual consoles as, 160
X client options from, 655–657
X Window configuration tools
    from, 673
command mode in vi, 9–10
command shell. *See* shells
commands. *See also* mount command
    administrative, 24–25
    alternatives, 599
    apachectl, 448, 800
    arp, 339–340, 800
    at, 358, 359, 800
    available in no mount linux rescue
        environment, 741
    awk, 24
    basic print, 26
    bzip2, 37–38
    cat, 21, 29
    cd, 20
    chage, 283–284, 801
    chattr, 801
    chcon, 709
    chgrp, 801
    chkconfig, 167, 169, 619, 801
    chmod, 30–31, 801
    chown, 801
    converting passwords to and from
        shadow files, 33–34

cp, 22
crontab, 36
df, 185–186, 751–752
dhclient, 632
dig, 575–576
dmesg, 29, 803
dumpe2fs, 754, 755, 803
e2label, 753–754, 755, 803
edquota, 294–298, 803
egrep, 23
env, 27
exportfs, 804
fdisk, 14, 15, 16, 186–187
find, 21, 804
fsck, 14, 17, 740, 755, 804
getfacl, 805
grep, 23
GRUB editing, 149
grub-install, 805
gzip, 37–38
head and tail, 22
host, 575
hosts.allow and hosts.deny, 694
hotswappable devices, 79–80
htpasswd, 805
ifconfig, 42, 333, 337–338, 339,
    742, 743, 806
ifup/ifdown, 333, 337
installation console, 128
ip6tables, 698
ipchains, 693
iptables, 48–49, 482, 698–700, 806
less, 21, 29
lftp, 51–53, 807
linux askmethod, 92, 93
ln, 22
locate, 21, 23, 807
lpc, 807
lpc status, 348
LPD, 347–349
lpq, 26, 348, 807
lpr, 26, 348, 808
lprm, 26, 349, 808
ls, 20
ls -Z, 706, 707
lsattr, 808
lvcreate, 417, 808
lvdisplay, 808
lvextend, 418, 808
lvremove, 808
make config, 397–398

make gconfig, 398–400
make help, 409
make menuconfig, 398, 399
make xconfig, 398, 399
man smb.conf, 529
mdadm, 808
mkbootdisk, 809
mkfs, 14, 15–17, 198–199,
    755, 809
mklabel, 191, 194
modprobe, 383–384, 809
more and less, 21
mount, 18–19, 185–186, 202, 203,
    521–522, 809
mount.cifs, 522, 809
mv, 22
netstat, 42, 338–339, 340, 809
nslookup, 575
partprobe, 195, 810
passwd, 32
ping, 41–42
print, 26
ps, 24
pvcreate, 417, 418, 811
pvdisplay, 811
pwd, 20
quota management, 294
quotacheck, 293, 294, 298, 811
quotaon, 811
repquota, 812
rescue, 90
resize2fs, 813
rndc, 575, 813
rpm -i kernel.rpm, 389, 390
rpm query, 228
rpm -U kernel.rpm, 389, 390
rpmbuild, 231, 813
sed, 23–24
service, 35
service httpd reload, 448
set, 29
setenforce, 708
setfacl, 814
showmount, 814
smbmount, 522
smbpasswd, 533, 534, 535, 814
smbumount, 522
sort, 23
startx, 666–669
su, 34
sudo, 34

switchdesk, 680–681, 746
switches for, 19
sync, 740
system-config-*, 815
system-config-display, 651
system-config-network, 334–336
system-config-samba, 536–537
system-config-securitylevel, 701
tar, 38
tmpwatch, 816
umask, 32, 816
umount.cifs, 522, 809
updatedb, 21, 23
useradd, 276, 277
usermod, 283, 816
vgcreate, 417, 816
vgdisplay, 816
vgextend, 418, 816
volume and volume group, 420–422
vsFTP configuration, 514
wc, 23
who and w, 24–25
xhost, 818
yum, 223, 238–241, 818
Common Internet File System (CIFS),
494, 519, 801
Common Unix Printing System.
See CUPS
communication channels, 5–6
compatibility
computer, 71–72
CPUs, 75
hardware, 70–74
Hardware Compatibility List, 72
media devices and filesystem, 12
compressing files, 37–38
computers
effect of multiple controllers on
older BIOS, 105
hard drive options for Linux, 7
Linux compatibility with, 71–72
planning IRQ layout for, 6
protecting, 693, 735
RAM requirements, 6–7, 76
updating kernel developments for
SMP, 75
.config file, 396–397
configuration files
allowing Web server to run while
reading changes to, 448

Apache, 450–451
backing up before editing,
293–294
booting system, 169–172
CUPS, 342
DNS client, 560
DNS server, 561–563
editing Samba, 523–524
/etc/exports for NFS servers, 497
/etc/pam.d/system-auth, 309
/etc/sysconfig/network, 331–332
finding errors in GRUB, 152–155
importance of DNS, 574
kickstart, 245
PAM, 306
Postfix main.cf, 598
sendmail, 592–593
shell, 287–290
Squid, 478–480
/tmp directory, 129
troubleshooting likely errors in,
730–731
using Red Hat Domain Name
Service configuration tool
with, 576
window manager, 287
xinetd, 616–618
X.org server, 658
Connect to CUPS Server dialog box,
343–344
consoles
installation, 127–129
virtual, 160
control flags for PAM, 306, 307
controllers for PC cards, 78
controlling services, 167–169
from command line, 167
Service Configuration tool for,
168–169
text-based services for, 168
verifying runlevel of activated
service, 169
copying files, 22
cp command, 22
cpuinfo file, 381–382
CPUs
compatible, 75
detecting information about with
cpuinfo file, 381–382
dual- and multi-core, 803

RPM packages for specific types
of, 223
virtualization and, 76
crackers
defined, 32
preventing spoofing by, 572
reviewing logins for activity
by, 274
Create New Logical Volume dialog
(GUI LVM Management tool), 427
Create New Samba User dialog (Samba
Server Configuration utility), 541
Create New User dialog (Red Hat User
Manager), 279–280
Create Samba Share dialog (Samba
Server Configuration utility), 539
cron daemon
about, 36, 354, 802
creating job settings, 357–358
routing messages with MAILTO
variable, 355
securing, 359–360
SELinux settings for, 357
setting up for users, 357
using crontab file, 355–357
crontab command
defined, 802
managing cron jobs with, 36
crontab file, 355–357
CUPS (Common Unix Printing
System), 341–354
about, 25–26, 330
Administration tab for,
350–351
configuration files for, 342
controlling with LPD commands,
347–349
defined, 802
installing and starting, 341
SELinux protection and, 354
tabs of, 349–350
using Red Hat Printer
Configuration tool, 342–347
verifying sharing, 351–353
Web-based interface for,
349–351
cylinders. *See also* hard drives
BIOS limits on reported, 105
defined, 96
Cyrus IMAP, 586

D

daemons
autofs, 206
controlling network services
with, 35
cron, 36
defined, 35, 802
disabling SELinux protection
for, 714
Samba, 520
data streams in Linux, 29
date
configuring with Date/Time
Properties tool, 171, 172
setting system, 123, 124
default desktops, 680–681
deleting
partitions, 188, 193
user accounts, 281
dependencies and RPM
installations, 224
depmod module, 383–384
desktops. *See also* GNOME Desktop
Environment; KDE Desktop
Environment
desktop environment package
groups, 111–112
GNOME and KDE, 677–680
managing default, 680–681
troubleshooting, 746
/dev directory
defined, 802
viewing devices in, 12, 14
development package groups, 114–115
devices
configuring for parallel ports,
77–78
hotswappable, 77–80
knowing name associated with
partitions, 98
serial port configurations for, 77
df command, 185–186, 751–752
dhclient command, 632
DHCP (Dynamic Host Configuration
Protocol), 627–633
about, 614
BOOTP protocol and, 627
client configuration for, 632–633
connecting server and client
computers, 633

defined, 802
exam coverage of, 615
finding MAC addresses for
clients, 631
getting server's IP address
information, 86–87
installing server and client
packages, 627
lab questions and answers,
641–642, 644–647
MULTICAST setting for
servers, 628
network configuration tool for
clients, 340
prerequisite skills for, 46
self test and answers,
640–641, 643
server configuration for,
628–631
summarized, 637
two-minute drill, 638
working with Windows clients, 631
DHCP clients
configuring, 632–633
connecting to server, 633
finding MAC addresses for, 631
installing client packages, 627
network configuration tool for, 340
troubleshooting, 632
DHCP servers
configuring, 628–631
connecting client to, 633
getting IP address information
from, 86–87
installing server packages, 627
MULTICAST setting for, 628
dig command, 575–576
direct memory address (DMA)
channels, 5, 6
directional brackets (< >), 451
directives for Apache, 452–455
directories. *See also* home directories;
root directory; shared directories; and
specific directories
absolute and relative paths for, 20
adding shared directory with NFS
Server Configuration tool,
499–502
/boot, 801
changing default permissions for
user, 289–290

checking shared Samba printers
and, 520–521
creating shared, 302–303
/dev, 12, 14, 802
/etc, 162, 287
exporting NFS, 496–499
filesystem, 12, 200–207
home, 285–286
init scripts hard linked to /etc, 162
kernel installation into /usr/src/
linux, 393–394
kernel module, 385–388
Linux, 12
mounting shared Samba, 521–523
reviewing SELinux security
for, 210
sharing with NFS clients, 509–512
source RPM build, 233
Squid, 477
structure of /usr/src/redhat, 231
/var/log, 362
disabled mode for SELinux, 707
disabling SELinux daemon
protection, 714
Disk Druid
defined, 802
LVM configuration with, 418
partitions with, 184, 185
disk quotas. *See* quotas
diskless NFS clients, 511
display managers
defined, 663, 802
gdm and kdm, 663–665
setting, 663–664
displays
configuring in Kickstart
Configurator, 259–260
configuring multiple X.org, 660
selecting with Display Settings
tool, 673
starting from remote clients,
675–676
Distributed Intrusion Detection
System, 274
DMA (direct memory address)
channels, 5, 6
dmesg command, 29, 803
DNS (Domain Name Service),
558–584
BIND, 561–577
defined, 558, 559, 803

DNS clients, 560–561
inverse DNS pointers in NFS, 504
lab questions and answers, 580,
582–584
named daemon for, 559
packages for, 559–560
prerequisite skills for, 45
reverse zone not delegated, 574
self test and answers, 579–580, 581
serial number errors in, 574
shortcomings of, 573–574
summarized, 577
topics on exam, 558
two-minute drill, 578
types of DNS servers, 561
DNS clients
configuration files installed with
RHEL, 559
configuring Linux computer as,
560–561
DNS servers
about localhost.zone file, 567
caching-only name servers, 561,
563–565, 801
configuration files for, 561–563
configuring with Red Hat Domain
Name Service tool, 561
exercise setting up, 576–577
forwarding-only name server, 561,
565–566
lack case sensitivity, 568
name servers suggested for exam
study, 567
packages required for, 559–560
reverse lookups with named.local
file, 567, 568
reverse zone not delegated, 574
searching named.ca for root DNS
servers on Internet, 566
slave name servers, 561, 565
starting named daemon, 573
timing for, 573–574
types of, 561
zone files for master, 570–572
documentation
access to during exams, 123
access to man pages during
exams, 123
kernel, 393
looking up Samba variables on
man pages, 529

man pages for xinetd configuration
variables, 618
PAM module, 305
Samba, 520
Domain Name Service. *See* DNS
domains
accepting mail from
unresolved, 595
configuring Samba server to
join, 533
configuring with master DNS
server, 567–569
names reserved for, 466
setting up Samba to share
directories on Microsoft, 525
DOS FDISK.EXE utility, 186
dot (.)
/etc/hosts.allow and /etc/hosts.deny
wildcard, 695
indicating hidden files, 286
double redirection arrows (> >), 30
Dovecot
about, 587, 589
activating, 590–591
configuring, 590
creating secure certificates for, 591
defined, 803
installing packages for, 589
lab questions and answers,
606–607, 609–611
self test and answers, 605–606,
608–609
SMTP used to send mail, 587–588
summarized, 603
two-minute drill, 604
downloading
kernel src.rpm package, 394–395
kernel tar files, 396
Red Hat Enterprise Linux,
53–55, 60
drivers
loading kernel, 158
options for kernel device,
403–407
selecting printer, 345, 346
dual-core CPUs, 803
dumpe2fs command, 754, 755, 803
DVD/CD drives
backups to, 37
compatible with filesystem, 12
Dynamic DNS, 558

Dynamic Host Configuration Protocol.
See DHCP
dynamic IP addresses, 39

E

e2label command
defined, 803
troubleshooting with,
753–754, 755
edquota command, 294–298, 803
egrep command, 23
electronic mail. *See* e-mail
elinks text browser, 51
emacs
defined, 803
errors starting in rescue mode, 8
e-mail, 586–611. *See also* e-mail clients;
sendmail
activating Dovecot, 590–591
exam topics on, 586
finding mail server packages, 589
installing mail server packages,
588–589
lab questions and answers,
606–607, 609–611
mail server components, 587
mail utility, 49–50, 600–601
overview, 586
Postfix, 598–599
reading mail messages, 601
reception with Dovecot,
589–591
selecting e-mail system, 599–603
self test and answers, 605–606,
608–609
sendmail configuration, 592–597
summarized, 603
two-minute drill, 604
e-mail clients, 600–602
command-line mail utility, 49–50,
600–601
configuration process for, 49
mail group "alias" lists, 50, 602
reading mail messages, 50, 601
enabling
firewall access for kernels, 705
IP masquerading, 704–705
ports for DNS communications,
564, 565
Telnet with xinetd, 620

encrypted communications and SSH, 621–622

enforcing mode for SELinux, 707, 709

environment variables
setting defaults with env command, 27
setting shell, 29

environments
defined, 803
hidden files in home directory, 285–287

error messages
found in troubleshooting scenarios, 733
requiring links package, 448
running partprobe command, 195

errors
common configuration file, 730–731
DNS, 573–574
finding GRUB configuration, 152–155
module errors in boot loader, 750–751
pico errors starting in rescue mode, 8
running yum command from local system, 239
troubleshooting Apache, 472–473
using /etc/exports files, 497–498

/etc directories
init scripts hard linked to, 162
system-wide configuration files located in, 287

/etc/auto.master file, 204
/etc/auto.misc file, 204–205
/etc/auto.net file, 205–206
/etc/bashrc file, 287
/etc/dovecot.conf file, 590
/etc/exports file
commands in NFS Server Configuration tool and, 500
creating shared directory in, 508–509
errors using, 497–498

/etc/fstab
activating disk quotas in, 293–294
defined, 803
mounting filesystems with, 200–201

options for mounting directories, 201, 202
remote directory mounting with NFS client during booting, 511

/etc/groups, 301
/etc/hosts file, 42–43, 560
/etc/hosts.allow file, 694, 695
/etc/hosts.conf file, 43
/etc/hosts.deny file, 694–696
/etc/inittab
configuring virtual consoles from, 160
defined, 803
determining runlevels with, 159–160
troubleshooting scenarios for, 731, 732
understanding boot process in, 164

/etc/ldap.conf file, 315
/etc/mail/sendmail.mc file, 594, 595
/etc/mail/sendmail.cf file, 594, 595
/etc/mail/submit.cf file, 594
/etc/named.caching-nameserver.conf file, 563
/etc/nologin file, 309
/etc/nsswitch.conf file, 43
/etc/openldap/ldap.conf file, 315
/etc/pam.d/login, 308–310
/etc/pam.d/system-auth file, 309
/etc/passwd file, 31–32, 275
/etc/profile.d/, 289
/etc/profile file, 288–289
/etc/rc.d files, 164
/etc/rc.dirc.sysinit files, 164
/etc/rc.sysinit script, 293
/etc/resolv.conf file, 43, 560
/etc/samba/smb.conf file
editing, 523–524
misspelled variables in, 533
testing changes to, 542
variables for, 529
/etc/shadow file, 33–34, 283–284
/etc/skel directory, 35, 285–287
/etc/squid/squid.conf file, 478–480
/etc/sysconfig directory
configuring files in, 169
configuring name resolution with /etc/sysconfig/network file, 42
exam tips for understanding of, 331
non-network files in, 170

/etc/sysconfig/iptables file, 700
/etc/sysconfig/networking/devices directory, 332
/etc/sysconfig/networking/profiles/ default directory, 332
/etc/sysconfig/network-scripts directory, 331, 332–333
/etc/sysconfig/selinux file, 707
/etc/sysconfig/squid file, 478
/etc/X11/prefdm file, 803
/etc/X11/xorg.conf file, 660–662
/etc/xinetd.conf file, 616
Ethernet Device dialog box, 335
exam. *See also* lab questions and answers; self test and answers
administrator login for, 273–274
based on x86 architecture, 75
books helpful for, 2
boot process topics, 144, 164
configuring client connections in NIS and LDAP, 313
creating partitions with care, 102
dealing with hardware problems, 158
desktop environment selection on, 112
device name associated with partitions, 98
DHCP knowledge required, 627
DNS topics on, 558, 567
e-mail topics on, 586, 600–602
filesystem administration on, 184
following instructions for IP addresses, 108
given credit only if changes survive reboot, 415
GUI access during Troubleshooting, 282
hardware issues in, 5
HTTP Web sites configured on, 458
importance of installation on, 70, 71, 88
index.html files to be created during, 469
installation and configuration requirements for, 272
installing GUI for, 120
kernel management, 376, 389, 393
kickstart preparation for, 222, 245

looking up Samba variables during, 529
LVM skills needed on, 376, 418
managing RPM packages, 222
mounting Zip drives, 203
network configuration tips for, 331, 337
network services on, 445, 495, 615
PAM configuration files on, 312
preparing for, 2–3
prerequisite skills for, 4
preventing unauthorized system access, 700
RAID on, 376, 412
Red Hat Network on, 234
reinstalls during, 126
RHCE troubleshooting skills, 748–759
RHCT troubleshooting skills, 742–748
runlevels of activated service for, 169
Samba configuration on, 524
Sample Exam 1, 768–781
Sample Exam 2, 784–782
SELinux topics on, 81, 184, 208, 708
setting up users, 125
source RPM familiarity for, 230
SSH, DHCP, and NTP network services on, 615
system administration tools used on, 330
system configuration during installation "dead time", 120
time server configuration on, 124
tips for users of other Unix-style systems, 255
troubleshooting skills, 728, 729, 742–759
upgrading kernels, 389
virtual hosts, 467, 470
when to install Virtualization package, 109
Xen, 377
X Window System on, 650, 651
executable virtual host files, 470
exim, 586
expanding logical volumes, 758
exportfs command, 804

exporting NFS directories
  activating list of exports, 498–499
  /etc/exports configuration file for, 497–498
  overview, 496
Express Cards, 78, 79, 804
Extended Internet Services Daemon. *See* xinetd

F

fdisk utility
  about, 14, 804
  commands for, 15, 186–187
  configuring new PC without partitions, 189
  creating partitions with, 188–189
  deleting partitions with, 188
  df and mount commands for, 185–186
  DOS FDISK.EXE vs., 186
  options for, 16
  overview, 185–186
  parted utility vs., 191, 192
  setting up swap partition, 190–191
  troubleshooting with, 745, 747–748, 752–753
  using, 185, 187
Fedora Core 5/6
  about, 53
  RHEL installation process vs., 92
  using, 54–55
Fedora Linux, 804
FHS (Filesystem Hierarchy Standard), 11, 57, 804
file locking, 504
file permissions, 30–31
file sharing. *See* network file sharing services
File Transfer Protocol. *See* FTP; vsFTP servers
files. *See also* configuration files; httpd .conf file; and specific files
  access control lists and permissions for, 208–210
  allowing and denying, 48
  Apache log, 471–472
  changing default user permissions for, 289–290

checking shared Samba, 520–521
compressing, 37–38
configuring SELinux Management Tool labeling options for, 714–715
contexts for SELinux, 706
corrupted, 755–756
creating, 22
crontab, 355–357
defaults for hidden, 285, 286
downloading kernel tar, 396
editing ks.cfg, 254
executable virtual host, 470
file permissions, 30–31
found in NFS nfs-utils and portmap RPM packages, 496
grub.conf, 390, 391–392
.htaccess, 463–464
index.html, 469
installing from, 92
key Squid, 477
linking, 22
list of /etc/profile.d/, 289
listing hidden, 286
localhost.zone, 567
managing system log, 38
meminfo, 381
modifying configuration, 162
modules.dep, 386
NFS file locking, 504
operating commands for, 19–22
/proc, 380–383, 811
reading, copying, and moving, 21–22
reverse DNS zone, 572–573
sample kickstart, 248–251
searching for, 20–21
sendmail configuration, 592–593
setting up executable, 28–29
sharing with Apache, 458–459
sorting, 23
spec, 815
symbolically linked NFS, 503
system configuration, 169–172
testing changes to /etc/samba/smb .conf, 542
/tmp directory configuration, 129
wildcards for searching for, 25
word count for, 23
zone, 570–572

filesystem device nodes, 11, 12, 13
Filesystem Hierarchy Standard (FHS),
    11, 57, 804
filesystems, 11–19, 184–219. *See also*
    partitions
    about, 11
    access control lists with, 208
    administrative tasks for, 210
    automounting, 203–207
    configuring on multiple
        partitions, 17–18
    converting LVM1 to LVM2, 430
    creating LVM partition, 18
    defined, 12, 804
    directories in, 12
    ext2/ext3 attributes for, 199
    formatting and checking, 14–17
    fsck command for unmounted, 740
    journaling, 197–198
    kernel configuration options
        for, 407
    lab questions and answers,
        213–214, 216–219
    local and remote network, 44
    logical volumes and, 97
    managing, 196–199
    media devices compatible with, 12
    messages when mounting ext2, 740
    mkfs command for creating,
        198–199
    mounting directory to, 200–207
    partitions mounted to, 18–19
    self test and answers for, 212–213,
        215–216
    setting up partitions with
        separate, 101
    standard formatting, 196–197
    troubleshooting, 747, 751–755
    two-minute drill, 211
    types of, 196
filtering files, 23–24
find command, 21, 804
fips (First Interactive Partition
    Splitter), 804
firewalls
    checking network communications
        with installation server, 87
    configuring during first boot, 122
    defined, 804
    enabling DNS ports for, 564, 565

Kickstart Configurator setup
    of, 259
maintaining configurations in
    iptables file, 700
packet filtering by, 697–698
packet IP address replaced with
    NAT, 703
running NFS through, 501
saving iptables configurations
    for, 700
setting up with Security Level
    Configuration tool, 701–703
Squid running with, 482
troubleshooting issues with, 756
using Apache with, 458
First Boot process, 120–126
    about, 120–121
    configuring regular user, 124
    firewall configuration during, 122
    installing software from Additional
        CDs window, 125
    kdump service setup, 123, 806
    licensing, 122
    password requirements in, 125
    SELinux configuration during,
        122–123
    setting system date and time,
        123, 124
    software updates configured
        during, 124
    testing sound card
        configuration, 125
    text-based steps for, 126
First Interactive Partition Splitter
    (fips), 804
firstboot, 804
floppy drives, 207
--force switch, 674
forward slash (/)
    end of Apache container indicated
        with, 452
    root directory indicated by, 12
forwarding-only name servers, 561,
    565–566
fsck command
    about, 14, 17
    defined, 804
    remounting filesystem with, 17
    troubleshooting filesystems with,
        754–755

using only with unmounted
    filesystems, 17, 740
FTP (File Transfer Protocol), 512–515.
    See also vsFTP servers
    basic vsFTP server
        configuration, 515
    configuring network installation
        server, 85–86
    defined, 805
    installing vsFTP servers, 512
    lab questions and answers,
        549–551, 553–556
    options in SELinux Management
        Tool for, 711
    prerequisite skills for, 45
    self test and answers, 548–549, 552
    SELinux support for vsFTP servers,
        512–513
    starting vsFTP servers on
        reboot, 513
    time-efficient installations via FTP
        servers, 94, 95
    two-minute drill, 546–547
    vsFTP server security
        configuration, 513–514

G

gateways, 805
gdm display manager, 663–665
General Options tab (Add NFS Share
    dialog), 499–500
geometrical positioning for X clients,
    656–657
getfacl command, 805
getty, 805
GIDs (group IDs). *See also* SGID bit
    about, 32
    creating with /etc/passwd, 275
    defined, 805
    Red Hat user private group
        scheme, 280–281, 301
global settings
    editing Samba, 537–538
    modifying Samba server, 524–529
globbing, 25, 498
glossary, 800–818
GNOME Desktop Environment,
    111, 112
    defined, 805
    features of, 677–679

gdm display manager for, 665
GUI printer management for, 349
illustrated, 678
Red Hat User Manager in,
277, 278
running Setroubleshoot Browser
in, 716
starting Red Hat Display Settings
tool with, 653
troubleshooting, 746
GParted, 194
GPG (GNU Privacy Guard), 805
GPG keys, 228
grace period for quotas, 295–297
graphic user interface. *See* GUI
grep command, 23
group IDs. *See* GIDs
groups. *See also* GIDs; SGID bit
about, 32
adding users to, 275–276
controlling ownership with SGID
bit, 303–305
creating and maintaining, 301–305
mail group "alias" lists, 50, 602
Red Hat user private group
scheme, 280–281, 301
sharing directories, 302–303
standard and Red Hat, 301–302
user private, 280–281, 301
GRUB (Grand Unified Boot) loader,
147–157
booting into runlevel of choice,
144, 164–167, 733
changing default boot stanza
in, 390
command line for, 155–157
commands for loading upgraded
kernels, 390
default option for Kickstart
Configurator, 257–258
defined, 805
editing commands for, 149
illustrated, 165
kernels loaded into memory
by, 377
passing parameters to, 149–150
password-protecting, 735
troubleshooting errors in
configuration file, 152–155
updating, 150–152, 391–392
using, 147–149

grub.conf file, 390, 391–392
grub-install command, 805
GUI (graphic user interface). *See also*
desktops; kernel configuration menu
options; X Window System
configuring with .xinitrc file,
667–669
exam coverage of, 650, 651
First Boot process with, 121
installing package group for, 120
modifying user accounts
independent of tools in, 282
Network Configuration utility,
333–334
parted tools for, 194
Service Configuration tool for
controlling service, 168–169
timesaving with text methods
vs., 281
tools for modifying system
configuration files, 171–172
virtual consoles in, 160
GUI LVM Management tool, 425–430
about, 425
adding logical volume with,
425–427
adding physical volume, 429, 430
illustrated, 426
opening, 426
removing logical volumes, 428, 429
resizing logical volumes, 428–430
volume group creation in, 426–427
gzip command, 37–38

H

hackers, 32
HAL (Hardware Abstraction Layer),
73–74
hard drives. *See also* partitions
adding SATA, 423–424
attaching external drive to parallel
ports, 78
backups using, 37
BIOS limits on reported
cylinders, 105
commands and options to
check, 755
compatible with filesystem, 12
configuring without partitions,
189, 193–194

disk space required for file servers,
103–104
installations from local,
87–88, 92
managing disk quotas, 290–301
naming partitions, 97–98
partitioning during installation,
99–101
planning partitions, 98
prerequisite skills for, 7
space needed for recompiling
kernels, 392
swap space on partitions,
104–105, 815
writing system changes from linux
rescue environment to, 740
hard limits, 296, 805
hardware. *See also* hard drives
ACPI and APM power
management, 74
basic knowledge required, 4–7, 57
compatibility of, 70–74
CPU requirements, 75–76
First Boot process, 120–126
floppy drives with
automounter, 207
hard drive options, 7
hotswap buses, 77–80
hotswappable RAID drives, 412
kernel device driver configuration
options, 403–407
lab questions and answers,
134–139, 141–142
Linux documentation for, 72
logical volumes, 97
plug and play and Hardware
Abstraction Layer, 73
RAID partitions, 96
RAM partitions, 6–7, 76
resolving conflicts with, 73
self test and answers, 133–134,
140–141
summary of installation on,
129–130
two-minute drill, 131–132
X Window System support for,
653–654
Hardware Abstraction Layer (HAL),
73–74
hash symbol (#), 524
head command, 22

hidden files, 285, 286
home directories
    about, 285–286, 805
    sharing Samba directory with
        Windows workstation,
        535–536
    Web access to pages placed on,
        462–463
/home partition, 415–417
host command, 575
hostnames
    characters allowed in, 568
    resolving problems for, 744
hosts. *See also* virtual hosts
    allowing security by, 694–696
    defining localhost addresses in
        sendmail, 595
    host-based security for
        Apache, 460
    secure virtual, 813
    securing with tcp_wrappers,
        694–696
    virtual, 466–468, 816
hotswap buses, 77–80
    commands for device management,
        79–80
    IEEE 1394, 78
    parallel ports and, 77–78
    PC Cards, 78–79
    serial ports and, 77
    types of hotswappable systems, 79
    USB support, 78
.htaccess files, 463–464
htpasswd command, 805
HTTP daemon, 444
HTTP installation servers
    configuring, 83–85
    time-efficient installations via,
        94, 95
HTTP Web sites for exam, 458
httpd.conf file
    about, 450
    Apache file global environment
        directives, 452, 453
    main server configuration
        directives, 452, 454–455
    virtual host configuration
        directives, 452, 455

I/O (input/output) addresses, 5, 6
ICMP (Internet Control Message
    Protocol), 806
ICP (Inter-Cache Protocol), 477
IEEE 1394, 78
ifconfig command, 42, 333, 337–338,
    339, 742, 743, 806
ifup/ifdown commands, 333, 337
IMAP4 (Internet Mail Access Protocol)
    about, 588, 589
    prerequisite skills for, 45, 586
index.html files, 469
init process, 159–160, 806
init scripts, 162
initial RAM disk, 806
inspecting system logs, 364
installation, 70–142. *See also* kickstart
    adding software from Additional
        CDs window, 125
    Apache, 447, 449–450
    boot loader configuration during,
        106–107
    booting options for exam, 88–89
    configuring network, 81–88,
        107–108
    console screens for, 127–129
    creating and using installation
        USB or CD/DVD, 89–90, 91
    CUPS, 341
    custom kernel compilation and,
        408–409
    customizing baseline packages in,
        108–110
    exam's focus on, 70, 71
    First Boot process, 120–126
    initiating with kickstart, 247
    installation log file, 127
    installing RPM packages, 224–225
    kernel source code, 394–395
    kernel upgrading vs., 389
    Kickstart Configurator methods
        for, 257
    lab questions and answers,
        134–139, 141–142
    Linux package groups available for,
        110–120
    mail server package for, 588–589

partitions added during, 99–101
    post-partition steps for, 106–120
    rebuild distributions for, 70
    redoing rather than fixing, 126
    remote installation of RPMs, 226
    Samba service, 517–518
    self test and answers, 133–134,
        140–141
    setting up from local hard drive,
        87–88, 92
    source RPM, 231
    summarized, 129–130
    system configuration during "dead
        time", 120
    time limits on exam, 71, 88
    time-efficient method for, 92–95
    timezones and root password
        setup, 108
    troubleshooting, 127–129
    two-minute drill, 131–132
    vsFTP server, 512
Installation and Configuration section
    Sample Exam 1, 776–781
    Sample Exam 2, 793–798
installation CDs, 53–54
installation consoles, 127–129
installation log file, 127
Inter-Cache Protocol (ICP), 477
Internet
    connecting multiple systems with
        IP masquerading, 703–705
    connections during exam, 123
Internet Control Message Protocol
    (ICMP), 806
Internet Mail Access Protocol. *See*
    IMAP4
Internet Printing Protocol (IPP), 26,
    341, 806
Internet SCSI (ISCSI), 806
interrupt request channels. *See* IRQ
    channels
inverse DNS pointers in NFS, 504
ip6tables command, 698
IP addresses
    assigning to specific network card,
        630
    checking if used to attack other
        systems, 274

configuring with Kickstart
  Configurator, 259
defining network with, 40–41
detecting problems with arp
  command, 339–340
DHCP and dynamic, 614
disguising with NAT, 703–705
following instructions for, 108
getting information from DHCP
  server, 86–87
IP forwarding, 382–383, 705, 806
IP numbers and address classes,
  39, 40
IPv4, 806
IPv6, 39, 806
locating domain name's address for
  DNS server, 566
solving hostname resolution
  problems, 744
time needed by DNS server to
  propagate changes, 573–574
translating host names to, 42–43
troubleshooting, 706
IP forwarding, 382–383, 705, 806
IP masquerading, 703–705
ipchains command, 693
IPP (Internet Printing Protocol), 26,
  341, 806
iptables command
  automating firewall configuration,
    701–703
  chain rule categories for, 699
  configuring, 698–700
  defined, 806
  effect on packets, 48–49
  enabling IP masquerading with,
    704–705
  format for, 698
  implementing packet filtering
    and/or NAT with, 482
  preventing computers from pinging
    your system, 699
  saving firewall configuration, 700
  uses for, 693
IPv4 addresses, 806
IPv6 addresses, 39, 806
IRQ (interrupt request) channels
  about, 5

conflicts with HAL configurations,
  73–74
planning layout for, 6
settings for, 5
ISCSI (Internet SCSI), 806
Itanium-based architecture, 75

jobs
  creating settings with cron
    daemon, 357–358
  running with at daemon, 358–359
joe editor, 8
journaling filesystems, 197–198

K

KDE Desktop Environment, 111, 112
  defined, 806
  features of, 677–678, 679–680
  illustrated, 678
  kdm display manager for, 665
  konsole command line terminal
    in, 254
  Red Hat User Manager in, 277
  starting Red Hat Display Settings
    tool with, 653
  troubleshooting, 746
kdm display manager, 663–665
Kdump service, 123, 806
kernel configuration menu options,
  400–408
  Block Layer options, 402
  Bus options, 402
  Code Maturity Level options, 401
  commands to make, 398–400
  Cryptographic options, 408
  Device Drivers options, 403–407
  Executable File Formats
    options, 402
  File Systems options, 407
  General Setup options, 401
  Instrumentation Support
    options, 407
  Kernel Hacking options, 407
  Library Routines options, 408
  Loadable Module Support
    options, 402

Networking options, 403
Power Management options, 402
Process Debugging Support
  option, 402
Processor Type and Features
  options, 402
Security options, 407
kernel log daemon (klogd), 360
kernel modules
  commands for loading, 378–379
  defined, 807
  directory structure for, 385–388
  finding, 393
  location for types of, 387
  removing, 387–388
  using, 383–385
Kernel-based Virtual Machine (KVM)
  technologies, 76
kernels, 376–409. See also kernel
  configuration menu options; kernel
  modules; recompiling kernels
  about, 377
  activating IP forwarding for,
    382–383
  analyzing messages when booting
    from GRUB, 158
  best practices for, 377–378
  changes in SMP limits for, 75
  compiling and installing custom,
    408–409
  configuring, 400–408
  defined, 807
  device driver options for, 403–407
  downloading tar files for, 396
  enabling firewall access for, 705
  exam preparation for, 376
  initialization and First Boot process
    for, 157–158
  installing, 393–395
  kernel modules, 383–385
  lab questions and answers,
    434–436, 438–442
  loading drivers for, 158
  monolithic vs. modular, 378–379
  patching, 390–391
  preventing ping of death, 383
  /proc filesystem and directory for,
    380–383

quota settings in, 291–292
recompiling, 396–408
required customization RPMs for, 395–396
self test and answers, 433–434, 437–438
setting up protection through firewalls, 693
sources for, 392–396
space needed for recompiling, 392
standard RHEL configuration, 401
stored in /boot partition, 379
summarized, 430
two-minute drill, 431–432
types of, 379, 380
updating, 226–227, 379
upgrading, 389–390
version numbers for, 388–389
Keyboard configuration tool, 171
keys
GPG, 228
private, 621, 811
public, 621–622, 811
RNDC, 569–570
utilities generating SSH, 623
kickstart, 244–260. *See also* Kickstart Configurator
about, 244, 807
configuring kickstart server, 246–247
creating configuration file for, 245
editing ks.cfg file on package to be installed, 254
exam preparation for, 245
partitioning options in file, 251–253
sample file, 248–251, 253
setting up boot USB containing, 245–246
starting installation with, 247
Kickstart Configurator
adding installation scripts to, 260
authentication protocols in, 259
Basic Configuration screen, 256, 257
boot loader options with, 257–258
configuring display in, 259–260
creating configuration file with, 245
firewall configuration in, 259

illustrated, 254, 256
installation methods with, 257
network configuration with, 259
Partition Options screen in, 258
selecting packages in, 260
using, 254–256
klogd (kernel log daemon), 360
.ko extension, 387
konsole in KDE Desktop Environment, 254
ks.cfg file, 254
KVM (Kernel-based Virtual Machine) technologies, 76

L

lab questions and answers
Apache and Squid, 487, 489–491
booting, 176–179, 181–182
DNS, 580, 582–584
e-mail, 606–607, 609–611
filesystem administration, 213–214, 216–219
hardware and installation, 134–139, 141–142
kernels, 434–436, 438–442
network file sharing services, 549–551, 553–556
NTP, 641–642, 644–647
package management, 264–266, 268–269
prerequisite skills, 63, 65–67
security, 721–722, 724–726
system administration tools, 368–370, 372–374
troubleshooting, 762–763, 765–766
user administration, 322–323, 325–327
X Window System, 685–686, 688–690
LDAP (Lightweight Directory Access Protocol)
about, 272, 807
configuring network clients, 314–315
database checks with Red Hat Authentication Configuration tool, 316–317
exam requirements for client connections in, 313

searching database with Name Service Switch file, 315–316
LDP (Linux Documentation Project), 72, 807
LE (logical extent), 808
less command, 21, 29
lftp command, 51–53, 807
/lib/modules/kernel_version/ directory, 385–388
licensing, 122
Lightweight Directory Access Protocol. *See* LDAP
LILO (Linux Loader), 147
Line Print Daemon. *See* LPD
Line Printer Next Generation (LPRng), 341
linking files, 22
Linux. *See* Red Hat Enterprise Linux
linux askmethod command, 92, 93
Linux Documentation Project (LDP), 72, 807
Linux editors, 8–11
availability of GUI-text editors during exam, 11
command mode in vi, 9–10
creating new user in vi, 10–11
Linux Hardware HOWTO document, 72
linux rescue environment, 735–742
illustrated, 736, 737, 738, 739
importance of, 728
no mount, 741–742
read-only, 741
standard, 738–740
testing troubleshooting scenarios with, 731
listing installed RPMs, 230
ln command, 22
local network file systems, 44
local NTP servers, 636–637
localhost.zone file, 567
localizing options for Squid, 480–481
locate command, 21, 23, 807
log files for Apache, 471–472
logical extent (LE), 808
Logical Volume Manager. *See* LVM
logical volumes. *See* LVs
logins
messages with /etc/nologin file, 309
mounting shared Samba directories during, 521–523

PAM user verification during, 306–308
reviewing recent for crackers, 274
using /etc/pam.d/login for configuring, 308–310, 312
logrotate command utility, 807
lpc command, 807
lpc status command, 348
LPD (Line Print Daemon)
about, 341
substituting for CUPS, 354
using LPD commands, 347–349
lpq command, 26, 348, 807
lpr command, 26, 348, 808
lprm command, 26, 349, 808
LPRng (Line Printer Next Generation), 341
ls command, 20
ls -Z command, 706, 707
lsattr command, 808
lvcreate command, 417, 808
lvdisplay command, 808
lvextend command, 418, 808
LVM (Logical Volume Manager), 417–430
about, 417–418
commands used with, 420–421
configuring during exam, 418
converting LVM1 filesystem to LVM2, 430
creating partition with, 18
creating physical volume, 418–419
exam preparation for, 376, 418
GUI LVM Management tool for, 425–430
one filesystem configured for multiple partitions, 17
RAID array used with, 417
setting up and using logical volumes, 419–420
summarized, 430
time required for partitions, 103
two-minute drill, 432
using, 97
volume group creation in, 419
lvremove command, 808
LVs (logical volumes)
adding, 423–424, 425–427, 757–758
/boot files unreadable on, 423
commands for managing, 421, 422

creating and using, 419–420
defined, 808
exam skills required for, 184
expanding, 758
filesystems and, 97
GUI LVM Management tool for adding, 425–427
partitioning utilities, 185–196
removing, 424, 428, 429, 759
resizing, 424–425, 428–430
troubleshooting, 756–759

M

macros for sendmail.mc file, 594
mail delivery agents, 587
mail group "alias" lists, 50, 602
mail readers, 601
mail server components, 587
mail transfer agents, 587
mail user agents, 587
mail utility
testing mail system from, 600–601
using from command line, 49–50
MAILTO variable, 355
main server configuration directives in httpd.conf, 452, 454–455
main.cf file, 598
make config command, 397–398
make gconfig command, 398–400
make help command, 409
make menuconfig command, 398, 399
make xconfig command, 398, 399
man pages
access to during exams, 123
looking up Samba variables, 529
xinetd configuration variable, 618
man smb.conf command, 529
managing filesystems, 196–199
creating with mkfs, 198–199
journaling filesystems, 197–198
list of standard filesystem types, 196–197
mounting directory to filesystem, 200–207
overview, 196
working with ext2/ext3 attributes for, 199
manually configuring SELinux, 708–709

masquerading, 808
Master Boot Record (MBR), 731, 732, 808
master DNS servers
about, 561
configuring simple domain with, 567–569
zone files for, 570–572
MBR (Master Boot Record), 731, 732, 808
md device, 410
mdadm command, 808
media devices. *See also* hard drives
compatible with filesystem, 12
listing of compatible, 14
referencing in /dev directory, 12, 14
meminfo file, 381
memory
loading kernels into, 377
measuring current system with meminfo file, 381
requirements for RHEL, 6–7, 72, 76
speed of hard drives and, 104
swap space based on system RAM, 104–105
messages. *See also* error messages
kernel messages when booting from GRUB, 158
reading mail, 601
routing with cron daemon, 355
when mounting ext2 filesystem, 740
Microsoft. *See* Windows
mirroring /home partition with RAID, 415–417
mkbootdisk command, 809
mkfs command
about, 14, 15–17
creating filesystems with, 198–199
defined, 809
formatting disk partitions with, 15, 17, 755
mklabel command, 191, 194
/mnt/sysimage file, 728–729
modprobe command, 383–384, 809
modular kernels, 378–379
modules. *See also* kernel modules
defined, 378
depmod, 383–384

PAM, 305
pam_listfile.so, 311–312
modules.dep file, 386
Monitor dialog (Display Settings tool), 673
monitors. *See* displays
monolithic kernels, 378–379
more command, 21
mount command, 18–19, 185–186, 202, 203, 521–522, 809
mount.cifs command, 522, 809
mounting
    automounting filesystems, 203–207
    ext2 filesystems, 740
    filesystems with /etc/fstab, 200–201, 202
    NFS directory from client with command line, 510
    options in SELinux Management Tool for, 711
    partitions from hard drive in rescue mode, 742
    remote directory with NFS client during boot, 511
    root directory in linux rescue environment, 738–740
    shared Samba directories, 521–523
    soft mounting option for NFS clients, 511–512
    USB keys and removable media, 201–203
moving files, 22
Mozilla Web browser, 50
MULTICAST setting for active network cards, 628
multi-core CPUs, 803
mv command, 22

N

name queries, 563
name resolution
    configuring, 42–43
    e-mail reliance on, 587
named daemon
    about DNS, 559
    starting, 573
named.ca file, 566
named.local file, 567, 568

names
    canonical, 802
    characters allowed in hostnames, 568
    NetBIOS, 519
    partitions, 97–98
    reserved domain, 466
    RPM package, 223
    WINS name resolution, 519, 528, 817
NAT (Network Address Translation), 703–706
    about, 703
    defined, 809
    IP forwarding, 705
    IP masquerading, 703–705
    prerequisite skills for, 48
    troubleshooting, 706
National Security Agency (NSA), 706
navigating files, 19–20
netstat command, 42, 338–339, 340, 809
network adapters. *See* NICs
Network Address Translation. *See* NAT
network configuration, 331–340
    arp command as diagnostic tool for, 339–340
    during installation, 107–108
    exam tips for, 331
    ifconfig command for, 42, 333, 337–338, 339, 742, 743, 806
    ifup/ifdown commands for, 333, 337
    installation for, 81–88
    netstat command for, 338–339, 340
    setting up network interface, 333–340
    system-config-network to modify interface, 334–336
    tool for DHCP clients, 340
    variables for /etc/sysconfig/network file, 331–332
Network Configuration utility, 333–334
    illustrated, 334
    modifying network interface with system-config-network in, 334–336
    tabs of, 336
    using during exam, 337

network file sharing services, 494–556. *See also* NFS servers; Samba
    configuring NFS server, 494–509
    creating Samba public access shares, 540–541
    file locking issues for NFS, 504
    FTP and vsFTPd, 512–515
    lab questions and answers, 549–551, 553–556
    major protocols for, 494
    performance tips for NFS, 504–505
    Samba services, 516–544
    self test and answers, 548–549, 552
    setting up for Samba servers, 529–533
    sharing NFS directories with client computers, 509–512
    statelessness of NFS, 502–503
    two-minute drill, 546–547
Network Information System (NIS), 810
network installation servers, 81–88
    configuring, 81
    FTP, 85–86, 94, 95, 512–515
    HTTP, 83–85, 94, 95
    NFS, 81–83, 494–509
    other requirements to setup, 86–87
Network Interface Cards. *See* NICs
Network Port options (SELinux Management Tool), 715
network security
    allowing and denying files, 48
    Extended Internet Services Daemon, 47
    iptables command, 48–49
    Network Address Translation, 48
    Network Information Service, 47
    overview of skills for, 47
    securing ports, 48
network services. *See* specific services
Network Time Protocol. *See* NTP
networks. *See also* network configuration; network services; system administration tools
    adding Linux to Windows, 528
    authenticating with NIS and LDAP, 313–317
    basic security for, 47–48
    configuring, 107–108, 331–340

controlling resource access with tcp_wrappers, 696–697
defining with IP addresses, 40–41
IP addressing configured with Kickstart Configurator, 259
knowing how to protect, 693
options in linux rescue mode, 736–737
packet handling on, 697
searching NIS and LDAP databases with Name Service Switch file, 315–316
security for, 47–49
setting up installation servers for, 81–88
solving problems with hostname resolution, 744
TCP/IP, 38–43
troubleshooting, 330, 742–743
X Window System designed for, 675
New Printer wizard, 344–346
New Volume Group dialog (GUI LVM Management tool), 427
nfs daemon, 497
NFS (Network File System). *See also* NFS clients; NFS servers
about, 44, 494–495
absolute and relative symbolic links, 503
activating list of exports, 498–499
adding shared directory, 499–502
command line configurations of, 506
configuring servers, 494–509
defined, 809
diskless clients, 511
/etc/exports configuration file for, 497–498
file locking issues for, 504
installations for exam, 495
inverse DNS pointers with, 504
lab questions and answers, 549–551, 553–556
options in SELinux Management Tool for, 713
performance tips for, 504–505
quotas on directories in, 299–300
reducing security risks for, 506

required RPM packages for, 496
root squash behavior of, 503
running through firewalls, 501
security risks for, 505–506
self test and answers, 548–549, 552
server startup configurations for, 496–497
sharing directories with clients, 509–512
statelessness of, 502–503
system processes for NFS clients, 510
troubleshooting hangs with, 503–504
two-minute drill, 546–547
using wildcards and globbing in, 498
working with SELinux, 502
NFS clients, 509–512
diskless, 511
hang when shutting down NFS server, 503–504, 507–508
mounting remote directory during boot process, 511
shared directory mounting via command line, 510
soft mounting, 511–512
system processes for, 510
troubleshooting NFS hangs, 503–504, 507–508
NFS file handle, 502
NFS Server Configuration tool, 499–502
activating shared directories at appropriate runlevels, 501
corresponding commands for /etc/exports, 500
creating shared directory with, 508–509
General Options tab, 499–500
illustrated, 499, 500
NFS servers, 494–509
about NFS standard, 494–495
activating list of exports, 498–499
client hangs when shutting down, 503–504, 507–508
configuring, 494–509
creating installation servers, 81–83

/etc/exports configuration file for, 497–498
exam topics on, 495
quirks and limitations of, 502–504
RPM packages required for, 496
running through firewalls, 501
startup configurations for, 496–497
time-efficient installations via, 92–95
using wildcards and globbing, 498
working with SELinux, 502
nfs-utils RPM package, 496
NICs (Network Interface Cards). *See also* network configuration
assigning IP addresses to specific, 630
configuring, 87, 88, 334–336
defined, 809
ifconfig switches for, 339
network scripts for, 332
setting up DHCP client, 632, 633
troubleshooting unrecognized second, 336
NIS (Network Information Service)
about, 272
checking database with Red Hat Authentication Configuration tool, 316–317
defined, 810
exam requirements for client connections in, 313
prerequisite skills for, 47
searching database with Name Service Switch file, 315–316
setting up network clients, 314
nmbd daemon, 520
no mount linux rescue environment, 741–742
nslookup command, 575
NTP (Network Time Protocol), 634–637
about, 614, 634, 809
client configuration for, 634–635
exam coverage of, 615
illustrated, 635
lab questions and answers, 641–642, 644–647
problems with SELinux and, 635
self test and answers, 640–641, 643

setting up local NTP server,
636–637
summarized, 637
two-minute drill for, 639
ntsysv configuration tool, 168

O

opening GUI LVM Management
tool, 426
operators for tcp_wrappers, 696
overriding inherited permissions with
.htaccess, 463–464

P

Package Manager utility. *See* pirut tool
Package Updater (Pup), 236, 811
packages, 222–269. *See also* Red Hat
Package Manager; source RPMs
about RPM, 223
adding, 111, 238–244
applications package groups,
113–114
automating installation with
kickstart, 244–260
Base System, 118–120
basic customization, 108–110
defined, 223
desktop environment, 111–112
development package groups,
114–115
DHCP, 627
DNS, 559–560
editing ks.cfg file before
installing, 254
elinks RPM, 448
finding mail server, 589
installed with Anaconda, 127
installing RPM, 224–225
lab questions and answers on,
264–266, 268–269
listing installed RPMs, 230
managing, 222–227
names of RPM, 223
overview of Linux package groups,
110–120
removing, 225, 238
required for NFS, 496
restoring missing X configuration
file for existing, 674

selecting in Kickstart
Configurator, 260
self test and answers on, 263–264,
267–268
Servers package group, 115–118
summary of package
management, 260
tarballs for distributing Linux, 23
testing RPM, 225
two-minute drill for, 261–262
updates for kernel RPM, 226–227
updating with Pup and Red Hat
Network, 234–238
using RPM queries, 227–228
validating signatures of, 228
verifying installed RPM, 229
packet filtering, 697–698
packets
chains for, 698
defined, 697
forwarding, 699, 700
iptables command effect on, 48–49
NAT handling of, 703
routing, 705
using iptables command to control,
698–700
PAM (Pluggable Authentication
Modules), 272, 305–313
authenticating halting and
rebooting computer, 706
configuring, 310–311
defined, 305, 810
documentation for, 305
limiting user access with, 311–313
location of configuration files, 306
types of modules and files for,
306–308
using /etc/pam.d/login for
configuring login, 308–310, 312
pam_listfile.so module, 311–312
parallel ports, 77–78
parameters
passing to GRUB, 149–150
shell, 27–28
xinetd, 619
parted utility, 191–196
defined, 810
deleting partitions with, 193
fdisk utility vs., 191, 192
making swap partition using,
195–196

mistakes using, 191
overview, 191
setting up new drive without
partitions, 193–194
troubleshooting with, 747,
752–753
using, 192–193
viewing commands for, 191–192
Partition Options screen (Kickstart
Configurator), 258
partitions. *See also* fdisk utility; parted
utility
adding during installation, 99–101
BIOS limits on cylinders
reported, 105
checking with dumpe2fs, 754
configuring one filesystem on
multiple, 17
converting LVM1 filesystem to
LVM2, 430
defined, 96
Disk Druid for, 184, 185
drive configured without, 189,
193–194
filesystem corruption on, 752–753
formatting with mkfs command,
15, 17, 755
installation steps after making, 106
kernels stored in /boot, 379
key commands and options to
check disks and, 755
kickstart file partitioning options,
251–253
knowing device name associated
with, 98
limitations on writing, 96, 187
LVM, 18
mirroring /home, 415–417
mounting from hard drive in rescue
mode, 742
mounting other, 18–19
naming, 97–98
options for Kickstart
Configurator, 258
planning, 98
RAID, 96
separate filesystems for, 101
stability and security of
multiple, 102
storage space required for RHEL,
103–104

swap, 190–191, 195–196, 747
swap space on, 104–105, 815
troubleshooting new, 747–748
using care creating exam, 102
utilities for creating, 185–196
partprobe command, 195, 810
passwd command, 32
passwords
    assigning user, 276–277
    changing user, 32
    configuring Web, 462
    creating with /etc/passwd, 275
    encrypting Samba server, 538
    importance of good, 277
    managing aging information from
        shadow file, 283–284
    managing Samba user, 534–535
    protecting Web sites and
        directories, 460–461, 464–466
    requirements in First Boot
        process, 125
    root, 108, 735
    shadow, 33
    tracing clear text, 624
    using corresponding Samba and
        Windows users and, 529, 533
PATA (Primary ATA), 810
patching kernels, 390–391
PATH variable
    checking, 28
    defined, 810
    setting and changing, 27
    using in crontab file, 355
paths, absolute and relative, 20
PC Cards (PCMCIA), 78, 79
PCI devices, 5
PDC (Primary Domain Controller), 810
PE (physical extent), 810
performance
    recompiled kernels and
        improved, 377
    Squid improvements of
        intranets, 481
    tips for NFS, 504–505
permissions
    access control lists, 208–210
    adding sticky bit to Samba, 542
    based on umask values, 32
    changing user file and directory
        default, 289–290
    executable script, 28–29

file, 30–31
    overriding inherited, 463–464
    setting Samba share, 539
    SUID and SGID, 32–33
permissive mode for SELinux, 707, 709
PGP (Pretty Good Privacy), 810
physical extent (PE), 810
physical volumes. See PVs
pico, 8
ping command
    preventing other computers from
        using, 699
    using, 41–42
ping of death, 383
piping data streams, 29
pirut tool (Package Manager utility)
    adding packages with, 111
    defined, 810
    illustrated, 243
    installing with, 243–244
    managing packages with, 242–243
Pluggable Authentication Modules.
    See PAM
PnP (plug and play), 73
Policy Module options (SELinux
    Management Tool), 715
POP3 (Post Office Protocol)
    about, 589
    prerequisite skills for, 45, 586
portmap daemon, 497, 505
portmap RPM package, 496
ports
    attaching devices to parallel,
        77–78
    compatible with filesystem, 12
    configuring for Apache, 458
    configuring with Security Level
        Configuration tool, 701–703
    enabling for DNS
        communications, 564, 565
    securing, 48
    serial, 77
    troubleshooting USB, 5
    typical numbers for xinetd,
        615–616
Post Office Protocol. See POP3
Postfix
    about, 586
    configuring and activating,
        598–599
    lab questions, 606–607, 609–611

prerequisite skills for, 45
    rebooting after modifying
        configuration, 598–599
    RPM packages for, 588–589
    selecting with alternatives
        command, 599
    self test and answers, 605–606,
        608–609
    summarized, 603
    two-minute drill, 604
    using system-switch-mail command
        to switch systems, 600
post-partition installations, 106–120
    configuring boot loader, 106–107
    customizing baseline packages in,
        108–110
    network configurations during,
        107–108
    overview of Linux package groups,
        110–120
    timezones and root password setup,
        107–108
power management, 74
prerequisite skills, 2–67
    accessing HTTP/HTTPS URLs
        with text or graphical browser,
        50–51
    basic hardware knowledge, 4–7
    books for reviewing, 2
    configuring e-mail clients, 49–51
    downloading Red Hat Enterprise
        Linux, 53–55, 60
    familiarity with network services,
        44–47, 59
    file operation commands, 19–22
    filesystem hierarchy and structure,
        11–19
    hard drives, 7
    Intel communication channels,
        5–6
    knowledge of architecture, 5
    lab questions and answers, 63,
        65–67
    Linux editors, 8–11
    network security, 47–48, 59
    preparing for RHCE and RHCT
        exams, 2–3
    printing, 25–26, 58
    RAM requirements, 6–7, 76
    security, 30–34, 58
    self test and answers, 61–62, 64–65

shells, 26–30, 58
summarized, 55–56
system administration, 34–38,
    58–59
TCP/IP networking, 38–43, 59
two-minute drill, 57–60
Unix-type operating systems and, 3
URL access via lftp command,
    51–53
Pretty Good Privacy (PGP), 810
Primary ATA (PATA), 810
Primary Domain Controller (PDC), 810
printers. *See also* CUPS; Red Hat Printer
Configuration tool
    adding, 26
    adding CUPS printer class,
        351, 352
    allowing user access to Samba
        shared, 530
    attaching to parallel ports, 77
    checking shared Samba directories
        and, 520–521
    controlling with LPD commands,
        347–349
    verifying CUPS sharing for,
        351–353
printing. *See also* CUPS
    basic commands for, 26
    configuration options in SELinux
        Management Tool for, 713
    configuring Samba client print
        services, 523
    prerequisite skills for, 25–26, 58
private key, 621, 811
/proc files, 380–383, 811
processes
    First Boot, 120–126
    listing running, 24
procmail, 586
ps command, 24
public access shares for Samba servers,
    540–541
public key, 621–622, 811
Pup (Package Updater), 236, 811
pvcreate command, 417, 418, 811
pvdisplay command, 811
PVs (physical volumes)
    adding with GUI LVM tool,
        429, 430
    commands for managing, 420

creating, 418–419
defined, 810
pwd command, 20

Q

QEMU, 76
QTParted, 194
queries
    using dig command for DNS, 576
    using RPM, 227–228
questions. *See* lab questions and answers;
    self test and answers
queues, lpc and print, 348
quota RPM package, 292–293
quotacheck command, 293, 294,
    298, 811
quotaon command, 811
quotas, 290–301
    activating in /etc/fstab, 293–294
    automating, 298
    configuring, 300–301
    defined, 811
    edquota command for setting,
        294–298
    generating reports on, 298–299
    grace period for, 295–297
    hard limits for, 296, 805
    managing, 294
    quota RPM package, 292–293
    quota settings in kernel, 291–292
    setting, 291
    soft limits for, 295, 815
    sysinit handling of, 293

R

RAID (Redundant Array of
    Independent Disks), 410–416
    about software RAID, 410
    configuring partitions for, 96
    creating RAID arrays, 412,
        414–415
    defined, 811
    exam preparation for, 376
    hard drive backups using, 37
    hotswappable hardware for, 412
    mirroring /home partition with,
        415–417
    modifying existing RAID
        array, 414

RAID 0, 410–411, 811
RAID 1, 411, 423, 811–812
RAID 4, 411
RAID 5, 411, 812
RAID 6, 411, 812
RAID 10, 412
    reviewing existing RAID array,
        413–414
    summarized, 430
    two-minute drill, 432
    using LVM with, 417
RAID 0, 410–411, 811
RAID 1, 411, 423, 811–812
RAID 4, 411
RAID 5, 411, 812
RAID 6, 411, 812
RAID 10, 412
RAM. *See* memory
reading
    mail messages, 50, 601
    text files with cat command, 21
read-only linux rescue
    environment, 741
rebooting
    Apache startup on, 447–449
    Postfix after modifying
        configuration, 598–599
    Squid server startup on, 477–478
    starting sendmail on, 596
    using chkconfig to verify service
        active after, 619
    vsFTP server startup on, 513
rebuild distributions
    configuring software updates on
        first boot, 124
    installation DVD for, 70
    studying for installation of, 71
    testing knowledge of, 4
recompiling kernels, 396–408
    advantages of, 377
    basic kernel configuration,
        400–401
    Block Layer menu options for, 402
    Bus menu options for, 402
    Code Maturity Level Options
        menu, 401
    compiling and installing custom
        kernels, 408–409
    configuration scripts for, 396–400
    configuring new kernel with make
        config, 397–398

creating .config file with make menuconfig, 398
Cryptographic menu options for, 408
Device Drivers menu options for, 403–407
Executable File Formats menu options for, 402
File Systems menu options for, 407
General Setup menu options for, 401
Instrumentation Support menu options for, 407
Kernel Hacking menu options for, 407
Library Routines menu options for, 408
Loadable Module Support menu options for, 402
making graphic configuration menus, 398–400
Networking menu options for, 403
options for kernel configuration, 400–408
Power Management menu options for, 402
Process Debugging Support option, 402
Processor Type and Features menu options for, 402
Security menu options for, 407
space needed for, 392
standard kernel configuration, 401
Red Hat Authentication Configuration tool, 316–317
Red Hat Certified Engineer exam. *See* RHCE exam
Red Hat Certified Technician exam. *See* RHCT exam
Red Hat Display Settings tool, 651, 670–673
Red Hat Domain Name Service configuration tool, 561, 576
Red Hat Enterprise Linux (RHEL). *See also* SELinux; third-party repositories
about, 53
adding to Windows network, 528
basic downloading steps for, 55

configuring Samba computer on Active Directory network, 526
development of, 444
differences from Unix, 3
DNS client configuration files installed with, 559
downloading, 53–54, 60
Dynamic DNS and, 558
Fedora Core 5/6, 54–55
Fedora Linux, 804
graphics support in, 653
GUI printer management for GNOME desktop, 349
Hardware Abstraction Layer, 73–74
Hardware Compatibility List, 72
Intel 32-bit architecture for, 5
kernel configuration for, 401
logging daemons in, 360
memory requirements for, 6–7, 72, 76
multiple monitors for X.org servers, 660
preventing unauthorized access to, 700
rebuild distributions, of, 4
reloading or restarting service with service command, 35
sharing Samba directory with workstation running, 535–536
single-user mode for, 814
software RAID, 410
source RPMs for, 54, 394
storage space for partitions, 103–104
system logs, 363
third-party repositories for, 54, 237, 241, 242
unable to open SELinux Management Tool if SELinux disabled, 83
using as DNS client, 560–561
Windows interoperability with Samba, 519
Red Hat Hardware Compatibility List (HCL), 72
Red Hat httpd Configuration tool for Apache, 475–476
Red Hat Network (RHN)
about, 234–235

benefits for remote systems with, 237–238
defined, 812
not included in Red Hat Exam Prep guide, 234
registration for, 235–236
Red Hat Package Manager (RPM), 222–227
automatic dependency resolution for updates, 237
building RHEL RPMs, 233–234
changing compile options for source RPM, 231–232
creating custom RPMs from source, 230, 232–233
custom source and binary RPMs, 232–233
defined, 223–224, 812
directory structure of /usr/src/redhat, 231
installing RPM packages, 224–225
listing installed RPMs, 230
queries for, 227–228
quota RPM package, 292–293
reference guides to RPM system, 232
remote installation of RPMs, 226
removing RPM packages, 225
source RPM installations, 230
summary of package management, 260
testing packages, 225
updating kernel RPM, 226–227
validating package signature, 228
verifying installed packages, 229
Red Hat Printer Configuration tool, 342–347
adding printers with, 26
choosing printer manufacturer, 344, 346
configuring remote and local printers, 343–344
illustrated, 347
printer and driver selection from, 345, 346
printer device options for, 344, 345
selecting type of connection in, 344, 345
using, 342–343

Red Hat User Manager, 277–280
    adding user with, 279–280
    illustrated, 279
    interface for, 277–278
    root user password required to
        run, 279
    starting, 278–279
redirection arrows (>), 29, 30
Redundant Array of Independent
    Devices. *See* RAID
refresh rate, 812
registration for Red Hat Network,
    235–236
reinstalling Linux during exam, 126
relative paths, 20
remote X applications
    starting display from remote
        clients, 675–676
    troubleshooting, 676–677
Remote Name Daemon Control
    (RNDC) key, 569–570
remote systems
    installation RPMs for, 226
    setting up filesystems for, 44
    using Red Hat Network with,
        237–238
removable media, mounting, 201–203
removing
    kernel modules, 387–388
    logical volumes, 424, 428, 429, 759
    RPM packages, 225
reports, quota, 298–299
repquota command, 812
rescue command, 90
rescue disk, 90
rescue environment. *See* linux rescue
    environment
reserved domain names, 466
resize2fs command, 813
resizing logical volumes, 424–425,
    428–430
reverse lookups, 567, 568
reverse zone
    about, 572–573
    defined, 813
    not delegated, 574
reviewing
    existing RAID array, 413–414
    recent logins, 274

RHCE exam. *See also* exam
    components of and requirements
        for, 768
    configuring Samba with smb.conf
        file, 524
    defined, 812
    diagnosing and correcting NFS
        network services, 508
    DNS topics on, 558, 563, 567
    e-mail topics on, 586, 587
    filesystem administration topics
        on, 184
    implementing packet filtering
        and/or NAT, 482
    Installation and Configuration
        exercises, 776–777, 778–781,
        793–794, 795–798
    installation topics on, 70, 71, 272
    knowledge of DHCP servers
        on, 627
    linux rescue environment, 735
    managing kernels, 376
    network services on, 445, 495
    NTP configuration and
        troubleshooting added to, 171
    reinstalls during, 126
    security topics on, 692
    skills addressed with system
        administration tools, 330
    slave name server configuration
        for, 565
    Troubleshooting and System
        Maintenance exercises,
        770–772, 773–776, 784–785,
        786–788, 789–792
    troubleshooting skills and
        objectives, 728, 729, 748–759
RHCT exam. *See also* exam
    Apache and Squid services not
        on, 445
    booting into runlevel of choice,
        733–735
    components of and requirements
        for, 768
    filesystem administration topics
        on, 184
    Installation and Configuration
        exercises, 776–778, 779–781,
        793–795, 796–798

    installation topics on, 70, 71, 272
    knowledge of DHCP clients
        on, 627
    managing kernels, 376
    NFS server topics, 495
    reinstalls during, 126
    skills addressed with system
        administration tools, 330
    Troubleshooting and System
        Maintenance exercises,
        769–770, 772–773, 785–786,
        788–789
    troubleshooting skills and
        objectives, 728, 729,
        742–748, 759
RHN. *See* Red Hat Network
rndc command, 575, 813
RNDC (Remote Name Daemon
    Control) key, 569–570
root, 813
root directory
    absolute path and, 20
    indicated by forward slash, 12
    mounting via linux rescue
        environment, 738–740
    standard subdirectories of, 13
root passwords, 108
root shell prompt (#), 741
root user account
    about, 273–274
    checking PATH for, 28
    logging in for exam as, 273
    NFS root squash behavior, 503
    password required to run Red Hat
        User Manager, 279
    running commands from, 15
    running yum command from, 239
/root/install.log file, 127
router, 813
routing, 705
routing tables, 338–339
rpm -i kernel.rpm command,
    389, 390
rpm command
    adding packages with, 111
    exam preparation for, 222
    query options for, 228
    yum command as supplement
        to, 223

RPM packages. *See* packages; Red Hat
   Package Manager; source RPMs
rpm -U kernel.rpm command, 389, 390
rpmbuild command, 231, 813
runlevels, 161–167
   about, 161, 813
   activating NFS directories at
      appropriate, 501
   booting into different, 144,
      164–167, 733
   determining with /etc/inittab,
      159–160
   functionality of, 161–162
   scripts for, 162–164
   verifying for activated
      service, 169

S

Samba, 516–544. *See also* Samba clients;
   Samba Server Configuration utility;
   Samba servers
   client configuration for, 520–523
   configuring with shares, 543–544
   defined, 813
   exam topics on, 495
   installing, 517–518
   interoperability with
      Linux/Unix, 519
   joining domains, 533
   lab questions and answers,
      549–551, 553–556
   managing users, 534–535
   misspellings of variables, 533
   overview, 516–517
   prerequisite skills for, 46
   self test and answers, 548–549, 552
   server configuration for, 523–533
   setting up SELinux support for,
      518, 713–714
   starting on Linux boot, 518
   testing changes to /etc/samba/smb.
      conf, 542
   two-minute drill, 546–547
   Windows and, 494, 519
Samba clients, 520–523
   checking file and print services,
      520–521
   configuring print services for, 523

mounting shared directories during
      login, 521–523
   types of, 520
Samba Server Configuration utility,
   536–541
   configuring users, 539–540
   creating public access shares,
      540–541
   modifying global settings with,
      537–538
   setting share permissions, 539
   starting, 517–518
   using, 537
Samba servers, 523–533
   Active Directory configurations
      for, 525–527
   adding sticky bit to permission
      values, 542
   configuring users, 533, 539–540
   directory sharing on Microsoft
      domains, 525
   editing /etc/samba/smb.conf file,
      523–524
   joining domains, 533
   looking up variables for, 529
   modifying global settings, 524–529
   public access shares for, 540–541
   setting share permissions for, 539
   share setting for, 529–533
   sharing home directories, 535–536
   using Windows passwords and
      usernames, 529, 533
Samba Users dialog (Samba Server
   Configuration utility), 541
Sample Exam 1, 768–781
   Installation and Configuration
      portion, 776–781
   Troubleshooting and System
      Maintenance portion, 768–776
Sample Exam 2, 784–782
   Installation and Configuration
      portion, 793–798
   Troubleshooting and System
      Maintenance portion, 784–793
sample kickstart file, 248–251, 253
SATA (serial ATA) drives
   adding, 423–424
   defined, 814
scientific method, 728–733

scripts
   adding Kickstart Configurator
      installation, 260
   disabling xinetd configuration, 618
   /etc/rc.sysinit, 293
   executing with permissions, 28–29
   importance of shell programming
      with, 27
   kernel configuration, 396–400
   runlevel 5 kill and start, 163
   startx, 666
searching for files, 20–21
Secure Shell (SSH) package, 620–626
   about, 614
   advantages of, 623–625
   configuring SSH server, 625–626
   encrypted communications and,
      621–622
   exam's focus on, 615
   lab questions and answers,
      641–642, 644–647
   overview, 620–621
   private keys, 621
   self test and answers,
      640–641, 643
   SSH client configuration, 626
   SSH services on Windows, 626
   summarized, 637
   two-minute drill, 638
   utilities generating keys, 623
secure virtual hosts, 468–469, 813
security, 30–34, 692–726. *See
   also* authentication; passwords;
   permissions
   allowing and denying files, 48
   at and cron daemons, 359–360
   Apache, 456–458, 460
   basic network, 47–48
   checking to see if system
      cracked, 274
   configuring iptables command,
      698–700
   file permissions, 30–31, 289–290
   firewalls and packet filtering,
      697–703
   implementing with SELinux, 209,
      210, 706–716
   kernel configuration options
      for, 407

lab questions and answers, 721–722, 724–726

maintaining firewall configurations in iptables file, 700

multiple partitions for, 102

NAT and, 48, 703–706

NIS, 47

overview, 58, 692–693

PAM, 306–308, 311–313

password, 277

preventing ping of death, 383

protecting network computers, 693

reducing NFS risks, 506

RHCE exam requirements for, 692

risks for NFS, 505–506

securing ports, 48

Security Level Configuration tool, 701–703

self test and answers, 720–721, 723–724

sendmail, 595–596

Setroubleshoot browser, 715–716

shadow passwords, 33

Squid Proxy Server options for, 482

SUID and SGID permissions, 32–33

summarized, 717

tcp_wrappers and packet, 693–697

two-minute drill, 718–719

used-based Apache, 460–461

users, groups, and masks, 31–32

vsFTP server, 513–514

xinetd and, 47

yum command for updating, 242

Security Enhanced Linux. See SELinux

Security Level Configuration tool, 701–703

illustrated, 701

modes for, 701

SELinux Management Tool vs., 709

setting up SELinux in Permissive mode, 707

Security tab (Samba Server Configuration utility), 537, 538

sed (stream editor), 23–24

selecting e-mail systems, 599–603

alternatives command for, 599

e-mail clients, 600–601

reading mail messages, 50, 601

system-switch-mail command to switch systems, 600

testing results of e-mail service, 600–601, 602–603

working with mail group "alias" lists, 602

self test and answers

Apache and Squid, 486–487, 488–489

booting, 175–176, 180–181

DNS, 579–580, 581

e-mail, 605–606, 608–609

filesystem administration, 212–213, 215–216

hardware and installation, 133–134, 140–141

kernels, 433–434, 437–438

network file sharing services, 548–549, 552

other networking services, 640–641, 643

package management, 263–264, 267–268

prerequisite skills, 61–62, 64–65

security, 720–721, 723–724

system administration tools, 367–368, 371–372

troubleshooting, 761–762, 764–765

user administration, 321–322, 324–325

X Window System, 684–685, 687

SELinux (Security Enhanced Linux), 706–716. See also SELinux Management Tool

about, 81, 706–707

added to Red Hat Exam Prep guide, 81, 184, 208

configuring during first boot, 122–123

CUPS protection disabled when configuring, 354

at daemon and, 359

defined, 813

development of, 209

diagnosing network services problems due to, 759

disabling during exam troubleshooting, 330

e-mail interference by, 586

exam configuration tips, 708

experimenting in Permissive mode, 707

file contexts for, 706

lab questions and answers, 721–722, 724–726

logging service protection disabled by, 360

making NFS work with, 502

manually configuring, 708–709

problems for NTP service with, 635

security implemented with, 210

Setroubleshoot browser, 715–716

setting up support for Samba, 518, 713–714

settings for cron daemon, 357

status configurations using /etc/ sysconfig/selinux, 707

support for vsFTP servers, 512–513

trouble opening SELinux Management Tool when disabled, 83

using SELinux Management Tool, 83, 709–715

SELinux Management Tool, 709–715

about, 708

advantages over Security Level Configuration tool, 709

configuring Boolean operations, 710–714

file labeling options, 714–715

illustrated, 710, 715

SELinux User options (SELinux Management Tool), 715

sendmail, 592–597

accepting mail from unresolved domains, 595

alternatives to, 586

basic operation of, 594–597

configuring and securing, 595–596

defined, 814

key configuration files for, 592–593

lab questions, 606–607, 609–611

macros for sendmail.mc file, 594

prerequisite skills for, 45

restarting modified, 596

RPM packages for, 588–589

selecting with alternatives command, 599

self test and answers, 605–606, 608–609

SMTP used to send mail, 587–588

summarized, 603

troubleshooting, 596–597

two-minute drill, 604

using system-switch-mail command to switch systems, 600

serial ATA. *See* SATA drives

serial number errors in DNS, 574

server certificates, 466

Server Settings (Samba Server Configuration utility), 537, 538

servers. *See also* DNS servers; network installation servers; Samba servers; servers; Squid

    Apache Web, 447, 449–450, 456–466, 474–475

    caching-only name, 561, 563–565, 801

    components of mail, 587

    configuring kickstart, 246–247

    defined, 814

    DHCP, 86–87, 627, 628–631, 633

    forwarding-only name, 561, 565–566

    FTP and vsFTP, 85–86, 94, 95, 512–515

    HTTP, 83–85, 94, 95

    network installation, 81, 86–87

    NFS, 81–83, 494–509

    NTP time, 634–637

    RAM requirements for Linux, 7

    Samba, 523–533

    securing host servers with tcp_wrappers, 694–696

    slave name, 561, 565

    SSH, 625–626

    storage space required for file, 103–104

    time-efficient method for installation from remote, 92–95

    using multiple X.org, 659–660

    X.org, 658–669

    X Window System, 651–653

Servers package group, 115–118

service accounts, 274

service command, 35

Service Configuration tool, 168–169

service httpd reload command, 448

Sessions dialog, 523

Sessions utility, 667

set command, 29

setenforce command, 708

setfacl command, 814

Setroubleshoot browser, 715–716

SGID (set group ID) bit

    controlling group ownership with, 303–305

    defined, 303, 814

    inheritance of group ID from, 302

    using SGID permissions, 32–33

Shadow Password Suite, 33–34, 814

share settings for Samba servers, 529–533

shared directories. *See also* network file sharing services

    activating NFS directories at appropriate runlevels, 501

    adding with NFS Server Configuration tool, 499–502

    creating, 302–303

    mounting from NFS client computer, 509–512

    reviewing and reading NFS, 205–206

    Samba, 520–523, 535–536

    sharing Samba directory on Microsoft domains, 525

sharing files with Apache, 458–459

shells. *See also* bash shell

    changing file and directory permissions for, 289–290

    checking PATH, 28

    configuration files for, 287–290

    defined, 26

    environment variables for, 29

    /etc/bashrc file for, 287

    /etc/profile file for, 288–289

    hidden files added to user shell configuration, 290

    managing data streams in, 29–30

    prerequisite skills for, 26–30, 58

    programming with scripts, 27

    script execution and permissions, 28–29

    variables and parameters for, 27–28

    wildcards in, 25

showmount command, 814

Simple Mail Transfer Protocol (SMTP), 587–588, 804

single quote ('), 595

single-user mode, 814

slave name servers, 561, 565

smbd daemon, 520

smbmount command, 522

smbpasswd command, 533, 534, 535, 814

smbumount command, 522

SMP computers, 75

SMTP (Simple Mail Transfer Protocol), 587–588, 804

SOA (Start of Authority), 814–815

soft limits for disk quotas, 295, 815

soft mounting option for NFS clients, 511–512

software RAID. *See* RAID

software updates. *See* updating

sort command, 23

sorting files, 23

sound card testing, 125

source RPMs

    building from tar archive, 230

    changing compile options for, 231–232

    creating custom, 230, 232–233

    defined, 815

    directory structure of /usr/src/redhat, 231

    installing, 230

    kernel, 394–396

    locating, 394

    required customization RPMs for kernels, 395–396

    RHEL 5, 54

spam protection, 714

spamassassin directory, 592–593

spec files, 815

SQL (Structured Query Language), 815

Squid, 476–483

    about, 444, 476–477

    advantages of, 481

    configuring /etc/squid/squid.conf file, 478–480

    defined, 815

    /etc/sysconfig/squid file, 478

    key files and directories, 477

    lab questions and answers, 487, 489–491

localizing options for, 480–481
options in SELinux Management Tool for, 714
proxy server configuration for, 482–483
security settings for, 482
self test and answers, 486–487, 488–489
starting on reboot, 477–478
summarized, 484
two-minute drill, 485
srm.conf file, 451
SRPMs. *See* source RPMs
SSH. *See* Secure Shell package
ssl.conf file, 450
standard error (stderr), 29
standard groups, 301–302
standard input (stdin), 29
standard linux rescue environment, 738–740
standard ouput (stdout), 29, 30
stanzas
about, 529–533
changing GRUB's default, 390
Start of Authority (SOA), 814–815
starting
X Window, 659
Squid, 477–478
Startup Programs tab (Sessions dialog), 523
startx command for X.org servers, 666–669
stateless protocol of NFS, 502–503
static IP addresses, 39
sticky bit for Samba permissions, 542
stream editor (sed), 23–24
Structured Query Language (SQL), 815
su command, 34, 284
subscriptions to Red Hat Network, 53
sudo command, 34, 284–285
SUID bit, 522, 815
SUID permissions, 32–33
superusers, 34, 815
swap partitions
making with parted utility, 195–196
setting up fdisk, 190–191
troubleshooting, 747
swap space, 104–105, 747, 815
switchdesk command, 680–681, 746

switches, 19
symbolically linked NFS files, 503
sync command, 740
syntax of virtual host containers, 470
syslog.conf log configuration file, 361
syslogd (system log daemon), 360–362
system administration tools, 330–374
about, 330
cron and at for automating administration, 354–360
CUPS, 341–354
exam objectives for, 330
lab questions and answers, 368–370, 372–374
network configuration, 331–340
self test and answers, 367–368, 371–372
summarized, 364
two-minute drill, 365–366
working with system logs, 360–364
system configuration files, 169–172
GUI tools for, 171–172
non-network /etc/sysconfig files, 170
system log daemon (syslogd), 360–362
system logs, 360–364
configuration file for syslogd, 360–362
inspecting, 364
logging daemons in RHEL, 360
managing, 38, 362
standard Red Hat, 363
system-config-* commands, 815
system-config-bind command, 561
system-config-display command, 651
system-config-network command, 334–336
system-config-samba command, 536–537
system-config-securitylevel command, 701

T

tabletype options for iptables command, 698
tail command, 22
tape backups, 37
tar command, 38
tar files, 396

tarballs, 23
TCP SYN attacks, 383, 700
TCP/IP networking, 38–43, 59
configuring name resolution, 42–43
defined, 815
defining network with IP addresses, 40–41
IP numbers and address classes, 39
IPv6 addressing, 39–40
network card configuration for, 87, 88
overview, 38–39
Samba and, 519–520
tools and commands for, 41–42
typical port numbers for, 615–616
tcp_wrappers, 693–697
configuring, 696–697
operators for, 696
securing users and host with, 694–696
Telnet
controlling resource access with tcp_wrappers, 695, 696–697
defined, 816
enabling with xinetd, 620
using Kerberos-based, 624
vulnerabilities of, 624
xinetd and, 614
testing. *See also* self test and answers
changes to /etc/samba/smb.conf, 542
disk quotas, 297
kickstart configuration, 248
mail system, 600–601, 602–603
RPM packages, 225
troubleshooting scenarios, 731
testparm utility for Samba, 542
text editors, 8–11. *See also* vi
about, 8
availability during exam, 11
configuring Samba with shares, 543–544
emacs, 803
vi, 8–10
text-based tools
accessing URLs with text browsers, 50–51
configuring Samba with shares in text editor, 543–544

controlling services with, 168
editing Apache configuration files
with, 475
GUI-text editors availability
during exam and, 11
learning command line
configurations for NFS, 506
modifying user accounts with, 282
running First Boot process
with, 126
Samba configuration in text
editor, 517
setting up network interface
with, 333
timesavings of, 281
third-party repositories
about, 54, 237
adding to system, 242
resynchronizing headers of, 241
tilde (~), 20
time
configuring timezones, 108
setting system date and, 123, 124
time synchronization. *See* NTP
timesavings
configuring system during
installation "dead time", 120
editing Apache configuration files
from command line, 475
installing via remote NFS server,
92–95
redoing installation rather than
fixing, 126
selecting correct desktop
environment, 112
setting Samba global
configurations from command
line, 537
testing mail system from command
line, 600–601
time required for LVM
partitions, 103
timing for DNS servers, 573–574
/tmp directory configuration files, 129
tmpwatch command, 816
tools. *See* system administration tools;
text-based tools; and specific tools
Translation options (SELinux
Management Tool), 715

troubleshooting, 728–766
about, 728
Apache errors, 472–473
boot failures, 144
boot loader, 749–750
booting into different runlevels,
733–735
cautions about removing RPM
packages, 225
checking partitions with
dumpe2fs, 754
configuration files, 162, 331
corrupted files, 755–756
desktop environments, 746
DHCP clients, 632
difficulties recognizing second
network adapters, 336
DNS configuration files, 574
e2label command for filesystem,
753–754, 755
errors in GRUB configuration file,
152–155
exam objectives for, 728, 729
fdisk and parted utilities for,
752–753
filesystems, 747, 751–755
fsck command for, 754–755
graphics hardware during boot
USB or CD/DVD
installation, 91
GUI-text editors for exam, 11
hostname resolution, 744
identifying problems during,
728–733
inspecting system logs for
problems, 364
installation, 127–129
IP addresses and NAT, 706
lab questions and answers on,
762–763, 765–766
linux rescue environment for, 728,
735–742
logical volumes, 756–759
module errors in boot loader,
750–751
network problems, 742–743
network service issues, 756, 759
new partitions, 747–748
NFS client hangs when shutting
down, 503–504, 507–508

partitioning mistakes using
parted, 191
remote X applications, 676–677
RHCT exam requirements for,
330, 742–748
scenarios and solutions for,
731–732
self test and answers, 761–762,
764–765
sendmail, 596–597
skills required for RHCE, 748–759
summarized, 759
swap partitions, 747
two-minute drill, 760
unable to open SELinux
Management Tool, 83
USB ports or PCI card from BIOS
menus, 5
using command line or text-based
tools for exam, 282, 748
yum command problems, 241
X clients and servers, 669
X Font Server, 674
X Window System, 666, 745
Troubleshooting and System
Maintenance section
exam objectives for, 728, 729, 759
Sample Exam 1, 768–776
Sample Exam 2, 784–793
two-minute drills
X Window System, 683
Apache and Squid, 485
booting, 173–174
DNS, 578
filesystem administration, 211
hardware compatibility and
installation, 131–132
kernels, 431–432
network file sharing services,
546–547
other networking services,
638–639
package management, 261–262
prerequisite skills, 57–60
security, 718–719
system administration tools,
365–366
troubleshooting, 760
user administration, 319.

U

UIDs (user IDs)
  about, 32, 816
  NFS and, 281
  SUID permissions, 32–33
umask command, 32, 816
umask file, 287
umask group settings, 302, 303
umount.cifs command, 522, 809
Unix-type operating systems
  development of Linux from, 444
  Red Hat differences from, 3
  Samba's interoperability between
    Windows and, 519
  tips for administrators of, 255
unmounting and remounting
  filesystems, 17
up2date
  automatic dependency resolution
    with, 237
  yum command replacing, 693
updatedb command, 21, 23
updating
  dependency resolution and
    RPM, 237
  GRUB, 150–152
  grub.conf file, 391–392
  kernels, 226–227, 379
  packages with yum command, 242
  with Pup, 236
  software in first boot, 124
upgrading
  kernels, 389–390
  RPMs, 224

  ss via lftp command, 51–53
  ng with text or graphical
    r, 50–51

    or, 78

      n, 91–92
      0

  20

User Access tab (Add NFS Share
  dialog), 500–501
user administration. See also users
  command line tools for, 274–277,
    283–284
  managing user environment,
    285–287
  overview of, 272
  Red Hat User Manager, 277–280
  self test and answers, 321–322,
    324–325
  shell configuration files, 287–290
  summarized, 317–318
  tips for managing user accounts,
    280–281
  two-minute drill, 319–320
  working with special groups,
    301–305
user IDs, 275
user interface. See also command line;
  GUI; X Window System
  CUPS Web-based, 349–351
  display managers, 663
User Mapping options (SELinux
  Management Tool), 715
user private groups
  configuring ownership and
    permissions for Samba home
    directory, 531
  creating group Samba directory,
    532–533
  Red Hat scheme for, 280–281, 301
User Properties dialog (Red Hat User
  Manager), 282, 283
useradd command, 276, 277
usermod command, 283, 816
users. See also root user account; UIDs
  about, 31–32
  adding, 273, 274–275, 276, 277,
    279–280
  Apache user-based security,
    460–461
  assigning password for, 276–277
  authenticating network, 313–317
  categories of, 273–274
  checking for authorized, 305–313
  configuring in first boot
    process, 124
  configuring Samba, 539–540

  creating in vi, 10–11
  deleting, 281
  disk quotas for, 290–301
  errors running yum command from
    local system, 239
  including in groups, 275–276
  limiting access to su and sudo
    commands, 284–285
  logging in for exam as root, 273
  managing, 280–281, 283–284,
    534–535
  modifying, 281–283
  POP, 589
  securing with tcp_wrappers,
    694–696
  security levels for, 693
  superusers, 34, 815
  using corresponding Samba and
    Windows, 529, 533
/usr/src/linux directory, 393–394
/usr/src/redhat directory, 231
uucp, 586

V

validating package signatures, 228
/var/log directory, 362
variables
  /etc/sysconfig/network file,
    331–332
  looking up Samba, 529
  MAILTO, 355
  misspellings of Samba, 533
  PATH, 27, 28, 355
  using environment vs. shell, 29
  xinetd configuration file, 618–619
verifying
  installed RPM packages, 229
  users with PAM, 306–308
versions
  Fedora Core, 53
  kernel version numbers, 388–389
very secure FTP servers. See vsFTP
  servers
vgcreate command, 417, 816
vgdisplay command, 816
vgextend command, 418, 816
VGs (volume groups)
  commands for managing, 421

configuration of, 422
creating, 419, 426–427
defined, 817
illustrated, 422
vi
basic text editing in, 10
command mode in, 9–10
creating new user in, 10–11
defined, 816
overview of, 8–9
video RAM requirements, 76
viewing filesystems list, 196
virtual consoles, 160
virtual hosts, 466–476
about, 466–468, 816
checking syntax of containers
for, 470
configuration directives in httpd.
conf for, 452, 455
executable files for, 470
log files for Apache, 471–472
secure, 468–469
troubleshooting Apache errors,
472–473
updating home page on Apache
server, 473
virtualization
CPUs and, 76
defined, 817
when to install package for, 109
VMware, 817
VMware Server, 92–93
volume groups. See VGs
volumes. See also LVs; PVs; VGs
defined, 12
exam skills required for logical, 184
logical, 808
physical, 810
removing logical, 759
volume groups, 817
vsFTP (very secure FTP) servers,
512–515
cautions using chroot_local_
user=YES command, 514
configuration commands, 514
configuring basic, 515
defined, 816
exam topics on, 495
installing, 512

lab questions and answers,
549–551, 553–556
self test and answers, 548–549, 552
SELinux support for, 512–513
setting up security for, 513–514
starting on reboot, 513
two-minute drill, 546–547

W

w command, 24–25
Web servers. See also Apache Web
servers
about, 444
allowing to run while reading
changes to configuration
files, 448
Apache access configuration,
456–466
changes in Apache 2.2, 446
exam focus on, 445
overview of Apache, 444–456
setting up virtual Apache, 474–475
virtual hosts with Apache,
466–476
Web service prerequisite skills, 46–47
Web sites
configuring passwords for, 462
creating index.html files during
exams, 469
protecting Web directory with
password, 464–466
updating home page on Apache
server, 473
virtual hosts for creating
multiple, 470
Web access to pages placed on
home directory, 462–463
who command, 24
wildcards
/etc/hosts.allow and /etc/hosts.
deny, 695
used in shell, 25
using with NFS /etc/exports, 498
winbindd daemon, 529
window managers
configuration files for, 287
defined, 677, 817
starting X server without, 654–655

Windows
configuring Samba on Active
Directory, 525–527
DHCP and, 631
interoperability with
Linux/Unix, 519
networking Linux with, 528
Samba's interaction with, 494
sharing Samba directories on
Microsoft domain, 525
SSH services on, 626
using same users and passwords as
Samba, 529, 533
workstations running shared
Samba directory, 529–530,
535–536
WINS (Windows Internet Name
Service) name resolution, 519,
528, 817
word count for files, 23

X

X clients
command line options for,
655–657
configuring to start with GNOME
desktop, 667
default, 654
defined, 817
troubleshooting scenarios for, 669
xterm program for, 657
X Display, 817
X Font Server, 674
X servers, 817. See also X.org servers
X Window System, 650–690
about, 650–651
clients and servers with, 651–653
command line options for X
clients, 655–657
defined, 817
desktops and window managers,
677–681
hardware supported for, 653–654
lab questions and answers,
685–686, 688–690
running remote X application
675–677
self test and answers, 684–

starting X server without window
   manager, 654–655
summarized, 682
tools for X.org configuration,
   670–674
troubleshooting, 666, 745
two-minute drill, 683
using customized .xinitrc file,
   668–669
XFree86 and X.org system, 650
X.org server configuration,
   658–669
xdm display manager, 663
Xen
   about, 377, 817
   Xen-based virtualization, 76, 109
XFree86, 650
xfs service script, 674
xhost command, 818
xinetd (Extended Internet Services
   Daemon), 614–620
   default settings in generic
      configuration file, 616–618
   defined, 818
   enabling Telnet with, 620
   lab questions and answers,
      641–642, 644–647
   network security and, 47

self test and answers, 640–641, 643
standard parameters for, 619
summarized, 637
two-minute drill, 638
typical port numbers for, 615–616
working with scripts and variables
   in, 618–619
/.xinitrc file, 667–669
X.org servers, 658–669
   configuration files for, 658
   configuring, 652
   defined, 818
   detailed examination of xorg.conf,
      660–662
   gdm and kdm display managers,
      663–665
   hardware support for, 654
   starting X Window, 659
   starting with text or graphical GUI
      access, 662
   starting without window manager,
      654–655
   startx command for, 666–669
   text login mode for, 662–663
   troubleshooting scenarios for, 669
   using multiple, 659–660
X.org system. See also X.org servers
   about, 650

command line tools for
   configuring, 673
configuring with Red Hat Display
   Settings tool, 670–673
X Font Server, 674
xterm program, 657

Y

ypbind, 818
ypserv, 818
yum command
   automatic dependency resolution
      for RPMs with, 237
   defined, 818
   installation commands for, 241
   installing kernel with, 227
   root account required to run, 239
   running, 238–240
   as supplement to rpm
      command, 223
   troubleshooting problems
      with, 241
   updates and security fixes with,
      242, 693

Z

zone files, 570–572